"I read *Obstacle to Peace* with great interest. Hammond is a knowledgeable and insightful writer. His analysis is sharp and original, refusing to allow mythology to supersede reality. We often discuss Israel-Palestine with too little attention to the central role of US policy. This book illustrates why such an omission is a terrible mistake."

—STEVEN SALAITA, Author of
The Holy Land in Transit: Colonialism and the Quest for Canaan

"Outstanding. This highly informative and meticulously researched book is a valuable resource for every scholar and activist. The flair with which the book has been written makes it accessible to those who are not as familiar with the Israel-Palestinian issue but who are eager to perfect their knowledge. Hammond's illuminating and invaluable book deserves a wide audience."

—SORAYA SEPAHPOUR-ULRICH, Independent Foreign Policy Analyst

"In *Obstacle to Peace*, Mr. Hammond provides a meticulously documented and compelling narrative of the long running Israel-Palestine conflict and the role that the United States has played in thwarting potential solutions. This work not only tells the story but also provides a valuable research vehicle for policy makers and commentators alike. It is a must for every bookshelf on this topic."

—DONALD LIEBICH, Author of
Fault Lines: The Layman's Guide to Understanding America's Role in the Ever-Changing Middle East

"When I first came to Palestine in 2003, I was naïve in many ways and had to start from the beginning. My previous work in South Africa helped to open up my eyes and see the deepening of apartheid in the Middle East, but what was missing was a book like *Obstacle to Peace*. The book is a bridge to a real peace process, unlike the vacuous diplomacy that continues while the colonization and theft does not stop and the apartheid is manifested. *Obstacle to Peace* helps those of us concerned with peace and justice to be firmly rooted when we speak out."

—MATS SVENSSON, Former Swedish Diplomat and Author of
Crimes, Victims and Witnesses: Apartheid in Palestine

OBSTACLE TO PEACE

The US Role in the Israeli-Palestinian Conflict

JEREMY R. HAMMOND

WORLDVIEW PUBLICATIONS

Published by
Worldview Publications
P.O. Box 181
Cross Village, Michigan 49723
www.ObstacleToPeace.com

Cover design by Peter O'Connor
Bespoke Book Covers
www.BespokeBookCovers.com

Publisher's Cataloging-in-Publication Data
provided by Five Rainbows Cataloging Services

Names: Hammond, Jeremy R.
Title: Obstacle to peace : the U.S. Role in the Israeli-Palestinian conflict / Jeremy R. Hammond.
Description: Cross Village, MI : Worldview Publications, 2016.
Identifiers: LCCN 2015907064 | ISBN 978-0-9961058-0-4 (hardcover) | ISBN 978-0-9961058-1-1 (pbk.) | ISBN 978-0-9961058-2-8 (Kindle) | 978-0-9961058-3-5 (EPUB)
Subjects: LCSH: United States--Foreign relations--Middle East. | Middle East--Foreign relations--United States. | Israel--Foreign relations--Palestine. | Palestine--Foreign relations--Israel. | Arab-Israeli conflict--Influence. | BISAC: POLITICAL SCIENCE / International Relations / Diplomacy. | POLITICAL SCIENCE / Peace. | HISTORY / Middle East / Israel & Palestine.
Classification: LCC DS119.76 .H3556 2016 (print) | LCC DS119.76 (ebook) | DDC 327.73056--dc23.

For Joanne, for believing, and Elijah, for being my daily reminder of why it's worth fighting for a better future.

CONTENTS

FOREWORD

BY RICHARD FALK*

T HERE IS A WIDENING public recognition around the world that diplomacy as it has been practiced with respect to resolving the conflict between Israel and Palestine has failed despite being a major project of the United States government for more than two decades. Actually, worse than failure, this stalled diplomacy has allowed Israel, by stealth and defiance, to pursue relentlessly its vision of a greater Israel under the unyielding protective cover of American support. During this period, the Palestinian territorial position has continuously worsened, and the humanitarian ordeal of the Palestinian people has become ever more acute.

An acknowledgement of this unsatisfactory status quo has led European governments belatedly to question their deference to American leadership in resolving the Israeli-Palestinian conflict. It has also persuaded more and more social activists in civil society in this country and elsewhere to rely on non-violent tactics of solidarity with Palestinian resistance, especially by way of the boycott, divestment, and sanctions (BDS) campaign that has been gathering momentum in the last year; and it is approaching a tipping point that seems to be making Israeli leaders noticeably nervous. Both of these challenges to the Oslo diplomatic approach are based on the belief that Israel has demonstrated its unwillingness to reach a political compromise with Palestine on the basis of a negotiated settlement even within a biased "peace process" overseen by the US as partisan intermediary. In effect, there will be no solution to the conflict without the exertion of greatly increased international pressures on Israel to scale back its territorial ambitions. Such an outlook reflects the influential view that the time has come to resort to coercive means to induce Israeli leaders and Zionists everywhere to rethink their policy options along more enlightened lines. The implicit goal is that by means of this pressure from without, a "South

---

* Richard Falk is a former UN Special Rapporteur on the situation of human rights in the Palestinian territories occupied since 1967.

African solution" will suddenly emerge as a result of an abrupt turnaround in Israeli policy.

Jeremy Hammond offers readers another approach, not incompatible with mounting pressure, and maybe complementary with it. In this meticulously researched, lucidly reasoned, and comprehensively narrated book, Hammond insists that not only has the Oslo "peace process" turned out to be a bridge to nowhere, but that the United States government, in criminal complicity with Israel, has actively and deliberately opposed any steps that could result in the establishment of an independent Palestinian state. Such an assessment poses a frontal challenge to the universally affirmed two-state supposed goal of these negotiations. Even Benjamin Netanyahu has, at times, given lip service to an endorsement of a Palestinian state—although in the heat of an electoral campaign in March 2015, he showed his true hand to the Israeli public by promising that no Palestinian state would come into being as long as he was prime minister. Netanyahu's flight from hypocrisy was further reinforced by appointing Danny Danon, a longtime extremist opponent of Palestinian statehood, as the next Israeli ambassador to the UN, which could also be interpreted as another slap in the face for US President Barack Obama. In this regard, it was the White House that did the heavy lifting to keep alive as long as possible the credibility of the flawed Oslo peace promise by insisting that this was the one and only path to ending the Israeli-Palestinian conflict.

In a refusal to adjust to this new Israeli posture, in Washington and at the UN, there is no departure from the consensus that a directly negotiated "two state solution" is the only path to peace, coupled with the totally fatuous tactical priority that what would alone be helpful is to persuade the parties to return to the negotiating table. Recent American presidents are all on record as devoting their maximum effort to reach these discredited goals and treat all other tactics employed on behalf of the Palestinians as "obstacles" that set back the prospect of ending the conflict. The US government joins with Israel in condemning all forms of international pressures to alter the status quo of the occupation, including Palestinian initiatives to be acknowledged as a full-fledged state within the UN system (a seemingly uncontroversial sequel to receiving diplomatic recognition as a state by more than 120 UN members) or to seek remedies for their grievances by recourse to the International Criminal Court. The United States has helped Israel use the Oslo peace process as a holding operation that gives Tel Aviv the time it needs to undermine once and for all Palestinian expectations of Israeli withdrawal and Palestinian sovereign rights. The whole Israeli idea is to make the accumulation of facts on the ground (that is, the unlawful settlement archipelago, its supportive Jews-only road network, and the unlawful separation wall) into "the new normal" that paves the way for a unilaterally imposed Israeli one-state solution combined with either Palestinian Bantustanization or third class citizenship in an enlarged Israel.

It is against this background that Hammond's book breaks new ground in ways that fundamentally alter our understanding of the conflict and how to resolve it. His abundantly documented major premise is that Israel could not proceed with its plans to take over the occupied territories of the West Bank and East Jerusalem without the benefits flowing from its "special relationship" with the United States. The perfidious reality that Hammond exposes beyond reasonable doubt is that the United States has been an essential collaborator in a grotesque double deception: falsely pretending to negotiate the establishment of a Palestinian state while doing everything within its power to ensure that Israel has the time it needs to make such an outcome a practical impossibility. This American role has included the geopolitical awkwardness of often standing alone in shielding Israel from all forms of UN censure for its flagrant violations of international law, which has included mounting evidence of an array of crimes against humanity.

As Hammond convincingly explains, the structures of government in the United States have been subverted to the extent that it is implausible to expect any alteration of this pattern of American unconditional support for Israel, at least in relation to the Palestinians, to come from within the government. Hammond also portrays the mainstream media as complementing this partisan governmental role, indicting particularly the *New York Times* as guilty of one-sided journalism that portrays the conflict in a manner that mostly accords with Israeli propaganda and sustains the malicious myth that the United States is doing everything possible to achieve a solution in the face of stubborn Palestinian rejectionism. In this regard, Hammond informs readers in his preface that *Obstacle to Peace* is explicitly written to wake up the American people to these overriding realities with the intention of providing the tools needed by the public to challenge the special relationship on behalf of justice and the national interests and values of the American republic. Without making the argument overtly, Hammond is providing the public with the sorts of understanding denied to it by a coopted media. What Hammond does for the reader is to show in painstaking detail and on the basis of an impressive accumulation of evidence what an objective account of Israeli-Palestinian relations looks like, including by correcting the gross misreporting of the interactions in Gaza that have led to a series of wars waged by the totally dominant armed forces of Israel against the completely vulnerable civilian population of Gaza. In an illuminating sense, if the media was properly doing its job of objective reporting, Hammond's book would be almost superfluous. Hammond's democratic major premise is that if Americans know the truth about Israeli-Palestinian relations, there will result a mobilization of opposition that produces a new political climate in which elected leaders will be forced to heed the will of the people and do the right thing.

In a fundamental respect, Hammond is hopeful as well as brave, as he seems firmly convinced that Israel could not continue with its unjust and criminal policies if it truly loses the United States as its principal enabler. It is in this primary sense, as conveyed by the book's title, that the United States is *the obstacle* to peace; but if this obstacle could be removed, then the shift in the power balance would force Israel to face the new realities and presumably allow the Palestinians to obtain their fully sovereign state and, with it, reasonable prospects for a sustainable peace. It needs to be appreciated that Hammond is writing as someone with a radical faith in the power of a properly informed citizenry to transform for the better the policies of the American republic, both with respect to the government and the media linkages that connect state and society with respect to the agenda of public policy.

In my view, *Obstacle to Peace* is the book we have long needed, utterly indispensable for a correct understanding of why the conflict has not been resolved up to this point, and further, why the path chosen makes a just and sustainable peace between Israel and Palestine a "mission impossible." Hammond goes further than this devastating exposure of past policy failures by offering guidelines for what he sensibly believes is the only viable way forward. Only the future will determine whether a grassroots movement can induce a repudiation of the dysfunctional special relationship, and if this should happen, whether it then leads Israel to act rationally to uphold its own security by finally agreeing to the formation of a Palestinian state. In Hammond's view, ending the occupation and securing Palestinian statehood is the immediate goal of a reconstructed diplomacy, but not necessarily the end point of conflict resolution. He defers consideration of whether a unified secular state is the best overall solution until the Palestinians as a state are able to negotiate on the basis of equality with Israel, and then to be in a position to rely on diplomacy to finally fulfill their right of return, which has been deferred far too long.

In the end, Hammond's extremely instructive book provides a fact-based overall account of the major facets of this complex relationship between Israel and Palestine and can be read as a plea to Americans to reclaim historical agency and act as citizens, not subjects. This plea is not primarily about the improper use of taxpayer revenues, but is concerned with activating the soul of American democracy in such a way that enables the country once more to act as a benevolent force in the world and, most concretely, to create the conditions that would bring peace with justice to the Palestinian people.

With the greatest admiration for Hammond's achievement in this book, I would point out finally that *Obstacle to Peace* is about more than the Israel-Palestine relationship and can be read beneficially with these larger concerns in mind. It is, above all, about the destruction of trust in the relationship between government and citizens, and about the disastrous failures of the media to serve as the vigilant guardian of truth and fact in carrying out its journalistic duties in a manner that befits a free society. *Obstacle to Peace* is a powerfully reasoned and fully evidenced case study and critique of the systemic malady of contemporary American democracy that threatens the wellbeing of the country as never before.

Richard Falk
Yalikavak, Turkey
August 2015

INTRODUCTION

BY GENE EPSTEIN*

"IN THE FOLLOWING PAGES, I offer nothing more than simple facts, plain arguments, and common sense; and have no other Preliminaries to settle with the reader, than that he will divest himself of prejudice and prepossession . . . ." That's Thomas Paine in his impassioned mini-book of 1776, *Common Sense.*

Paine was advocating revolutionary war, while Jeremy Hammond in this book is merely urging that the US and Israeli governments stop being obstacles to peace so that peaceful relations can be established between Israelis and Palestinians. Paine, however, probably had an easier time getting past the prejudice and prepossession of the audience he was addressing. In Hammond's case, people who would benefit most from reading his book will put up a wall of resistance against the simple facts, plain arguments, and common sense he offers.

I know, because over the years I've spoken with many of these people. Their identity as Jews and as Americans—or identification with Jews or with Americans—seems to depend on a certain false narrative that is difficult for them to abandon. The falsity can often be demonstrated, as Hammond shows, not by citing sources critical of Israel, but by citing journalists, historians, and politicians who are themselves Jews, Zionists, or Israelis—a fact that, perhaps perversely, makes me proud of being a Jew. We are a candid people, who tell it like it is.

I found *Obstacle to Peace* quite convincing, but my pride in being Jewish and American, and my identification with many Israelis, remains intact. That should not be a difficult feat. If Zionists and Israelis committed unjust and even heinous acts, that hardly makes them unique in light of what Winston Churchill once called "the dark and lamentable catalogue of human crime." Nor does it make the history of Israel very different from that of many other nations, including the US. My pride in being Jewish is not diminished by knowl-

* Gene Epstein is Economics and Books Editor at *Barron's*, the financial weekly.

edge of these facts, just as my contempt for Jew-haters is not diminished when they cite the crimes of Israel to justify their anti-Semitism.

People have told me that I "don't support Israel" because of my views. They might as well level that accusation against the Israeli Peace Now movement, Shalom Achshav, established in 1978, and its sister organization, Americans for Peace Now. Those who subscribe to the mythic version of events are in effect condemning Israelis and Palestinians to a permanent state of war. With supporters like that, neither side may need antagonists.

* * *

Confronting a few key myths and accepting a few shocking facts helps pave the way to read *Obstacle to Peace*.

Start with facts about the origins of Israel. There was never any illusion among Zionists that Palestine, according to the legendary slogan, was "a land without a people for a people without a land." At the outset, the Zionist view was that non-Jewish residents had to be dispossessed of their land in order to establish a Jewish state.

Theodore Herzl, known as the father of modern Zionism, wrote in his diary in 1895, "We shall have to spirit the penniless population across the border, by procuring employment for it in the transit countries, while denying it any employment in our own country. Both the process of expropriation and the removal of the poor must be carried out discreetly and circumspectly."

Herzl's proposed discretion and circumspection eventually proved unworkable. David Ben-Gurion, later to become Israel's first prime minister, declared in 1938, "My approach to the solution of the question of the Arabs in the Jewish state is their transfer to Arab countries." By way of clarification, Ben-Gurion said, "I am for compulsory transfer. I do not see anything immoral in it."[1]

Since the areas where Jews had legally purchased land amounted to less than 7 percent of the territory of Palestine, compulsory transfer became viewed as the only option. According to the candid account of former Israeli Foreign Minister Shlomo Ben-Ami in *Foreign Affairs*, "the noble Jewish dream of statehood was stained by the sins of Israel's birth." Those sins involved "the often violent expulsion of 700,000 Arabs as Jewish soldiers conquered villages and towns throughout Palestine."

Quoting Ben-Gurion as declaring in October 1948, "The Arabs of the Land of Israel have only one function left to them—to run away," Ben-Ami notes, "And run they did; panic-stricken, they fled in the face of massacres in Ein Zeitun and Eliabun, just as they had done in the wake of an earlier massacre in Deir Yassin. Operational orders, such as the instruction from Moshe Carmel, the Israeli commander of the northern front, to 'attack in order to conquer, to kill among the men, to destroy and burn the villages,' were carved into the col-

lective memory of the Palestinians, spawning hatred and resentment for generations."

Ben-Ami adds, "Palestinian refugees were forced into the wilderness of exile, with no guarantee of a new national home and no prospect of returning to
their native land. The yearning for return thus became the Palestinian's defining
national ethos."[2]

Israeli historian Benny Morris has opined, "Ben-Gurion was right. . . . A
Jewish state would not have come into being without the uprooting of 700,000
Palestinians. Therefore it was necessary to uproot them."[3]

A revisionist story about the Palestinian Arabs was promulgated in 1984 by
American journalist Joan Peters in her book, *From Time Immemorial*. According to Peters, a large share of these people were not indigenous to Palestine, but
were themselves immigrants—lured by the economic opportunities created by
the Zionist settlers—and therefore had no more right to the land than the Jews
who migrated to Palestine.

Peters' work was exposed as fraudulent by scholars, most notably Norman
Finkelstein and the Israeli historian Yehoshua Porath—another case of Jews
telling it like it is. But even if not fraudulent, it would hardly justify the violent
expulsion that Ben-Gurion had ordered.

Similarly problematic is another myth: that the Palestinians fled voluntarily
because they were exhorted to do so by Arab states, which needed them gone
in order to clear the field for their invading armies. Even if that were true, it
could hardly justify preventing the Palestinians from returning to their land
once the shooting stopped. Citing the "scrupulous research" of Benny Morris,
former minister Ben-Ami writes that "the 1948 expulsion of the Palestinian
Arabs was in no small measure driven by a desire for land among Israeli settlers,
who grabbed it and then actively pressured the Arab refugees from returning to
their villages."[4]

One solution to the Palestinian problem that I have frequently heard is that
the Palestinians must all move to Jordan, Lebanon, or other places where Arabs
reside. If Jordan opens its doors, and if the Palestinians decide to move there,
no one could object. By similar logic, no one could object if the US offers open
immigration to the Israeli Jews and they respond by moving en masse to the
US—where, after all, many Jews have prospered. But forcible transfer in either
case is a very different matter.

* * *

Based on the above facts, we are left with the tragic irony that ethnic cleansing
has been perpetrated on the Palestinian Arabs by Jews, who had themselves
been victims of ethnic cleansing for centuries. Recall Israeli foreign minister
Ben Ami's acknowledgement that these horrors "were carved into the collective

memory of the Palestinians." There must be Palestinians still alive whose collective memory is drawn from first-hand experience of the awful events. There is no way for Jews, of all people, to justify these crimes—or to maintain that they were justified by the greater good of creating a Jewish state.

Historian Benny Morris makes that very argument, going so far as to assert that Ben-Gurion's only "mistake" was that the ethnic cleansing was not total. "If the end of the story turns out to be a gloomy one for the Jews," Morris said in an interview, "it will be because Ben-Gurion did not complete the transfer in 1948."[5] And in *My Promised Land*, a best-seller in the US, Israeli journalist Ari Shavit takes a similar position.

Citing in *My Promised Land* the forcible expulsion in 1948 of 30,000 Palestinians from the town of Lydda, Shavit acknowledges that what happened was a "human catastrophe" that offered grounds to be "horrified." But he still asserts that "the conquest of Lydda and the expulsion of Lydda were . . . an inevitable phase of the Zionist revolution that laid the foundation for the Zionist state." Therefore, he concludes, "when I try to be honest about it, I see that the choice is stark: either reject Zionism because of Lydda, or accept Zionism along with Lydda."

Shavit chooses to "accept Zionism along with Lydda," based on Zionism's transcendent goal of establishing a haven for Jews. As noted, the morality of that viewpoint should be especially repugnant to Jews, whose ancestors have been victimized by countless Lyddas over their history.

In any case, another tragic irony is that the haven dream has been an abject failure. We Jews of New York City arguably live in safer circumstances than our counterparts in Jerusalem. Even Shavit seems to agree. The first sentence of *My Promised Land* reads, "For as long as I remember, I remember fear," by which he means fear of Israel's enemies. Later, he writes, "The Jewish state is a frontier oasis surrounded by a desert of threat."[6] *Obstacle to Peace* amply demonstrates that the metaphor is a caricature and that Israel has posed a greater threat to its neighbors than vice versa; but Israel's policies have indeed served to escalate the threat of terrorism against Israeli Jews.

* * *

It doesn't have to be this way. Hammond argues in this book for a two-state solution, with Israel withdrawing to its pre-1967 borders, and with a Palestinian state comprising Gaza, the West Bank, and East Jerusalem.

"Pre-1967" refers to the 1967 war, when land was taken by Israel through conquest. Any such reference touches a nerve: Didn't Israel fight that war because the army of Nasser's Egypt was about to attack and invade? In fact, the real history of Israel's conflicts with Arab governments is far more complex than the conventional history makes it out to be.

On the origins of the 1967 war, we have it on the authority of Israeli Prime Minister Menachem Begin, who was a member of the cabinet at the time, that Israel started that war. "The Egyptian army concentrations in the Sinai approaches do not prove that Nasser was really about to attack us," observed Begin in a 1982 talk delivered at Israel's National Defense College. "We must be honest with ourselves. We decided to attack him."[7]

But let's even accept the myth that the Arab governments were always the irrational aggressors in these conflicts. There is an absurd non sequitur I have often heard that conflates the actions of the Palestinians with those of Arab governments, and thus characterizes the Palestinians as irrational aggressors. But, obviously, these governments acted in their own interests and could hardly be expected to care very much about, or be very influenced by, the interests of a weak and stateless people.

Apart from that, there is the deep-seated conviction among so many skeptics I've spoken with that the Palestinian Arabs who threaten Israel are in general so depraved, and so intractable, that negotiating with them is next to impossible. Is not Hamas—a name that is practically synonymous with "terrorist"—bent on the destruction of Israel? How could Israel possibly consider sharing a border with a state that is populated with such people?

Regarding the two-state solution, a friend asked me, "Does Israel have a legitimate concern that it might be attacked by a Palestinian state if it has an army?" He clearly thought the answer was "Yes." But the question assumes that the Palestinians are inherently prone to violence, since no violent acts on their part could have been reactive, defensive, or motivated by grievances about having long been denied their rights.

But let's imagine that even after the Palestinians' legitimate claims are met, the worst and most violent elements take control of the Palestinian state, and it then launches a foolhardy attack on Israel. Given the balance of power, the outcome of such a conflict would be similar to the US having to deal with an attempt at military invasion by Mexico. And once you read *Obstacle to Peace*, you might think that the risks of a two-state solution are mainly on the other side.

I was once told by an Israeli immigrant to the US—a quite sophisticated entrepreneur—that the ethical code of the Palestinians is stuck in the 19th century. I did not want to spoil our social evening, and so did not point out that any random sampling of statements from Israeli settlers in the West Bank—a highly influential group—makes it clear that their own moral code dates back to ancient times.

According to an article in *Haaretz*, a West Bank rabbi named Yitzhak Shapiro has published a book called *The King's Torah*, based on "passages quoted from the Bible, to which he adds his opinions and beliefs." Among his opinions: "If we kill a Gentile who has sinned or has violated one of the seven commandments—because we care about the commandments—there is nothing wrong with the murder." The article adds that the book has "had wide dissemination and the enthusiastic endorsements of prominent rabbis."[8]

We speak of Islamic fundamentalism, but Old Testament fundamentalism gives it stiff competition. Menachem Begin, for example, was a fervent advocate of the right of the Israeli settlers to take over the West Bank based on divine providence. As *Mother Jones* has noted, "The active alliance between evangelical Christians, American Jewish organizations, and conservative Israeli leaders dates to the tenure of Prime Minister Menachem Begin, who took office in 1977. Begin and his Likud Party used religious arguments to justify confiscation of Arab land . . . ."[9]

Begin had been head of the Irgun, a terrorist organization that blew up the King David Hotel in Jerusalem in 1946. Another Israeli prime minister, Yitzhak Shamir, had been one of the leaders of another terrorist group, the Stern Gang. Together with the Irgun, the Stern Gang had participated in the infamous massacre in 1948 of Palestinians in the village of Deir Yassin.[10]

I have been told by another critic, a quite brilliant quant in the investment field, that Palestinian militants target civilians, while Israel's military tries to minimize civilian casualties. His willingness to believe such claims about Israel's intentions seems to be inseparable from his view that, unlike the Palestinian economy, the Israeli economy has spawned tech start-ups. It is not very likely that any government officials would baldly state their intention to kill civilians. But as Hammond points out, given Israel's clear aim in these conflicts to terrorize the population, together with its targeted destruction of civilian infrastructure, we can hardly call it coincidence that the civilian death toll attributed to Israel is orders of magnitude higher than any attributed to the Palestinians.

Hamas should certainly expunge from its charter inflammatory rhetoric calling for the elimination of Israel, and all Palestinian groups should repudiate all terrorist acts inflicted on Israel. But then, Israeli leaders should publicly repudiate their own tradition of religious fundamentalism, ethnic cleansing, hate-mongering—and the far greater terrorism that has marked its own actions.

A case can be made that the Palestinians have met the Israelis more than halfway on these issues. As Hammond reports, when Prime Minister Benjamin Netanyahu demanded that the Palestinians recognize Israel as a "Jewish state"—a racially-tinged statement that seems to codify the second-class status of Israel's non-Jewish citizens—the Palestinian Authority replied, "We officially demand that the US administration and the Israeli government provide a map of the borders of the state of Israel which they want us to recognize. . . . If this map is based on the 1967 borders and provides for the end of the Israeli occupation over all Palestinian lands . . . then we recognize Israel by whatever name it applies to itself in accordance with international law."[11]

As Hammond notes, it is quite possible that a Palestinian state would be led by the Palestinian Authority rather than by Hamas. He points out that Israel's policies serve to empower Hamas at the expense of the PA every time Israel launches a military operation against Gaza. So the idea that a Palestinian state might be dominated by Hamas is not a reason to continue existing Israeli policies, but a very strong argument for changing them.

Even Hamas has been misrepresented by the media. As Hammond writes in this book, "contrary to the obligatory claim that it sought Israel's 'destruction,' Hamas had in fact long declared its intention of seeking a Palestinian state *alongside Israel*—a position Hamas has reiterated constantly over the years." He then provides examples. No such reciprocal statements have been made by the Israeli government.[12] But that does not mean Israel's policies cannot change.

In *Common Sense*, Thomas Paine famously claimed for the American Revolution that "The sun never shined on a cause of greater worth." In *Obstacle to Peace*, Jeremy Hammond's claims are more modest. "The goal of this book," he writes, is to help "achieve an end to what is undoubtedly the most infamous of the world's longstanding international conflicts." As readers will find, *Obstacle to Peace* is filled with common sense.

Gene Epstein
November 2015

PREFACE

ON MAY 19, 2011, US President Barack Obama gave a speech outlining his administration's policy with regard to the Israeli-Palestinian conflict. In his speech was one sentence that the mainstream media found particularly remarkable: "We believe the borders of Israel and Palestine should be based on the 1967 lines with mutually agreed swaps, so that secure and recognized borders are established for both states."[1] Notwithstanding the fact that previous administrations had made similar statements, the consensus among American mainstream political commentators was that Obama's remarks constituted a "shift" in US policy.[2] What was truly remarkable about this episode, however, was how well it illustrated the extraordinary institutional myopia and cognitive dissonance among the American intelligentsia.

It requires no extensive knowledge of the subject to be able to see it. All one need know is that there is something called "the two-state solution" to the Israeli-Palestinian conflict, according to which a final agreement on borders between Israel and an independent state of Palestine should be based on what are called the "1967 lines", also known as the 1949 armistice lines or the "Green Line" for the color with which it was drawn on the map. With no additional knowledge, one may draw an obvious corollary to the claim that Obama's statement marked a change in US policy. Logically, this must mean that until this policy "shift" occurred, the US had *rejected* the idea that an agreement on borders should be based on the 1967 lines. Incredibly, mainstream media commentators declared this shift even while universally maintaining the belief that US policy had *always* been supportive of the two-state solution.

Indeed, pretense to the contrary notwithstanding, the US has long joined Israel in rejecting the two-state solution, in favor of which there is otherwise a consensus in the international community.[3] Moreover, US policy has remained rejectionist under the Obama administration. Obama's celebrated reference to the "1967 lines" must be understood within the context of the events and developments of recent years, as well as within the historical context of what is known as the US-Israel "special relationship". It is only by separating Obama's rhetoric from the facts on the ground that political commentators are able to announce that his words demonstrate a US policy commitment to the establishment of a viable independent state of Palestine in accordance with the international consensus on a two-state solution. If, however, one assesses US policy based on the ancient wisdom "You will know them by their fruits" and analyzes the Obama administration's policy based on deeds rather than rhetoric, it becomes clear that his remarks represented absolute continuity of the longstanding US policy of rejecting the two-state solution for the Israeli-Palestinian conflict.

Indeed, it is clear just from Obama's "1967 lines" rhetoric alone, if one knows how to decipher his very careful choice of wording, that US policy is rejectionist in nature. By the time you are done reading this book, you will be able to do so.

The mainstream American media maintain the pretense that the role of the US in the conflict is an indispensable one. It is an article of faith that the US government seeks a peaceful two-state resolution and acts out of benevolence to achieve that end. Yet it should be plainly obvious to any rational observer that, far from being an "honest broker" in what is dubbed "the peace process", the US is one of the primary obstacles to a peaceful resolution and, arguably, *the* primary obstacle (hence this book's title, borrowed from the euphemistic description used variously by government officials to describe either Israel's illegal settlement activities or the Palestinian leadership). Indeed, setting aside illusions, the so-called "peace process" is transparently intended to *prevent* the implementation of the two-state solution. US and Israeli government officials may speak favorably of *a* two-state solution, yet they vigorously oppose *the* two-state solution. It must be understood that the "solution" the US and Israel are trying to enforce is *not* consistent with the international consensus. Their policies are not premised on the equal rights of all human beings and are not intended to achieve the fulfillment of a just settlement through application of international law. Rather, their policies are designed to subjugate Palestinians to their will through political force and violence. It is a foundational assumption of the US and Israeli governments that the Palestinians must surrender their rights under international law and bow to their demands.

While this reality should be self-evident, academics and mainstream media commentators dutifully choose not to see it, preferring instead to propagate a fictional narrative in which the US government is hailed for its benevolence and indispensable efforts to achieve peace. The media thus effectively serve to manufacture consent for US policy. The media's propaganda is highly effective. When I witnessed the response to Obama's "1967 lines" speech, I began writing this book in earnest to be able to provide an antidote.

The purpose of this book is to systematically deconstruct the US mainstream narrative about the Israel-Palestine conflict and to reconstruct a proper framework for discussion moving forward. It is to empower with knowledge anyone who is truly interested in seeing peace and justice prevail. Whether you are a peace activist, a blogger, a journalist, an academic, a politician, or just a concerned citizen of the world, this book provides you with the knowledge required to make a difference and help change the nature of the debate. The goal of this book is to effect the paradigm shift necessary to be able to achieve an end to what is undoubtedly the most infamous of the world's longstanding international conflicts.

The common view is that the Israeli-Palestinian conflict is intractable. There is some truth to this. Under the existing framework, it *is*. But it needn't be. A peaceful solution to the conflict need not be a distant dream. It can be realized. But for that to happen, government policy, as well as the very nature of the mainstream discussion about the conflict, needs to change. *You* can help make that happen by consuming the knowledge contained in this book and then *acting* on it. Any caring individual can use their own unique knowledge and skills to play a role in the collective effort to raise awareness about the true nature of the conflict, the reasons for its persistence, and what needs to happen for peace to be achieved. Without individuals choosing to accept that critical role, peace will remain elusive. Government isn't going to get the job done. Bringing peace to the Middle East is up to *us*.

While I set out writing this book after witnessing the media's reaction to Obama's "1967 lines" speech, it had its origins several years prior. At the end of June 2008, I wrote that the six-month ceasefire between Israel and the Palestinian group Hamas would end with a full-scale military assault by Israel on the Gaza Strip. I commented about how Israel had engaged in numerous actions that "seem designed to bring about hostile response which would give Israel a *casus belli* to invade Gaza. In the event of any such invasion, Israel will claim that it had exhausted diplomacy. Israel has made sure that the cease-fire is unsustainable. But it is beneficial as it would be used as political cover for future military action."[4] When Israel commenced "Operation Cast Lead", I continued to write about events as they unfolded. This work ultimately led to my receipt of a Project Censored award for my focus on the US role in supporting Israel's assault on Gaza.[5] As I watched the establishment media create an at best misleading and at times wholly fictitious narrative of unfolding events, I became determined to write a book to set the record straight.

But to do that, I thought, I would need to explain to readers the historical context and examine the roots of the conflict and major events since, such as the watershed 1967 Arab-Israeli war. So I set out further researching and writing about the conflict's origins, which led me to splinter my original concept and publish a short book titled *The Rejection of Palestinian Self-Determination: The Struggle for Palestine and the Roots of the Israeli-Arab Conflict.*[6] I wrote a paper titled "The Myth of the UN Creation of Israel" that received some attention in the Israeli media when the newspaper *Arutz Sheva* asked Hebrew University lecturer Dr. Mordechai Nisan to respond to it. His response was particularly remarkable for the fact that he dismissed the paper as "a sophist-style 'scholarly' refutation of the international foundation for Israel's establishment in 1948", while at the same time admitting that my paper's thesis is *correct*.[7]

As events unfolded under the Obama administration, I kept my original book idea in mind, but it evolved and expanded. Then came Obama's "1967 lines" speech, and I was compelled to finally put pen to paper (figuratively speaking; more literally, finger to keyboard), not only to set the record straight on Israel's assault on Gaza and the US's support for Israel's war crimes during that operation, but also to examine the broader role of the US in the ongoing conflict.

Among the countless other challenges in taking on such an ambitious project, I faced difficult decisions about how to organize the prodigious amount of material I wanted to cover. It was not my intent to write a comprehensive history of the conflict from its origins until today, or to retread ground already covered extensively by other authors. Yet, I knew the book would still need to provide crucial historical context. How could that be done? I decided rather than starting in the past and working my way forward through events chronologically, I would begin with more recent events and insert historical background where necessary for understanding the past's influence on the present.

As another example, I knew the first part of the book would focus on Operation Cast Lead, but how would I compile the information? I could weave all my source materials together to tell the story of what actually happened; but I felt it was just as important to tell the story of how it was reported. There is a tendency to view the media as apart from the conflict, as though sources like the *New York Times* were merely passive observers providing consumers with the knowledge required to have an informed opinion. I wanted to shatter this illusion. The media did not merely provide source material, but was itself an essential part of the story that needed to be told. Hence, I decided to produce a narrative almost entirely from material available *at that time*. For example, one important source is the UN Fact-Finding Mission on the Gaza Conflict, popularly known as "the Goldstone Report", which I did not use as a source for the chapter on Operation Cast Lead (Chapter 2). The Goldstone Report, too, was not merely an informational resource, but an important part of the story that deserved a chapter of its own (Chapter 5).

Similarly, I initially considered having a chapter specific for certain aspects of the conflict. I could have written, for example, a single chapter dedicated to Operation Cast Lead, one to the "peace process", one to Israel's siege of Gaza, one to the role of the media, and so on. But to so divide the book into such neat sections would be to try to separate aspects of the conflict that in reality are intertwined and must be understood not apart from each other, but in a greater context as a whole. How could one understand the "peace process" and Israel's illegal settlements as something distinct and separate from, say, Israel's assault on Gaza or its attack on the humanitarian flotilla in May 2010? How could one understand the role of the media *separately* from what happened during Operation Cast Lead, when the media's role was such a significant part of the story that needed to be told? Etc.

Accordingly, I chose early on to tell the story chronologically not in terms of what exactly happened and when, but rather in terms of *how* the fictional mainstream narrative I was setting out to deconstruct had been shaped. Thus, instead of confining various topics to particular chapters, I return to them throughout the book. Likewise, instead of providing historical context first and then moving on to recent events, the narrative jumps into the past as appropriate or necessary to provide the background. Organizing material this way would also serve to remind how history remains relevant for understanding the present (something mainstream commentators often seem conveniently forgetful of).

This book covers a lot of material. It has often overwhelmed me in writing it. It is my hope that I have put it all together in a way that does not do the same to the reader. Although it would certainly help, I have tried to write the book so as not to require an extensive prior knowledge of the subject to be able to understand it. I also wanted it to be accessible to a broader audience, including those who may have only the most basic understanding (or misunderstanding) about the conflict, but who are willing to commit the time to developing a well-informed opinion. The nature of the material, as well as the sizeable commitment of the government and mainstream media to preventing such, has not made this an easy task. But I have done my best. The reader may judge whether I've succeeded.

CHAPTER 1

THE RISE OF HAMAS IN GAZA

I N DECEMBER 1987, A MASS uprising of the Palestinian people began against the military occupation of their territory by the state of Israel that became known as the first "intifada", an Arabic word meaning "throwing off". In September 1988, the *New York Times* reported on "the first serious split of the nine-month-old Palestinian uprising". The previous month, a new organization had published its charter. The group went by the name "Hamas", an acronym for Harakat al-Muqawama al-Islamiya, or Islamic Resistance Movement, and it had quickly become "a major force in the Gaza Strip". Hamas was critical of the Palestine Liberation Organization (PLO) and posed a threat to its secular leadership under Yasser Arafat. This was complicating efforts to pressure Arafat to negotiate a peace agreement with the occupying power.

Nevertheless, the Israeli government had "taken no direct action against Hamas", which led to a belief among many Palestinians that Hamas was "being tolerated by the Israeli security forces in hopes of splitting the uprising". This was a tactic, the *Times* noted, that Israel had used before.[1] Reportedly, Israel had even funded Hamas's parent organization, Mujama al-Islamiya, which was legally registered in Israel by Hamas founder Sheikh Ahmed Yassin nearly a decade before.[2] The US State Department observed how "some Israeli occupation officials indicated that Hamas served as a useful counter to the secular organizations loyal to the PLO."[3] As a result, the US conceded, "Israeli forces may be turning a blind eye to Hamas activities".[4]

Hamas would go on to deserve its reputation as a terrorist organization. In April 1994, Hamas claimed responsibility for the first Palestinian suicide bombing, carried out in retaliation for the murder of twenty-nine Muslims in a mosque in Hebron by Baruch Goldstein, a Jewish settler armed with an assault rifle.[5]

While it might at first seem inexplicable that Israel would lend its tacit sup-port for Hamas's rise, there is a logical explanation: the main problem confront-ing Israel was the threat of peace. The PLO had changed course, renouncing ter-rorism in favor of political engagement. It had dangerously joined the interna-tional consensus on the two-state solution for the Israeli-Palestinian conflict.

This international consensus is based on the principle of international law that it is inadmissible for a state to acquire territory by war. Consequently, Israel is required by law to withdraw from the territories occupied during the June 1967 "Six Day War", which include the Palestinian territories of the West Bank and the Gaza Strip. In the aftermath of the 1967 war, this requirement was emphasized in United Nations Security Council Resolution 242, as well as numerous subsequent resolutions, including Resolution 338 (which called for a ceasefire to end the October 1973 Arab-Israeli war, or the Yom Kippur War, as it is known in Israel).

While initially it was presumed that the occupied West Bank and Gaza Strip would return to the states under whose administration they had previously been subject (Jordan and Egypt, respectively), in accordance with the right to self-determination explicitly recognized in the UN Charter, the consensus quickly evolved to envision the establishment of an independent Palestinian state along-side Israel on the basis of the pre-June 1967 boundaries (also known as the 1949 armistice lines, or the "Green Line" for the color in which it was drawn on the map), with minor and mutually agreed revisions to the final border.

The primary threat to Israel, given its goal of retaining as much of the oc-cupied territory as politically feasible, was manifest on November 15, 1988, when the legislative body of the PLO, the Palestinian National Council (PNC), proclaimed the independent state of Palestine in Algiers, Algeria. The PNC attached a political communiqué to the declaration accepting UN Security Council Resolutions 242 and 338 as the basis for a peace settlement.[6] "We totally and absolutely renounce all forms of terrorism", Arafat declared the fol-lowing month, "including individual, group and state terrorism."[7]

When Arafat was invited to address the General Assembly at the UN head-quarters in New York City, the US refused to issue him a visa. So he was invited to address the Assembly instead from Geneva, Switzerland, where he called on the international community to stand by the Palestinian people in their struggle to exercise the right to self-determination, as well as to uphold the right of Arab refugees expelled from Palestine in 1948 to return to their homeland—rights rejected by Israel as contrary to both its colonial project in the occupied ter-ritories and its domestic character as a "Jewish state". Arafat said that Palestine, for its part, was "a state which believes in the settlement of international and regional disputes by peaceful means in accordance with the charter and reso-lutions of the United Nations." He again reiterated the PLO's acceptance of Resolutions 242 and 338 as the basis for a peace agreement.

As a legal basis for its declaration of independence, the PLO also cited UN General Assembly Resolution 181 of November 29, 1947. The declaration characterized this resolution as having "partitioned Palestine". In his address to the Assembly, Arafat described Resolution 181 as "the only birth certificate" for the state of Israel and reminded that it had called for the establishment of *two* states.[8]

However, it must be emphasized that the popular claim that the UN created the state of Israel by partitioning Palestine is a myth.[9]

UN General Assembly Resolution 181

Resolution 181 was a product of the United Kingdom's attempt to extract itself from the conflict situation that its policies had helped create under the League of Nations' Palestine Mandate, which effectively recognized the UK as the occupying power in Palestine after World War I. At the request of Britain to intervene, the UN General Assembly on May 15, 1947, adopted Resolution 106, which established the UN Special Committee on Palestine (UNSCOP) to investigate "the question of Palestine" and make recommendations.[10]

On September 3, UNSCOP issued its report to the General Assembly, stating its majority recommendation that Palestine be partitioned into separate Jewish and Arab states. The report noted that the population of Palestine at the end of 1946 was estimated to be almost 1,846,000, with 1,203,000 Arabs (65 percent) and 608,000 Jews (33 percent). Growth of the Jewish population had been mainly the result of immigration, while growth of the Arab population had been "almost entirely" due to natural increase. It observed that there was "no clear territorial separation of Jews and Arabs by large contiguous areas". Even in the Jaffa district, which included Tel Aviv, Arabs were a majority.[11]

Moreover, the Jewish population in the area of the proposed Jewish state was 498,000, while the number of Arabs was 407,000, plus an estimated 105,000 Bedouins, bringing the total Arab population to approximately 512,000. "In other words," noted the report of a subcommittee established by the General Assembly to follow up on UNSCOP's recommendation, "at the outset, the Arabs will have a majority in the proposed Jewish State." The subcommittee also noted that population distribution was closely connected with "the factor of land ownership in the proposed Jewish State"—meaning that even *within* the borders of the "Jewish State", Arabs would own more land than Jews.[12]

An UNSCOP survey of land ownership cited 1943 statistics showing that of Palestine's total land area (26,320,505 dunams), Arabs and other non-Jews owned nearly 94 percent (24,670,455 dunams). By contrast, the Jews owned only 5.8 percent (1,514,247 dunams).[13] Land ownership statistics for 1945 likewise showed that Arabs owned more land than Jews in every single district in Palestine. The district with the highest percentage of Jewish ownership was

Jaffa, where 39 percent of the land was owned by Jews, compared to 47 percent owned by Arabs. Jews owned less than 5 percent of the land in eight out of the sixteen districts.[14] Even by the end of the Mandate in 1948, according to the Jewish National Fund (a quasi-governmental organization founded in 1901 to purchase land for Jewish settlement), the Jewish community had acquired only about 6.9 percent (1,820,000 dunams) of the total land area of Palestine.[15]

As the UNSCOP report noted, "The Arab population, despite the strenuous efforts of Jews to acquire land in Palestine, at present remains in possession of approximately 85 percent of the land."[16] And as the subcommittee report observed, "The bulk of the land in the Arab State, *as well as in the proposed Jewish State*, is owned and possessed by Arabs" (emphasis added).[17]

UNSCOP nevertheless made the prima facie inequitable recommendation that the Arab state be constituted from about 44 percent of the whole of Palestine, while the Jews would be awarded more than 55 percent for their state.[18] In other words, the partition plan called for expropriating land from Arabs in order to redistribute it to Jews. Whatever the Arabs might have thought about this plan was not given much consideration. In fact, the UNSCOP report *explicitly rejected* the right of self-determination for the Arab Palestinians, despite it being a universal right recognized under the UN Charter. The "principle of self-determination" was "not applied to Palestine," the report stated, "obviously because of the intention to make possible the creation of the Jewish National Home there. Actually, it may well be said that the Jewish National Home and the *sui generis* Mandate for Palestine run counter to that principle."[19]

The members of UNSCOP were thus perfectly cognizant of the fact that the partition proposal was a violation of the rights of the Arabs, as well as contrary to the very Charter under which they were acting. This didn't stop a majority from pushing through their recommendation for partition—an indication of the colonial and racist framework within which these countries' respective policymakers were still operating. The very composition of UNSCOP reflected this. The UN at the time consisted of fifty-five members, including Egypt, Iraq, Lebanon, and Syria; yet, no representatives from any Arab nation were included. Palestine remained the only one of the formerly Mandated Territories not to be recognized as an independent state. Egypt, Iraq, Syria, Lebanon, and Saudi Arabia requested that the termination of the Mandate and recognition of Palestine's independence be placed on the UN agenda, but this motion was rejected. The Arab Higher Committee, the central political body of the Arab community in Palestine, announced that it would not participate in the Palestinians' own disenfranchisement by collaborating with UNSCOP. Officials from neighboring Arab states, on the other hand, did agree to meet with UNSCOP representatives.[20]

The UK issued a statement saying that it agreed with the partition recommendation, but that it could not be implemented unless it was agreed to by both sides.[21] Being inherently unjust, the plan was doomed from the start. The Arab Higher Committee naturally rejected it and maintained that the independence of Palestine must be recognized and a democratic state formed "which would respect human rights, fundamental freedoms and equality of all persons before the law, and would protect the legitimate rights and interests of all minorities whilst guaranteeing freedom of worship and access to the Holy Places." This proposal, which mirrored the minority recommendation of the UNSCOP report, was rejected by the Zionist leadership. (The political movement to establish a national homeland for the Jewish people is known as Zionism. The Austro-Hungarian journalist Theodor Herzl first outlined this project in a pamphlet titled *The Jewish State* in 1896 and is considered the movement's founder).[22]

After receiving the UNSCOP report, the General Assembly established the Ad Hoc Committee on the Palestinian Question, which echoed UNSCOP's minority recommendation by appropriately rejecting the partition plan as being "contrary to the principles of the [UN] Charter". It recommended instead that Palestine's independence be recognized. The UN had "no power to give effect to" the partition plan and could not "deprive the majority of the people of Palestine of their country and transfer it to the exclusive use of a minority in the country".[23]

The General Assembly nevertheless proceeded to adopt Resolution 181, which recommended that the partition plan be implemented. To that end, it referred the matter to the Security Council, *where it died*. On February 24, 1948, the US ambassador to the UN, Warren Austin, likewise observed that the only way the plan could be implemented was through the use of force, and the Security Council had no authority to use force to partition Palestine against the will of the majority of its inhabitants.[24] On March 19, Austin further observed that war was brewing and expected to erupt when the British Mandate over Palestine came to an end on May 14. He argued that the UN *did* have authority to intervene, with force if necessary, to prevent this foreseen breach of international peace.[25]

The Security Council, however, took no action. Ethnic cleansing operations by the Zionist forces had already been underway for several months. By the time the Mandate came to an end, 200 Arab towns and villages had been destroyed and a quarter of a million Palestinians had fled or been forcibly expelled.[26] The same day the Mandate expired, May 14, 1948, the Zionist leadership under David Ben-Gurion unilaterally declared the existence of the State of Israel, citing Resolution 181 as constituting "recognition by the United Nations of the right of the Jewish people to establish their State".[27] It bears reemphasizing that contrary to popular misconception, Resolution 181 neither partitioned Palestine nor conferred upon the Zionist leadership any legal authority to declare the state of Israel.

As anticipated, the violence erupted into full-scale war as the neighboring Arab states mustered armed forces to intervene. By the end of the Israeli campaign of conquest and ethnic cleansing, more than 750,000 Palestinians—over half of Palestine's Arab population—had fled or were driven from their homes. When the armistice lines were drawn in 1949, Israeli territory exceeded that allotted to it under the partition recommendation, leaving the Arabs in possession of merely 22 percent of the land in Palestine. To Israelis, this was a "War of Independence". To the Palestinians, it was the "*Nakba*"—their "catastrophe".[28]

The Threat of Peace

The PLO's citation of Resolution 181 in its own declaration of independence was arguably a regrettable strategic error. It unwittingly undermined the Palestinians' position by perpetuating the false belief that Israel was established by the UN through a legitimate political process. It also implied that Palestinian self-determination was *derived* from this resolution when it must rather be recognized as a natural right—a right that had, in fact, been explicitly rejected under the inequitable partition plan. On the other hand, citing Resolution 181, just as the Zionists had done, served to remind Israel that the General Assembly had recommended the establishment of *two* states. Israel could not without hypocrisy reject this rationale since it was relied upon as the legal basis for its own founding document.

Regardless of the wisdom of citing Resolution 181 as a legal basis for Palestinian statehood, it should be stressed that the PLO's declaration of independence represented a major concession on the part of the Palestinians. The PLO was effectively agreeing to accept Israel's existence on land formerly belonging mostly to Arabs as a fait accompli and to establish their own state in just 22 percent of the remaining former territory of Palestine comprising East Jerusalem, the West Bank, and the Gaza Strip.[29]

The PLO's accession to the two-state solution on the basis of the 1949 armistice lines posed a threat to Israel's occupation and colonization project. Thus, Israel's support for Hamas as a force to counter the PLO followed from the political calculus that the ultimate threat to Israel was not that of terrorism, but the possibility of having to give up the dream of establishing *Eretz Yisrael*, the Land of Israel, in all of the territory of former Palestine. From the beginning, the key dilemma for the Zionists was how to establish this "Jewish state" in the fullest extent of land possible *without* the Palestinians, whose very existence posed an obstacle to this goal simply in terms of demographics; hence the initial ethnic cleansing of Palestine, as well as the subsequent ongoing displacement under the occupation regime that has been in place since 1967.

That the real threat to Israel has been that of peace achieved through implementation of the two-state solution is well evidenced by its policies and their predictable consequences. This is oftentimes the only rational explanation for Israel's actions. Its continued occupation, oppression, and violence toward the Palestinians have served to escalate the threat of terrorism against Israeli civilians, but this is a price Israeli leaders are willing to pay. Indeed, the threat of terrorism has often served as a necessary pretext to further goals that would not be politically feasible absent such a threat.

That Israel's policies have been counterproductive in terms of mitigating the threat of terrorism is hardly a controversial observation, but has long been recognized among Israel's own leadership. In October 2003, for example, the Chief of Staff of the Israel Defense Forces (IDF), Moshe Ya'alon, notably criticized the policies of Prime Minister Ariel Sharon because they served to increase hatred of Israel and strengthen terrorist organizations. The following month, four former chiefs of Israel's domestic security service, the Shin Bet, similarly spoke out, saying that Israel was headed in the direction of "catastrophe" and would destroy itself if it continued to take steps "that are contrary to the aspiration for peace", such as the continued oppression of Palestinians under Israeli occupation. "We must admit that there is another side," said Avraham Shalom, Shin Bet director from 1980 to 1986, "that it has feelings and that it is suffering, and that we are behaving disgracefully."[30]

But the policies continued, with Israel often acting violently to provoke a violent response, including its use of extrajudicial killings. On March 22, 2004, Israel assassinated Hamas founder Sheikh Ahmed Yassin, a quadriplegic. "I could not recognize the sheikh, only his wheelchair," said one witness to the attack. Palestinian Prime Minister Ahmed Qurei called it "a crazy and very dangerous act" that "opens the door wide to chaos" because "Yassin is known for his moderation, and he was controlling Hamas".[31] Analysts predicted that the assassination would "likely lead to increased violence against Israel in the form of retaliation attacks". Critics included members of Sharon's own government, such as Interior Minister Avraham Poraz, who made similar observations.[32]

Other predicted consequences also point to a much different rationale for the decision than the claimed pretext of fighting terrorism. Some experts argued that the assassination was in part "intended to build domestic support for a planned Israeli withdrawal from Gaza and part of the West Bank." But more importantly, the attack had "devastated prospects for a peace settlement in the Middle East".[33] That the true goal of the assassination was to undermine prospects for peace is further underscored by the fact that Yassin had just a short time prior said that "Hamas could accept a Palestinian state in the West Bank and Gaza Strip". He had also recently offered a long-term truce in exchange for withdrawal from the territories, described by the British newspaper *The Independent* as "a major shift in policy from Hamas"—a new policy that moved Hamas, like the PLO before it, closer to acceptance of the two-state solution.[34]

The Political Ascension of Hamas

While the Palestinian Authority (PA) under the presidencies of Yasser Arafat and his successor, Mahmoud Abbas, was increasingly seen as corrupt and ineffectual, willing to do the bidding of Israel and the US, Hamas was increasingly seen as a viable alternative that would clean up the corruption and more faithfully defend the rights of Palestinians as they pursued the goal of statehood. While the PA often seemed willing to put Palestinian rights on the negotiating table, Hamas refused the euphemistic demands of the US and Israel to give up the right to armed resistance against occupying military forces ("renounce violence") and to accede that the unilateral declaration of the establishment of the state of Israel in May 1948 and the ethnic cleansing of Palestine had been legitimate (recognize Israel's "right to exist").

In January 2005, the London *Guardian* reported "a turning point in Hamas's strategy" as it again suggested entering a long-term ceasefire with Israel and expressed the desire to achieve its aims through engagement in the political process.[35] With municipal elections scheduled to occur at the end of the month, the US State Department reported that Hamas was "Neck and Neck" with Fatah (the largest faction of the PLO and the political party of Mahmoud Abbas, who was elected president on January 9, two months after the death of Yasser Arafat). It also noted that "a majority of both Fatah and Hamas supporters" backed "a continuation of the ceasefire, ongoing talks with Israel, and a two-state solution." Hamas was largely seen by Palestinians "as more qualified to clean up corruption, resist occupation, and uphold societal values". Furthermore, the "lack of hope in the peace process may also contribute to support for Hamas."[36]

As the elections approached, Hamas also agreed to cease firing rockets and mortars into Israel while President Abbas negotiated a more comprehensive ceasefire that would end the Second Intifada, which had been ongoing since September 2000.[37]

On January 28, 2005, the election results were announced. It was an overwhelming victory for Hamas, which gained 75 out of 118 seats in ten local councils, with Fatah winning only 39 seats. Hamas continued to gain council seats in municipal elections in May. The ceasefire was concluded the following month. Hamas, while not a party to the agreement, said it would nevertheless maintain the cessation of hostilities.[38]

Rather than encouraging Hamas's engagement in the political process, however, Israel continued to seek to isolate the group. Instead of encouraging Hamas to moderate its behavior, Israel continued to attempt to provoke the group into a violent response. Israel sent the message to Hamas that its steps towards moderation and political engagement would bear no fruit. When Hamas cleaned the streets, Israeli bulldozers and tanks destroyed them, and when Hamas erected streetlights, Israeli soldiers shot them out.[39]

In August, Israel implemented its planned withdrawal from the Gaza Strip, demolishing its settlements rather than leaving the homes for Palestinians' use. The IDF completed evacuation of the settlements and withdrew by mid-September.[40]

Palestinians celebrated in the streets, and for nearly a week, no rockets were fired into Israel from Gaza. The ceasefire seemed to be holding. But on September 23, Israel launched a raid into a West Bank village, killing three members of Islamic Jihad for allegedly planning to fire rockets or mortars at Israeli settlements. President Abbas called the raid a "dangerous and unjustified action. We are exerting efforts to maintain the ceasefire and they are doing this action without any reason."[41]

Members of the Al-Quds Brigades, Islamic Jihad's military wing, retaliated by firing rockets into Israel from Gaza, the first such attack since the withdrawal. Issuing a statement accepting responsibility for the rocket fire, Islamic Jihad also reported an IDF Apache helicopter hovering over Gaza City. In nearby Jabaliya, Hamas was holding a rally celebrating the Israeli withdrawal when a truck exploded, killing 19 people and injuring more than 120. Israel denied responsibility, but Hamas claimed that an IDF helicopter had fired into the rally and proceeded to launch rockets into Israel. President Abbas and the Fatah Central Committee publicly blamed the deaths on Hamas, saying the blast was an accidental explosion of rockets on display in the back of the truck. Hamas insisted that the rockets were dummies containing no explosives. The Al-Aqsa Martyrs Brigades—a group that emerged as an offshoot of Fatah during the Second Intifada—likewise blamed Israel and accused the PA of treason. Israel responded to Hamas's rocket attacks by launching airstrikes into Gaza, killing four Hamas members. It also arrested over 200 Palestinians in the West Bank, mostly members of Hamas and Islamic Jihad. After two days of attacks, on September 25, Hamas announced that it would return to the ceasefire.[42]

Shortly thereafter, another round of municipal elections were held in the West Bank, with Hamas receiving nearly a third of the votes.[43] Parliamentary elections were scheduled for January 25, 2006. As they drew near, Hamas published a manifesto that Western news agencies found remarkable for its absence of any mention of a goal to eliminate Israel. Hamas candidate Ghazi Hamad said it reflected the group's position of seeking a Palestinian state along the 1967 lines. He said Hamas would not recognize that Israel had a "right to exist", but that it was seeking to shift strategy away from armed struggle to engagement in the political process. "Having Hamas inside the system is a positive development," said Palestinian cabinet minister Ghassan Khatib, "whereby they have to abide by the rules of the majority and respect the arguments of the administration they are part of, which includes a state built on 1967 borders. It will take time but Hamas will no longer have their own militia. It will be solely a political force."[44]

Israel and the US, however, had other plans and other goals. Israel initially announced that it would prevent Palestinians from casting ballots in occupied East Jerusalem, but then changed its position. Under the new rules dictated by the Occupying Power, Palestinians would be allowed to vote, but Hamas candidates couldn't appear on the ballot or campaign there. Three candidates who tried to do so were arrested.[45] The US spent $1.9 million through a program run by the US Agency for International Development (USAID) in an effort to bolster Fatah, a violation of Palestinian election law. USAID mission director for the Palestinian territories, James Bever, nevertheless characterized the program as an effort "to support the democratic process".[46] When the results of the election were in, despite US and Israeli efforts to sway the vote, Hamas had won 76 of 132 seats in the legislature.[47]

An editorial in the *New York Times* sensibly urged the US government to engage Hamas to encourage its evolution. It criticized the US and the European Union for having "equivocated" with the self-contradictory policy of pressing Israel "to allow Hamas to participate in the elections" while having also "threatened to cut aid and ties to a Hamas-dominated Palestinian Authority." Arguing that this was counterproductive, the *Times* continued:

> Hamas's participation in Palestinian politics is not necessarily a bad thing, and resisting it is very likely to do more harm than good. As a political party, Hamas revealed itself to be disciplined, pragmatic and surprisingly flexible. It fielded well-regarded candidates, including doctors and academics. In some cases, Hamas aligned itself with independents once affiliated with the secular Fatah party. And although the Hamas charter calls for the destruction of Israel and the liberation of Palestine "from the river to the sea," the party's campaign manifesto made no mention of these goals.

The US's refusal to engage in diplomacy with Hamas "will only further legitimize the party" and "could even give rise to violence", the *Times* foretold. Furthermore, "cutting off aid to the Palestinian Authority, which is already in a fiscal crisis and enormously dependent on foreign aid, could bankrupt it, further destabilizing the region."[48]

But the US and Israel had already set their course. Despite the predicted consequences, acting Israeli Prime Minister Ehud Olmert announced that Israel "will not negotiate with a Palestinian administration if even part of it is an armed terrorist organization calling for the destruction of the state of Israel".[49] Former Israeli Foreign Minister Shlomo Ben-Ami similarly assured that the election results "have definitely brought an end to the peace process".[50]

Rather than calling for Israel's destruction, however, the top Hamas official in Gaza, Mahmoud al-Zahar, said that if Israel was ready to withdraw from the occupied territories, release their prisoners, stop its aggression, and make a "geographic link between the Gaza Strip and West Bank," then Hamas was ready to accept the establishment of an independent state of Palestine along the 1967 lines and to enter a long-term truce to see what Israel's "real intention" was.[51]

Hamas was "ready to make a just peace," wrote the head of Hamas's political bureau, Khaled Meshal, in an op-ed in the British newspaper *The Guardian*. However,

> The day Hamas won the Palestinian democratic elections the world's leading democracies failed the test of democracy. Rather than recognize the legitimacy of Hamas as a freely elected representative of the Palestinian people, seize the opportunity created by the result to support the development of good governance in Palestine and search for a means of ending the bloodshed, the US and EU threatened the Palestinian people with collective punishment for exercising their right to choose their parliamentary representatives. . . . We shall never recognize the right of any power to rob us of our land and deny us our national rights. . . . But if you are willing to accept the principle of a long-term truce, we are prepared to negotiate the terms. Hamas is extending a hand of peace to those who are truly interested in a peace based on justice.[52]

The US and Israel weren't interested in such a peace. Israel announced that it would not transfer tax funds that it collected in occupied Palestine on behalf of the PA, effectively stealing Palestinian taxpayers' money. The US asked the PA to return $50 million in funds given for infrastructure projects. Abbas consented.[53]

A team of Israeli officials—including Foreign Minister Tzipi Livni; the prime minister's senior advisor, Dov Weissglass; the director of the Shin Bet; and senior generals—met to discuss what policy course should be taken in response to Hamas's election victory. It was agreed that Israel's reply would be to punish the Palestinians for voting the wrong way by implementing an economic blockade of the Gaza Strip. "It's like an appointment with a dietician", Weissglass joked during the meeting. "The Palestinians will get a lot thinner, but won't die."[54]

The US and Israel were also "discussing ways to destabilize the Palestinian government so that newly elected Hamas officials will fail and elections will be called again," noted the *New York Times*. "The intention is to starve the Palestinian Authority of money and international connections to the point where, some months from now, its president, Mahmoud Abbas, is compelled to call a new election."[55]

Hamas official Nasser Abdaljawad responded that the Muslim world would provide for Palestinians' needs and that Hamas would save money by ending the corruption that existed under Abbas. Hamas spokesman Farhat Assad laughed, "First, I thank the United States that they have given us this weapon of democracy. But there is no way to retreat now. It's not possible for the US and the world to turn its back on an elected democracy."[56]

On this latter point, the Hamas spokesman was clearly mistaken. The US cut off all aid to the new government. Secretary of State Condoleezza Rice announced, "The principle is very clear. We're not going to fund a Hamas-led government."[57]

Abbas, for his part, proved willing to do the bidding of the US and Israel by issuing the ultimatum to Hamas that it must accept existing agreements between Israel and the PLO or he would replace Ismail Haniyeh, the Hamas candidate expected to become prime minister, and possibly even call for new elections—even though he had no authority to do so.[58]

Prior to Hamas's parliamentary election victory, Abbas had tried to have the Fatah-controlled Palestinian Legislative Council (PLC) grant him special authorities, including the power to appoint judges to a constitutional court without seeking legislative approval. This would have allowed judges appointed by Abbas to decide whether laws passed under the incoming parliament were constitutional. The new Hamas-controlled parliament proceeded to revoke those special powers. As that session began, Fatah members walked out, while Fatah gunmen near the parliament building in Gaza City fired shots into the air in an apparent attempt to intimidate the decision. Tayeb Abdel-Rahim, a senior aid to Abbas, afterward responded by describing the move by Hamas as "a coup attempt". But as Hamas legislator Mahmoud Ramahi correctly pointed out, "The law is very clear. It gives us the right to endorse or reject the resolutions or the decisions of that [previous] session."[59]

As expected, Hamas senior member Ismail Haniyeh was appointed Prime Minister. In an interview with the *Washington Post* near the end of February, he was asked whether Hamas would accept the conditions placed upon it by the US: to recognize Israel, abide by existing agreements, and renounce violence. He responded by asking why these conditions weren't also placed on Israel. "Which Israel should we recognize?" he shot back. "The Israel of 1917; the Israel of 1936; the Israel of 1948; the Israel of 1956; or the Israel of 1967? Which borders and which Israel? Israel has to recognize first the Palestinian state and its borders and then we will know what we are talking about." He said that if Israel stopped its incursions and assassinations, Hamas would be able to convince Palestinian militant groups to abide by the ceasefire. He reiterated Hamas's willingness to enter into a long-term truce if Israel were to withdraw to the 1967 lines. If Israel accepted a Palestinian state and respected their rights, "then we are ready to recognize them", he added. "We do not have any feelings of animosity toward Jews. We do not wish to throw them into the sea. All we seek is to be given our land back, not to harm anybody."[60]

But while the US and EU were demanding that Hamas renounce violence, as the *Washington Report on Middle East Affairs* pointed out, "Israel was busy killing Palestinians." In the month since the election, "Israeli forces using air strikes and ground fire killed at least 27 Palestinians in Gaza and the West Bank," including "a 9-year-old girl who had strayed into a 'forbidden area' in Gaza"—a wide strip of land in Gaza along its entire border with Israel that the Israeli military enforced as off-limits.[61]

Hamas, however, continued to strictly observe the ceasefire. It had been doing so for sixteen months when, on June 9, 2006, Israel launched artillery into Gaza, killing seven Palestinians having a picnic on the beach and injuring dozens of others. Hamas retaliated with rocket fire that caused no casualties, the *New York Times* reported, as "nearly all of them appeared to land inside Gaza".[62] The group's adherence to the ceasefire up until that point was well recognized by the Western mainstream media. CNN reported that while other groups had been responsible for firing rockets, "Hamas has stuck to the cease-fire it announced in February 2005".[63] The Associated Press (AP) said that Hamas militants "have largely stuck to the truce". The BBC noted that Hamas "has been observing a self-imposed ceasefire for more than a year".[64]

The *New York Times*, too, acknowledged that Hamas "had officially been abiding" by the ceasefire when Israel "killed seven civilians at a beachside picnic", which provoked retaliatory rocket fire from Hamas. But that wasn't the message the American newspaper delivered with its headline. Instead, the headline read, "Hamas Fires Rockets at Israel After Calling Off Truce", thus leaving any readers just gleaning headlines or skimming the article with the *false* impression that it was *not Israel* that violated the ceasefire.[65]

'Operation Summer Rains'

On June 24, 2006, Israeli soldiers raided Gaza and abducted two Palestinian brothers, Osama and Mustafa Abu Muamar, whose father was a member of Hamas, but who were not themselves members. They disappeared into Israel's prison system, joining thousands of other Palestinian prisoners, including children and hundreds held indefinitely and without charge in what is known as "administrative detention".[66]

The following day, Hamas militants entered Israel through a tunnel; killed two Israeli soldiers; and captured a third, Corporal Gilad Shalit. In response, Israel launched a military operation in Gaza code-named "Summer Rains", destroying three bridges and bombing the only power plant, cutting electricity to half of the Strip. This assault on civilian infrastructure constituted a violation of international law that "raised the specter of a humanitarian crisis" (Associated

Press).[67] The Israeli human rights organization B'Tselem concluded that the objective of the attack "was to collectively punish the entire Palestinian population" and condemned it as "a war crime".[68] Amnesty International likewise called on Israel to end its "wanton destruction and collective punishment" as its forces proceeded to abduct sixty-four Palestinian legislators and eight ministers.[69]

The US mainstream media's treatment of the situation was epitomized by a *New York Times* editorial determining that "responsibility for this latest escalation rests squarely with Hamas" because of its attack on soldiers in Israel. There was no mention of Israel's abduction of two Palestinian civilians the day before, or of Israel's violation of the ceasefire that killed seven civilians on the beach. "Ironically," the *Times* added, "Hamas has chosen this bleak moment to finally endorse a document that implicitly recognizes Israel within its pre-1967 borders." But this didn't represent progress, in the editors' view, because "Hamas's military wing has crossed those very borders". There was no mention that Israel had crossed those very borders the day before—or, for that matter, that Gaza had been under nearly four decades of Israeli occupation. Nor was there any mention of Israel's policy of collectively punishing the civilian population of Gaza. The *Times* tacitly endorsed Israel's military assault by stating that Israel "needs to be delivering" the message to Hamas that "things must not be allowed to go on like this".[70]

Israel was at the same time also involved in military operations in Lebanon. By July 18, Steven Erlanger reported in the *New York Times*, the "asymmetry in the reported death tolls" was "marked and growing: some 230 Lebanese dead, most of them civilians, to 25 Israeli dead, 13 of them civilians." In Gaza, 103 Palestinians had been killed, including at least 30 civilians. One Israeli soldier was also killed by friendly fire. Erlanger commented: "The cold figures, combined with Israeli air attacks on civilian infrastructure like power plants, electricity transformers, airports, bridges, highways and government buildings, have led to accusations . . . that Israel is guilty of 'disproportionate use of force' in the Gaza Strip and Lebanon and of 'collective punishment' of the civilian populations." Erlanger proceeded to go on at length with Israeli denials of any wrongdoing before quoting Israeli Ambassador to the UN Dan Gillerman responding to the criticisms that Israel was using unlawful force by saying, "You're damn right we are."[71]

As columnist Gideon Levy remarked in the Israeli newspaper *Haaretz*, Israel was "rampaging through Gaza—there's no other word to describe it—killing and demolishing, bombing and shelling, indiscriminately." He likened Gaza to "a prison" and deplored the "disgraceful and shocking collective punishment" that Israel was inflicting on the Palestinians, noting that the US also bore responsibility. Two months after Israel began its military operations, "224 Palestinians, 62 of them children and 25 of them women", were dead. "A day doesn't go by without deaths, most of them innocent civilians."[72]

The Israeli government was delivering a message, just as the *New York Times* had urged. By mid-September, according to the International Federation of Human Rights, 307 Palestinians had been killed in Gaza since the capture of Gilad Shalit on June 25, with civilians accounting for 80 percent of the casualties.[73]

The Hamas 'Coup' in Gaza

In contrast to the policies of their government, a poll showed that 56 percent of Israelis would support negotiations with a Palestinian unity government that included Hamas, and 67 percent believed this was required to achieve a peace agreement.[74] Mahmoud Abbas, for his part, continued to serve the interests of Israel and the US by relaying their demands that Hamas must accept the Oslo Accords and recognize the state of Israel before a unity government could be formed. Abbas's policy was likewise contrasted by public opinion among the Palestinians, a majority of whom agreed with Hamas that the government should not recognize Israel. The US, of course, did *not* demand that Israel recognize Palestine.[75]

By October 2006, the possibility of a civil war in Gaza was being discussed in the media. As the talks between Hamas and Fatah broke down, violent clashes began occurring—a situation worsened by a financial crisis brought about by Israel's withholding of PA tax revenues, the cessation of aid by the US and its allies, and the continued blockade of Gaza. *The Guardian* pointed out that this left "hundreds of young men, who have ready access to weapons, without salaries."[76]

Abbas again threatened to dismiss the Hamas government and call for new elections, while the US had a $42 million campaign underway to bolster Fatah in the event Abbas made good on his threat. The US effort included training and arming Force 17, Abbas's special guard. The US had already sent weapons to Fatah in May in an arms transfer Prime Minister Olmert said he had approved. "I did this because we are running out of time and we need to help Abu Mazen," Olmert said, referring to Mahmoud Abbas by his nickname. Meeting with Condoleezza Rice, Abbas requested more arms from the US, which Rice said would likely be granted, according to a senior PA official.[77] Abbas had plenty of support from the US and Israel, but he failed to garner the support needed from Fatah leaders, most of whom opposed his move to illegally dismiss the Hamas government. Talks on a unity government resumed.[78]

On November 26, as part of a new cease-fire agreement with Hamas, Israel withdrew its troops from Gaza.[79]

In mid-December, with no progress on a unity government and Hamas less than a year into its four-year parliamentary term, President Abbas announced that he would call for early elections. Hamas rejected the move, saying it would not participate in new elections and correctly asserting that any such move by Abbas would be illegal. Under Palestinian law, the president had the power to dismiss the prime minister only with legislative approval, and he had no authority to call for early parliamentary elections.[80] By February 2007, the deadlock nevertheless appeared to be coming closer to a resolution, with Hamas and Fatah said to be close to signing an agreement to form a national unity government.[81]

In March 2007, Arab leaders sought to revive the Arab Peace Initiative, a 2002 peace plan that offered normalization of diplomatic relations if Israel withdrew from the territories occupied in 1967 in compliance with Resolution 242, accepted a Palestinian state within the 1967 lines, and agreed to seek a "just solution" for Palestinian refugees. Israel rejected the offer to revive the initiative, with Deputy Prime Minister Shimon Peres calling it a "diktat" and insisting that "negotiation" between the Palestinians and the Occupying Power was "the only way to overcome our differences".[82]

Israel's policy, of course, remained one of refusal to enter into negotiations with the elected Palestinian government. Though it should go without saying, it would perhaps be remiss not to also point out that Israel's obligation to respect international law and human rights is non-negotiable.

During the ceasefire that followed Israel's withdrawal from Gaza in November 2006, other Palestinian militant groups fired rockets at Israel, but Hamas fired none. Israel, however, claimed that the ceasefire did not apply to the West Bank and continued operations there. Then, in April 2007, Israel launched a series of raids into Gaza and the West Bank, killing nine Palestinians. Hamas responded by firing rockets into Israel for the first time since the ceasefire began. The *New York Times* headline once again simply read, "Hamas militants declare end to cease-fire with Israel".[83]

Israel then began launching regular assaults on Gaza. By the end of May, forty-seven Palestinians—including fifteen civilians, seven of whom were children—had been killed in Israeli attacks, while one Israeli woman had been killed by a rocket attack. Israel also arrested thirty-three Palestinians in the West Bank, including a cabinet minister, three legislators, and three mayors.[84]

With the collapse of the ceasefire also came the breakdown of relations between Hamas and Fatah, and factional violence once again escalated. After more than fifty Palestinians had been killed in the fighting, Abbas and Haniyeh met to discuss how to restore the peace with each other and with Israel.[85] But the US and Israel sought to foment the factional violence. "If you look at exit scenarios for what's going on there now," said one Israeli official, referring to the US program, "you could have a force loyal to Abbas in northern Gaza that could be highly useful to Israel."[86]

Hamas was not unaware of how the US and Israel were pressuring Abbas to overthrow their government and providing him the means to do so violently. Hamas seized a shipment of US arms intended for Fatah, prompting one official to say, "We obtained the US weapons and will keep hijacking any assistance the Americans provide to Fatah. Our fighters are aware of the American and Israeli conspiracies to topple our government."[87] The following month, the *New York Times* reported that the US wanted to send another arms shipment to Abbas's Presidential Guard, but Israeli officials were worried the weapons would just be seized by Hamas, as the previous shipment had been.[88]

In June, Abbas's US-trained presidential guards fired rocket-propelled grenades at Haniyeh's home near Gaza City. Hamas militants retaliated by firing mortars at Abbas's presidential office compound.[89] A Fatah spokesman claimed that "Hamas is seeking a military coup against the Palestinian Authority", while Hamas spokesman Sami Abu Zuhri correctly pointed out that Fatah had "relations with the US administration and Israel" and was involved in "an international and regional plan aiming to eliminate Hamas."[90]

Despite US and Israeli backing, Fatah gunmen were defeated by Hamas, which consolidated its control over Gaza.[91] Abbas declared a state of emergency, dismissed the unity government, appointed Salam Fayyad as the new prime minister, and said he would seek early elections.

"Prime Minister Haniyeh remains the head of the government even if it was dissolved by the president," responded Sami Abu Zuhri.[92] Haniyeh issued a statement saying that Abbas's actions had "no basis in law" and declaring that the national unity government remained in charge.[93] Indeed, under the Palestinian Basic Law, while the president had the authority to dismiss the government, the dismissed government should have remained in place until a vote of the Legislative Council. Since Abbas's appointment of Fayyad to replace Haniyeh was done without the approval of the Legislative Council, in which Hamas held a majority of seats, his action was illegal.[94]

Fatah's claim that it was *Hamas* that had instigated "a coup against the Palestinian Authority" nevertheless became the narrative adopted by the US government and mainstream media.[95]

Following the illegal ouster of the Hamas government by Abbas, the US immediately lifted its embargo on his new government. The *Washington Post* noted that "analysts have questioned the legality under Palestinian law of Abbas's dismissal of the Hamas-dominated government", but the George W. Bush administration "brushed aside such concerns". Condoleezza Rice remarked that the resumption of aid to Abbas was in part to "support his efforts to enforce the rule of law". Hamas was seeking "to divide the Palestinian nation"—a behavior, she declared, that the US rejected.[96]

The irony didn't go unnoticed by the *New York Times*, which commented on how the Bush administration "essentially threw its support behind the dismantling of a democratically elected government."[97] That, of course, was precisely the plan. In April 2008, *Vanity Fair* reported on documents it had obtained showing "a covert initiative, approved by Bush and implemented by Secretary of State Condoleezza Rice and Deputy National Security Adviser Elliot Abrams, to provoke a Palestinian civil war. The plan was for forces led by ['Fatah's resident strongman in Gaza' Muhammad] Dahlan, and armed with new weapons and supplied at America's behest, to give Fatah the muscle it needed to remove the democratically elected Hamas-led government from power." But the plan "backfired" and "inadvertently provoked Hamas to seize total control of Gaza." David Wurmser, a former Middle East adviser to Vice President Dick Cheney, candidly admitted that "what happened wasn't so much a coup by Hamas but an attempted coup by Fatah that was pre-empted before it could happen."[98]

Following the attempted overthrow of the democratically-elected government and the Hamas takeover of Gaza, Israel escalated its blockade policy and proceeded to place Gaza under a state of total siege, preventing Palestinians from leaving the territory and blocking humanitarian aid and other essential goods from entering.[99] The purpose of the blockade was to punish the civilian population for having voted the wrong way and for continuing to have Hamas as their leadership despite the US and Israel's failed effort to remove the group from power. On November 3, 2008, the US embassy in Tel Aviv cabled to Secretary Rice, "Israeli officials have confirmed to Embassy officials on multiple occasions that they intend to keep the Gazan economy functioning at the lowest level possible consistent with avoiding a humanitarian crisis." The cable reiterated: "As part of their overall embargo plan against Gaza, Israeli officials have confirmed to econoffs [US Embassy economic officers] on multiple occasions that they intend to keep the Gazan economy on the brink of collapse without quite pushing it over the edge".[100]

Israel's "collective punishment of Gaza" resulted in a "humanitarian crisis", reported John Dugard to the UN Human Rights Council (UNHRC) on January 21, 2008, in his capacity as UN Special Rapporteur on the situation of human rights in the Palestinian territories occupied since 1967. Israel also remained "in serious violation of its legal obligations" with its continuing construction of settlements and a separation wall in the West Bank.[101]

The 2008 Ceasefire

In early June 2008, Israeli Prime Minister Ehud Olmert warned that Israel was planning a military operation in Gaza with the ostensible objective of stopping rocket and mortar attacks. Olmert told reporters that "the pendulum is closer to a decision for a serious operation." Israeli Defense Minister Ehud Barak similarly stated that a military attack on Gaza was "closer than ever." Isabel Kershner reported in the *New York Times*, "There have been plans for broad military action for months."[102] Palestinian President Mahmoud Abbas urged Israel to instead consider an Egyptian-brokered ceasefire agreement with Hamas.[103] Under the ceasefire, Hamas would cease rocket attacks and Israel would ease its blockade of Gaza. The proposal was met with acceptance, but a senior Israeli official warned that if it broke down, "there will not be another attempt at a cease-fire. There will be a large-scale Israeli operation".[104]

The ceasefire went into effect on June 19, and Israel immediately and repeatedly violated it. After the first week of the ceasefire, the UN reported that Israel had violated the truce on at least seven occasions with soldiers shooting at Palestinian farmers attempting to reach their own land near the border fence. Two elderly Palestinians, one seventy and the other eighty-two years old, were wounded.[105]

On June 24, Israel killed two Palestinians, one a member of Hamas and the other of Islamic Jihad, in the West Bank city of Nablus. Islamic Jihad issued a statement saying that "the reprisal for this noble blood will be in the depths of the Zionist entity, God willing", and later took credit for three rockets fired from Gaza that struck the Israeli city of Sderot that afternoon. Hamas's response was to urge "all Palestinian factions to abide by the calm agreement".[106] Islamic Jihad then announced, "We have confirmed to our friends in Hamas that we have decided to respect the ceasefire," but added that there would be reprisals in the event of any further attacks from Israel.[107]

Defense Minister Ehud Barak reacted by ordering the closure of all border crossings and preventing much-needed goods from entering Gaza. This was "a violation of the deal for calm in Gaza", noted a Hamas spokesman.[108] Mark Regev, the spokesman for Prime Minister Olmert, announced that Israel would hold Hamas responsible for any attacks by other militant factions and that "the truce applies only to the Gaza Strip and not to the West Bank".[109] In other words, Israel was free to assassinate members of Islamic Jihad or other militant groups in the West Bank, but any response from their brethren in Gaza would be considered a violation of the ceasefire by Hamas, even though Hamas itself was honoring the agreement.

By such means, Israel made apparent its intent to provoke a violent response from militants in Gaza, a not unfamiliar modus operandi for Israel. As Isabel Kershner observed in the *New York Times*, "Previous cease-fire understandings in Gaza have fallen apart over continuing Israeli raids in the West Bank and the inability of Palestinian leaders to contain the smaller groups." She noted that it was Islamic Jihad that had fired the rockets while Hamas had urged the group to abide by the ceasefire, but the headline nevertheless adopted Israel's narrative and declared, "Rockets Hit Israel, Breaking Hamas Truce".[110]

On June 26, a fourth rocket was fired from Gaza, by the Al-Aqsa Martyrs Brigades, which issued a statement saying the attack was "a response to Israeli Zionist violations, for there has been no Israeli adherence to the truce."[111] Senior Hamas official Mahmoud al-Zahar, however, announced that Hamas would take action against any factions that threatened the preservation of the ceasefire. Hamas official Taher Nunu said that the Hamas government "will not allow anyone to violate this agreement". Prime Minister Haniyeh stated, "We expect everyone to respect the agreement so that the Palestinian people achieve what they look for, an end to this suffering and breaking the siege".[112]

On June 30, another rocket fired from Gaza landed in Israel.[113] The *New York Times* editors commented that there were "risks" to the truce because "Hamas may not respect or enforce the cease-fire; there have been almost daily violations." In fact, in the week and a half since the ceasefire had gone into effect, there had been only three instances in which Palestinians had fired rockets at Israel. It was true that there had been "almost daily violations"—but by *Israel*, not Hamas. The *Times* likewise saw fit to omit the fact that Hamas had fired zero rockets and was urging those responsible to cease. Likewise omitted was the fact that Gaza remained under siege, with Israel collectively punishing the civilian population by preventing food and other humanitarian supplies from entering. Instructively, the editorial was titled "Israel's Diplomatic Offensive".[114]

Israel's "Diplomatic Offensive" was a policy transparently intended to provoke a violent response from Palestinian militants that would serve as a casus belli for its planned invasion of Gaza, at which time Israel predictably would proclaim that it had exhausted diplomatic efforts to maintain the peace.[115] That point was driven home the next day, as Israel announced that it would continue to fire "warning shots" at any Palestinians who came within several hundred meters of the border fence, into what it called a "special security zone", thus preventing farmers from accessing their own land.

Hamas once again pledged to maintain the truce, despite the provocations and violations by Israel. Ismail Haniyeh told reporters, "We still say that maintaining the calm is a national interest, but the Israelis must commit to lifting the siege and opening the crossings".[116] Hamas officials also said that they had arrested several militants for intending to fire rockets into Israel. Israel proceeded to shut down four Hamas charities in the West Bank, including a clinic, an orphanage, an Islamic school for girls, and a mosque.[117]

On July 10, Israeli soldiers shot and killed an unarmed eighteen-year-old Palestinian in Gaza who was looking for scrap metal along the border, according to his family. The teenager was a member of the Al-Aqsa Martyrs Brigades, members of which responded by launching two Qassam rockets into Israel. Hamas arrested two militants responsible for firing the rockets. Israel proceeded to abduct twelve Hamas members in the West Bank.[118]

Meanwhile, the siege continued. Amnesty International issued a report in July titled "Gaza Blockade—Collective Punishment". "A humanitarian crisis is engulfing Gaza", it stated, that was "not the result of a natural disaster but entirely man-made and avoidable." Israel's blockade had

> left the population, 1.5 million Palestinians, trapped and with few resources. They are surviving, but only just. Some 80 percent depend on the trickle of international aid that the Israeli government allows in. Even patients in dire need of medical treatment not available in Gaza are often prevented from leaving; more than 50 of these have died [since June 2007]. . . . In the first five months of 2008 some 380 Palestinians, more than a third of them unarmed civilians and including more than 60 children, were killed by the Israeli army, almost all of them in the Gaza Strip. In the same period 25 Israelis, 16 of them civilians, were killed by Palestinian armed groups.[119]

In October, the IDF warned Hezbollah that it would apply its "Dahiya Doctrine"—a reference to the destruction in Beirut during Israel's 2006 war on Lebanon, in which an entire district was flattened—if any rockets were fired at Israel during the planned Gaza operation. "What happened in the Dahiya quarter of Beirut in 2006 will happen in every village from which Israel is fired on," the head of the IDF's northern division, Major General Gadi Eisenkot, told the Israeli newspaper *Yedioth Ahronoth*. "We will apply disproportionate force on it and cause great damage and destruction there. From our standpoint, these are not civilian villages, they are military bases. . . . This is not a recommendation. This is a plan. And it has been approved."[120]

A report by retired Colonel Gabriel Siboni published by the Israeli Institute for National Security Studies bluntly titled "Disproportionate Force" stated that the "Dahiya Doctrine" would also apply to Gaza. The "challenges" faced by "the IDF's response to a large scale conflict both in the north and in the Gaza Strip" could be "overcome by adopting the principle of a disproportionate strike against the enemy's weak points as a primary war effort. . . . With an outbreak of hostilities, the IDF will need to act immediately, decisively, and with force that is disproportionate to the enemy's actions and the threat it poses. . . . This approach is applicable to the Gaza Strip as well." The deliberate use of "disproportionate force" was for "instilling proper expectations of the IDF response among the civilian population".[121]

The announcement of the "Dahiya Doctrine", in other words, was an open declaration of Israel's intent to commit war crimes in order to inflict punishment on the Palestinian civilian population during its planned attack on Gaza.

Senator Obama's 'Unshakeable Commitment' to Israel

The Israeli military openly declaring its intention to commit war crimes did not deter US presidential candidate Senator Barack Obama from endorsing the planned assault on Gaza. Nor did the illegality of Israel's attempts to annex East Jerusalem deter him from endorsing this Israeli policy.

Following the June 1967 war and the occupation of the Gaza Strip and West Bank, Israel passed measures to effectively annex East Jerusalem. In May 1968, the UN Security Council passed Resolution 252, declaring Israel's annexation to be "invalid" under international law. In July 1969, the Council passed Resolution 267, reaffirming "the established principle that acquisition of territory by military conquest is inadmissible" and confirming that Israel's annexation was "invalid". Resolution 271 of September 1969 censured the ongoing "military occupation" by Israel of Jerusalem. Resolution 298 of September 1971 deplored Israel's continued violation of UN resolutions and confirmed that Israel's attempts to annex Jerusalem "are totally invalid". Resolution 446 of March 1979 affirmed "once more that the Fourth Geneva Convention . . . is applicable to the Arab territories occupied by Israel, including Jerusalem", and determined "that the policy and practices of Israel in establishing settlements in the Palestinian and other Arab territories occupied since 1967 have no legal validity". Resolution 452 of July 1979 emphasized again that Jerusalem was included in "the occupied Arab territories" and that Israel's annexation "has no legal validity and constitutes a violation of the Fourth Geneva Convention". Resolution 465 of March 1980 reaffirmed that Israel's annexation attempts "have no legal validity". Resolution 471 of June 1980 again reiterated the applicability of the Fourth Geneva Convention "to the Arab territories occupied by Israel since 1967, including Jerusalem". Resolution 476 of June 1980 deplored Israel's continued violation of international law, reaffirmed "the overriding necessity to end the prolonged occupation of Arab territories occupied by Israel since 1967, including Jerusalem". It also reaffirmed that Israel's annexation measures "have no legal validity and constitute a flagrant violation of the Fourth Geneva Convention" and were thus "null and void". Resolution 478 of August 1980 again confirmed that Israel's annexation of Jerusalem was "null and void" and called on member states "that have established diplomatic missions at Jerusalem to withdraw such missions from the Holy City". Security Council Resolutions 592 (December 1986), 605 (December 1987), 607 (January 1988), 636 (July 1989), 694 (May 1991), 726 (January 1992), and 799 (December 1992) all again reaffirmed the applicability of the Fourth Geneva Convention to occupied Palestinian territory, including Jerusalem.[122]

In July 2004, the International Court of Justice (ICJ) issued an advisory opinion at the request of the UN General Assembly that reaffirmed that "all these territories (including East Jerusalem) remain occupied territories and that Israel has continued to have the status of occupying Power". The ICJ also determined that Israel's settlements in the West Bank, including Jerusalem, "have been established in breach of international law."[123]

On July 23, 2008, US Senator Barack Obama was in Sderot, Israel, where he gave a speech professing his "unshakeable commitment to Israel's security". The US, he said, was a "friend and ally" that "will always stand by the people of Israel." Illustrating what that would mean if he were elected president, he proceeded to declare how the US would back Israel in its violations of international law, insisting to his Israeli audience that "Jerusalem will be the capital of Israel". To make clear that he was referring to *all* of Jerusalem, including occupied Palestinian territory, he emphasized that "it is important that we don't simply slice the city in half". The status of Jerusalem was an issue that would need to be resolved through negotiations with the Palestinians, he said. But what this meant to Obama was that the city's status could not be determined through application of international law. Rather, it could only be determined through US-moderated talks between Israel and the Palestinians, until and during which Israel would continue its theft of Palestinian land, and in the event of which, as he had just stated explicitly, Obama as president would support the Israeli position.

Emphasizing again his "commitments" to Israel, Obama told his audience, "Now, in terms of knowing my commitments, you don't have to just look at my words; you can look at my deeds." Among his "deeds", Obama cited his support for Israel's 2006 war on Lebanon ("The Second Lebanon War" in Israel, the First Lebanon War having been Israel's devastating 1982 invasion) and accompanying assault on Gaza (Operation Summer Rains). Obama also sought to assuage Israeli "concerns" about him "pressuring them into concessions" by assuring his audience that they had nothing to fear in that regard. In other words, an Obama administration would fully back Israel's position and pressure only the Palestinians to make any and all concessions necessary to achieve what Israel wanted.

When asked whether he thought Israel should talk with Hamas, Obama replied, "If somebody was sending rockets into my house where my two daughters sleep at night, I'm going to do everything in my power to stop that. And I would expect Israelis to do the same thing." These words would subsequently be used by Israeli officials to justify their implementation of the Dahiya Doctrine in Gaza.

Obama naturally also endorsed Israel's policy of refusing to talk with Hamas, reiterating the usual euphemistic preconditions that it "recognize Israel's right to exist and renounce violence as a tool to achieve its aims." Israel, on the other hand, need not recognize Palestine's "right to exist" or renounce violence as it continued to receive billions in US military aid.[124]

The day after Obama's speech, Israel's Defense Ministry announced its approval for the illegal construction of additional Jewish homes in a settlement in the Jordan Valley.[125]

As the US presidential campaign season carried on, Senator Barack Obama's acquaintance with a Palestinian-American scholar became a campaign issue, resulting in a competition of sorts between the Obama camp and that of his main contender for the presidency, Senator John McCain. Both campaigns boasted of their unquestionable commitment to Israel while competing to distance themselves from even the appearance of having any kind of sympathies for the Palestinians. The issue arose because Obama had once spoken at a dinner in honor of Rashid Khalidi, the Edward Said Professor of Modern Arab Studies at Columbia University, editor of the *Journal of Palestine Studies*, and a prolific author who was critical of Israel and US foreign policy.

At the dinner in 2003, Obama said that his many talks with Khalidi and his wife had been "consistent reminders to me of my own blind spots and my own biases". Five years later, during the presidential campaign season, the *Los Angeles Times* ran a report about the dinner, commenting how Obama "expresses a firmly pro-Israel view of Middle East politics, pleasing many of the Jewish leaders and advocates for Israel whom he is courting in his presidential campaign." Obama's own people underscored that point: "Aides say that Obama's friendships with Palestinian Americans reflect only his ability to interact with a wide diversity of people, and that his views on the Israeli-Palestinian conflict have been consistent. Obama has called himself a 'stalwart' supporter of the Jewish state and its security needs. He believes in an eventual two-state solution in which Jewish and Palestinian nations exist in peace, which is consistent with current US policy."[126]

But just the fact of having associated with a Palestinian-American caused many to question Obama's commitment to Israel. His acquaintance with Khalidi was manufactured into a scandal in October, when Republican presidential candidate John McCain compared the dinner in Khalidi's honor with a "neo-Nazi outfit". His vice presidential pick, Sarah Palin, scolded Obama for having attended an event where "Israel was described . . . as the perpetrator of terrorism rather than the victim."[127]

The Obama campaign instructively responded by putting out a statement emphasizing that Obama had been "clear and consistent on his support for Israel", that Khalidi was not an advisor to him or his campaign, "and that he does not share Khalidi's views." "Instead of giving lectures on media bias," a campaign spokesman said, "John McCain should answer why, under his own chairmanship, the International Republican Institute repeatedly funded an organization Khalidi founded."[128] Given such competing rhetoric, a casual observer would have to be forgiven for presuming that that Khalidi must have been a member of some kind of terrorist organization, and not merely a respected scholar who co-founded the Center for Palestine Research and Studies, which received a $448,873 grant from the IRI in 1998 for work in the West Bank.[129]

After firing back at his political opponents, the Obama campaign underscored where his administration would stand on the issue of the Israeli-Palestinian conflict. Obama's vice presidential nominee, Senator Joe Biden, did his part by meeting with the Israeli Ambassador to the US, Sallai Meridor, in late October, to reiterate the Obama-Biden campaign's "unshakeable commitment" to what is commonly referred to as the "special relationship" between the US and Israel.[130]

The Collapse of the Ceasefire

On November 4, 2008, the day of the US presidential election, Israel violated the ceasefire by launching airstrikes and a ground incursion into Gaza that killed six members of Hamas, following which Hamas resumed rocket attacks against Israel. Israel claimed Hamas was digging a tunnel under the border in order to launch a raid into Israel, but offered no evidence of a tunnel, much less of intent by Hamas to violate the ceasefire it was so carefully adhering to.[131]

Until Israel's violation, the ceasefire had proved remarkably effective at mitigating rocket attacks. As Reuters had reported in August, "Rocket firings have become rare since an Egyptian-brokered truce between Hamas and Israel took effect in June."[132] Hamas's observance of the truce had been absolute, as a report from the Meir Amit Intelligence and Terrorism Information Center acknowledged. "Hamas was careful to maintain the ceasefire", the report stated, which had "brought relative quiet". In the six months preceding the truce, 2,278 rockets and mortar shells had been launched at Israel. By contrast, from the start of the truce until November 4, only twenty rockets and eighteen mortar shells were fired at Israel (five of the mortar shells landed in Gaza). None were fired by Hamas.[133] Amnesty International similarly noted that the ceasefire "has been the single most important factor in reducing civilian casualties and attacks on civilians to the lowest level since the outbreak of the uprising (intifada) more than eight years ago." That relative calm had now been threatened as a result of the "killing of six Palestinian militants in Gaza by Israeli forces in a ground incursion and air strikes on 4 November", which "was followed by a barrage of dozens of Palestinian rockets on nearby towns and villages in the south of Israel."[134]

Israel's violation effectively ended the ceasefire, precipitating chaotic violence as both sides engaged in daily tit-for-tat attacks. In mid-November, Ehud Barak announced that Israel was considering carrying forward its planned full-scale military assault on the Gaza Strip.[135]

The UN Relief and Works Agency (UNRWA) in Gaza warned later that month of an impending humanitarian catastrophe as a result of the ongoing

Israeli siege.[136] The Israeli human rights organization Gisha issued a report finding that Israel's restrictions were "aimed at civilians and undertaken for purposes of collective punishment—and are therefore illegal."[137] Amnesty International also reported in early December on Israel's collective punishment of the civilian population of Gaza, stating that "the supply of humanitarian aid and basic necessities" had been "reduced from a trickle to an intermittent drip." The water and sanitation infrastructure was collapsing, and there were fuel and electricity shortages, with hospitals "struggling to power life-saving machinery". Israel had frequently denied passage of patients requiring medical treatment not available in Gaza, resulting in scores of preventable deaths. Amnesty also noted that Israeli forces had killed about twenty Palestinians, including two children, since its November 4 ceasefire violation. No Israelis had been killed in rocket attacks.[138]

The UN Special Rapporteur on the situation of human rights in the Palestinian territories occupied since 1967, Richard Falk (who had succeeded John Dugard earlier that year), also issued a statement calling attention to the blockade. He observed that Israel was "allowing only barely enough food and fuel to enter to stave off mass famine and disease." This "policy of collective punishment" was a "flagrant and massive violation" of Article 33 of the Fourth Geneva Convention. "The truce was maintained by Hamas", he observed, "despite the failure of Israel to fulfill its obligations under the agreement to improve the living conditions of the people of Gaza. The recent upsurge of violence occurred after an Israeli incursion that killed several alleged Palestinian militants in Gaza." Falk also condemned the firing of rockets at Israel as "a criminal violation of international law".[139]

Israeli authorities subsequently jailed and then expelled Falk from the country for his "hostile position toward Israel".[140]

With the ceasefire due to expire on December 19, a poll published midmonth showed that 74 percent of Palestinians and 51 percent of Israelis wanted to see it extended. Hamas indicated its willingness to renew the ceasefire if Israel would open the border crossings.[141]

What Ethan Bronner reported in the New York Times on December 20, however, was that Hamas "declared in a statement that the ceasefire had expired, saying the truce would not be renewed" because Israel failed to uphold its commitments under the agreement. Bronner acknowledged that Hamas had been "largely successful" in preventing other armed groups, such as Islamic Jihad and Al-Aqsa Martyrs Brigades, from firing rockets into Israel, and that "Hamas imposed its will and even imprisoned some of those who were firing rockets". He also candidly observed that Hamas's job was made all the more difficult because "Israeli forces continued to attack Hamas and other militants in the West Bank, prompting Palestinian militants in Gaza to fire rockets." Neither Bronner nor anyone else at the *Times*, however, informed their readers that Hamas *did* offer to renew the ceasefire, but that this offer *was rejected by Israel*.[142]

On December 22, the Hamas leadership expressed its seriousness about extending the ceasefire by ordering a 24-hour stand-down to allow Israel time to accept its offer and open the borders to allow humanitarian supplies into Gaza.[143] Writing in the *Jerusalem Post* on December 24, Larry Derfner said that "Hamas is offering Israel a cease-fire if Israel lifts the siege on Gaza—and Israel should take it." Israel's siege was intended "to make life for Gazan civilians so miserable that they turn Hamas out", and a "new, terrible Middle East war" was looming. "The way out of such a war is for Israel to lift the blockade" in return for the ceasefire. If Israel refused Hamas's offer, he wrote, "Our arrogance and blindness will get a lot of innocent people killed."[144]

Prime Minister Ehud Olmert's response to Hamas's offer was to demand not only that militants unilaterally cease firing while Israeli attacks continued, but also that the civilian population of Gaza rid itself of the Hamas government. It was an effective declaration that one of the goals of Israel's planned military offensive was regime change. To achieve this, Israel would pay the cost of provoking the very rocket fire the military operation was ostensibly intended to put a stop to, in order to create the necessary pretext for its own resort to violence. This was accomplished by first violating and then refusing to renew the ceasefire agreement. As Reuters forecast, the impending military assault on Gaza "could result in heavy casualties" as well as "fuel a humanitarian crisis."[145]

Israel's "Diplomatic Offensive" was over. "Operation Cast Lead" would commence. The "Dahiya Doctrine" would be applied.

CHAPTER 2

'OPERATION CAST LEAD'

"**I**AF STRIKE ON GAZA is Israel's version of 'shock and awe'," read the headline in *Haaretz* on December 27, 2008. The newspaper described the bombardment by the Israeli Air Force as "the harshest IDF assault on Gaza since the territory was captured during the Six-Day War in 1967." It was a "massive attack much along the lines of what the Americans termed 'shock and awe' during their invasion of Iraq in March 2003." The attack had been in the planning for months, and "little to no weight was apparently devoted to the question of harming innocent civilians."[1] Indeed, Israel timed the launch of its surprise "shock and awe" bombing campaign to coincide with a busy hour when the streets were full of children leaving their schools after morning lessons.[2]

UNRWA commissioner Karen AbuZayd expressed shock at Israel's onslaught and revealed that Israel had told the agency it would evaluate Hamas's offer to renew the ceasefire. "They said they would wait 48 hours", she disclosed. "That was on Friday morning, I believe, until Sunday morning, and that they were going to evaluate. . . . There was only one rocket that went out on Friday, so it was obvious that Hamas was trying, again, to observe that truce to get this back under control." Israel had nevertheless commenced the bombing at 11:30 a.m. that Saturday morning. When a reporter asked her whether Gazans were aware that Israel's operation was a consequence of Hamas having unilaterally ended the cease-fire and launching rocket attacks, she replied, "Well, I don't think that they think that the truce was violated first by Hamas. I think they saw that Hamas had observed the truce quite strictly for almost six months," but received nothing in return. The crossings were not opened, and it was Israel, she informed the reporter, that violated the ceasefire.[3]

UN Special Rapporteur Richard Falk issued a statement condemning both Israel and Hamas for violations of international law. Israel had engaged in the collective punishment of 1.5 million people, targeted civilian areas in one of the most densely populated strips of land in the world, and was engaged in a disproportionate military response. Israel had struck non-military targets such as police stations, and hundreds had already been killed and injured in the airstrikes. Palestinian rocket attacks against civilians in Israel were illegal, but this did not relieve Israel of its own obligations under international law. In addition, far from making Israeli civilians safer, Israel's assault had prompted a barrage of retaliatory rocket fire that had killed one Israeli, the first since before the ceasefire had gone into effect. Israel had also ignored Hamas's diplomatic initiative to renew the ceasefire. Alluding to the US role, Falk added, "The Israeli airstrikes today, and the catastrophic human toll that they caused, challenge those countries that have been and remain complicit, either directly or indirectly, in Israel's violations of international law. That complicity includes those countries knowingly providing the military equipment including warplanes and missiles used in these illegal attacks, as well as those countries who have supported and participated in the siege of Gaza that itself has caused a humanitarian catastrophe."[4]

The reported death toll on the first day included 230 Palestinians and one Israeli civilian. "Hospital morgues were already full", reported *The Independent*. "The dead were piled on top of each other outside."[5] Amnesty International condemned rocket attacks by Palestinian militants as well as the "disproportionate use of force by Israel", including its killing of scores of unarmed Palestinian civilians and police who were not participating in hostilities.[6]

The US government, on the other hand, condemned only the violence committed by Palestinians while giving its blessing to Israel's onslaught. "The United States strongly condemns the repeated rocket and mortar attacks against Israel and holds Hamas responsible for breaking the ceasefire and for the renewal of violence in Gaza," announced Secretary of State Condoleezza Rice.[7]

President-elect Obama conveyed that he was monitoring the situation but had nothing to say about it. "There is one president at a time", his spokeswoman offered as explanation—a fact that, curiously, had not prevented Obama from commenting on any other political issue. The *New York Times* recalled that while in Sderot in July, "Mr. Obama made statements that sounded similar to those issued by the Bush administration"—condemning Hamas's violence while endorsing Israel's.[8]

With the US's backing, Israel rejected international calls for a ceasefire and justified its actions by invoking the US "war on terrorism". Defense Minister Ehud Barak said that asking Israel to cease its operations was "like asking you to have a cease-fire with Al-Qaeda".[9]

After two days, the "massive and unprecedented bombardment of Gaza" (*Jerusalem Post*) had resulted in 250 Palestinian deaths and some 1,450 injuries. The IDF's targets included the Islamic University in Gaza City, the offices of Al-Aqsa TV, the Gaza Interior Ministry, a mosque, and police stations.[10]

The UN Security Council issued a statement calling "for an immediate halt to all violence".[11] Israel again rejected calls for a ceasefire, with Ehud Barak announcing that Israel's military assault "will be extended and deepened as we find necessary."[12] The Israeli defense minister also invoked Obama's speech in Sderot as justification for Israel's onslaught: "Obama said that if rockets were being fired at his home while his two daughters were sleeping, he would do everything he could to prevent it".[13] The *New York Times* likewise reminded that when Obama was in Israel, "he all but endorsed the punishing Israeli attacks now unfolding."[14]

As Israel inflicted its punishment on the population of Gaza, Obama remained silent. "There's only one president who can speak for America at a time", repeated his senior adviser, David Axelrod.[15]

Israel proceeded to drop bunker-buster bombs supplied by the US on Gaza, according to the *Jerusalem Post*. The first shipment of the GBU-39s had arrived just in time for Israel to deploy them in its assault. IDF officials said that Israel would "not hesitate to target the homes of civilians who protected Hamas terrorists throughout the operation. 'We will go after every Hamas operative, no matter where he is,' one official said."[16]

After the first two days of Israel's onslaught, the Gaza Health Ministry reported that all nine hospitals in Gaza were "overwhelmed". The reported Palestinian death toll had risen to 315, at least 51 of whom were civilians, including seven children under age fifteen.[17] The estimate of civilian deaths was "likely to be conservative", said UNRWA spokesman Christopher Gunness, "and it is certainly rising".[18]

In *The Independent*, Johann Hari reminded that "The Gaza Strip is smaller than the Isle of Wight but it is crammed with 1.5 million people who can never leave. . . . When bombs begin to fall—as they are doing now with more deadly force than at any time since 1967—there is nowhere to hide."[19]

The US mainstream media, however, revealed little sympathy for the Palestinians. On the contrary, Israel's version of "shock and awe" was at times described with outright reverence, as with the obsequious *New York Times* headline, "Israel Reminds Foes That It Has Teeth". In that piece, Ethan Bronner uncritically parroted the implausible Israeli pretext that its bombardment was "aimed primarily at forcing Hamas to end its rocket barrages and military buildup". Israel was "gambling that its aggressive military posture will not alienate the new administration" and found Obama's "unwavering expressions of support" to be an encouraging sign. Not once did Bronner mention that scores of Palestinian civilians had already been killed.[20]

Palestinian correspondent Taghreed El-Khodary, the only *Times* journalist actually on the ground in the Gaza Strip, was the lead author of another *Times* article published the same day that helped to fill in some of the gaps left by Bronner. She reported that Gaza's hospitals were "stretched to the breaking point after 18 months of Israeli sanctions" and "on the verge of collapse as they struggled to care for the more than 600 people wounded in two days". Israel, meanwhile, was preparing to expand its assault with a ground operation.[21]

By Tuesday, December 30, four days into Operation Cast Lead, three Israeli civilians had been killed by rocket fire. UNRWA reported the Palestinian death toll at 364, including at least 62 civilians. The hospitals in Gaza were so overwhelmed that they were "turning away all but the most seriously wounded", reported *The Guardian*.[22] Taghreed El-Khodary relayed in the *Times* how "residents pulled relatives from the rubble of prominent institutions leveled by waves of Israeli F-16 attacks as hospitals struggled to keep up with the wounded and the dead and doctors scrambled for supplies."[23]

The F-16 fighter jets, of course, had been provided to Israel by the US, along with Apache gunship helicopters and other military hardware. The US continued to call upon only Hamas to cease violence while blessing the assault being carried out in large part with arms it had supplied to Israel. "Israel is going after terrorists who are firing rockets and mortars into Israel, and they are taking the steps that they feel are necessary to deal with the terrorist threat," said a White House spokesman. "In order for the violence to stop, Hamas must stop firing rockets into Israel and agree to respect a sustainable and durable ceasefire."[24]

While the US was defending its own complicity in the onslaught by mischaracterizing Israel's attacks as being strictly aimed at legitimate military targets, a former top adviser to Israel's domestic security service, Matti Steinberg, candidly told the *Boston Globe* that "Hamas's civilian infrastructure is a very, very sensitive target. If you want to put pressure on them, this is how."[25]

Hasbara

As with the case for war in Iraq and the false claims about its possession of weapons of mass destruction (WMD), the US mainstream media during Operation Cast Lead simply parroted the US government's official line, the actual facts being relegated to irrelevancy.

"Israel must defend itself", began a December 30 editorial in the *New York Times*. "And Hamas must bear responsibility for ending a six-month cease-fire this month with a barrage of rocket attacks into Israeli territory." It declined to inform readers that Gaza had for years been under an illegal Israeli blockade that collectively punished the civilian population (it made only a passing reference to the "punishing embargo on Gaza"). There was no mention of Israel's repeated violations throughout the ceasefire, including the wounding of two elderly men and the killing of an unarmed teenager. There was no mention of the fact that Hamas had strictly observed the ceasefire until Israel ended it with its November 4 violation. Nor was there any mention of Hamas's offer to renew the ceasefire and Israel's rejection of that offer.[26]

By now, the facts could simply be brushed aside, swept down the memory hole, not worthy of even a footnote, with the *New York Times*, America's "newspaper of record," setting the tone for the rest of the media. Thus, under the fawning headline "Despite Strikes, Israelis Vow to Soldier On", which similarly omitted all of the same relevant context, Isabel Kershner reported simply that "Israel began its devastating aerial bombardment of Hamas targets in Gaza with the stated goal of stopping the incessant rocket fire that has plagued Israeli towns and villages close to the border for years". That there had even *been* a ceasefire—much less that *Israel* had been the party that violated it—could now also be entirely forgotten.[27]

The media didn't only deceive by omission, but often simply made it up as they went along, spinning yarns with flagrant disregard for the truth, such that when the ceasefire *was* mentioned, it was only to blame Hamas for violating and refusing to renew it. A piece filed under the category of "news analysis" in the *Times* begged the question, "Why did Hamas end its six-month cease-fire on Dec. 19?" The simple answer provided for readers was that Hamas preferred the "way of armed force" and rejected negotiations. Never mind the facts.[28]

Just as the propaganda campaign in the run-up to the 2003 invasion of Iraq had been effective in manufacturing consent for war, so did US media reporting on the situation in Gaza serve to manufacture consent for the government's policy of supporting Israel's criminal activities. A poll taken at the time showed that 44 percent of Americans believed Israel was right to resort to force against the Palestinians in Gaza; 55 percent believed the Palestinians were to blame for the situation, while only 13 percent placed primary responsibility on Israel.[29]

Israel was successfully fighting its own propaganda war, noted the *Jewish Chronicle*. The assault on Gaza was "the first major demonstration of Israel's total overhaul of its 'hasbara' operation following the Second Lebanon War", the article explained. The Hebrew word "*hasbara*" literally means "explaining" and commonly refers to Israel's public relations (PR) efforts. The hasbara operation included "a new forum of press advisers" that had been "working for the past six months on a PR strategy specifically geared to dealing with the media during warfare in Gaza." The *Chronicle* offered several examples of how it worked:

> The international media were directed to a press center set up by the Foreign Ministry in Sderot itself so that foreign reporters would spend as much time as possible in the main civilian area affected by Hamas rockets. When the IDF was represented on the international TV networks, it was by Major Avital Leibovich to project a feminine and softer image. Ministers have been ordered by the Cabinet Secretary not to give interviews without authorization so as not to repeat the PR disaster

of a year ago, when Deputy Defense Minister Matan Vilnai threatened the Palestinians with a "holocaust".

One of the officials involved, former Israeli Ambassador to Italy and France Avi Pazner, elucidated on the necessity for the propaganda offensive, as well as its effectiveness: "Whenever Israel is bombing, it is hard to explain our position to the world. . . . The coverage is definitely less hostile than what we saw during the Second Lebanon War two-and-a-half years ago."[30] It also helped that Israel was able to control the media narrative about events in Gaza by virtue of having blocked journalists from entering the Strip since early November.[31]

Numerous Israeli reporters, however, showing considerably more honesty than their American counterparts, challenged their government's propaganda efforts. Barak Ravid reminded in *Haaretz* that preparations for Operation Cast Lead had been underway since the beginning of the ceasefire, which Israel violated on November 4. When Hamas offered to renew the ceasefire, "Israel continued to send out disinformation" by responding that it would take several days to consider the matter only to take advantage of the opportunity to catch Hamas off-guard by launching its planned military operation.[32]

US media reporting was also contrasted by other international media, including in the UK. In an example worth quoting at length, William Sieghart wrote the following in an op-ed for the London *Times*:

> Last week I was in Gaza. While I was there I met a group of 20 or so police officers who . . . were eager to know whether foreigners felt safer since Hamas had taken over the Government? Indeed we did, we told them. Without doubt the past 18 months had seen a comparative calm on the streets of Gaza; no gunmen on the streets, no more kidnappings. They smiled with great pride and waved us goodbye.
>
> Less than a week later all of these men were dead, killed by an Israeli rocket at a graduation ceremony. Were they "dangerous Hamas militant gunmen"? No, they were unarmed police officers, public servants killed not in a "militant training camp" but in the same police station in the middle of Gaza City that had been used by the British, the Israelis and Fatah during their periods of rule there.
>
> The distinction is crucial because while the horrific scenes in Gaza and Israel play themselves out on our television screens, a war of words is being fought that is clouding our understanding of the realities on the ground. . . .

The political leadership of Hamas is probably the most highly qualified in the world. Boasting more than 500 PhDs in its ranks, the majority are middle-class professionals—doctors, dentists, scientists and engineers. Most of its leadership have been educated in our universities and harbor no ideological hatred towards the West. It is a grievance-based movement, dedicated to addressing the injustice done to its people. It has consistently offered a ten-year ceasefire to give breathing space to resolve a conflict that has continued for more than 60 years.

The Bush-Blair response to the Hamas victory in 2006 is the key to today's horror. Instead of accepting the democratically elected Government, they funded an attempt to remove it by force; training and arming groups of Fatah fighters to unseat Hamas militarily and impose a new, unelected government on the Palestinians. Further, 45 Hamas MPs are still being held in Israeli jails. . . .

Two months ago the Israeli Defense Forces broke the ceasefire by entering Gaza and beginning the cycle of killing again.[33]

Such commentary would have been considered heresy, had anything like it appeared in the US mainstream media. As it turned out, there were few heretics among American commentators possessing honesty or journalistic integrity enough to even *question* the official narrative, much less seriously challenge it.

Israel's Rejection of a Ceasefire

"US Presses Israel on Cease-Fire", declared one headline in the *New York Times* on December 30. "Amid a Buildup of Its Forces, Israel Ponders a Cease-Fire", declared another. The gist of the story, as the American media presented it, was that the US and Israel both wanted a ceasefire, but Hamas continued to reject any peaceful resolution in favor of violence.[34]

While the *Times* didn't bother to specify, the headlines alluded to a French proposal for a 48-hour ceasefire in part to allow humanitarian assistance into the Gaza Strip. Also unreported in both articles was Israel's actual response: "There's no such thing as a 'humanitarian cease-fire'." An aide to Prime Minister Ehud Olmert delivered the message that "Gaza is not undergoing a humanitarian crisis. We're constantly supplying it with food and medications, and there's no need for a humanitarian cease-fire."[35]

Nor did the *Times* clarify for its readers that what the US was seeking in terms of a ceasefire was actually contrary to the French proposal. While the French plan called for *both* parties to halt violence, the White House had made clear its position that Hamas alone should lay down its arms. The Bush administration was seeking a "durable" ceasefire for which "the most important thing is that Hamas respect it", explained White House spokesman Gordon Johndroe. Claiming that Hamas "failed to renew the cease-fire", he summed up, "The onus is on Hamas."[36]

This US policy stood in stark contrast to the response of the international community and human rights organizations, which joined France in demanding that both sides cease fire. Amnesty International called on Israel to "stop all unlawful attacks", such as had occurred on the first day of Operation Cast Lead when seven students who had just left a UN-run school after finishing lessons were killed in an Israeli bombardment. Amnesty warned Israel against a ground invasion with the reminder that "there are no 'safe' places in Gaza for civilians to seek shelter".[37]

On December 31, the UN Security Council convened to address the matter. UN Secretary-General Ban Ki-moon condemned the violence on both sides, urged all parties to uphold international humanitarian law, and stressed the importance of bringing about a ceasefire. Numerous delegates similarly condemned both Palestinian rocket attacks and Israel's military operation and called for a ceasefire. Israel's UN ambassador, Gabriela Shalev, however, insisted that Israel was only targeting "the terrorists and their infrastructure", that it was doing the "utmost to minimize civilian casualties", and that Hamas bore "the sole responsibility for the current escalation and for any civilian casualties" because it "stores weapons and explosives in homes, schools, mosques and hospitals."[38] Siding with Israel, US Ambassador to the UN Zalmay Khalilzad blamed the violence entirely on Hamas on the basis of the lie that Hamas had broken the ceasefire. "We support an immediate ceasefire that is sustainable and implemented by all," he told the Council. "Specifically, this means that Hamas must stop its rocket attacks." The message to Israel was clear: while the rest of the world was demanding that Israel, too, cease its violence, Israel could carry on with the knowledge that it had the full backing of the world's most powerful government.[39]

Predictably, Israel rejected the proposal for a 48-hour humanitarian ceasefire, having never seriously considered it in the first place (*New York Times* headlines notwithstanding).[40] Israel maintained that there was no need. IDF commander Col. Moshe Lev boasted that "Hamas is trying to create the appearance of a humanitarian crisis, but together with the international organizations, we are preventing this from happening"—news that must have come as great surprise to groups like Human Rights Watch and Amnesty International, not to mention agencies of the United Nations.[41] Israeli Foreign Minister Tzipi Livni similarly announced that a ceasefire was unnecessary because "there is no humanitarian crisis in the Strip, and therefore there is no need for a humanitarian truce." The humanitarian situation in Gaza, insisted Livni, was "completely as it should be".[42]

The head of the Arab League, Amr Moussa, replied, "I am greatly surprised by, and I reject, the words of the Israeli foreign minister. . . . And this is an astonishing thing, that after more than 450 victims and more than 2,000 injured . . . then it is said there is no humanitarian crisis. . . . There may be those that sympathize with such a remark. This is something we must condemn, and we must say there is a major humanitarian crisis. . . ."[43]

Livni also claimed that Israel had achieved its ostensible goal of stopping rocket fire, but that the IDF's operation must continue in order to end weapons smuggling into Gaza through tunnels under its border with Egypt. Indeed, an IDF analysis a week into Operation Cast Lead assessed that the threat posed to Israel by Hamas's ballistic capabilities had been overstated.[44] In addition, Livni pointed to Israel's "common interests and values" with the US and assured that "Obama's administration is not a threat to Israel" because the President-elect "also does not want to give legitimacy to terror". With this ongoing US support, she assured, the collective punishment of the civilian population of Gaza would continue in furtherance of the larger ostensible goal of removing Hamas from power.[45]

"Israel Rejects Cease-Fire, but Offers Gaza Aid", read the exonerating headline in the *New York Times*. Written by Ethan Bronner, the lead paragraph relayed Israel's assurances that it would "expedite and increase humanitarian aid" and work with "its allies"—meaning the US—on "a durable, long-term truce." Bronner noted that Israel had bombed the parliament and other government buildings, universities, and mosques with the curious remark that such targets were "once considered off limits"—an instructive example of how the media accommodates the US government's standard that international law just doesn't apply when it comes to the actions of Washington or its partners.

Bronner relayed how the Palestinian death toll, according to "overwhelmed hospital officials" and UN estimates, had risen past 390, a quarter of whom were civilians, including 25 women and 38 children. But it was not concern for the welfare of Palestinians that prompted Israel to announce that it was "seeking ways to increase humanitarian aid"—which Israel could have easily enough accomplished by simply ceasing to block it. Rather, as Bronner paraphrased from a senior Israeli official, it was "so that its military endeavor could continue without further pressure to stop."[46]

Defending Israel's War Crimes

While Ethan Bronner suggested that Israel's targeting of civilian objects was no longer "off limits", another *Times* article asserted, "In the debate over civilian casualties, there is no clear understanding of what constitutes a military target." It was an "ambiguity" that was "evident at the intensive care ward in Shifa Hospital" in Gaza City.[47]

Indeed, the "ambiguity" was evident throughout the Gaza Strip. The same day, January 1, Israel bombed the home of fifty-two-year-old Nizar Rayan, a leading Hamas official in Gaza. The Associated Press reported that the attack "flattened Rayan's apartment building" and "heavily damaged several neighboring buildings". Rayan's four wives and nine of his children, four of whom were under eighteen, were also killed.[48]

This supposed "ambiguity" disappears, however, when one sets aside Washington's rules and examines what international law actually has to say about the matter. The Geneva Conventions and their Additional Protocols are explicit in their definitions of legitimate military targets and of civilian persons and objects that have protected status. Article 50 of the Protocol I additional to the Geneva Conventions states, "In case of doubt whether a person is a civilian, that person shall be considered to be a civilian". Additionally, "The presence within the civilian population of individuals who do not come within the definition of civilians does not deprive the population of its civilian character."[49] Rayan's wives and children were unambiguously civilians, and their home was unambiguously a civilian target. His mere presence in his own home did not deprive that household of its civilian character under customary international law. Israel's assassination of Rayan was therefore, unambiguously, a war crime.

Haaretz reported the killing of Nizar Rayan and his family in their home as "a significant development" not only because of Rayan's high-ranking position, "but also because of the message his assassination sends to the Palestinians." The message that Israel would indiscriminately bomb women and children in their homes was delivered as the IDF was preparing to launch a ground invasion in which "many civilian casualties can be expected."[50]

In the US media, much column space was provided to prominent defenders of Israel's war crimes. Charles Krauthammer wrote in the *Washington Post* that the violence was not "morally complicated" because "Israel is so scrupulous about civilian life that, risking the element of surprise, it contacts *enemy* noncombatants in advance to warn them of approaching danger." He cited an Associated Press report that informed how, on the first day of the bombing, "thousands of Gazans received Arabic-language cell-phone messages from the Israeli military, urging them to leave homes where militants might have stashed weapons."[51] Krauthammer may also have been alluding to what the IDF code-named "roof knocking", in which residents of buildings were warned that they had ten minutes to leave before the place was bombed. The killing of Rayan and his family was reportedly an example of "roof knocking" in action.[52] The falla-cious assumption inherent in Krauthammer's argument was that issuing warn-ings to civilians to leave a targeted building relieved Israel of its responsibility under international law not to engage in indiscriminate warfare and justified deliberately bombing them. It did not.

The remainder of his defense of Israel's war crimes consisted of a repetition of the standard Israeli hasbara: "Hamas . . . started this conflict with unrelent-ing rocket and mortar attacks on unarmed Israelis"; "Hamas hopes that inevi-table collateral damage—or, if it is really fortunate, an errant Israeli bomb—will kill large numbers of its own people for which, of course, the world will blame Israel"; Hamas had rejected "an extension of its often-violated six-month cease-fire (during which rockets never stopped, just were less frequent)"; etc.[53]

Harvard law professor Alan M. Dershowitz similarly defended Israel's actions in the *Wall Street Journal* as "justified under international law". Israel "should be commended" for what it was doing to the Palestinians in Gaza, in his view. He, too, invoked Obama's remarks in Sderot as justification. The President-elect's words showed that he "understands how the terrorists exploit the morality of democracies." Citing Article 51 of the UN Charter, Dershowitz observed that every nation has the right to self-defense against armed attack, but that "its ac-tions must satisfy the principle of proportionality." As evidence that Israel was satisfying this requirement of international law, he offered an anecdote related to him by a former head of the Israeli air force, according to whom the IDF declined to bomb one house because, after issuing a warning for civilians to evacuate, Hamas "sent mothers carrying babies to the house" because it "knew that Israel would never fire at a home with civilians in it"—a belief proven false the previous day with the killing of Rayan's family.[54]

Dershowitz's argument was a reiteration of Israeli hasbara that Hamas was fully responsible for the deaths of Palestinian civilians in Israeli attacks because the group was using civilians as "human shields". Turning again to what inter-national law actually has to say about it, the explicit prohibition of the use of human shields is found in Article 51 of the Protocol I additional to the Geneva Conventions: "The presence or movements of the civilian population or indi-vidual civilians shall not be used to render certain points or areas immune from military operations, in particular in attempts to shield military objectives from attacks or to shield, favor or impede military operations. The Parties to the con-flict shall not direct the movement of the civilian population or individual civil-ians in order to attempt to shield military objectives from attacks or to shield military operations." The definition of human shields does *not* include civilians who, for example, chose to remain in their homes despite warnings from Israel to flee. And, again, issuing such warnings did not relieve Israel of it obligation to respect the prohibition of indiscriminate attacks, which include: "(a) those which are not directed at a specific military objective; (b) those which employ a method or means of combat which cannot be directed at a specific military objective; or (c) those which employ a method or means of combat the effects of which cannot be limited as required by this Protocol; and consequently, in each such case, are of a nature to strike military objectives and civilians or civilian objects without distinction." Included within the definition of "indiscriminate attacks" is the disproportionate use of force, codified in Article 51(5)(b) as "an attack which may be expected to cause incidental loss of civilian life, injury to civilians, damage to civilian objects, or a combination thereof, which would be excessive in relation to the concrete and direct military advantage anticipated."

It is difficult to imagine that a professor of law at Harvard could be so unfamiliar with the Geneva Conventions and its additional Protocols. Yet Dershowitz proceeded to argue that Israel's attacks were "Perfectly 'Proportionate'," as the title of his op-ed declared. His argument was: "The claim that Israel has violated the principle of proportionality—by killing more Hamas terrorists than the number of Israeli civilians killed by Hamas rockets—is absurd." He didn't cite anyone making that absurd argument, for the obvious reason that nobody had. Dershowitz proceeded at some length and with much gusto to tear this strawman to pieces. Following that, he pointed out that "proportionality is not measured by the number of civilians actually killed, *but rather by the risk posed*" (emphasis added). Of course, it was precisely according to this measure that Israel had repeatedly been criticized by the international community and human rights organizations. But by employing the strawman argument, Dershowitz was able to relieve himself of having to actually address any of the numerous specific cases being cited as examples of disproportionate attacks, including Israel's deliberate bombing of police stations, mosques, schools, and homes.[55]

The US's Rejection of a Ceasefire

On January 2, as efforts were underway at the UN to achieve a ceasefire, Condoleezza Rice agreed that it "should take place as soon as possible," but only under the US condition that it be "durable and sustainable." President Bush elaborated on the meaning of this in a repetition of the standard propaganda narrative:

> The United States is leading diplomatic efforts to achieve a meaningful cease-fire that is fully respected. Another one-way cease-fire that leads to rocket attacks on Israel is not acceptable. And promises from Hamas will not suffice—there must be monitoring mechanisms in place to help ensure that smuggling of weapons to terrorist groups in Gaza comes to an end. . . . This recent outburst of violence was instigated by Hamas—a Palestinian terrorist group supported by Iran and

Syria that calls for Israel's destruction. . . . Eighteen months ago, Hamas took over the Gaza Strip in a coup, and since then has imported thousands of guns and rockets and mortars. Egypt brokered a cease-fire between Hamas and Israel, but Hamas routinely violated that cease-fire by launching rockets into Israel.[56]

In fact, the US was impeding diplomatic efforts to achieve a meaningful ceasefire, as illustrated the following day, when it blocked a Security Council statement calling for an immediate ceasefire (meaning both sides must cease fire, the only "one-way" ceasefire proposal being the US's).[57] The US's main precondition for the cessation of Israel's onslaught was the verifiable end of weapons smuggling into Gaza, with a UN monitoring mechanism to ensure compliance. This is what a "durable" and "sustainable" ceasefire meant. Needless to say, there was no equal demand for monitoring mechanisms to ensure that arms were not transported to Israel.

As far as Hamas's military capabilities were concerned, the IDF had already acknowledged its overestimation of Hamas's firepower, and the truth remained that it was Israel that violated the ceasefire, no matter how many times the lie to the contrary was repeated. As for what Bush described as a "coup" by Hamas, investigative historian and journalist Gareth Porter reminded that,

> Until mid-2007, there was a serious political obstacle to a massive conventional war by Israel against Hamas in Gaza: the fact that Hamas had won free and fair elections for the Palestinian parliament and was still the leading faction in a fully legitimate government. But the George W. Bush administration helped Israel eliminate that obstacle by deliberately provoking Hamas to seize power in Gaza. That plan was aimed at getting Palestinian President Mahmoud Abbas to dissolve the democratically elected Hamas government. . . . Rice demanded that Abbas dissolve the Haniyeh government. When Abbas didn't follow through, the Bush administration instructed him to declare a state of emergency and form an emergency government, while also encouraging the director of Fatah's paramilitary forces, Muhammad Dahlan, to attack Hamas, which responded to the US effort to see it overthrown by expelling Fatah from Gaza.[58]

Finally, contrary to the obligatory claim that it sought Israel's "destruction", Hamas had in fact long declared its intention of seeking a Palestinian state *alongside Israel*—a position Hamas has reiterated constantly over the years. To cite a few examples, in early 2005, Hamas issued a document outlining the idea of a unity government with Fatah that "for the first time in its existence," *Haaretz* reported, "unequivocally recognizes the 1967 borders and adopts the main principle guiding Fatah: the establishment of a Palestinian state with Jerusalem as its capital."[59] In early 2006, Hamas official Mahmoud al-Zahar publicly stated that Hamas was seeking a Palestinian state and would accept a long-term truce with Israel if it withdrew from the territories occupied in 1967.[60] Ismail Haniyeh, as already noted, reiterated to the *Washington Post* in February 2006 that Hamas would accept an agreement for "the establishment of a Palestinian state with Jerusalem as its capital with 1967 borders".[61] In December 2006, Khaled Meshal said that "all the Palestinian factions agree to a return of Israel's borders to pre-1967 designations. . . . We accept the need for two countries to exist, but Israel has no legitimacy so long as the occupation continues."[62] Meshal repeated the following month that Hamas was "with the consensus of the necessity of establishing a Palestinian state on the June 4 borders, including (East) Jerusalem, the right of return and the withdrawal of Israel to these borders." When asked whether this presupposed the existence of Israel, he answered,

> The problem is not that there is an entity called Israel. The problem is that the Palestinian state is non-existent. There is a reality that Israel exists on Palestinian territory. . . . There will remain a state called Israel. This is an issue of fact, but the Palestinians should not be required to recognize Israel. . . . As a Palestinian today I speak of a Palestinian and Arab demand for a state on 1967 borders. It is true that in reality there will be an entity or a state called Israel on the rest of Palestinian land. . . . We are demanding a Palestinian state on the 1967 border including Jerusalem and the right of return.[63]

Former US President Jimmy Carter met with Hamas officials in April 2008 and relayed their acceptance of a Palestinian state on the 1967 lines and willingness to "accept the right of Israel to live as a neighbor next door in peace" if it withdrew.[64] Hamas's "ultimate goal", Carter said, "is to see Israel living in their allocated borders, the 1967 borders, and a contiguous, vital Palestinian state alongside."[65] Meshal at the same time repeated, "We accept a state on the June 4 line with Jerusalem as capital, real sovereignty and full right of return for refugees but without recognizing Israel. . . . We have offered a truce if Israel withdraws to the 1967 borders, a truce of 10 years as proof of recognition."[66] *Haaretz* explained that "Meshal used the Arabic word hudna, meaning truce, which is more concrete than tahdiya—a period of calm—which Hamas often uses to describe a simple cease-fire. Hudna implies a recognition of the other party's existence."[67] On November 8, 2008, four days after Israel's violation of the ceasefire, Haniyeh once again reiterated his government's willingness to accept a Palestinian state within the 1967 lines.[68]

On January 4, 2009, Israel launched its ground invasion of Gaza, which was "likely to increase the civilian toll", the *New York Times* dryly noted. The fact that the US had blocked a UN statement calling for a ceasefire the day before was deemed unfit to print by the *Times*. Serving its usual role of manufacturing consent for US policy, the article stated that the Israel-Hamas ceasefire "began to break down in November"; naturally, the *Times* declined to explain why. The lead reporter in the byline, incidentally, was Isabel Kershner, who had reported Israel's November 4 violation the day it occurred, before the conscious decision was made to toss this inconvenient detail down the memory hole. Likewise, in the same sentence about the ceasefire, the *Times* repeated the by now standard refrain that "Hamas declared it over on Dec. 19", the relevant facts in that regard, too, being deemed unfit to print.[69]

As the IDF continued its operations, it destroyed the American International School in Beit Lahiya and damaged several others. It struck a market in Gaza City, killing five civilians and wounding many others.[70] It struck the Ibrahim al-Maqadmah mosque in Beit Lahiya while more than two-hundred people were inside praying, killing fifteen and injuring dozens more.[71]

Responding to international criticism of the IDF's attacks on mosques, Shin Bet director Yuval Diskin claimed that Hamas militants were storing weapons and hiding themselves inside on "the assumption that Israel will avoid attacking Muslim houses of worship"—a plainly mistaken belief, if any Hamas members were so naive as to espouse it. The Israeli government offered no evidence to support its claim as officials openly declared that mosques were being *deliberately* targeted.[72]

The number of Palestinian deaths rose to 491, with approximately 2,400 injured. According to the UN Office for the Coordination of Humanitarian Affairs (OCHA), "at least 20 percent of the fatalities and 40 percent of the injuries are women and children".[73] Israel refused to allow a medical team from the International Committee of the Red Cross (ICRC) into Gaza to help hospitals cope with the masses of injured people overwhelming Palestinian medical personnel.[74] UN Secretary-General Ban Ki-moon continued to urge the Security Council to bring about an immediate end to the violence—a vain effort, given US opposition.[75]

Israel continued to reject calls for a ceasefire, instead invoking what the *New York Times* had dubbed its "Diplomatic Offensive" as justification for continuing its military operation. "For many months," Prime Minister Ehud Olmert said, "we gave the cease-fire a chance in the hope of avoiding a wide-ranging military operation. Our hopes were dashed."[76]

US government officials praised Israel for its refusal to consider a ceasefire. As the IDF targeted civilian infrastructure and indiscriminately killed hundreds of civilians, Senate Republican leader Mitch McConnell opined that what Israel was doing was "very important".[77] Vice President Dick Cheney explained, "We think, if there's to be a ceasefire, you can't simply go back to the status quo ante, what it was a few weeks ago, where you had a ceasefire recognized by one side but not adhered to by the other."[78] It was true, of course, that only one side had adhered to the ceasefire—just not in the way Cheney meant. State Department spokesman Sean McCormack reiterated in a press briefing the US's demands for "a sustainable, durable cease-fire", the green-light from Washington for Israel to continue its killing and destruction until such time as a UN mechanism was in place to prevent smuggling into Gaza through the tunnels from Egypt, a vital lifeline through which much-needed civilian goods were also imported in defiance of Israel's ongoing illegal blockade.[79]

Illuminating just how isolated the US was in its efforts to block a ceasefire, British Prime Minister Gordon Brown openly split with the Bush administration by saying, "We need an immediate ceasefire. The blame game can continue afterwards, but this dangerous moment, I think, requires us to act."[80] As a further illustration of the kind if difficulty the US was having rationalizing its position of blocking an immediate ceasefire resolution, it's worth quoting at length from the transcript of McCormack's briefing:

> QUESTION: If it's true, as you say, and I think that you agree because you do say this humanitarian situation is dire, that lives are at stake, that there have been civilian casualties despite the efforts to minimize them.
>
> MR. MCCORMACK: Right.
>
> QUESTION: What's wrong with an immediate cease-fire that doesn't have to be sustainable and durable if, during the pause that you get from an immediate cease-fire, something longer-term can be negotiated?
>
> MR. MCCORMACK: Well—
>
> QUESTION: I don't understand the calculus. If you say you want to save lives and protect people, why not accept something that is less—
>
> MR. MCCORMACK: Right.
>
> QUESTION: —than perfect if you can get to that point?
>
> MR. MCCORMACK: Right.
>
> QUESTION: If you can use that to get to a point that is (inaudible)?

MR. MCCORMACK: I guess the calculation is, Matt, fundamentally that you're not going to get to that point under those circumstances.

QUESTION: How do you—how do you figure? How do you—

MR. MCCORMACK: Well, you know, we've gone through circumstances like this before, and it—look, it's—well, there are no sureties in these things. You know, you take a look at the facts, you take a look at history, and you make your best set of calculations and you do what you think is right in order to achieve the objectives that you have laid out. And it doesn't—it perhaps helps the situation in the immediate term—

QUESTION: Well, if this is something that can perhaps do that, what's wrong with that?

MR. MCCORMACK: Well, you know, the question is, Matt, you know, are you trading off against lives in the future just for, you know, an immediate cease-fire? You don't want to get to the point—you don't want to get—

QUESTION: Do you want to save lives or not?

MR. MCCORMACK: Of course, Matt. Of course. Of course—

QUESTION: Well, if you can perhaps do that, what's wrong with that?

MR. MCCORMACK: That's exactly my point, Matt. Are you trading off against lives in the future that will be lost if you don't go for a durable, sustainable cease-fire? We're not willing to do that.[81]

Thus, the Bush administration's argument was that the lives of many Palestinian civilians had to be deliberately sacrificed today so that, hypothetically, the lives of a few Israeli civilians could be saved in the future.

At the same briefing, another reporter broke ranks and noted that Hamas had offered to extend the truce with Israel, but that Secretary Rice had refused to be involved. When asked whether, in retrospect, refusing to engage in an effort that might have avoided bloodshed was a wise choice, McCormack stammered, "No, I—look, to lay the—lay the blame for what has happened at the doorstep of anyone else than Hamas is, I think, misguided."[82]

Facts be damned!

The message from the Bush administration was unambiguous: the US's support for Israel's military assault was unconditional. The US would do everything in its power to defend Israel's actions and block efforts to end the violence in order to permit Israel to finish the job of punishing the civilian population for the crime of having Hamas as Gaza's governing authority.

'No Humanitarian Crisis'

"Gaza Hospital Fills Up, Mainly With Civilians", read a headline in the *New York Times* on January 5. Taghreed El-Khodary reported from Gaza that "The casualties at Shifa [Hospital] on Sunday—18 dead, hospital officials said, among a reported 30 around Gaza—were women, children and men who had been with children." Most casualties "appeared to be civilians." El-Khodary quoted Israel's cabinet secretary, Oved Yehezkel, repeating that "there is no humanitarian crisis in Gaza"; however, she added, "Many here would dispute that."[83]

Israel had begun raining white phosphorus down on Gaza, incendiary munitions intended to be used on the battlefield as a smokescreen or for illumination, but a war crime under international law if used against civilian persons or objects. Israel denied that it was using phosphorus shells, but the London *Times* reported that "the tell-tale shells could be seen spreading tentacles of thick white smoke to cover the troops' advance."[84]

The World Health Organization (WHO) reported that the Palestinian death toll had risen to 548, including 44 women and at least 120 children. Women and children thus accounted for a third of the dead, as well as nearly half of the injured. Three mobile clinics were destroyed. A paramedic was killed and two injured while trying to evacuate a patient when their ambulance was struck by Israeli munitions. Six medical staff had been killed and three ambulances struck since the Israeli operation began. All hospitals in Gaza were operating on backup generators for the third day in a row.[85]

"The humanitarian crisis caused by the current violence in Gaza is hitting children and women the most," said a statement from the United Nations Children's Fund (UNICEF). "Children form over half of Gaza's population of nearly 1.5 million and are bearing the brunt of the conflict."[86] CNN reported the frightened and tearful reaction of Palestinian children to the devastation they were experiencing and concluded that "the violence children are witnessing will sow the seeds for future violence." One young boy was quoted as saying, "When the Jews bomb us when we are asleep . . . We get scared". The boy had told Hamas TV, "When we will grow up, we will bomb them back".[87]

Israel arrested two Palestinian journalists and continued to block reporters from entering Gaza, leading Aidan White, the General Secretary of the International Federation of Journalists (IFJ), to express "concerns that there is a systematic attempt to prevent scrutiny of actions by the Israeli military. . . . The eyes of the world are on Gaza, but Israel is trying to censor the news by keeping the media at bay."[88] The Geneva-based Press Emblem Campaign issued a statement condemning Israel for deliberately targeting Hamas-run media installations, including Al-Aqsa TV, Al-Resalah newspaper, and Sawt al-Aqsa radio.[89] Ethan Bronner was also moved to publicly criticize that Israel "should be ashamed" for restricting reporters' access to Gaza.[90]

"Warnings Not Enough for Gaza Families", stated the headline of another *Times* report from Taghreed El-Khodary on January 6. The lead paragraph read:

> GAZA—The Samouni family knew they were in danger. They had been calling the Red Cross for two days, they said, begging to be taken out of Zeytoun, a poor area in eastern Gaza City that is considered a stronghold of Hamas. No rescuers came. Instead, Israeli soldiers entered their building late Sunday night and told them to evacuate to another building. They did. But at 6 a.m. on Monday, when a missile fired by an Israeli warplane struck the relatives' house in which they had taken shelter, there was nowhere to run. Eleven members of the extended Samouni family were killed and 26 wounded, according to witnesses and hospital officials, with five children age 4 and under among the dead.[91]

Offering another glimpse into the reality on the ground, Ethan Bronner reported how the IDF was issuing warnings to Gazans: "While phones rang with the recorded threats against Hamas, leaflets dropped from airplanes littered the streets, saying: 'Hamas is getting a taste of the power of the Israeli military after more than a week and we have other methods that are still harsher to deal with Hamas. They will prove very painful. For your safety, please evacuate your neighborhood.' But many in Gaza said they had no place to go because many neighborhoods received the same message."[92]

Heeding the IDF's warnings, many civilians fled to the shelter of UNRWA-run schools, several of which the IDF proceeded to bomb. The previous night, the UN-run Asma Elementary School in Gaza City had received a direct hit, killing three civilians. An entire family of seven—five children and their parents—had also been wiped out the previous day when the IDF shelled their home. "These deaths", stated Maxwell Gaylard, the UN coordinator for humanitarian and development activities in the occupied territories, "highlight the tragic reality of the situation in Gaza that for civilians, neither homes nor UN shelters are safe."[93]

Forty-two civilians were killed on January 6 when Israel attacked an UNRWA school in Jabaliya, bringing to 619 the estimated number of dead Palestinians, 41 percent of whom were children.[94] It was the third UN school that the IDF had struck, in addition to an UNRWA health center. "The locations of all UN facilities have been communicated to the Israeli authorities and are known to the Israeli army", noted UN Secretary-General Ban Ki-moon in a statement.[95]

The UN High Commissioner for Refugees (UNHCR), António Guterres, further noted that "this is the only conflict in the world in which people are not even allowed to flee".[96] It was the "civilian population of Gaza", reiterated OCHA, that "was continuing to bear the brunt of the violence."[97] Ban Ki-moon also continued to emphasize the urgent need for a ceasefire to end the violence, describing the situation in Gaza as a "humanitarian crisis".[98] The ICRC likewise described the consequence of Israel's blockade and military operation as a "full-blown humanitarian crisis".[99]

In response to reports that it had hit the UNRWA school in Jabaliya, the IDF initially claimed that "mortar shells were fired from within the school at IDF forces. The IDF returned fire."[100] John Ging, the UNRWA director of operations in Gaza, rejected Israel's claim, stating that "militants have not violated the sanctity of UN facilities".[101] He relayed the assurances of his staff that "there were no militants in the schools" and challenged anyone claiming to have evidence to the contrary to produce it. "The school was clearly marked as a UN building", he added, "and GPS coordinates for the site had been provided to Israeli forces."[102] Christopher Gunness similarly stated that "after an initial investigation, we at UNWRA are 99 percent certain that there were no militants at that school when this instance took place."[103]

The *Washington Post* nevertheless disingenuously reported, "UN officials said they did not know whether fighters had been in the school, and wanted the matter investigated."[104] By contrast, a *Haaretz* headline reported, "UN rejects IDF claim Gaza militants operated from bombed-out school".[105] At the same moment that article was published on the *Post's* website, it was hosting an online discussion with UNRWA spokesman Johan Erickson, who repeated, "We can say categorically that at the moment of the shelling there were no militants inside the school compound."[106]

Christopher Gunness subsequently issued an official statement saying that the IDF had admitted "in private briefings with diplomats" that the alleged rocket fire had come "from outside the UNRWA school compound, not from inside it." The IDF had therefore acknowledged that its initial allegation was "entirely baseless."[107] The IDF still publicly maintained, however, that mortar shells were fired at Israeli forces "from within the Jabaliya school. In response to the incoming enemy fire, the forces returned mortar fire to the source."[108]

Impervious to the facts on the ground, the US remained staunchly in support of Israel's onslaught. When White House Press Secretary Dana Perino was asked, given the climbing number of civilian deaths, whether Israel was "being as cautious as the US has been urging them to be", she responded,

> We have counseled our ally Israel to be very cautious about protecting innocents, and I do think that the Israelis take great care to do so. I saw the reports about the school. I don't have any information about that. I think that we should not jump to conclusions, and we should wait to find out what the evidence says. What we do know is that Hamas often hides amongst innocents, and uses innocent people, including children, as human shields. So I think we need to wait and find out all the facts before we make a judgment as to what happened in this incident.

Thus, in the view of the Bush administration, the benefit of the doubt belonged not to the innocent victims of the attack, but to its perpetrators. In accordance with this standard, the US needn't wait for any evidence from the IDF to support its claims that Hamas was using civilians as "human shields", but could rather jump to the conclusion that this was so by taking the IDF's word for it strictly as a matter of faith.

When asked what President Bush's response would be to Ban Ki-moon's "call to reign in the Israelis", Perino asserted that "the pictures and the stories are gut-wrenching—on both sides. I mean, you have casualties on the Israel side, as well." Adding that "Hamas has been terrorizing Israel" since 2007 and citing the example of a rocket that struck a vacant Israeli school the day before, she answered that Bush would "make that case on behalf of the Israelis, as well."[109] As Perino was attempting to draw equivalence between the suffering "on both sides", the ratio of Palestinian women and children killed for each Israeli civilian was *eighty-four to one*.[110]

At the UN, Condoleezza Rice once again boasted how the US was "working around the clock to try to end the violence"—by continuing to block any efforts in the Security Council to call for an immediate ceasefire.[111]

A spokeswoman for the President-elect, meanwhile, repeated that Barack Obama was monitoring the situation, but that "there is one president at a time, and we intend to respect that."[112] Obama broke his silence only with the meaningless comment, "The loss of civilian life in Gaza and Israel is a source of deep concern for me, and after January 20, I'm going to have plenty to say about the issue."[113]

By then, the massacre in Gaza—carried out with US arms and Washington's blessing—would be over.

'They Are Doing Good'

As part of its ongoing efforts to limit the information coming out of Gaza, Israel continued to prevent journalists from entering. Israel was "seeking to entirely control the message and narrative", Bronner noted in the *Times*. "For the truth to get out," he quoted John Ging saying, "journalists have to get in."[114] By banning journalists from Gaza, the world was largely dependent on reports from the IDF, with Palestinian reporters living in Gaza facing the often prohibitive danger of venturing out to gather information to share with the world.[115] Cameraman Basel Faraj became the second journalist to be killed on January 6, following the earlier killing of photographer Hamza Shahin. "Israel is making a mockery of its status as a democratic country by violating international law," criticized Aidan White of the IFJ, "ignoring its own Supreme Court and showing contempt for the United Nations by defying its obligations under Resolution 1738 to protect journalists in conflict zones."[116]

Some of the most scathing and honest criticisms of Israel's assault, the likes of which could not be found in the US mainstream media, continued to come from Israeli commentators. It is worth quoting a few examples at length. In *Haaretz*, Gideon Levy wrote,

> Everything is permitted, legitimate and just. The moral voice of restraint, if it ever existed, has been left behind. . . . They liquidated Nizar Rayan? Nobody counts the 20 women and children who lost their lives in the same attack. There was a massacre of dozens of officers during their graduation ceremony from the police academy? Acceptable. Five little sisters? Allowed. Palestinians are dying in hospitals that lack medical equipment? Peanuts. . . . Here lie their bodies, row upon row, some of them tiny. Our hearts have turned hard and our eyes have become dull.[117]

Avi Shlaim, who served in the Israeli army in the 1960s, wrote in *The Guardian*,

> Eight months before launching the current war on Gaza, Israel established a National Information Directorate. The core messages of this directorate to the media are that Hamas broke the ceasefire agreements; that Israel's objective is the defense of its population; and that Israel's forces are taking the utmost care not to hurt innocent civilians. Israel's spin doctors have been remarkably successful in getting this message across. But, in essence, their propaganda is a pack of lies. A wide gap separates the reality of Israel's actions from the rhetoric of its

spokesmen. It was not Hamas but the IDF that broke the ceasefire. It did so by a raid into Gaza on 4 November that killed six Hamas men. Israel's objective is not just the defense of its population but the eventual overthrow of the Hamas government in Gaza by turning the people against their rulers. And far from taking care to spare civilians, Israel is guilty of indiscriminate bombing and of a three-year-old blockade that has brought the inhabitants of Gaza, now 1.5 million, to the brink of a humanitarian catastrophe.[118]

Gideon Lichfield wrote in *Haaretz*,

> I frequently get asked by Israelis, "why aren't we winning the PR war? Why don't people understand that this is what we have to do?" Many are convinced that there is something wrong with Israeli hasbara (public advocacy), that the spokespeople aren't effective enough, or that the Palestinians have a huge and demonically efficient propaganda machine. When I hear this I have to explain that Israeli hasbara is so sophisticated that there is still no adequate word for it in English; that some of Israel's spokespeople could talk the hind legs off a donkey and then persuade the donkey to dance the hora. . . . So why isn't Israel winning the PR war? Partly, of course, it's because the numbers are against it. Six hundred Palestinians dead versus nine Israelis, as of today's figures: There's just no way to make that proportion look pretty. Retired generals can drone on all they like about what 'proportionality' really means in the laws of war, ambassadors can helpfully point out that many more Germans were killed than British in the Second World War, but these are theoretical notions; on television, what looks bad looks bad. (Nor do I really buy the argument that if Israel's casualties were more visibly bloody—if, say, the media showed the gory pictures of the few people who have been hit by Qassams instead of holding them back to keep the home front from getting agitated—then you could counter the stream of barbaric images from Gaza. There's just no competition.)[119]

The prevailing attitude in Israel, however, was exemplified by a *Jerusalem Post* editorial that asked, "How do Israelis feel when our artillery strikes a UN-run school building, killing dozens of people? The answer is: deeply shaken, profoundly distressed, sorrowful at the catastrophic loss of life. But we do not feel guilt. We are angry at Hamas for forcing this war on us; for habitually using Gaza's civilians as human shields; and—in this latest outrage—for transforming a center where people had sought refuge into a shooting gallery and weapons depot." There remained, of course, no evidence that Hamas had done any such thing. UN officials had firmly rejected the claim rockets were fired from the school in Jabaliya, and not even the IDF had claimed that it was being used as a "weapons depot". As was also so often true for the US media, facts didn't much matter.

The *Post* editorial went on to complain, instructively, that too many news agencies had engaged in "propagandistic" reporting, such as when a BBC camera "took us inside" Al-Shifa Hospital, providing "a voyeuristic, nearly pornographic, view from inside emergency rooms, operating theaters and morgues". It wasn't that the BBC was fabricating images or exaggerating the severity of the situation on the ground; its journalistic sin, rather, was that it provided an actual firsthand glimpse into the very real devastation and human suffering that Israel was inflicting on Palestinian civilians in Gaza.[120]

In Israel, on a hill overlooking the Palestinian town of Beit Hanoun, Jews gathered to watch the smoke rising from the Israeli bombardment. "Avi Pilchick took a long swig of Pepsi and propped a foot on the plastic patio chair he'd carried up the hillside to watch the fighting", relayed McClatchy reporter Shashank Bengali. "'They are doing good,' Pilchick, 20, said of Israeli forces battling Palestinian militants in Gaza, 'but they can do more.'"[121]

On the prevailing attitude of her fellow Israeli citizens, *Haaretz* correspondent Amira Hass lamented, "What luck my parents are dead. . . . What luck that they are not alive to hear Ehud Barak and Tzipi Livni explaining that we have nothing against the Palestinian people, and the cabinet secretary explaining that there is no humanitarian crisis and this is just Hamas propaganda. . . . How lucky they are not here and cannot hear the crowd roaring in the coliseum."[122]

Israel Ignores a UN Ceasefire Resolution

By January 7, the Palestinian death toll reached 680, with women and children accounting for 45 percent of fatalities.[123] UNICEF reported that "Gaza's water and sewage system is on the verge of collapse due to the lack of fuel and power."[124] OCHA reiterated that civilians continued to "bear the brunt of the violence" with "no safe space in the Gaza Strip" to find shelter. The Israeli army was dropping leaflets, broadcasting radio and TV messages, and phoning Gazans to order them "to evacuate their homes and go to urban areas." Far from indicating an Israeli desire to avoid civilian casualties, its actions put people at greater risk, causing civilians to panic and flee "amidst gunfire and shelling."[125]

Under international pressure to allow humanitarian assistance into Gaza, Israel agreed to a three-hour daily halt to its operations. "When you are trying to feed 750,000 people a day in Gaza as we are," responded Christopher Gunness, "you need a permanent ceasefire. You can't do that in a three-hour window".[126] The halt offered only a "brief moment of relief for the civilian population", informed UNRWA spokesman Johan Erickson, in which they could "bury their dead" and "rush out to get food, water, etc." Furthermore, the "humanitarian corridor" Israel had promised to facilitate "did not materialize", and UNRWA remained unable "to distribute food and medicine and water to all the hundreds of thousands of Gazans who desperately need it at this time." Additionally, while the US had been rejecting calls for an immediate ceasefire on the hypothetical grounds that it wouldn't be observed by Hamas, Erickson noted that the temporary cessation of operations "was respected by both sides."[127]

Setting in motion developments that would lead to a UN investigation that produced what is popularly known as the Goldstone Report, the Human Rights Council, upon the formal request of thirty-three of its forty-seven members, announced that it would hold a special session to address "the grave violations of human rights in the Occupied Palestinian Territory including the recent aggression in the occupied Gaza Strip".[128]

On January 8, the Palestinian death toll stood at 758, including 56 women and 257 children, according to OCHA. The killing was reaching "alarming proportions", said the organization Medicins Sans Frontiers (Doctors Without Borders), with the "extreme violence indiscriminately affecting civilians."[129] The UN Bureau of the Committee on the Exercise of the Inalienable Rights of the Palestinian People issued a statement expressing its concern that Israel's assault was "being carried out with a rather scant regard for the life of the Palestinian civilian population". Contrary to its continued denials, Israel was "perpetuating a humanitarian crisis in the Gaza Strip".[130]

Due to Israel's blockade, there was a "severe shortage" of gas needed for cooking, as well as the diesel fuel required to run the generators that hospitals were relying on for power. The Independent described the shortage as "the biggest problem facing Shifa and other medical facilities in Gaza."[131]

The London Times reported that photographic proof of Israel's use of white phosphorus munitions had emerged "despite official denials" by the IDF. The Times had identified munitions bearing the designation M825A1, made in the USA. "This is what we call a quiet shell—it is empty," lied an IDF spokeswoman when confronted with the evidence; "it has no explosives and no white phosphorus. There is nothing inside it".[132]

During the three-hour time period when the IDF was supposed to be implementing a lull and facilitating a corridor for aid to get through, it instead attacked a UN convoy. In separate incidents, two UNRWA staff members were killed, bringing to four the total number of staff killed since Israel's operation began. As a consequence of the attacks, which were condemned by the Secretary-General, UNRWA was forced to suspend food distribution.[133]

Amnesty International made note of reports that Israeli forces were using Palestinians as human shields.[134]

Uncovering one of the most horrific atrocities of Operation Cast Lead, the ICRC and Palestine Red Crescent Society (PRCS) finally arrived in Zeytoun, where members of the Samouni family had been terrorized for days by Israeli forces. The rescue team had been trying since January 3 to reach the neighborhood, but was prevented from doing so by the IDF. When they got there, they "found four small children next to their dead mothers in one of the houses. They were too weak to stand up on their own. One man was also found alive, too weak to stand up. In all there were at least 12 corpses lying on mattresses." More dead and injured were found in other homes. Israeli soldiers ordered them to leave the area, but the rescue team refused. "The Israeli military must have been aware of the situation but did not assist the wounded," said Pierre Wettach, the ICRC's head of delegation for Israel and the Occupied Palestinian Territories. "Neither did they make it possible for us or the Palestine Red Crescent to assist the wounded." The ICRC concluded that the IDF had "failed to meet its obligation under international humanitarian law to care for and evacuate the wounded."[135]

At the UN Security Council, a ceasefire resolution was finally passed, but only after incorporating language to satisfy the US.[136] Resolution 1860 condemned "all violence and hostilities directed against civilians" and called for "an immediate, durable and fully respected ceasefire, leading to the full withdrawal of Israeli forces from Gaza". The resolution incorporated the US demand that the ceasefire be "durable" by calling upon member nations to make efforts "to prevent illicit trafficking in arms and ammunition" into Gaza. It also emphasized "the need to ensure sustained and regular flow of goods and people through the Gaza crossings" and called for "the unimpeded provision and distribution throughout Gaza of humanitarian assistance, including food, fuel, and medical treatment."[137]

The resolution passed in the fifteen-member Council with fourteen votes in favor. The US, knowing that Israel would interpret the call for a "durable" ceasefire precisely as US officials had repeatedly defined it, abstained. Speaking after the vote, Condoleezza Rice called it "a step towards our goals" and proceeded to succinctly reiterate the main talking points of the fictional official narrative:

> We must establish an international consensus that Gaza must never again be used as a launching pad for rockets against Israeli citizens, because it is important to remember how this crisis began. Violence in Gaza was instigated by Hamas, a terrorist group that has called for the destruction of Israel. Eighteen months ago, Hamas took over the Gaza Strip in a coup, and since then thousands of guns, rockets and mortars have

been smuggled into Gaza. Hamas refused to extend the *tah-diya* [ceasefire agreement], and continued armament is a root cause of the current situation and has gravely endangered the residents of both Gaza and southern Israel. Hamas's commitment to violence is an attack not only on Israel, but also on the two-State solution.[138]

Following the vote, a diplomatic row broke out between the US and Israel when Ehud Olmert publicly boasted that he had pressured the US not to vote in favor of the resolution, leaving Condoleezza Rice "shamed" because she had "prepared and arranged" the draft, but "in the end she did not vote in favor." As Olmert told the story,

> In the night between Thursday and Friday, when the secretary of state wanted to lead the vote on a ceasefire at the Security Council, we did not want her to vote in favor. I said "get me President Bush on the phone". They said he was in the middle of giving a speech in Philadelphia. I said I didn't care. "I need to talk to him now". He got off the podium and spoke to me. I told him the United States could not vote in favor. It cannot vote in favor of such a resolution. He immediately called the secretary of state and told her not to vote in favor.

State Department officials denied Olmert's story, saying it was the US's plan all along to abstain.[139] The official reason given was that the US "thought it important to see the outcomes of the Egyptian mediation," a reference to an initiative by Egypt and France to mediate a ceasefire outside of the UN. No rationale was offered for why interest in the outcome of that effort should preclude a US vote in favor of the UN ceasefire resolution.[140] Rice subsequently charged that Olmert's account was "fiction" and emphasized that she and President Bush had discussed "the importance of allowing the Council to send a signal even though the United States believed that the resolution was premature."[141]

A *Haaretz* report, however, offered additional insights into the incident leading to the conclusion that Olmert's version was "closer to the truth" than Rice's. Israel was not worried, the newspaper explained, because it was clear that the US was going to veto a ceasefire resolution that had been drafted by Libya.

> But then, Palestinian Authority Prime Minister Salam Fayyad, a former senior World Bank official, decided that this was the moment to make use of his Washington connections. Fayyad persuaded the Americans to support a softened version of the resolution, which called for a prompt cease-fire, hoping that such a resolution would speed up the ongoing truce talks. He

asked the British and French for help, and they agreed. Rice signaled her French and British counterparts, Bernard Kouchner and David Miliband, that she was on board. European diplomats, UN officials and a senior PA official all said Thursday that as of last Friday night it was clear to almost everyone that the US, like the other 14 Security Council members, would vote for the softened resolution. They said Rice had promised as much to her European colleagues.

Then came the phone call and the US reversal—an instructive example of how the US government often acts to accommodate Israel even if in contradiction to its own declared policy.[142]

The day after the UN passed the ceasefire resolution, the US Senate passed a resolution "Recognizing the right of Israel to defend itself against attacks from Gaza and reaffirming the United States' strong support for Israel in its battle with Hamas, and supporting the Israeli-Palestinian peace process". The next day, the US House of Representatives passed its own version of the bill. Their sponsors willfully oblivious to the facts on the ground, both resolutions praised Israel for facilitating humanitarian aid to Gaza and condemned only the violence committed by Hamas. The House resolution exonerated Israel and blamed Hamas alone for all civilian casualties for its use of "human shields", an allegation for which there remained no evidence.[143]

"Despite repeated calls to the offices of the resolutions' principle Democratic sponsors," wrote Stephen Zunes, author and Professor of Politics and International Studies at the University of San Francisco, "not one of them could provide a single example of this actually occurring during the current wave of fighting." He noted that similar accusations made by Democratic leaders in a 2006 resolution during Israel's war on Lebanon "were later systematically rebuked in a detailed and meticulously researched 249-page report by Human Rights Watch." The Congress, by "attempting to redefine just what constitutes human shields", was setting a dangerous precedent:

> Despite this desperate effort to rationalize the large-scale killing of Palestinian civilians by Israeli forces, the fact that a Hamas leader lives in his own private home, attends a neighborhood mosque and seeks admittance in a local hospital does not constitute the use of human shields. . . . In short, [Speaker of the House Nancy] Pelosi and other congressional leaders appear to be advancing a radical and dangerous reinterpretation of international humanitarian law that would allow virtually any country with superior air power or long-range artillery to get away with war crimes. . . . It is also important to note that, even if Hamas were using human shields in the legal definition

of the term, it still does not absolve Israel from its obligation to avoid civilian casualties.[144]

With the US having abstained from the UN vote on Resolution 1860 despite it incorporating Washington's demand for a "durable" ceasefire, and with both houses of Congress explicitly endorsing Operation Cast Lead, the message to Israel was unambiguous. Having received loud and clear the message from Washington, Israel had the green light it needed to be able to continue with impunity its military assault on the helpless civilian population of the Gaza Strip.

It's 'Hard' for Israel Not to Kill Civilians

"Gaza bloodshed continues despite UN calls for ceasefire", read the headline in *The Guardian* on January 9, as Operation Cast Lead entered its fourteenth day.[145] Prime Minister Olmert dismissed the UN ceasefire resolution as "unworkable".[146] The IDF would "continue to act in order to attain the objectives of the operation," proclaimed the Israeli government. *Haaretz* astutely observed that Israel's interpretation of the UN resolution was consistent with what the US had intended a "durable" ceasefire to mean: Israel "would not accept any cease-fire" and "the IDF would not withdraw from Gaza until the establishment of a mechanism that would ensure a halt to weapons-smuggling from Egypt into the Hamas-ruled territory."[147]

It appeared, however, that Hamas was not well able to rearm itself via the tunnels. The IDF suggested as much when it admitted several days later that Hamas was suffering ammunition shortages and that there had been "a dramatic drop in the ability of Hamas to launch rockets against Israel".[148]

As Israel's operation continued, OCHA reported 758 Palestinians dead, including 56 women and 257 children, and at least 3,100 injured, including 452 women and 1,080 children.[149] The IDF targeted a media office building.[150] The population was traumatized and sleep-deprived, reported John Ging. UN Emergency Relief Coordinator John Holmes said that the daily three-hour cessation of operations provided some relief from Israel's bombardment, but did not permit the population access to basic services for long enough to be meaningful.[151] UNRWA remained unable to resume its operations because,

> On numerous occasions in recent days, humanitarian convoys have come under Israeli fire even though their safe passage through clearly designated routes at specifically agreed times had been confirmed by the Israeli liaison office. Although UNRWA's protests were met with renewed promises that there would be no further coordination failures, humanitarian access continued to be impeded by live-fire incidents. Given the

nature, severity and frequency of these incidents, UNRWA decided that the risks to its staff exceeded the threshold required for operational safety.[152]

In Washington, DC, when asked whether Israel was living up to its obligations under international law, Condoleezza Rice defended its actions by saying it was "very difficult" for Israel to do so in Gaza, "which is a very densely populated area." It was also "hard" for Israel not to kill civilians, she argued, because "Hamas participates in activities like [using civilians as] human shields".[153]

By January 10, the Palestinian death toll was at 833, including at least 85 women and 284 children.[154] Israel continued its indiscriminate use of white phosphorus munitions "in densely populated areas", reported Human Rights Watch, which "violates the requirement under international humanitarian law to take all feasible precautions to avoid civilian injury and loss of life."[155] B'Tselem similarly observed that Israel's use of white phosphorus in civilian areas was "absolutely prohibited" under international law since the munitions "cannot distinguish between combatants and civilians" and "by their nature cause unnecessary suffering."[156]

Despite the fact that the distinctive air-bursting munitions had been photographed streaming their burning wafers over populated areas, the IDF continued to deny that it was using white phosophorus munitions.[157] "I can tell you with certainty," an IDF spokesperson had lied the week before, "that white phosphorus is absolutely not being used". Israel continued to maintain that any munitions it might be firing were being used "in accordance with international law".[158]

The implausibility of Israel's denials did not stop the Western media from treating its use of the weapon as merely an unproven claim. "Group accuses Israel of firing white phosphorus into Gaza," read a CNN headline, despite the article being accompanied online with an image of the weapon in use—clear photographic proof that the "accusation" was true.[159] In a similar fashion, a BBC article was accompanied by a photograph unmistakably showing white phosphorus munitions bursting over a residential area with the caption: "Human Rights Watch says pictures like this point to white phosphorus use, but Israel denies this". The article disingenuously asserted that there was "no way independently to explain the contradiction between the Israeli military's denial" and reports of its use of the weapon. Unimaginatively, the BBC failed to realize the simplest and most obvious explanation, given their own photographic proof: that Israeli officials were lying.[160]

A letter published on January 11 in the London *Sunday Times* and signed by twenty-seven scholars and academics—including Richard Falk (a professor at Princeton, as well as UN Special Rapporteur) and Professor of International Law Christine Chinkin (who would later join the UN fact-finding mission that produced the so-called Goldstone Report)—rejected Israel's contentions that its actions could be justified as "self-defense" and criticized both Israel and Hamas for committing war crimes.[161]

The US media continued to downplay the death and destruction Israel was inflicting on the Gaza Strip by characterizing the IDF as taking great care not to harm civilians, blaming all civilian deaths on Hamas or the "fog of war", and otherwise echoing Condoleezza Rice's statement that it was "hard" for Israel not to kill civilians despite its best efforts. In a *New York Times* article titled "A Gaza War Full of Traps and Trickery", Steven Erlanger reported that Hamas had turned Gaza into "a deadly maze of tunnels, booby traps and sophisticated roadside bombs". Hamas was hiding weapons "in mosques, schoolyards and civilian houses," and "the leadership's war room" was "a bunker beneath Gaza's largest hospital". In support of these claims, Erlanger cited "Israeli intelligence officials". The sourcing for the rest of the article followed suit: "According to an Israeli journalist embedded with Israeli troops . . .", "Israeli officials say . . .", ". . . the Israelis say . . .", "The Israelis say . . .", etc. Erlanger referred to Hamas's "use of civilians as shields in Gaza" as though it was a fact, rather than an unproven Israeli claim. He uncritically relayed Israel's assertion that its killing of over forty civilians in the attack on the Jabaliya UN school was return fire "in response to mortar shells fired at Israeli troops". Erlanger then offered his judgment that "[s]uch an action is legal" despite understatedly and contradictorily acknowledging in the same sentence that there were "questions" about whether the attack was "proportional".[162]

Subsequent *Times* articles would repeat these claims, but without any kind of caveat as to the source. Thus, Ethan Bronner could subsequently report as fact, without caveat, that "Hamas booby-traps schools, apartment buildings and the zoo, and its fighters hide among civilians".[163]

B'Tselem reported on the result of a preliminary IDF inquiry into its attack on the Jabaliya school:

> The report indicated that rocket fire from a building next to the school had been identified. For unclear reasons, firing from the air "was not possible" so the decision was made to direct fire "towards the source of the shooting." The standard deviation of these mortar shells is a few dozen meters. Soldiers fired three shells, one of them hitting the school. Army officers told *Haaretz* that, in retrospect, "the choice of the means of response was faulty," and that the army should have used a precise weapon. It was also reported that apparently, the school was marked on maps that had been given to paratroopers operating in the area. . . . Under these circumstances, a weapon with this range of deviation constitutes a weapon that does not

distinguish between civilian and military objects. Accordingly,
it violates the principle of distinction in international humanitarian law and its use must be absolutely prohibited.[164]

That is, contrary to Steven Erlanger's suggestion that the attack was "legal", it
was yet another unambiguous war crime.

On January 12, the death toll was at 884 dead, including 93 women and
275 children.[165] The medical journal *The Lancet* published a statement signed
by 760 American medical students expressing their outrage at Israel's "violent
assault on a civilian population" and for causing a "humanitarian disaster" in
Gaza. "We are embarrassed at US complicity", the statement added, "and regret
that many of the weapons fired come from our own country."[166]

The UN Human Rights Council passed a resolution strongly condemning
Israel's military operation, which had resulted in "massive violations of human
rights of the Palestinian people and systematic destruction of the Palestinian
infrastructure". It decided to dispatch an independent fact-finding mission "to
investigate all violations of international human rights law and International
Humanitarian Law by the occupying Power, Israel, against the Palestinian people throughout the Occupied Palestinian Territory, particularly in the occupied
Gaza Strip, due to the current aggression".[167] The resolution passed with thirty-
three votes in favor, thirteen abstentions, and one vote against, from Canada,
which argued that the resolution was not balanced because it did not condemn
Hamas rocket attacks against Israel. (The reason there was no nay vote from the
US was that it was not a member of the Council; it would later join under the
Obama administration.)[168]

On January 13, the Palestinian death toll was at 971.[169] UNICEF conveyed that some Palestinian children were "so shocked that they are unable
to speak".[170] ICRC President Jakob Kellenberger visited Al-Shifa Hospital and
related the "shocking" scene he saw there. It was "unacceptable to see so many
wounded people."[171] The ICRC and Red Crescent Movement issued a joint
statement deploring Israel's abandonment of wounded people "left to suffer
alone, unable to reach hospitals and inaccessible to ambulances and medical
workers", which was in violation of Israel's obligation under international law
"to collect, care for and evacuate the wounded, without delay or discrimination."[172] Ban Ki-moon pleaded, "My message is simple, direct and to the point:
the fighting must stop. To both sides, I say: Just stop, now. Too many people
have died. There has been too much civilian suffering. Too many people, Israelis
and Palestinians, live in daily fear of their lives. And in Gaza, the very foundation of society is being destroyed: people's homes; civic infrastructure; public
health facilities; and schools."[173]

Human Rights Watch published a report condemning Israel for causing a
"humanitarian crisis" with its ongoing blockade of Gaza and military opera-

tions. Noting that Egypt was complicit for refusing to open the Rafah border crossing, the group stated that the blockade was "a form of collective punishment in violation of international law". The report detailed the horrendous suffering of the civilian population from the military operations: IDF forces denying medical teams access, leaving the injured and sick to die; "dire shortages of food, water, cooking gas, fuel and medical care"; the electricity, water, and sewage infrastructure "stretched to a breaking point"; medical facilities "completely overwhelmed"; hospitals running on generators dependent on fuel denied to them by Israel; people traumatized, with children, who comprised more than half the population, being particularly vulnerable; and casualty estimates that were likely conservative "because some of them have not been able to reach hospitals or be brought to morgues."[174]

The IFJ issued a statement again condemning Israel's efforts to control the flow of information out of Gaza, including its continued detention of two Palestinian journalists and attacks on media offices. "Israel makes plain its intention to prevent proper and objective coverage of the conflict in Gaza," said Aidan White. "The situation speaks more about unashamed intimidation and manipulation of media than about security consideration on the part of Israel."[175]

An ICRC official confirmed to the Associated Press that Israel was using white phosphorous munitions. His comments made headlines in the US, however, because he also said that it was "not very unusual to use phosphorus to create smoke or illuminate a target. We have no evidence to suggest it's being used in any other way." The widely published AP article was deceptively titled "ICRC: Israel's use of white phosphorus not illegal"—even though the official quoted, Peter Herby, hadn't said that. He had merely indicated that additional information was required before a judgment could be made as to whether Israel's use of the weapon was legal. He specifically stated that "evidence is still limited because of the difficulties of gaining access to Gaza", but this portion of his comments wasn't reported until the third-to-last paragraph. The distinction between the false headline and what Herby actually said was no doubt lost upon many readers, even among those who actually read past the title.[176]

In a particularly instructive example of how the media obfuscated the truth in such a manner as to manufacture consent for the US's support for Israeli crimes, the *Christian Science Monitor* repeated Herby's comments under the headline, "Red Cross: No evidence Israel is using white phosphorus illegally". Further down the page, however, one could read: "Monitor staff writer Robert Marquand reported yesterday that human rights groups have witnessed white phosphorus munitions exploding over populated areas of Gaza." No attempt was made to reconcile the blatant contradiction for readers.[177]

Moreover, in a separate article published the same day, Marquand quoted Chief of Staff Gabi Ashkenazi lying that the IDF "does not use white phosphorus". But a senior military analyst for Human Rights Watch, Marc Garlasco, had been on the northern border of Gaza for five days watching the munitions exploding over "the Jabaliya refugee camp, one of the most crowded areas in Gaza." Garlasco told the *Monitor*, "I can see them; we are very certain, whatever the Israeli Defense Forces may say, that white phosphorus is being used." Garlasco also told the *Monitor* that such use of the munitions over populated areas was illegal. But there was no headline informing "Human Rights Watch: Israel is using white phosphorus illegally". Instead, the title was "Israel under fire for alleged white phosphorus use"—as though it was still a question whether Israel was even *using* the munitions, much less whether it was doing so legally.[178]

On the ground in Gaza, Taghreed El-Khodary reported for the *New York Times* that large numbers of Palestinians were "fleeing their homes for makeshift shelters in schools, office buildings and a park as the Israeli Army continues to press its military campaign deeper into Gaza City." The IDF continued to drop leaflets warning families to evacuate, but as the killing of over forty people at the UN school in Jabaliya had demonstrated, "the shelters are not completely safe". Among the reasons Palestinians were fleeing was the IDF's use of "a noxious substance that burns skin and makes it hard to breathe." Reporters in Gaza City were shown the source of this substance, a "metal casing with the identifying number M825A1", a white phosphorus munition. The article concluded:

> When exposed to air, it ignites, experts say, and if packed into an artillery shell, it can rain down flaming chemicals that cling to anything they touch. Luay Suboh, 10, from Beit Lahiya, lost his eyesight and some skin on his face Saturday when, his mother said, a fiery substance clung to him as he darted home from a shelter where his family was staying to pick up clothes. The substance smelled like burned trash, said Ms. Jaawanah, the mother who fled her home in Zeytoun, who had experienced it too. She had no affection for Hamas, but her sufferings were changing that. "Do you think I'm against them firing rockets now?" she asked, referring to Hamas. "No. I was against it before. Not anymore."[179]

The M825A1 munitions were, of course, supplied to Israel by the US—a fact that the *Times* instructively declined to inform its readers.[180]

More proof still was needed, however, for El-Khodary's colleague Ethan Bronner to report that Israel was using white phosphorus. Two days later, in the only other mention of it by the *Times* throughout Israel's entire military operation, he wrote that ICRC President Jakob Kellenberger had seen "no evidence of the use of white phosphorus" during a visit to Gaza. "Palestinians say Israel is using it", Bronner added.[181] Thus, all of the relevant facts Bronner saw fit to sweep down the memory hole, to be replaced by a meaningless citation of one individual who happened not to have personally witnessed white phosphorus being used, along with the characterization of its use by Israel as nothing more than a *claim* made by *Palestinians*. The repeated statements from human rights organizations like Human Rights Watch and B'Tselem condemning its documented use, confirmations by the ICRC and UN, the photographic proof published in media outlets around the world, and even his own colleague's on-the-ground reporting from Gaza of the finding of shells marked "M825A1". . . . None of this did Bronner consider relevant information to bestow upon his readers.

Remarkably, following the end of Operation Cast Lead, Bronner penned an article defending his record and proclaiming that his reporting did not have a pro-Israel bias. His argument was the non sequitur that since he was also accused of being too pro-Palestinian by Israel's defenders, therefore his reporting must be balanced. After so settling the matter, Bronner had the chutzpah to accuse his critics of being the ones lacking objectivity. They were victims of their own prejudice, he argued, which explained why they couldn't recognize that his articles were perfectly "neutral". Despite his best efforts at denial and deflection, examples of his bias riddled the article. The clearest instance was how he mischaracterized critics of Israel's operation—which included reputable Israeli journalists, the UN, the ICRC, Amnesty International, Human Rights Watch, B'Tselem, Gisha, etc.—as being apologists for indiscriminate Palestinian rocket attacks. Bronner then pitted this bogus representation of Israel's critics against the positions held by Israel's defenders: Israel was not the aggressor; Hamas used human shields; and the IDF was exercising restraint, trying to avoid civilian casualties, and allowing in humanitarian aid despite being at war—a summary of pro-Israel talking points that could have been pulled from the headlines of Bronner's own newspaper. Oblivious to the irony, Bronner concluded by expressing his agreement with one critic who wrote him to say, "You should not be a reporter if you are not telling the whole story, not just the parts that sell."[182]

It truly must have been "hard", as Condoleezza Rice had put it, for Israel to avoid civilian casualties while using white phosphorus in heavily populated areas and otherwise engaging in indiscriminate attacks, intentionally targeting civilian objects, preventing medical teams from helping the wounded, and enforcing a policy of deliberate collective punishment against the trapped and defenseless population of Gaza. It is understandable that US government officials like Rice would seek to downplay Israel's crimes, given their complicity in them.

The 'Education' of Hamas

The US government's complicity in Israel's crimes also goes a long way toward explaining the nature of the reporting in the US mainstream media. Commentary ranged from self-censorship that served to obfuscate the nature of Israel's military assault to openly praising Israel's attacks on civilians. In perhaps the most astonishing example of the latter, *New York Times* columnist Thomas L. Friedman on January 13 lauded Israel's military operation in Gaza, encouraging the IDF to inflict even more "pain" on the Palestinian civilian population. He began by posing his only question about Israel's operation: "What is the goal? Is it the education of Hamas or the eradication of Hamas?" He hoped that it was the former. Then he explained why. Operation Cast Lead was like Israel's 2006 war on Lebanon, in which Israel's strategy was "to use its Air Force to pummel Hezbollah and, while not directly targeting the Lebanese civilians with whom Hezbollah was intertwined, to inflict substantial property damage and collateral casualties on Lebanon at large." This deliberate use of indiscriminate force by the IDF to punish the civilian population was "the education of Hezbollah". Israel's policy "was not pretty, but it was logical." Friedman continued: "In Gaza, I still can't tell if Israel is trying to eradicate Hamas or trying to 'educate' Hamas, by inflicting a heavy toll on Hamas militants and heavy pain on the Gaza population. If it is out to destroy Hamas, casualties will be horrific and the aftermath could be Somalia-like chaos. If it is out to educate Hamas, Israel may have achieved its aims."[183]

In sum, Friedman expressed his hope that Israel's goal was to "educate" Hamas, which he defined as a policy of intentionally inflicting "heavy pain" on the civilian population—as in Lebanon, where the policy had been to deliberately cause destruction of civilian property and civilian casualties. In other words, the three-time Pulitzer Prize-winning columnist for the *New York Times* was explicitly praising Israel's "logical" military policy of committing what he, as a former war correspondent, must certainly have understood were war crimes.

Despite the rising Palestinian death toll, the media was apparently effective in manufacturing consent for the US policy of supporting Israel's criminal actions. A poll showed that 44 percent of Americans still supported Israel's use of force, compared to only 36 percent who thought it "excessive". Furthermore, 44 percent said Hamas was fully responsible for the violence, compared to only 14 percent who held Israel responsible and just 9 percent who said both parties shared in the blame.[184]

Public opinion in Israel also remained strongly supportive of Israel's murderous violence. An editorial in the *Jerusalem Post* commented that "the world must be wondering, do Israelis really believe that everybody is wrong and they alone are right? The answer is yes." In the *New York Times*, Ethan Bronner noted that dissenting voices were rare, "at least among the Jewish population". The caveat was appropriate; further into the article, he noted that for many of the 1.4 million Israelis who were Arab, about one-fifth of Israel's population, the violence had "produced a very different feeling, a mix of anger and despair."[185]

Indeed, a poll in Israel showed that 94 percent of Israeli Jews supported the military assault on Gaza, while 85 percent of Israeli Arabs opposed it.[186]

In Washington, at her Senate confirmation hearing on January 13, President-elect Obama's choice for Secretary of State, Hillary Clinton, defended Israel's onslaught. She and Obama were both "reminded of the tragic humanitarian cost", but "deeply sympathetic to Israel's desire to defend itself". She hollowly added that they were "pained by the suffering of Palestinians and Israeli civilians."[187] As she spoke, the latest casualty figures were at least 387 Palestinian women and children killed, compared to three Israeli civilians—a ratio of 129 to 1.[188]

By January 14, the Palestinian death toll was at 1,013, including 76 women and 322 children.[189] In a briefing to the UN Security Council, John Holmes—with apparently intended irony—said he was sure that the Israeli government was doing everything possible to minimize civilian casualties, but that it was "clearly not succeeding." The US representative, Rosemary A. DiCarlo, said the US was concerned about the humanitarian situation, while reiterating the US's green-light for continued Israeli violence (the need for a "durable" ceasefire, as per the US's unilateral interpretation of Resolution 1860). She also lectured the other delegates that they "must not forget . . . that this outburst of violence was instigated by Hamas". It was Hamas alone who was responsible for any civilian deaths, she asserted, on the grounds that Hamas was using them all as human shields.[190]

In an unprecedented move, Amnesty International called for the UN Security Council to enact an arms embargo on *all* parties, pointing out that a shipment of US arms was on its way to Israel. The US Department of Defense said the arms were being delivered "to the US stockpile in Israel" and were not intended for Israel to use in its military operations. However, as Amnesty pointed out, an agreement between the two countries "has allowed US munitions stockpiled in Israel to be transferred to the Israeli Defense Force in 'an emergency.'" The arms shipment had been approved by the Pentagon four days after the start of Israel's military operation and included white phosphorus munitions.[191]

On January 15, the estimated Palestinian death toll was 1,086, including 79 women and 346 children; 4,900 had been wounded, including 724 women and 1,709 children. An additional number of Palestinians were treated for shock. The Israeli death toll remained at three Israeli civilians and nine Israeli soldiers, four of whom were killed by friendly fire. The main UNRWA compound in Gaza City, the Al-Wafa Hospital, the Al-Fata Hospital, and the Al-Quds Hospital all took direct hits in IDF attacks. Two ambulances were also hit. The UNRWA compound was targeted with white phosphorus, causing a fire that destroyed a workshop and the main warehouse, where hundreds of tons of humanitarian supplies were being stored and 700 Palestinians were taking refuge. Israel also attacked the Al-Shorouq Tower in Gaza City, which housed main offices and studios of local and international media, resulting in the wounding of two journalists from Abu Dhabi TV.[192]

While Israel continued to deny using white phosphorus, John Ging told a news conference how it was used against the UNRWA compound. "It looked like phosphorous, it smelled like phosphorous and it burned like phosphorous, so that's why I'm calling it phosphorous," he said. "The place went up in flames. Our workshop was the part that was hit most severely. It went on fire, as did part of the warehouse. Of course, we had to take cover until we got reassurances that there wouldn't be further firing." The fire service was delayed because of the fighting in the area, and by the time they got there, "it was too late to save the warehouse", where "hundreds of tons of food and medicine" were to be dispatched that day to UNRWA's health and food centers.[193]

Israel claimed that its attacks on the UNRWA warehouse were in response to Hamas fire from the vicinity. John Ging, however, emphasized that no militants had fired from the compound and questioned why Israeli liaison officers never reported to UN officials that Hamas militants were in the area, despite having been in constant contact. "They should tell us if there are militants operating in our compound or in our area," he said. "The fact that they don't, we take as indicative of the fact that there wasn't."[194] Christopher Gunness similarly replied, "Their credibility is hanging in rags." The IDF, he said, had privately acknowledged that the alleged source of fire was several hundred yards away from the UNRWA compound.[195] John Holmes also condemned the use of white phosphorus in civilian areas, saying that Israel's disproportionate use of force was unjustified and in violation of international humanitarian law.[196]

In response to the criticisms, Tzipi Livni defended Israel's actions as necessary "to defend its citizens."[197] Prime Minister Olmert said Israel was sorry for destroying the warehouse, but tacitly acknowledged that it had been deliberately targeted by claiming that "Hamas fired from the UNRWA site." It was "absolutely true", he insisted, that Israeli forces "were attacked from that place".[198]

When Secretary of State Condoleezza Rice was asked whether she had submitted a protest to Israeli officials about the attack on the UN compound, she answered that they had discussed "the difficulties that this had caused and the need to try to avoid such incidents". Then she proceeded to defend the attack as demonstrative of "the very dangerous nature of the kind of fighting that is going on"—a reiteration of the basic theme that Hamas, not Israel, was responsible for the deaths that occurred when the IDF targeted locations where it could expect civilians to be present.[199]

The willingness of the US government to defend the attack on the UNRWA compound was contrasted by that of even its closest allies. UK Prime Minister Gordon Brown called it "indefensible".[200] The president of the European Parliament, Hans-Gert Pöttering, condemned it as an example of Israel's "contempt for international law".[201] The Parliament passed a resolution expressing its shock at the suffering of the population; deploring attacks on Palestinian civilians and UN targets; and calling on both sides to respect UN Resolution 1860, which meant that Israel must lift its blockade and allow in humanitarian aid to "fulfill its obligations under international law and international humanitarian law".[202]

Nine Israeli human rights groups called for an investigation into possible Israeli war crimes, including the Israel section of Amnesty International, B'Tselem, Gisha, and Physicians for Human Rights-Israel.[203] Amnesty International additionally called for an investigation specifically into Israel's attack on the UNRWA headquarters.[204]

By January 16, the toll was 1,115 Palestinians dead, one-third of them children. Of the 5,015 injured, more than one-third were also children.[205] Israel struck a home in Jabaliya refugee camp, killing Hamas Interior Minister Saeed Seyyam, along with his son, his brother, and six others.[206] UNICEF reported that 840,000 children in Gaza had been traumatized by the ongoing violence and warned of the long-lasting psychological consequences. "We do not want to assume it will create a generation of hate," said Sigrid Kaag, Regional Director for the Middle East and North Africa. "But it definitely—the social trauma, the impact, the loss children have suffered—be it of a sibling, be it of a parent, be it of their closest friend, be it their auntie—this is an immense, immense negative impact on anybody's life, even in the best of circumstances."[207]

Under increased international pressure, the IDF announced that it would increase its daily operational halt from three to four hours. The World Food Program (WFP) welcomed the additional hour, but noted that "it is still insufficient time for WFP to meet the needs of its beneficiaries. This will only be possible when the fighting stops."[208] Human Rights Watch condemned rocket attacks from Palestinians as war crimes and called on Israel to cease its indiscriminate use of heavy artillery in residential areas of Gaza City. The rights group further observed that the IDF had been "broadcasting warnings that told people, among other things, that 'For your own safety, you are required to leave your homes immediately and move to the city centers.' Despite these warnings, the IDF has launched attacks against the Gaza city center, causing civilian casualties."[209]

The UN General Assembly, in an emergency special session, passed a resolution supporting Security Council Resolution 1860 and its call for an immediate ceasefire and an end to the blockade. The resolution passed 142 to 4. Three of the nay votes were from Israel, the US, and the Pacific island nation of Nauru. The fourth was from Venezuela, which had broken diplomatic relations with Israel in protest over its onslaught. The Venezuelan government explained that its intent had been to abstain because it felt the resolution wasn't critical enough of Israel's failure to meet its obligations under international law, but that its vote was recorded as a nay due to technical difficulties.[210]

Israel criticized the resolution as one-sided because it did not condemn Hamas's alleged use of schools, mosques, and hospitals to conduct military operations or its smuggling of arms into Gaza through the tunnels. But as Marc Garlasco of Human Rights Watch pointed out the day of the vote, Israel was "very quick to say" that Hamas was using civilian locations for military purposes in order to justify its killing of civilians, "but very short on proof."[211] The resolution also did not condemn Israel's well-documented (and indeed admitted) attacks on homes, schools, hospitals, or UN facilities; or its use of white phosphorus munitions over populated areas; or the fatality ratio of 124 Palestinians killed for each Israeli (excluding the four Israeli soldiers killed by friendly fire), etc. Needless to say, these omissions were not cited by the US and Israel as reasons to reject the resolution as "one-sided".

The rationale offered by the US for its vote was that the basic framework for a ceasefire had already been established with Security Council Resolution 1860 so a separate General Assembly resolution was "neither necessary, nor useful". The US deputy ambassador to the UN, Alejandro D. Wolff, said that the Assembly "must be careful not to complicate efforts to seek a solution or undermine ongoing diplomatic activity to halt the violence in Gaza". He offered no explanation for how a General Assembly resolution expressing support for Resolution 1860 would "undermine" efforts to implement it.[212]

Tzipi Livni had in the meantime flown to Washington, where she and Condoleezza Rice signed a memorandum of understanding (MOU) describing steps the US and Israel would take to stop arms from being smuggled into Gaza.[213] As Rice and Livni spoke in Washington of the need to prevent Hamas from rearming, US-made F-16s, Apache helicopters, and white phosphorus munitions continued to rain death and destruction on Gaza. "Over the past few decades," *Salon* fortuitously reported the same day the MOU was signed, "the US has provided about $53 billion in military aid to Israel." In addition, "US taxpayers have paid to supply over 500 million gallons of refined oil products—worth about $1.1 billion—to the Israeli military". US taxpayers had paid the shipping costs, too. Thus, the US appeared to be "providing most, or perhaps even all, of the Israeli military's fuel needs." On the other hand, the US Congress hadn't "shown much interest" in helping with the fuel shortage in Gaza for purposes such as cooking or running hospital generators.[214]

The day after the MOU was signed, the IDF struck another UNRWA-run school, in Beit Lahiya. Ban Ki-moon condemned the attack, which occurred two days after Israeli leaders had apologized and assured him that UN sites would be respected. He demanded an investigation and "punishment of those who are responsible for these appalling acts."[215] In its attack on the school, the IDF had once again employed white phosphorus. John Ging informed that two brothers, aged five and seven, were killed, and fourteen others wounded. Christopher Gunness implored, "Where you have a direct hit on an UNRWA school where about 1,600 people had taken refuge, where the Israeli Army knows the coordinates and knows who's there, where this comes as the latest in a catalogue of direct and indirect attacks on UNRWA facilities, there have to be investigations to establish whether war crimes have been committed."[216] More than fifty UN facilities had sustained damage since the assault began.[217] Sixteen health facilities had been damaged by Israeli attacks, which constituted a "grave violation of international humanitarian law," said the head of the WHO mission in Gaza, Tony Laurance.[218]

The editors of *The Lancet* condemned Israel's slaughter:

> We find it hard to believe that an otherwise internationally respected, democratic nation can sanction such large and indiscriminate human atrocities in a territory already under land and sea blockade. The heavy loss of civilian life and destruction of Gaza's health system is unjustified and disproportional, despite rocket attacks by Hamas. The collective punishment of Gazans is placing horrific and immediate burdens of injury and trauma on innocent civilians. These actions contravene the fourth Geneva Convention.[219]

In a separate special report, the British medical journal also related the conditions at Al-Shifa Hospital:

> The best-equipped medical facility in the Gaza Strip resembled a charnel house. Corpses were strewn on the floor after morgue refrigerators inside Al-Shifa—a 585-bed hospital in Gaza City—were packed to capacity in the first week of the Israeli military offensive in the Palestinian enclave. Doctors were reduced to treating the injured on the floor and doing surgery by flashlight.... "These are scenes out of Dante's Inferno. Many arrive with extreme amputations, with both legs crushed, [what] I suspect are wounds inflicted by very powerful explosives called DIME", Mads Gilbert, a visiting Norwegian surgeon at Al-Shifa, told reporters.... Even before Israel's aerial assault began on Dec. 27, the public-health infrastructure inside the Gaza Strip was precarious because an 18-month blockade has created a dearth of drugs and spare parts for crucial medical equipment. Fuel shortages put hospital patients, dependent on backup generators for hours at a time, at grave risk. Without sufficient fuel for ambulances, donkey carts often haul the wounded. But 3 weeks of bombardment and tank fire has put the health services on the brink of collapse.[220]

On January 18, two days before Barack Obama was sworn in as President of the United States, as a result of an Egyptian mediation initiative, Israel announced an end to Operation Cast Lead. Hamas also declared a ceasefire, accompanied with a warning that Israel had one week to evacuate its forces from Gaza.

The Palestinian Ministry of Health reported that 1,300 Palestinians had been killed, including 104 women and 410 children; 5,300 had been injured, including 795 women and 1,855 children. An undetermined number of adult male civilians were among the casualties. Additional bodies continued to be recovered from areas where Israel had withdrawn. The Israeli casualty figures remained at three civilians killed and nine soldiers, four by friendly fire. Eighty-four Israeli civilians had been injured.[221]

Before the fighting ended, a tragedy played out live on Israel's Channel 10 news when Dr. Izzeldin Abuelaish, a Palestinian doctor who worked at the Sheba Medical Center in Israel and had been reporting daily for the station, frantically told reporters by phone that an Israeli attack on his home in the Jabaliya refugee camp had killed three of his daughters, Bisan (age twenty), Mayar (age fifteen), and Aya (age fourteen), as well as his niece, Nur (age seventeen). Surviving members of his family were injured, trapped in their home, and unable to get help. On live television, the Israeli reporter speaking with Dr. Abuelaish made phone calls to try to get help to his family. As a result of the reporter's effort, the IDF allowed an Israeli ambulance through to take the wounded to an Israeli hospital. "Everybody in Israel knows that I was talking on the television and on the radio," Dr. Abuelaish said, "that we are at home, that we are innocent people. Suddenly, today, when there was hope for a ceasefire, on the last day, I was talking to my children, [and] suddenly they bombed us. Is that how you treat a doctor who takes care of Israeli patients? Is that what's done? Is this peace?"[222]

The IDF dealt with the tragedy by claiming that a sniper had opened fire on its troops from Dr. Abuelaish's building. "The Israeli Defense Forces does not target innocents or civilians, and during the operation the army has been fighting an enemy that does not hesitate to fire from within civilian targets," said an IDF spokesman.[223] Later, as Dr. Abuelaish spoke on camera to reporters, an Israeli woman who had three sons in the IDF shouted and pointed her finger at him, demanding to know why there were weapons in his home. Afterward, she told reporters that the IDF would not have attacked his home "without good reason".[224] The IDF, however, later retracted its claim that there had been sniper fire from the building.

"I raised my children to work, and to be soldiers of peace. I believed medicine could be a bridge for peace between Israelis and Palestinians," said Dr. Abuelaish. "Why did they destroy my hopes? My children? I want a reason, give me a reason." He expressed his belief that "Violence is never the right way. My daughters and I were armed with nothing but love and hope."[225] Dr. Abuelaish, the lead paragraph of a *New York Times* article informed, had "devoted his life to medicine and reconciliation between Israelis and Palestinians." Further down the page, the *Times* explained:

> Dr. Abuelaish is a rarity: a Gazan at home among Israelis. He describes himself as a bridge between the two worlds, one of the few Gazans with a permit to enter Israel because of his work. "I wanted every Palestinian treated in Israel to go back and say how well the Israelis treated them," he said. "That is the message I wanted to spread all the time. And this is what I get in return?" Later, sitting on a plastic chair near his daughter's hospital room, Dr. Abuelaish spoke with the prayer of so many parents who have buried their children as part of the Israeli-Palestinian conflict. "I hope that my children will be the last price."[226]

Israel remained unapologetic. "These claims of war crimes are not supported by the slightest piece of evidence," said a Foreign Ministry spokesman as the international community called for investigations into Israel's military conduct. Testimony collected by B'Tselem from residents in the village of Khuza'a included claims that Israeli forces had "attempted to bulldoze houses with civilians inside", "killed civilians trying to escape under the protection of white flags", "opened fire on an ambulance attempting to reach the wounded", and "used indiscriminate force in a civilian area and fired white phosphorus shells." B'Tselem noted that this was consistent with other testimony that it had gathered. One of the first Western journalists to get into Gaza following the ceasefire, photographer Bruno Stevens reported, "What I can tell you is that many, many houses were shelled and that they used white phosphorus. . . . It appears to have been indiscriminate."[227]

The "education" of Hamas—or, translated from Thomas Friedman's euphemistic terminology, the collective punishment of the entire civilian population of Gaza—was complete.

CHAPTER 3

THE 'PEACE PROCESS'

"I T MAY NOT BE very clear who actually won this conflict, if that concept means anything in Gaza," John Ging told reporters at an UNRWA press conference on January 19, 2009, "but it's pretty clear who lost, and that's the civilian population of Gaza, and to a much lesser extent the civilian population of southern Israel".[1]

John Holmes reported to the UN Security Council that 21,000 homes had been destroyed or badly damaged. "Widespread destruction was caused to Gaza's economic and civil infrastructure," he informed. "I saw, for example, an entire industrial and residential area in East Jabaliya that had been systematically bulldozed. . . . Damage to power, water, sanitation, medical, education and agricultural infrastructure was widely visible." There was a critical need for humanitarian assistance for Gaza, but Israel was "continuing the effective collective punishment of the civilian population" by allowing only "a limited trickle of items into Gaza". One consequence was that the population relied on the tunnels for daily essential goods, the existence of which Israel then pointed to as a rationale for continuing the siege that made the tunnels necessary in the first place.

Karen AbuZayd had a similar message for the Council: "In my tours around Gaza since the ceasefire of 18 January, I have been deeply saddened to see what appears to have been systematic destruction to schools, universities, residential buildings, factories, shops and farms."[2]

By January 28, the estimated Palestinian death toll had risen to 1,366, including 430 children and 111 women, not including those who had died due to lack of access to health care; 5,380 Palestinians had been injured, including 800 women and 1,870 children.[3] With detailed information about the names, ages, and circumstances of their deaths, B'Tselem subsequently put the final figure at 1,391 Palestinians killed, at least 759 of whom were civilians, including 108 women and 318 minors. In addition, 248 police officers not participating in hostilities were killed in Israeli bombings of police stations. Hence, more than 72 percent of Palestinians killed in Operation Cast Lead were civilians.[4]

An Amnesty International investigative team arrived in Gaza and reported finding evidence of the widespread use of white phosphorus munitions, including still-burning wedges of phosphorus, in heavily populated areas.[5] Amnesty documented additional Israeli violations of international law, including extensive destruction of civilian homes and property, deliberate blocking and impeding of humanitarian assistance to the civilian population, and collective punishment of the civilian population.[6] As its fact-finding mission continued, Amnesty reported evidence that Israelis had shot Palestinian children carrying a white flag.[7] Israel had also used flechettes against civilians during its operations. Flechettes are four-centimeter metal darts, thousands of which are packed into shells that explode in the air, scattering the darts over an area 300 meters wide and 100 meters long. "An anti-personnel weapon designed to penetrate dense vegetation, flechettes should never be used in built-up civilian areas", Amnesty noted.[8] In addition, Amnesty found that "Emergency medical rescue workers, including doctors, paramedics and ambulance drivers, have repeatedly come under fire from Israeli forces in the Gaza conflict while carrying out their duties."[9]

The *Washington Post* followed up on the story of the Samouni family in Zeytoun, reporting that in all, twenty-nine members of the family were killed by Israeli forces who refused to allow ICRC ambulances through to evacuate the wounded.[10]

Israeli soldiers began to speak out about their experiences in the operations. Troops were ordered to "Fire on anything that moves in Zeytoun". "We pounded Zeytoun into the ground," a soldier told the London *Times*. "We were to shoot first and ask questions later."[11] Soldiers had left behind racist graffiti on walls, such as "Arabs need 2 die", "1 is down, 999,999 to go", "Die you all", "Death to Arabs", "Arabs must die", and "The Only Good Arab is a Dead Arab".[12] Reuven Pedatzur commented in *Haaretz* on how Israel's senior commanders had "decided to avoid endangering the lives of soldiers, even at the price of seriously harming the civilian population." What happened in Gaza "was no war", he explained, because "in reality, not a single battle was fought during the 22 days of fighting."[13]

On January 20, Barack Obama was inaugurated as President of the United States. The position his administration immediately took with regard to Israel's massacre in Gaza was that Israel should investigate itself, rather than having an independent investigation under the auspices of the UN. "We expect Israel will meet its international obligations to investigate and we also call upon all members of the international community to refrain from politicizing these important issues," said Susan Rice, the administration's newly appointed ambassador to the UN, in her first speech before the Security Council—"politicizing" being her euphemism for condemning Israel's war crimes.[14]

Obama appointed George Mitchell as his special envoy for Middle East peace and dispatched him to the region as Israel continued air strikes on the tunnels in Gaza. On the day Mitchell arrived in Israel, the Israeli group Peace Now released a report finding that Israel's illegal settlement construction in the West Bank had increased by almost 60 percent in 2008.[15]

As Mitchell was meeting with officials from Israel and the PA, Hamas once again reiterated its willingness to enter into a long-term truce with Israel. "We want to be part of the international community," said Hamas official Ghazi Hamad. "We accept a state in the '67 borders. . . . We are not talking about the destruction of Israel."[16] It nevertheless remained obligatory for US government officials and media commentators to state that Hamas refused to recognize Israel's "right to exist". The Obama administration continued the policy of refusing diplomatic relations with Hamas and demanding that it accept the US's preconditions for negotiations. Hamas must "renounce violence", "recognize Israel", and "agree to abide by prior agreements", Secretary of State Hillary Clinton reiterated in February. Needless to say, no reciprocal demands were made of Israel.[17]

George Mitchell, a former US Senator, was not new to the conflict. He had been appointed under the Bill Clinton administration to lead a fact-finding commission to make policy recommendations. The Sharm El-Sheikh Fact-Finding Committee Report, also known as the Mitchell Report, was submitted to the Bush administration in April 2001. The report called on both sides to end the violence and on Israel to "freeze all settlement activity, including the 'natural growth' of existing settlements." It referred to previous negotiations under the so-called "peace process", including in Madrid in 1991 and in Oslo in 1993. The latter round of talks had resulted in the signing of the first Oslo Accord, which stated that the goal was to arrive at "a permanent settlement based on Security Council Resolutions 242 and 338." The Mitchell Report noted that under the Oslo agreement, "the integrity and status" of Gaza and the West Bank "as a single territorial unit" was to be "preserved during the interim period". In addition to Israel having agreed to this, "customary international law, including the Fourth Geneva Convention, prohibits Israel (as an occupying power) from establishing settlements in occupied territory pending an end to the conflict." Israeli settlement construction, the report further noted, had nevertheless continued. "A cessation of Palestinian-Israeli violence", it emphasized, "will be particularly hard to sustain unless the GOI [government of Israel] freezes all settlement construction activity."[18]

Mitchell's previous role undoubtedly fed apprehensions among Israeli policy makers that the Obama administration would try to pressure Israel to halt its illegal settlement activity. Avigdor Lieberman, a prominent member of Israel's legislature, the Knesset, proclaimed that there was "no connection" between the settlements and Israel's conflict with the Palestinians and declared that Mitchell's mission had "absolutely no chance" of succeeding.[19]

But while US officials expressed rhetorical opposition to Israel's colonization of the West Bank, in practice, US policy was effectively supportive of it. And while the US expressed rhetorical support for a two-state solution based on Resolution 242, in practice, US policy effectively undermined that goal. In order to understand the role the US has played in the Israeli-Palestinian conflict, it is necessary to examine the historical context of the so-called "peace process" and its rejectionist framework, within which US policy would continue to operate under the Obama administration.

Resolution 242

One of the key documents comprising the legal foundation for the two-state solution is UN Security Council Resolution 242, which was passed unanimously on November 22, 1967, following the June "Six Day War", during which Israel invaded and occupied the Syrian Golan Heights, the Egyptian Sinai Peninsula, and the Palestinian territories of the West Bank and Gaza Strip (the latter of which had until then been under the administration of Jordan and Egypt, respectively). The preamble and first operative clause of the resolution reads:

> The Security Council,
>
> *Expressing* its continuing concern with the grave situation in the Middle East,
>
> *Emphasizing* the inadmissibility of the acquisition of territory by war and the need to work for a just and lasting peace in which every State in the area can live in security,
>
> *Emphasizing* further that all Member States in their acceptance of the Charter of the United Nations have undertaken a commitment to act in accordance with Article 2 of the Charter,
>
> 1. *Affirms* that the fulfillment of Charter principles requires the establishment of a just and lasting peace in the Middle East which should include the application of both the following principles:
>
> (i.) Withdrawal of Israel armed forces from territories occupied in the recent conflict;

> (ii) Termination of all claims or states of belligerency and re-
> spect for and acknowledgment of the sovereignty, territorial
> integrity and political independence of every State in the area
> and their right to live in peace within secure and recognized
> boundaries free from threats or acts of force. . . .[20]

The Israeli interpretation of Resolution 242 rests primarily on two arguments. First, there is the claim that the absence of the definite article "the"
before "territories occupied" in sub-paragraph (i.) of the first operative clause
means that the Security Council did not intend for Israel to withdraw from *all*
of the territory occupied. Second, there is the claim that sub-paragraph (i.) is
conditional upon sub-paragraph (ii.), meaning that there is to be no withdrawal
until "secure and recognized boundaries" are established through negotiations.[21]
Thus, the Israeli position is that the Palestinians must negotiate a final settlement on borders while remaining under foreign military occupation and while
Israel continues to prejudice the final outcome of those negotiations with its
ongoing colonization of the West Bank.

The call for the withdrawal of Israeli
forces must be understood within the context of the emphasized principle of
international law that it is inadmissible to acquire territory by war. As a basic
point of fact with regard to English grammar, the absence of the article "the"
before the noun "territories" has no effect on the meaning of the sentence insofar as the *extent* of withdrawal is concerned. The Golan Heights, the West
Bank, the Gaza Strip, and the Sinai Peninsula are all "territories", plural, that
were occupied during the war, and therefore "territories", plural, from which
Israel must withdraw, according to the plain and unambiguous language of
Resolution 242.

The Israeli argument absurdly maintains that the text cannot be understood
to read "*the* territories" and so must be understood to read "*some of the* territories"—patently fallacious and self-defeating logic. To further illustrate the
prima facie absurdity of the Israeli interpretation, the second operative clause
of Resolution 242 affirms the necessity "For guaranteeing freedom of navigation through international waterways in the area", which is a clear reference to
Egypt's closing of the Straits of Tiran and Suez Canal to Israeli vessels prior to
the war. According to the logic of the Israeli argument, since this clause doesn't
include the definite article "the" before "international waterways", it must be
understood to mean that Egypt could continue to blockade Israeli shipping in
some waters, just not *all* international waterways through which Israeli shipping
occurred. Israel would surely reject such preposterous reasoning in this regard,
yet employs the same fallacy in an effort to justify its ongoing occupation and
theft of Palestinian land.

Israel had made its interpretation of the draft resolution known before the vote, prompting French Ambassador to the UN Armand Berard to point out another reason why Israel's argument was moot: the equally authentic French version of the text *does* contain the definite article. He observed that, "on the point which the French delegation has always stressed as being essential—the question of withdrawal of the occupation forces—the resolution which has been adopted, if we refer to the French text which is equally authentic with the English, leaves no room for any ambiguity, since it speaks of withdrawal '*des territoires occupés*', which indisputably corresponds to the expression 'occupied territories'."[22]

As for the claim that the first sub-clause is conditional upon the second, as a simple point of fact, the extent of the withdrawal called for in sub-clause (i.) is *not* determined by sub-clause (ii.), but is rather determined independently from it by the words "from territories occupied", which means the territories beyond the 1949 armistice lines that Israel occupied during the June war. The resolution states that "both" withdrawal *and* secure and recognized boundaries are a requirement for peace, conditioning neither one upon the other.

To support the Israeli interpretation, its proponents also often quote statements by American or British officials made years after the resolution was passed. However, it is not for member states to individually interpret the meaning of UN resolutions. Unilateral interpretations have no legitimacy under international law. Rather, resolutions must be understood and interpreted according to the will of the Security Council as a whole. Furthermore, the relevant documentary record for understanding the will of the Council is not that from years afterward, but that prior to and up until the time of the resolution's passage.

Before the vote on the resolution, which was drafted by the UK, British Foreign Secretary George Brown stated:

> The attitude of the British Government is clear. . . . I should like, if I may, to set out certain principles which I believe should guide is in striving collectively for a lasting settlement. Clearly, such principles must derive from the United Nations Charter. Article 2 of the Charter provides that "All Members shall refrain in their international relations from the threat or use of force against the territorial integrity or political independence of any State. . . ." Here the words "territorial integrity" have a direct bearing on the question of withdrawal, on which much has been said in previous speeches. I see no two ways about this; and I can state our position very clearly. In my view, it follows from the words in the Charter that war should not lead to territorial aggrandizement.[23]

He reiterated this point prior to the adoption of the resolution by stating, "I should like to repeat what I said when I was here before: Britain does not accept war as a means of settling disputes, nor that a State should be allowed to extend its frontiers as a result of war. This means that Israel must withdraw."[24]

Lord Caradon, the British representative at the UN who was principally credited with drafting the resolution, also reiterated his government's position during deliberations on the text: "As to the first operative paragraph, and with due respect for fulfillment of Charter principles, we consider it essential that there should be applied the principles of both withdrawal and security, and we have no doubt that the words set out throughout that paragraph are perfectly clear."[25] Two days before the vote, Lord Caradon reiterated, "If I had to sum up the policy which has been repeatedly stated by my Government, I would go back to the words used by my Foreign Secretary in the General Assembly less than a month ago." After quoting George Brown's words, he emphasized, "In our resolution we stated the principle of the 'withdrawal of Israel armed forces from territories occupied in the recent conflict' and in the preamble we emphasized 'the inadmissibility of the acquisition of territory by war'. In our view, the wording of those provisions is clear."[26]

This view was shared at the time by every other member of the Security Council, *including the United States.* In the emergency special session of the General Assembly that was called following the June war, the US and the Union of Soviet Socialist Republics (USSR) jointly drafted two resolutions, the second of which affirmed "the principle that conquest of territory by war is inadmissible under the UN Charter, and consequently that the withdrawal by the parties to the conflict to the positions they occupied before June 5, 1967 is expected."[27] The US Ambassador to the UN, Arthur Goldberg, stated the US position before the General Assembly that "One immediate, obvious and imperative step is the disengagement of all forces and the withdrawal of Israeli forces to their own territory."[28] At the Security Council in August, the US sought to "stick with the formula that Arthur worked out and discussed with the Russians". As a result, Goldberg drafted a resolution calling "Without delay" for "withdrawal by the parties to the conflict of their forces from territories occupied by them in keeping with the inadmissibility of the conquest of territory by war".[29]

Prior to the vote on the UK draft, the representative of the Soviet Union said, "We understand the decision taken to mean the withdrawal of Israel forces from all, and we repeat, all territories belonging to Arab States and seized by Israel following its attack on those States on 5 June 1967."[30]

The Indian representative noted that "there was universal agreement among the membership of the United Nations" that "the principle of non-acquisition of territory by military conquest" meant "the withdrawal of Israel armed forces to the positions they held prior to the outbreak of the recent conflict on 5 June 1967." On that basis, the Indian delegate continued,

> It is our understanding that the draft resolution, if approved by the Council, will commit it to the application of the principle of total withdrawal of Israel forces from all the territories—I repeat, all the territories occupied by Israel as a result of the conflict which began on 5 June 1967. In other words, the draft commits the Council to the withdrawal of Israel forces from the whole of Sinai, Gaza, the Old City of Jerusalem, Jordanian territory west of the Jordan River [the West Bank] and the Syrian territory [the Golan Heights]. This being so, Israel cannot use the words "secure and recognized boundaries", contained in sub-paragraph (ii) of operative paragraph 1 of the United Kingdom draft resolution, to retain any territory occupied in the recent conflict. Of course, mutual territorial adjustments are not ruled out, as indeed they are not in the three-Power draft resolution co-sponsored by India. This is our clear understanding of the United Kingdom draft resolution.[31]

The US had known that India was going to make this statement and was also aware that if it was challenged, the resolution might be vetoed by the Soviet Union. The US did not challenge it.[32] That interpretation is the only legitimate and legally valid reading of Resolution 242.[33]

UN Security Council Resolution 242 has been reaffirmed by numerous subsequent resolutions, including Resolution 338 of October 22, 1973. In its 2004 advisory opinion on the legal consequences of Israel's separation wall in the West Bank, the International Court of Justice reiterated that "All these territories (including East Jerusalem) remain occupied territories". It affirmed "the illegality of territorial acquisition resulting from the threat or use of force". It also affirmed that the Fourth Geneva Convention "is applicable in the Palestinian territories". Accordingly, the ICJ determined that "the Israeli settlements in the Occupied Palestinian Territory (including East Jerusalem) have been established in breach of international law." It also determined that the "tragic situation can be brought to an end only through implementation in good faith of all relevant Security Council resolutions, in particular Resolutions 242 (1967) and 338 (1973)."[34]

Resolution 242 was framed in the aftermath of a war in which Israel took over control of the West Bank from Jordan and the Gaza Strip from Egypt. It was initially assumed that these territories would return to their administration. The US had assured King Hussein of Jordan, for example, that it was "prepared to support a return of the West Bank to Jordan with minor boundary rectifications".[35] However, since the mid-1970s, there has been an international consensus on a two-state solution that comprises recognition of the right of the Palestinian people to self-determination, envisioning the creation of an independent state of Palestine based on the pre-June 1967 lines, with minor and mutually agreed changes to the border.[36]

In February 1971, Egyptian President Anwar Sadat offered Israel a peace treaty along the lines of the international consensus, with recognized borders based on the pre-June 1967 lines, but it was rejected by Israel.[37] The US joined Israel in its rejection, and, as Noam Chomsky has observed in his seminal treatise on the conflict:

> In January 1976, the US was compelled to veto a UN Security Council Resolution calling for a settlement in terms of the international consensus, which now included a Palestinian state alongside of Israel. The resolution called for a settlement on the 1967 borders, with "appropriate arrangements . . . to guarantee . . . the sovereignty, territorial integrity and political independence of all states in the area and their right to live in peace within secure and recognized boundaries," including Israel and a new Palestinian state in the occupied territories.[38]

US policy has since remained rejectionist, meaningless rhetoric to the contrary notwithstanding. The so-called "peace process" is in reality the process by which the US and Israel have blocked implementation of the two-state solution.

To be clear, one must distinguish between *a* two-state solution, as proposed by the rejectionists and furthered via the "peace process", and *the* two-state solution, as per the international consensus and in accordance with international law. They are emphatically *not* the same, despite being nearly universally treated as identical by the thought-controlling American intelligentsia, the high priests of the state religion who dutifully perform the function of manufacturing consent for US foreign policy.[39]

Additionally, Resolution 242 affirmed the necessity "For achieving a just settlement of the refugee problem". This alludes to another key document comprising the foundation of the two-state solution, UN General Assembly Resolution 194, to which we will now turn our attention.

Resolution 194

On November 29, 1948, Israel formally requested membership in the UN, declaring that it "unreservedly accepts the obligations of the United Nations Charter and undertakes to honor them from the day when it becomes a Member of the United Nations."[40]

The Arab states naturally objected to the request. Syria expressed its view that "the application did not merit consideration" and drafted a General As-

sembly resolution requesting the ICJ to issue a legal opinion about Israel's contention that it had authority under Resolution 181 "to partition Palestine for
the creation of a Jewish sovereign State, against the wishes of the majority of the
Palestine population".[41]

Two days after Israel submitted its membership request, its representative at
the UN, Moshe Shertok, effectively declared to the General Assembly that Israel
intended to annex Jerusalem by rejecting any notion of withdrawal and describing Israel's control over the city as a fait accompli. He likewise dismissed any
notion that expelled Palestinians should be allowed to return to their homes,
asserting that the "final solution" for the refugee problem "could be worked out
only after the peace settlement had been concluded".

Also invited to speak was Henry Cattan, the representative of the Arab
Higher Committee. Cattan said that the Arabs "were not prepared to consider
any solution which was based on the partition of Palestine", and he "could not
concede the right of the so-called Government of Israel to represent any part
of Palestine. Palestine belonged to its inhabitants and to those who owned the
land, but the Jews owned only 7 percent of the territory and did not represent
the majority of the population even in the area which they controlled." Nor
could he agree that the UN "could admit to membership the Government of a
State which had come into being through the expulsion of the majority of the
rightful inhabitants of the territory it claimed and which had a terrible record of
atrocity and pillage." Israel's admission to the UN, he foresaw, "would destroy
all hope of establishing normal peaceful conditions in the Middle East."

Israel's membership was "premature", said the Syrian delegate, unjustified by
the UN Charter and international law. How could Israel be considered eligible
for admission, he inquired, when its borders had yet to be legally defined? Furthermore, its actions had shown "that it was not a peace-loving State".

The Lebanese delegate warned that admitting Israel as a member to the
UN would have "dire consequences" and "would come as a bombshell to the
50 million Arabs of the Middle East." Theodor Herzl, he recalled, "had said that
if a Jewish State was created in Palestine, it would constitute a bulwark of European civilization against barbarism. If the civilization which the Jews wished
to protect was epitomized by the regime which they had set up in Palestine with
all its atrocities, then the Arabs of the Middle East, together with all the other
countries of Asia, would almost certainly prefer barbarism."

The representative from Iraq perceived that the proposal to admit Israel
while the question of borders was still under discussion "was an attempt to
prejudge the issue". He inquired of his fellow delegates, "Would it not be more
correct to ask the people of Palestine, who were directly concerned, whether the
Jewish State was acceptable to them before proposing such action?"

As far as many UN members were concerned, however, the answer to his
question had already been provided in the form of UNSCOP's explicit rejection

of the right of the Arab inhabitants of Palestine to self-determination. Following the discussion, the Assembly took a vote on Syria's proposal to obtain an advisory opinion from the ICJ. It was rejected by a vote of twenty to twenty, with eight abstentions (a two-thirds majority being required for adoption).[42]

The Western prejudice against the Palestinian Arabs was similarly illustrated two months earlier in a report of the UN Mediator for Palestine, Count Folke Bernadotte. "The Jewish State was not born in peace as was hoped for" in Resolution 181, the report stated, "but rather, like many another State in history, in violence and bloodshed." The partition of Palestine was now a fait accompli, Bernadotte wrote, notwithstanding the fact that "this was accomplished by a procedure quite contrary to that envisaged for the purpose in the resolution." The UN's appointed "mediator" made no effort to hide his admiration for the Zionist leadership for their accomplishment of having established their "Jewish State" by force and ethnic cleansing. "In establishing their State within a semi-circle of gunfire," he lauded, "the Jews have given convincing demonstration of their skill and tenacity."

Bernadotte urged the international community "to be more understanding of the Arab viewpoint" and explained that the Arabs had "consistently advocated" the solution of a single independent state of Palestine "with full rights and guarantees for the Jewish minority". Then he immediately dismissed this solution as "unrealistic", declaring that "the cantonal and federal state schemes have no practical merit which would make them worthy of consideration."

He observed that the means by which Israel was established had brought the "new and difficult element" of hundreds of thousands of Arab refugees into the "Palestine problem". He pronounced that "the right of the refugees to return to their homes if they so desire must be safeguarded". Then he immediately dismissed the practicability of them ever doing so. "It is futile to assume that the Jewish community could undergo a rapid change of heart", he needlessly stated. There was "no possibility whatsoever of persuading or inducing the Jews to give up their present separate cultural and political existence and accept merging into a unitary Palestine in which they would be a permanent minority." The false choice he presented to the Assembly was to either legitimize the Zionists' territorial gains and ethnic cleansing or "to wipe out the Jewish State and its Provision Government by force."[43]

Bernadotte signed his report to the General Assembly on September 16, 1948. The following day, he was murdered in Jerusalem along with UN Observer Colonel André Serot. The perpetrators of his assassination were Jewish terrorists from the Zionist group Lehi, otherwise known as the Stern Gang. One of the leaders of Lehi at the time was Yitzhak Yezernitsky, who later became known as Yitzhak Shamir, Prime Minister of Israel.[44]

In accordance with Bernadotte's recommendation, the General Assembly paid lip service to the internationally recognized right of refugees to return to their homeland. On December 11, 1948, the Assembly passed Resolution 194, which resolved "that the refugees wishing to return to their homes and live at peace with their neighbors should be permitted to do so at the earliest practicable date, and that compensation should be paid for the property of those choosing not to return and for loss of or damage to property which, under principles of international law or in equity, should be made good by the Governments or authorities responsible. . . ." The resolution also established a Conciliation Commission for Palestine to take over the work of the assassinated UN Mediator.[45] The US joined the 59 percent majority of countries that voted in favor of the resolution.[46]

Also in accordance with Bernadotte's recommendations, the Assembly proceeded to summarily dismiss the views and legitimate concerns of the Arabs and to prejudice the rights of the Palestinian refugees. Syria again submitted a draft resolution, this time in the Security Council, questioning the legitimacy of the "creation of a Jewish sovereign state" in Palestine "against the wishes of the majority of its population" and deciding "to request an advisory legal opinion of the International Court of Justice" about whether General Assembly Resolution 181 conferred any legal authority for the establishment of the state of Israel "without consulting the lawful inhabitants of the country in securing their consent".[47] The resolution failed, with only Belgium joining Syria in favor, and the nine other voting members, including the US, abstaining.[48]

Also failing to pass were draft resolutions from the UK and France deciding to postpone consideration of Israel's membership in the UN until the Conciliation Commission had completed its work. The US, which favored admitting Israel as a member, abstained from both votes. The UK's Sir Alexander Cadogan presciently noted that the US representative had "expressed the belief that the admission of Israel to the United Nations would facilitate the negotiations which are to take place on the subject of the ultimate fate of Palestine. He did not give any particular reasons for that, and I beg to doubt whether, in fact, that would be the effect. I am rather inclined to the belief, or the fear, that negotiations might be found to be rather more difficult if Israel were at this moment admitted to the United Nations."[49] History, needless to say, proved the UK representative's view to be the correct one.

Cadogan also expressed his government's view that it was "necessary for the Council to assure itself that the authorities were complying with resolution 194", as well as the Security Council's own various resolutions. He noted that other states' applications for membership had long been held up and opined that "it seems extremely rash of the Security Council to take a decision for the admission of Israel at this stage. I cannot quite understand the reason for this very great haste with which we are invited to vote for this admission."[50]

Sir Cadogan was presumably feigning naiveté for diplomatic purposes, as the reason was perfectly self-evident: admitting Israel would prejudice the rights of the Palestinians and cement Israel's territorial gains illegitimately acquired through the use of force. That was the transparent goal as far as the Provisional Government of Israel was concerned. Numerous UN members, including the US, contented themselves—for varying reasons relating to their own prejudices, perceived self-interests, and geostrategic considerations—to go along with the plan to disenfranchise the Palestinians.[51]

In the months that followed, Israel continued to reject the right of Palestinian refugees to return to their homeland. Speaking to the Assembly on February 7, 1949, Moshe Shertok was adamant in reiterating Israel's position that the subject of Arab refugees must be excluded from any discussions on a peace agreement. The refugees should forget about returning to their homes, he suggested, and just resettle elsewhere.[52] The Chairman of the Conciliation Commission, Claude de Boisanger of France, adopted the Zionists' position, urging a solution requiring the refugees to give up the hope of ever returning home. He favored a solution that could be "worked out practically and not by adhering to rigid law and principle."[53]

In a meeting with the Conciliation Commission on February 24, 1949, Shertok again rejected outright that refugees had a right "to return to their homes if they wished to do so".[54] The Commission proceeded to draw up an outline of the practical considerations related to any possible return of refugees to their homes. It stated that "Jewish intransigence" on the question of refugees was "likely" due to "their unwillingness to relinquish the land that belonged to the refugees"; it expressed the fear "that the land of the returning refugees will be expropriated by the Israeli Government whenever this becomes necessary to their plans".[55]

Israel also passed measures to extend its civil jurisdiction to Jerusalem, a move the Conciliation Commission deemed "extremely regrettable, and indeed contrary to the spirit, if not the letter" of Resolution 194 and the duty of parties concerned "to abstain from undertaking any action tending to alter the *status quo* of the City."[56] The Commission nevertheless took the view that any solution to the problem must be "mutually acceptable" to the interested parties—which is to say that it adopted a position that Israel's goals must be accommodated regardless of being contrary to international law and its obligations under the Charter as an applicant to UN membership, as well as being prejudicial to the equal rights of the Palestinians.[57]

On the right of return, a subsequent report of the Conciliation Commission noted that during its meetings with Arab governments between March 21 and April 5, 1949, "The Arab delegations pointed out that, up to the present, the Government of Israel not only had not accepted that principle but had endeavored to create a de facto situation which would render the practical application of the principle more difficult or even impossible." The Commission "had no difficulty in recognizing the truth of the Arab contention" that Israel intended to disallow refugees from returning. Indeed, their fears in this regard were "well founded". Despite visiting several refugee camps and seeing for themselves "the deplorable material and moral situation of the refugees", the Commission maintained the view that Israel should effectively be allowed a veto power over any proposed solutions to the refugee problem, as well as over the question of territorial boundaries.[58]

On March 4, 1949, the US submitted a draft resolution to the Security Council judging that "Israel is a peace-loving State and is able and willing to carry out the obligations contained in the Charter" and recommending that the General Assembly admit Israel as a member to the UN.

Illustrative of the attitude of the resolution's supporters, Norway's representative expressed doubts about whether Israel's membership was justified, particularly given its lack of legally defined borders, but said that he would nevertheless vote in favor on the blind hope that Israel would fulfill its Charter obligations. The Soviet representative more enthusiastically supported Israel's admission, countering with the *false* claim that Israel's borders were legally defined by Resolution 181 and declaring despite all evidence to the contrary that Israel was already "loyally complying with its obligations to the United Nations". He then provided insight into how he managed to arrive at this conclusion by proclaiming that the questions of Jerusalem and the Arab refugees could not be linked to the question of Israel's membership.

The UK was alone in sitting on the fence. Sir Terence Shone expressed that his government was "disturbed at statements which have been made by responsible Israeli representatives, which suggest that the Israeli Government does not intend to pay attention to certain United Nations resolutions." He referred to the status of Jerusalem, as well as the plight of the refugees, who were "still dying in hundreds" and were "likely to continue to do so until some further decisive action can be taken to help them." Israel had a responsibility in this regard, he continued, and until Israel "clarified" its position, the UK could not take a definite stand on the question of its admission. "We hope that the Israeli Government will be able to make clear that it intends to abide by United Nations resolutions and does not intend to flout them, as utterances which bear the stamp of responsible statements suggest may be the case."

Egypt's representative, Mahmoud Fawzi Bey, was the lone voice determined to uphold the principles of the Charter and international law. In his plea to the Council, he quoted a news report filed from Tel Aviv the previous month that stated, "It is obvious that most of the displaced Arabs cannot return, because their homes and in some cases even their villages, no longer exist." UN observers had also reported "that demolition of the homes of the displaced Arabs has been carried out systematically, with the intention and premeditation, so that those Arabs, once having left their homes, cannot return." He chastised Council members for their willingness to have the UN act as accomplice in the injustices perpetrated against the Arabs of Palestine: "Yes, chase away the Arabs, demolish their old homes, build new ones, take their lands and settle there, and make the conquest complete. Make it an all-around *fait accompli*. This is legal currency in the eyes of some people—the *fait accompli*. It is legal tender, accepted, unfortunately so often, in recent months." He urged the Council not to act "against the principles of justice, against the principle of self-determination for the people, and against the precepts of human rights, which the United Nations, only a short while ago, approved."

His eloquent pleas fell on deaf ears. With Egypt casting the only negative vote, the resolution was adopted with nine in favor (the UK abstained).[59] The text of the resolution was transmitted to the General Assembly three days later in a letter from the provisional government of Israel.[60]

In the Assembly debate on May 5, Charles Malik reiterated Lebanon's opposition to Israel's UN membership. Surely, the UN General Assembly, by adopting Resolution 181, had "not intended that the Jewish State should rid itself of its Arab citizens. . . . Surely the Jews, who claimed that they had always been an uprooted people whose homelessness had driven them to fight for their ancient home, could not in all justice and conscience seek to remedy that uprooting by inflicting it upon others." Given Israel's rejection of the right of refugees to be repatriated, to admit Israel would effectively reward it for defying the will of the UN. It "would be tantamount to a virtual condemnation of one million Arabs to permanent exile" and would ensure "the perpetuation of the homelessness of the Arab refugees." Additionally, to admit Israel before the question of borders and the status of Jerusalem had been legally settled "was equivalent to giving it a blank cheque to draw its frontiers wherever it wished. In effect, it meant condoning, by a solemn act of the United Nations, the right of conquest." He could not understand the attitude of favoring Israel's request "in the hope that it would ultimately abide by the Assembly's earlier decisions, in view of the fact that Israel had demonstrated in advance its unwillingness to abide by those decisions."

Taking his turn, the Israeli representative then reiterated his government's position precisely as Malik had just outlined: Israel's control over Jerusalem was a fait accompli, and its government would not accept any responsibility for the plight of Arab refugees apart from accepting an obligation "to make compensation for abandoned lands." They would not be allowed to return.[61]

In subsequent debates, the Arab states reiterated the concerns about Israel's attitude towards the Arab refugees and the lack of legally recognized borders. The idea of a "Jewish state" itself was contrary to the spirit of the UN Charter, Yemen's representative noted on May 7. "The theory of national homogeneity", he said, "could not be supported by the United Nations."[62]

But the states supporting Israel's membership could not be reasoned with and continued to content themselves in willful ignorance of the actual situation.

On May 9, for example, Norway's representative expressed his government's attitude that it was enough to favor Israel's membership "on the assumption" that Israel "would do its utmost to arrive at a solution" to the refugee problem. Colombia remained unsatisfied with Israel's attitude towards the refugees and supported their right to return. It rejected the notion that a state could unilaterally establish its own borders through the use of force. Yet it favored admitting Israel nevertheless. Denmark took a slightly different view, arguing bizarrely that, to gain membership, Israel was not required to respect the right of Arab refugees to return to their homes in accordance with the principle of customary international law and UN Resolution 194.

The UK alone dissented from the views of non-Arab member states. Sir Terence Shone agreed with the Arabs that it was indeed "desirable to examine the applicant's qualification in the light of its record, particularly in connection with its willingness to comply with any existing relevant resolutions of the United Nations." Israel's intentions "did not appear to be entirely in accordance with" UN resolutions, he understatedly observed. "It would be deplorable", he further stated, "if the plight of the refugees were used as a bargaining factor" in negotiations over a formal peace settlement.[63]

The final debate on the matter occurred on May 11. Warren Austin expressed the US government's equal disregard for Israel's actual deeds and contrary declarations; it was enough that "Israel had solemnly pledged its word to carry out the obligations of the Charter". The Netherlands, Canada, New Zealand, and Iceland all expressed their like view. Israel could be "trusted" to honor its responsibilities and obligations (Canada), and there was "no doubt" that it would do so (Iceland). Bolivia proclaimed that Israel had "fulfilled the conditions" required for membership under Article 4 of the UN Charter. Peru argued that once Israel was admitted, "it would be under greater moral obligation" to accept the will of the UN. Guatemala adopted the US's puzzling argument that admitting Israel "would contribute greatly to the solution". France and Uruguay expressed their support, the latter by invoking the Holocaust and expressing the belief that the problems of persecution, refugees, and racial discrimination "would disappear" with international acceptance of the state of Israel—a statement obviously intended to apply to the Jews, but not the Arabs, who were evidently regarded as something less than human by Western policymakers. With no less hypocrisy, Ecuador lectured the Arab states that they "would benefit from the admission of Israel" and could adopt "the democratic spirit" by accepting the Assembly's inevitable decision to grant Israel's request—the "democratic spirit" again being inapplicable to the Arabs, whose equal right to self-determination had already been summarily dismissed. The Cuban government also invoked the Holocaust and adopted the Soviet Union's position that the question of Israel's admission "was completely divorced" from the matters of Jerusalem, borders, and Arab refugees. It was "inappropriate", in Cuba's view, to consider these issues when addressing the question of whether to admit Israel. By means of so willfully ignoring the Israeli government's actual deeds and candid declarations of intent, Cuba could declare that Israel was "proving its love of peace" and its willingness to fulfill its obligations as a Charter member.

The Arab states pleaded with the other members of the Assembly to consider their own obligations under the UN Charter. The Iraqi delegate had to remind members once more that, having only recently adopted the Convention on Prevention and Punishment of the Crime of Genocide and the Universal Declaration of Human Rights, they "should be mindful of the plight of three-quarters of a million human beings."

The Syrian representative lamented that "never before in history had the forcible invasion of a country and the expulsion of its original inhabitants been welcomed by countries professing their attachment to justice and peace. It would not be a happy omen for the United Nations if it were to reward aggression by approval and admit to membership a Government which had not only disregarded the wishes of the United Nations, but had also indicated its intention to continue to do so."

Charles Malik excoriated the UN for its "perpetual meetings for the purpose not of bringing reality into conformity with the will of the United Nations, but of revising and transforming that will in order to adapt it to the independently developing reality. Thus, the United Nations could only stand by helplessly and take note of events; it remained powerless to determine them." He noted further that the International Refugee Organization, established by the UN in 1946 in light of the refugee crisis created by World War II, "was spending millions of dollars on the resettlement of Jews in Palestine. By that very act, it was contributing to the unsettling of as many Arabs outside Palestine."

The Yemen delegate similarly noted that admitting Israel would prejudice the rights of displaced Arabs and equate to "the sanctioning of aggression and injustice".

Sheikh Ahmed Jabbar, the representative of Saudi Arabia, noted that the same powers that had pushed for the adoption of UNSCOP's partition plan—which had explicitly rejected the rights of the majority of its inhabitants—was now pressing for the admission of a state "artificially created through terrorism and aggression. There was no limit to prejudice when certain great Powers found it expedient to adopt a policy regardless of whether or not it was in conformity with the principles of the Charter."

Following the futile debate, by a vote of thirty-seven in favor, twelve against, and nine abstentions (including the UK), the General Assembly admitted Israel as a member of the United Nations on the grounds that it was "a peace-loving State which accepts the obligations contained in the Charter and is able and willing to carry out those obligations".[64]

Article 4 of the UN Charter states that "Membership in the United Nations is open to all other peace-loving states which accept the obligations contained in the present Charter and, in the judgment of the Organization, are able and willing to carry out these obligations."[65] As the ICJ has pointed out, this establishes five requisite conditions for UN membership: "an applicant must (1) be a State; (2) be peace-loving; (3) accept the obligations of the Charter; (4) be able to carry out these obligations; and (5) be willing to do so."[66]

The attributes of statehood defined under the 1933 Montevideo Convention on the Rights and Duties of States include having "a defined territory".[67] As the unilaterally-declared state of Israel had no legally defined territory, it did not meet the first requirement under Article 4 for UN membership. As the territory within the *de facto* boundaries of Israel was acquired through the use of force in contravention of international law and the UN Charter, including by ethnically cleansing Palestine of most of its Arab population, Israel patently did not meet the second requirement for membership. As the Israeli leadership repeatedly proclaimed its intent to annex territory acquired by force, including Jerusalem, and rejected the internationally recognized right of refugees to return, it patently did not meet the fifth requirement for membership, rendering the third and fourth requirements moot.

That is to say, the adoption on May 11, 1949, of UN General Assembly Resolution 273 (III), the US-sponsored resolution that admitted Israel as a UN member, was a violation of the very Charter under which the Assembly was purporting to operate and is thus illegal, null and void.

The Oslo Accords

In 1978, Egyptian President Anwar Sadat and Israeli Prime Minister Menachem Begin met with US President Jimmy Carter at Camp David to negotiate a peace treaty. The talks resulted in two agreements together known as the Camp David Accords, signed on September 17. The first, The Framework for Peace in the Middle East, stated that "The agreed basis for a peaceful settlement of the conflict between Israel and its neighbors is UN Security Council Resolution 242 in all its parts"—a resolution, of course, that Israel interpreted as it pleased. The agreement stated that Israel should negotiate with "the representatives of the Palestinian People" and foresaw "transitional arrangements for the West Bank and Gaza for a period not exceeding five years". But the PLO was neither invited to Camp David nor party to the agreement. Instead, Israel agreed that "The delegations of Egypt and Jordan may include Palestinians", but only "as mutually agreed", meaning that Israel itself would determine which "representatives of the Palestinian People" could participate in future negotiations, during which Israel would further seek to determine "modalities for establishing the elected self-governing authority". In other words, Israel refused to negotiate with the existing PLO leadership and would only do so once a governing authority *approved by Israel* was established. (The eventual product of this process was the Palestinian Authority.) The second agreement, A Framework for the Conclusion of a Peace Treaty between Egypt and Israel, led to the signing of the Treaty of Peace between the Arab Republic of Egypt and the State of Israel on March 26, 1979. The treaty reaffirmed the "Framework" agreements and invited "the other Arab parties to this dispute to join the peace process with Israel".[68]

In December 1987, Israel's intelligence services were caught off guard when a spontaneous eruption of mass resistance against the occupation began. The First Intifada was "a reminder to Israelis", as the BBC has appropriately noted, "of what their first Prime Minister David Ben-Gurion had said in 1938: 'A people which fights against the usurpation of its land will not tire so easily.'"[69]

In 1991, as the intifada continued, the US-led "peace process" was renewed in Madrid, Spain, which led in 1993 to another round of talks in Oslo, Norway. The first talks in which the PLO was allowed to directly participate, the Oslo negotiations resulted in the Declaration of Principles on Interim Self-Government Arrangements (or the Oslo I Accord), the purpose of which was effectively to block implementation of the two-state solution and perpetuate the Israeli occupation. As former Israeli Foreign Minister Shlomo Ben-Ami has observed, "One of the meanings of Oslo was that the PLO was . . . Israel's collaborator in the task of stifling the intifada and cutting short what was clearly an authentically democratic struggle for Palestinian independence."[70] Natan Sharansky, a former Member of the Knesset and Chair of the Shalem Center's Institute for Strategic Studies, similarly explained in 2008 that "the idea of Oslo was to find a strong dictator to . . . keep the Palestinians under control."[71]

These observations are not merely hindsight. Dr. Israel Shahak, a retired professor from Hebrew University and Chairman of the Israeli League of Human and Civil Rights, at the time wrote an article titled "Oslo Agreement Makes PLO Israel's Enforcer". He explained that from the beginning of the occupation, Israel had found "Palestinian collaborators to rule the territories on its behalf", a role that had been played by the "so-called 'notables,' those figures influential in Palestinian society even before the conquest". However,

> Between 1981 and 1983, Ariel Sharon demolished the power of the notables and tried to replace them with his "Village Leagues," often composed of the dregs of the society. After the start of the intifada, however, this method failed. Israel had to undertake the task of ruling the Palestinians on every level by use of its own manpower. This form of direct rule was much less efficient and more corrupt and burdensome. The Israeli establishment has wanted for quite some time to restore the old method of indirect rule, especially in the Gaza Strip, on

Israeli terms. This is the real meaning of the Oslo Agreement
as Israel perceives it.

In its new role as "Israel's Enforcer", the PLO would be "rewarded by a lot of
money, by a much greater degree of honor than the notables enjoyed, and by
some vague verbal concessions that will lead to further stalemates in negotiations. . . . But if [Yasser] Arafat and his henchmen really hope that, in return
for doing efficiently the job [Israeli Prime Minister Yitzhak] Rabin had assigned
them, they will be treated as the rulers of a sovereign state, they are deluding
themselves and their people."[72]

Furthermore, Shahak explained, during the 1991 Madrid talks, the US had
conceded to Israel that it could interpret Resolution 242 however it pleased and
assured that the UN itself would play no role in the "peace process". As envisioned in 1978, the approved Palestinian leadership was to negotiate "interim
self-government arrangements" with the Occupying Power while putting off a
final settlement based on Resolution 242. There was no reference to the principle of Palestinian self-determination, and the Israelis would not meet with an
autonomous Palestinian delegation, but instead with a Jordanian-Palestinian
delegation that *excluded the PLO*, recognized internationally as "the sole legitimate representative of the Palestinian people".[73]

Camille Mansour elucidated in a 1993 paper published in the *Journal of
Palestine Studies* that,

> By inviting the Palestinians to the negotiations under these
> conditions, US officials, who had in fact adopted almost all
> the conditions set by former Prime Minister Yitzhak Shamir
> for the convening of the conference, were in a way sending the
> following message to the PLO, the official Palestinian leader-
> ship. The PLO, which had been wanting to take part in nego-
> tiations since 1974, was called upon to put aside its Novem-
> ber 1988 declaration of a state, supported by the vast majority
> of the Palestinians and recognized by more than 100 countries
> around the world. It was invited to postpone for at least five
> years any solution for the Palestinian refugees, who constitute
> the majority of the Palestinian people and a portion of whom,
> in Lebanon and Kuwait, were in urgent need of an equitable
> solution. It was asked to give its green light to a process that
> expressly sought to marginalize it in favor of a yet-to-be-estab-
> lished authority in the West Bank and Gaza Strip which would
> have only certain powers, during a five-year period, relating to
> daily life and under the overall control of Israel's military occu-
> pation, without any guarantee about the principles governing
> the permanent settlement.

Israel had also continued to pursue an aggressive settlement policy throughout the negotiations, establishing "facts on the ground" prejudicial to the final outcome of any negotiated settlement on borders, without fear of being reproved by the US. The US's disinclination to take any meaningful steps to pressure Israel to halt its illegal settlement activities, Mansour further observed, was inconsistent with its promise to "act as an honest broker" and with its position that "no party should take unilateral actions that seek to predetermine issues".[74]

Immediately following the signing of the Declaration of Principles, Israel reiterated its rejection of the international consensus that a final settlement be based on UN Resolution 242, with a withdrawal of Israeli forces from occupied Palestinian territory and the establishment of a Palestinian state with minor and mutually agreed changes to the pre-June 1967 boundaries. "We agree to a confederated formula between Jordan and the Palestinians in the West Bank," declared Israeli Deputy Foreign Minister Yossi Beilin, "but we will not return to the pre-1967 borders. United Jerusalem will remain the capital of the State of Israel."[75]

In May 1994, Israel and the PLO signed the Agreement on the Gaza Strip and the Jericho Area (or the Gaza-Jericho Agreement), which established the Palestinian Authority as the administrative body under the PLO that would fulfill the role of "Israel's Enforcer". Under the agreement, responsibility "for all the legislative and executive powers and responsibilities" within its limited jurisdiction was "transferred" to the PA, which was tasked with establishing "a strong police force" to keep the Palestinians in line in areas where Israel would assign it administrative and security duties. To this end, the PA's security forces would enforce a monopoly on violence and see to the strict disarmament of the Palestinian public on Israel's behalf.[76]

In September 1995, the next step in the "peace process" was initiated. Dubbed "Oslo II", it resulted in the Israeli-Palestinian Interim Agreement on the West Bank and the Gaza Strip. The agreement stated that the process would continue within the framework of the Madrid negotiations while putting off any negotiations on permanent status that might "lead to the implementation of Security Council Resolutions 242 and 338", as unilaterally interpreted by Israel, which interpretation the entire US-led "peace process" was designed to get the Palestinians to acquiesce to.

Oslo II referred to the newly created PA as the "Interim Self-Government Authority", which would nominally be elected by the Palestinian people but would require the US and Israel's approval to receive recognition. Israeli military forces within the West Bank would be redeployed according to the division of the territory into three separate zones, while Israel would "continue to carry the responsibility for external security" in the entire West Bank, "as well as the responsibility for the overall security of Israelis and Settlements". In Area A, the PA would have both administrative and security jurisdiction. In Area B, it would have administrative duties while Israel retained "security" control. Israel would exercise total control over Area C, which included all settlements and constituted about 70 percent of the West Bank.[77]

In a speech to the Knesset on October 5, 1995, Prime Minister Yitzhak Rabin made explicit the rejectionist policy that Israel and the US were further-ing by means of the Oslo agreements:

> In our view, the permanent solution lies in the territory of
> the State of Israel made up of Eretz Yisrael as it was under the
> British Mandate—although that does not refer to the Golan
> Heights, of course—and alongside it, a Palestinian entity that
> will be the home of the majority of the Palestinian residents
> of the Gaza Strip and West Bank. We want the entity to be
> less than a state and we want it to independently manage the
> lives of the Palestinians under its jurisdiction. The borders of
> the State of Israel under the permanent agreement will exceed
> the borders that existed prior to the Six-Day War. We will not
> return to the lines of 4 June 1967.

Rabin also said that Israel would retain all of Jerusalem and the settlement blocs, as well as maintain a military presence along the Jordan River, which was in Area C. Thus, Israeli military forces would completely surround the West Bank and totally control the borders of the Palestinian non-state "entity". The whole of the occupied territories would not be annexed into Israel, Rabin ex-plained, because that would mean a binational state with a sizeable Palestin-ian population, which would demographically undermine Israel's existence as a "Jewish state". He reminded his audience "that we made a commitment to the Knesset not to uproot a single settlement within the framework of the interim arrangement and not to freeze building and natural growth."[78]

The Palestinian "entity" was thus relegated by Oslo II to a series of small, non-contiguous, Bantustan-like zones separated by Jewish-only highways, within which zones the PA would exercise limited authorities largely on behalf of the Occupying Power, which would maintain total control over a military security zone comprised of most of the West Bank.

In late 1997, with Israel continuing its colonization of Palestine, the US attempted to revive the stalled Oslo process by determining a timeline for the implementation of Oslo II. The result was the Wye River Memorandum, signed by Israeli Prime Minister Benjamin Netanyahu and PLO Chairman Yasser Ara-fat on October 23, 1998. The memorandum called for the resumption of per-manent status negotiations and determined that "neither side shall initiate or take any step that will change the status of the West Bank and the Gaza Strip in accordance with the Interim Agreement."[79] The US separately assured Arafat in a letter that "the United States will continue to make clear the importance of avoiding unilateral steps that would prejudge or preempt the issues reserved for the permanent status negotiations."[80]

However, the State Department also privately informed Tel Aviv what that actually meant: specifically, the US would oppose any "unilateral declaration of statehood" by the Palestinian leadership.[81] The US also confidentially assured Israel that it interpreted the matter of permanent status negotiations in terms of Israel's "security" needs; the State Department emphasized, "Only Israel can determine its own security needs and decide what solutions will be satisfactory." In other words, in terms of the US-Israeli interpretation of Resolution 242, only Israel could determine where the "secure and recognized boundaries" of Israel would be—an unambiguous green light for Israel to continue its illegal colonization.[82]

In remarks during a press conference following the signing of the memorandum, President Bill Clinton praised Israel for taking steps to allow the Palestinians "to breathe a little easier" and promised "a package of aid to help Israel meet the security costs of redeployment"—which effectively meant that the US would directly finance Israel's occupation regime in order to help sustain it. To the same end, Israel was also assured that aid would be provided to the PA to help it meet the costs of acting as Israel's Enforcer.[83]

Affirming that Israel perfectly understood the US interpretation of the Wye River Memorandum, the Israeli cabinet approved it with the understanding that in any negotiations on Gaza and "Judea and Samaria" (Israel's term of reference for the West Bank), the government would "preserve the vital national interests of the State of Israel". These included: "security areas, the areas around Jerusalem, the areas of Jewish settlement, infrastructure interests, water sources, military and security locations, the areas around north-south and west-east transportation arteries, and historic sites of the Jewish people." The cabinet also affirmed its understanding that no "unilateral steps which will change the status of the area" should be taken. In accordance with the Clinton administration's letters of assurance, this naturally excluded Israel's settlement activities and referred specifically to the possibility of a "unilateral declaration by the Palestinian Authority on the establishment of a Palestinian state" (the PLO having effectively nullified its own previous declaration of independence by agreeing to the Oslo Accords).[84]

Predictably, Israel continued to bulldoze Palestinian homes in the West Bank, confiscate Palestinian land, and expand Jewish settlements. As Amnesty International observed in a 1999 report, Oslo II not only didn't halt this process, but *didn't even slow it down*: "between 1995 and 1999, house demolitions in the West Bank including East Jerusalem remained at the same high level."[85]

Camp David

In July 2000, President Clinton held a summit at Camp David with Israeli Prime Minister Ehud Barak and PLO Chairman Yasser Arafat. Arafat reluctantly agreed to the negotiations only after Clinton had assured him he would not be blamed for the failure if the talks did not succeed; they did not, and Clinton publicly blamed Arafat anyway.[86]

There has been widespread disagreement about what Israel actually proposed at Camp David, and no official map was ever publicly released. The standard narrative in the US media has been that Israel "offered extraordinary concessions" (*Washington Post*) to the Palestinians, but that "Arafat's recalcitrance" (*Los Angeles Times*) and "Palestinian rejectionism" (*US News & World Report*) led to the failure of the talks and Arafat's rejection of Israel's "generous peace terms" (*Los Angeles Times*).[87] A 2008 Congressional Research Service report parroted that "Israel was willing to cede more than 90% of the West Bank" to a Palestinian state—the verb "cede" implying that *Israel* would be giving up land to the *Palestinians*, when the truth was precisely the opposite.[88]

That the standard narrative consists of such fictions is illustrative of the how the media simply adopts the framework in which US policy operates, structuring the discussion not in terms of what Israel has a *right* to under international law, but in terms of what Israel *wants*. Under international law, every inch of the West Bank, including East Jerusalem, is "Occupied Palestinian Territory" (ICJ) to which Israel has no legal claim. Thus, within the proper framework of international law, the amount of Israel's "concessions" was negative; *all* concessions were demanded of the Palestinian side, which had already conceded the 78 percent of the land beyond the 1967 lines, agreeing to establish a state on the 22 percent of historic Palestine comprised of Gaza and the West Bank. Thus, what is dubbed Israel's "generous" offer in newspeak in fact consisted of demands for the Palestinians to make even more extraordinary concessions and cede a significant amount of additional land to Israel.

According to Dr. Ron Pundak, who served as a member of the official Israeli negotiating team during the Oslo process and was also involved in the Camp David and later Taba negotiations, the map Israel initially presented "included an annexation of approximately 12% of the West Bank without territorial compensation". By the end of the talks, Israel was still demanding annexation of 9 percent with only 1 percent in compensation. "The version presented in retrospect by Israeli spokespersons," Pundak noted, "claiming that Barak at Camp David offered 95% and an additional 5% in compensation, or alternatively 97% and another 3% compensation, is an attempt at rewriting history." Pundak published a map of what was proposed, showing enormous swaths of land cutting deep into the West Bank to annex major settlement blocs and dividing the West Bank in two with a "temporary" Israeli "security zone" along the Jordan River.[89]

A detailed firsthand account of the Camp David summit was recorded by Akram Haniyeh, a close adviser to Arafat and a member of the Palestinian team. He observed that the faulty assumption of the Israeli and American negotiating teams was that, "given the weakness of their situation, the Palestinian leadership needed an achievement such as statehood and would be willing to pay a high price for it." The Clinton administration "was simply following what had become the traditional American role vis-à-vis the Palestinian-Israeli conflict": to advocate on behalf of Israel to get the Palestinians to acquiesce to its demands. To this end, "the American team concentrated all its pressure on the Palestinian delegation", while making "no attempt to exercise any pressure on the Israelis."

What the Israelis offered the Palestinians at Camp David was not a serious attempt to achieve a peaceful settlement. They presented maps "showing Israeli annexations ranging from 10 to 13.5 percent of the West Bank", which were connected in "such a way as to control Palestinian water resources in the West Bank." The Israeli goal was "to cement the gains from the 1967 War, to restructure and legalize the occupation." Israel denied responsibility for the 1948 Nakba—the ethnic cleansing of three-quarters of a million Arabs from Palestine—and rejected the right of refugees to return. Israel's insistence on annexation of occupied East Jerusalem was another non-starter for the Palestinians. On July 19, a clearly frustrated Arafat told Clinton,

> The Palestinian leader who will give up Jerusalem has not yet been born. I will not betray my people or the trust they have placed in me. Don't look to me to legitimize the occupation! Of course, it can continue longer, but it can't last forever. No one can continue indefinitely to impose domination by military force—look at South Africa. . . . I was elected president on a clear platform, and our political line has been laid down by our leadership bodies. Our people will not accept less than their rights as stated by international resolutions and international legality.[90]

Essentially confirming Haniyeh's account of what transpired at Camp David, Ehud Barak afterward declared: "I did not give away a thing. I made clear and I am proud of it, that in exchange for an end to the conflict and giving up the right of return, 80 percent of the settlers under Israeli sovereignty, recognitions of the security needs of Israel and of Israel's affinity to the holy places, we will be ready for painful, defined concessions that lead to a Palestinian state."[91]

Taba

On September 28, 2000, Knesset Member (and later Prime Minster) Ariel Sharon marched on the Temple Mount (Haram al-Sharif) in Jerusalem, the location of Al-Aqsa Mosque, with over 1,000 Israeli police, despite having been warned by both Palestinian and US officials that his planned visit would be a provocation. Palestinians engaged in mass protests that Israel attempted to put down by force, killing several and wounding hundreds. The uprising that followed became known as the Al-Aqsa Intifada or Second Intifada.[92]

In another effort to mediate, on December 23, 2000, President Clinton proposed parameters for a final settlement at a meeting with Israeli and Palestinian representatives at the White House. He suggested that all of Gaza and approximately 95 percent of the West Bank should become a "non-militarized" Palestinian state, with Palestinians being compensated for some of the annexed territory in a land swap. He suggested that Jerusalem should become the capital of two states, with Arab areas going to Palestine and Jewish areas to Israel. On the refugee problem, Clinton proposed that most of the refugees could return to live in the Palestinian state, rather than return to their former homes in what is now Israel.[93]

From January 21 to 27, 2001, Israeli and Palestinian negotiators met in Taba, Egypt, where they continued discussions on a permanent settlement based largely on the Clinton parameters, but without US involvement. The talks were ultimately called off by Israel; but in a joint statement, the parties expressed their view that the talks had been positive and productive, bringing them closer to an agreement than ever before. They expressed their "shared belief that the remaining gaps could be bridged with the resumption of negotiations" following upcoming Israeli elections.[94]

At the request of the parties, the EU's special envoy to the Middle East, Miguel Angel Moratinos, compiled a document summarizing their positions at the end of the talks. The Moratinos Non-Paper, as it was called, noted the agreement that borders would be based on the pre-June 1967 lines in accordance with Resolution 242. Contradictorily, however, the Israelis insisted on annexing settlement blocs and maintained that Israel was "entitled to contiguity between and among their settlements". They sketched a map proposing annexation of about 6 percent of the West Bank, while the Palestinians expressed a willingness to cede about 3 percent of their land to Israel in the context of a land swap. Both sides accepted in principle Clinton's suggestion that Jerusalem would become the capital of two states, with the Palestinian team expressing a willingness to accept Israeli annexation of existing Jewish settlements in occupied East Jerusalem. The Israelis maintained that the Palestinian state would be "nonmilitarized", while the Palestinians said they were "prepared to accept limitations on its acquisition of arms and be defined as a state with limited arms." Israel wanted "overriding Israel control" over the airspace of the Palestinian state and "requested access to Palestinian airspace for military operations and training", which the Palestinians rejected.

On the matter of Palestinian refugees, Israel expressed agreement that "a just settlement of the refugee problem in accordance with UN Security Council Resolution 242 must lead to the implementation of UN General Assembly Resolution 194" of December 11, 1948. But the Israelis paradoxically agreed only to a phased absorption of a limited number of refugees into Israel, and they rejected the idea of restitution for refugees' lost property.[95]

While there was still a great deal of disagreement on a number of key issues, the talks at Taba nevertheless resulted in broad series of agreements that represented the closest the Israelis and Palestinians had ever been to reaching a final settlement. It was an unprecedented and historic series of negotiations that received relatively little attention. However, it must be emphasized that, within the framework of what both sides were entitled to under international law, every single concession discussed at Taba was expected and made from the Palestinian side, and none from Israel.

But the US and Israel would subsequently take steps to roll back even this limited progress. On January 20, 2001, George W. Bush was sworn in as President of the United States. His administration declared that the Clinton parameters "were no longer United States proposals". On February 6, Ariel Sharon was elected Prime Minister of Israel. His government declared that the negotiations at Taba were "null and void" and that Jerusalem was to be the undivided capital of Israel. On April 13, Sharon said he could accept a disarmed Palestinian state, but only on the condition that Palestinians accept Israeli annexation of 58 percent of the West Bank.[96]

The Road Map

On June 24, 2002, President Bush gave a speech declaring that new Palestinian leadership and "a new constitutional framework" would be required before the US would support the creation of a Palestinian state. Further conditioning US support for the Palestinians' right to self-determination, Bush added that the PA must engage in "a sustained fight against the terrorists" and successfully "dismantle their infrastructure" before the US would support Palestinian statehood, thus demanding the impossible task of ending terrorism while perpetuating its root causes. Paying lip service to the recommendations of the Mitchell Report, Bush said that "Israeli settlement activity in the occupied territories must stop". He then rendered this meaningless by reiterating the US acceptance of Israel's unilateral interpretation of Resolution 242: "the Israeli occupation that began in 1967 will be ended through a settlement negotiated between the parties, based on UN Resolutions 242 and 338, *with Israeli withdrawal to secure and recognize borders*" (emphasis added).[97]

In sum, the policy of the Bush administration was that Palestinians must negotiate with Israel while remaining under its military occupation; Israel would not be expected to withdraw until there was a final agreement on borders, until which time Israel would continue prejudicing the outcome; and Israel would only be expected to negotiate with a Palestinian government that met with US and Israeli approval, which is to say a leadership that would be willing to make the enormous concessions to Israel that Arafat had been unwilling to make.

In a move largely interpreted as an attempt to garner international support in the prelude to the US invasion of Iraq, the Bush administration cooperated with the EU, Russia, and the UN Secretariat (together known as the "Quartet") in an attempt to revive the "peace process". The US produced a draft document titled Elements of a Performance-Based Road Map to a Permanent Two-State Solution to the Israeli-Palestinian Conflict (or simply the Road Map), which was effectively an attempt to undo the progress that had been made at Taba, picking up instead where Oslo II had left off.

Presented in April 2003, "Phase 1" of the Road Map called on Palestinians—but not Israelis—to "immediately undertake an unconditional cessation of violence". The Road Map thus obligated Palestinians to cease even legitimate armed resistance to foreign military occupation, while the party responsible for the preponderance of the violence was given an effective green light to continue to use force to achieve its aims, with a few limitations that Israel could comfortably feel free to ignore (i.e., no "deportations, attacks on civilians; confiscation and/or demolition of Palestinian homes and property, as a punitive measure or to facilitate Israeli construction; destruction of Palestinian institutions and infrastructure"). The Palestinians were called on to recognize "Israel's right to exist in peace and security", but Israel was not called on to reciprocate. To fulfill the Bush administration's goal of finding a new, more compliant leadership, the Road Map called for a new Palestinian constitution to be approved following elections. The Road Map also called on Israel to freeze all settlement activity—a repetition of principle no more meaningful than its incarnation in Bush's speech the previous year.

Under "Phase 2", efforts would be "focused on the *option* of creating an independent Palestinian state with *provisional* borders and *attributes* of sovereignty, based on the new constitution, as a way station to a permanent status settlement" (emphasis added). This "option", the Road Map said, could not be achieved until the Palestinian leadership acted "decisively against terror" and was "willing and able to build a practicing democracy based on tolerance and liberty." Furthermore, whether or not this "option" would be implemented was to be "based upon the consensus judgment of the Quartet of whether conditions are appropriate to proceed".

"Phase 3" of the Road Map would also be "based on consensus judgment of [the] Quartet" and consist of final status negotiations between Israel and the

Palestinians. In other words, before final status negotiations could even *begin*, the Palestinians must meet all of the US's preconditions, with the US wearing the judge's robe on the question of whether or not those preconditions had been met.[98]

In short, the Road Map was a means by which the US would exercise an effective veto power over the creation of a viable, sovereign, independent Palestinian state.

Even this appeasement, however, was unacceptable to the Sharon government, which refused to accept the Road Map because it also placed some obligations on Israel (i.e., a settlement freeze). As a result, on May 23, Secretary of State Colin Powell and National Security Adviser Condoleezza Rice issued a statement accepting that Israel had "significant" and "real concerns" about its obligations under the Road Map and promising to "address them fully and seriously" in its "implementation"—the only meaningful interpretation of which is that there would be no substantial consequences if Israel chose to simply ignore its end of the bargain.[99] With this understanding clearly in mind, Sharon replied that, "in view of the US promise to address those concerns fully and seriously", his government was "prepared to accept the steps set out in the road map."[100]

The Israeli cabinet in turn endorsed Sharon's carefully worded acceptance of the "steps set out in" the Road Map by making explicit its interpretation of what that meant:

> The character of the provisional Palestinian state will be determined through negotiations between the Palestinian Authority and Israel. The provisional state will have provisional borders and certain aspects of sovereignty; be fully demilitarized, with no military forces, but only with police and internal security forces of limited scope and armaments; be without the authority to undertake defense alliances or military cooperation; and [allow] Israeli control over the entry and exit of all persons and cargo, as well as of its air space and electromagnetic spectrum.

If the Palestinians refused these Israeli preconditions under "Phase 2", Israel would never have to enter "Phase 3" negotiations on a final settlement.

Another condition Israel unilaterally placed upon the Palestinians was that they must accept "Israel's right to exist as a Jewish state". This effectively meant that the Palestinians must accept that the Zionist's unilateral declaration of the existence of the state of Israel in May 1948 and the ethnic cleansing of Palestine were legitimate, and also that they must officially recognize Arab-Israelis, one-fifth of Israel's population, as second-class citizens. Consequently, Palestinians must also waive "any right of return for Palestinian refugees to the State of

Israel." Additionally, the issue of settlements "in Judea, Samaria, and Gaza" was "not to be discussed".[101]

In short, Israel's "acceptance" of the Road Map consisted of an explicit rejection of most of its key terms as they related its own obligations, along with its unilateral imposition of additional demands never agreed to by the other party. Accordingly, Israel proceeded apace with further expansion of its illegal settlements, as well as with the illegal construction of the separation wall in the West Bank that would serve to further the de facto annexation of major swaths of Palestinian territory into Israel.[102]

The Bush administration's response to Israel's unilateral and illegal actions "was almost totally symbolic", as the *New York Times* put it. The US had extended $3 billion in annual loan guarantees to Israel, which was additional to the $1.4 billion in unused guarantees from the previous fiscal year that would roll over. The administration reduced this total of $4.4 billion in loan guarantees by $289.5 million. "Even as the administration imposed the financial penalty on Israel, though," the *Times* noted, "the United States was vetoing a United Nations Security Council resolution demanding that Israel end threats to exile Yasser Arafat," whom Condoleezza Rice described as "an obstacle to peace."[103]

The State Department acknowledged that this "totally symbolic" move "did not reflect the total cost of Israel's settlement building and fence construction". When asked whether the amount deducted corresponded with the amount Israel spent on its settlements and the wall, spokesman Richard Boucher responded that "it's obviously not because the fence cost a lot more than $289.5 million."[104] The US "penalty" therefore consisted of rewarding Israel with $4.1 billion in loan guarantees for the fiscal year, a significant financial incentive to continue its illegal policies.

As the Institute for Research: Middle Eastern Policy (IRmep) noted in a 2005 report, while not directly funding the settlements, the US aid allowed Israel to free up resources that were "pouring into settlement development and infrastructure building designed to partition key Palestinian territories and annex others to the state of Israel." Additionally, the US government had given tax-exempt status to non-profit organizations that were "directly and indirectly financing the coordination of illegal settlement building, encroachment, and violence against Palestinians."[105]

This trend has continued. The *Washington Post* reported in March 2009, three months after President Obama was sworn in, that organizations granted tax-exempt status by the US government were financing illegal activities such as "demolitions of Palestinian homes" (which Secretary of State Hillary Clinton deemed merely "unhelpful").[106] The *New York Times* reminded in July 2010 about the continuing practice of "many groups in the United States using tax-exempt donations to help Jews establish permanence in the Israeli-occupied territories—effectively obstructing the creation of a Palestinian state, widely seen as a necessary condition for Middle East peace." In what the *Times* deemed a "surprising juxtaposition", while US officials rhetorically opposed Israeli settlements, "the American Treasury helps sustain the settlements through tax breaks on donations to support them."[107]

Sharon's 'Disengagement Plan'

In December 2003, Prime Minister Ariel Sharon gave a speech providing the first outlines of Israel's planned withdrawal from the Gaza Strip, dubbed the "disengagement plan".[108] In April 2004, he sent a letter to President Bush providing the details of his plan, which included accelerating construction of the illegal separation wall in the West Bank and continuing, with only a few "limitations", the "growth of settlements".[109] The "disengagement plan" was transparently designed to gain for Israel the political leverage necessary—primarily meaning US backing—for its escalation of illegal colonization in the West Bank.

Bush's letter of reply to Sharon restated the US commitment to the Road Map and its rejection of the Palestinian right of return. He endorsed Israel's illegal wall by accepting the Sharon government's hollow statements that it "should be a security rather than political barrier, should be temporary rather than permanent, and therefore not prejudice any final status issues including final borders". Bush also said that because of "new realities on the ground", it would be "unrealistic to expect that the outcome of final status negotiations will be a full and complete return to the armistice lines of 1949". A final status agreement could "only be achieved on the basis of mutually agreed changes that reflect these realities."[110]

Thus, the Bush administration gave Israel an implicit green light to continue expanding settlements, explicit support for Israel's desire to annex illegally-constructed settlement blocs, and an endorsement of the illegal annexation wall conditioned only upon the understanding that Israel wouldn't *portray* it *as* such. As for the Palestinians, they would just have to accept the "new realities on the ground", meaning that they must agree as a precondition to cede major swaths of the West Bank to Israel during any future negotiations. Since Yasser Arafat would never agree to do so, new Palestinian leadership would be required, as laid out explicitly in Bush's speech on June 24, 2002, and again in the Road Map. (After Arafat's death in November 2004, Mahmoud Abbas would emerge as the approved Palestinian leader.) The letter conveyed the overall message that the US accepted Israel's unilateral interpretation of the Road Map, a fulfillment of the previous promise that it would "fully and seriously" address Israel's "real concerns" about its implementation.

Israeli officials made no pretense about the meaning of the planned withdrawal from Gaza. "The significance of the disengagement plan is the freezing of the peace process," Sharon's senior adviser Dov Weissglass proclaimed that October.

> And when you freeze that process, you prevent the establishment of a Palestinian state, and you prevent a discussion on the refugees, the borders and Jerusalem. Effectively, this whole package called the Palestinian state, with all that it entails, has been removed indefinitely from our agenda. And all this with authority and permission. All with a [US] presidential blessing and the ratification of both houses of [the US] Congress. . . . The disengagement is actually formaldehyde. It supplies the amount of formaldehyde that is necessary so there will not be a political process with the Palestinians.[111]

The *Washington Post* reported how "Some of Sharon's top aides suggested that once Gaza was evacuated, the whole process would go in a deep freeze for many years—leaving Israel in control of the West Bank, where its most populated and richest settlements were located."[112] A *New York Times* editorial similarly acknowledged that "Mr. Sharon is sacrificing Gaza in return for the world's acceptance of Israel's 'de facto annexation of 7 percent of West Bank territory,' as a political columnist, Nahum Barnea, theorized in Yedioth Ahronoth, a Hebrew-language daily." This was a plan, the *Times* editors opined, that should not be embraced "with anything other than enthusiasm."[113]

In July 2004, at the request of the UN General Assembly, the International Court of Justice issued its advisory opinion affirming that the separation wall and all Israeli settlements in the West Bank, including in East Jerusalem, were illegal under international law. The ICJ noted that "the wall's sinuous route has been traced in such a way as to include within that area the great majority of the Israeli settlements in the occupied Palestinian Territory (including East Jerusalem)." It judged that "the construction of the wall and its associated régime create a 'fait accompli' on the ground that could well become permanent, in which case, and notwithstanding the formal characterization of the wall by Israel [as being 'temporary' and built only for 'security' purposes], it would be tantamount to *de facto* annexation." The chosen route "gives expression *in loco* to the illegal measures taken by Israel with regard to Jerusalem and the settlements". The wall's construction "severely impedes the exercise by the Palestinian people of its right to self-determination, and is therefore a breach of Israel's obligation to respect that right."

Israel had destroyed or confiscated property for the wall, and its construction imposed severe restrictions on the movement of Palestinians in the West Bank. The city of Qalqiliya, for example, with a population of 40,000, was completely surrounded and effectively imprisoned, with the only point where residents could enter or exit being an Israeli military checkpoint. Nearly 25,000 acres of agricultural land had been confiscated and destroyed during just the first phase of the wall's construction. The wall had "further led to increasing difficulties for the population concerned regarding access to health services, educational establishments and primary sources of water." Cut off from their own land and water resources, many Palestinians would be forced to leave their homes.

The ICJ rejected Israel's claim that the wall was "necessary to attain its security objectives", stating that "The wall, along the route chosen, and its associated régime gravely infringe a number of rights of Palestinians residing in the territory occupied by Israel, and the infringements resulting from that route cannot be justified by military exigencies or by the requirements of national security or public order. The construction of such a wall accordingly constitutes breaches by Israel of various of its obligations under the applicable international humanitarian law and human rights instruments."

The ICJ affirmed that Israel had a right and a duty to protect its citizens, but that the "measures taken are bound nonetheless to remain in conformity with applicable international law. In conclusion, the Court considers that Israel cannot rely on a right of self-defense or on a state of necessity in order to preclude the wrongfulness of the construction of the wall. . . . The Court accordingly finds that the construction of the wall, and its associated régime, are contrary to international law."[114]

Despite the ICJ ruling, the construction of the wall continued, with explicit White House approval. In November 2005, Senator Hillary Clinton—wife to former President Bill Clinton and later President Obama's Secretary of State—toured a section of the wall and openly declared her support for it. "This is not against the Palestinian people," she asserted, dismissive of international law, the judgment of the ICJ, and the facts on the ground. "This is against the terrorists."[115] Shortly after Clinton made her comments, Tzipi Livni stated, "One does not have to be a genius to see that the fence will have implications for the future border". In keeping with the message Bush had sent and the understanding between the US and Israel, she immediately added, "This is not the reason it was built, but it could have political implications."[116]

Accelerating construction of the illegal wall was an integral part of Sharon's "disengagement plan", which, he declared in February 2005, could "pave the way to implementation of the roadmap" in accordance with Israel's unilateral interpretation of it. "Only actions and not words," Sharon professed, could "attain the vision of two states living side by side in peace and tranquility."[117]

Israel's actions had indeed spoken loudly: declaring the Taba talks "null and void"; conditioning its "acceptance" of the Road Map on rejection of the obligations it placed on Israel, as well as the unilateral placement of additional preconditions on the Palestinians; continuing settlement expansion in the West Bank; constructing an illegal separation wall to effectively annex major swaths

of Palestinian territory; and withdrawing from Gaza while maintaining restrictive control over its borders, territorial waters, and airspace.

The US Ambassador to Israel, Daniel Kurtzer, reiterated in an interview with
Israel's Channel 10 the following month that it was the Bush administration's
view that major settlement blocs "should remain within the State of Israel."
This was the policy that had been communicated the year before in Bush's letter
to Sharon, he pointed out. He repeated unequivocally that it was US policy to
support "the retention by Israel of major Israeli population centers as an outcome of negotiations. It is very, very clear to both the United States and Israel
what this means."[118]

Kurtzer's remarks caused "a diplomatic furor" for the State Department,
compelling Secretary of State Condoleezza Rice to meaninglessly reassure that
Israel's settlement expansion was "at odds with American policy." The *New York
Times* correctly observed that Sharon had "justified his plan" to withdraw from
Gaza "on the basis of his belief that Washington will support Israel's intention
to keep its main settlement blocs" in the occupied territory, including East
Jerusalem. The *Times* described the contradiction between the US government's
rhetorical opposition to the colonization and the actual policy of effective sup-
port for it as "[d]iplomatic ambiguities".[119]

There was no ambiguity about the matter in Israel, where, as Kurtzer had
noted, officials had been made "very, very clear" about it. "We can't expect to
receive explicit American agreement to build freely in the settlements," Sharon
sympathetically explained to his cabinet. The US's implicit green light would
suffice. So the growth of settlements would continue, and they would "remain
in Israel's hands and will fall within the (separation) fence". Israel, Sharon assured, had "made this position clear to the Americans."[120]

Commentators in the US media feigned mystification over the ostensible
"ambiguities" of US policy. Acknowledgment of the meaninglessness of the
US's rhetorical opposition to Israel's illegal activities only occasionally slipped
through the cracks, such as when Jackson Diehl commented in the *Washington
Post* that Sharon had a "bold agenda" to "obtain support of President Bush
for a unilateral Israeli solution" that was premised on abandoning negotiations
and the Road Map. The plan was for Israel "to withdraw from the Gaza Strip,
then impose a border of Israel's choosing in the West Bank, fortified by walls
and fences." Sharon had been straightforward in explaining that "his whole
purpose" was "to avoid the result of a negotiated settlement"—a plan to which
"Bush signed on." Administration officials "understand very well what Sharon's
goals are but choose not to notice them". The consequence for the Palestinians
was that they would be "left with Gaza and several enclaves separated from each
other by Israeli roads and settlements"—and "whether that is someday called a
state" was of "secondary concern for the Israeli prime minister."[121]

Following the Israeli withdrawal from Gaza in the summer of 2005, *The Independent* provided a concise summary of the "disengagement plan" with the headline, "Sharon pledges to expand West Bank settlements as last Israelis leave Gaza".[122] Underscoring another key element of the plan, *Haaretz* reported on September 13, prior to the annual General Debate of the General Assembly, that the "main message" Sharon would deliver to the UN was that "Israeli responsibility for the Gaza Strip has come to an end." Sharon had "adopted the Foreign Ministry's position that it would be out of place to declare 'the end of the occupation' in Gaza, at least as long as the Palestinians do not control the border crossings, airspace and territorial waters. Instead, the ministry prefers 'the end of Israeli responsibility.'" Taking a cue from Pontius Pilate's vain symbolic act, Israel was washing its hands of the consequences its policies inflicted upon the civilian population in Gaza.[123]

Following the General Debate, the UN General Assembly passed a resolution recalling relevant Security Council resolutions, including Resolution 242, as well as the ICJ's advisory opinion. It reaffirmed the principles of "equal rights", "self-determination", and "the inadmissibility of the acquisition of territory by war"; reaffirmed the illegality of Israeli settlements, actions to change the status of Jerusalem, and construction of the wall; and demanded "that Israel, the occupying Power, comply with its legal obligations under international law". The resolution passed with 156 votes in favor, 9 abstentions, and 6 opposed (the US, Israel, Australia, the Marshall Islands, Palau, and the Federated States of Micronesia).[124]

"These resolutions are purely symbolic," US Ambassador to the UN John Bolton told reporters in an attempt to rationalize the US's ritualistic opposition to the international community's annual reaffirmation of the two-state solution. "It is one reason why many people say the UN is not really useful in solving actual problems. We have been making enormous progress toward solutions in the Arab-Israeli conflict, and that progress has benefited from UN participation, but it does not benefit from needless repetition of meaningless resolutions in the General Assembly."[125]

Annapolis

In July 2007, President Bush called for a peace conference to be chaired by Secretary of State Condoleezza Rice and held at the US Naval Academy in Annapolis, Maryland, in November.[126] Israeli leaders met in advance with members of the PA to work out the terms of a joint agreement. When the Palestinian side suggested that international law should be included in the terms of reference, according to the leaked minutes from the meeting, Israeli Foreign Minister Tzipi Livni retorted, "NO. [*sic*] I was the Minister of Justice. I am a lawyer. . . . But I am against law—international law in particular. Law in general." Her alternative suggestion was, "If we want to make the agreement smaller, can we just drop some of these issues? Like international law, this will make the agreements easier." The PA team understandably protested Livni's assertion "that Palestinians don't really need international law."[127]

A joint statement was finally agreed upon, less than an hour before the Annapolis conference was opened. It simply reiterated both sides' commitment to the Road Map, without any reference to Resolution 242 or international law, and reiterated that the US would "monitor and judge the fulfillment of the commitment of both sides of the road map"—which is to say that the US would unilaterally determine whether or not the Palestinians could have a state.[128]

President Bush then issued a statement expressing that Israel must "bring an end to the occupation that began in 1967 through a negotiated settlement"—another reiteration of the US's acceptance of the Israeli interpretation of UN Security Council Resolution 242.[129]

Prime Minister Ehud Olmert (who replaced Sharon in early 2006) stated that "previous agreements" would be "a point of departure" for future negotiations. He specifically cited Resolution 242 and the Road Map; but in the same breath, he also cited Bush's letter to Sharon outlining specific ways in which future talks would depart from both international law and previous agreements with the Palestinians.[130]

Tzipi Livni insisted that she "did not come here today to argue about rights". By this, she meant *Palestinians'* rights, which could not serve as any "point of departure" for negotiations. At the same time, she made sure to assert "the Jewish nation's right to all of the Land of Israel", inclusively meaning the West Bank and Gaza. Within this framework of how "rights" would apply to future negotiations, she expressed that the Road Map was "not an obstacle to the process", but "the right way to advance it".[131]

Olmert and Livni subsequently briefed the Israeli cabinet on what had been achieved at Annapolis, which further illuminates precisely why they believed the Road Map was "the right way" to "advance" the so-called "peace process". Olmert explained that the "most important thing in the joint statement" was that "any future arrangement and agreement will be operationally subject to fulfilling all of the road map commitments, including all of its stages and outlines. In other words, *Israel will not have to carry out any commitment stemming from the agreement* before all of the road map commitments are met" (emphasis added). In other words, Israel expected the Palestinians to fulfill all of their commitments under the Road Map (and then some), while fulfilling none of its own.[132]

Livni likewise bragged how they had "succeeded in meeting the goals" that the Israeli government had set for itself at Annapolis. Israel's commitments under the Road Map would be "conditional on an examination of actual implementation on the ground of the first phase"—meaning, again, that Israel would not have to meet any of its own obligations until there was a new Palestinian government that was able to reign in militant groups, would renounce the right to armed resistance against occupation, and would accede the legitimacy of the Zionist's unilateral declaration of the state of Israel and ethnic cleansing of Palestine. Since no elected Palestinian leader could be expected to meet those preconditions and retain his legitimacy in the eyes of his own people, Israel could confidently preclude the possibility of any final status negotiations.

Furthermore, even hypothetically speaking, "within the framework of the negotiations" envisioned under the Road Map, "Israel's hands will not be tied" since there would be "no inclusion of issues problematic for Israel"—international law, for example. This stalling on negotiations, which would allow Israel to continue to prejudice their outcome in the meantime, could continue indefinitely. The Israelis refused to be bound by or commit to "a timetable that will bring direct international pressure to bear on Israel." They had "made it emphatically clear that the entire dialogue must be bilateral", with "no direct involvement of the international community" throughout the process. "It was not easy to achieve this," Livni bragged, "but we insisted."[133]

As Israel planned to construct 300 housing units in the Har Homa settlement in occupied East Jerusalem, Condoleezza Rice offered the feeble criticism that it didn't help to build the "confidence" necessary to move forward under the Road Map. "Secretary of State Rice should be blessed for her efforts in the relaunching of the peace process," quipped Israeli Housing Minister Ze'ev Boim in reply, "but it cannot be that on every occasion this will be tied together with the cessation of construction in Jerusalem."[134]

With regard to settlement policy and East Jerusalem, *Haaretz* pointed out that Israel had no "no good answer" to the US's rhetorical objections. It had only a "ridiculous" claim of sovereignty when "No one in the world recognizes Israel's annexation of East Jerusalem." The editorial concluded that, "At this rate, and with this sagacity, the Annapolis conference will prove no more than a barren footnote."[135]

That, of course, was precisely the point, as far as the Israeli government was concerned. In this sense, Annapolis was par for the course in the US-led "peace process", the entire purpose of which was to relegate international law and the internationally recognized rights of the Palestinians to no more than a barren footnote.

CHAPTER 4

OBAMA'S 'NEW BEGINNING'

WHILE ISRAEL'S ASSAULT ON Gaza was "extremely damaging for Israel's international image and standing", the *Jerusalem Post* observed in February 2009, shortly after Barack Obama's inauguration, it hadn't "yet manifested in any major diplomatic crises". This was true even though "questions about Israel's disregard for human rights, excessive use of force, possible war crimes, and indiscriminate attacks on international facilities are high on the international agenda."[1] The simple explanation was that such questions were *not* high on Washington's very different agenda, which remained consistent across administrations.

This did not go unnoticed in the Arab world. Egyptian author Alaa al-Aswany wrote in an op-ed for the *New York Times* that the Muslim world had "welcomed" Obama "with almost total enthusiasm until he underwent his first real test: Gaza. Even before he officially took office, we expected him to take a stand against Israel's war on Gaza. We still hope that he will condemn, if only with simple words, this massacre that killed more than 1,300 Palestinians, many of them civilians. (I don't know what you call it in other languages, but in Egypt we call this a massacre.) . . . But Mr. Obama has been silent."[2]

Elections were held in Israel in February, with a foreboding outcome. "President Obama's ambition to move quickly on Israeli-Palestinian peace suffered a significant setback", the *Washington Post* reported, when the right-wing Likud party of Benjamin Netanyahu more than doubled its seats in the Knesset. The ultra-nationalist party, Yisrael Beiteinu, also made gains, thus "increasing the prospect that a government uninterested in peace talks will emerge from the post-election efforts to form a governing coalition." Aaron David Miller, a former adviser to the US Secretary of State who had participated in negotiations, told the *Post*, "This is like hanging a 'closed for the season' sign on any peace-making for the next year or so."[3]

The head of the Yisrael Beiteinu party was Knesset member Avigdor Lieber-man, a former member of Kach, a group founded by Meir Kahane and listed by the US State Department as a terrorist organization.[4] The head of the Kadima party, Tzipi Livni, also had a right-wing background, with both of her parents having been "key figures" in the Zionist terrorist organization Irgun, accord-ing to a BBC profile. Irgun was responsible for the 1946 bombing of the King David Hotel in Jerusalem and participated with Lehi (or the Stern Gang) in the infamous 1948 massacre of Palestinians in the village of Deir Yassin. Livni shared her parents' Zionist beliefs, if not Irgun's methods, having once told the *New York Times*, "I believe, like my parents, in the right of the Jewish people to the entire land of Israel"—meaning also the occupied West Bank and Gaza Strip.[5]

The head of Irgun at the time of the King David Hotel bombing, inciden-tally, was Menachem Begin, who went on to become Israeli prime minister.[6] As already noted, another prime minister, Yitzhak Shamir, had likewise been a leading member of the terrorist group Lehi.[7]

Although completely unfounded, there were growing fears in Israel that the Obama administration would pressure the Israeli government to freeze settle-ment construction. The new administration was "likely" to "cut the equivalent sum of the latest investments in settlements from the remaining budget for US guaranteed loans", *Haaretz* wrongly predicted.[8]

Amnesty International was meanwhile calling for the US to suspend its military aid to Israel. "Israeli forces used white phosphorus and other weapons supplied by the USA to carry out serious violations of international humanitar-ian law, including war crimes," said Donatella Rovera, the head of Amnesty's fact-finding mission to southern Israel and Gaza. Amnesty noted that the US had agreed to provide $30 billion in military aid to Israel over a 10-year period. "To a large extent," observed the group's Middle East director, Malcolm Smart, "Israel's military offensive in Gaza was carried out with weapons, munitions and military equipment supplied by the USA and paid for with US taxpayers' money. . . . As the major supplier of weapons to Israel, the USA has a particular obligation to stop any supply that contributes to gross violations of the laws of war and of human rights. The Obama Administration should immediately suspend US military aid to Israel."[9]

US-supplied arms used by Israel in its operations included F-16 combat aircraft, Apache helicopters, Hellfire missiles, MK-82 500-pound bombs, M825A1 white phosphorus munitions, flechettes, and 120 mm tank rounds. Other arms supplied to Israel by the US included Black Hawk combat helicop-ters, Bell Cobra gunships, armored vehicles, missile launchers, GBU-39 bombs, artillery rounds, and M4 carbine assault rifles. "Put simply," an Amnesty report on foreign arms supplies to Israel stated, "Israel's military intervention in the Gaza Strip has been equipped to a large extent by US-supplied weapons, munitions and military equipment paid for with US taxpayers' money."

Amnesty noted that under the US Foreign Assistance Act, "no security assistance may be provided to any country the government of which engages in a consistent pattern of gross violations of internationally recognized human rights"—but this could be circumvented under the US Export Administration Act if the President determined that "extraordinary circumstances" existed. Under the US Arms Export Control Act, US military equipment and training could only be supplied for "legitimate self-defense" or in participation with UN peacekeeping operations or other purposes consistent with the UN Charter. Under the Leahy Law, the US is prohibited "from providing most forms of security assistance to any military or police unit when there is 'credible evidence' that members of the unit are committing gross human rights violations."

In addition to calling on the US to suspend its military assistance to Israel, Amnesty repeated its call for "a comprehensive UN Security Council arms embargo on Israel, Hamas and other Palestinian armed groups until effective mechanisms are in place to ensure that weapons or munitions and other military equipment will not be used to commit serious violations of international human rights law and international humanitarian law."[10]

The Obama administration instead sought to reassure Israel that no cuts in military aid would occur.[11] It was a clear reaffirmation of the "special relationship" in which the US materially supports Israel's violations of international law, including military actions amounting to war crimes, as during Operation Cast Lead.

American and Israeli Exceptionalism

The "special relationship" in the aftermath of Israel's Gaza massacre posed a special problem for the intelligentsia dedicated to the idea of American exceptionalism, in which framework the US occasionally makes benign "mistakes", but only ever with the most benevolent of intentions—an assumed quality that is often naturally projected upon its closest partner in the Middle East, as well. The simple solution for the apologists of the military-industrial complex and US foreign policy was to simply dismiss any suggestion that Israel had committed war crimes.

In one instructive example, worth examining at length, Anthony H. Cordesman—the Arleigh A. Burke Chair in Strategy at the Center for Strategic and International Studies and a national security analyst for ABC News—wrote a report published several weeks after the end of Operation Cast Lead that concluded "Israel did not violate the laws of war." Rather, it had used "decisive force to enhance regional deterrence and demonstrate that it had restored its military edge"—all perfectly legal. Israel, he proclaimed, had only targeted "legitimate military objectives in spite of their very real humanitarian costs."

Tellingly, Cordesman prefaced his analysis by remarking that it "has to be written largely from an Israeli perspective" because Hamas had offered "few details" apart from "propaganda statements". Declarations from the IDF, on the other hand, he considered credible. Indeed, he reproduced page after page throughout his report of verbatim IDF summaries of its operations, which he relied heavily upon to arrive at his conclusion that Israel committed no violations of international law.

He further prefaced his assessment by emphasizing that it only examined the question of disproportionate force "in the context of fighting and winning asymmetric wars and not as legal or moral issues". The reason for this, he explained, was that "analysts without training in the complex laws of war" should not examine the legal issues because of the risk they might become politicized and manipulated and "used as a basis for propaganda". How could he declare that Israel committed no war crimes while at the same time stating that his own analysis did not consider Israel's actions in the context of their legal or moral legitimacy and, further, that analysts without legal training should not issue such judgments? The contradiction is easily reconciled. Cordesman was simply applying the usual hypocritical standard of the US government: invoking international law for the purpose of exonerating the US's Middle East partner was fine, but to do so for the purpose of critically examining Israel's actions such that the wrong conclusion might be drawn just would not do. Note that according to this standard, the word "propaganda" is a euphemism simply meaning any conclusion contrary to the one desired.

Cordesman's application of this standard was evident throughout his paper. For instance, he criticized Hamas for using the ceasefire period to allegedly rearm and prepare for armed conflict while *praising* Israel for doing the same thing. He lauded with admiration how Israel launched its operation "after months of detailed planning" involving "high levels of secrecy and compartmentation to ensure that its war plans did not leak."

Cordesman admitted that the "immediate trigger of the war" was Israel's violation of the ceasefire on November 4. Yet his analysis was premised on the assumption that "Hamas must bear responsibility" because it was "Hamas actions that triggered the fighting, the Israeli actions that followed". He reconciled his apparent self-contradiction by simply moving the timeline forward from November 4 to December 19 and beginning his analysis from there. On that date, Cordesman argued, the ceasefire was ended by Hamas. He could not have been unaware, as he was writing this, that the ceasefire was officially six months in duration, December 19 marking its official expiration *by agreement*.

But *some* rationalization was needed to be able to premise his analysis in a way that would allow him to arrive at his desired conclusions; the deception that

Hamas had somehow ended the ceasefire unilaterally would suffice. Cordesman was also no doubt aware that Hamas had offered to renew the ceasefire, and that this offer was *rejected by Israel*; indeed, he alluded to this by lauding the effectiveness of "Israel's deception plan" in catching Hamas by surprise with the IDF's military operation.

Cordesman insisted that Israel made "a systematic effort to limit collateral damage". As evidence for this, he cited the fact that the IDF had detailed maps, including "the location of sensitive facilities like schools, hospitals, and religious cites [*sic*, i.e., 'sites']"—all of which, as Cordesman acknowledged, Israel proceeded to systematically bomb. He excused such attacks on "sensitive facilities"—his euphemism for civilian objects with protected status under international law—with the remark that "IDF forces almost certainly were correct in reporting that Hamas used mosques and other sensitive sites in combat." He offered no evidence to support this assumption, but accepted it as a matter of faith. By his own account, there was "no way to determine" whether the IDF's claims in this regard were true or whether such locations "were not actually being used by Hamas". Even if the IDF's claims were false, he argued further, systematically bombing schools, hospitals, and mosques could be justified on the grounds that they occurred in "the heat and uncertainty of combat"—his euphemism "combat" meaning a scenario in which one of the world's most advanced and powerful militaries rained down bombs on a totally defenseless and impoverished population imprisoned in a tiny strip of land from which Israel prevented them fleeing.

Cordesman recognized the suffering caused to the civilian population by Israel's bombing, as well as its ongoing blockade of goods and people into and out of Gaza. But having declared Israel's bombardment of civilian objects legal, he further dismissed its responsibility for their suffering on the grounds that "States do not have an obligation to provide humanitarian relief to their enemies or to enemy populations in wartime". On the contrary, under the Fourth Geneva Convention, Israel did in fact have "the duty of ensuring the food and medical supplies of the population" (Article 55). Perhaps we may attribute Cordesman's false statement to his admission that he found the laws of war to be "complex" and his view that therefore "analysts without training" shouldn't examine the legal issues; unless, of course, it is to declare that "Israel did not violate the laws of war."

He described at some length how the IDF deliberately targeted "sensitive facilities"; yet he nevertheless declared that there was "little evidence that the IAF struck deliberately against civilian targets, or that the air campaign deliberately violated the laws of war." His rationale for this irreconcilable self-contradiction was, again, essentially that since the IDF hadn't publicly admitted that there was no military justification for its intentional targeting of civilian objects, therefore its actions must have been in accordance with the laws of war.

The death toll among Palestinian civilians, including women and children, might seem to suggest otherwise, Cordesman acknowledged. He dealt with this problem by asserting that only the IDF's own estimates of civilian casualties were reliable. There were "no credible estimates" apart from the IDF's own. Palestinian sources such as the Ministry of Health and the Palestinian Center for Human Rights (PCHR)—a well-respected organization based in Gaza City whose affiliations included the International Commission of Jurists and which was funded by Oxfam, the EU, Christian Aid, and CARE International, among others—could not be trusted. As for casualty estimates from UN agencies, "many Israelis feel that such UN sources are strongly biased in favor of the Palestinians." So Israel's claims about the extent of its own killing should be accepted on faith, while estimates from agencies of the United Nations must be considered unreliable because certain Israelis said so.

Cordesman allowed that "Palestinian civilians suffered far more than either the IDF or Hamas", but deemed "exact numbers" to be "less important" than the fact that "images of civilian deaths and suffering were seen throughout the world for some three weeks", which affected "perceptions" about Israel's operation. In other words, the only significance Cordesman attributed to the massive suffering of the Palestinian civilian population was that it made Israel look bad.

Cordesman acknowledged again that the IDF "did hit some purely civilian targets, including important UN targets like an UNRWA school where 42 Palestinians died". But he adopted the US government's standard that the benefit of the doubt belonged not to the victims of the massacre, but to its perpetrators. It was "not clear", he argued, "that Hamas or other combatants were *not* in or near such targets" (emphasis added), and international law required only "an effort to discriminate—not perfect success". So, as long as Israel *claimed* to have a military justification, even if it was lying, then its attacks were justified. As for just what "effort to discriminate" the IDF had ostensibly made when it massacred over forty civilians at a UN-run school, Cordesman left it open to the reader's imagination.

There was "no evidence" of Israeli "abuses", he concluded, "aside from a few limited cases", the "only significant" example of which was "the possible misuse of 20 phosphorus shells in built up areas". So the massacre of over forty civilians was too insignificant to be called abuse and warrant outrage. "War is inherently horrible", he offered as an excuse for the Palestinians' intense suffering at the hands of Israel. To translate into the vernacular: shit happens. Sure, Israel made "mistakes", but they were no worse "than NATO did in Kosovo or that the US and its allies made in dealing with targets in populated areas in Iraq and Afghanistan."[12] And, of course, the US might from time to time make "mistakes", but that its intentions are always benign and its actions justified is axiomatic.

Any analysis that doesn't accept this unquestionably as a matter of faith is by definition nothing more than "propaganda".

'The Most Moral Army in the World'

Insistent denials that Israel committed war crimes were further challenged in March 2009, when the Israeli military academy at Oranim Academic College published more testimonies from Israeli soldiers who participated in Operation Cast Lead.

A non-commissioned officer related a case in which a commander ordered troops to shoot an elderly woman crossing a road: "I don't know whether she was suspicious, not suspicious, I don't know her story. . . . I do know that my officer sent people to the roof in order to take her out. . . . It was cold-blooded murder."[13] He described the rules of engagement: "When we entered a house, we were supposed to bust down the door and start shooting inside and just go up story by story. . . . I call that murder. Each story, if we identify a person, we shoot them. I asked myself—how is this reasonable?"[14]

A squad leader testified, "At the beginning the directive was to enter a house with an armored vehicle, to break the door down, and start shooting inside and—I call it murder—to shoot at everyone we identify. In the beginning I asked myself how could this make sense? Higher-ups said it was permissible because everyone left in the city [Gaza City] is culpable because they didn't run away." A later directive was to enter a home warning its residents through a loudspeaker, "you have five minutes to run away and whoever doesn't will be killed."[15]

In another case, Israeli soldiers had set up a sniper position on the roof of a Palestinian family's home, and, as another infantry squad leader recalled,

> The platoon commander let the family go and told them to go to the right. One mother and her two children didn't under-stand and went to the left, but they forgot to tell the sharp-shooter on the roof they had let them go and it was okay, and he should hold his fire and he . . . he did what he was sup-posed to do, like he was following his orders. . . . The sharp-shooter saw a woman and children approaching him, closer than the lines he was told no one should pass. He shot them straight away. In any case, what happened is that in the end he killed them. I don't think he felt too bad about it, because after all, as far as he was concerned, he did his job according to the orders he was given. And the atmosphere in general, from what I understand from most of my men who I talked to . . . I don't know how to describe it. . . . The lives of Palestinians,

let's say, is something very, very less important than the lives of our soldiers. So as far as they are concerned they can justify it that way.[16]

According to other testimony, literature passed out to soldiers by army rabbis "had a clear message—we are the people of Israel, we came by a miracle to the land of Israel, God returned us to the land, now we need to struggle to get rid of the gentiles that are interfering with our conquest of the land".[17]

Haaretz reported on another practice within the IDF:

> Dead babies, mothers weeping on their children's graves, a gun aimed at a child and bombed-out mosques—these are a few examples of the images Israel Defense Forces soldiers design these days to print on shirts they order to mark the end of training, or field duty. The slogans accompanying the drawings are not exactly anemic either: A T-shirt for infantry snipers bears the inscription "Better use Durex," next to a picture of a dead Palestinian baby, with his weeping mother and a teddy bear beside him. A sharpshooter's T-shirt from the Givati Brigade's Shaked battalion shows a pregnant Palestinian woman with a bull's-eye superimposed on her belly, with the slogan, in English, "1 shot, 2 kills."

One soldier, "Y.", described to *Haaretz* a shirt he had designed after Operation Cast Lead for Battalion 890 of the Paratroops. It depicted "a King Kong-like soldier in a city under attack. The slogan is unambiguous: 'If you believe it can be fixed, then believe it can be destroyed!'" Asked what the depicted soldier was holding in his hand, "Y." replied:

> A mosque. Before I drew the shirt I had some misgivings, because I wanted it to be like King Kong, but not too monstrous. The one holding the mosque—I wanted him to have a more normal-looking face, so it wouldn't look like an anti-Semitic cartoon. Some of the people who saw told me, "Is that what you've got to show for the IDF? That it destroys homes?" I can understand people who look at this from outside and see it that way, but I was in Gaza and they kept emphasizing that the object of the operation was to wreak destruction on the infrastructure, so that the price the Palestinians and the leadership pay will make them realize that it isn't worth it for them to go on shooting. So that's the idea of "we're coming to destroy" in the drawing.

"Humor of this kind" was condemnable, said an IDF spokesman. He added that the shirts were civilian clothing to which military regulations did not apply, while promising that the IDF would take action to put an end to this "phenomenon." Yet, as *Haaretz* observed, "According to Y., most of these shirts are worn strictly in an army context, not in civilian life"; and it had been a long-standing practice within the IDF that had often been met with the approval of commanding officers.[18]

In response to media reports relaying the soldiers' testimonies to the public, Defense Minister Ehud Barak repeatedly declared that the IDF was "the most moral army in the world".[19] In one repetition of the mantra, Barak justified Israel's actions by comparing them to the US's own use of force in international affairs: "The Israeli Army is the most moral in the world, and I know what I'm talking about because I know what took place in the former Yugoslavia, in Iraq."[20] This was perhaps intended as a message to the Obama administration, implying—with considerable merit—that the US could not join in the criticism of Israel's military conduct without hypocrisy. It was a variation of Israel's theme of invoking the US's "war on terrorism" as justification for its own actions.

While Israel announced that its military would investigate its own conduct, IDF Chief of Staff Lt. Gen. Gabi Ashkenazi responded, "I don't believe that IDF soldiers cold-bloodedly targeted Palestinian civilians. We will wait for the results of the investigation, but my impression is that the IDF behaved in a moral and ethical manner." Any "incidents" that might have occurred, he insisted, were "isolated". He then expressed what a "great privilege" it was to head the IDF and proudly boasted, "We received a mission and fulfilled it."[21]

Gideon Levy in *Haaretz* lambasted the IDF's "propagandistic and ridiculous responses", which were "shameless lies" intended "to deceive the public". Israel "will not seriously investigate anything", he predicted. "Until we recognize Palestinians as human beings, just as we are, nothing will change."[22]

Fulfilling Levy's prediction, in late March, the IDF announced the completion of an investigation into the conduct of its soldiers based on the released testimonies. It declared that it had found no evidence of wrongdoing and that no charges would be brought against any soldiers. The testimonies had been "purposely exaggerated", the IDF said. It denied the account of the mother and her children being killed and said that the soldier who testified about an elderly woman being gunned down by a sniper "was only repeating a rumor he had heard". Yes, the IDF acknowledged, the "rumor" was true. She had indeed been shot. But, the IDF insisted, the sniper had "no choice" but to gun the unarmed old lady down.

The IDF did manage to find at least one victim in its investigation, as indicated by the Chief Military Advocate General (MAG), Brigadier General Avichai Mendelblit, who expressed his anger at the soldiers who had given their testimonies. "It will be difficult to evaluate the damage done," he scolded, "to the image and morals of the Israel Defense Forces and its soldiers".[23]

Israel's declarations of no wrongdoing failed to persuade the UN and human rights organizations, which proceeded to systematically dismantle them. The Israeli branch of Physicians for Human Rights issued a report criticizing Israel for preventing the evacuation of injured civilians during Operation Cast Lead.[24] Human Rights Watch published a report documenting Israel's illegal use of US-supplied white phosphorus munitions "over populated areas, killing and injuring civilians, and damaging civilian structures, including a school, a market, a humanitarian aid warehouse and a hospital". Doctors described patients who had been scorched to the bone with chemical burns. In the case of the attack on the UNRWA headquarters, "the IDF kept firing white phosphorus despite repeated warnings from UN personnel about the danger to civilians." If the IDF's purpose had been to create a smoke screen, it could have done so by using the 155 mm smoke projectiles in its inventory without the risk of fires or burn injuries to civilians. Israel's choice "strongly suggests that the IDF was not using the munition for its obscurant qualities, but rather for its incendiary effect." Furthermore, there was "no evidence of Hamas using human shields in the vicinity at the time of the attacks."[25]

Richard Falk submitted a 26-page report to the Human Rights Council stating that Israel had committed grave war crimes in Gaza. Israel continued to control Gaza's borders, territorial waters, and airspace, and thus remained Occupying Power. Its blockade of Gaza was illegal, a violation of Article 33 of the Fourth Geneva Convention, which prohibited collective punishment, and Article 55, which obligated Israel to provide food and health care to the population. The full might of Israel's military had been "directed at an essentially defenseless society of 1.5 million persons." In addition to the civilian casualties, which included hundreds of women and children, 21,000 homes had been damaged or destroyed. The "scale and nature" of Israel's attacks were irreconcilable with the requirement of international law to distinguish between military targets and civilian persons and objects. Additionally, Israel's resort to military force was unlawful since diplomatic and peaceful alternatives had not been exhausted. Palestinian rocket attacks were also "a clear violation of international law", but the ceasefire had been very effective in mitigating them, and it was Israel's violations of the ceasefire—such as its November 4 invasion of Gaza—that were primarily responsible for its collapse. Moreover, Hamas had repeatedly proposed renewing the ceasefire, but Israel had refused. Falk's report concluded by calling for a UN investigation into possible war crimes headed up by independent experts.[26]

A 43-page report by the UN Secretary-General's special representative for children and armed conflict, Radhika Coomaraswamy, presented an account of how Israel used an 11-year-old Palestinian boy as a human shield in the neighborhood of Tal al-Hawa on January 15. The boy had been forced to walk in front of soldiers and to enter buildings before the troops. This was "just one of the hundreds of incidents that have been documented and verified" by UN officials in Gaza.[27]

Israel's ambassador to the Human Rights Council, Aharon Leshno Yaar, dismissed the UN reports as part of a pattern of "demonizing Israel".[28]

The Obama administration, meanwhile, in a characteristic example of the kind of "pressure" it would exert on Israel, protested some of the restrictions Israel placed on Gaza, but not the blockade policy itself. As a result, Reuters related, Olmert said he would "lift restrictions on food items, such as pasta and cheese". But it remained "unclear whether restrictions on deliveries of other harmless items, such as toilet paper, soap and toothpaste, would also be lifted." Cigarettes and chocolates remained forbidden to Gazans, as did the cement and steel they required to rebuild after the US-supported devastation of their property.[29]

In April, the UN Human Rights Council appointed Richard J. Goldstone to head its fact-finding mission to investigate whether war crimes were committed during Israel's twenty-two-day assault on Gaza. A well-respected international jurist, Goldstone had on his resume the role of Chief Prosecutor of the International Criminal Tribunals for the former Yugoslavia and Rwanda. Joining Goldstone were Christine Chinkin, Professor of International Law at the London School of Economics and Political Science; Hina Jilani, Advocate of the Supreme Court of Pakistan and former Special Representative of the Secretary-General on Human Rights Defenders; and Desmond Travers, a retired Irish Army Colonel and member of the Board of Directors of the Institute for International Criminal Investigations.[30]

Israel immediately announced that it would not cooperate with the UN investigation.[31]

As the UN investigation was announced, Physicians for Human Rights-Israel released the report of its own fact-finding mission, which concluded that "The underlying meaning of the attack on the Gaza Strip, or at least its final consequence, appears to be one of creating terror without mercy to anyone. . . . It appears that the wide range of attacks with sophisticated weaponry was predominantly focused on terrorizing the population. . . . There is absolutely no doubt that the number of medical institutions such as hospitals and mobile clinics were specifically targeted, including a large number of ambulances." Children in particular "were disproportionately affected by the attack". In addition to the deaths and injuries, many children suffered "severe psychological damage". Israel's attacks had "left the population of the Gaza Strip without any hope for the future." Operation Cast Lead, the report concluded, had been a "severe military attack on a predominantly civilian population".[32]

On April 22, the IDF announced the conclusions of an initial series of self-investigations (apart from the probe into the soldiers' testimonies). Unsurprisingly, the IDF again declared that it had "operated in accordance with international law" and "maintained a high professional and moral level while facing an enemy that aimed to terrorize Israeli civilians whilst taking cover amidst uninvolved civilians in the Gaza strip and using them as human shields." There had been "a very small number of incidents in which intelligence or operational errors took place during the fighting", but they were "unavoidable and occur in all combat situations, in particular of the type which Hamas forced on the IDF, by choosing to fight from within the civilian population." Hamas had booby trapped homes and fired from schools, the IDF claimed, presenting no evidence. It touted as proof of its goodwill towards civilians the fact that it dropped over two million leaflets warning them to flee to safety, as well as its "extensive use of accurate munitions, wherever and whenever possible, to minimize harm to civilians."

With regard to the killing of over forty civilians at the UNRWA school in Jabaliya on January 6, the IDF claimed that militants had launched mortars eighty meters from the school—an acknowledgment that Israel's original claim that fire had originated from *within* the school compound was false. It justified its indiscriminate killing of dozens of civilians by describing it as "unintentional".

The burning down of the UNRWA warehouse was cited as an example of "the unfortunate result of the type of warfare that Hamas forced upon the IDF". The IDF claimed its forces "did not intend, at any stage, to hit a UN facility." Yet it failed to explain why Israel had chosen to use white phosphorus munitions, either in that attack or elsewhere over densely populated areas. It offered no explanation for how, if not intentional, the compound had taken numerous direct hits despite its precise GPS coordinates being known to the IDF; why the IDF continued to bombard the facility even after repeatedly notified that it was being struck; or why Prime Minister Olmert had admitted that the compound *was* targeted on the false grounds that Hamas had fired from that location.

The IDF admitted that it had attacked UN aid convoys. It first declared that in no such instance was there a "deliberate intention to hit a UN vehicle or facility"—a claim it then immediately contradicted by asserting, without evidence, that in one such instance, a UN vehicle *was* targeted because it "was being used for terrorist operations." It also admitted to targeting medical facilities and ambulances, which it attempted to justify by asserting that Hamas had used hospitals, including Al-Shifa, as command centers or weapons storage facilities and ambulances "as cover for terrorist operations". It provided no evidence to support these claims.

The IDF attempted to justify its attack on the home of Nizar Rayan that killed four of his wives and nine of his children by claiming that a "weapons

storage facility" had been located there. It offered no evidence. The IDF justified its attack on the house of Dr. Abuelaish that killed three of his daughters
and his niece on the basis that its forces had "identified suspicious figures on the
third floor of the building". No explanation was provided as to what made the
"figures" purportedly seen there "suspicious". The IDF further attempted to justify both of these attacks on civilians in their home by saying that the occupants
had been warned to leave but chose to stay—as though that relieved the IDF of
its obligation under international law not to engage in indiscriminate attacks.

On January 6, numerous civilians were killed in an Israeli attack on a home
in the Zeytoun neighborhood of Gaza City. The IDF claimed that its target
had been "a weapons storage facility" in a building next door. It described this
as "a professional mistake of the type that can take place during intensive fighting in a crowded environment against an enemy that uses civilians as cover for
its operations." So nobody would be held accountable. No evidence was offered for the existence of the alleged "weapons storage facility" next door to the
home where this "professional mistake" had resulted in the deaths of more than
twenty members of the Daya family.

The IDF claimed that the Ibrahim al-Maqadmah mosque in Beit Lahiya
"was not attacked at all"—which it then immediately contradicted by stating
that "the casualties of the attack were in fact Hamas operatives killed while
fighting against the IDF." Naturally, there was no explanation for how an attack
that didn't occur could possibly have caused casualties. As we will return to,
both of these claims—that the mosque was not attacked and that the victims
were not civilians—were false.[33]

Upon the release of the IDF's report, Ehud Barak trumpeted that Israel's
willingness to investigate itself "once again proves that the IDF is one of the
most moral armies in the world."[34]

International human rights organizations remained unpersuaded. B'Tselem
said the IDF inquiry failed to satisfy the requirements for an independent inquiry and emphasized the importance of Israel cooperating with the UN fact-
finding mission headed by Richard Goldstone.[35]

Amnesty International pointed out that the IDF "lacks credibility" and was
repeating claims it had made since the beginning of its operations, "but without providing the necessary evidence to back up the allegations." There was "a
strikingly large gap between the 'very small number' of mistakes referred to in
the IDF's briefing paper and the killing by Israeli forces of some 300 Palestinian
children and hundreds of other unarmed civilians". The IDF's conclusions did
"not even attempt to explain the overwhelming majority of civilian deaths nor
the massive destruction caused to civilian buildings in Gaza." Given the lack of
evidence supporting Israeli claims, the IDF's self-investigation appeared to be
"more an attempt to shirk its responsibilities than a genuine process to establish
the truth". Amnesty detailed many of the IDF's misleading statements, factual

errors, and errors of omission. It also noted that the IDF had refused to respond to its requests to meet with officials to discuss concerns about violations of international law and similarly urged Israel to cooperate with the UN fact-finding mission.[36]

Facts didn't matter so much in the US, where the media continued to play its usual role of manufacturing consent for government policy and whitewashing the US's complicity in Israel's war crimes. In an article titled "Israeli Military Says Actions in Gaza War Did Not Violate International Law", the *New York Times* uncritically parroted the IDF's conclusions. It was not until the very last paragraph of the 1,067 word article that one could read even the slightest hint that perhaps the investigation might not be very credible: "Israeli and international human rights groups rejected the Israeli military's internal investigations as inadequate. Human Rights Watch called Wednesday's statement by the military 'an insult to the civilians in Gaza who needlessly died.' The army leadership, the group said, is 'apparently not interested, willing, or able to monitor itself.'"[37]

Meanwhile, Israel's siege of Gaza continued, also with US support. "Instead of downplaying the consequences of this blockade," Human Rights Watch urged in a letter to Secretary of State Hillary Clinton, "we ask that you use the influence of the United States and your office to press Israel to end this policy which purposefully punishes civilians as a way to pressure Hamas." The US government was "Israel's most important political, military and financial backer" and therefore had "an obligation to strongly criticize and dissociate itself from policies that constitute unlawful collective punishment."[38]

But the US continued to back Israel, Ethan Bronner candidly acknowledged in the *New York Times*, despite the fact that the well-recognized purpose of Israel's blockade policy was "to keep Gaza at subsistence" in order to teach Palestinians to "realize their mistake" of having voted for Hamas.[39]

On May 5, the UN released the summary of a report of a Board of Inquiry into attacks on UN personnel and facilities in Gaza. It found that Israel had not made sufficient efforts to avoid civilian casualties, with examples including the IDF's "direct and intentional strike" on the UNRWA-run Asma Elementary School in Gaza City on January 5 and its attack on the UNRWA school in Jabaliya on January 6. In the latter case, the UN rejected the IDF's initial claim that Hamas had fired from within the school compound—an allegation that remained on the Israeli Ministry of Foreign Affairs' website at the time the report was drafted. The UN was unable to determine whether Hamas had fired mortars from the vicinity outside of the school, but even if this was the case, the IDF's choice of 120 mm high explosive mortar rounds meant it could not maintain "an adequate safety distance between whatever its target point may have been and the school", meaning that the attack had been indiscriminate.

Further examples were an IDF attack that damaged an UNRWA health center on January 6, attacks on the aid convoy on January 8, and the attack on the UNRWA compound on January 15. The UN found "no evidence" that any fire had originated from within the compound and stressed that the UN staff "stated that they heard no gunfire from within the compound or from the immediate area". Furthermore, Israel's decision to use white phosphorus in its attack on the compound "was grossly negligent, amounting to recklessness." The report drew similar conclusions with regard to Israel's attack using white phosphorus on the UNRWA Beit Lahiya Elementary School on January 17.[40]

"Israel rejected the inquiry's findings," noted *The Guardian*, "even before the summary was released, as 'tendentious' and 'patently biased'."[41] Israeli spokeswoman Mirit Cohen fell back on the hopeless assertion that its self-investigation "proved beyond doubt that the IDF did not intentionally fire at the UN installations".[42]

The US had already been hard at work behind the scenes to protect Israel from being held accountable for its attacks on UN facilities—a task in which it found a willing accomplice in its Quartet partner the UN Secretary-General. Ambassador Susan Rice had spoken with Ban Ki-moon three times on May 4 to express the US's concerns over the Board of Inquiry's report. Washington was particularly worried about its recommendations to investigate other incidents involving UN premises and personnel that were not included in the Board's terms of reference, as well as incidents unrelated to the UN that involved civilians. According to a leaked State Department cable, Rice "underscored the importance of having a strong cover letter that made clear that no further action was needed and would close out this issue." Ban Ki-moon told Rice that he "was constrained in what he could do since the Board of Inquiry was independent", and he could not alter their report and recommendations. He assured Rice that his staff was, however, "working with an Israeli delegation on the text of the cover letter." Rice thanked him "for his exceptional efforts on such a sensitive issue."[43]

After the Secretary-General transmitted the report, cover letter, and summary to the Security Council the following day, Rice followed up with another cable to Washington. She noted that his cover letter "underscored that Boards of Inquiry do not consider questions of legality nor make legal findings" and that he would "seek no further inquiry into matters the Board addressed" that were outside of its terms of reference—specifically, its recommendation for further investigations. While the US couldn't prevent the Security Council from discussing the matter, Rice informed Washington, it could block a press statement or a resolution. The concern was that this might isolate Washington. "If the US were the sole delegation to block a statement," Rice noted, "that information would quickly be known publicly." There was also a concern about the General

Assembly taking up the matter. "We cannot block such a session", she worried, "nor a product (which we expect is likely) from such a session."[44]

When the Security Council did discuss it on May 13, Ambassador Alejandro Wolff "made clear the United States would not support any product from the Council on this matter."[45]

Under Ban Ki-moon's leadership, the UN ultimately received $10.5 million in compensation from Israel for damages, which "concluded" the matter as far as he was concerned. Amnesty International criticized the Secretary-General for securing compensation for the UN "without securing compensation for any of the actual victims of the attacks"—despite the Board of Inquiry's specific recommendation that the UN seek compensation for civilian victims of attacks not involving UN facilities or personnel. "Surely, the acceptance of this sum for damage to UN buildings can only be the first step in repairing the damage caused by the conflict," Amnesty said in a letter to the Secretary-General. "The UN cannot ignore the lack of reparations to the hundreds of women, men and children who were killed, injured or the thousands who lost property during the Gaza conflict in attacks that violated international humanitarian law."[46]

Following the release of the summary of the UN Board of Inquiry's report, Human Rights Watch issued a report documenting the killing of twenty-nine civilians, including eight children, by Israeli aerial drones during Operation Cast Lead. Despite being "one of the most precise weapons in Israel's arsenal", drones "killed civilians who were not taking part in hostilities and were far from any fighting". Such attacks were "in violation of the laws of war".[47]

Indeed, as the UN and human rights organizations continued their investigations into Operation Cast Lead, evidence that the IDF's conduct was consistent with it being "the most moral army in the world" would prove very hard to come by. But having benefactors in positions of power, Israel could rest assured that it would not be held accountable for its war crimes.

US Policy on Israel's Settlements

The actual facts notwithstanding, the media reinforced the perception that the Obama administration was taking a "tougher" stance toward Israel, which fed fears among Israelis that it would pressure the Netanyahu government to freeze settlement construction.[48] None of the US's enormous amount of leverage, however, was applied for this purpose. On the contrary, the Obama administration, like its predecessor, tacitly communicated its green light for Israel to continue with its illegal policies. In April 2009, for example, the Obama administration again assured that a $30 billion military assistance program begun under the Bush administration would continue.[49]

Cited as evidence of the administration's "tougher" stance, Vice President Joe Biden opined that "Israel has to work toward a two-state solution".[50] Obama's special envoy, George Mitchell, told Israel's new Foreign Minister, Avigdor Lieberman, that the US "favors" a two-state solution. Lieberman dismissed even this modest rhetorical support for Palestinian statehood by saying that "new ideas" must be found.[51] Netanyahu reiterated his demand that the Palestinians must "first recognize Israel as a Jewish state before talking about two states for two peoples."[52] He said that Israel was "prepared to resume peace negotiations without any delay and without any preconditions"—meaning without a settlement freeze.[53]

In contrast to the Israeli government's position, a poll showed that 78 percent of Israelis, along with 74 percent of Palestinians, supported a two-state solution.[54] Khaled Meshal, too, reiterated to the *New York Times* that Hamas "has accepted a Palestinian state on the 1967 borders including East Jerusalem, dismantling settlements, and the right of return based on a long term truce."[55]

In early May, in advance of a meeting with Prime Minister Netanyahu, President Obama met with Israeli President Shimon Peres. The *Washington Post* reported that "Peres and Obama agree that the creation of a Palestinian state alongside Israel—roughly along the lines of the pre-June 1967 borders—is the best way to preserve Israel's security and character as a Jewish and democratic state." However, the *Post* explained, Peres was "representing an Israeli government that does not share his views".[56]

On the day of Obama's meeting with Netanyahu, the private intelligence company Strategic Forecasting, Inc., or Stratfor, published an article typifying the institutional myopia of American political analysts. Every single one of the obstacles to the two-state solution came from the Palestinian side, according to its author, company CEO George Friedman. The main obstacle was "Arab hostility to such an outcome." Preposterously suggesting that Netanyahu was committed to "the two-state formula", Friedman dealt with the fact that the Arab states and Palestinian leadership had long joined the international consensus by dismissing it on the grounds that nations "frequently claim to favor various things they actually are either indifferent to or have no intention of doing anything about"—an accurate observation, but one Friedman neglected to apply to the two most obvious and relevant examples: the US and Israel.[57]

The day before Obama's meeting with Netanyahu, the *New York Times* headline read, "World Watches for US Shift on Mideast".[58] The world would be disappointed. Following the meeting on May 18, Obama publicly reaffirmed the US-Israeli "special relationship". He said that settlements must stop, but in the context of the Road Map and the need to create circumstances conducive to negotiations, rather than in the context of international law and human rights. He said "the humanitarian situation in Gaza has to be addressed", but, again, only in terms of *Israel's* interests. If Gazans had no hope, he reasoned, "then that is not going to be a recipe for Israel's long-term security or a constructive track to move forward."

When it came Netanyahu's turn to speak to the press, he reiterated his pre-condition that the Palestinians must "recognize Israel as a Jewish state" for the "peace process" to move forward.

Indicating his acceptance of this demand, Obama responded that it was "in US national security interests to assure that Israel's security as an independent Jewish state is maintained."[59]

There was not the slightest indication of any "shift" in US policy—at least, not in the direction the world had been watching for.

Less than a week later, Netanyahu told his cabinet that, while there were no plans to build any new settlements, Israel would continue construction and expansion of its existing colonies in the West Bank, which it dubbed "natural growth".[60] "I want to say in a crystal clear manner that the current Israeli government will not accept in any fashion that legal settlement activity in Judea and Samaria be frozen," declared Transport Minister Yisrael Katz—referring to government-approved settlements as being "legal" under Israeli law, irrespective of the fact that they violated the Fourth Geneva Convention.[61] When Israel referred to "illegal outposts", this meant settlement camps that had not been authorized by the Israeli government. Israel was obligated to dismantle such camps under the Road Map, in addition to freezing "legal" settlements. When Israeli security forces evacuated the Maoz Esther "outpost" in the West Bank in late May, Ehud Barak plausibly assured settlers that there was "no connection" between its decision to remove such settlements and "American pressure".[62]

At the end of May, Secretary Clinton said that the administration "wants to see a stop to settlements—not some settlements, not outposts, not 'natural growth' exceptions. . . . That is our position. That is what we have communicated very clearly."[63] Just as clearly, the administration's words were belied by its actions, which sent Israeli policymakers the very different message that there would be no consequences if it continued to ignore the Obama administration's empty rhetoric.

Having already met with Netanyahu, Obama also had a much-less-talked-about meeting with Mahmoud Abbas later that month.[64] According to the chief Palestinian negotiator, Saeb Erekat, who accompanied Abbas to Washington, Abbas asked Obama if he was serious about achieving the two-state solution. If so, it was incomprehensible that the US would allow Israel to continue settlement construction in the West Bank. The alternatives were a one-state solution or extremism and violence. Obama had the choice of applying international law or exercising double standards, Abbas said, which would undermine "moderates" like himself and encourage extremism. Only the US was capable of making Israel stop its colonization as necessary for permanent status negotiations to resume.

Obama answered Abbas by promising that he was personally committed to the establishment of a Palestinian state. But instead of acknowledging Israel's obligations under international law, he kept it about Israel's interests and the importance of talks between Fatah and Hamas on a unity government, with the usual preconditions that Hamas renounce violence, recognize Israel's "right to exist", and uphold the very same prior agreements that Israel insisted on perpetually violating.[65]

His actual policies notwithstanding, Obama himself came under criticism from senior Israeli officials and American political commentators for failing to uphold a prior agreement: Bush's letter to Sharon expressing the US's policy of supporting Israel's annexation of major settlement blocs under any negotiated peace deal.[66] Elliot Abrams in a *Wall Street Journal* op-ed criticized the Obama administration for denying that such an agreement with Israel existed.[67] In the *Washington Post*, Abrams asserted that Bush's letter had "largely resolved the issue". He further argued that Israel's colonization was not creating "insurmountable barriers to peace" because it was willing to make a "territorial compromise". Instead, it was the Palestinians who were the obstacle, having rejected the "generous offer" Ehud Barak made at Camp David of "approximately 94 percent of the West Bank, with a land swap to make up half of the 6 percent Israel would keep". More recently, the recalcitrant Palestinians rejected Ehud Olmert's offer of "93 percent, with a one-to-one land swap".[68]

As with Israel's demands at Camp David, Abrams was grossly mischaracterizing what Olmert had actually offered the previous year. Olmert initially proposed in August that Israel would annex 6 percent of the West Bank with a 5.5 percent land swap in which Israel would keep the good land it wanted and in exchange give the Palestinians desert territory next to the Gaza Strip.[69] By December, Olmert's proposal was slightly revised to include Israeli annexation of 6.3 percent of the West Bank corresponding largely with the route of the separation wall and a 5.8 percent swap for land in the Judean Desert.[70] Moreover, illustrating the lack of seriousness with which Olmert's proposal was made, a key aspect was its inclusion of the precondition that the PA must oust Hamas and regain control of Gaza. "There is going to be no agreement, period," an Israeli official explained to *Haaretz*. Olmert was merely concerned with establishing his legacy. Abbas's spokesman appropriately called Olmert's proposal a "waste of time" and reiterated the PA's adherence to the international consensus on a two-state solution: complete Israeli withdrawal and a Palestinian state along the pre-June 1967 boundaries, with East Jerusalem as its capital.[71]

Washington Post columnist Charles Krauthammer similarly criticized the Obama administration for refusing to endorse the Bush letter, even though Obama "piously insists that all parties to the conflict honor previous obligations." Like Abrams, he rejected the idea that Israel's illegal colonization was an obstacle to peace. He did so on the same fictional grounds that the Palestinians had "rejected every offer of independence and dignity" from Israel because they would rather choose "destitution and despair" than accept less than "the extinction of Israel."[72]

Dan Kurtzer—the former ambassador who had explicitly reiterated the Bush administration's policy of support for Israel's annexation of major settlement blocs—responded to Krauthammer with his own *Post* op-ed. He defended the Obama administration by saying it was "pursuing policies that every administration since 1967 has articulated", which included the position that "settlement activity should stop". As for an agreement on Israel's annexation of existing settlements, "there was no such understanding" because Bush's letter had expressed support for annexation only in terms of "mutually agreed changes". Kurtzer left out what this actually *meant* in the context of the letter: that the Palestinians would have to come to their senses and accept the "realities" on the ground by agreeing under US coercion to Israeli annexation of large portions of their territory.[73]

The Cairo and Bar-Ilan Speeches

On June 4, 2009, President Obama gave a much-anticipated speech in Egypt at Cairo University. He said he was there "to seek a new beginning between the United States and Muslims around the world" while reaffirming "America's strong bonds" and "unbreakable" relationship with Israel. He vowed that the US would not turn its back on the Palestinians' aspirations "for dignity, opportunity, and a state of their own". Then he rendered this promise meaningless by laying down the usual three euphemistic demands of the Palestinians: renounce the right to armed resistance against foreign military occupation ("abandon violence"), commit to a framework for negotiations that excluded the applicability of international law ("recognize past agreements"), and accede that the unilateral declaration of Israel's existence and ethnic cleansing of Palestine had been legitimate ("recognize Israel's right to exist"). He went so far as to lecture the Palestinians that armed resistance was "wrong"—a moral judgment he applied selectively, needless to say.[74] (He was later awarded the Nobel Peace Prize and used his acceptance speech to defend the US's own frequent resort to violence, saying that "force may sometimes be necessary" and the "non-violence practiced by men like Gandhi and King may not have been practical or possible in every circumstance".[75])

Obama told his Cairo audience that Palestine's "right to exist cannot be denied", despite his own government refusing to recognize Palestine as an independent state. His administration would subsequently attempt to block further international recognition of Palestinian statehood.

It bears emphasizing that the concept of the "right to exist" of a state is meaningless. No state has a "right to exist". Individuals have rights; governments and politically-defined territories with boundaries drawn on the map do not. The proper framework for discussion is not a state's "right to exist", but people's right to self-determination—a right denied to the Palestinians by Israel, not vice versa. The need for Israel to reframe the issue in terms of a "right to exist" thus becomes obvious. Unfortunately, it has done so with incredible success, such that the meaningless framework of its "right to exist" has been universally adopted, with extreme prejudice toward the rights of the Palestinians.

Obama said that the US "does not accept the legitimacy of continued Israeli settlements" and that it was "time for these settlements to stop". But, as ever, this criticism of Israel came only in the context of violating "previous agreements", with no reference to international law or Palestinians' rights. His administration would later veto an uncontroversial UN Security Council resolution censuring Israel for this illegal activity.

Obama criticized Israel's siege of Gaza in the same vein. Rather than condemning the blockade as an illegal act of collective punishment and calling directly upon Israel to end it, he advised that the "continuing humanitarian crisis in Gaza does not serve Israel's security". Of trivial consideration were international law and the rights of the Palestinians, which were only relevant inasmuch as gratuitous abuses drew unwanted international criticism.[76]

On June 14, at Bar-Ilan University in Tel Aviv, Netanyahu gave his own speech in which he invited Arab leaders to meet with him to "make peace". Then he outlined what would be required for the "peace" he desired to occur. He reiterated his demand that the Palestinian leadership must "begin peace negotiations without prior conditions"—meaning while Israel continued to take illegal actions prejudicial to the outcome of said negotiations. Israel, he declared, was "committed to international agreements, and expects all sides to fulfill their obligations". The "root of the conflict" was not Israel's occupation, colonization, and rejection of Palestinian self-determination, but rather the refusal of the Palestinians "to recognize the right of the Jewish People to its own state". Then he declared that the illegal colonization of Palestinian land would continue; reiterated Israel's rejection of the internationally recognized right of Palestinian refugees to return to their homeland; and announced that any "area in Palestinian hands", whether or not it was called a "state", would need to be defenseless. Palestinians could not have an army, could not control their own air space, and could not enter "military treaties". If the Palestinians would agree to these preconditions to surrender their rights and sovereignty, he was "ready to agree to a real peace agreement, a demilitarized Palestinian state side by side with the Jewish state."[77]

The *Washington Post* reported Netanyahu's explicit rejection of the two-state solution under the headline, "Netanyahu Backs 2-State Goal: Endorsement Comes With Prerequisites for Palestinians".[78] The *New York Times* headline likewise announced: "Netanyahu Backs Palestinian State, With Caveats".[79] In similar Orwellian fashion, President Obama responded to Netanyahu's speech with praise, calling it an "important step forward" that showed how "committed" Netanyahu was to a two-state solution.[80] It was a "positive" step, Obama told the press, while taking the occasion to emphasize once more that "Israel's security is non-negotiable"—unlike Israel's obligation not to violate international law or Palestinians' rights, including the right to self-determination and the right of return, which were very much matters to be negotiated away in the framework of the "peace process".[81]

In stark contrast to Netanyahu's explicit rejectionism, Ismail Haniyeh again reiterated Hamas's willingness to accept a solution more along the lines of the international consensus. "If there is a real project that aims at resolving the Palestinian cause on establishing a Palestinian state on 1967 borders, under full Palestinian sovereignty," Haniyeh said, "we will support it." Haniyeh met again with Jimmy Carter, who reported that "Hamas leaders want peace and they want to have reconciliation not only with their Fatah brothers, but also eventually with Israelis, to live side by side, with two nations, both sovereign nations recognized by each other and living in peace".[82]

Obama offered no comment praising Hamas for expressing commitment to a two-state solution or lauding Haniyeh's remarks as a positive step. There were no headlines in the *New York Times* or the *Washington Post* proclaiming how Hamas backed the two-state goal.

Punishing Gaza

Concerned only with "Israel's security", the absence in Obama's Cairo speech of any consideration for what the ongoing siege of Gaza meant *for the Palestinians* was a stark testimony to the nature of the US's policy of complicity in Israel's crimes against humanity.

Shortly after Obama announced his "new beginning" with the Arab world, the ICRC issued a report noting that, six months after the end of Israel's military assault on Gaza, the siege was "making it impossible for Gazans to rebuild their lives." The amount of goods Israel was allowing into Gaza fell "well short of what is required to meet the population's needs." Israel refused to allow in the cement, steel, and other building materials required for reconstructing neighborhoods that looked "like the epicenter of a massive earthquake". The inability to restore water and sanitation services represented "a major threat to public health."

Israel was also preventing Palestinians from leaving to get health care that Gaza's hospitals could not provide, as well as hampering the supply "of even the most basic items". Hospitals were still running on backup generators several hours a day, and limited fuel supply remained a serious concern.

Unemployment was soaring at 44 percent as a consequence of Israel's restrictions, which resulted in 96 percent of industrial operations in Gaza being shut down, translating into a loss of about 70,000 jobs. The economy had collapsed, leading to "a dramatic increase in poverty", with over 70 percent of the population living in poverty conditions. Up to 40 percent of Gazan families lived on a monthly income of less than $120, with each working individual on average having to support six or seven members of their immediate family. "The likely consequences" of the diet Palestinian children were forced to live on included "stunted growth of bones and teeth, difficulty in fighting off infections, fatigue and a reduced capacity to learn."

Gaza's farmers, comprising over a quarter of the population, were also suffering. Israel had "uprooted thousands of citrus, olive and palm groves" and "destroyed irrigation systems, wells and greenhouses." Many farmers could not reach their own land because of Israel's "no-go" zone, which included at least 30 percent of the arable land in Gaza. Farmers who dared to work their land in this area risked "being shot at". Gaza's fishing industry was likewise suffering as Israel restricted fishermen to operating within three nautical miles from shore in Gaza's territorial waters.

The ICRC concluded:

> Over the last two years, the 1.5 million Palestinians living in the Gaza Strip have been caught up in an unending cycle of deprivation and despair as a result of the conflict, and particularly as a direct consequence of the closure of the crossing points. . . . Under international humanitarian law, Israel has the obligation to ensure that the population's basic needs in terms of food, shelter, water and medical supplies are met. The ICRC once again appeals for a lifting of restrictions on the movement of people and goods as the first and most urgent measure to end Gaza's isolation and to allow its people to rebuild their lives. . . . The alternative is a further descent into misery with every passing day.[83]

But none of this mattered to Barack Obama. The important question to his administration was not one of legality or morality, but simply whether or not the collective punishment of 1.5 million people served "Israel's security".

On June 30, the day after the ICRC released its report on the impact of the siege, the Israeli Navy intercepted a boat intending to deliver humanitarian supplies to Gaza. The boat, sponsored by the Free Gaza Movement and dubbed *The Spirit of Humanity* for the voyage, was boarded in international waters by Israeli forces and redirected under threat of violence to Ashdod, Israel. Its passengers, including former US Congresswoman Cynthia McKinney and Nobel Peace Prize laureate Mairead Corrigan Maguire, were imprisoned before being deported.[84] An IDF spokesman said that the boat was captured because "it was illegally attempting to enter the Gaza Strip."[85]

"In fact, *The Spirit of Humanity* was in international waters when it was illegally seized by the Israeli navy in an act of piracy", McKinney said in a radio interview conducted by phone while she was imprisoned in Israel. "The Israelis hijacked us because we wanted to give crayons to the children of Gaza," she said in a recorded statement that was posted to the video-sharing website YouTube. "This is an outrageous violation of international law against us," she relayed from jail. "We're asking the international community to demand our release so we can resume our journey."[86]

Also from jail, Mairead Maguire spoke with Amy Goodman of *Democracy Now!*. "Our little boat was boarded by the navy combat soldiers, and they came in full riot gear onto our boat when we were just twenty-five miles off the shore of Gaza." She emphasized, "the tragedy is that the American government, the UN and Europe, they remain silent in the face of the abuse of Palestinian human rights".[87]

"We would be concerned", came the response to the hijacking from the British Foreign Office, "if the stories of the Israeli Navy boarding the boat in international waters were true".[88] The "stories" *were* true; the British government expressed *no* concern. Neither, of course, did the US government, which remained completely silent. The US media did provide some coverage of the incident, but only to characterize the humanitarian activists, rather than Israel, as having been guilty of some kind of "violation". CNN reported, "The Israeli navy took control of a boat that violated an Israeli blockade and crossed into Gazan waters" after "[d]isregarding all warnings" from Israel.[89] The *New York Times* said Israel had "seized control of" or "commandeered" the boat, taking care not to use the word "hijacked" to describe what occurred. The only hint the *Times* offered that Israel's actions were a violation of international law was a passing reference to a statement from Richard Falk that "the seizure of the boat was unlawful".[90]

In commentary, the hijacking was met with sentiment ranging from indifference to outright hostility—again, toward Cynthia McKinney, not Israel. David Lewkowict wrote a blog post on the *Fox News* website titled "Cynthia Mckinney [*sic*] Does it Again". He pointed out that this was the second boat McKinney had been on that had been "seized for violating the Israeli blockade."[91] Mary Ann Akers of "The Sleuth" blog at the *Washington Post* wrote a post similarly titled, "Cynthia McKinney Strikes Again". She lamented, "Somehow we didn't think we had seen the last of Cynthia McKinney." After explaining how McKinney had "resurfaced" by getting herself "arrested" by Israeli forces, Akers launched into a mockery of her political career, saying she had been defeated in 2006 "not long after she was accused of punching a Capitol Police officer". McKinney had previously "made a brief comeback" after a 2002 defeat, "at which time her father said he blamed the 'J-E-W-S' for his daughter's defeat."[92]

The incident with the officer, according to McKinney, was instigated by him inappropriately laying his hands on her after failing to recognize her as a Congresswoman as she walked past a security checkpoint. The Capitol Police Chief, Terrance Gainer, while blaming McKinney, acknowledged that the officer had indeed grabbed her.[93] And while Akers left her readers to draw the conclusion that McKinney's father was a conspiratorial anti-Semite, in fact, McKinney had indeed been defeated by a challenger "who received substantial support from Jewish donors" as the *Washington Post* observed, including from board members of the American Israeli Public Affairs Committee (AIPAC), the influential "pro-Israel" lobby, which targeted her for speaking out against Israel's violations of international law and human rights abuses.[94]

The caricature the media sketched of McKinney was thus one of a reckless hothead from an anti-Semitic family who had been lawfully "arrested" by Israeli authorities—as opposed to a courageous woman who was kidnapped in international waters while on a humanitarian mission to draw attention to the plight of the suffering civilian population of the Gaza Strip.

Following the ICRC's condemnation of Israel's illegal blockade, Amnesty International released a 105-page report titled "Operation 'Cast Lead': 22 Days of Death and Destruction". It reminded that of the approximately 1,400 Palestinians killed, about 300 were children, in addition to hundreds of other unarmed civilians. Two-hundred unarmed male civilians were killed, as well as 240 police officers who were not participating in hostilities. Amnesty documented numerous cases of Israel's indiscriminate use of force. As for Israel's claim to have done everything possible to avoid civilian casualties, the IDF had indeed dropped leaflets, made telephone calls, and issued radio broadcasts warning people to leave their homes—only to then attack UN schools or other locations where civilians had gone to seek shelter. Israel also redefined civilians as military targets by claiming that any person or institution associated with Hamas could be legitimately attacked, which was contrary to the definitions of combatants and civilians under international law. Whether or not they were members of Hamas, individuals not directly taking part in hostilities were civilians whose killing by Israel was unlawful. Attacks on ministries, the parliament building, media outlets, and mosques likewise violated the laws of war.

Amnesty examined the case of the Israeli attack that killed dozens of civilians just outside the UNRWA school in Jabaliya on January 6, pointing out how Israel had changed its story constantly, with each different account containing inaccuracies. Israel had also claimed that two Hamas militants had fired rockets from the location, naming them as Imad and Hassan Abu Askar. But Imad was "a 13-year-old schoolboy" who was killed in the street outside the school along with other civilians, and there was no "Hassan" in the family.

In addition to indiscriminate attacks against civilians, Israel engaged in "wanton destruction" of Palestinian property, destroying and vandalizing houses "for no apparent reason". There were "large areas of Gaza" that had been "razed to the ground, leaving many thousands homeless and the already dire economy in ruins." Israeli forces had "defaced the wall with racist and threatening graffiti, deliberately smashed and soiled furniture and possessions, and often left excrement all over the houses when they left." Factories, animal pens, greenhouses, and orchards were also wantonly destroyed. In some areas, fields "were littered with dead cows, goats and sheep, some crushed by bulldozers, others seemingly killed as they ran away." In Zeytoun, the Sawafeary chicken farm "was likewise flattened and 65,000 chickens were crushed to death or buried alive. The tracks of tanks and armored bulldozers were clearly visible where the vehicles had driven over the cages and coops, crushing thousands of chickens." (Perhaps Hamas was hiding amongst the poultry, using the fowl as shields?)

Hamas had also committed war crimes with its indiscriminate rocket fire into Israel, which killed three Israeli civilians. However, Amnesty "found no evidence that Hamas or other Palestinian fighters directed the movement of civilians to shield military objectives from attacks." On the other hand, the group documented how, "In several cases Israeli soldiers also used civilians, including children, as 'human shields', endangering their lives by forcing them to remain in or near houses which they took over and used as military positions. Some were forced to carry out dangerous tasks such as inspecting properties or objects suspected of being booby-trapped. Soldiers also took position and launched attacks from and around inhabited houses, exposing local residents to the danger of attacks or of being caught in the crossfire." Finally, Amnesty urged Israel to cooperate with the UN fact-finding mission headed by Richard Goldstone.[95]

Israel and Hamas both rejected the Amnesty report for being unbalanced. Israel dismissed it on the grounds that it ignored the efforts of the IDF to try to minimize harm to innocent civilians—notwithstanding the fact that Amnesty had specifically criticized the means by which the IDF ostensibly had done so.[96]

Highlighting the US's complicity in Israel's war crimes, the day after Amnesty's report was published, the *Jerusalem Post* informed that Israel was negotiating with the US on the possible sale of Lockheed Martin F-35 Joint Strike Fighter jets (also known as the Lightning II) to Israel. Additionally, Israel hoped the US would agree to allow Israel to resell its US-provided F-22 fighter jets to other countries. Negotiations were also underway for the purchase of additional Apache Longbow attack helicopters.[97]

The UK was also a supplier of military equipment to Israel. Later that month, it revoked five export licenses for equipment used in Israeli Saar naval gunships. The reason given was that during Operation Cast Lead, Israel violated the UK's export criteria that such equipment not be used for "internal repression". Other British-made components used by Israel during Operation Cast Lead were first exported to the US and then resold to Israel. "The vast majority of arms imports to Israel come from the US", noted Richard Burden, chairman of the Britain Palestine All-Party Commons Group, "and unless any new policy addresses that issue it will simply not be effective."[98]

On the heels of the ICRC and Amnesty reports, an organization of Israeli veterans called Breaking the Silence released additional testimonies from soldiers who had participated in Operation Cast Lead. The testimonies showed "that the massive and unprecedented blow to the infrastructure and civilians of the Gaza Strip were a direct result of IDF policy". Soldiers described the IDF's wanton destruction, indiscriminate use of force, and use of Palestinians as human shields.

The testimonies described how homes were destroyed on the grounds that there might be explosive charges planted inside. Orchards were razed on the grounds that they could be used as cover by snipers. One soldier explained that "whole neighborhoods were simply razed because four houses in the area served to launch Qassam rockets. . . . It's disproportionate."

Another soldier disclosed that they "actually received orders" that they were to take high ground and "raze as much as possible of the area". This meant demolishing homes that were "not implicated in any way" as being used for military purposes; their "single sin" was the fact that they were "situated on top of a hill in the Gaza Strip." When asked whether there was any fighting occurring in his area, the soldier replied, "No, usually we did not see a living soul."

One soldier related how "most of the mosques" in his area "were demolished". He said a brigade commander "explicitly told us we should not hesitate to target mosques. Nothing is immune, nothing and no area."

Another solider related a commander's remarks to his battalion: "'[W]e're a democracy, so we can't demolish Gaza to the extent that we'd really like. . . . Fortunately the hospitals are full to capacity already, so people are dying more quickly.' Then someone answered him, one of the soldiers replied cynically: 'So kill the doctors.' The commander replied dismissingly, not understanding his cynical intent, twice: 'We're a democracy, we can't do things the way we would like to do them.'"

When asked what bothered him most, one soldier replied, "Many things. Firstly, all that destruction. All that fire at innocents. This shock of realizing with whom I'm in this together. My mates, really, and that's how they're behaving. It was simply amazing. Inconceivable."

Asked what the attitude of the troops was when they occupied people's homes, one soldier answered, "The guys would simply break stuff. Some were out to destroy and trash the whole time. They drew a disgusting drawing on the wall. They threw out sofas. They took down a picture from the wall just to shatter it. They really couldn't see why they shouldn't." When troops entered homes, "the assumption is that everyone is a terrorist, and then it's legitimate to do just anything we please."

Other testimonies related how the army rabbinate distributed pamphlets with the stamp of the IDF on them: "Like writing, for example, that the Palestinians are like the Philistines of old, newcomers who do not belong in the land, aliens planted on our soil which should clearly return to us." A rabbi told one group of soldiers that they were "conducting the war of 'the sons of light' against 'the sons of darkness.'"

A battalion commander told his troops not to worry, that "everyone will have taken plenty of people down" and there would be "plenty of terrorists for everyone."

Another soldier related a speech from his battalion commander: "He defined the operation goals: 2,000 dead terrorists, not just stopping the missiles launched at (Israeli) communities around the Gaza Strip. . . . As for rules of engagement, the army's working assumption was that the whole area would be devoid of civilians. . . . Anyone there, as far as the army was concerned, was to be killed."

"We were to shoot to kill anyone within our lines, no second thoughts", said one soldier. Troops were told it was "better [to] hit an innocent than hesitate to target an enemy." They were told "that if we suspect someone, we should not give him the benefit of the doubt. Eventually this could be an enemy, even if it's some old woman approaching the house. It could be an old woman carrying an explosive charge."

"The goal was to carry out an operation with the least possible casualties for the army," said one soldier, "without its even asking itself what the price would be for the other side. This was the thrust of things that we heard from more than one officer."

A battalion commander told his troops, "You see something and you're not quite sure? You shoot." The rules of engagement were summarized: "In urban warfare, anyone is your enemy. No innocents."

The understanding one soldier took away from a briefing was "that it's better to shoot first and ask questions later."

"The soldiers were made to understand that their lives were the most important," testified another, "and that there was no way our soldiers would get killed for the sake of leaving civilians the benefit of the doubt. We were allowed to fire in order to spare our lives."

One testified how his commander burst into a home and opened fire indiscriminately, killing "an elderly guy" who was hiding there with babies and other family.

The rule of engagement was to "Shoot as we enter a room."

If a warning was given for residents of a home to leave, and nobody came out, "whoever is left inside is a dead man." Soldiers were ordered to enter homes with live fire.

Soldiers described an overall picture of encountering little to no resistance to their operations. There was occasional mortar or sniper fire, but they saw few combatants. One soldier said: "Nearly no one ran into the enemy. I know of two encounters during the whole operation. The soldiers, too, were disappointed for not having any encounters with terrorists. The defined situation was that sparing our forces was of primary importance. This means that if we detect anyone, we disconnect, summon a helicopter and take down the house."

One soldier testified, "One guy said he just couldn't finish this operation without killing someone. So he killed someone, apparently some sort of lookout. There was an order that if you see someone on the lookout at our building, he should be taken down." They were told "that if anyone is out on a street where the IDF is currently present, and he's holding a cell phone—he must be a lookout." He continued: "I don't remember exactly whether it was a cell phone. Could be. I can definitely say he was not armed. I can definitely say the soldier regarded this as some children's game and was delighted and laughing after this. I think that a normal person, even having killed an armed terrorist, would not be amused."

Other testimony corroborated accounts of Israeli soldiers using Palestinian civilians as human shields. One soldier said that it was "ludicrous" that the IDF had said "that the matter was investigated and there are no testimonies on the ground and that the Israeli army is a moral army."

One soldier described using Palestinians as "Johnnies"—the code word for "using Palestinian civilians as human shields during house searches".[99]

When the testimonies from the Breaking the Silence report hit the news, IDF spokeswoman Lt. Col. Avital Leibovich dismissed them as "hearsay and word of mouth."[100] Defense Minister Ehud Barak maintained that "The IDF is one of the most moral armies in the world and behaves in accordance with the highest ethical code."[101]

US Aid to Israel

Neither the emerging facts about Israel's war crimes during Operation Cast Lead nor its ongoing illegal colonization deterred the Obama administration from continuing US support for its criminal policies. On July 15, Secretary of State Hillary Clinton gave a speech at the Council on Foreign Relations in which she characterized the situation as one wherein the US and Israel alone were taking positive steps toward peace, while the Palestinians were failing to live up to their responsibilities; the Obama administration was "working with the Israelis to deal with the issue of settlements", but "progress toward peace cannot be the responsibility of the United States or Israel alone."[102] A week later, US State Department spokesman P. J. Crowley reassured the Netanyahu government that US support for its policies would continue. "There's been some reporting that the United States is contemplating financial or economic pressure against Israel," he noted. "We are not contemplating such action."[103]

UN Secretary-General Ban Ki-moon at the same time called on Israel to cease all settlement activity, which was "contrary to international law" and "a strong international consensus".[104] The Israeli government, however, with backing from the US, knew it could continue to violate international law in defiance of the international community. After consulting with the State Department on the plan to continue Israeli settlement construction in East Jerusalem, Israeli Ambassador to the US Michael B. Oren assured his fellow citizens that "there is no crisis" in US-Israeli relations. "We are talking about an extremely deep alliance," he consoled.[105] Israeli Finance Minister Yuval Steinitz assured that there were no "limitations on the horizon" with regard to US financial and military support. "It's not time to be concerned about that".[106]

The US government's support for Israel continued despite being contrary to the spirit, if not the letter, of its own laws. Under US law, arms provided to foreign nations may only be used for "internal security", for "legitimate self-defense", or for purposes pursuant to the UN Charter. The law states that "a principal goal of the foreign policy of the United States shall be to promote the increased observance of internationally recognized human rights by all countries". Consequently, "no security assistance"—including "military assistance"—"may be provided to any country the government of which engages in a consistent pattern of gross violations of internationally recognized human rights." There is a very large loophole, however, stating that such assistance *may* be provided to such a country if "the President certifies in writing to the Speaker of the House of Representatives and the chairman of the Committee on Foreign Relations of the Senate that extraordinary circumstances exist warranting provision of such assistance."[107]

As a Congressional Research Service report has noted, Israel has received more US aid since World War II than any other country. From 1976 until 2004, Israel received more aid annually than any other nation, and thereafter came second only to Iraq, where the US in 2003 initiated a war of aggression to overthrow the regime of Saddam Hussein on a pretext of lies.[108] Since 1985, the US has provided about $3 billion in grants to Israel annually. Most US financial support for Israel is in the form of military aid, which is "designed to maintain Israel's 'qualitative military edge' (QME) over neighboring militaries" and has "helped transform Israel's armed forces into one of the most technologically sophisticated militaries in the world." On top of the annual $3 billion in grants, the US provides loan guarantees to Israel, which enables Israel to borrow at lower interest rates, and which also means that if the Israeli government was to ever default on its loans, the American taxpayers would be on the hook to bail it out.

In 2003, Congress authorized $9 billion in loan guarantees to Israel under a law stipulating that this amount could be reduced according to the amount Israel spent on settlements. As already discussed, the Bush administration deducted $289.5 million in 2003 and an additional $795.8 million in 2005, for a total of just over a $1 billion deduction. Just how meaningless this "penalty" was has also already been briefly discussed, but becomes even clearer in light of the fact that *Israel had only requested $8 billion in the first place.* Thus, even after the "penalty" deduction of $1 billion from the $9 billion authorized, the US was still fully meeting Israel's request and providing more than enough funding for Israel's projected budgetary requirements to sustain its occupation and illegal settlement regime.

Furthermore, in August 2007, the Bush administration announced that it would increase military aid to Israel by $6 billion over the following decade, with incremental annual increases until 2011, when total military aid alone reached $3 billion (economic grants have been gradually reduced while military grants have increased; by 2008, the economic grants were completely phased out out).

Nicholas Burns, the Under Secretary of State for Political Affairs, who signed the Memorandum of Understanding between the US and Israel on the military assistance, described it as "an investment in peace".

Most of the grant money to Israel is used to purchase US military hardware—effectively a US taxpayer subsidy to the military industrial complex.

In addition to military grants and loan guarantees, the US provides Israel with tens of millions in additional financial aid, including the Migration and Refugee Assistance fund and the American Schools and Hospitals Abroad Program. From 2000 to 2010, total US aid to Israel amounted to $31,748,550,000, or an average of about $3.17 billion annually. Although under US law, aid to Israel technically cannot be used for projects beyond the pre-June 1967 lines, US grants and loan guarantees "free up domestic Israeli funds for other uses."

In other words, meaningless declarations to the contrary aside, the US has long supported Israel's illegal activities—financially, militarily, and diplomatically.[109]

The Obama administration, for its part, re-approved loan guarantees worth $3.8 billion, with no deductions for the costs of Israel's illegal construction activities.[110] Additionally, the administration moved to increase military cooperation. For instance, Israel had requested GBU-28 Hard Target Penetrators, or bunker-buster bombs, in 2005, but the arms deal was frozen out of concern that Israel was sharing US military technology with China. Obama lifted the hold and delivered the bombs shortly after taking office. In a meeting with Jewish community leaders, Obama assured, "Look, we have some very smart people on this. Don't think that we don't understand the nuances of the settlements issues. We do." He offered the additional reassurance that his chief of staff, Rahm

Emanuel, whose father had been a member of the Zionist terrorist organization Irgun, "understands the politics there, and he explains them to me."[111]

Rhetoric aside, Obama's "new beginning" bore no slight resemblance to the old status quo. What he delivered instead was perfect continuity of the US's longstanding rejectionist policy, which included pressuring the Palestinians to return to the "peace process" by which the US and Israel blocked implementation of the two-state solution, financially supporting Israel's illegal colonization and human rights abuses under the occupation regime, militarily supporting Israel's aggression and war crimes, and diplomatically protecting Israel from international censure and efforts to hold it accountable for its perpetual violations of international law.

An extraordinary example this latter aspect of the US-Israeli "special relationship" was manifest in the administration's response to the report of the UN Fact-Finding Mission on the Gaza Conflict, more popularly known as the Goldstone Report, to which we now turn our attention.

CHAPTER 5

THE GOLDSTONE REPORT

IN JULY 2009, ISRAEL ISSUED a paper stating additional findings from its ongoing self-investigations and claiming that Operation Cast Lead was "both a necessary and a proportionate response to Hamas' attacks". Despite acknowledging the "unfortunate effects" the operation had "on Gaza's civilian population", it insisted that the IDF did not violate international law. The justification offered was that Hamas used "the civilian population in Gaza to shield its military operations"; it was Hamas, therefore, that was responsible for all civilian casualties. The numerous international human rights organizations and UN agencies that had reached contrary conclusions had done so "without waiting for the evidence". They were guilty of a "rush to judgment" and "propaganda and prejudice".

The paper repeated the familiar claims that "Hamas stored explosives and weapons in and around schools, mosques, UN facilities and homes", "used medical facilities and ambulances for military purposes", "repeatedly fired mortars and other weapons from locations adjacent to UN schools and medical facilities, and from the roofs of residential apartment buildings", "used individual civilians as human shields", and "turned civilian neighborhoods into battlefields, by digging warrens of tunnels lined with explosives and booby-trapping residential buildings in order to cause their collapse at the outset of any IDF incursion." By such means, the paper argued, Hamas sought to increase "the likelihood of harm to the citizens and homes of Gaza" in order "to score propaganda coups and vilify Israel" when "unintended civilian casualties resulted."

Israel also again invoked "the NATO bombings of the former Yugoslavia and operations in Afghanistan and Iraq by the United States" as further justification for its own actions resulting in "civilian casualties and damage to public and private property."[1]

On the question of the legal justification for its resort to armed force (*jus ad bellum*), the paper asserted that Hamas had used the ceasefire period "to rearm and prepare for the next round of hostilities". To prove that the "arms buildup by Hamas is indisputable", the paper offered images of Hamas militants with various weaponry all dated well prior to the ceasefire, mostly from 2007, including one of a masked militant with a light machine gun described in the caption as an "anti-aircraft" weapon. In its attempts to pin all responsibility on Hamas for the conflict, the paper lied that Hamas had "unilaterally terminated" the ceasefire on December 19.[2]

The paper naturally omitted the relevant facts: that Israel had continuously violated the ceasefire agreement, that Hamas had fired no rockets until Israel's November 4 violation, that the ceasefire had been extremely effective in limiting the number of rocket attacks against Israel by other militant groups, that Hamas offered to renew the ceasefire and halted rocket attacks in order to give Israel time to consider that offer, and that it was Israel who rejected that offer in favor of a resort to armed force with a surprise attack on the Sabbath. Since any consideration of these facts would lead incontrovertibly to the conclusion that Israel had plenty of alternatives to violence and therefore that its resort to force was unlawful, the reason for Israel's willful omission of them is understandable.

On the question of its conduct during hostilities (*jus in bello*), as evidence for its claim that Hamas had used "human shields", the paper offered alleged statements from a couple of captured and interrogated Palestinians containing admissions that Hamas operatives "frequently carried out rocket fire from schools . . . precisely because they *knew* that Israeli jets would not fire on the schools"—an obviously erroneous assumption, if any Hamas members were actually so naive as to believe so.[3]

Even if one considered Israeli interrogation reports to constitute credible evidence, such admissions would not constitute justification for the IDF's numerous attacks on schools. For starters, turning to the interrogation report cited in the paper, the two detainees' statements supposedly acknowledging that Hamas fired from schools were from interrogations conducted on January 11 and thus could not possibly have constituted actionable intelligence underlying the many attacks on schools *prior* to that date, including numerous UN-run schools and the American International School.[4] Furthermore, if the interrogations revealed true confessions of attacks originating from schools prior to the detainees' capture, it would not justify specific incidences of attacks on schools *following* their interrogation; for example, an admission that rockets were fired from a specific school on January 10 would not constitute justification for bombing it on January 12, when there no longer remained any military advantage at all, much less one outweighing the potential harm to civilians or damage to civilian property. And, needless to say, it wouldn't justify bombing some *other* school.

The credibility of this section of the paper also wasn't helped by the documented record of Israel's abuses against detainees, including the use of torture during interrogations.[5]

The report of prisoners' interrogations was not the only source the paper cited as evidence. It also cited a statement from a Hamas official made on February 29, 2009—more than a month *after* Operation Cast Lead had ended (a claim to *ex post facto* justification, apparently)—and a report of the UN Secretary-General from March that "confirmed receiving reports of Hamas using children and others as shields".[6]

That UN report did indeed point out that there were "*concerns* that Hamas *reportedly* used children as shields and *may have* used schools and hospitals or areas in their proximity to launch rockets" (emphasis added). However, it pointed out that there was a lack of corroborating evidence that such reports—originating, of course, from the Israeli government—were *true*. Rather, the UN concluded that Israel's claims "must be further investigated." Continuing to the very next paragraph in that same UN document, one could read:

> On 15 January, in Tal al-Hawa, south-west of Gaza City, an 11-year-old boy was made to accompany IDF for a number of hours during a period of intense operations. As the soldiers entered the Palestinian Red Crescent Society building, the boy was made to enter first, in front of the soldiers. While moving through the town the boy was made to walk in front of the group, even when the IDF soldiers met with resistance and were fired upon. On arrival at Al-Quds Hospital, the boy remained in front of the soldiers, but then was subsequently released. This appears to be in direct contravention of a 2005 Israeli High Court ruling on the illegality of the use of human shields.[7]

Thus, Israel's own source not only *didn't* support its claim that Hamas had used civilians as human shields, but in fact documented how *the IDF* had done so. The fact that Israel had to cherry-pick so deceptively from the documentary record in this manner in order to produce its best "evidence" that Hamas had used human shields is exceedingly instructive.

It's worth also noting that the UN report was referring to a 2005 decision by the Israeli Supreme Court in which it ruled that the IDF's routine practice of using of Palestinians as human shields was illegal. At the time, as reported by *Ynetnews* (the online English-language sister publication of the Israeli daily *Yedioth Ahronoth*), defense officials protested this ruling on the grounds that the IDF "made use of the 'human shield' procedure on 1,200 occasions over the last five years, and only on one occasion did a Palestinian civilian get hurt." The reference was to an 18-year-old Palestinian who was killed while being used as a human shield by Israeli soldiers in 2002.[8]

Several questions concerning legality naturally arise: Upon what information did IDF commanders base their decisions to launch admittedly deliberate attacks on schools? What evidence or intelligence information were they in possession of *at the time of those decisions* that Hamas was using those specific schools as bases from which to launch attacks? How was the determination made that the military advantage sought outweighed the potential risk to civilians? Israel's paper answered none of these questions and offered not even the slightest actual evidence to support its declarations that the numerous intentional attacks on schools were in accordance with the requirements of international law.

While failing to offer any evidence to support its claim that civilians killed in IDF attacks were at the time being used as human shields, the paper did offer some evidence that Hamas had placed civilians at risk by firing from within populated areas. In one example, it cited a report from *Newsweek* documenting a case where Hamas militants launched a rocket from between four apartment buildings full of refugees on January 17.[9] But the same *Newsweek* article also said there were "plenty of examples" to support claims that "Israel was using indiscriminate force with complete disregard for civilians", such as when "an entire neighborhood" in Jabaliya was bombed and then "methodically demolished house-by-house" by Israeli forces. "In several hours of interviews," the article stated, "every one of the residents interviewed in eastern Jabaliya insisted that there had been no provocation from the area, no resistance fighters, and no rocket launchings."[10]

Thus, we again see that one of Israel's own sources contradicted the purpose for which it was being cited: to exculpate the IDF of responsibility for committing war crimes by engaging in indiscriminate use of force.

Israel also presented photographs claiming to show weapons discovered "in a mosque in Jabaliya", but no further information was offered, such as which mosque the photos were allegedly taken at, its precise location, or even the date the photos were taken. It cited another prisoner who allegedly confessed during interrogation that Hamas stored weapons in mosques, as well as video footage allegedly showing secondary explosions from weapons stored in a mosque after it was bombed by the IDF.[11] If one examines the video released by the IDF, however, it is apparent that the second explosion was the result of *a second Israeli bomb* dropped on the mosque.[12]

Although one would never know it from listening to US government officials, Israel's continued efforts to justify its massacre in Gaza were not taken seriously outside of Washington, DC. International organizations such as the UN and human rights groups continued to document the Israeli government's illegal policies and war crimes. In August, OCHA published a report noting the UN estimate of 1,383 Palestinians killed during Operation Cast Lead, including 333 children. Thousands of homes had been destroyed or severely damaged, and Gazans remained unable to rebuild due to Israel's ban on construction materials. The amount of goods allowed through the crossings remained "negligible" in terms of the needs of the population, whose livelihoods were devastated as a result.

The fishing industry had collapsed, with an accompanying rise in prices for fish, as Israel continued to deny Gazans access to their own territorial waters. More than 40 percent of the workforce was unemployed. Farmers remained unable to work their own land anywhere within at least 300 meters and as far as 1,000 meters from the border with Israel as IDF troops opened "warning fire" at Palestinians who entered the "security zone". Since Israel escalated its blockade policy following Hamas's 2006 election victory, thirty-three Palestinian civilians, including eleven children, had been killed in such shootings. Sixty-one had been injured, including thirteen children.

The education system had largely collapsed, with many schools having been destroyed or damaged. The schools that remained open were over-crowded. Israel continued to delay or deny educational materials, and most students were prevented from accessing universities outside of Gaza.

As a result of Israel's blockade, the population was malnourished, with a "high prevalence of stunting" among children aged six to sixteen and "alarming" levels of anemia among babies and pregnant women. Ninety percent of the population continued to be without power for four to eight hours a day, with the remaining 10 percent having no electricity at all. Ten thousand Palestinians remained without access to running water, and the inability to maintain the wastewater infrastructure had resulted in 80 million liters of sewage being discharged into the environment. Only 5 to 10 percent of the water extracted from the aquifer met WHO safety standards. The health system remained crippled, with hospitals continuing to rely extensively on generators. Under these conditions, the tunnels under the border with Egypt were an essential lifeline for the people of Gaza, allowing for the limited provision of essential goods such as construction materials, livestock, fuel, and food. Israel's blockade, OCHA concluded, both on land and at sea, was "collectively punishing the entire Gazan population."[13]

Human Rights Watch issued another report documenting seven incidents in which Israeli soldiers fired on civilians carrying white flags during Operation Cast Lead, resulting in the killing of eleven civilians, including five women and four children. At best, this was indiscriminate use of force, and, "At worst, the soldiers deliberately fired on persons known to be civilians." There was "no evidence that the civilian victims were used by Palestinian fighters as human shields or were shot in the crossfire between opposing forces." On the contrary, in each case, "civilian victims were in plain view and posed no apparent security threat." The IDF's self-investigation "failed to include any of the incidents documented in this report, even though Human Rights Watch had sent details of these attacks to the IDF in early February 2009, including GPS coordinates of the incidents, names of those killed and wounded, and the circumstances of their deaths."[14]

B'Tselem published a report on the findings of its investigation into the casualty figures for Operation Cast Lead, which the IDF had refused to cooperate with. While the IDF claimed that 1,166 Palestinians were killed, of whom 709 were "terrorists" and 295 civilians, B'Tselem found that 1,387 Palestinians were killed, of whom 773 were civilians, including 320 under age eighteen and 107 women. An additional 248 police officers who were not taking part in the hostilities were killed when Israel systematically targeted police stations, including 42 cadets killed while standing in formation at the police headquarters in Gaza City on the first day of the bombing. Only 330 of those killed—less than 25 percent of the total—were confirmed combatants. On the Israeli side, thirteen were killed, including three civilians and ten members of the security forces, four of whom were killed by friendly fire. The report pointed out that while the IDF claimed only 89 of those killed were under age sixteen, B'Tselem had obtained "copies of birth certificates and death certificates along with other documentation regarding the vast majority of the minors who were killed" and confirmed the deaths of 252 children under sixteen years of age.[15]

Such reports serve to illustrate a fact that warrants particular emphasis as we proceed to examine the so-called "Goldstone Report" and the manufactured controversy it elicited: well before the report of the UN fact-finding mission was released, the credibility of Israel's self-exonerations was already hanging in tatters amidst the overwhelming evidence of Israeli war crimes.

The Report of the UN Fact-Finding Mission on the Gaza Conflict

In September 2009, the UN Human Rights Council released its 452-page Report of the United Nations Fact-Finding Mission on the Gaza Conflict, more popularly known as the Goldstone Report. The Mission's mandate was of a limited scope, requiring it to examine "any actions by all parties that might have constituted violations of international human rights law or international humanitarian law". It did not address the question of whether Israel's military operation itself had been legal. That is to say, it examined the legality of conduct during the conflict (*jus in bello*), but not whether Israel's resort to armed force was justified in the first place (*jus ad bellum*).[16]

The report noted that estimates of Palestinian fatalities from non-governmental organizations were "generally consistent", ranging from 1,387 to 1,417. The number of deaths raised "very serious concerns about the way Israel conducted the military operations in Gaza."[17] One consequence was the psychological trauma of the population. Twenty percent of children in Gaza suffered from post-traumatic stress disorders. The conditions they experienced were "likely to increase the readiness to embrace violence and extremism."[18]

The Mission recognized that Israel's assault on Gaza and its impact must be evaluated within the context of the blockade that was imposed following Hamas's election victory in 2006. The living conditions of Palestinians had already been dire and were worsened by Israel's operation, during which the IDF "destroyed a substantial part of the economic infrastructure", including factories, farmland, greenhouses, water wells, and fishing boats. "Levels of stunting and thinness in children and of anemia prevalence in children and pregnant women were worrying even before the military operations," and the IDF's destruction of homes and resulting displacement particularly affected women and children. The destruction of water and sanitation infrastructure further aggravated the situation. The blockade and military assault had together left most Gazans "destitute" and unable to rebuild. The Palestinians' inability to reconstruct the civilian infrastructure of Gaza, such as in the areas of health, sanitation, and water, constituted a major public health threat. The amount of goods and humanitarian aid Israel permitted into Gaza even before its assault was "wholly insufficient to meet the humanitarian needs of the population", and the blockade "significantly contributed to an emergency situation that became a full-fledged humanitarian crisis after the military operations".[19]

The Mission was "shocked to learn how badly educational facilities and activities in the Gaza Strip have been affected as a result of the blockade and the recent military operations." At least 280 schools were destroyed or damaged. Eighty-six children and teachers were killed at UNRWA schools, and 402 children and 14 teachers were injured.[20]

The Mission concluded that the continuing blockade violated Israel's obligation under Article 23 of the Fourth Geneva Convention to allow free passage of food, clothing, and medical supplies. Additionally, the Mission concluded that Israel's destruction of civilian infrastructure served "the specific purpose of denying sustenance of the civilian population", the consequences of which were further aggravated by Israel "actively preventing reconstruction efforts". The nature of Israel's blockade and military assault "cumulatively indicate the intention to inflict collective punishment on the people of the Gaza Strip" in violation of Article 33 of the Convention.[21]

The report discussed how the "Dahiya doctrine" had emerged during Israel's war on Lebanon in 2006, "involving the application of disproportionate force and the causing of great damage and destruction to civilian property and infrastructure, and suffering to civilian populations". It concluded "from a review of the facts on the ground that it witnessed for itself that what was prescribed as the best strategy appears to have been precisely what was put into practice."[22] It was evident that Operation Cast Lead "was a deliberately disproportionate attack designed to punish, humiliate and terrorize a civilian population".[23]

The Mission cited Israeli political and military leaders' statements prior to and during Operation Cast Lead on the implementation of the "Dahiya doctrine", such as Major General Gadi Eisenkot's remark that it was a "plan" that had been "approved" and retired Colonel Gabriel Siboni's remark that the doctrine applied to Gaza as well as Lebanon. On January 6, Deputy Prime Minister Eli Yishai said that it would be "possible to destroy Gaza, so they will understand not to mess with us." The ongoing assault was "a great opportunity to demolish thousands of houses of all the terrorists, so they will think twice before they launch rockets." Yishai later said that Israel "should hit their infrastructure, and destroy 100 homes for every rocket fired." On January 13, Tzipi Livni said that Israel was a country that "responds by going wild—and this is a good thing." Such statements, the report concluded, "leave little doubt that disproportionate destruction and violence against civilians were part of a deliberate policy."[24]

Israel had attempted to justify its targeting of the Palestinian Legislative Council building and the Gaza main prison on the grounds that they were part of the "Hamas terrorist infrastructure". The Mission rejected this argument, pointing out that there was "no evidence" that either building had "made an effective contribution to military action." As a result, they "constituted deliberate attacks on civilian objects" in violation of international law. Israel had employed the same justification for its attacks on police stations, which the Mission similarly rejected. Noting that "the Gaza police were a civilian law-enforcement agency", it determined that Israel's systematic targeting of police stations on the first day of bombing "violated international humanitarian law."[25]

The Mission examined the question of whether Israel had met its obligation to take feasible precautions to protect civilians and civilian objects. Israel had warned the population of coming attacks through the use of telephone calls, leaflets, and radio broadcasts, but the effectiveness of these warnings was undermined by their "lack of specificity and thus credibility". "The credibility of instructions to move to city centers for safety", the Mission stated, "was also diminished by the fact that the city centers themselves had been the subject of intense attacks during the air phase of the military operations." The Mission determined that issuing such warnings "does not relieve commanders and their subordinates of taking all other feasible measures to distinguish between civilians and combatants." Furthermore, the IDF had been "systematically reckless" in using white phosphorus munitions and negligent in its use of inherently indiscriminate flechettes in populated areas.[26]

The Mission concluded that Israel's attack on the UNRWA compound on January 15 violated international law. The IDF's "sustained shelling" of the compound with white phosphorus continued for several hours despite the fact that it was fully notified that it was hitting a UN site. UNRWA officials had made numerous calls to Israeli officials. John Ging, who was in Jerusalem at the time, made twenty-six calls to the IDF's Humanitarian Coordination Center in Tel Aviv "to demand that the shelling be stopped". He was met with assurances that it would be, "but it was clear when he relayed this message back to

Gaza that shelling was continuing." The Mission rejected Israel's justification for the attack—that the IDF had "not anticipated" that the compound would be hit—on the simple and obvious grounds that "The Israeli armed forces were told what was happening. It no longer had to anticipate it." Furthermore, Prime Minister Olmert himself had stated that the IDF targeted the compound deliberately because Palestinian militants had fired from within it. Israel subsequently changed its story, claiming that the source of the alleged rocket fire was nearby the compound. This claim was contradicted by UNRWA staff, who reported no such fire in the area at the time. But even giving Israel the benefit of the doubt, the IDF's choice of white phosphorous munitions was disproportionate, an act of "reckless disregard" that was compounded by its decision to continue its shelling despite having been alerted by UN staff. The attack on the compound "violated the customary international law requirement to take all feasible precautions" to avoid civilian casualties and damage to civilian objects.[27]

Israel also attacked the Al-Quds Hospital on January 15 with white phosphorus munitions and at least one high explosive shell. Israel did not reply to the Mission's inquiries about this attack. The only reference to it in the reports of Israel's self-investigations was a citation from a *Newsweek* article, which read, "Talal Safadi, an official in the leftist Palestinian People's Party, said that resistance fighters were firing from positions all around the hospital." Yet that same article also quoted the hospital director general, Dr. Khalid Judah, as saying, "I know for a fact that no one was using the hospital." Furthermore, Israel had not suggested that the hospital itself was being used by armed groups. The hospital "could not be described in any respect at that time as a military objective", yet it was "the object of a direct attack" by the IDF in violation of Article 18 of the Fourth Geneva Convention. "Even in the unlikely event that there was any armed group present on hospital premises," the report noted, the attack was made without warning, in violation of Article 19 of the Convention.[28]

The Mission drew similar conclusions about Israel's attacks on the Al-Wafa Hospital on January 5 and 16, both of which had similarly occurred without any clear military objective and without specific warning that the hospital would be made the object of attack.[29]

Regarding the January 6 attack on the UNRWA school in Jabaliya, the Mission stated that it could not exclude the possibility that Palestinian armed groups had fired from the vicinity, but found no evidence to support that allegation. It considered "the credibility of Israel's position damaged by the series of inconsistencies, contradictions and factual inaccuracies in the statements justifying the attack." Recognizing that "very genuine dilemmas" may arise in combat situations concerning the military objective versus the requirement that attacks be proportionate, "The Mission does not consider this to be such a case. The firing of at least four mortar shells to attempt to kill a small number of specified individuals in a setting where large numbers of civilians were going about their daily business and 1,368 people were sheltering nearby cannot meet the test of what a reasonable commander would have determined to be an acceptable loss of civilian life for the military advantage sought." While Israel claimed that it had killed "two senior Hamas militants" in the attack, Imad Abu Askar and Hassan Abu Askar, Imad was in fact a 13-year-old boy who "was not a Hamas operative." There was no "Hassan" in the family; the second victim was Imad's 19-year-old brother, Khaled. Israel's decision to use mortars in the attack "appears to have been a reckless one" since "they are incapable of distinguishing between combatants and civilians. A decision to deploy them in a location filled with civilians is a decision the commander knows will result in the death and injuries of some of those civilians." The Mission determined that the attack was therefore "indiscriminate, in violation of international law".[30]

Eleven incidents in which the IDF launched direct attacks against civilians were also investigated by the Mission, all but one of which was a situation where IDF forces "must have been aware of their civilian status". The one possible exception was Israel's bombing of the Daya family's home. In most of these cases, Israel also refused "to allow the evacuation of the wounded or to permit access to ambulances." In no case "were there any grounds which could have reasonably induced the Israeli armed forces to assume that the civilians attacked were in fact taking a direct part in the hostilities". In every case, Israel had violated international law.[31]

The Mission investigated several incidents in Zeytoun, where twenty-nine members of the Samouni family were killed. On January 4, Israeli soldiers entered the home of Ateya al-Samouni, shot him dead, and injured several others, including four-year old Ahmad al-Samouni. Israeli soldiers ordered members of the family to relocate to the home of Wa'el al-Samouni, which was then attacked on January 5, killing twenty-one and injuring nineteen. Israeli forces prevented PRCS ambulances from entering the area to evacuate the wounded. It wasn't until January 7 that the ICRC and PRCS were allowed through. By that time, it was too late for young Ahmad, who had died ten hours after being shot three days before, a fact that suggested "he might have had a good chance of survival" had Israel not prevented an ambulance from getting through. When some members of the family tried to leave for Gaza City on January 5, Israeli soldiers shot Iyad al-Samouni, still in handcuffs after his home was invaded, in both his legs. Israeli troops then prevented his family from evacuating him. A PRCS staff member found his body there three days later. The Mission concluded that the Israeli forces had "shot deliberately at a civilian who posed no threat to them" and "deliberately let him bleed to death."[32]

In another incident, Israeli soldiers sitting atop a tank eating a snack opened fire on members of the Abd Rabbo family (a grandmother, husband, wife, and three daughters), who were all carrying white flags. The grandmother, Hajja Souad, and three young daughters—Souad (age nine), Samar (five), and Amal (three)—were all shot. When they called to their neighbor, who happened to be an ambulance driver, for help, the Israeli soldiers obstructed him and then forced him to leave the area. They then crushed his ambulance with a tank or bulldozer. Amal and Souad died of their wounds. The family, with the help of neighbors, then managed to carry Samar and her grandmother to Al-Shifa Hospital. Samar suffered a spinal injury that doctors said would leave her paralyzed for the rest of her life.[33]

The report noted Israel's self-contradiction in claiming that it didn't attack the al-Maqadmah mosque near Beit Lahiya on January 3 while at the same time claiming that those killed in the attack were "Hamas operatives". In fact, the Mission found, the mosque was attacked while a large number of people were gathered inside for evening prayers. At least fifteen people were killed and around forty injured. Notably, the IDF had not suggested "that the al-Maqadmah mosque was being used at the time to launch rockets, store weapons or shelter combatants". Therefore, considering "the absence of any explanation as to the circumstances that led to the missile strike on the al-Maqadmah mosque", the Mission concluded that "the mosque was intentionally targeted by the Israeli armed forces"—a finding "strengthened in the face of the unsatisfactory and demonstrably false position of the Israeli Government."[34]

The Mission investigated the case of Israel's F-16 airstrike on the Daya family home in Zeytoun on January 6, which killed twenty-two members of the family, including twelve children under ten years old. Israel claimed the attack was an "error" because it had intended to hit a neighboring building it claimed was a "weapons storage facility". The Mission found this version of events "to be unsatisfactory". Even giving Israel the benefit of the doubt, "The fact that target selection had gone wrong at the planning stage does not strip the act of its deliberate character." The Mission concluded that Israel's "lack of due diligence" constituted "a violation of the right to life as set out in article 6 of the International Covenant on Civil and Political Rights, to which Israel is a party."[35]

The Mission investigated another case in which Israel on January 5 attacked condolence tents for Arafa Abd al-Dayem, a first-aid volunteer who died from injuries sustained when his ambulance was struck with a flechette missile the day before in the Izbat Beit Hanoun area in northeast Gaza. "The tents were struck three times in two hours," the Mission noted, "again with flechettes missiles." At least twenty people were injured, five of whom died of their injuries, including two boys, ages thirteen and sixteen. Israel had not addressed this case in its investigation reports and, furthermore, had denied that flechettes were an indiscriminate choice of weaponry. The Mission reminded that flechettes were "by their nature lacking in discrimination." Moreover, there was "nothing at all" indicating any military objective. The attacks seemed rather "designed to kill and maim the victims directly and otherwise to terrify the people in the area" and were "a grave breach" of international law.[36]

Incidents involving "the destruction of industrial infrastructure, food production, water installations, sewage treatment plants and housing" were investigated, including an attack on the Al-Bader flour mill, the only such mill still in operation in Gaza. The Mission found that the mill's destruction "had no military justification. The nature of the strikes, in particular the precise targeting of crucial machinery, suggests that the intention was to disable the factory's productive capacity" and "to deny sustenance to the civilian population".

The IDF had "systematically flattened" 31,000 chickens with bulldozers at farms in Zeytoun that had supplied over 10 percent of the Gaza egg market, "a deliberate act of wanton destruction".

The wall of "one of the raw sewage lagoons of the [Sheikh Ijlin] Gaza wastewater treatment plant" was struck by Israeli forces, causing "the outflow of more than 200,000 cubic meters of raw sewage onto neighboring farmland. The circumstances of the strike suggest that it was deliberate and premeditated."

The Namar wells complex in Jabaliya, which provided drinking water for residents of Gaza, had been systematically destroyed in Israeli airstrikes on the first day, with no possible justification.

Israel's "systematic destruction" of residential buildings "was carried out in the absence of any link to combat engagements with Palestinian armed groups or any other effective contribution to military action" and constituted a violation of international law.

Israel's systematic destruction of the civilian infrastructure included the "only cement-packaging plant in Gaza (the Atta Abu Jubbah plant), the Abu Eida factories for ready-mix concrete, further chicken farms and the Al-Wadiyah Group's food and drinks factories."

The facts indicated "that there was a deliberate and systematic policy on the part of the Israeli armed forces to target industrial sites and water installations."[37]

The Mission also investigated the conduct of Palestinian armed groups, focusing on allegations that they had violated the sanctity of schools, mosques, hospitals, and other civilian locations, and also used human shields. It emphasized that Israeli forces seemed to have been met with little to no actual resistance during the invasion. There were "relatively few reports of actual crossfire between the Israeli armed forces and Palestinian armed groups. This would also appear to be reflected in the low number of Israeli soldiers killed or injured during the ground offensive." It was also a common theme among soldiers' testimonies collected by Breaking the Silence "that they had no encounters with Palestinian combatants."

With regard to Israel's claim that Hamas had booby-trapped homes, the Mission could not discount the possibility that this occurred, but pointed out that there was "no basis to conclude" from the reports alleging such activity "that civilian lives were put at risk". It found no evidence that armed groups had used mosques for military purposes. It "did not find any evidence to support the allegations" that hospitals were used by armed groups for military purposes. It pointed out that the PRCS, during its own investigations, had found that there were no instances of their ambulances being used by Palestinian combatants. It determined conclusively that armed groups had not used any UN facilities.

Furthermore, the Mission "did not find any evidence of civilians being forced to remain in their houses by Palestinian armed groups". It found "no evidence" that "combatants mingled with the civilian population with the intention of shielding themselves from attack". It "found no indication" that civilians were forced "to remain in areas under attack from the Israeli armed forces". And it "found no evidence" that "armed groups either directed civilians to areas where attacks were being launched or forced civilians to remain within the vicinity of the attacks."

However, Palestinian armed groups *had* fired rockets or mortars from urban areas and thus potentially put civilians at risk, which constituted a violation of customary international law.[38] Additionally, rocket and mortar fire by Palestinian armed groups was "incapable of being directed towards specific military objectives and have been fired into areas where civilian populations are based." Such attacks "constitute a deliberate attack against a civilian population" that amounted to "war crimes" and possibly "crimes against humanity." The Mission found that "one of the primary purposes of the rocket and mortar attacks is to spread terror among the Israeli civilian population, a violation of international law."[39]

While finding no evidence that Palestinian militants had used human shields, the Mission further documented how *Israeli* forces had done so: "The Mission investigated four incidents in which the Israeli armed forces coerced Palestinian civilian men at gunpoint to take part in house searches. . . . The men were blindfolded and handcuffed as they were forced to enter houses ahead of the Israeli soldiers. . . . The Mission concludes that this practice amounts to the use of Palestinian civilians as human shields and is therefore prohibited by international humanitarian law." It was "cruel and inhuman treatment" that constituted "a war crime."[40]

The Mission stressed that there is "a clear obligation for States to investigate and, if appropriate, prosecute allegations of serious violations by military personnel". Any failure to do so was itself a violation of international law. Such investigations must be independent, effective, prompt, and impartial. The "system put in place by Israel", the Mission found, "does not comply with all those principles" and "is not effective in addressing the violations and uncovering the truth."

Ilan Katz, a former Deputy Military Advocate General, had himself criticized "the use of operational debriefings by commanders in order to prevent criminal investigations". Katz said, "Even if a decision is made by the Military

Advocate General to order the opening of criminal investigations, investigation is usually nearly impossible at that point". Katz's statement seemed an admission "that the system does not comply with the requirement of promptness". Katz's criticisms were also "consistent with other assessments", such as from Human Rights Watch. The Mission determined that "Operation debriefing, to review operational performance, is not an appropriate tool to conduct investigations of allegations of serious violations of human rights and humanitarian law. It appears to the Mission that established methods of criminal investigations such as visits to the crime scene, interviews with witnesses and victims, and assessment by reference to established legal standards have not been adopted." The IDF's self-investigations "appear to have relied exclusively on interviews with Israeli officers and soldiers" and thus "did not comply with required legal standards."

Additionally, while Israel had opened some thirteen criminal investigations, there was an "undue delay" of six months to start them. The Mission concurred with the determination of Amnesty International that Israel's self-investigations were wholly inadequate. It concluded that Israel was in "violation of its obligation" to investigate allegations of war crimes and other violations of international law. It added that "there are serious doubts about the willingness of Israel to carry out genuine investigations in an impartial, independent, prompt and effective way as required by international law."[41]

Among the Mission's recommendations was that the Security Council should require Israel "to launch appropriate investigations that are independent and in conformity with international standards", as well as establish an independent committee of experts to assess Hamas's responsibility to do the same. In the absence of good-faith investigations, the Security Council should, "acting under Chapter VII of the Charter of the United Nations, refer the situation in Gaza to the Prosecutor of the International Criminal Court pursuant to article 13 (b) of the Rome Statute".[42]

Upon the report's release, Richard Goldstone wrote an op-ed for the *New York Times* relaying the Mission's findings that both Israel and Hamas had committed war crimes and reiterating its recommendation that both parties must investigate alleged abuses. "Unfortunately," he wrote, "both Israel and Hamas have dismal records of investigating their own forces." While Israel had "begun investigations into alleged violations by its forces in the Gaza conflict," they were "unlikely to be serious and objective."[43]

The Response from the US and Israel

The US response to the report at the Human Rights Council in Geneva, Switzerland, was delivered by the Assistant Secretary of State for Democracy, Human Rights and Labor, Michael Posner. It was a blanket dismissal of the report based entirely on ad hominem argumentation that failed to substantively address any of its factual findings; indeed, it was apparent that Posner hadn't bothered to actually read the report before carrying out his instructions to denounce it. He made it clear that Israel's disproportionate use of force was of no concern to the US; rather, it was the Human Rights Council whose behavior was "grossly disproportionate", for the amount of attention it paid to Israel. The Council employed a "double standard" and was "unfair" to Israel. He lauded Israel's "well-established commitment to the rule of law". The US government was "confident" that Israel could "carry out robust investigations" into its own conduct. Posner defended the IDF's conduct by repeating Israel's baseless claims that Hamas had used human shields and used schools, hospitals, and mosques for storing weapons and firing rockets. The US also had "very serious concerns about the recommendations spelled out in this report, especially that these allegations be taken up by the UN Security Council and then possibly referred to the International Criminal Court."[44]

The US's "very serious concerns" in this latter regard were understandable, given the extent of its complicity in Israel's crimes, which would extend now to blocking any effort to seek accountability. The US Permanent Representative to the UN, Susan Rice, similarly accused the Mission of having a mandate that was "unbalanced, one sided and basically unacceptable." She suggested that the international community should not focus on the tragic events and violations of international law that occurred during Israel's twenty-two-day full-scale military assault on Gaza because "we need to be focused on the future".[45]

Amnesty International described Rice's comments as "deeply disappointing".[46]

Thirty-two members of the US Senate, meanwhile, urged Secretary of State Clinton to take action "to block the report from reaching the UN Security Council" and "to denounce any punishment against Israel". They dismissed the report's "flawed findings" as "misleading and unacceptable" and criticized the Mission's mandate as "one-sided". The letter dealt with the fact that it had also found Hamas guilty of war crimes by falsely claiming that it had "exceeded" its mandate in doing so; it further complained that "the vast majority of the report focuses on Israel's conduct, rather than that of Hamas."[47]

The fact that the vast majority of the violence, death, and destruction had been perpetrated by Israel was apparently of no relevance as the Senators implied that the report should have devoted an equal number of pages to Hamas's conduct. As Stephen Zunes retorted, "the ratio of civilian casualties inflicted by the Israelis relative to those inflicted by Hamas was more than 250:1. This would seem to indicate a legitimate reason to focus primarily on Israel." Zunes also commented on the absurdity of the Senators' accusation of anti-Israeli bias by noting that, in addition to being a well-respected international jurist and expert on international law, Goldstone was "Jewish, a longtime supporter of Israel, chair of Friends of Hebrew University, president emeritus of the World ORT

Jewish school system and the father of an Israeli citizen."[48] He thus couldn't very credibly be accused of "anti-Israeli" bias, much less, for that matter, of "anti-Semitism"—another charge regularly leveled at critics of Israeli policies by its defenders.

The Senate letter claimed that the Goldstone Report didn't recognize Israel's right to self-defense under Article 51 of the UN Charter. Actually, the Mission didn't address the question of whether or not Israel's resort to force had been lawful or not, but only examined its conduct during its operations. That Israel had a right to defend itself was taken for granted, and the Mission's recognition of this right was a consideration implicit or explicit throughout its report, including in its conclusion that, "While the Israeli Government has sought to portray its operations as essentially a response to rocket attacks in the exercise of its right to self-defense, the Mission considers the plan to have been directed, at least in part, at a different target: the people of Gaza as a whole."[49]

The Senators claimed that the report "ignores the fact that Israel acted in self-defense only after its civilian population suffered eight years of attacks by rockets and mortars fired indiscriminately from Gaza." It was the Senators, however, who were ignoring the fact that it was *Israel* who violated the ceasefire and refused to renew it, as well as the fact that the Mission *had* taken the rocket and mortar attacks on Israel into consideration. Indeed, the report offered a historical overview of the conflict that explicitly noted, "The firing of rockets and mortars from Gaza into Israel began in 2001. Israeli sources report that as many as 3,455 rockets and 3,742 mortar shells were fired into Israel from Gaza until mid-June 2008."[50]

Finally, the Senators stated that "the report does not adequately recognize the extraordinary measures taken by the Israel Defense Forces to minimize civilian casualties". In fact, the Mission had documented at great length Israel's failure to uphold its obligations in that regard, including an examination of Israel's "warnings" to civilians, which were found to be lacking in credibility and effectiveness, particularly given the fact that in numerous instances, Gazans were ordered to evacuate to locations that were then deliberately targeted by the IDF.

The denunciations of the report by Israeli government officials were even more hysterical than the US Senate's. Netanyahu condemned the Mission as "a kangaroo court against Israel, whose consequences harm the struggle of democratic countries against terror".[51] He demanded the world leaders "Reject the findings of this commission" and "condemn this report and act to quash its consequences now".[52] He rejected the report's recommendation that Israel credibly investigate allegations of war crimes by vowing that "No soldiers or officers will be brought before a commission of inquiry."[53] President Shimon Peres likewise decried the report as "a mockery of history" that failed "to distinguish between the aggressor and a state exercising its right for self-defense" and that granted "legitimacy to terrorism". Deputy Foreign Minister Danny Ayalon similarly denounced it as "a dangerous attempt to harm the principle of self-defense by democratic states and provides legitimacy to terrorism."[54] Tzipi Livni contended that the report was "based on a distorted system of values."[55]

In the *Jerusalem Post*, Larry Derfner criticized the reaction of Israeli officials with scathing sarcasm:

> How dare anyone deny us the right to self-defense! How dare anyone deny us the right to fight back against terrorism! . . . And there are no limits on our right to self-defense. There is no such thing as "disproportionate." We can blockade Gaza, we can answer Qassams with F-16s and Apaches, we can take 100 eyes for an eye. We can deliberately destroy thousands of Gazan homes, the Gazan parliament, the Ministry of Justice, the Ministry of Interior, courthouses, the only Gazan flour plant, the main poultry farm, a sewage treatment plant, water wells and God knows what else. *Deliberately*. After all, we're acting in self-defense. By definition. And what right do the Palestinians have to defend themselves against this? None. Why? Because we are better than them. Because we're a democracy and they're a bunch of Islamo-fascists. Because ours is a culture of life and theirs is a culture of death. Because they're out to destroy us and all we are saying is give peace a chance. One look at the ruins of Gaza ought to make that plain enough. . . . The Goldstones of the world call this hypocrisy, a double standard. How dare they! Around here, we call it moral clarity.[56]

B'Tselem issued a statement rejecting the Israeli government's criticisms of the Goldstone Report, which was "the result of a serious, professional investigation, reflecting a deep and genuine commitment to ensure that justice is done."[57]

The US's similar response to the report, Human Rights Watch noticed, "sends a message that serious laws-of-war violations will be treated with kid gloves when committed by an ally". The US had "resorted to calling the report 'unbalanced' and 'deeply flawed, but provided no real facts to support those assertions". On the contrary, the report was "a sober, careful assessment of the violations committed by both sides in the conflict, which closely corresponds to the findings by Human Rights Watch and other independent groups."

"The US effort to dismiss the Goldstone report", said the group's Geneva director, Juliette de Rivero, "was downright shameful for an administration that claims to promote the rule of law and accountability for war crimes." The US's insistence that Israel could investigate itself "reflects a disappointing refusal to confront reality," she added. The US was also "missing an important opportunity" because "by letting Israel off the hook, it's also letting Hamas of the hook."[58]

On September 25, Egypt, on behalf of the Non-Aligned Movement (which includes Palestine as a member) and other state organizations, submitted a draft resolution to the UN Human Rights Council endorsing the Fact-Finding Mission Report and referring it to the General Assembly.[59] On October 1, the day before the vote on the draft was supposed to occur, Netanyahu declared that to refer the report to the Assembly would "strike a severe blow to the war against terrorism", "afford total legitimization to terrorists", "condemn the victim", and "strike a fatal blow to the peace process".[60] The US opposed the resolution on the grounds that Israel would reject peace talks if it passed. President Abbas agreed under pressure from Washington to defer the vote until March, sparking protests against his leadership among Palestinians and condemnation of him in the Arab media.[61] Hamas described Abbas's decision as "collusion" with Israel.[62]

On October 9, his administration's policies notwithstanding, the Norwegian Nobel Committee announced its decision to award the Nobel Peace Prize to President Barack Obama "for his extraordinary efforts to strengthen international diplomacy and cooperation between peoples."[63] In his statement accepting the honor, Obama said that peace would require "an unwavering commitment that finally realizes . . . the rights of all Israelis and Palestinians to live in peace and security in nations of their own."[64]

Holding him to his words, Human Rights Watch urged Obama to "use the weight and authority of his Nobel Peace Prize to put the peace process on the right track . . . by demanding justice for serious crimes by all sides in the Gaza war." His administration was doing the opposite, however, by trying to kill efforts to forward the Fact-Finding Mission report to the UN General Assembly or Security Council.[65]

After Obama received the Nobel Prize, Abbas reversed himself and, defying Washington, Palestine as a non-member state joined Egypt and other nations in submitting a resolution to the Human Rights Council. Juliette de Rivero of Human Rights Watch responded to the US's argument that the resolution would "derail peace efforts" by saying that "persistent impunity, not the prospect of justice, was the greater threat to peace". Patrizia Scanella of Amnesty International similarly urged that without accountability and an end to impunity, there could be no peace in the Middle East.[66]

The resolution passed on October 16 with twenty-five votes in favor and eleven abstentions. It condemned Israel's land confiscation, home demolitions, construction of settlements and the separation wall, and refusal to cooperate with the Fact-Finding Mission. It endorsed the recommendations of the report and advised the General Assembly to take them into consideration. Five countries joined the US in voting against the resolution, which the US said was "not balanced" and "could only exacerbate" the situation.[67]

Former US ambassador to the UN John Bolton wrote a *Wall Street Journal* op-ed criticizing the resolution as biased on the grounds that it "lacerated Israel", but not Hamas. Bolton declined to point out that what the resolution criticized Israel for was its refusal to cooperate with the Fact-Finding Mission—something it couldn't very well condemn Hamas for, since Hamas *had* cooperated. Bolton condemned the Human Rights Council for "concentrating on Israel and the US rather than the world's real human rights violators". So the US and Israel's human rights violations were mere figments of the world's imagination. He also scolded Obama for joining the Council rather than sticking to the previous administration's policy of "shunning the HRC and attempting to delegitimize it". Bolton's further remarks were instructive:

> The Goldstone Report has important implications for America. In the UN, Israel frequently serves as a surrogate target in lieu of the US, particularly concerning the use of military force pre-emptively or in self-defense. Accordingly, UN decisions on ostensibly Israel-specific issues can lay a predicate for subsequent action against, or efforts to constrain, the US. Mr. Goldstone's recommendation to convoke the International Criminal Court is like putting a loaded pistol to Israel's head—or, in the future, to America's.

The US should withdraw from the Council, he argued, because "next time" it might have "Washington as its unmistakable target."[68]

Bolton's concern was understandable, given the US's own frequent resort to unlawful use of force, such as its war of aggression against Iraq. Crimes within the ICC's jurisdiction include the crime of aggression, war crimes, crimes against humanity, and crimes against the UN and associated personnel.[69] Indeed, Israel and the US both had good reason to worry about the possibility of Israel's actions being referred to the ICC.

Attacking the Messenger

In an interview on *PBS NewsHour* on September 15, 2009, Richard Goldstone answered criticisms of the Fact-Finding Mission Report. He corrected the false claims that the Mission's mandate was to investigate only Israel and pointed out the invalidity of criticizing the report as biased because it didn't devote an equal number of pages to Hamas as to Israel. He noted further that there wasn't any dispute that indiscriminate rocket and mortar attacks by Palestinian armed groups were war crimes. The Mission had also fully taken into account Israel's version of events. It was "disappointing" that there was such "simple rejection of the report on grounds that don't begin to deal with the merits or the facts."

The next guest on the program was the Israeli Ambassador to the US, Michael B. Oren, who ironically proceeded to reject the report on grounds that didn't begin to deal with the merits or the facts. Oren repeated the standard talking points about Israel doing "its utmost" to avoid civilian casualties and having "no choice" but "to defend itself" in response to "years" of rocket fire. He went so far as to lie that "Israeli leaders begged Hamas to extend a cease-fire". He defended Israel's refusal to cooperate with the UN Mission by calling it "a farce of justice" and calling the Human Rights Council "hardly an impartial body". That the Mission was biased was evidenced by its lack of necessity, since Israel had already "cleared" itself "of virtually all of" the "complaints of irregularities"—his euphemism for war crimes.

When the show's host, Gwen Ifill, pointed out that the Mission had concluded that Israel's self-investigations fell short of the requirements of international law and lacked credibility, the best response Oren could muster was, "I think that, once you start establishing the precedent that democratic countries can't investigate themselves, I think you've got a problem." Desperately, he fell back on his talking points, calling the report "a victory for terror" and again invoking the US's "war on terrorism" to justify Israel's actions with the undoubtedly true remark, "I don't think the United States would like to see a similar report mounted against its conduct of its operations in Afghanistan."[70]

Goldstone elsewhere responded to the Obama administration's dismissal of the report as "flawed" by saying, "I have yet to hear from the Obama administration what the flaws in the report that they have identified are. I would be happy to respond to them, if and when I know what they are." He had "no doubt" that "many of the critics—the overwhelmingly majority of critics—have not read the report". This was obvious since "the level of criticism does not go to the substance of the report. There still have not been responses to the really serious allegations that are made." Hinting at an explanation for the vitriolic attacks on the report from Israeli officials, he offered the insight that "People generally don't like to be accused of criminal activity."[71]

In an interview with Bill Moyers on PBS, Goldstone discussed his reasons for accepting the mission despite the pressure he knew he would come under. He could not decline the position, he explained, because "being Jewish was no reason to treat Israel exceptionally, and to say because I'm Jewish, it's all right for me to investigate everybody else, but not Israel." He knew his decision would antagonize many of his own friends, such as at Hebrew University, where he sat on the board. But the criticisms of the report lacked substance and were "a knee-jerk reaction to attack the messenger rather than the message."

When Moyers said the report "basically accuses Israel of waging war on the entire population of Gaza", Goldstone responded simply by saying, "Correct."

Moyers followed up with the question of whether the Mission had found evidence that Israeli attacks on civilian persons and objects were deliberate. Goldstone replied, "Well we did. We found evidence in statements made by present and former political and military leaders, who said, quite openly, that there's going to be a disproportionate attack. . . . You know, one thing one can't say about the Israel Defense Forces is that they make too many mistakes. They're very, a sophisticated army. And if they attack a mosque or attack a factory, and over 200 factories were bombed, there's just no basis to ascribe that to error. That must be intentional."

He was asked about Israel's argument, which was accepted by the US, that bombing the Palestinian legislative assembly building was legitimate because it was part of the "Hamas infrastructure". In reply, Goldstone reasoned that if the US was at war, "it would be legitimate to bomb the Pentagon; I would suggest it would be illegitimate to bomb the Congress." The "only logical reason" for Israel's destruction of Gaza's infrastructure, he elucidated, "is collective punishment against the people of Gaza for voting into power Hamas, and a form of reprisal for the rocket attacks and mortar attacks on southern Israel. . . . I think they were telling the people of Gaza that if you support Hamas, this is what we're going to do to you."

On a more personal note, Goldstone confided, "I was, quite frankly, nervous going into Gaza. I had nightmares about being kidnapped. You know, it was very difficult, especially for a Jew, to go into an area controlled by Hamas. . . . On the contrary, I was struck by the warmth of the people, that we met and who we dealt with in Gaza. You know, my fears were put aside." For other Jews to suggest that he had betrayed his people by accepting the mission was "a form of racism. Why should my being Jewish stop me from investigating Israel? . . . I think true friends criticize their friends when they do wrong things. . . . The only thing they can be afraid of is the truth. And I think that is why they're attacking the messenger and not the message."[72]

A Case Study in Congressional Hypocrisy

The same day Goldstone's interview aired, a resolution was introduced into the US House of Representatives illustrating his point. The draft resolution contained numerous falsehoods, beginning with its refrain that the mandate of the UN Fact-Finding Mission had "pre-judged" Israel's guilt and called for investigations only into Israel's, but not Hamas's, conduct.[73] Its reference to the "mandate", however, was to the Human Rights Council resolution of January 12, 2009, which had called for a fact-finding mission to be established to investigate possible Israeli war crimes. In fact, the actual mandate ultimately adopted by the Mission and accepted by Goldstone was "to investigate *all* violations of international human rights law and international humanitarian law that *might have* been committed at any time in the context of the military operations that were conducted in Gaza during the period from 27 December 2008 and 18 January 2009, whether before, during or after" (emphasis added).[74] This fact was reflected in the report itself, which we may recall stated that the Mission's mandate required it to examine "any actions *by all parties* that *might have* constituted violations of international human rights law or international humanitarian law" (emphasis added).

The House resolution also meaninglessly criticized the Human Rights Council's resolution of January 12 for including "no mention of the relentless rocket and mortar attacks" against Israel. It naturally did not object to the Council's resolution on the equivalent grounds that it didn't mention Israel's relentless siege of Gaza, its violation of the ceasefire, etc. Nor did it point out the far more relevant fact that the Goldstone Report *did* discuss the history of such attacks on Israel and condemned them as war crimes.

The House resolution criticized Christine Chinkin's membership in the Mission with the argument that she had prejudged Israel's guilt by signing the letter published in the *Sunday Times* on January 11, 2009, describing Israel's actions as "war crimes".[75] The same letter, of course, also said rocket attacks on Israel were war crimes, but the resolution's drafters refrained from criticizing Chinkin for having "prejudged" Hamas's guilt.[76]

The House resolution dismissed the UN Mission's finding that civilians had been deliberately attacked by Israeli soldiers as "unsubstantiated", with no elaboration as to how the Goldstone Report's hundreds of pages of detailed case studies had failed to substantiate its conclusions.

The resolution lied that in the Goldstone Report, the Mission's members had written, "we did not deal with the issues . . . regarding the problems of conducting military operations in civilian areas and second-guessing decisions made by soldiers and their commanding officers 'in the fog of war'" (ellipsis in original).[77] In fact, those words did *not* appear in the report. The quote was actually taken from an e-mail by Richard Goldstone to one Maurice Ostroff that was published online. Ostroff had written Goldstone to ask why the Mission did not invite the testimony of Colonel Richard Kemp, "the former commander of British forces in Afghanistan and an adviser to the UK cabinet, who has expert knowledge of warfare in conditions similar to that in Gaza."[78]

Ostroff offered no explanation of what knowledge Kemp was supposed to have of the actual situation *in Gaza* that would warrant his being interviewed by the Mission. But we may turn to Kemp's outspoken views on the matter to get an idea. Several months after Operation Cast Lead ended, Kemp gave an address to the Jerusalem Center for Public Affairs (JCPA) in which he compared Israel's actions in Gaza to the US and UK's actions in Afghanistan and Iraq. He argued that civilians were sometimes mistakenly killed due to the "fog of war" and parroted Israel's claims that Hamas had used human shields, as well as used "mosques, schools and hospitals" as military "strongholds". He further reasoned that if women and children were killed, it was only because they were "trained and equipped to fight". He cited the IDF's warnings to civilians of its impending attacks as evidence of it having met its "obligation to operate within the laws of war". He claimed that "the IDF allowed huge amounts of humanitarian aid into Gaza", and boasted that "during Operation Cast Lead the IDF did more to safeguard the rights of civilians in a combat zone than any other Army in the history of warfare". His entire speech was in essence a reiteration of Israeli leaders' contention that the IDF was "the most moral army in the world".[79]

In an interview with the BBC during the midst of Israel's assault, after the UN had passed its ceasefire resolution, Kemp said the "civilian deaths" were "absolutely tragic", but that "Israel doesn't have any choice" except to go on with the killing. The exchange that followed is instructive:

> HOST: And so to what extent does the impact on civilians—
> on people who have nothing to do with Hamas, but live in a
> heavily populated area [and] so can't escape—to what extent
> does their fate factor in considerations?
>
> KEMP: I think—I would say, from my knowledge of the IDF
> and from the extent to which I've been following the cur-
> rent operation, I don't think there has ever been a time in the
> history of warfare when any army has made more efforts to
> reduce civilian casualties and the deaths of innocent people
> than the IDF is doing today in Gaza. Um—when you look at
> the number of civilian casualties that have been caused, that
> perhaps doesn't sound too credible. I will accept that. How-
> ever—um—Hamas has been trained extensively by Iran and
> by Hezbollah to fight among the people, to use the civilian
> population in Gaza as a human shield. . . . It's impossible. It is
> impossible to stop [civilians deaths from] happening when the
> enemy is using them as a shield.
>
> HOST: Indeed. . . . But people watching this will think, "Well
> there is also the criticism from UN eyewitnesses who talk of
> the house where people were advised to move to safety [and]
> 24 hours later, was bombed by Israel."
>
> KEMP: Well . . . Of course, I can't really comment on—on
> the detail of that. I don't have any of the facts available on that.
> I've no doubt that any allegations like that will be looked into
> very seriously by Israel.[80]

Kemp later gave a statement to the Human Rights Council repeating the same talking points and condemning the Goldstone Report. He was speaking in his capacity as a spokesman for the group UN Watch, an affiliate organization of the American Jewish Committee, which proudly boasts on its website having been called by *Salon* "the most powerful pro-Israel lobby in the United States."[81]

Returning to the House resolution, recall its use of an ellipse in the quote from Goldstone taken from his e-mail to Ostroff. Following is the relevant text from Goldstone's reply (emphasis added to portions omitted by the House): *"I would also mention that there was no reliance on Col. Kemp mainly because in our Report* we did not deal with the issue *he raised* regarding the problems of conducting military operations in civilian areas and second-guessing decisions made by soldiers and their commanding officers 'in the fog of war'. *We avoided having to do so in the incidents we decided to investigate."*[82] His meaning, of course, was that in all but one of the eleven specific incidents the Mission investigated involving direct attacks on civilians, the IDF "must have been aware of their civilian status". Such attacks included Israel's targeting of the home of Wa'el al-Samouni on January 5, the very same attack mentioned by the BBC reporter that Kemp admitted he didn't know anything about (right after he acknowledged that his thesis about the benevolence of Israel's conduct didn't sound too credible, given the actual number of civilians killed).

As a further illustration of the point Goldstone was making, recall the Mission's finding that while "very genuine dilemmas" about the question of proportionality may arise in combat situations, it did not consider Israel's attack on the UNRWA headquarters on January 15 to be such a case.

The House resolution proceeded to quote Goldstone out of context as saying, "If this was a court of law, there would have been nothing proven".[83] In the article from which the quote was taken, Goldstone went on to say he hoped Israel and the Palestinians would conduct their own credible investigations, in which case the report would serve as "a useful road map." The article continued:

> He recalled his work as chief prosecutor for the international war crimes tribunal in Yugoslavia in 1994. When he began working, Goldstone was presented with a report commissioned by the UN Security Council based on what he said was a fact-finding mission similar to his own in Gaza. "We couldn't use that report as evidence at all," Goldstone said. "But it was a useful roadmap for our investigators, for me as chief prosecutor, to decide where we should investigate. And that's the purpose of this sort of report."[84]

The House resolution asserted that there was "a great body of evidence" that Palestinian combatants had used mosques, schools, and hospitals, as well as humans, to shield their military operations. It criticized the Goldstone Report for having "repeatedly downplayed or cast doubt upon that claim". The report had indeed cast doubt upon that claim, for the simple reason that no such "great body of evidence" was to be found.

The drafters concluded that the Goldstone Report was "irredeemably biased and unworthy of further consideration or legitimacy"—a perfect description of their own resolution.[85]

In reply, Goldstone sent a letter to leading members of the House Committee on Foreign Affairs noting that the draft included "serious factual inaccuracies and instances where information and statements are taken grossly out of context". He provided a detailed rebuttal listing many of its falsehoods and misleading statements, as well as correcting the record about the Mission's mandate.[86]

The House nevertheless adopted a version of the resolution that was nearly identical to the draft, with a few minor revisions. It dropped the lie that Goldstone's comments from his e-mail about Richard Kemp had come from "the body of the report itself", only to replace it with the wording "the authors of the report admit . . ." and retaining the out-of-context and misleadingly truncated quote. It thus simply exchanged one lie for another (the other three members of the Mission, of course, had nothing to do the e-mail). Text was also added referring to "a so-called broadened mandate" that "was never officially endorsed by a plenary meeting of the UNHRC". This was added in an attempt to maintain the characterization of the Mission's mandate as "one-sided" regardless of the fact that the mandate actually carried out was to investigate the conduct of both parties to the conflict. The adopted text also called on the Obama administration to oppose—including through use of its veto power in the Security Council—any UN resolution that endorsed the report and called for implementation of its recommendations.[87]

Such a resolution was adopted by the General Assembly on November 5. In it, the Assembly expressed its appreciation to the Fact-Finding Mission, requested that the Secretary-General transmit the report to the Security Council, and called upon both parties to the conflict to undertake investigations into violations of international law. The resolution passed 114 to 18, with 44 abstentions.[88] The US representative explained Washington's nay vote by repeating the substanceless charge that the Mission's report "was deeply flawed and had an unbalanced focus on Israel".[89]

The US was not alone in trying to prevent Israeli leaders from being held accountable for war crimes. The UK abstained from the General Assembly resolution, but a diplomatic row erupted the following month. Former Israeli Foreign Minister Tzipi Livni was due to address a Jewish National Fund conference in

London, but a British court issued a warrant to arrest her for war crimes. The "deeply embarrassed" British Foreign Office issued an apologetic statement saying that it was looking into the case and stressing how important it was that Israeli leaders be able to go to the UK "to promote peace".[90]

As an indication of what it meant for Livni to "promote peace", her office issued a statement that she was "proud of all her decisions connected to Operation Cast Lead", a massive military operation against the defenseless population of Gaza that had "achieved its goal".[91] The British ambassador was summoned by the Israeli Foreign Minister "to receive a formal dressing down over the affront", as the London *Times* put it. The Palestinians represented in the lawsuit that led to the arrest warrant were "radical elements", Israel's Foreign Ministry charged. It urged the British government to "prevent an abuse of the British legal system against Israel and its citizens by anti-Israel elements."[92]

"We will not agree", protested Netanyahu, "that IDF commanders and soldiers, who—heroically and in a moral fashion—defended our citizens against a brutal and criminal enemy, will be condemned as war criminals. We object this absurdity outright." Livni complained that "The problem starts when they equate terrorists and Israeli soldiers."[93] Israeli Foreign Minister Avigdor Lieberman bemoaned that "classic anti-Semitism" was "being used to incite hatred against Jews, and to delegitimize the State of Israel". The anti-Semitic efforts to "delegitimize" Israel included the General Assembly's endorsement of the Goldstone Report's recommendations and request to forward it to the Security Council.[94]

The British government responded by pledging to reform the law that allowed judges to issue arrest warrants for former government officials no longer protected by diplomatic immunity. Such an attempt to hold Israeli leaders accountable for war crimes was, in British Foreign Secretary David Miliband's view, "insufferable".[95]

Washington was no doubt pleased to see London acting on the basis of their shared values.

The 'Illegal but Legitimate' Doctrine

Richard Goldstone posed a serious problem for defenders of Israel's war crimes. He could not plausibly be dismissed as "anti-Israeli" or an "anti-Semite", or even as "anti-Zionist". "I'm certainly a friend of Israel", he once said in an interview. "I don't mind being called a Zionist; it depends on the definition."[96]

Nor was he someone who could reasonably be accused more broadly of standing in the way of Western interests, as narrowly defined by Washington, DC. On the contrary, he had in the past played an instrumental role in establishing a doctrine used to justify US military intervention, which earned him a certain kind of credibility that made his participation in the UN Fact-Finding Mission all the more troublesome for the US and Israel. Among other accomplishments on his résumé, Goldstone was one of the heads of the Independent International Commission on Kosovo, which was established on the initiative of the Prime Minster of Sweden, Göran Persson, in the aftermath of the 1999 Kosovo War.

The NATO bombing of Kosovo was characterized in the West as a "humanitarian intervention" despite the fact that it resulted in an escalation of atrocities on the ground in the former Yugoslavia and a higher civilian death toll in its first three weeks than had occurred during the three months prior. In the year before the bombing, some 2,000 people were killed and several hundred thousand became refugees, according to NATO. Most of the victims were ethnic Albanians. According to US intelligence, the number of internally displaced was 250,000. The UN High Commissioner for Refugees reported a similar figure of 230,000. But after less than two weeks of bombing, the UNHCR reported that 350,000 refugees had fled Kosovo just since the start of the NATO campaign. By the time it stopped, the estimated number of refugees was 671,500.[97]

NATO Commanding General Wesley Clark afterward announced that it had been "entirely predictable" that the bombing would result in an escalation of violence on the ground.[98] "I can't say I'm surprised by any of this," Clark said of Serbian President Slobodan Milosevic's response to the bombing. "The military authorities fully anticipated the vicious approach that Milosevic would adopt, as well as the terrible efficiency with which he would carry it out." President Clinton similarly admitted, "We knew he would do this". The chairman of the House Intelligence Committee, Porter Goss, likewise acknowledged that US intelligence had predicted that ethnic cleansing would be a consequence of the bombing:

> Our intelligence community warned us months and days before this happened that we would have a virtual explosion of refugees over the 250,000 that was expected as of last year, that the Serb resolve would increase, that the conflict would spread, and that there would be ethnic cleansing. . . . One of the consequences surely would be that if you stick in this nest, you're going to stir it up more, and that was one of the things that might have happened and in fact that is one of the things that did happen because Milosevic did in fact, instead of caving in, he reacted by striking back harder against the Kosovars, harder, more quickly, more ruthlessly.

The intelligence community's predictions in this regard "were very accurate", Goss observed.

When asked whether it would have influenced the NATO campaign if they had known Milosevic would respond by implementing the systematic "cleansing" of ethnic Albanians from Kosovo, Wesley Clark candidly replied, "Well we knew that to be the case at the time. We were operating, however, under the instructions from the political leadership. It was not designed as a means of blocking Serb ethnic cleansing. It was not designed as a way of waging war against the Serb and mob forces in Kosovo in any way. There was never any intent to do that. That was not the idea."[99]

In addition to the predictable humanitarian disaster the bombing precipitated, some 500 civilians were also killed directly by NATO in its airstrikes.[100]

The result of the commission Goldstone was invited to co-chair was called The Kosovo Report. It concluded that the NATO bombing was in violation of international law because it was neither an act of self-defense against armed attack nor authorized by the UN Security Council (the only two conditions under international law in which the use of force is permissible). The Commission nevertheless argued that the bombing was justified as a "humanitarian" intervention despite having understatedly "failed to achieve its avowed aim of preventing massive ethnic cleansing." Thus was born the new Western doctrine of "illegal but justified" use of force in international affairs.[101]

The doctrine would subsequently be invoked to justify further US military interventions, such as the illegal war on Iraq launched in March 2003. For instance, Anne-Marie Slaughter, a professor of politics and international affairs at Princeton University and a former Director of Policy Planning for the US State Department (and a recipient of the department's Distinguished Service Award), wrote in the *New York Times* on March 18—the day before President Bush announced the war's commencement—that the US abandonment of "efforts to get United Nations approval" wasn't as bad as it looked because Bush had "started on a course that could be called 'illegal but legitimate'" and eventually could win UN acceptance, "though only after an invasion." So the war would violate international law, but that was fine, because the ends could justify the means; and, despite the global opposition to the war, it might gain international approval after the fact. The "relevant history" was "from Kosovo", Slaughter observed, asserting that the Kosovo doctrine would apply to Iraq, as well. She confidently declared that after invasion, US forces would "find irrefutable evidence that Saddam Hussein's regime possesses weapons of mass destruction". Her prophecy didn't come to pass. Iraq's alleged possession of weapons of mass destruction (WMD) was, of course, the proclaimed pretext for the war, despite the complete lack of credible evidence presented by the US government prior to the invasion to support its claims that Iraq still possessed WMD. The US later admitted that it had invaded Iraq on a false pretext, acknowledging that the UN had already successfully disarmed the country and that Iraq had unilaterally destroyed the remaining unaccounted-for stockpiles in 1991. Exuding slightly less confidence in the declared pretext, Slaughter added that even without finding proof of WMD post-invasion, the war on Iraq could still be justified if the Iraqi people welcomed US forces and the UN helped "to rebuild the country" after its destruction by the US—neither of which occurred to any significant extent, either. The US was "still playing by the rules", Slaughter concluded; it was just that, "depending on what we find in Iraq, the rules may have to evolve, so that what is legitimate is also legal."[102]

To take a more recent example of the application of the doctrine, which evolved into what is sometimes referred to as the "responsibility to protect" (often abbreviated "R2P"), it has also been applied to the NATO bombing of Libya. After an armed rebellion erupted in the country in February 2011 and the regime of Muammar al-Gaddafi responded with force to suppress the insurrection, the UN Security Council passed a resolution authorizing the use of force "to protect civilians and civilian populated areas". The US and its allies then violated the UN Charter by immediately exceeding the resolution's mandate and proclaiming their policy of regime change, which included openly arming and supplying the rebel forces.[103]

Naturally, the bombing campaign was sold to the public as a "humanitarian intervention". Just prior to the commencement of bombing, Obama declared that if the US did not intervene, "Many thousands could die. A humanitarian crisis would ensue. The entire region could be destabilized. . . ." All of which *did* end up occurring, but as a direct *consequence* of NATO's intervention.[104] Shortly after the bombing began, Obama defended his policy by saying that without intervention, the rebel stronghold of Benghazi "could suffer a massacre that would have reverberated across the region and stained the conscience of the world."[105] Secretary Clinton declared, "We have every reason to fear that, left unchecked, Gaddafi will commit unspeakable atrocities."[106]

However, as observed by Alan Kuperman, an associate professor at the University of Texas's Lyndon B. Johnson School of Public Affairs, Gaddafi "did not massacre civilians in any of the other big cities he captured—Zawiya, Mistrata, Ajdabiya—which together have a population of equal to Benghazi. Yes, civilians were killed in a typical, ham-handed, Third World counterinsurgency. But civilians were not targeted for massacre as in Rwanda, Darfur, Burundi, the Democratic Republic of Congo, Bosnia, or even Kosovo after NATO intervention." When *Chicago Tribune* editor Steve Chapman inquired with the White House about what hard evidence it was basing its claims of imminent genocide on, the Obama administration "declined to comment". This was "a surprising omission," Chapman observed, "given that a looming holocaust was the centerpiece of the president's case for war."[107] In an article based on testimony he had given to the Senate Committee on Foreign Relations, President of the Council on Foreign Relations Richard N. Haass similarly noted that "The evidence was not persuasive that a large-scale massacre or genocide was either likely or imminent."[108]

That it would serve to prolong the conflict was implicit in another of the principle arguments presented by proponents of the bombing. The consensus was that without intervention, the armed rebellion would likely have been crushed in a matter of weeks. Anne-Marie Slaughter wrote in the *New York Times* on March 13, before the bombing began, that the rebels were "ragged groups of brave volunteers who barely know how to use the weapons they have". Therefore, "action that will change the situation on the ground" was required. Arming the rebels was not enough; bombing was necessary. Otherwise it was "quite likely that Colonel Gaddafi will have retaken or at least besieged Benghazi" by the time arms arrived.[109] In *Foreign Affairs* on March 16, Robert E. Hunter argued in favor of intervention by writing that Gaddafi was "now closing in on a final campaign to defeat the rebels".[110] On March 18, a day after the UN Security Council passed a resolution authorizing a no-fly zone to protect civilians, the *New York Times* reported on how the Obama administration had pushed for intervention because Gaddafi's forces were "turning back the rebellion that threatened his rule". The administration's position "was forced largely" by "the crumbling of the uprising", which "raised the prospect that Gaddafi would remain in power".[111] Thus, it was perfectly well understood by the advocates of military intervention that it would not end, but *prolong* the violence. Far from being a "humanitarian" intervention, the resulting excess deaths would simply be an acceptable cost of Washington's regime change policy.

The bombing began on March 19, the anniversary of the invasion of Iraq in 2003. The goal of ensuring that the violence would not be cut short was fully realized. The *New York Times* observed that the rebel forces had been "battered and routed", but as soon as NATO bombs started dropping on Libya, the armed rebels "began to regroup".[112] Writing in *Foreign Affairs*, Professor Michael W. Doyle commented that "Gaddafi probably would have been able to conquer the rebel capital Benghazi with his air force, artillery, and armor, but the commencement of allied intervention will destroy the air force and protect the civilian population from large-scale ground attacks." (Note the euphemistic use of "civilian population". The true purpose of the bombing was, after all, to protect rebel forces, whereas civilians could be expected to die in increasing numbers as a result of deliberately prolonging the violence. Such intentional blurring of the distinction between civilians and armed rebels was standard at the time.)[113] The Commander of the United States Africa Command (AFRICOM), General Carter F. Ham, announced at the end of the month that while the Gaddafi regime had vast military superiority over the rebels and "possesses the capability to roll them back very quickly", the bombing campaign was "the major reason that has not happened."[114]

The consequences were predicted. Stewart Patrick, for instance, writing in *Foreign Affairs* less than a week after the bombing started, accurately foresaw that "The conflict could settle into a bloody, inconclusive stalemate" and "victorious rebel forces could launch their own round of score-settling."[115] It is difficult to know how many people were killed in the conflict. Prior to the bombing, estimates of the numbers killed by Gaddafi's forces in the thousands were offered by opposition sources and parroted widely in Western media, but unverifiable. Human Rights Watch provided a conservative number of about 300 confirmed deaths since the rebellion began towards the end of February.[116] One month after the bombing started, the opposition claimed that the death toll had risen to 10,000.[117] By the end of April, the US State Department estimated that as many as 30,000 had been killed in the escalating violence.[118] By the end of August, the opposition claimed the death toll was as high as 50,000.[119] By mid-September, according to Amnesty International, tens of thousands of civilians had been made refugees and over 672,000 foreign nationals had fled the country; 4,500 Libyans had fled to Egypt, and another 187,000 to Tunisia.[120]

There were atrocities by both sides. The UNHCR reported in August that rebel forces were targeting sub-Saharan Africans.[121] The Western-backed rebel forces, whose ranks included members of Al-Qaeda, engaged in massacres, executing Gaddafi loyalists and black Africans.[122] The rebels ethnically cleansed entire towns, such as Tawargha, where the residents were mostly black. Rebels "forced the entire population of some 30,000 to flee and looted, vandalized and burned down their homes and properties", Amnesty International noted in a later report.[123] In October, Gaddafi was captured and executed by the rebels.[124] The ICRC reported that mass graves were being uncovered. Toward the end of the month, what the *New York Times* described as "one of the worst massacres of the eight-month conflict" was discovered in Sirte, where, according to Human Rights Watch, fifty-three Gaddafi supporters had been executed by rebel forces.[125]

By the time the NATO bombing campaign ended, 17,939 sorties had been flown. A UN inquiry into the conflict found that NATO airstrikes killed civilians and damaged civilian infrastructure. Of the twenty airstrikes it investigated, the UN documented the deaths of sixty civilians, as well as fifty-five injuries. In two of the airstrikes where civilian infrastructure was damaged, "no military target could be identified." The worst case uncovered was in the town of Majer, where on August 8, "NATO bombs killed 34 civilians and injured 38. After the initial airstrike killed 16, a group of rescuers arrived and were hit by a subsequent attack, killing 18." The UN inquiry concluded that "NATO's characterization of four of five targets where the Commission found civilian casualties as 'command and control nodes' or 'troop staging areas' is not reflected in evidence at the scene and witness testimony."[126] A *New York Times* investigation involving visits to more than twenty-five strike locations revealed that scores of civilians had been killed by NATO bombings, despite denials. A Human Rights Watch report said that at least seventy-two civilians had been confirmed killed in NATO airstrikes, one-third of them children.[127]

According to the UN, following the toppling of the Gaddafi regime, the rebels continued to hold some 7,000 people prisoner. Amnesty International reported that there was "widespread torture" and prisoner deaths at locations across Libya.[128] A year after the rebellion began, Amnesty reported that the Western-backed militias were "out of control" and committing "widespread human rights abuses with impunity", including arbitrary detentions, torture, revenge attacks, and forcible displacement.[129] The transitional government held its first elections in July 2012, in a vote that was made more difficult, the *New York Times* noted, due to the "prevailing lawlessness".[130] Frederic Wehrey noted in *Foreign Affairs* that the election resulted in "an Islamist landslide" and warned of the danger that "armed militias could destabilize the state" as "low level violence" continued in the west and south of the country.[131] A researcher for the Libyan Observatory for Human Rights who had opposed the Gaddafi regime and had been imprisoned numerous times under his rule told the press that "The human rights situation in Libya now is far worse than under the late dictator Muammar Gaddafi".[132]

It was not all despair, however. There was the occasional positive news coming out of Libya. "Western Companies See Prospects for Business in Libya", read one headline in the *New York Times* in October. The article reported,

> The guns in Libya have barely quieted. . . . But a new invasion force is already plotting its own landing on the shores of Tripoli. Western security, construction and infrastructure companies that see profit-making opportunities receding in Iraq and Afghanistan have turned their sights on Libya, now free of four decades of dictatorship. Entrepreneurs are abuzz about the business potential of a country with huge needs and the oil to pay for them, plus the competitive advantage of Libyan gratitude toward the United States and its NATO partners.

The "Libyan gratitude", of course, referred not to the general public, but to the country's new leadership, the Transitional National Council, who met with delegations from Western companies. The article noted how the British defense minister, Philip Hammond, had "urged British companies to 'pack their suitcases' and head to Tripoli." The US might also "benefit from the Libyan authorities' appreciation of NATO's critical air support for the revolution", the *Times* added, and "Western companies hope to have some advantage over, say, China, which was offering to sell arms to Colonel Gaddafi as recently as July."[133]

The hopes of Western corporations of a rapid stabilization of the situation and return to business-as-usual were undoubtedly dampened as lawlessness continued to reign in Libya and the entire region was destabilized. The British security service, MI5, warned that Libya now offered "a permissive environment for Al-Qaeda", which had established the country as a base of operations—as also predicted.[134] Chaos and lawlessness reigned in Libya as rival militias claimed authority in areas across the country. Mali was destabilized as thousands of fighters fled there and the country was flooded with arms.[135] Ross Douthat commented in a *New York Times* column that "Mali today looks a bit like Libya did in early 2011, except with a more obvious jihadi presence", which was "only one example of the spillover from Colonel Gaddafi's ouster".[136] Yahia H. Zoubir in *Foreign Affairs* wrote about how Libya's neighbors feared that the conflict "would pry the lid off Tripoli's sizeable weapons cache and lead to the dispersal of arms across the region. It turns out that they were right to be worried." A "weapons bonanza" had resulted from the conflict, as well as "disappearing money, and a wave of refugees". With newly acquired arms, jihadist groups were also destabilizing Algeria. The fallout in Mali led to hundreds of thousands more refugees fleeing that country. This placed "a heavy burden on countries that can barely sustain their own populations, which are suffering from drought and hunger." It was "doubtful", Zoubir concluded, "that NATO's celebrated 'successful operation' will bring prosperity to the new Libya and stability to the region."[137]

Comparisons to Kosovo were customary, and warranted—just not necessarily in the manner intended. John Mueller wrote in *Foreign Affairs* shortly after the bombing commenced that the campaign seemed to be "following the pattern" of Kosovo, including how "the bombing buoyed domestic support for the previously unpopular demon-in-charge", who did not capitulate as intended, so "the campaign had to be continued for months." Another consequence of the bombing of Kosovo "was a monumental refugee crisis for which the administration and the world were utterly unprepared—something that may be in progress in Libya."[138] Michael O'Hanlon, in another *Foreign Affairs* piece supportive of the intervention in Libya, reminded that the NATO bombing in Kosovo "is considered a success," even though "it was initially disastrous in its net effect on the population".[139]

The "illegal but legitimate" doctrine was invoked. Writing in *Foreign Policy*, Eric A. Posner pointed out that the US-led bombing campaign in Libya violated international law, which presented a "conundrum". It was another application of the "illegal but legitimate" doctrine, "a near contradiction which comes close to saying that governments should disregard law when they have, or think they have, legitimate moral or political aims. But given that governments always believe that their aims are legitimate," Posner reasonably wondered, "what force can law possibly have when it comes to arms?"[140]

Michael W. Doyle, in his aforementioned *Foreign Affairs* piece, also acknowledged that NATO's bombing had greatly exceeded the UN mandate, which authorized a no-fly zone to protect civilians, "not the ouster of Gaddafi that US President Barack Obama has called for and which is most likely to resolve the crisis politically." This presented "questions" about the legality and "ethical legitimacy" of NATO's actions because "when foreigners seek to liberate a country whose people have been unable to liberate themselves, they often fall into one or more of three traps." The first trap was an eruption of "civil strife" following "the liberating invasion." The second was a new regime that was unpopular with its own people and thus only able to "remain in power thanks to ongoing foreign support", which "renders the country a client state rather than a free nation." The third was "when the leadership learns that it can only govern as the previous dictator did—by force." Doyle argued that "Foreign states must sometimes override or disregard these traps"—all merely accidental outcomes, of course—when so "liberating" nations. In other words, the West must sometimes resort to the unlawful use of force regardless of the predictable disastrous consequences for the very people they ostensibly wished to "liberate", as in Kosovo, Iraq, and Libya. In the latter case, the US intervention "may simply set the stage for a prolonged and costly civil war." The NATO bombing "strains against the letter of the UN Charter law", and its "ethical and legal justifications" were "murky", but the "illegal but legitimate" doctrine nevertheless applied. The fact that the policy of regime change had been carried out under the cover of a UN resolution had encouragingly "narrowed the divide between legitimacy and legality."[141]

Such was the nature of the discussion among the American intelligentsia. Such is the role of the US in world affairs.

'An Evil, Evil Man'

While they could not credibly resort to the usual charge of "anti-Semitism" in response to criticisms of Israel's actions, defenders of its war crimes spared no effort in attacking Richard Goldstone's character and attempting to discredit the UN report. Prominent among them was Harvard law professor Alan Dershowitz, who went so far as to call Goldstone a traitor to the Jewish people and to describe the report as "a defamation written by an evil, evil man."[142]

Dershowitz went to great lengths to try to prove his case in a paper published on the Harvard University website titled "The Case Against the Goldstone Report: A Study in Evidentiary Bias". (A summary of his central accusations therein was later published in the *Jerusalem Post*.[143]) An examination of this paper, considered by Harvard to be a "scholarly article", illustrates just how impossible it was proving for Israel's defenders to substantively challenge the report's central findings. Dershowitz's own difficulty in this regard could be gleaned just from the paper's introduction, where he began with a series of ad hominem arguments. He attacked Goldstone as "biased" without even attempting to substantiate the charge. He dismissed the report itself as "a shoddy piece of work, unworthy of serious consideration by people of good will, committed to the truth." Among his complaints was that it was "poorly written" with "overall poor craftsmanship".[144]

Dershowitz rejected the report's conclusion that a primary purpose of Operation Cast Lead was to punish the civilian population and insisted that Israel's goal was to stop Hamas's rocket attacks. In order to sustain this assertion, he naturally made no mention anywhere in his forty-nine-page paper of the fact that it was Israel that violated the ceasefire and refused Hamas's offer to renew it, etc. Rather than addressing the substance of the report, Dershowitz from the start created a strawman argument that served as the foundation for his entire paper. He lied that the report concluded that Israel's primary purpose "was to target innocent Palestinian civilians—children, women, the elderly—for death". He repeated this falsehood throughout his paper: "the report accuses the Jewish state of having implemented a policy in Gaza that borders on genocide"; "its real purpose: namely the killing of Palestinian civilians"; "a carefully planned and executed policy of deliberately targeting innocent civilians for mass murder"; "a governmental policy of deliberately maximizing civilian deaths"; "the explicit policy of the IDF to target Palestinian civilians and to maximize civilian deaths", etc. He proclaimed that "the report presents no hard evidence to support its serious accusations of a governmental policy of deliberately maximizing civilian deaths". Focusing his energy on arguing this strawman allowed him to attack the report in an attempt to discredit it while avoiding altogether the need to address the report's *actual* conclusions.[145]

To support his lies about the report, Dershowitz willfully and deliberately quoted portions of it out of context. For instance, he wrote that "The report found these serious charges 'to be firmly based in fact' and had 'no doubt' of their truth."[146] Neither of these two quotes from the report, however, was in reference to a conclusion that Israel set out to deliberately kill as many civilians as possible. The first quote rather referred to the finding that "the operations were in furtherance of an overall policy aimed at *punishing* the Gaza population for its resilience and for its apparent support for Hamas, and possibly with the intent of forcing a change in such support" (emphasis added). The second came from a sentence noting that the Mission was left with "no doubt that responsibility lies in the first place with those who designed, planned, ordered and oversaw the operations"—hardly a controversial finding.[147]

Self-conscious that he was employing a strawman fallacy, Dershowitz went out of his way to assure readers: "Lest there be any doubt that this is the accusation being made, read the words of the report itself." (Underlined emphasis in all instances is Dershowitz's.) He proceeded to quote the report's finding that, "While the Israeli Government has sought to portray its operations as essentially a response to rocket attacks in the exercise of its right to self-defense, the Mission considers the plan to have been directed, at least in part, at a different target: the people of Gaza as a whole."[148] This supposed proof of Dershowitz's, if one bothers to take his advice and actually read *all* the words of the report *in context*, reveals the full extent of his intellectual dishonesty. The very next sentence in the report—omitted by Dershowitz for the obvious reason—was the finding noted above that it was Israel's intent to *punish* the civilian population, *not* to commit mass killing on a genocidal scale. The very next page of the report reiterated that Israel's operation "was a deliberately disproportionate attack designed to *punish, humiliate* and *terrorize* a civilian population" (emphasis added).[149]

This conclusion was one Dershowitz didn't trouble himself to challenge. He argued, "If Israel's intention was truly to kill civilians, why was the combatant to civilian casualty ratio only one to less than two? Certainly if one of the world's most advanced military forces intended to kill civilians it could have made that ratio one to five or even one to ten." In other words, the fact that "only" "1.885" Palestinian civilians were killed for every combatant, "even according to one of the most biased and skewed sources available" (by which he meant the Palestinian Center for Human Rights), proved that Israel didn't set out to commit genocide, since civilians would have accounted for an even greater proportion had that been the case.[150] Of course, the fact that nearly twice as many civilians were killed as combatants would very much suggest a disproportionate use of force intended to *punish* and *terrorize* the population. The reason Dershowitz found it necessary to resort to strawman argumentation in his effort to debunk the report becomes painfully obvious.

In another enlightening example, he wrote (italicized emphasis added):

> The report's final argument, made implicitly at various points in the document, goes something like this: Israel deliberately targeted non-human civilian targets, such as a flour mill and a wastewater plant; this proves that the IDF wanted to punish civilians who relied on these facilities; *it follows therefore that the IDF deliberately intended to hit human civilian targets and kill as many civilians as possible.* . . . But even if it were true that Israel sought to punish the civilian population of Gaza by attacking food and sewage facilities, it would not follow that Israel intended to kill civilians. . . . Just as American sanctions against Iran would cause the Iranian "people [to] suffer," so too do Israeli sanctions. But it is a far cry from sanctions to murder, and it is a non-sequitur to argue that the destructions of non-human civilian targets proves an intention to target human beings for death.[151]

Notice that everything up to the emphasized clause is accurate, but by falsely attributing a logical fallacy of his own invention to the UN Fact-Finding Mission, Dershowitz avoided having to substantively address the report's *actual* findings, including that Israel deliberately targeted the civilian infrastructure—which he tacitly acknowledged—and that this was done *to punish the population*—which he allowed might also be true.

A further illustration of Dershowitz's intellectual bankruptcy (emphasis added):

> Reasonable people may disagree as to whether the deaths that resulted from Israel's military objects were proportional or disproportional to risks its civilians feared from Hamas rockets. Reasonable people could also disagree about whether Israel's policy of destroying Hamas buildings, tunnels and industry should be permissible under international law. *But that is not the essence of what the report accuses Israel of deliberately planning—namely the deliberate targeting and killing of hundreds of innocent Palestinian women and children.*[152]

Dershowitz thus acknowledged that the report's *actual* conclusions, that Israel engaged in a disproportionate use of force and that its destruction of the civilian infrastructure was a war crime, were indeed *reasonable*. Once again, the reason he felt it necessary to employ strawman argumentation is palpable. Such dishonesty was the essence of Dershowitz's "scholarly" paper.

In yet another example, he falsely claimed that "the Goldstone Report takes the alleged instances of Israeli soldiers intentionally targeting civilians and claims it was the *policy* of Israel to intentionally target civilians". Again we see that employing his strawman allowed him to deny that this was a matter of policy without actually addressing the report's conclusion that there were clear instances in which IDF forces intentionally targeted civilians.[153]

Elsewhere, Dershowitz inadvertently confirmed conclusions of the Goldstone Report. He acknowledged, for instance, that Israel's "Dahiya Doctrine" was implemented in Operation Cast Lead. He admitted that it was a policy consisting of the deliberate use of "disproportionate force". But he claimed this policy was solely "intended to destroy infrastructure" and "says nothing about specifically targeting civilians for death". Of course, the admitted fact that Israel deliberately engaged in disproportionate force with the intent of destroying civilian infrastructure said a great deal indeed about the validity of the report's conclusion that Israel's purpose was to *punish* the civilian population.

He insisted that the numerous quotes in the report from Israeli officials declaring their intent to use disproportionate force only referred to destroying infrastructure and killing members of Hamas. "Ordinary people, civilians, are not mentioned" in the quotes, Dershowitz lied. "Their exclusion is significant. Yet the report misused this doctrine and these quotes to try to prove that the object of Operation Cast Lead was the killing of civilians."[154]

In truth, what the report rightly used these quotes to prove was that Israel's policy was one of deliberate use of disproportionate force to punish the civilian population—a fact that, as just noted, Dershowitz admitted. As for his claim that civilians were not mentioned in the quotes, firstly, this is a perfectly meaningless observation since disproportionate force by definition includes any use of force that puts civilians at risk of death or injury in a manner disproportionate to any military objective. Secondly, Dershowitz was not merely making a disingenuous argument; he was lying outright. There was in fact explicit mention of civilians accompanying the Israeli declarations of intent to punish them. For example, Retired Major General Giora Eiland, who was also a former head of Israel's National Security Council, was quoted as saying that one of Israel's goals, in addition to "the destruction of the national infrastructure", was to create "intense suffering among the population" and cause "the suffering of hundreds of thousands of people".[155]

"The report itself admits that it does not know 'whether Israeli military officials were directly influenced by these writings'", Dershowitz continued. "But it reaches the conclusion that 'What [sic] is prescribed as the best strategy appears to have been precisely what was put into practice.' Yes! The destruction of <u>physical</u> infrastructure. Not the targeting of civilians."[156] Examining the full paragraph of the report from which Dershowitz was selectively and inaccurately quoting, one finds (portions he omitted emphasized): "*The Mission does not have to consider* whether Israeli military officials were directly influenced by these writings. *It is able to conclude from a review of the facts on the ground that it witnessed for itself that* what is prescribed as the best strategy appears to have been precisely what was put into practice."[157] But even more significant than the dishonest means by which he attempted to discredit the report was his enthusiastic acknowledgment that the Mission's actual conclusion was indeed valid. Were the quotes from Israeli officials evidence of Israel's intent to commit war crimes by engaging in the deliberate and systematic destruction of civilian infrastructure in Gaza? "Yes!"

His argument descended from there even further into absurdity. He made completely nonsensical statements such as that Israel's proclaimed intent to use "disproportionate" force "does not constitute an admission that <u>unlawfully</u> disproportionate force would be employed under the standards of international law". Of course, outside of the rabbit hole the Harvard law professor had dug for himself, disproportionate force was *by definition* a war crime.

As the ICRC points out, "The principle of proportionality in attack is codified in Article 51(5)(b) of Additional Protocol I, and repeated in Article 57."[158] As a reminder, that clause prohibits any attack "which may be expected to cause incidental loss of civilian life, injury to civilians, damage to civilian objects, or a combination thereof, which would be excessive in relation to the concrete and direct military advantage anticipated." Again, disproportionate force is included within the definition of "indiscriminate attacks", all of which are war crimes. Drawing on Article 51 of Additional Protocol I, the Rome Statute of the International Criminal Court defines as "war crimes" grave breaches of the Geneva Conventions, including "Extensive destruction and appropriation of property, not justified by military necessity and carried out unlawfully and wantonly". Other serious violations of international law include: "Intentionally directing attacks against civilian objects, that is, objects which are not military objectives"; "Intentionally launching an attack in the knowledge that such attack will cause incidental loss of life or injury to civilians or damage to civilian objects . . . which would clearly be excessive in relation to the concrete and direct overall military advantage anticipated"; "Attacking or bombarding, by whatever means, towns, villages, dwellings or buildings which are undefended and which are not military objectives".[159]

Dershowitz himself correctly explained that "the harm collaterally inflicted on civilians must not be disproportionate to the military objective". But he nevertheless attempted to deny that the quotes from Israeli officials showed unlawful intent with the gibberish argument that "there is no prohibition against using overwhelming—that is disproportionate—military force against a legitimate military object." His use of the word "disproportionate" here was, of course, meaningless and irrelevant. One may stipulate that there is no prohibition of "overwhelming" force against military targets. Yet it remains true that, under international law, *disproportionate* attacks are by definition *not* limited to military objects and constitute war crimes.[160]

Dershowitz himself referred to the statement from Major General Gadi Eisenkot that "in every village from which Israel is fired on", Israel would "apply disproportionate force on it and cause great damage and destruction there. From our standpoint, these are not civilian villages, they are military bases." So, to further his argument, Dershowitz simply adopted Israel's own standard of redefining *entire villages* as "a legitimate military object". We observe further that, setting aside the Orwellian redefinition and considering what international law actually has to say about it, the kinds of attacks that Dershowitz *admitted* Israel carried out *with intent* were indistinguishable from "war crimes".

For a forty-nine-page paper purporting to debunk the Goldstone Report, Dershowitz included astonishingly few references to the specific incidents in which the UN Mission concluded that Israel had committed war crimes. In the few instances where Dershowitz did actually cite such incidents, he contented himself with simply parroting Israel's position. He mentioned the case of the Abd Rabbo family, for example. He naturally didn't bother to explain the details—that the grandmother and three daughters were shot while carrying a white flag—but simply referred to the "incident" and the Mission's finding that "the Israeli armed forces were not engaged in combat or fearing an attack at the time of the incident." He rejected this finding by citing a *Time* magazine article in which the reporter relayed that most residents insisted "there were no Hamas fighters in the area at the time". One resident farmer, however, took him aside "and said, in a near whisper, that Hamas had been firing rockets from the vicinity where the episode took place." Dershowitz didn't relay the first sentence of that same paragraph in the *Time* article, which said, "Whether the Israeli troops believed they were under threat when they opened fire is unclear."[161]

Just taking the *Time* report on its face, even if it was true that Hamas had fired rockets *where* the incident took place, did the farmer mean that they were firing rockets *when* it happened? It seems that the reporter misinterpreted and that the farmer was referring to an earlier time. While it may have been unclear at the time to the reporter whether the Israeli forces felt under threat, any ambiguities were dispelled by investigations into the incident from not only the UN Mission, but also Amnesty International and Human Rights Watch.

The father, Khaled Abd Rabbo, told Amnesty that Israeli forces had moved into the area around his home on January 3. Four days later, the Israeli forces called through a megaphone in Arabic to order everyone to leave their homes. A tank was parked ten meters from their door, with two other tanks nearby. Two soldiers were standing in their garden "eating chips and chocolate". The family stood there for a while, waiting to be told what to do, when a soldier emerged from the top of the nearest tank, took aim at them, and opened fire. Khaled's mother told Amnesty the same story.[162]

Other residents likewise told Human Rights Watch that Israeli forces had been in control of the area since January 3, the day Israel launched its ground operation. Initially, Palestinian militants engaged the IDF, but "quickly retreated to the west as Israeli armor approached together with air support." Fighting continued in the area over the following days, but was "concentrated a few hundred meters to the west" of the Abd Rabbo home. Seven neighborhood residents told Human Rights Watch "that major fighting in the area had stopped by the morning of January 7", when the family emerged from their home on the instruction of a soldier calling for them to do so through a megaphone. Waving white flags, they awaited further instructions. After several minutes, a soldier opened fire on them. The nine-year-old, Souad, was killed instantly. The grandmother described how the three-year-old girl, Amal, "was hit in the chest and abdomen and her intestines came out." She was taken inside, but died there "because the ambulance could not come." Samar lived, but was paralyzed. (Human Rights Watch also documented three cases in which the IDF detained male residents of the neighborhood and used them as human shields to search Palestinian homes.)[163]

Witnesses also told the UN Mission about the Israeli soldiers eating a snack at the time, including one who specifically said they were eating chips and chocolate.[164] The *Time* article cited by Dershowitz, incidentally, also quoted one witness as saying, "Two Israeli soldiers were beside their tank, eating chocolate and potato chips".[165] This would seem very odd behavior indeed for Israeli soldiers under threat from nearby combatants. Moreover, Israel itself had never claimed that Hamas was firing from the vicinity at the time of the attack or otherwise that the Abd Rabbo family was attacked mistakenly in the "fog of war".

The evidence is rather clear that an Israeli soldier intentionally fired directly at the family.[166]

In reply to the UN Mission's request that Israel cooperate with its investigations, Israel's UN ambassador, Aharon Leshno Yaar, stated in a letter, "Reports that the members of the Mission were accompanied at every stage of their visit to Gaza by Hamas officials gives serious reason to doubt that any true picture of the situation in Gaza . . . can possibly emerge." Goldstone replied to this charge by writing that such reports were untruthful and categorically denying "the allegation that Hamas officials accompanied Members of the Fact Finding Mission at all, let alone 'at every stage of their visit to Gaza.'" This exchange of letters was included in an appendix of the Goldstone Report.[167] Dershowitz charged that Goldstone "lied about the role Hamas played in escorting and presenting evidence to the Mission." After quoting the relevant portion from Goldstone's reply letter, Dershowitz asserted, "The actual truth is quite different." To support this, he cited a news report alleging that "Hamas security often accompanied his team during their five-day trip to Gaza". How did Dershowitz rule out the hardly farfetched possibility that the news report was indeed simply parroting misinformation, as Goldstone credibly contended? He didn't, of course, but that was no obstacle for him to draw the desired conclusion.[168]

Dershowitz elsewhere in his paper seemed to borrow from the US House of Representatives' resolution denouncing the Goldstone Report. But whereas that resolution had taken out of context Goldstone's remark, "If this was a court of law, there would have been nothing proven", Dershowitz took the distortion a step further by lying that "Goldstone has himself acknowledged that there is no actual 'evidence' that the report's conclusions are correct".[169]

He also parroted the House resolution's criticism that the Mission "deliberately chose to ignore" the "expert testimony" of Richard Kemp. He quoted Goldstone's remark about how the Mission "did not deal with the issues he raised" concerning problems arising from "the fog of war". Then he declared, "That is a willful lie. The report dealt specifically with precisely that issue." Of course, it was Dershowitz who was willfully lying, deliberately choosing to ignore the very next sentence of Goldstone's e-mail, in which he explained that the Mission "avoided having to do so" in the incidents of direct attacks on civilians that it decided to investigate since in each case there was no possible military objective.[170]

Dershowitz falsely attributed to the Mission the logic that "because the IDF uses such advanced weaponry, whenever civilians were killed, they must have been killed intentionally". He criticized that its report "paints the IDF as a military force that, unlike any other military force in the world, simply does not commit errors." In fact, it was not the UN Mission that painted this image of the IDF. Rather, the Mission had merely observed that Israel itself had in only one instance attributed the deaths of civilians to "error".

This was abundantly clear from Dershowitz's own supporting example, where he took issue with the Mission's statement that Israel's January 6 attack on the Daya family's home in Zeytoun "appears to be the only incident that has elicited admission of error by the Israeli authorities". This statement was "not made in good faith", he argued, because "the Israeli government claims that an attack on an oxygen truck that killed four civilians and four Hamas militants was a mistake of fact error. The IDF erroneously believed the oxygen canisters to be rockets and targeted the truck for destruction."[171] So his charge of bad faith on the part of the UN Mission boiled down to Israel having attributed not one but *two* incidents involving civilian deaths to "error".

Moreover, the fact that it was Dershowitz who was arguing in bad faith is evident in the fact that the Mission *did* discuss the incident with the truck and *explicitly clarified* why it was considered different in this regard from the attack on the Daya home. Israel in its own self-investigatory reports had admitted that, "In fact, the truck was carrying oxygen tanks and not rockets." Yet Israel *defended the attack as reasonable* because of the truck's alleged "proximity to terrorist sites used for rocket launches". And with that, Israel dismissed the incident and said there were "no grounds to open a criminal inquiry".[172] The UN Mission observed that Israel's comments about the attack on the truck were "somewhat more equivocal" than its explanation for the attack on the Daya home. Israel had not attributed the civilian deaths to its "error" of mistaking oxygen tanks for rockets, but rather to the location of the truck. In the case of the Daya home, Israel described the attack as a "mistake". In the case of the truck, what Israel described as an "error" was *not* the attack itself, which it rather attempted to justify.[173]

Unable to come up with any other examples where Israel had admitted that it killed Palestinian civilians in error, Dershowitz irrelevantly added, "Four out of the nine IDF deaths were caused by friendly fire. Of course these deaths were errors. Surely there were many more errors, as there always are in war." Then he nonsensically remarked, "To assume that all deaths caused by errors were, in fact, deliberate, begs the critical question and reflects the bias of the report."[174] The Mission had made no such assumptions, and it was, of course, Dershowitz who was again begging the question by treating as axiomatic that "all deaths" were "caused by errors". One can hardly fault the Mission for observing that in only one case did the government of Israel itself attribute civilian deaths to an attack it judged to be a "mistake", or for understanding this to mean that Israel "does not consider the other strikes brought to its attention to be the result of similar or other errors."[175]

Dershowitz repeatedly parroted Israel's own untenable positions throughout his paper as though fact, such as proclaiming that the Gaza police not engaging in hostilities were legitimate military targets. "It is sad that so many innocents died during the Gaza war," he wrote, "but numbers alone do not prove that

Israel intended to kill civilians, especially in light of how Hamas used civilians as shields." He decried the Mission's "half-hearted findings" in this regard and argued that its bias was indicated in its choice of language. "The Mission only 'believes' that there are 'indications' of firing from urban areas", he wrote. "It only 'suffices to say' that 'in some cases' there 'was evidence.'" Following these selected partial quotations, he continued at great length to argue that Hamas fired from urban areas.[176] He need not have troubled himself so much, as Hamas's firing of rockets from urban areas was in fact regarded by the Mission as uncontroversial. As stated in the Goldstone Report, "The Mission finds that the presence of Palestinian armed fighters in urban residential areas during the military operations is established."[177]

He took issue with the Mission describing as a "possibility" that combatants had fired from nearby the UN school in Jabaliya, rather than accepting it as hard fact. He cited three news reports of witnesses saying there was rocket fire from nearby the school. "Although two of these three sources are cited in the report," he argued, "little credence is granted to them because, according to the interviews the Mission conducted, 'No witness stated that he had heard any firing prior to the Israeli armed forces' mortars landing.'"[178] Dershowitz declined to provide the very next sentence from the Goldstone Report, which continued, "*On the other hand*, the Mission is aware of at least two reports that indicate local residents had heard such fire in the area" (emphasis added).[179] We thus see that, contrary to Dershowitz's accusation that the Mission simply dismissed them, it was in fact entirely on the basis of those two reports—both of which cited anonymous witnesses—that the Mission concluded that, despite the unanimous testimony to the contrary from its own interviews, it was possible that militants had fired from the vicinity. Even more instructive than Dershowitz so deceitfully quoting the report out of context was the fact that he declined to address the Mission's main findings with regard to the attack on the UN school in Jabaliya: the IDF's repeated claim that the alleged firing had come from within the school compound and its claim that two "senior Hamas militants" responsible for the alleged rocket fire were killed in the attack were both categorically *false*.

"Unsurprisingly," Dershowitz complained further, "the report does not address Hamas' clear pattern of using schools to launch attacks. It makes a single mention of a rocket fired from a school."[180] In the mention he was referring to, the Mission was citing Amnesty International, which interviewed residents who said they witnessed militants firing a rocket from a school, but "at a time when the schools were closed." The Amnesty report had also said "that it had seen no evidence that rockets had been launched from residential houses or buildings *while civilians were still in them*" (emphasis added).[181] Dershowitz offered no evidence to the contrary in support of his assertion that there was a "clear pattern" of Hamas using civilians as human shields by firing from schools.

Dershowitz further charged that the report "ignores evidence that hospitals *may* have been used for military purposes" (emphasis added). He thus tacitly acknowledged that there was no proof that hospitals were used by Hamas for military purposes. What evidence did the Mission ignore, according to Dershowitz? "The Mission," he wrote, "even though it is in possession of a Newsweek article suggesting otherwise, does not make factual findings whether there were militants operating in the vicinity of the Al-Quds Hospital when it was attacked by Israeli forces."[182] He was referring to the *Newsweek* article cited by Israel in its attempt to justify attacking the hospital. Of course, the Mission didn't *need* to make any factual findings about whether militants were operating "in the vicinity of" the hospital, only whether they were operating from the hospital grounds itself, since it was apparent that the hospital itself had been "the object of a direct attack by the Israeli armed forces"—and Israel did not claim that the hospital had been hit in error.[183]

Beyond that, he attempted to characterize as sinister the fact that the Mission did not investigate Israel's claim that the Al-Shifa Hospital was used by Hamas as a military base of operations, asking why it would "avoid" investigating "one of Israel's most serious allegations". How he judged that this was among the "most serious" of Israel's claims when it was virtually obligatory for Israel to claim that any civilian objects struck were targeted because Hamas was operating there is something he made no attempt to elucidate. It was enough for him to attribute this to some malevolent intent to willfully ignore evidence, rather than accepting that the Mission couldn't possibly investigate every single such allegation made by Israel—or that it was unnecessary to do so in light of Israel's failure to present evidence to support them in the first place.

Dershowitz further criticized the report for concluding that, if there were any incidents of militants using ambulances during their operations, it was "the exception, not the rule." He ended this section of his paper by noting that the report cited "an article in which an ambulance driver says militants 'ordered me to get them out, to put them in the ambulance and take them away. . . . And then one of the fighters picked up a gun and held it to my head, to force me.'"[184] He offered no further comment, apparently figuring that this would suffice to prove that the Mission was being willfully dishonest in its conclusion. That it was yet again Dershowitz who was being dishonest becomes apparent by turning to the actual context in the Goldstone Report. After relaying this incident of the attempted hijacking of an ambulance, the Mission observed that the same news article

> also describes how the PRCS ambulance teams managed to avert this misuse of ambulances. According to this report, relied on by the Israeli Government, the attempts of Palestinian combatants to exploit ambulances as shield for military opera-

tions were not successful in the face of courageous resistance of the PRCS staff members. This is consistent with the statements of representatives of the Palestinian Red Crescent Society in Gaza who, in interviews with the Mission, denied that their ambulances were used at any time by Palestinian combatants. Finally, in a submission to the Mission, Magen David Adom [Israel's national emergency medical service, a member of the International Federation of Red Cross and Red Crescent Societies] stated that "there was no use of PRCS ambulances for the transport of weapons or ammunition . . . (and) there was no misuse of the emblem by PRCS."[185]

Dershowitz similarly accused the Mission of "willful blindness" for investigating "only one instance in which the Israelis alleged mosques were used for military purposes. Had they been interested in the truth, surely the Mission would have performed more investigations."[186] Unsurprisingly, Dershowitz commented no further on that one incident, which was Israel's attack on the Ibrahim al-Maqadmah mosque, a case in which Israel had *not* argued that the mosque was being used for military purposes, but simply denied that any such attack occurred while contradictorily and falsely claiming that those killed in the attack were not civilians. (As we will come to, Israel later admitted to attacking the mosque.) The Mission explained that while it was "not able to investigate the allegation of the use of mosques generally by Palestinian groups for storing weapons", there was in this particular case "no evidence that this mosque was used for the storage of weapons or any military activity by Palestinian armed groups."[187] Had he been interested in the truth, surely Dershowitz would have at least briefly mentioned the facts about the one case that the Mission *did* investigate.

As "hard evidence" that Hamas fighters stored weapons in mosques, Dershowitz cited US media reports written by journalists who weren't even *in* Gaza—two filed their reports from Jerusalem and the third from Sderot. Both journalists were simply following the customary procedure of uncritically parroting the unsubstantiated claims made by government officials.[188] The rest of his "hard evidence" consisted of claims from the IDF that could not be independently verified. The potentially most damning example he presented was a video showing a rocket being fired from just outside a mosque in Gaza on January 7, 2009, *according to the IDF*.

He cited a second video showing what Israel *claimed* were "secondary explosions" from weapons stored inside a mosque it attacked on December 31, 2008. However, in the video, the aerial view of the mosque was obscured by cloud cover, and there may just as well have been additional bombs dropped on it.

A third video he cited was the same one discussed previously, in which a second bomb can be seen dropping on the mosque and causing the secondary explosion that Israel *falsely claimed* was from weapons stored inside.

The fourth was a video of Israeli soldiers *claiming* they were fired on from a mosque. The video and accompanying photographs *claimed* to show weapons inside a mosque, such as an anti-aircraft gun stored in a dimly lit stairwell and rockets in a dark room with concrete walls, but with nothing to indicate that the location where the video was shot was actually even a mosque in Gaza.

Fifth, he cited a report showing photographs of a single AK-47 and ammunition laid out on the floor of a mosque near a pulpit where the IDF *claimed* the weapon had been found.

His sixth piece of evidence was an aerial photograph showing a mosque where the IDF *claimed* there was a rocket-launching site nearby.

His seventh was another photograph, taken from a much higher altitude (such that buildings are tiny and roads thin lines) and marked with labels and variously colored triangle symbols shown in the key as "Bunker", "Hidden Position", "Rigged Explosives", etc.—images amusingly reminiscent of the satellite images that Secretary of State Colin Powell presented to the UN Security Council in February 2003 as "evidence" that Iraq had WMD.

Dershowitz's final piece of "damning evidence", which he humorously described as "particularly convincing", was the IDF's *claim* to have in its possession "a seized Hamas intelligence map", which was nothing more than a rough sketch of buildings and streets marked up with various colored lines allegedly showing "areas of operation" and dots the IDF *claimed* were locations where Hamas had planted explosives throughout the neighborhood depicted in the drawing.[189]

All of these videos could be said to be "hard evidence" only so long as one was willing to take the IDF's word for everything.

Dershowitz also made much of the report's statement that "The Mission found no evidence that members of Palestinian armed groups engaged in combat in civilian dress". He argued that "the hard evidence contradicts the report's conclusion." But the Mission in that very same paragraph also stated, "Their failure to distinguish themselves from the civilian population by distinctive signs is not a violation of international law in itself. . . . What international law demands, however, is that those engaged in combat take all feasible precautions to protect civilians in the conduct of their hostilities."[190] Dershowitz proceeded to cite numerous examples from media reports where reporters said militants were dressed in civilian clothing, only two of which suggested the combatants were engaged in hostilities with civilians nearby. Of those two, neither were written by reporters who were actually in Gaza. Both were filed from Jerusalem. Both were simply doing what most mainstream journalists who know what is good for their careers do, which is to unquestioningly parrot whatever official narrative is handed to them from government officials.[191]

Dershowitz rejected the Mission's statement that it was presented with no evidence that Hamas had used human shields. "Here, again," he wrote, "the hard evidence points to the opposite conclusion." To support this contention, he cited a London *Times* report of a man whose family was forced to stay in their home while Hamas militants set up a position on their rooftop. The man was instructed, "If soldiers come, you must send your children to warn us. Tell them there is no one here and we will escape somewhere else."[192] That same article also happened to tell the story of another male civilian who was used as a human shield—*by Israeli soldiers*. "There were maybe a dozen of us being used", the man told the *Times*. "Different men were doing different things for soldiers. We were forced to hammer holes through walls, then check rooms to see if there were any fighters." He was sent on one "special mission" where he was forced by Israeli soldiers to go out and confirm kills for them and bring back the weapons of the Palestinian militants they had shot. "There is no way to verify independently either man's story", the *Times* noted.[193] There was naturally no mention by Dershowitz of what, by his own standard, constituted "hard evidence" that Israeli soldiers had used human shields.

His next exhibit was a Knight Ridder news report in which a woman told her story about how the IDF warned four brothers who were members of Hamas that their home would be a target. The article stated, "Leaders at the local mosque urged neighbors to converge on the apartment building and act as human shields, she added. *No one heeded the call, however, so the Hamas militants fled*" (emphasis added). Dershowitz had no explanation for how a case in which it is clear that there was no actual use of civilians to shield military operations could at the same time constitute "hard evidence" to the contrary.[194]

His only other two pieces of "hard evidence" were edited videos from the IDF. Both were uploaded to the IDF's YouTube channel on September 17, 2009. The first showed what appeared to be a rocket being fired from the roof of a building. The video then cut to a different angle to show a man emerging from the door of the building. A nearby group of seven people, including children, ran to him and followed him back into the building. The IDF claimed in a caption that this man was the militant who fired the rocket, and that what is seen in the video is him calling the civilians "to help him leave the house"— both of which claims are impossible to determine from the video, particularly given how it was edited. It seems a dubious proposition that the civilians would have so willingly hurried to join the man inside had he actually been calling to them to shield him from an Israeli counterstrike immediately after having fired a rocket from the roof. Surely, he could just as well have been calling the others inside for shelter from the Israeli aircraft spying down on them from above. It was only after another cut to a more distant shot that the group of people was seen to emerge and, in contrast to their earlier race to get inside, began walking rather nonchalantly down the road. The IDF caption claimed that "the terrorist" was among them, which was also impossible to determine from the video given the distance.

The second video showed a man running down a road and then through a farm field. There was nothing to suggest he was a combatant except the IDF's caption claiming he was a "terrorist". At one point, he ran past three other people, apparently children. He appeared to stop for a moment as if speaking to them. Then they all ran off in different directions as he resumed his run across the field. Having left the children some distance behind, he tripped and fell, while the IDF's caption read, "Terrorist feigns being wounded." (Had it been more imaginative, the IDF could have also informed in a caption how the children had been instructed to wait in the field for the runner, who passed them a series of communiques with instructions to relay them to different Hamas commanders stationed nearby.) Rather strangely, for someone supposed to be faking an injury, the man quickly picked himself up again and continued running past some cows (bovine shields, perhaps?). He slowed as he neared a building and, just before the video faded out, another person the caption identified as an "innocent bystander"—*not* to be automatically presumed a fellow terrorist, mind you (far be it from the IDF to consider *every* Palestinian a "terrorist")—walked to meet him. The video, in sum, was evidence of absolutely nothing.[195]

Dershowitz accused the Mission of having "applied totally different standards" in its evaluation of Israel's intent as compared with Hamas's. He argued that the Mission was "content to rely on extremely weak circumstantial evidence to infer Israeli intent" to perpetrate a "mass murder" that "borders on genocide". On the other hand, its conclusion that Hamas "did not intend to use Palestinian civilians as human shields" depended on the much higher standard of lacking "direct evidence" to the contrary. Let us dissect this argument. One, Dershowitz falsely attributed said conclusions to the Mission (his usual strawman). Two, the Mission's actual conclusion that Israel's intent was to use disproportionate force was emphatically not inferred on "extremely weak circumstantial evidence". Three, the Mission had not made any judgment about whether Hamas members ever *intended* to use human shields, only whether they had actually *done* so—something Dershowitz's argument tacitly acknowledged there was no "direct evidence" of.

Continuing in this vein, he criticized the Mission for refusing to infer intent on the basis of a Hamas official's statement after the end of Operation Cast Lead that the Palestinian people "have formed human shields of the women, the children, the elderly, and the mujahideen, in order to challenge the Zionist bombing machine." But neither had the Mission inferred the intent of Israeli officials solely on the basis of their declarations that the IDF would use disproportionate force. As the report explained, it "did not have to" since it was apparent from "the facts on the ground" that a deliberate policy of disproportionate use of force to punish the civilian population is "precisely what was put into practice".

Delving even more deeply into the absurd, he next criticized the Mission for not considering incidents of Hamas firing rockets from mosques and hospitals *prior* to Operation Cast Lead as proof that Hamas did so *during* that operation.

Finally, he quoted the report's statement that, "While reports reviewed by the Mission credibly indicate that members of Palestinian armed groups were not always dressed in a way that distinguished them from civilians, the Mission found no evidence that Palestinian combatants mingled with the civilian population with the intention of shielding themselves from attack." He then launched into a tirade about this "maddening reasoning", and rhetorically asked what *other* reason combatants could have had for mingling among the civilian population in civilian dress.[196] The attentive reader will notice that this wasn't actually what the Mission said, there being not a trivial difference between "members of Palestinian armed groups", who may *or may not have been* participating in hostilities, and "combatants", who by definition must have been. In the sentence just prior to the one Dershowitz quoted here, the Mission explained that there were no clear and specific cases from the information it had of combatants in civilian dress engaging in "combat activities in urban residential areas *that would have placed the civilian population and civilian objects at risk of attack*" (emphasis added).[197] To illustrate the point, recall the example cited by the Mission of militants firing rockets from a school that was *unoccupied*.

Dershowitz concluded by accusing the members of the Mission of being "biased 'experts'" with "limited experience" who "lack the expertise" as well as "the neutrality and objectivity" to make legal determinations. The UN as a whole, he further charged, was "an organization with a long history of anti-Israel bigotry", and "the methodology employed in this report is fundamentally flawed".[198]

Given Dershowitz's hypocrisy, himself being guilty in abundance of the dishonesty and bias he projected onto Richard Goldstone and the UN Mission, and applying his own standard, one must conclude that the Harvard law professor is "an evil, evil man" indeed.

CHAPTER 6
'SERIOUS ABOUT PEACE'

As the US was defending Israel's war crimes and its own complicity in them, the Obama administration was demanding that the Palestinians return to the "peace process" by resuming negotiations "without preconditions"—a euphemism meaning without obligating Israel to cease its colonization of the West Bank. The Obama administration's occasional rhetorical opposition notwithstanding, this constituted an unambiguous green light for Israel to continue this illegal activity.

This implicit US support for Israel's settlement activity was reiterated frequently, such as in a White House statement on September 4, 2009. The administration expressed "regret" that Israel had planned to approve additional construction projects and that it did not accept the "legitimacy" of settlements. It urged Israel to stop because "such actions make it harder" to "create a climate in which negotiations can take place". Thus, the White House framed the question of a settlement freeze not as a legal obligation but merely a voluntary show of good faith. The reassuring message to Israel was that there would be no consequences if it chose to ignore such rhetoric, required from time to time in order to maintain a public illusion of US opposition to the Israel's illegal colonization. Driving home the message, the Obama administration emphasized that its "commitment to Israel's security is and will remain unshakeable"—a promise that the US would continue to back Israel financially, militarily, and diplomatically, despite its ongoing criminal activities.[1]

Israel's response indicated that it understood the Obama administration's message perfectly well. Netanyahu paid his respects to Obama by agreeing to consider temporarily refraining from authorizing additional projects while making clear that East Jerusalem and existing projects throughout the West Bank would be excluded from any such settlement "freeze". This was accompanied by an announcement from Ehud Barak that the Defense Ministry was authorizing another 450 housing units to be built illegally in the West Bank.[2]

This was enough of a gesture of respect to satisfy the Obama administration, since it lent the US the ability to propagandize that Netanyahu was taking the "unprecedented" step of agreeing to "freeze" settlement activity, thus proving that Israel was willing to compromise in order to make peace. And if the Palestinians refused to negotiate despite this "freeze", it would prove they weren't interested in resolving the conflict.

Every September, the UN General Assembly holds its General Debate, during which heads of state address the global body in part to persuade it to adopt certain agendas. In the case of the Obama administration, the agenda was to persuade the world's nations either to get behind the "peace process" or stay out of the way so that the US could pursue its existing policies without interference. On September 23, 2009, Obama told the Assembly that the US had "worked steadily and aggressively to advance the cause of two states". He then elucidated how it would continue doing so. He reiterated that the US "does not accept the legitimacy of continued Israeli settlements" while refusing to acknowledge their illegality and again calling for "negotiations without preconditions". He said that the US goal was to have two states: a "viable and independent Palestinian state" alongside "a Jewish state of Israel"—an implicit endorsement of Netanyahu's racist demand that the Palestinians recognize Israel as a "Jewish state". Furthermore, Obama said that the establishment of the Palestinian state would be a step toward ending "the occupation that began in 1967"—another reiteration of the US's acceptance of Israel's unilateral interpretation of Resolution 242. With no lack of irony, Obama added that the world "must decide whether we are serious about peace, or whether we will only lend it lip service."[3]

An illustration of where his own administration stood with regard to that question came the following day during a meeting between George Mitchell's team and Palestinian negotiators. The chief PA negotiator, Dr. Saeb Erekat, said that any exclusion of East Jerusalem from a settlement "freeze" was "a nonstarter". He asked, "When the US president says settlements are 'illegitimate', what are the consequences of that? Will anything change?"

David Hale, a member of the US team, replied that "from the beginning" the US had "treated Jerusalem and settlements as separate issues"—the only meaningful interpretation of which is that the US supported Israel's illegal annexation and colonization of East Jerusalem. Hale said he understood that the Palestinians were "unhappy" that any settlement freeze would have "imperfections" but that they "just won't get" what they wanted. In other words, Israel's illegal colonization in East Jerusalem would continue, with the US's tacit blessing. Making plain that the US's position going into any negotiations was synonymous with Israel's, Hale added that currently existing construction projects would also not be part of any such freeze.

When Jonathan Schwartz on the US team asked the Palestinians if they would be willing to accept Obama's remarks to the UN as terms of reference for negotiations, they responded as one: "No", said Erekat; "He said 'the Jewish state'", interjected Akram Haniyeh; "Which is indirectly taking a position on refugees," finished Rami Dajani. That is, to recognize Israel as a "Jewish state" would not only be to accept the consignment of the fifth of Israel's population that is Arab to second-class citizenship, but also to effectively surrender the internationally recognized right of Palestinian refugees to return to their homeland.

"That's our position", Mitchell adamantly replied—a confirmation that Obama the day before had indeed intended his description of Israel as "a Jewish state" to signal that the US stood fully behind Netanyahu's demand that the Palestinians surrender the right of return.[4]

The Americans met with the Palestinians again on October 1. Erekat repeatedly asked why the US would not explicitly join the international consensus and endorse the two-state solution, with a Palestinian state on the pre-June 1967 lines with minor and mutually agreed revisions to the border. Mitchell's revealing response was that this would mean "taking a new position."[5]

The following day, Erekat again pressed Mitchell on the issue of borders. Referring to the Annapolis process, he said that the Bush administration had already agreed to use the 1967 lines as a term of reference for negotiations. Mitchell responded, "Again I tell you that President Obama does not accept prior decisions by Bush. . . . Countries are bound by agreements, not discussions or statements."

"But this was an agreement with [Secretary of State Condoleezza] Rice," Erekat replied.

Mitchell shot back, "It is not legally binding—not an agreement."

"For God's sake," a frustrated Erekat retorted, "she said to put it on the record. It was the basis for the maps."[6]

In sum, while Obama was paying lip service to peace, Mitchell was reiterating privately to the Palestinians that the US as a matter of policy rejected the international consensus on a two-state solution.

The Settlement 'Freeze'

Already under heavy criticism for having caved to US pressure to defer the vote on the draft resolution in the UN Human Rights Council, President Abbas held firm that there would be no negotiations without a full cessation of settlement construction. The US held just as firm in its demand that negotiations must occur "without preconditions".[7]

In continued talks with Mitchell's team, Erekat expressed his frustration at the Obama administration's unwillingness to pressure Israel to accept the 1967 lines as a starting point for border negotiations with an air of defeat. "The Palestinians know they will be a country with limitations", he said. They "won't have an army, air force or navy", he continued—thus acquiescing to the Israeli demand that Palestinians surrender their collective right to self-defense. They also "know that 5 million refugees will not go back" to the homes and land from which they were expelled, he added—thus acquiescing to the Israeli demand that Palestinians surrender the right of return.

Erekat's resignation of the rights of his people was not good enough for Mitchell, however, who responded by once again expressing the Obama administration's rejection of a full settlement freeze. Seemingly forgetful of the fact that his own 2001 report and the subsequent Road Map both determined that Israel must halt its settlement activity, Mitchell argued that the Palestinians had in the past "negotiated without a freeze all the time", so they should have no problem with doing so again this time around. When Erekat reiterated that Mahmoud Abbas "cannot go back to negotiations with settlements and business as usual", Mitchell firmly replied, "Then there will never be negotiations."

A clearly frustrated Erekat then pointed out that the Obama administration's continued support for the Israeli position was costing it credibility in the Arab world. "People in the Middle East are not taking Barack Obama seriously", he said. Mitchell remained unmoved.[8]

On October 31, 2009, Hillary Clinton praised as "unprecedented" what Netanyahu was now offering in terms of "restraint": a ten-month moratorium on authorizations for new settlement projects in the West Bank that excluded East Jerusalem and existing construction projects. Repeating the obligatory call for talks "without preconditions", she emphasized that the so-called "freeze" Netanyahu was offering was not and "has never been a pre-condition". Rather it had "always been an issue [to be dealt with] within negotiations".[9]

Her comments were understandably not very well received in the Arab world. "Pressuring Palestinians to make further concessions to accommodate Israeli intransigence is not the answer," replied Saeb Erekat. "Palestinians cannot accept continued settlement construction . . . in violation of international law. . . . Negotiations for their own sake . . . provide a cover behind which Israel will further entrench its occupation, and continue to create 'facts on the ground' that foreclose any prospect for a two-state solution."[10]

"The result of Israel's intransigence and America's back-peddling," said Nabil Abu Rdainah, a spokesman for Mahmoud Abbas, "is that there is no hope for negotiations on the horizon."[11]

Ziad Abu Zayyad, a former minister, said that Palestinians could not participate in "negotiations over land when Israel is changing the land and building on it and deciding before the fact what the results of the negotiations will be."[12]

"If there is no freeze on settlements," said Arab League chief Amr Moussa, "there is no wisdom: What are you negotiating? Why build more settlements? Why create another fait accompli? It is not serious." Furthermore "more settlements" would mean that "a viable state" for the Palestinians "will not be possible".[13]

"It is not reasonable or acceptable," said Egyptian Foreign Minister Ahmed Abul Gheit, "to conduct negotiations with the continuation of settlements."[14]

"The current Israeli government does not want peace," responded Syrian President Bashar al-Assad. "There is no partner for peace in Israel."[15]

The response in Israel to the policy outlined by Clinton, on the other hand, was euphoric. Netanyahu naturally agreed that "the place to resolve differences of opinion is around the negotiating table." Israel was "prepared to start peace talks immediately," he said, and proceeded to condescendingly scold the Palestinians to "get on with it and get with it."[16]

"There is no question," praised Israeli Deputy Foreign Minister Danny Ayalon, "that the United States are our staunchest friends and that Israel's firm stance on its positions pays off".[17]

"The US administration understands," commented Science and Technology Minister Daniel Hershkowitz, "what we have always said—that the real obstacle to negotiations are the Palestinians."[18]

The headline and subtitle in the British daily *Telegraph* read, "US drops demand for Israeli settlement freeze: US credibility in the Arab world has suffered a serious setback after Hillary Clinton dropped demands for a halt to Jewish settlement expansion in the West Bank".[19] This was misleading, since, as Clinton had correctly pointed out, the Obama administration had never called for a settlement freeze from Israel as a "precondition" for talks, and the "demands" were never anything more than weak suggestions that Israel properly understood it was welcome to ignore.

In the US media, the even more misleading caricature was painted of an Israel going out of its way to achieve peace, but having its efforts frustrated by intransigent Palestinians who refused to reason. "Israel putting forth 'unprecedented' concessions, Clinton says," read the headline in the *Washington Post*, above a subtitle adding, "But Palestinians reject Netanyahu's offer on settlements".[20]

On November 25, Netanyahu officially announced the 10-month moratorium on new settlement projects in the West Bank, excluding East Jerusalem, public buildings, and the nearly 3,000 illegal housing units that the Israeli government had already approved for construction.

It was "significant", said George Mitchell, that Israel was implementing a settlement freeze for "the first time ever" because it "could have substantial impact on the ground". Such remarks from US government officials served to obfuscate the fact that Israel's colonization would in fact continue under the misleadingly labeled "moratorium" or "freeze".[21]

Negotiations 'Without Preconditions'

In late August 2009, acting Palestinian Prime Minister Salam Fayyad announced a plan "to establish a de facto state apparatus within the next two years". It was immediately denounced by Israeli officials. The plan was "contrary to all the agreements signed between the sides", Finance Minister Yuval Steinitz scolded, an act of "unilateralism" constituting "threats" to Israel.[22]

Israel was becoming increasingly concerned that the Palestinians might take their case to the international community and seek recognition of statehood from the UN. Netanyahu in November reportedly asked Obama to veto any such proposal if it ever reached the Security Council. The administration subsequently promised to do just that.[23]

To prevent the Palestinians from going to the UN, they had to be persuaded to return to the "peace process", which was proving increasingly difficult given Israel's ongoing colonization. The Palestinians continued to insist that the foundation for negotiations be international law, with the inclusion of the 1967 lines as a term of reference.

"We would prefer language that does not predetermine the outcome before negotiations start," came Ambassador Oren's hypocritical rebuttal—with Israel doing its best to predetermine the outcome with far more than just "language".[24]

Mahmoud Abbas's response to Israel's precondition that Palestinians be willing to negotiate while the colonization of their land continued was to threaten to resign.[25]

Israeli officials called his bluff and doubled down. "If the Palestinian side," replied Israeli Finance Minister Yuval Steinitz, "instead of accepting our outstretched hand, continues to give us the cold shoulder, attack us internationally and advance the Goldstone Report, we will return to the security cabinet to reconsider the freeze." That is, if the Palestinians refused to accept a framework for talks in which international law was deemed irrelevant, Israel would begin authorizing new settler housing projects in the occupied West Bank just to spite them. "We won't turn our cheek," Steinitz added melodramatically, "and continue to make down payments and receive in return nothing but incitement and a cold shoulder."[26]

Abbas backed down on his threat to resign, but stood firm on insisting that before meaningful negotiations could occur, Israel must cease acting contrary to its obligations under the Road Map and cease violating international law.[27]

"Anyone who sets such conditions," responded Israeli Foreign Minister Avigdor Lieberman, "is just trying to escape reality and avoid negotiations and a peaceful solution."[28]

Israeli Deputy Foreign Minister Danny Ayalon wrote an op-ed in *Haaretz* criticizing the Palestinians for their rejection of Israel's terms. Comparing the situation to the Camp David and Annapolis negotiations, he complained how

Israel had "offered the Palestinians everything possible for peace", only to be met with stubborn intransigence.[29] (Ayalon's comparison to past talks during the "peace process" was not altogether inappropriate. As Shlomo Ben-Ami, a former Foreign Minister and participant in the Camp David and Taba talks, put it, "Camp David was not the missed opportunity for the Palestinians, and if I were a Palestinian I would have rejected Camp David, as well."[30])

While the US was demanding that the Palestinians stop insisting that Israel cease violating international law, the Palestinian position did have some backing from the European Union. On December 8, the EU issued a statement reiterating "that settlements, the separation barrier where built on occupied land, demolition of homes and evictions are illegal under international law, constitute an obstacle to peace and threaten to make a two-state solution impossible." The EU urged Israel "to immediately end all settlement activities, in East Jerusalem and the rest of the West Bank and including natural growth".[31]

The *Financial Times* noticed in an editorial that "Washington was silent on the EU policy paper", which it naively interpreted as the Obama administration "seeing it as a helpful nudge towards the two-state solution". The editors also commented on what they perceived as an optimistic legacy of Operation Cast Lead: "The increased and brutal frequency of war in this volatile region has shifted international opinion, reminding it is not above the law. Israel can no longer dictate the terms of the debate."[32] Of course, there was another, more credible, interpretation of Washington's silence, which was that the EU's call for a full settlement freeze contradicted the US policy of calling for negotiations "without preconditions" and was thus seen as unwanted interference in the US goal of getting the Palestinians back to the "peace process", in which Israel very much could dictate the terms of the debate.

On December 16, Abbas insisted that if Netanyahu would implement a full settlement freeze, final-status talks could be completed within six months. "They tell me I had not previously demanded a construction freeze in the settlements," he said. "True, in 1993 we didn't do so, but then there were no agreements about a freeze. Now, there is the road map." The Palestinians had lived up to their obligations under that agreement, he said, and Israel should do the same.[33]

At the UN Security Council two days later, the special coordinator for the Middle East peace process, Robert Serry, similarly pointed out that the moratorium fell well short of Israel's commitments under the Road Map.[34]

In January 2010, George Mitchell was asked in an interview about the possibility of the US withholding loan guarantees to pressure Israel to halt settlement construction. "Under American law," he acknowledged, "the United States can withhold support on loan guarantees to Israel". However, he emphasized, the Obama administration had no plans to do so.[35]

This mere *acknowledgment* that removing a financial incentive for Israel to continue violating international law was an option available to the Obama administration was treated as completely out of line and met with a fury of reassurances that this was not open for consideration.

"Any attempt," declared Senator Joseph Lieberman, "to pressure Israel, to force Israel, to the negotiating table by denying Israel support will not pass the Congress of the United States".

"We disagree, obviously, with that comment," said Senator John McCain, "and I am sure that you will see the administration in the future say that is certainly not the administration's policy."[36]

McCain was correct. US State Department spokesman P. J. Crowley swiftly assured that Mitchell "wasn't signaling any, you know, particular course of action", and that the Obama administration was not "wielding that particular tool at this particular time."[37]

Israeli Finance Minister Steinitz similarly sought to put to rest any fears in his own country stemming from Mitchell's statement, comforting that there was "no indication that there is any intention to pressure us through the guarantees".[38]

The message from the Obama administration was perfectly unambiguous: Israel could continue its illegal policies, and the Palestinians must accept as a precondition that negotiations *not* operate within a framework of international law.

Leading Palestinians to Certain Conclusions

While the US vowed to continue rewarding Israel for its refusal to abide by the conditions of the Road Map and its persistent violations of international law, the Palestinians continued to suffer the consequences.

Amnesty International issued a report noting that Israel used 80 percent of the water from the only aquifer in the West Bank while denying Palestinians access. "Israeli settlers, who live in the West Bank in violation of international law," Amnesty stated, "have intensive-irrigation farms, lush gardens and swimming pools. Numbering about 450,000, the settlers use as much or more water than the Palestinian population of some 2.3 million." Donatella Rovera, Amnesty's researcher on Israel and the Occupied Palestinian Territories, explained that "Israel allows the Palestinians access to only a fraction of the shared water resources, which lie mostly in the occupied West Bank, while the unlawful Israeli settlements there receive virtually unlimited supplies. In Gaza the Israeli blockade has made an already dire situation worse."[39]

In addition to humanitarian supplies and reconstruction material, goods blocked by Israel included school supplies like textbooks, notebooks, and pens. "What possible justification can there be for blocking school supplies, which effectively deprives children of their right to an education?" asked Sarah Leah Whitson, the Middle East and North Africa Director at Human Rights Watch. The organization pointed out that the blockade was in violation of international law, amounting to collective punishment. Israel's restrictions on school supplies also violated Article 50 of the Fourth Geneva Convention, which required the Occupying Power to "facilitate the proper working of all institutions devoted to the care and education of children." The group also drew attention to the role of the US "as Israel's most important political, military and financial backer", and it once again called on the US "to dissociate itself from the blockade and to speak out against it."[40]

B'Tselem reported that "extensive areas in the Gaza Strip have yet to be rebuilt" because of Israel's siege, which was keeping 1.5 million people "imprisoned".[41]

UNRWA conveyed that "the quality of life among Palestinians living in Gaza continues to deteriorate as a result of the Israeli economic blockade of Gaza." John Ging expressed the organization's concern that "the blockade, which amounts to collective punishment of the Palestinians in Gaza, has prompted the collapse of the private sector, and created unprecedented unemployment, poverty and food insecurity."[42]

Fifty-four members of Congress dissented from the Obama administration's policy by signing a letter urging President Obama to put pressure on Israel to ease the siege. The letter expressed that Israel must address its security concerns "without resulting in the de facto collective punishment of the Palestinian residents of the Gaza Strip."[43]

Like the similar call from Human Rights Watch, it was ignored, and the administration's policy of complicity in the collective punishment of the people of Gaza continued.

The nature and full impact of Israel's siege was systematically self-censored from the US media, which, rather than condemning the illegal blockade, tended to instead blame its victims. The *Washington Post* offered lessons for the Palestinians by relating the story of Yousef Barakat. When Yousef was thirteen, his father had instructed him not to participate in protests at the Erez border crossing, but the rebellious youth had gone to one in October 2000 anyway, where he was shot and blinded in his right eye by a rubber bullet. Now twenty-two, Yousef had "no clear sense of what will follow his upcoming graduation" from Al-Quds University. "Under the strategy that Israel has employed in Gaza," the *Post* lectured, "that lack of opportunity should lead the young man to certain conclusions: reject Hamas, reconcile with the rival government in the West Bank and then with Israel, and see Gaza reopened to the world." The moral of the story was thus that the suffering of the Palestinians was their own fault, and to end it, all they had to do was to cease their troublesome rebelliousness, surrender their rights, and bow to the will of the Occupying Power and

Washington, DC. With Israel having "choked off the economy in Gaza, increasing poverty and despair among its 1.5 million people", the people of Gaza must just accept the Israeli punishment and learn obedience, and then their self-inflicted suffering could come to an end.[44]

Israel's 'Cast Lead' Self-Exoneration: Update

In January 2010, Israel released a paper providing an update on its self-investigations into the IDF's conduct during Operation Cast Lead. It asserted that the UN Fact-Finding Mission Report contained "serious inaccuracies and misstatements."[45]

Israel's report said that a further review by the Military Advocate General of incidents in which UN facilities, ambulances, and hospitals had been attacked "found no basis to order criminal investigations".[46] It declared that the IDF's use of white phosphorus munitions "was consistent with Israel's obligations under international law."[47] For their role in attacking the UNRWA compound on January 15, 2009, two officers were "disciplined", an action one IDF official described to the London *Times* as a "slap on the wrist". The fact that they chose to attack the UN facility with inherently indiscriminate white phosphorus munitions was mentioned in neither the report nor their reprimand.[48] The IDF meanwhile altogether denied "that two of its senior officers had been summoned for disciplinary action", *Haaretz* reported.[49]

Israel was not entirely unwilling, however, to hold anyone accountable for criminal behavior during Operation Cast Lead. One soldier was indicted and convicted to seven months in prison for stealing a credit card from a home in Gaza. His court martial declared, "The crime of looting is harmful to the moral duty of every IDF soldier to keep human dignity".[50]

Israel acknowledged that the location of the Namar wells complex in Jabaliya had been deliberately targeted on the first day of Israel's airstrikes. The report boasted that all the IDF's strikes on the compound "were accurate". To justify the attack, it claimed that the wells were located inside a "Hamas military compound", which was "a legitimate military target", and that "the IDF did not know of the existence of the water wells" at the time of the attack. It did not explain how the IDF—which was intimately familiar with Gaza from decades of military occupation—had failed to anticipate that there might be wells at a complex operated by the Gaza Coastal Municipalities Water Utility, or in what way such a facility constituted a "Hamas military compound".[51]

It's useful to also contrast Israel's findings with those of the UN Fact-Finding Mission, which "addressed questions to the Government of Israel with regard to the military advantage pursued in attacking the Namar wells group, but received no reply." The Mission had visited and photographed the site, which belonged "to the civil administration", and "found no grounds to suggest that there was any military advantage to be gained from hitting the wells." But at least Israel's paper had finally answered the Mission's question "as to whether the Israeli air strikes on the Namar wells group were deliberate or made in error".[52] As Israel acknowledged, it was quite deliberate.

In the case of the Sheikh Ijlin wastewater treatment plant in Gaza City, Israel denied that it had been responsible for the destruction of the lagoon wall that flooded the surrounding area with raw sewage. The paper allowed that the MAG "could not definitively rule out the possibility that IDF activity had caused the damage to the wall"; but "he could also not dismiss the possibility that the damage to the basin might have resulted from a deliberate action by Hamas as part of a defensive plan to hamper the movement of IDF forces in the area."[53]

One may again compare Israel's disavowal of responsibility for the damage with the findings of the UN Fact-Finding Mission: Israeli forces "had taken control of the plant and the surrounding area" before the damage occurred and were in control of it at the time, and it was therefore "highly unlikely that Palestinian armed groups could have taken up positions in or around the lagoon".[54]

With regard to the Al-Bader flour mill, Israel claimed that "the immediate area in which the flour mill was located was used by enemy armed forces" in order "to attack IDF troops". The paper cited two examples: one of an alleged Hamas ambush of an IDF squad "200 meters south of the flour mill", and the other of an engagement with "enemy forces" "500 meters east of the flour mill". Israel admitted that IDF commanders had "identified the flour mill as a 'strategic high point'", but they did not attack it until "IDF troops came under intense fire from different Hamas positions in the vicinity of the flour mill"— with "vicinity" evidently meaning anywhere from 200 to 500 meters away. The IDF forces "returned fire" by firing tank shells not at the source of the alleged fire, but at the flour mill, deemed "a legitimate military target" apparently by the sole virtue of it having been made the object of a direct attack by the IDF. After acknowledging that the mill was deliberately struck, the paper somewhat needlessly noted that the MAG "could not conclusively determine that the flour mill was in fact used by Hamas's military operatives".[55]

In essence, Israel actually confirmed the Fact-Finding Mission's conclusions that the attacks on the mill were "intentional and precise", and that there was "no suggestion that the Israeli armed forces considered the building to be a source of enemy fire" at the time of the attack—thus rendering it a war crime.[56]

Finally, the paper addressed an IDF attack on the home of Muhammad Abu Askar by claiming without evidence that it was "a legitimate military target" because it was "used to store weapons and ammunitions".[57]

The UN Fact-Finding Mission, by contrast, noted that Mr. Abu Askar was a member of Hamas who served on a number of administrative committees, that he held a master's degree in education and was pursuing a PhD, and that he "denies any involvement in armed militant activities."[58]

Israel touted the paper as proof of its commitment to "full compliance with the Law of Armed Conflict, and to investigating every allegation of violations, irrespective of the source of the allegation."[59] As Israel submitted the paper to the UN, Defense Minister Barak once again decried the Fact-Finding Mission Report as "distorted, false, and irresponsible". He declared that Israel's own investigation emphasized that "the IDF is like no other army, both from a moral standpoint as well as from a professional standpoint."[60]

Human rights groups remained unconvinced. Amnesty International issued a statement describing Israel's update as "totally inadequate" and blasting it for not credibly addressing critical questions about the IDF's conduct, including its use of white phosphorus; attacks on UN and other civilian buildings and infrastructure; and direct attacks on civilians, including ambulance crews.[61] Human Rights Watch issued a report titled "Turning a Blind Eye: Impunity for Laws-of-War Violations during the Gaza War", which pointed out that Israel's self-investigations "have fallen far short of international standards". All of its investigations had been conducted by the IDF itself, with no independent review. Of the 150 investigations Israel said it had opened, around 120 were "limited to 'operational debriefings' that consider testimony from the soldiers involved but not from witnesses or victims." Israel had also failed to investigate culpability among the political and military leadership who authorized policies such as the targeting of the Gaza police, the use of white phosphorus, and rules of engagement. Human Rights Watch also pointed out that while the only conviction was for the theft of a credit card, two other soldiers had been indicted for using a Palestinian boy as a human shield.[62]

"Yes," Israeli minister Yuli Edelstein repented, "I am ashamed of the soldier who stole some credit cards".[63]

A 'Hiccup' in US-Israeli Relations

In mid-March 2010, an incident occurred that sparked what Israeli Ambassador Michael B. Oren theatrically described as "a crisis of historic proportions": US Vice President Joe Biden arrived in Israel as part of an effort to restart the "peace process" as Israel simultaneously announced its approval for the additional construction of 1,600 housing units in the Jewish settlement of Ramat Shlomo.[64]

Israel's Interior Ministry said it was just a coincidence that the announcement was made while Biden was in the country. Meir Margalit, a member of Jerusalem's City Council, however, told a different story:

This is the interior minister's initiative, which is meant to sabotage the announcement that Netanyahu issued today regarding the renewal of indirect negotiations with the Palestinians. It is also a kind of slap in the face of the American administration. [Interior Minister Eli] Yishai could have waited two or three days after US Vice President Biden left the country, but instead of waiting, he chose to do this while he is here, in order to signal to the Obama administration that there [are] large forces in Israel that will not allow him to promote any peace talks.[65]

Biden responded to the announcement with the statement, "I condemn the decision by the government of Israel to advance planning for new housing units in East Jerusalem. The substance and timing of the announcement, particularly with the launching of proximity talks, is precisely the kind of step that undermines the trust we need right now and runs counter to the constructive discussions that I've had here in Israel."[66]

The problem for the US was not that Israel was expanding an illegal settlement. After all, it was demanding that the Palestinians enter negotiations "without preconditions". The problem was, rather, as Biden indicated, the "timing" of the announcement, which was objectionable because it underscored the fact that settlement activities were ongoing with the US's approval. The US media did its part in misinforming Americans as to the true nature of the administration's policy by taking its declarations at face value while ignoring the actions that belied its rhetoric. The headline in the *Washington Post* read, "US condemns Israel's plans to build housing in east Jerusalem". By contrast, the incident was accurately reported in *Haaretz* under the headline, "US gave green light for East Jerusalem construction".[67]

Writing in *Foreign Policy*, Mark Perry expounded on the true nature of the problem. "Biden's embarrassment" was "not the whole story". In January, a team of senior military officers had been dispatched by the US Central Command (CENTCOM) commander, General David Petraeus, to brief the Chairman of the Joint Chiefs of Staff, Admiral Michael Mullen, on the Israeli-Palestinian conflict. In their briefing, they "reported that there was a growing perception among Arab leaders that the US was incapable of standing up to Israel". The concern for the military was that this was undermining its efforts to enforce US hegemony over the region. A Pentagon officer familiar with the briefing told *Foreign Policy*, "America was not only viewed as weak, but its military posture in the region was eroding." Biden reportedly told Netanyahu, "What you're doing here undermines the security of our troops who are fighting in Iraq, Afghanistan and Pakistan. That endangers us and it endangers regional peace."[68]

Petraeus similarly told the Senate Armed Services Committee,

The enduring hostilities between Israel and some of its neighbors present distinct challenges to our ability to advance our
interests in the AOR [CENTCOM Area of Responsibility].
Israeli-Palestinian tensions often flare into violence and large-
scale armed confrontations. The conflict foments anti-Ameri-
can sentiment, due to a perception of US favoritism for Israel.
Arab anger over the Palestinian question limits the strength
and depth of US partnerships with governments and peoples
in the AOR and weakens the legitimacy of moderate regimes
in the Arab world. Meanwhile, Al-Qaeda and other militant
groups exploit that anger to mobilize support.[69]

A former Israeli Ambassador to the UN, Dore Gold responded to the affair
by taking note of Petraeus's concern that Arab "perceptions" of a bias toward
Israel could cause problems for the US "in the Arab street" and among its "Arab
military partners." He argued that it was wrong, however, to consider Israel a
"strategic liability" rather than a "strategic asset". He proceeded to detail how
the US benefited from "Israel's strategic partnership", including shared intelligence and technology.[70]

It was a "strategic partnership" that Alexander Haig once described by saying, "Israel is the largest, most battle-tested and cost-effective US aircraft carrier
that cannot be sunk, does not carry even one US soldier, and is located in a
most critical region for US national security."[71]

Haaretz observed that Netanyahu had erred not by violating international
law or taking actions to prejudice the outcome of negotiations, but by committing the much more heinous sin of "damaging the standing of the US in the
Middle East and the Muslim world".[72]

In sum, the problem wasn't that the Palestinians were being denied their
right to self-determination or that Israel was violating international law. Rather,
the problem was one of restoring US "credibility" among Arab leaders (who
had their own publics to manage) in order to maintain its hegemony over the
region. It thus boiled down to a problem of Arab "perception", which needed to
be managed, which was difficult to do when Israel made bold public announcements drawing attention to certain aspects of the US-Israeli relationship that
the US did not wish to be highlighted.

In an effort to limit the damage to US "credibility" and to manage the "perception" that it supported Israel's illegal policies, the US and its Quartet partners issued a statement calling on Israel and the Palestinians "to act on the basis
of international law and on their previous agreements and obligations". It stated
that "unilateral actions taken by either party cannot prejudice the outcome of
negotiations", reiterated the obligations of both sides under the Road Map, and
urged Israel "to freeze all settlement activity, including natural growth". The

Quartet also said it was "deeply concerned by the continuing deterioration in Gaza, including the humanitarian and human rights situation of the civilian population". It stressed "the urgency of a durable resolution" that "addresses Israel's legitimate security concerns, including an end to weapons smuggling into Gaza".[73]

But given the Obama administration's endorsement of continued settlement activity and assurances that there would be no consequences if Israel continued its violations of international law, the Netanyahu government understood that it was free to ignore the Quartet statement. Furthermore, lacking an explicit demand by the Quartet for Israel to end its illegal blockade, the logical implication was that *until* a mechanism was in place to ensure there were no weapons being smuggled into Gaza through the tunnels, Israel could continue the siege. This was in accordance with the US-Israeli interpretation of Security Council Resolution 1860 calling for a "durable" ceasefire, which allowed Israel to ignore that resolution, as well.

Writing in advance of another scheduled meeting between Obama and Netanyahu, George Friedman of Stratfor accurately highlighted the problem for the US with the timing of Israel's pronouncement. The US "wants one thing from Israel now: for Israel to do nothing that could possibly destabilize the western balance of power or make America's task more difficult" elsewhere in the region. The US "has interests in the broader region that are potentially weakened by this construction at this time." Therefore, "Obama's task is to convince Netanyahu that Israel has strategic value for the United States, but only in the context of broader US interests in the region." The fact that Israeli policy violated international law and the rights of the Palestinians was of absolutely no consideration—thus receiving no mention in Friedman's analysis.[74]

The real problem for the administration was also manifest in a public opinion survey taken at the time showing that a majority of Americans believed that the supposed "inability" of the US to get Israel to stop its settlement activity made the country less respected internationally.[75]

But the Obama administration was hardly helpless to stop it. If it wanted the activity to end, it could have—as an obvious first step—just stopped supporting it. It could have ended the financial aid that incentivized the settlement policy. It could have ended its complicity in Israeli war crimes and human rights violations by ending US military assistance. It could have chosen to *not* protect Israel against being held accountable at the UN. It could have referred to the settlements as being not merely of questionable "legitimacy", but illegal under international law. It could have insisted that Israel end this criminal activity, rather than insisting that the Palestinians must accept its continuance. It could have insisted that it was a non-negotiable obligation of Israel to comply with international law, rather than insisting that Israel's compliance was something that Israel could negotiate and disregard at its own choosing.

It takes no great imagination to come up with additional actions that the US could have taken, and if ceasing support for Israel's criminal policies didn't do the trick to end them, then one could go on from there; but it hardly seems useful to enter that hypothetical realm so long as the support continues. Choosing not to see this simple and obvious truth must take a great deal of self-discipline on the part of the American intelligentsia, who choose rather to frame the issue as one of Arabs having what we are supposed to understand to be merely a "perception" that the US is not an "honest broker", that it rather supports Israel at the expense of the rights, lives, and legitimate aspirations of the Palestinians.

Such a self-disciplined approach to foreign policy analysis allowed for the mainstream discussion to continue in its usual surreal framework. Thus it was, even to the extent that Obama could be roundly criticized for being *too hard on Israel*. David Frum, a resident fellow at the American Enterprise Institute and former speechwriter for President George W. Bush, lamented how "not so long ago", "even-handedness was diplomatic code for anti-Israel animus. Those now look like the good old days. The Obama administration has tilted so far against Israel that even-handedness looks like up from down here."[76] David Horowitz and Jacob Laksin, in a booklet titled "Obama and the War Against the Jews", decried how Vice President Biden had delivered a "punishment" against Israel for its "routine" announcement of additional construction in East Jerusalem, which "was hardly an issue to create any sort of problem, let alone to cause a rupture between allies." The "punishment" the authors were referring to was Biden's having arrived late at Netanyahu's home for dinner.[77]

No less self-disciplined, nearly 300 members of Congress signed a letter to Secretary of State Clinton reaffirming "the unbreakable bond that exists between our country and the State of Israel" and dismissing the incident as the normal course of affairs, in which there were bound to be "occasional misunderstandings" of this sort. The letter expressed no concern over the illegality of Israel's actions, but merely noted that Netanyahu had promised that "such surprises"—again, the problem being merely the *timing* of Israel's announcement—would "not recur". Israel was a peaceful nation, the letter asserted, which was "constantly having to defend itself from attack" throughout its existence, even though it had always upheld the pledge contained in its May 14, 1948 founding document to extend its hand in "peace and good neighborliness"—as clearly evidenced by the concurrent ethnic cleansing of 750,000 Arabs from Palestine; or its "Cast Lead" massacre in Gaza, ongoing collective punishment, and illegal colonization of Palestinian land (to take examples from either end of Israel's historical timeline). "Our valuable bilateral relationship with Israel needs and deserves constant reinforcement", the letter expressed, with the hope and expectation that the US and Israel would "move beyond this disruption quickly".[78]

Obama met again with Netanyahu on March 23, with the *Washington Post* observing that their meeting was "shrouded in an unusual news blackout, with no statement issued after the meeting".[79]

Soon after, Nita Lowey, the Chairwoman of the US House Appropriations Subcommittee on Foreign Operations, which oversees US aid to Israel, proclaimed that the recent affair concerning Biden's visit was just a "hiccup" and that the two allies "must move forward" rather than "dwell on disagreements". She reassured Israel that US financial and military support would continue uninterrupted.[80]

Meanwhile, *Haaretz* reported that, "Even as Prime Minister Benjamin Netanyahu received the full wrath of the Obama administration, the Defense Ministry and Pentagon were concluding yet another huge deal." Israel would purchase three C-130J Super Hercules transport aircraft under the deal, which "goes to show" that the "diplomatic crisis" had yet "to make itself felt as far as defense relations are concerned."[81]

Indeed, the "full wrath" of the Obama administration proved much more purr than roar.

Getting 'Tough' on Israel

The day after Obama's meeting with Netanyahu, the UN Human Rights Council adopted a resolution that recalled Security Council Resolution 242 and other relevant resolutions, as well as "the conclusion of the International Court of Justice, in its advisory opinion of 9 July 2004, that the construction of the wall by Israel, the occupying Power, in the Occupied Palestinian Territory, including East Jerusalem . . . severely impedes the right to the Palestinian people to self-determination". It reaffirmed "the inalienable, permanent and unqualified right of the Palestinian people to self-determination, including their right to live in freedom, justice and dignity and to establish their sovereign, independent, democratic and viable contiguous State". It also reaffirmed its "support for the solution of two States, Palestine and Israel, living side by side in peace and security". The resolution was adopted with a vote of forty-five to one and no abstentions.[82]

The US explained its lone opposition to the Council's affirmation of the Palestinians' right to self-determination by dismissing it as being among "a slate of resolutions so replete with controversial elements and one-sided references that they shed no light and offer no redress for the real challenges of the region". Instead of passing "highly politicized" and "divisive" resolutions, the US lectured, the world should be "supporting and encouraging continuing talks between the two parties" within the rejectionist framework of the US-led "peace process".[83] The rest of the planet, of course, didn't consider there to be anything "controversial" about recognizing that Palestinians have rights, too.

The next day, the Human Rights Council adopted a resolution deciding to establish a committee of independent experts to monitor and assess the obligation of both Israel and Hamas to investigate any alleged violations of international law during Operation Cast Lead, "including the independence, effectiveness, [and] genuineness of these investigations and their conformity with international standards".[84] The resolution was adopted with a vote of twenty-nine to six, with eleven abstentions. Hungary, Italy, the Netherlands, Slovakia, and Ukraine joined the US in opposition. In explanation for its nay vote, the US offered the circular logic that it "cannot support international oversight of these domestic legal processes absent any indication that they are manifestly failing to deal seriously with alleged abuses."[85] The very purpose of the proposed committee, of course, was to determine whether the parties were doing so.

Understandably, the US could not come out and say, "We oppose this resolution because we do not think Israel should be held accountable for its crimes, and we do not want international scrutiny of Israel's crimes because we are complicit in them." So this was the best alternative explanation the US could come up with. A more cogent (albeit self-defeating) argument would have been to point out that such a committee was unnecessary, as it had already been well-established that Israel's record of investigating its own conduct was "dismal" (Justice Goldstone), that its investigations into its Gaza operations were "totally inadequate" (Amnesty International), and that its self-acquittals were contradicted by many reports from numerous human rights organizations (Amnesty, Human Rights Watch, B'Tselem, etc.), numerous UN bodies, and the Fact-Finding Mission Report itself.

The US's sole nay vote notwithstanding, the Council forged ahead, later announcing the members of the committee: Christian Tomuschat, a Professor Emeritus at Humboldt University in Berlin who had served as a member of the UN Human Rights Committee, as president of the International Law Commission, and as chair of the Guatemalan Historical Clarification Commission; Mary McGowan Davis, a justice of the Supreme Court of the State of New York and a federal prosecutor in New York City; and Param Cumaraswamy, a former President of the Malaysian Bar Association and member of the International Commission of Jurists who served for nearly a decade as the UN Special Rapporteur on the independence of judges and lawyers.[86]

The Obama administration, with help from the compliant media, kept up the ridiculous façade that the US government had attempted to pressure Israel to freeze settlement activity, but, despite its best efforts, couldn't get Netanyahu to budge. Obama said in April that the Israelis and Palestinians "may say to themselves, 'We are not prepared to resolve these issues no matter how much pressure the United States brings to bear.'" Peace might not be achieved "even if we are applying all of our political capital," Obama added.[87] One could just as well interpret this remark as an acknowledgment that his administration had *not* actually bothered to try applying any meaningful pressure on Israel—but mainstream commentators universally kept to the script.

The following day, on April 14, Obama gave a speech that the *New York Times* said signaled a "shift" in US policy. The ostensible "shift" came when Obama said that resolving the Israeli-Palestinian conflict was a "vital national security interest of the United States". True, Secretary of State Condoleezza Rice had similarly said that a peace deal was of "strategic interest" to the US, and "glimmers of daylight between United States and Israeli interests" had begun to appear during the Bush administration. "But President Bush shied away from challenging Israeli governments", the *Times* asserted. The truth, of course, was just the opposite: Bush went so far as to deduct $1 billion from loan guarantees to Israel—an "almost totally symbolic" gesture, as the *Times* described it at the time, but nevertheless far more than anything Obama had ever done. Setting aside the selective amnesia, the *Times* continued on to say that "tougher policies toward Israel" might "flow from" Obama's "new thinking"—thus making clear that the supposed "shift" in US policy was merely a hypothetical possibility, and not yet a tangible reality.[88]

Obama had campaigned under the slogans of "Hope" and "Change", but, needless to say, the foreseen "shift" in US policy would never actually materialize. *The Guardian* shortly thereafter reported that the US had privately told the PA that if it entered negotiations with Israel, the US would "consider" not vetoing any UN Security Council resolution condemning ongoing Israeli settlement activity.[89] That is to say, if the PA did not accept the Obama administration's ultimatum to accept negotiations "without preconditions", the US would continue to use its veto to protect Israel against international censure for its colonization of Palestinian land; but if the PA agreed to accept this continued illegal activity, then the administration might "consider" allowing a resolution critical of Israel to pass—but with no guarantee that it wouldn't go ahead and continue its habitual use of its veto anyway.

The Israeli government was not totally insensitive to the Obama administration's "credibility" problem stemming from the US's support for Israel's crimes. The *Washington Post* reported in May that Netanyahu made a "tactical" decision not to convene its housing planning committee, as a "temporary gesture", in the wake of the Biden scandal, "to appease US officials". The *Post* obsequiously reported that Israel was in a "battle" to achieve "sovereignty and international legitimacy" for its settlements because its annexation of Jerusalem was "not recognized by the international community"—the standard euphemistic phrase by which the US media alludes to the fact that the world had repeatedly and universally upheld, including through a great many UN Security Council resolutions, that Israel's annexation was illegal, null and void.[90]

The American public was inundated with a propaganda narrative that often manifested itself as nonsensical drivel completely devoid of reality. One could read in *US News & World Report*, for instance, under the headline "Israel Is a Key Ally and Deserves US Support", the saga of how "The Israelis are clearly prepared to live with a Palestinian state along their borders. The trouble is precisely that the Palestinians are not." One could listen to the tale of how Israel was "demoralized about the potential of negotiations" because of "the hostility President Obama has shown to Israel from the start". One could hear the legend of how Israel had offered "territorial concessions" in the past, but was unable to do so now given Obama's lack of "a basic commitment to Israel, or sympathy for it." And, of course, one could be handed the prescription that the US must support Israel in its rejection of any peace talks that include the pre-June 1967 lines as a term of reference because such borders would be "neither secure nor defensible".[91]

That the Obama administration could draw criticism for being "hostile" to Israel and for not going far enough in its rejection of the two-state solution is a remarkable testimony to the nature of what is considered acceptable and serious political commentary in the US mainstream media, the effect of which is to manufacture consent for the US's policy of financially, militarily, and diplomatically supporting Israel's routine violations of international law.

CHAPTER 7

MURDER ON THE HIGH SEAS

I N APRIL 2010, THE ICRC reported that hospitals continued to suffer power outages while Israel continued to hinder the delivery of essential medical equipment and supplies into Gaza, risking the health of thousands of Palestinians.[1]

The WHO reported the following month that standards of health care were declining. Infant mortality was up. Unemployment, poverty, and environmental standards were worsening as Israel continued to block essential goods and humanitarian supplies.[2]

The UN Development Program (UNDP) also issued a report in May providing an update on the situation in Gaza. "Depriving people from their right to pursue a dignified life should raise an issue of conscience," the report regrettably found it necessary to say—undoubtedly due to the fact that it *hadn't* raised an issue of conscience in Washington, DC. While the Quartet had welcomed an announcement by Israel that it would allow more goods into Gaza, "the quantity and relevance of the goods permitted does not address the nature and scale of the needs." The unemployment rate in Gaza remained "among the highest in the world."

In spite of the blockade, Gazans had managed to repair about 25 percent of the infrastructure damage from Operation Cast Lead. This was "first and foremost" a result of the "resilience and ingenuity" of the people of Gaza. They were "producing building blocks from crushed rubble and cement", which were then "loaded on to old trucks and donkey carts and hauled off to repair damaged homes." They had "maximized the use of locally available resources", such as repairing roads "with the rubble of destroyed houses" and using recycled crushed rubble mixed with cement imported from the tunnels, which remained a lifeline for Gazans. The Palestinian electricity and telecommunications companies had "performed most of their repairs using available spare parts and us-ing imaginative and unorthodox solutions." As for international relief efforts, Gaza had "benefited from greater support from Arab donors and Islamic inter-national NGOs and organizations" than from UN organizations and Western non-governmental organizations.

The report noted that "psychological distress and pathology are among the most significant health consequences of the blockade and the Cast Lead opera-tion, affecting virtually the entire Gaza population." Symptoms of psychological trauma included "continuous crying for no reason, fear of loneliness and dark-ness, exaggerated fear of blood, sleep disturbances, eating disorders and weight loss or gain, frustration and depression, nervousness, obsession with death, bed wetting, and lack of self-care and child-care. Children were, in particular, se-verely affected by the psychological trauma of the military operations." More than half of the children in Gaza (61.5 percent) showed symptoms of severe post-traumatic stress disorder (PTSD).[3]

The Israeli rights group Gisha released a partial list of items Israel prohibited from entering Gaza. Banned goods included: sage, cardamom, cumin, corian-der, ginger, jam, halva, vinegar, nutmeg, chocolate, fruit preserves, seeds and nuts, biscuits and sweets, potato chips, gas for soft drinks, dried meat, fresh meat, plaster, tar, wood for construction, cement, iron, glucose, industrial salt, plastic/glass/metal containers, industrial margarine, tarpaulin sheets for huts, fabric, flavor and smell enhancers, fishing rods, various fishing nets, buoys, ropes for fishing, nylon nets for greenhouses, hatcheries and spare parts for hatcheries, spare parts for tractors, dairies for cowsheds, irrigation pipe systems, ropes to tie greenhouses, planters for saplings, heaters for chicken farms, musi-cal instruments, size A4 paper, writing implements, notebooks, newspapers, toys, razors, sewing machines and spare parts, heaters, horses, donkeys, goats, cattle, and chicks.[4]

The list of banned goods was attained by Gisha under a freedom-of-infor-mation lawsuit. The Defense Ministry refused to explain why such items were prohibited "on security grounds". The government sought to deny Gisha's on-going lawsuit, which was seeking clarification on the criteria for banning such goods on the grounds that they would "harm national security and possibly even diplomatic relations."[5]

In an attempt to draw the world's attention to the plight of the Palestinians and break Israel's illegal blockade, a flotilla organized by the Free Gaza Move-ment, in cooperation with the Turkish Foundation for Human Rights and Free-doms and Humanitarian Relief (IHH), set sail for Gaza carrying 10,000 tons of humanitarian aid. Seven-hundred human rights activists representing fifty nationalities participated in the "Freedom Flotilla", including 1976 Nobel Prize laureate Mairead Maguire (who had also been on *The Spirit of Humanity* with Cynthia McKinney); Holocaust survivor Hedy Epstein; Swedish writer Henning Mankell; a number of European legislators; and Israeli citizens, including Knesset member Hanin Zoabi.

In late May, Obama held a White House reception in honor of Jewish American Heritage Month, where he reaffirmed once more that "in pursuing peace between Israelis, Palestinians, and Arabs, our bond with Israel is unbreakable." This "bond" included unconditional support for Israel, regardless of its criminal policies and actions, as events would soon prove yet again.[6]

Four days later, on May 31, Israel attacked the Freedom Flotilla in international waters forty miles off the coast of Gaza. The flagship of the flotilla, the *Mavi Marmara*, was boarded by Israeli commandos who stormed the Turkish vessel with live fire. Nine peace activists were killed in the violence that erupted on board, with some of the passengers rejecting nonviolent resistance and choosing to exercise self-defense against the Israeli attack in an attempt to prevent the ship from being hijacked and redirected to the Israeli port of Ashdod. Israel's attack on the flotilla was a "brazen act of piracy", an editorial in the *Financial Times* observed, which was perpetrated to enforce "the illegal blockade of Gaza". It was an act that "lays bare the country's slide into contempt for international law".[7]

Israel acknowledged that it attacked the ships in international waters, but nevertheless attempted to characterize its deadly assault as an act of "self-defense", falsely suggesting the flotilla was carrying arms to Gaza. "They were mobbed, they were clubbed, they were beaten, stabbed, there was even a report of gunfire", said Prime Minister Netanyahu. "And our soldiers had to defend themselves." He preposterously declared that it was Israel's policy to "let humanitarian aid, any kind of goods that are meant for peace, to the civilian population of Gaza", and that the goal of its blockade was to "prevent weapons and war materials from coming into Gaza, and allowing humanitarian aid to go the population of Gaza."[8] Deputy Foreign Minister Danny Ayalon announced, "We couldn't allow the opening of a corridor of smuggling arms and terrorists [into Gaza]."[9] The IDF issued a statement saying that it had taken control of "ships that tried to violate the naval blockade" and claiming that its "soldiers encountered serious physical violence by the protestors, who attacked them with live fire."[10] IDF spokeswoman Avital Leibovich announced, "This happened in waters outside of Israeli territory, but we have the right to defend ourselves."[11] The Ministry of Foreign Affairs issued a statement likewise claiming that "demonstrators onboard attacked the IDF naval personnel with live fire and light weaponry including knives and clubs. Additionally two of the weapons used were grabbed from an IDF soldier." The Israeli commanders had merely acted to defend themselves against "this life-threatening and violent activity".[12] Government spokesman Mark Regev claimed, "Live fire was used against our forces. They initiated the violence, that's 100% clear."[13]

Such declarations of self-justification could hardly be taken seriously. In an emergency special session of the UN Security Council, a consensus that Israel's actions were in violation of international law emerged. Assistant Secretary-General for Political Affairs Oscar Fernandez-Taranco called for "a full investigation", stressed "the importance of all parties strictly adhering to the framework of international law", and criticized that "today's bloodshed would have been avoided if repeated calls on Israel to end the counterproductive and unacceptable blockade of Gaza had been heeded." The representative from Lebanon, who was also President of the Security Council, described Israel's attack as "piracy" and said it was "a flagrant violation of the Charter of the United Nations, international law, international humanitarian law and the law of the sea." Israel continued "in an act of collective punishment to impose an illegal blockade". It had claimed the blockade was "legal", but "their law is the law of the jungle, which the United Nations has declared must be combated." Turkish Minister of Foreign Affairs Ahmet Davutoğlu called Israel's attack "tantamount to banditry and piracy." UK Ambassador Sir Mark Lyall Grant reminded Israel of its obligation to lift the blockade under Resolution 1860, as did the Japanese and Nigerian representatives. The representative from Mexico condemned the attack as "contrary to international law". The representative from Brazil condemned the attack, for which there could be "no justification". The Austrian representative said Israel's legitimate security concerns could not "in any way justify what has happened today." The Russian representative condemned the attack as "a gross violation of the norms of international law" and called for "a prompt cessation of Israel's blockade". The Ugandan and Chinese representatives condemned the attack. The French representative condemned Israel's "disproportionate use of force and a level of violence that nothing justifies" and called for "the lifting of the blockade, which is unsustainable and illegal." The representative from Gabon condemned the attack and said that the "new situation reminds us once again of the urgency of lifting the Gaza blockade, in accordance with resolution 1860". The representative from Bosnia and Herzegovina condemned the attack as "a grave breach of international humanitarian law and a violation of the United Nations Convention on the Law of the Sea."

The entire Security Council spoke with one voice in condemning Israel's attack on the flotilla and calling once again for Israel to lift its illegal blockade of Gaza. Two lone voices stood out in rejecting that international consensus.

Israel's Deputy Ambassador to the UN, Don Carmon, repeated that "there is no humanitarian crisis in Gaza" and declared that Israel's assault on the flotilla had been "in accordance with international law". He claimed that the passengers were "not peace activists", that some had "known terrorist histories", and that their purpose was "to send a message of hate and to implement violence." The Turkish humanitarian group, the IHH, had supported Hamas and Al-Qaeda, and Israel had merely acted "to counter illegal breakage of the blockade."

The US Ambassador to the UN, Alejandro Wolff, said the US was "deeply disturbed by the recent violence and regrets the tragic loss of life and injury". But instead of condemning Israel for killing nine civilians, he blamed the victims of the attack, who, he lectured, should have chosen "non-provocative and non-confrontational mechanisms" by delivering their aid to Israel, which itself would then have ostensibly delivered it to Gaza. It was not Israel's illegal assault on a civilian vessel in international waters, but the flotilla's effort to break the illegal blockade that was "neither appropriate nor responsible", in the view of the US government.[14]

As a result of US opposition to any criticism of Israel, the Security Council issued a watered-down statement that did not reflect the strong remarks made during the emergency session, but instead merely expressed deep regret for "the loss of life and injuries resulting from the use of force during the Israeli military operation in international waters against the convoy sailing to Gaza". It was only "in this context"—vague context indeed—that the statement condemned "those acts which resulted" in the loss of civilian lives. It called for an investigation into the incident, emphasized the importance of implementing Resolution 1860, and reiterated its "grave concern at the humanitarian situation in Gaza".[15]

At the UN Human Rights Council, where the US couldn't exercise its veto power, a resolution was passed that more closely reflected the consensus of the international community. It condemned "in the strongest terms the outrageous attack by the Israeli forces against the humanitarian flotilla of ships, which resulted in the killing and injuring of many innocent civilians from different countries". It called upon "the occupying Power, Israel, to immediately lift the siege on occupied Gaza". It also announced the Council's decision "to dispatch an independent, international fact-finding mission to investigate violations of international law" resulting from the attack. It passed thirty-two to three, with nine abstentions. Italy and the Netherlands joined the US in voting against the resolution.[16]

State Department spokesman P. J. Crowley explained the US vote by saying that the resolution was "a rush to judgment" because it put "complete responsibility on Israel" rather than blaming the victims, as the US government preferred to do. The US also opposed any independent, international investigation. "We continue to believe that Israel is in the best position to lead that investigation," Crowley added, still unconvinced by its "dismal" record (Goldstone) and "totally inadequate" self-investigations into the IDF's conduct during the assault on Gaza (Amnesty International).[17]

The Israeli response to the international community's condemnation of its attack consisted of continued denials that its blockade was illegal, insistence that there was no need for humanitarian aid in Gaza, and characterizations of the Freedom Flotilla as somehow constituting a threat to Israel's security, including by preposterously suggesting it might have been attempting to smuggle weapons. Israeli Foreign Minister Avigdor Lieberman called the world's condemnation of Israel's deadly attack "two faced".[18] Netanyahu similarly replied, "Once again, Israel faces hypocrisy and a biased rush to judgment." He disingenuously implied that the flotilla had been carrying arms by saying, "If the blockade had been broken, dozens and hundreds more ships carrying weapons could have come." He declared once again that Israel's policy was "very simple. Humanitarian and other goods can go in, and weapons and war material cannot. And we do let civilian goods get into Gaza. There is no humanitarian crisis in Gaza."[19]

The US response followed a similar narrative, characterizing any criticism of Israel as being a prejudicial rush to judgment. White House spokesman William Burton said, "The United States deeply regrets the loss of life and injuries sustained, and is currently working to understand the circumstances surrounding this tragedy."[20] When asked why the Obama administration hadn't condemned Israel for killing nine peace activists on board a humanitarian vessel in international waters, White House spokesman Robert Gibbs replied, "Nothing can bring them back." He instead offered the meaningless comment: "We condemn the loss of life and regret it deeply."[21] So it was not Israel but the Grim Reaper himself who alone deserved condemnation for the killings.

Eric Cantor, a leading Republican in the US House of Representatives, called on the Obama administration "to veto any biased UN resolutions reining in Israel's right to defend itself." He didn't bother to explain how an attack on an unarmed ship on a humanitarian mission in international waters that resulted in the killing of nine civilians could possibly constitute an act of "self-defense".[22]

In an instructive interview with Charlie Rose on PBS, Vice President Joe Biden parroted Israel's own defense by ludicrously suggesting that the ships might have been carrying arms to Gaza. He said that Israel "has a right to know whether or not arms are being smuggled in." Israel had offered to deliver the aid to Gaza itself, "So what's the big deal here? What's the big deal of insisting it go straight to Gaza? Well, it's legitimate for Israel to say, 'I don't know what's on that ship.'" Not wishing to appear entirely callous and indifferent to the suffering of the people of Gaza, he added that "one thing we have to do is not forget the plight of the Palestinians there", and "we have to put as much pressure and as much cajoling on Israel as we can to allow them to get building materials in . . ."

As he was saying this, Rose interrupted him to point out that the flotilla was trying to do just that.

Biden replied, "Yes, we know that, but they could have easily brought it in here and we'd get it through." (One might be curious why he would describe Israel as "here" despite being in the US. Perhaps shedding some light on this was his use of the pronoun "we", alluding to the US-Israeli partnership in punishing the civilian population in Gaza. It might also be helpful to point out that Biden once declared, "I am a Zionist", which could help explain his choice of words, which any English-speaking alien visiting Earth for the first time would naturally assume must be coming from the vice president of the place called "Israel".) Biden offered no further comment on how he could argue on one hand that Israel was justified in its attack because the flotilla might have been shipping arms to Gaza while on the other admitting the he *knew* the ships were only carrying humanitarian aid.

When he said there needed to be "a transparent and open investigation of what happened", Rose inserted that it should be an international investigation. Biden rejected this, clarifying that he meant "an investigation run by the Israelis". So it was up to Israel once again to investigate its own conduct and, no doubt, declare itself innocent of any wrongdoing.[23]

With the US already having protected Israel from being held accountable for its criminal assault on Gaza and its ongoing colonization of the West Bank, the significance of the US's position on the flotilla was perfectly understood in Israel. The *Jerusalem Post* reported that according to a top Israeli Navy commander, "Israel will use more aggressive force in the future to prevent ships from breaking the sea blockade of the Gaza Strip".[24]

The US media also played its usual role. Isabel Kershner wrote in the *New York Times* that "Israel faced intense international condemnation" for "enforcing what Israel says is a legal blockade". Why not instead write ". . . for enforcing what the international community says is an illegal blockade"? The rest of the article similarly relied almost entirely upon the Israeli narrative:

> Israel said . . . . An Israeli official said . . . . The Israelis had planned . . . . The [Israeli] military said . . . . Another [Israeli] soldier said . . . . But the forces "had to open fire in order to defend themselves," the [Israeli] navy commander, Vice Adm. Eliezer Marom, said. . . . At least seven [Israeli] soldiers were wounded, one of them seriously. The [Israeli] military said that some suffered gunshot wounds; at least one had been stabbed. . . . Israeli officials said that international law allowed for the capture of naval vessels in international waters if they were about to violate a blockade. . . . Israel says it allows enough basic supplies through border crossings to avoid any acute humanitarian crisis.

Kershner's report offered more details about how Israeli commandos were injured than about how nine civilians were killed. She was apparently not unaware of the conspicuous bias and attempted to excuse it by writing, "There were no immediate accounts available from the passengers of the Turkish ship," who had been detained or sent to Israeli hospitals. But this hardly explained how she could relay the Israeli assertions that the blockade was lawful and the flotilla raid a "legal" act of "self-defense" while choosing *not* to disclose how the international community had long condemned the siege as an act of collective punishment in violation of international law and UN Resolution 1860, as well as condemned Israel's deadly attack as disproportionate and completely devoid of legal justification.[25]

An account of the attack in the *Washington Post* dispensed with even the pretense of objectivity, opening with, "This is the Israeli version of the deadly raid on an aid ship bound for Gaza."[26] The *Post* never followed up with a piece beginning, "This is the passengers' version of the deadly raid . . . ."

Passenger accounts of the attack were reported, but one generally had to turn to the international media to find them. *Al Jazeera* reporter Jamal Elshayyal, who was on board the *Mavi Marmara*, in his last report before Israel cut off the ship's communications, said that Israeli troops were using live ammunition during its assault.[27] Other passengers began speaking to reporters after being deported from Israel, similarly asserting that Israeli forces had used live fire even before boarding the flagship.[28]

Illustrating the mainstream Israeli view, the *Jerusalem Post* was critical of the IDF not for attacking a civilian ship in international waters and killing nine peace activists, but for being "caught unprepared and without an adequate response" to international media reports on the attack, thus leaving "the Israeli PR machine . . . scrambling for damage control". This failure of Israel's "PR machine" had not been for lack of preparation, the *Post* admitted. The IDF spokesman's office and Foreign Ministry had conducted meetings "in the weeks leading up to Monday's operation" to coordinate hasbara efforts for the planned attack. The propaganda effort had tried to "undermine the flotilla's legitimacy" even before it set sail by claiming the IHH was "a radical Islamic group" that "had ties with Hamas". The Israeli propaganda machine had also gone "out of its way to prove that there was not a humanitarian crisis in the Gaza Strip." During the attack, the IDF "had hoped to obtain a complete media blackout and planned to jam the signals from the *Mavi Marmara*." Passengers had nevertheless "successfully transmitted images throughout most of the takeover", which "enabled the activists to get their message out about the Israeli 'aggression.'" As a result of this failure of Israel's "PR machine", "the media was full of one-sided reports" making Israel look bad.[29] If only Israel had better handled its propaganda war and been more successful at preventing the truth from getting out . . . .

The Israeli Ministry of Foreign Affairs released photos on its official Flickr page (a photo sharing website) that it said were taken of items found aboard the *Mavi Marmara* following the raid. Astute commenters on the Flickr page and bloggers pointed out, however, that the metadata embedded in the digital photos showed that many of them had been taken much earlier. A photo of bullet-proof vests, one of an electric saw, and another of night-vision goggles and a rifle scope had all actually been taken in 2006. A photo of an axe and another photo of cans of pepper spray had both been taken in 2003.[30]

The IDF posted a press release on its website with a heading that declared, "Attackers of the IDF soldiers found to be Al-Qaeda mercenaries". It cited as evidence the claim that passengers "were equipped with bullet proof vests, night vision goggles, and weapons." When asked by reporters what evidence they had that any of the passengers had links to Al-Qaeda, the IDF's response was: "We don't have any evidence. The press release was based on information from the [Israeli] National Security Council." The IDF website subsequently replaced its original headline with "Attackers of the IDF Soldiers Found Without Identification Papers", although the title meta tag of the page—the title that appears in internet browsers and search engine results—continued to declare an Al-Qaeda link.[31]

On June 2, the *New York Times* offered op-ed space to both Daniel Gordis, vice president of the Shalem Center in Jerusalem, and Ambassador Michael B. Oren. Gordis's op-ed echoed the *Jerusalem Post's* criticisms, bewailing the fact that Israel had "utterly failed to convince the world" that Operation Cast Lead "was a defensive effort", but that, "despite widespread criticism at the way the raid was conducted, few here doubted that stopping the flotilla was the right thing to do." He repeated the Israeli talking point that "there is no humanitarian crisis in Gaza" before contradictorily blaming Hamas for the admitted shortage of food, shelter, and medicine. "Israel will, of course, endure tremendous international condemnation for this week's events," he wrote. "Sadly, though, we Israelis are becoming somewhat inured to such criticism. And we know that we dare not capitulate now. . . . Israelis are resigned to the fact that reason will not shake the world's blatant double standard."[32] Clearly, since in truth Israel's only shortcoming was its inability to convince the world of its magnanimity, the fact that it was so universally criticized for its actions could only mean that the world was populated with anti-Semitic hypocrites. What other conclusion could a reasonable person possibly draw?

Oren's contribution was titled "An Assault, Cloaked in Peace". The "assault" he was referring to, naturally, was not Israel's murder of civilians, but the flotilla's peaceful effort to break the illegal blockade. In his Orwellian account, a "mob" that was "paid and equipped to attack Israelis" had "assaulted Israeli special forces on the deck" of the *Mavi Marmara*, and Israeli forces proceeded to kill nine civilians only in "self-defense"—a right exclusive to Israel, and not afforded to the passengers whose ship was stormed by a mob of armed commandos paid and equipped to attack their ship in international waters. Oren suggested that passengers had carried firearms and used them against Israeli commandos, claimed that the IHH had been "linked to Islamic extremists" by Israeli intelligence, and said that "the real purpose" of the flotilla was to "allow the flow of seaborne military supplies to Hamas". He wrote that "Israel has a right and a duty to defend itself from Hamas and its backers" and that the flotilla passengers were "supporting the terrorists".[33]

In an outrageous display of dishonesty and prejudice, the *Times* editors accompanied both op-eds online with an image depicting a colossus of a man standing on a shore with an outstretched arm, motioning firmly for a ship at sea to stop. The ship in the illustration was loaded to the brim not with humanitarian supplies or peace symbols, but missiles.[34]

Israel's 'Passionate Defenders'

Israel's attack on the flotilla presented a similar problem for the US as the "hiccup" in US-Israeli relations after Biden's March visit. Netanyahu had planned to travel to Washington to meet again with Obama on June 1, the day after the attack, but the meeting was canceled because, as *Haaretz* put it, "under the current circumstances it would be a bad photo-op".[35] Meir Dagan, the head of Israel's Mossad intelligence agency, warned the Knesset's Foreign Affairs and Defense Committee that "Israel is gradually turning from an asset to the United States to a burden."[36]

One primary concern in the US was that Israel's attack would complicate the Obama administration's efforts to get back to the "peace process".[37] The *Washington Post* commented also on how "the administration increasingly faces a difficult balancing act as Israel's diplomatic isolation deepens"—an allusion to the difficulty arising from trying to balance its support for Israel's continual violations of international law while attempting to combat "perceptions" in order to maintain "credibility".[38] This was indeed an arduous task, given the full extent of US support for Israel's crimes. The editors of the *New York Times* advised Obama to describe the attack as "unacceptable", support an international investigation, and finally join the international community in "urging Israel to permanently lift the blockade". This would "lessen the suffering of the people of Gaza" so as to "give the United States more credibility" in its efforts "to negotiate a peace deal".[39]

Times columnist Nicholas D. Kristof similarly opined that Israel was "antagonizing its support base in the United States" and "depleting America's international capital as well as its own". He recalled Gen. Petraeus's comments two months before about "the perception that the United States favors Israel breeds anti-Americanism and bolsters Al-Qaeda", as well as Dagan's statement that Israel was becoming a "burden" to the US. Most of his column was a discussion of this damage to the US's "credibility", although he did manage to dedicate a whole sentence to the fact that Israel's siege "has accomplished nothing—except to devastate the lives of 1.5 million ordinary Gazans". Obama should "push hard for an end to the Gaza blockade", Kristof wrote, his primary consideration being not the Palestinian suffering, but the international image of the US and its Middle Eastern ally. "Above all," Kristof closed, "he needs to nudge Israel away from its tendency to shoot itself in the foot, and us along with it."[40]

In a similar vein, Anthony Cordesman suggested that actions such as Israel's murderous attack on the *Mavi Marmara* "unnecessarily make Israel a strategic liability when it should remain asset". The US, he added, "does not need unnecessary problems in one of the most troubled parts of the world". Unlike Kristof, Cordesman didn't waste space in his analysis with any bleeding-heart acknowledgment of the devastated lives of 1.5 million Gazans.[41]

After its deadly attack, the Israeli government press office distributed a link to a video on YouTube mocking the flotilla activists. The spoof video, set to the tune of "We Are the World", featured Israelis dressed as Arabs—led by the managing editor of the *Jerusalem Post*, Caroline Glick—waving weapons and singing, "We con the world, we con the people." Government spokesman Mark Regev said, "I called my kids in to watch it because I thought it was funny." The daily *Yedioth Ahronoth* praised the video, saying it "defended Israel better than any of the experts". The government was later forced to apologize under heavy public criticism for having distributed a video that so insensitively mocked the deaths of nine civilians.[42]

At the same time, the IDF repeated claims for which it had already admitted there was no evidence: that flotilla passengers were "Linked to Al-Qaeda, Hamas and Other Terror Organizations". The IDF named six of the "terrorists": Fatimah Mahmadi, a member of Viva Palestina, a British charity established by Member of Parliament George Galloway; Ken O'Keefe, a former US Marine who served in the Gulf War and whom the IDF deemed an "operative of the Hamas Terror organization" who had "attempted" to "form and train a commando unit" for Hamas (O'Keefe had gone to Gaza to try to broker a ceasefire between Hamas and Israel, which naturally entailed meeting with Hamas officials, and which proposal included bringing 10,000 international observers into Palestine to deter Israeli aggression and document any human rights violations); Hassan Iynasi, whom the IDF accused without evidence of financing Islamic Jihad; Hussein Urosh, whom the IDF accused of participating "to assist in smuggling Al-Qaeda operatives" into Gaza; and Ahmad Umimon, whom the IDF accused of being "an operative of the Hamas Terrorist organization".[43]

The German magazine *Spiegel Online* noted that the IDF offered "no evidence" and made allegations that were "almost impossible to verify because the Israeli government appears to be basing them on secret intelligence information, if indeed there is a foundation for their claims." Furthermore, it was not Israel's practice to release and deport terrorists, as had been done with the flotilla participants, which "implicitly casts doubt on the veracity of the allegations." Israel's claims of IHH links to terrorist organizations, including Al-Qaeda, were "similarly complicated"—meaning also entirely without an evidentiary basis.[44]

The US went into damage control mode. The day after the attack, Israeli Ambassador Michael B. Oren and National Security Adviser Uzi Arad had a series of meetings at the White House, including with US National Security Adviser James L. Jones. "The meetings focused on how to contain the immediate diplomatic fallout from the raid," the *Washington Post* reported, mentioning again how the administration "faces a difficult balancing act" between continuing its support for Israel "while not letting Arab anger over the raid . . . undercut its outreach to the Muslim world." While there were "questions about the legality" of Israel's attack, the *Post* added, "Allen Weiner, a former State Department lawyer and legal counsel at the US Embassy at The Hague, said Israel was technically operating legally." The *Post* quoted Weiner asserting as much. No legal expert was cited to provide the consensus view of the world community that the blockade constituted illegal collective punishment and the attack on the flotilla unlawful use of force.[45]

A *New York Times* editorial stated that an Israeli self-investigation was "not going to suffice" and alluded to Israel's lack of credibility by remarking how its claims that ship passengers were armed and had shot at Israeli commandos were "being ignored by everyone except its most passionate defenders."[46] The position of the US government, of course, remained that there should be no international inquiry into the attack.

It emerged the same day that one of the nine civilians killed aboard the *Mavi Marmara* was an American citizen. Furkan Doğan, a nineteen-year-old American of Turkish descent, had been "shot at close range, with four bullets in his head and one in his chest", according to an autopsy conducted after the bodies had been returned to Turkey.[47] *The Guardian* obtained the autopsy results of the nine men, who had been "peppered with 9 mm bullets, many fired at close range", and "shot a total of 30 times". Five of the men "were killed by gunshot wounds to the head". Doğan had been shot five times from a distance of less than forty-five centimeters, "in the face, in the back of the head, twice in the leg and once in the back." Sixty-year-old İbrahim Bilgen "was shot four times in the temple, chest, hip and back." Two of the other men "were shot four times, and five of the victims were shot either in the back of the head or in the back".[48]

Another ship, the *Rachel Corrie* (named for an American peace activist who was killed by an IDF bulldozer driver who ran her over in the Gaza Strip on March 16, 2003), had planned to sail with the flotilla, but was delayed due to technical problems. Having set sail from Malta carrying fifteen passengers, Israel vowed to intercept any additional ships approaching Gaza. Netanyahu decried the effort as "a terrorist operation."[49] Among the passengers was Mairead Maguire, who had received the Nobel Peace Prize for her "passionate desire to make a stand against all violence and terror". Little wonder that nobody except Israel's "most passionate defenders" took its hysterical claims and self-justifications seriously.[50]

The *Rachel Corrie* never reached Gaza, but was intercepted on June 5.[51]

Among Israel's "passionate defenders", Thomas Friedman lamented how "agonizing" it was for him "to watch the disastrous clash between Israeli naval commandos and a flotilla of 'humanitarian' activists" (his quotation marks implying that they were not *really* humanitarian activists) and how "painful" it had been for him to hear Turkey's Prime Minister, Recep Taayip Erdoğan, "lash out with ever-greater vehemence at Israel over its treatment of the Palestinians in Gaza." Thus, what pained Friedman wasn't Israel's collective punishment of Gazan civilians, but *criticisms* of that policy. He had a "big problem" with such criticisms because he considered them hypocritical. The "concern for Gaza and Israel's blockade" was "out of balance" with "other horrific cases in the region", and so "it is not surprising Israelis dismiss it as motivated by hatred"—a reiteration of the theme that any criticisms of Israel were inherently hypocritical and perhaps bordering on anti-Semitic.

Friedman proceeded to defend Israel's actions by charging that it was the victim of "a setup". The only faults he found in Israel's actions were that it "failed to fully appreciate who was on board" and "failed to think more creatively about how to avoid the very violent confrontation that the blockade-busters wanted." So it would have been better for Israel if no high-profile figures had participated, since less attention might then have been drawn to the attack. And Israel could had been more imaginative in planning its attack so that it didn't have to shoot nine civilians, who had "wanted" Israeli soldiers to storm their ship and had practically begged the commandos to execute them as part of their devious plot to make Israel look bad.

As for the siege of Gaza, it was "surely not all Israel's fault". Hamas must also bear the blame for Israel's policy because it refused "to recognize Israel or prior peace agreements" and launched "missile attacks on Israel", thus leaving Israel with no choice but to implement a policy of collective punishment against the civilian population. Friedman did advocate "ending this Gaza siege", but only because it was not "in Israel's interest" "to have a whole new generation grow up in Gaza with Israel counting how many calories they each get". Ergo, in Friedman's view, as long as it was "in Israel's interest" to do so, then collectively punishing the entire civilian population of Gaza in violation of international law would be just fine.

The human rights and well-being of the Palestinians factored into Friedman's equation only indirectly: Israel's siege was eroding "its own moral fabric" in the eyes of civilized humanity concerned with quaint ideas about human rights and international law, thus increasing Israel's "international isolation". But in the end, it "may be that Hamas will give Israel no other choice" but to continue the siege. Israel, for its part, should "show a lot more initiative in determining if that is really so". Thus, if Israel was in some undefined way to show more "initiative" in determining for itself that it had no choice but to punish the civilian population of Gaza, then it couldn't be legitimately criticized for doing so—though such "initiative" would surely not stop the hypocrites and anti-Semites from laying blame on Israel for such trivial deeds as violating international law.[52]

Another of the "passionate defenders", renowned French philosopher Bernard-Henri Lévy similarly called upon the world to "stop demonizing Israel" with its "flood of hypocrisy". He opined in a *Haaretz* op-ed that the "manner" in which Israel had attacked the flotilla was "stupid", but the "flood of hypocrisy, bad faith and, ultimately, disinformation" was "by no means acceptable." He proceeded with no shortage of hypocrisy and in bad faith to brazenly lie that "the blockade concerns only arms and the material needed to manufacture them" and "aid has never stopped passing into Gaza".[53]

Israel's Deputy Minister of Foreign Affairs, Danny Ayalon, penned an op-ed for the *Wall Street Journal* with the same theme, stating that "those that participate in these flotillas reek of hypocrisy." This was because there were "100 armed conflicts and dozens of territorial disputes around the world" and "millions of people killed and hundreds of millions live in abject poverty without access to basic staples". Therefore, to focus one's attention on Israel's crimes against the Palestinians was hypocritical. Ayalon, incidentally, also took the time in his op-ed to criticize Lebanon for its abuses against resident Palestinians, which was apparently *not* hypocritical, even though it was equally true that there were many conflicts and disputes around the world and many killed and living in poverty in places *other* than Lebanon. Ayalon's criteria for whether or not criticism was hypocritical, therefore, clearly boiled down to whether or not it was leveled *at Israel*, which must be exempt by definition from any international censure. Humankind must sort out all of the rest of the world's problems before it could fairly and reasonably turn any of its attention to *Israel's* behavior.

Ayalon also charged that the goal of the Nobel laureate and other peace activists aboard the flotilla was to "hand money to Hamas that will never reach the innocent civilians of Gaza". Such touching compassion for the welfare of Palestinians might have seemed less contrived had it not come from someone whose whole purpose in writing was to defend Israel's enforcement of an illegal blockade that collectively punished those very same people. Ayalon naturally downplayed the impact of Israel's siege, touting that Gaza had "just opened a sparkling new shopping mall" and that "a new Olympic-sized swimming pool was recently inaugurated and five-star hotels and restaurants offer luxurious fare."

Clearly, the UN bodies and human rights organizations that focused their attention on the detrimental effects of the siege on the overwhelming majority of Gazans who were impoverished and dependent upon humanitarian assistance for survival, rather than on the indulgences of the tiny class of wealthy elites, were at best misguided—and perhaps likewise guilty of "hypocrisy" and "delegitimizing Israel".[54]

Israel's Legal Argument

Israel's arguments for why its blockade and attack on the *Mavi Marmara* were legal were summarized in an article titled "The Legal Basis of Israel's Naval Blockade of Gaza" written by Ruth Lapidoth, Professor Emeritus of International Law at the Hebrew University of Jerusalem, and published by the JCPA. It is instructive to examine the arguments at length, inasmuch as doing so reveals the extent of the intellectual dishonesty of those who chose to defend Israel's murderous actions.

Lapidoth began by arguing that "the rules of the laws of armed conflict apply" to the "armed conflict" between Israel and Hamas. From this, Lapidoth drew the conclusion that "Israel may control shipping headed for Gaza—even when the vessels are still on the high seas." Lapidoth explained how she arrived at this conclusion: "The rules on blockade are based on customary international law, as there is no comprehensive international treaty on this subject. . . . The customary rules on blockade can be found in the manuals of the laws of war issued by certain Western countries such as the United States and Britain. In addition, there is a manual prepared by an international group of experts in 1994 called the San Remo Manual."[55]

By claiming that we must depend upon *customary* international law to decide whether or not a blockade is legal or not, Lapidoth implied that the body of *formal* international law is somehow irrelevant and inapplicable. Lapidoth was thus able to ignore, for example, Article 2 of the UN Charter, which states: "All Members shall settle their international disputes by peaceful means in such a manner that international peace and security, and justice, are not endangered. . . . All Members shall refrain in their international relations from the threat or use of force against the territorial integrity or political independence of any state, or in any other manner inconsistent with the Purposes of the United Nations."

Article 33 of the Charter provides the prescription for seeking remedy to an international dispute or grievance: "The parties to any dispute, the continuance of which is likely to endanger the maintenance of international peace and security, shall, first of all, seek a solution by negotiation, enquiry, mediation, conciliation, arbitration, judicial settlement, resort to regional agencies or arrangements, or other peaceful means of their own choice."

For Member states, without prejudice to their inherent right to self-defense, it is up to the UN Security Council to "determine the existence of any threat to the peace, breach of the peace, or act of aggression", and to "make recommendations, or decide what measures shall be taken in accordance with Articles

41 and 42, to maintain or restore international peace and security" (Article 39). If the Security Council finds that such a situation exists, it may authorize the use of force "as may be necessary to maintain or restore international peace and security", including the implementation of a "blockade" (Article 42).[56]

Thus, Israel had a legal obligation to bring any grievances it had to the UN Security Council, which could authorize a blockade if deemed necessary. Yet Israel rather implemented its blockade unilaterally, without UN authorization. This is not to say that a naval blockade may not be implemented under any circumstances without UN authorization. Again, nations have an inherent right to self-defense, and a blockade may be implemented as a legitimate measure to defend against an "armed attack", but any such measures "shall be immediately reported to the Security Council" (Article 51).

Simply announcing a blockade, which Israel did not formally do until 2009, is not enough to make it lawful. Even if it may be considered an act of self-defense against armed aggression, it must still comply with the rules of international law; furthermore, Israel had additional obligations as Occupying Power. Far from receiving UN sanction for its imposed blockade, Israel continued it in *violation* of Security Council Resolution 1860, which called for "the unimpeded provision and distribution throughout Gaza of humanitarian assistance, including of food, fuel and medical treatment".

Israel is also a party to the Fourth Geneva Convention, which prohibits any acts constituting collective punishment of a civilian population: "No protected person may be punished for an offence he or she has not personally committed. Collective penalties and likewise all measures of intimidation or of terrorism are prohibited" (Article 33). Israel is legally obligated to allow humanitarian shipments into Gaza: "To the fullest extent of the means available to it, the Occupying Power has the duty of ensuring the food and medical supplies of the population; it should, in particular, bring in the necessary foodstuffs, medical stores and other articles if the resources of the occupied territory are inadequate" (Article 54). Additionally, "If the whole or part of the population of an occupied territory is inadequately supplied, the Occupying Power shall agree to relief schemes on behalf of the said population, and shall facilitate them by all means at its disposal", including "consignments of foodstuffs, medical supplies and clothing." Israel is obligated to "permit the free passage of these consignments" and to "guarantee their protection" (Article 59).[57]

Lapidoth acknowledged that "A blockade has to permit the passage of humanitarian assistance if needed"; but, she argued, "the San Remo Manual includes two conditions (in Article 103): first, the blockading party may decide where and when and through which port the assistance should reach the coast. In addition, the state may require that a neutral organization on the coast should control the distribution of the items."[58] However, these conditions would only apply in cases where there was a legitimate and lawful blockade to begin with, and thus didn't apply to Israel's unilateral blockade that the ICRC and other international bodies and human rights organizations had declared to be an illegal act of collective punishment.

It is useful to further examine what the San Remo Manual actually has to say about the matter. It applies to "armed conflict at sea" (Article 1). Yet there was no armed conflict at sea in this case. Gaza had no navy (nor an army or air force, for that matter). Attacks against Israel were limited to rockets and mortars fired by militant groups from land against targets on land. Nevertheless, we may for the sake of argument allow that the San Remo Manual was applicable. It explicitly states that the "principles of necessity and proportionality apply equally to armed conflict at sea" (Article 3) and that "Parties to the conflict shall at all times distinguish between civilians or other protected persons and combatants and between civilian or exempt objects and military objectives" (Article 39). It defines "military objectives" as "those which . . . make an effective contribution to military action" (Article 40). Any attacks must be "limited strictly to military objectives", and merchant vessels not making a military contribution "are civilian objects" (Article 41). Any attacks that "are of a nature to cause superfluous injury or unnecessary suffering" or that "are indiscriminate" because they "are not, or cannot be, directed against a specific military objective" are strictly "forbidden" (Article 42). A further obligation is to "take all feasible precautions in the choice of methods and means in order to avoid or minimize collateral casualties or damage". Also forbidden is any attack that "may be expected to cause collateral casualties or damage which would be excessive in relation to the concrete and direct military advantage anticipated from the attack as a whole" (Article 46). Additionally, among the vessels that "are exempt from attack" are "vessels engaged in humanitarian missions, including vessels carrying supplies indispensable to the survival of the civilian population, and vessels engaged in relief actions and rescue operations", as well as "passenger vessels when engaged only in carrying civilian passengers" (Article 47). Finally, any blockade that "has the sole purpose of starving the civilian population or denying it other objects essential for its survival", or which causes "damage to the civilian population" that "is, or may be expected to be, excessive in relation to the concrete and direct military advantage anticipated from the blockade", is strictly "prohibited" (Article 102).[59]

It is eminently clear that according to the very document Lapidoth cited to justify Israel's actions, the attack on the *Mavi Marmara* was illegal. Lapidoth did acknowledge in passing that "there is the condition that a state may not starve the civilian population", but offered no further comment. Even if one could argue that blocking humanitarian supplies was not Israel's "sole" purpose, the fact remained that the continued suffering of the civilian population was a known consequence of the blockade, which was by any rational measure indiscriminate, disproportionate, and otherwise excessive in relation to any possible military objective.

Ignoring all of the above, Lapidoth argued further that a "merchant ship may be visited, searched, or captured", and that "it may be attacked" if it "resists". She asserted that any ship "that clearly intends to breach" a lawful blockade could be "dealt with while it is still on the high seas." From this, she concluded that Israel's capture of the flotilla ships "in international waters" was "legal".[60]

But, again, this assumes a lawful blockade to begin with, and, furthermore, the San Remo Manual explicitly states that the "visit and search" of "merchant vessels" may occur only when "there are reasonable grounds for suspecting that they are subject to capture" (Article 118). No such grounds existed with regard to ships Lapidoth acknowledged were "engaged in humanitarian missions" and which were thus exempt from attack regardless of the lawfulness of the blockade itself. Furthermore, the flotilla ships were forcibly redirected to Israel, while the San Remo Manual specifically states that only "with its consent" may a merchant vessel "be diverted from its declared destination" (Article 119).[61]

Lapidoth cited previous blockades, such as during the Korean War and the Iran-Iraq War, without explaining what relevance those instances had to this case. She again proclaimed that Israel "acted in compliance with international law because it has fulfilled all the conditions for a lawful blockade", including having "notified the relevant authorities of its blockade in Gaza". But by "all the conditions", she just meant those she had cherry-picked, the obvious reason for her omission of all the *other* conditions being that Israel *hadn't* met them, which would have proved problematic for the conclusion she desired to arrive at.

Finally, Lapidoth addressed the question of whether Israel was the legal Occupying Power in Gaza. "Some say that since Israel is still in control of Gaza's airspace and adjacent sea, Israel is still the occupier", she wrote, without bothering to identify who "Some" were, i.e., UN bodies, the ICRC, human rights organizations, etc.; essentially, the entire international community. "According to another opinion," i.e., Israel's, "under the Hague Regulations of 1907 (Respecting the Laws and Customs of War on Land), occupation has to include full control of the area. ('Territory is considered occupied when it is actually placed under the authority of the hostile army. The occupation extends only to the territory where such authority has been established and can be exercised.'—Article 42), and of course Israel does not control the whole territory of Gaza. Therefore, it is not responsible for what happens there." She concluded, "In my opinion, since Israel is not in control of Gaza, it is not the occupier, but in those areas in which Israel still has control—which means sea and airspace—Israel is responsible."[62]

Yet all one must do to recognize the fallacy of this argument is to read what Article 42 actually says, which she conveniently quoted for us. It simply does *not* say that a country must "control the whole territory" for it to be considered occupied. It is extraordinary that Lapidoth could proclaim that Israel was in control "only" of Gaza's sea and airspace, as if there was no sign of its blockade policy at Gaza's *borders*. Israel cannot on one hand place Gaza's land, sea, and airspace under its military control while on the other maintaining that the conditions of occupation do not exist, that "it is not responsible for what happens there."

Apologists for the Israeli attack on the *Mavi Marmara* have claimed that the nine activists were killed in an Israeli act of "self-defense" against passengers aboard the ship who attacked Israeli commandos with clubs and knives. However, it must be recognized that: (a) the inherent right to self-defense against armed aggression belongs not to commandos illegally storming peaceful vessels on humanitarian missions in international waters, but to the civilian passengers aboard; and (b) the Israeli attack, being against a civilian and not a military target and in enforcement of an unlawful blockade of Gaza, was a war crime in and of itself, with the murder of nine peace activists being an additional crime for which there is no justification under international law. To illustrate the absurdity of the logic of Israeli apologists, we may contemplate a simple thought experiment: an armed robber who has broken into a home and killed the homeowner argues before the court that he committed no crime because the homeowner attacked him with a knife, and therefore his act of killing was an exercise of his right to self-defense. Would any self-respecting judge or jury member take this legal defense seriously?

A 'Good Deal' for Gaza

The Freedom Flotilla failed to break the siege, but it did succeed in its goal of focusing international attention onto the issue. As Hamas lawmaker Aziz Dweik later put it, "The Gaza flotilla has done more for Gaza than 10,000 rockets."[63]

On June 9, 2010, Israel announced under intense international criticism that it would allow a greater number of goods into Gaza. The items Israel removed from its list of banned goods were illustrative of just how little the blockade had to do with security; they included juice, jam, halva, spices, shaving cream, potato chips, cookies, and candy.

The UN humanitarian coordinator in the Palestinian territories, Maxwell Gaylard, responded, "A modest expansion of the restrictive list of goods allowed into Gaza falls well short of what is needed."[64] Hamas spokesman Sami Abu Zuhri dismissed it as insignificant and not worth commenting on.

"Yes, we have allowed some chocolate and other snacks through today, but Hamas has rejected them," Ambassador Oren pouted. "They rejected our chocolate."[65]

The day of Israel's announcement, President Obama met with President Abbas and was afterward asked whether he would "take a tougher line with Israel". He replied by saying he had discussed with Abbas how to "actually allow more goods, more services into Gaza", that the PA was "already doing a number of things inside Gaza", and that the US "is already providing assistance". (So, essentially, "No.") His only criticism of Israel's collective punishment of the Palestinians was that it was "inherently unstable", presumably because it forced the US into the "difficult balancing act" of supporting Israel's actions while managing "perceptions" and maintaining "credibility".[66]

The media nevertheless persisted in the charade that the Obama administration was being "tough" on Israel. The Associated Press bewilderingly reported that Obama had called "for sharply limiting Israel's blockade". Obama had done no such thing.[67]

While the administration criticized the flotilla organizers for trying to break the siege instead of taking their humanitarian goods to Israel for its government to deliver to Gaza, the *New York Times* observed that the seized goods were—unsurprisingly—still "sitting at the border in Israel". Israel's excuse for why it wasn't delivering the goods to Gaza as promised was that it was "trying to find a more appealing partner" than the Hamas government "to distribute it"—which, the *Times* added, "may prove difficult."[68]

On June 14, the ICRC issued a press release reiterating that Israel's blockade "constitutes a collective punishment imposed in clear violation of Israel's obligations under international humanitarian law." It detailed the detrimental effect on the health and livelihood of the Palestinians and stated that "the dire situation in Gaza cannot be resolved by providing humanitarian aid." Rather, it was imperative that the blockade be lifted completely.[69]

The ICRC's statement was widely reported in the international media, but almost completely ignored in the US. The only mention of it on the *New York Times* website was the inclusion of two paragraphs taken from a 639-word Reuters article attached to the foot of another article about how Israel had announced a government-appointed commission to investigate its own conduct during the flotilla raid. While the Reuters article had detailed at length the ICRC's condemnation of the blockade as an illegal act of collective punishment, the *Times* selected for inclusion only two paragraphs: the lead, which noted the ICRC's judgment "that Israel's blockade of the Gaza Strip violated the Geneva Conventions", and the one that began, "Israel is entitled to impose restrictions on military material for security reasons . . . ."[70]

On June 20, Israel took "another small step" (*Los Angeles Times*) to ease the siege by agreeing to allow additional truckloads of goods into Gaza, while continuing to block imports of construction materials and raw materials for industry and food production, to block exports, and to prevent Palestinians from entering or leaving.[71]

Even that "small step" went too far for some Israeli officials. Yoel Hasson, a Knesset member from the Kadima party, described the Netanyahu government's agreement to allow more truckloads of goods into Gaza as "a victory for terror".[72]

UNRWA spokesman Christopher Gunness responded to Israel's measure by pointing out—as the ICRC had—that, "Even if the blockade is eased it remains illegal under international law as it is a collective form of punishment on a civilian population."[73] British Prime Minister David Cameron also dismissed the measure as not enough, saying that "Gaza cannot and must not be allowed to remain a prison camp."[74]

George Mitchell, on the other hand, described Israel's announcement as welcomed "progress". He defended the blockade on the grounds that "Israel has legitimate security concerns".[75] The *Washington Post* remarked in a considerable understatement that "Israel lacks international support" for its policy. But "No matter how alone Israelis have felt in the past," the *Post* also noted, "they have routinely found comfort in unconditional US support."[76]

As with Israel's Gaza massacre, the US sought to block an international investigation into Israel's attack on the flotilla. The US favored an Israeli investigation by a three-member committee led by former Supreme Court Justice Jacob Turkel that was handpicked by Netanyahu, had no subpoena power, and would not be able to question IDF soldiers or compel members of the military to provide evidence. All it could do was to request documents and summaries from the IDF's inquiries into its own conduct. UN Secretary-General Ban Ki-moon pointed out that the Turkel Commission was "not sufficient enough to have international credibility". *Haaretz* described it as "a farce".[77]

Marc Lynch, an associate professor of political science and international affairs at George Washington University and a blogger at *Foreign Policy*, commented that the Israeli decision had come "in exchange for American support for a whitewash of the investigation of the flotilla incident". This was "a good deal" for Gazans, he argued, because a real investigation would not "produce anything of any particular value". The US's willingness to defend Israel's murder of nine peace activists in exchange for a slight easing of the siege was therefore "the right move", for which members of the Obama administration "deserve some real credit".[78]

Lynch offered no comment on why, if the US wanted Israel to ease its siege, it couldn't have just used its enormous influence to pressure Israel to do so, or why an effort to seek accountability would be of no particular value to anyone—least of all the victims' families.

One thing was certain: it was a very good deal for Israel. Accordingly, Israel continued to act with impunity. The day after it announced the decision to allow in more goods, it granted preliminary approval for additional demolitions of Palestinian homes and illegal settlement construction in East Jerusalem.[79]

It also ordered the deportation from East Jerusalem of three members of the Palestinian parliament and a former minister.[80] B'Tselem issued a report in July finding that the number of Israelis living in the settlements was half a million. With Israel controlling 42 percent of the West Bank, there was a "continuous pilfering of land from Palestinians". In addition to taking land for "military needs", Israel had provided a "cloak of legality" to its "ongoing theft" by declaring Palestinian property to be "state land" under the Ottoman Land Law of 1858.[81]

Obama and Netanyahu rescheduled their meeting for July 6 to allow some time for the outcry over Israel's murderous attack on the *Mavi Marmara* to blow over. Prior to the meeting, Eliot L. Engel, a Democratic representative from New York, criticized Obama for "appearing to put public pressure on Israel while appearing not to put the same type of intense pressure on Palestinians."[82] Obama illustrated just how delusional that suggestion was in his remarks to the press following the meeting. He praised Netanyahu for continuing the slightly-eased siege, as well as for being prepared to enter peace talks, without once mentioning the issue of settlements. He repeated how the US's "commitment to Israel's security" was "unwavering" and cited examples of the importance of their "special relationship": "economic, military-to-military, issues related to Israel maintaining its qualitative military edge, intelligence-sharing, how we are able to work together effectively on the international front", etc. When asked whether he thought it would be "helpful for Israel to extend the partial settlement moratorium", which was due to expire in September, Obama responded by praising Israel for having "shown restraint" that was "conducive" to peace talks, which he hoped would occur "well before the moratorium has expired".

His tone changed entirely when it came to the Palestinians. It was "very important", he lectured, that they "not look for excuses for incitement, that they are not engaging in provocative language; that at the international level, they are maintaining a constructive tone, as opposed to looking for opportunities to embarrass Israel."

He had no words for Israel about any behaviors it should not be engaged in or tone of language it shouldn't be using.[83]

A headline in the *Washington Post* summed up the meeting: "Netanyahu hears no discouraging words from Obama". In the article, Dana Milbank attempted to reconcile the image of Obama as being "tough" on Israel with his failure to hold Netanyahu accountable for his actions by explaining that Obama *wanted* to be tough, but just *couldn't* due to overwhelming political pressure to be nice to Israel. In response to the administration's previous complaints over Israel announcing settlement construction during Joe Biden's visit, "The Israel lobby reared up, Netanyahu denounced the administration's reactions, Republican leaders sided with Netanyahu, and Democrats ran for cover." While Obama had been "positioning himself as more of an honest broker", "he has now learned the painful lesson that domestic politics won't allow such a stand."[84] The message was that, since Obama was unable to get "tough" on Israel due to factors simply beyond his control, therefore he couldn't fairly be criticized for doing the opposite. Another *Post* article the same day optimistically described Obama's meeting with Netanyahu as a "makeup session" and positive effort to "thaw relations".[85]

The "crisis of historic proportions", as Ambassador Oren had described it, had passed. The US and Israel had survived the "hiccup" in their "special relationship", which Obama could thankfully be credited for salvaging. What this happy makeup meant in terms of the consequences *for the Palestinians* was a question mainstream American commentators couldn't be troubled to consider.

One obvious result was the continuation of the collective punishment of the civilian population of Gaza. A joint report of OCHA and the World Food Program in August 2010 examined Israel's restrictions on Palestinians' access to their own land. Israel had gradually expanded the "security zone" over the years so that Palestinians were prevented from accessing land from 1,000 to 1,500 meters from the border, accounting for 17 percent of the total land mass of Gaza and 35 percent of its agricultural land. Israel also restricted Palestinians' access to their own waters to three nautical miles from shore. Israel enforced its restrictions "by opening live fire on people entering the restricted areas". Since the end of Operation Cast Lead, 22 civilians had been killed under these circumstances and 146 injured, including at least 27 children. Israel also discouraged access through "the systematic leveling of farm land and the destruction of other private property located in restricted areas."[86]

On November 30, a group of twenty-five international organizations, including Amnesty International, Christian Aid, Oxfam International, and Save the Children, published a report titled "Dashed Hopes: Continuation of the Gaza Blockade". While Israel had in June announced under international pressure "a set of measures to 'ease' its illegal blockade", "five months later, there are few signs of real improvement on the ground". The report called on Israel to "fully lift its blockade of the Gaza Strip."

The UN estimated that 670,000 truckloads of reconstruction material would be required to repair the destruction from Operation Cast Lead, but Israel was permitting only about 715 truckloads per month, keeping the inflow at "a mere 11% of pre-blockade levels", a rate at which "it would take many decades to build the needed homes".

Israel continued to ban all exports. There had been an increase in the amount of food allowed in, but Israel continued to deny permits for many items not on its list of banned goods, and items on the list banned as "dual use"—meaning it could theoretically have military as well as civilian applications—went "far beyond the international definition of dual-use items". Factories remained without the raw materials required to reopen. Gaza's unemployment rate was at 39 percent, with 80 percent of the population dependent on international aid for survival.

There had been no easing of restrictions on fuel imports. Gaza's only power plant remained limited to 68 percent of its capacity. Cooking gas imports were about half of what was required for average needs, and there was "almost no diesel and petrol allowed for [the] commercial sector." One consequence was "a chronic lack of electricity and regular blackouts, affecting provision of essential services, including water supply, sewages treatment, and health services."

Gazans remained unable to access 35 percent of their farmland and 85 percent of their territorial waters because they risked being shot if they entered Israel's "buffer zone". Since the "easing" of the blockade, Israeli soldiers had shot and killed six civilians, including two children, and injured fifty-seven others, including ten children. Under the Oslo Accords, Israel agreed to respect Palestinians' right to access their own waters up to twenty nautical miles from shore; but in practice, it limited Gazans to three nautical miles, sometimes opening fire on fishing boats even within this limit, causing casualties. This had devastated the fishing industry and caused the poverty rate among fishermen to soar to 90 percent.

Israel continued to deny to Palestinians freedom of movement, and although it had promised to improve the process for entry and exit permits, there had to date been "no tangible improvement in practice." Patients needing medical treatment unavailable in Gaza were among the few allowed to leave, but they required permits that were "frequently delayed or denied by Israeli authorities". The delays meant missed hospital appointments, which meant the permit process would need to begin all over again. These restrictions on exit permits preventing Palestinians from getting the medical care they needed had caused thirty-three patient deaths since 2009.

The report concluded that Israel's blockade policy "constitutes a collective punishment of the entire civilian population of Gaza and is in clear violation of international law". It was implemented to punish Palestinians for electing Hamas to power, but "upholding the rights and needs of civilians in Gaza must not be conditional on other political objectives." Fully lifting the blockade "remains a legal, economic and political imperative for those seeking a lasting resolution to the Israeli-Palestinian conflict." The international community had a responsibility to ensure the "complete lifting of the blockade", and the UN Security Council should thus take action to ensure the implementation of Resolution 1860.

In an apparent allusion to the US policy of refusing to do so, the report called on the international community to "State explicitly that the ongoing blockade is illegal under international law."[87]

In another report reiterating many of these same points, the Palestinian Center for Human Rights also pointed out that "the diplomatic initiatives sponsored by the Quartet . . . merely focus on the increase of the volume of goods' exchanges" and "fail to address the inherent illegality of the closure and the detrimental effects it has on the local populations' human rights." Israel's "alleged easing is in fact purely cosmetic and does not represent any substantial change to the intrinsic illegality of the closure." As John Ging had put it, there was "no tangible change for the people on the ground here with regard to their condition, dependence on aid, the absence of any recovery or reconstruction." While Israel had apparently removed such goods as "sage, cardamom, cumin, coriander, ginger, jam, ketchup, biscuits and potato chips" from its list of banned items, "other seemingly innocuous goods, such as dried fruit, fresh meat, notebooks, toys, musical instruments, fishing nets, irrigation pipe systems, donkeys and goats continued to remain prohibited, along with potential 'dual use goods', which include virtually all construction materials."

Additionally, the Israeli government had openly admitted in a case before the Supreme Court that its policy was one of "Targeting the economy itself", which it described as "a legitimate means of warfare" and "a relevant consideration" when deciding what goods to permit into Gaza.[88]

Evidence that the people of Gaza had gotten a "good deal" out of the Obama administration's decision to block any efforts to hold Israel accountable for its actions remained conspicuously lacking.

Israel's 'Cast Lead' Self-Exoneration: Second Update

While the "makeup session" between Obama and Netanyahu was taking place in early July 2010, in an apparently coordinated effort, Israel announced indictments and disciplinary actions resulting from its self-investigations. The *New York Times* reported that a staff sergeant had been indicted for manslaughter for killing a civilian carrying a white flag, and a battalion commander faced a charge of "deviating from 'authorized and appropriate' army behavior" for ordering the use of a Palestinian man as a human shield. A third officer who ordered the strike on the Ibrahim al-Maqadmah mosque received "disciplinary action": he was told he "would not serve in similar positions of command in the future" and was "rebuked". A criminal investigation was also ordered into the attack on the Samouni family home in Zeytoun. The *Times* also reminded that Israel had earlier "reprimanded" a brigadier general and a colonel for the attack on the UNRWA compound, charged two staff sergeants for using a nine-year-old boy as a human shield, and convicted a soldier of stealing a Palestinian's credit card.[89]

Israel later that month released its second update on its self-investigations into Operation Cast Lead, in which the IDF for the most part acquitted itself of wrongdoing. It justified its attacks on police stations by pronouncing that "Hamas's 'police' force" performed "significant military functions" and that Gaza's police stations were "legitimate military targets". At the same time, the paper implicitly confirmed the findings of the UN Fact-Finding Mission, B'Tselem, and Amnesty International that the police were not engaged in hostilities at the time they were killed, stating in a footnote that "police have been observed performing this function during *past* operations of the IDF in the Gaza Strip" (emphasis added)—but evidently *not* during Operation Cast Lead.[90]

In the case of the attack that killed over forty civilians just outside the UNRWA school in Jabaliya on January 6, Israel said the deaths were "regrettable", but determined that "the anticipated collateral damage" was "not excessive" and that the IDF's choice of mortar rounds was "appropriate".[91] That is to say, Israel found it "appropriate" to launch mortar rounds toward a school where civilians were taking shelter despite admittedly having anticipated that doing so would likely result in civilian deaths. Whether the number of civilians actually killed exceeded the number anticipated, Israel didn't say. Nor did it clarify whether it would agree that over forty qualified as excessive.

With regard to Israel's attacks on the UNRWA compound on January 15, the paper said that two senior commanders had been "disciplined" for authorizing "the use of high explosive shells", but that no criminal charges were filed against them because the shells were allegedly "aimed at military targets". It claimed that the IDF "needed" to use white phosphorus munitions "to protect Israeli forces" and that their use "complied with the requirements of proportionality" under international law. The paper offered no explanation for how, if "aimed at military targets", multiple rounds managed instead to hit the UN compound, including white phosphorus shells that burned down the warehouse. Nor did it explain why the bombardments continued even after the IDF had been repeatedly informed that the compound was being hit, or why Olmert had publicly stated that the compound was indeed directly targeted. The paper also stated that the damage to the UN site "was more extensive than the IDF had anticipated", thus contradicting itself with an admission that the IDF had indeed *anticipated* that its bombardments would damage the compound.[92]

Israel finally admitted—after long having denied it—that the IDF hit the Ibrahim al-Maqadmah mosque on January 3, "resulting in a large number of casualties inside the mosque". It claimed that the target had been "two terrorist operatives" who "belonged to" a group that had launched rockets at Israel—but who were evidently not themselves engaged in hostilities. Israel admitted that a captain knew the building was a mosque and faulted him for not informing his superiors, who supposedly "were not aware" of this and "did not anticipate" the deaths of civilians inside. The commanding officers had "used a more powerful missile than they had been directed to use", supposedly because "the requested missile was not available". The captain was "disciplined by means of a severe reprimand", and two other officers were "sanctioned" for having "exercised poor professional judgment" in their choice of weapon.[93]

The paper acknowledged an incident discussed in the UN Fact-Finding Mission Report in which a civilian was killed while "walking with a group of civilians carrying white flags" in Juhr ad-Dik on January 4. The soldier who pulled the trigger had been indicted "on the charge of manslaughter".[94]

With regard to another case studied by the Mission, in which a woman named Rouhiyah al-Najjar was shot in the head while walking with a group of women and children carrying white flags, Israel acknowledged the killing. But it claimed that the soldiers' concern that the women and children "could conceal a gunman or suicide bomber" justified firing a "warning shot", which killed Najjar by "richochet"—a determination apparently made on the sole basis of the testimony of the soldier who fired the fatal shot. Since the killer had not confessed to murder, Israel saw no reason to investigate the plausibility of this explanation any further, much less file any charges.[95]

Regarding the case discussed in the Fact-Finding Mission Report of the shooting of members of the Abd Rabbo family on January 7 while they were carrying white flags, Israel claimed that "the evidence was insufficient to initiate criminal proceedings". It arrived at this conclusion by dismissing the testimony of numerous Palestinian witnesses on the puzzling basis, lacking in detail, that there were "discrepancies" between their testimonies and "the findings of the investigation"—apparently another case of determining that since the killers hadn't confessed to the murders, there was no reason for disciplinary action; and since the witness testimonies didn't match the IDF debriefings, they must be dismissed. Instructively, Israel did *not* claim there were any discrepancies *between the testimonies of eyewitnesses* to the shootings.[96]

Regarding the case where flechettes were used in an attack on condolence tents in Beit Lahiya on January 5, Israel claimed that a tank crew, from nearly a mile away, "had visually identified a squad of terrorist operatives in open terrain, loading a 'Grad' rocket onto a launcher". The soldiers "did not identify any civilians in the vicinity", and "the harm to the civilians" occurred "incidentally". Furthermore, flechettes were "not prohibited under international law".[97] Israel thus failed to address the relevant question of whether its actual *use* of the weapon was indiscriminate, as all evidence indicated. As the UN Mission had pointed out, when used in residential areas where civilians may be expected to be present, flechettes are "by their nature lacking in discrimination".

With regard to the destruction of the Sawafeary chicken farms in Zeytoun on January 3, the paper asserted that the "chicken coops were destroyed" in order "to allow a clean line of sight for protection of IDF forces." Israel declared that it was "not intended to deny the civilian population in Gaza access to essential commodities". The destruction of private property and killing of tens of thousands of chickens was "justified by military necessity."[98]

Israel's paper claimed that the Atta Abu Jubbah cement-packaging plant "may have" been damaged from shelling by soldiers who "believed"—incorrectly, evidently—"that the plant was being used by Hamas operatives". The soldiers fired at unspecified and perhaps equally imaginary "military targets near the factory". Other "incidental" damage to the plant was caused by "IDF tanks and bulldozers" that "entered the plant" allegedly in order to "locate and destroy an intricate tunnel system that was dug by Hamas". Whether this alleged tunnel system was actually found in the plant Israel didn't disclose—a curious omission, indeed, had it been real.[99]

Israel similarly justified the destruction of the Al-Wadiyah Group's factories on the grounds that Hamas had been "in the area". Since there was a "concern" that the factories posed a "threat", "the IDF forces decided to demolish the buildings." Israel's investigation "concluded that the demolition of the buildings was lawful" on the grounds of "military necessity."[100]

With regard to the Al-Bader flour mill, the paper noted that since Israel's first update on its investigations, the media had reported "that the UN was in possession of evidence that contradicted the findings of the IDF investigation. Specifically, it was reported that an unexploded IAF bomb was found in the mill, even though the command investigation had concluded there had been no aerial strike." Israel's response to the UN's evidence was to insist that the mill "had not been intentionally targeted". The IAF had conducted attacks "in the vicinity of the mill", but "none of them could have resulted in a hit on the flour mill." At the same time, Israel admitted that, indeed, "the ordnance had found its way into the mill". No alternative explanation was provided. Had it grown legs and walked?[101]

The two staff sergeants charged with "compelling a Palestinian minor to assist them in a manner that put the minor at risk" were later found guilty. The Israeli military justice system determined that stealing a credit card was a greater crime than using a nine-year-old boy as a human shield: the thief was sentenced to seven-and-a-half months in prison, while the two staff sergeants were demoted to the rank of sergeant and given suspended three-month sentences. "The slap on the wrist for these soldiers", said Human Rights Watch's Middle East director, Sarah Leah Whitson, "is another slap in the face for the victims of violations during Operation Cast Lead."[102]

Israel's refusal to punish soldiers for war crimes was certainly nothing new. B'Tselem had issued a report the previous month noting how, since the beginning of the Second Intifada in 2000, Israel's military justice system "effectively grants immunity to soldiers and officers, with the result that soldiers who kill Palestinians not taking part in hostilities are almost never held accountable for their misdeeds." The group documented how "the army allows soldiers and officers to violate the law, encourages a trigger-happy attitude, and shows gross disregard for human life."[103]

On September 23, 2010, the UN report of the committee of independent experts to monitor and assess investigations into the Gaza conflict by Israel and the Palestinians was released. It noted that any investigation that was not "impartial, thorough, effective and prompt" must be viewed as "no more than a maneuver of artful deceit." The committee had "concerns about the investigations conducted into the Gaza conflict thus far." It criticized Israel's refusal to cooperate and expressed "reservations as to whether investigations were sufficiently prompt", given the long delays in launching investigations and interviewing witnesses.[104]

The committee also noted that at the center of Israel's military justice system was the Military Advocate General, who was appointed by the Minister of Defense and acted in a legal advisory role, leading to "dual responsibilities" that "raise concerns of a lack of impartiality." The MAG "gave legal advice . . . to commanders at all levels leading up to and during the Gaza conflict"; and Israel had publicly stated that its "lawyers examined the legality of planned targets, participated in the operational planning process, helped direct humanitarian efforts and took part in situation assessments, exercises and simulations." The lack of impartiality was also manifest in the fact that, despite "the seriousness of the allegations, the military investigations thus far appear to have produced very little." Israel appeared not to have investigated all of the allegations of serious violations of international law documented in the UN Fact-Finding Mission Report and had "not conducted a general review of the military doctrine regarding legitimate military targets."[105]

The committee further stated:

> Finally, Israel has not conducted investigations into decisions made at the highest levels about the design and implementation of the Gaza operations. A core allegation in the [UN Fact-Finding Mission] report was that the systematic and deliberate nature of the destruction in Gaza left the Mission "in no doubt that responsibility lies in the first place with those who designed, ordered and oversaw the operations". Those alleged serious violations go beyond individual criminal responsibility at the level of combatants and even commanders, and include allegations aimed at decision makers higher up the chain of command.[106]

The UN committee concluded that the role of the MAG's office in investigating the IDF's conduct while itself intimately involved in operational planning and execution—including by offering legal advice with respect to chosen targets—constituted "a conflict of interest" that raised a serious concern about the credibility of its inquiries. Israel's failure to investigate its military and political leadership was also a failure of its obligations under international law;

and, in any event, "the military justice system would not be the appropriate mechanism to undertake such an investigation, given the military's inherent conflict of interest."[107]

The committee also found that while Hamas had established a committee to undertake investigations, its report "did not seriously address the recommendations by the Fact-Finding Mission to the de facto Gaza authorities."[108]

With regard to the role of Israel's Military Advocate General, the US Embassy in Tel Aviv noted in a diplomatic cable to Secretary Clinton: "A long-standing joke in the Israeli military relates to the need for an attorney as an essential component of the combat soldiers [sic] assault equipment." But the MAG's plan to "take the troops through the treacherous minefields of international law" was "a promise that now seems overly optimistic."[109]

The Report of the UN Fact-Finding Mission on the Gaza Flotilla Incident

The Turkel Commission, Israel's self-investigation into its deadly attack on the *Mavi Marmara*, was at the time also underway. Mark Steel reported in *The Independent* on some of the facts emerging from the inquiry, including the testimony of "Sgt S", who was responsible for shooting six of the nine civilians killed aboard the ship and who justified his actions by saying they "were without a doubt terrorists". "And he produced evidence to back this up," Steel quipped, "which was: 'I could see the murderous rage in their eyes'." According to the IDF, the activists aboard the ship were "well-trained and likely ex-military". Evidence was produced for this, too, which was: "each squad of the mercenaries was equipped with a Motorola communication device, so they could pass information to one another". Explaining why none of these "terrorists" had any firearms, the IDF said they preferred to use "bats, metal bars and knives, since opening fire would have made it blatantly clear they were terrorists and not peace activists". At the same time, the IDF insisted that the passengers *had* brought guns aboard, but that "the mercenaries threw their weapons overboard after the commandos took control of the vessel".[110]

In sum, one could look into the eyes of the passengers aboard the *Mavi Marmara* and see that they were terrorists with murderous intent, which was also confirmed from the fact that they were equipped with cell phones. But they were clever enough to try to disguise the fact that they were terrorists by throwing their guns into the sea and instead grabbing whatever else they could find on board to use against the armed Israeli soldiers storming their ship.

Defense Minister Ehud Barak defended his role by telling the Turkel Commission that, while he was responsible "for the orders given on the political level", the IDF was responsible for how the operation was actually carried out. "The politicians determined the 'what' and the IDF worked out the 'how'," he explained. While careful to pin responsibility for the operation's "complica-tions" on the military, rather than the political leadership, Barak praised the attack on the flotilla as a "success", saying that its goal "was achieved."[111]

IDF Chief of Staff Lieutenant-General Gabi Ashkenazi told the commis-sion that his soldiers' actions during the attack had been "proportionate and correct", and that they had "exhibited calm, bravery and morality". They had "legitimately opened fire and shot those they needed to shoot and not those they didn't need to shoot." Their only "mistake" was that, "to reduce the risk" to themselves, they "should have used precise fire to incapacitate" passengers on the deck who were "preventing" them "from boarding the boat". In other words, the commandos' sole "mistake" was that they only shot and killed civil-ians *after* storming the ship and hadn't shot any *before* landing on deck.[112]

In August, the UN Secretary-General announced his formation of a Panel of Inquiry to investigate Israel's attack on the flotilla, separate from the Human Rights Council's fact-finding mission into the incident. The Panel was to consist of former New Zealand Prime Minister Geoffrey Palmer and Colombia Presi-dent Alvaro Uribe, along with one member each from Israel and Turkey.[113]

In September, the Center for Constitutional Rights, a legal advocacy or-ganization based in New York, issued a report emphasizing that the attack on the flotilla must be assessed in light of the fact that Israel's blockade was "il-legal under international law". Furthermore, the attack was "disproportionate" and therefore "illegal" regardless of the legality of the blockade. Additionally, Israel's claim that there were weapons aboard was entirely without merit, and the boats, which had variously left ports in Turkey, Greece, and Cyprus, had all been searched before departure.[114]

With the expectation that the UN's fact-finding mission would reach similar conclusions, the Israeli Foreign Ministry denounced it even before publication as "biased and as one-sided as the body that has produced it". The matter had been "amply and sufficiently investigated as it is" by the Turkel Commission. "All additional dealing with this issue is superfluous and unproductive."[115]

Released on September 27, the UN report of the fact-finding mission on the flotilla attack detailed the effects of Israel's blockade on the civilian popula-tion. It had caused a "severe humanitarian situation in Gaza, the destruction of the economy and the prevention of reconstruction". It was "inflicting dis-proportionate damage upon the civilian population" amounting to "collective punishment" in violation of Article 33 of the Fourth Geneva Convention. As such, Israel's interception of the flotilla "could not be justified and therefore has to be considered illegal." Alluding to the US's apologetic description of the situ-ation in Gaza, the mission stated that to characterize the "humanitarian crisis" in Gaza as merely "unsustainable" was "totally intolerable and unacceptable in the twenty-first century."[116]

Under international law, and according to the San Remo Manual that Israel had cited as justification, "the only lawful basis" for such actions "would be a reasonable suspicion" that the vessels were "making an effective contribution" to war or posed an imminent threat to Israel that it had no other means to prevent. In this case, Israel was rather "motivated by concerns about the possible propaganda victory that might be claimed by the organizers of the flotilla." The evidence given at the Turkel Commission itself had made it "clear that there was no reasonable suspicion" that the flotilla posed any kind of military threat. "Thus, no case can be made for the legality of the interception and the Mission therefore finds that the interception was illegal." The passengers aboard "were civilians" who "must be considered protected persons", and consequently there could be no justification for the use of military force against them.[117]

The report documented the facts and circumstances of the attack at length. It noted that while the flotilla organizers had intended "to deliver humanitarian assistance and supplies to Gaza", their primary objectives were "to draw international public attention to the situation in the Gaza Strip and the effect of the blockade" and "to break the blockade". The *Mavi Marmara* had left from the port in Antalya, Turkey, where "stringent security" measures were implemented "and all items taken on board were checked. Passengers and their luggage were subjected to security checks similar to those found in airports before boarding, including body searches." The other boats in the flotilla had similarly been subject to "meticulous security checks".[118]

Israel had openly planned "to intercept, board and commandeer the ships. Details of the Israeli plans had been published in an Israeli newspaper." Flotilla participants became aware of the Israeli plans while assembling near Cyprus. As a result, some passengers aboard the *Mavi Marmara* took it upon themselves to prepare "to defend the ship against any boarding attempt." Using tools from the ship's workshop, they sawed sections of railings and removed chains between them. "When the ship's crew discovered this, the tools were confiscated and locked in the radio room on the bridge." It was evident from the fact that "last minute efforts to fashion rudimentary weapons" occurred that "no weapons were brought on board the ship." Passengers aboard the other boats had discussions about engaging in passive resistance and adhering to nonviolence in the expectation that Israeli forces would attempt to board.[119]

As the flotilla approached Gaza, Israeli naval forces radioed the boats and warned them that they were approaching a blockade, ordering them to change course to Ashdod, Israel. The captains of the flotilla ships replied that their purpose was to deliver humanitarian aid to Gaza, that the Israeli blockade was illegal, and that Israel had no authority to order them to change course. Israeli forces first attempted to board the *Mavi Marmara* from zodiac boats by attaching ladders to the hull, but passengers repelled the soldiers with water hoses, chairs, sticks, and other objects. A helicopter was then used to drop soldiers by rope onto the deck. The Mission determined that "live ammunition was used from the helicopter onto the top deck prior to the descent of the soldiers."

When the first soldiers landed on the deck, fighting broke out and soldiers were disarmed by the passengers and their weapons thrown into the sea. One American passenger, former US Marine Ken O'Keefe, disarmed a soldier by seizing and unloading his 9 mm pistol, which was "then hidden in another part of the ship in an attempt to retain evidence." There was "no evidence to suggest that any of the passengers used firearms" against the Israeli soldiers, who continued to use live ammunition while storming the deck. Three soldiers were subdued, brought inside the ship, and released after Israeli forces had taken over control of the ship. During the initial fifteen minutes of the attack, four passengers were fatally wounded, and at least nineteen others injured, fourteen with gunshot wounds. "Given the relatively small number of passengers on the top deck during the incident," the report said, "the Mission is driven to the conclusion that the vast majority were in receipt of gunshot wounds."[120]

The Mission found that:

> Israeli soldiers continued shooting at passengers who had already been wounded, with live ammunition, soft baton charges (beanbags) and plastic bullets. Forensic analysis demonstrates that two of the passengers killed on the top deck received wounds compatible with being shot at close range while lying on the ground: Furkan Doğan received a bullet in the face and İbrahim Bilgen received a fatal wound from a soft baton round (beanbag) fired at such close proximity to his head that parts such as wadding penetrated his skull and entered his brain. Once the Israeli forces had secured control of the top deck they undertook measures to move down to the bridge deck below in order to take over the ship's bridge and thus take control of the ship. . . . Israeli soldiers fired live ammunition both from the top deck at passengers on the bridge deck below, and after they had moved down to the bridge deck. At least four passengers were killed, and at least nine injured (five with firearms injuries) during this phase. None of the four passengers who were killed, including a photographer who at the time of being shot was engaged in taking photographs and was shot by an Israeli soldier positioned on the top deck above, posed any threat to the Israeli forces.[121]

Other ships in the flotilla were also forcefully boarded, with soldiers using stun grenades and firing plastic bullets and paint balls at passengers engaged in passive resistance. The Mission concluded that, "Insofar as the Israeli interception of the flotilla was unlawful . . . the use of force by the Israeli forces in seizing control of the *Mavi Marmara* and other vessels was also *prima facie* unlawful since there was no legal basis for the Israeli forces to conduct an assault and interception in international waters." Furthermore, even given "a justifiable belief of an immediate threat to life or serious injury of certain soldiers which would have justified the use of firearms against specific passengers", "lethal force was employed by the Israeli soldiers in a widespread and arbitrary manner which caused an unnecessarily large number of persons to be killed or seriously injured. . . . The circumstances of the killing of at least six of the passengers were in a manner consistent with an extra-legal, arbitrary and summary execution."[122]

Since the interception of the flotilla was unlawful, "the detention of passengers on board each of the vessels was also *prima facie* unlawful." After being forcefully redirected to Ashdod and imprisoned, Israelis attempted to coerce passengers to sign a form stating in Hebrew that "the signatory admitted to having entered Israel illegally and consented to deportation and [to] be banned from re-entering Israel for a 10-year period." Most refused to sign "on the basis that they had been brought to Israel from international waters against their will or because they did not want to sign a document they did not understand." Some passengers were threatened with a "lengthy detention period pending court proceeding", "threatened with physical violence", or "beaten or physically abused" in an effort to coerce them into signing the document. As passengers were in the process of being deported, some witnessed an older passenger being treated roughly and protested his treatment, for which they were "charged by soldiers using batons. In the foray, around 30 passengers were beaten to the ground, kicked and punched in a sustained attack by soldiers."[123]

On September 29, the Human Rights Council adopted a resolution welcoming the report of the committee of independent experts, condemning Israel's refusal to cooperate, and renewing the committee's mandate to assess the self-investigations of Israel and Hamas into their conduct during Operation Cast Lead. The resolution was adopted by a vote of twenty-seven to one.[124] The Council also passed a resolution welcoming the report of the fact-finding mission on the attack on the flotilla, regretting Israel's non-cooperation, endorsing the report's conclusions, and recommending that the General Assembly consider the report. It passed by a vote of thirty to one.[125] The explanation offered by the US for its solitary nay vote was that the "language, tone and conclusions" of the fact-finding mission report were "unbalanced", meaning that it was critical of the perpetrators of the crime rather than the victims.[126]

The Turkel Commission: Another Israeli 'Whitewash'

Israel publicly released the final report of the Turkel Commission in January 2011. It pointed out that Gisha and B'Tselem had argued that Israel remained the occupying power in Gaza because it "controls movement to and from the Gaza Strip via land crossings", "exercises complete control over Gaza's airspace and territorial waters", "controls movement within Gaza through periodic incursions and a 'no-go zone'", "controls the Palestinian population registry", "exercises control over Gaza's tax system and fiscal policy", and "exercises control over the Palestinian Authority and its ability to provide services to Gaza residents". The commission didn't dispute any of these facts, but nevertheless concluded that "Israel does not have 'effective control' in the Gaza Strip", thus that it was not an Occupying Power, and thus that the Fourth Geneva Convention did not apply. It cited an Israeli Supreme Court decision further concluding that Israel "does not have a general duty to ensure the welfare of the residents of the Gaza Strip". So Israel was free to punish the civilian population as it saw fit.[127]

The Turkel Commission argued further that the naval blockade was legal under international law, citing the San Remo Manual and repeating the fallacious arguments already discussed. It admitted that a direct result of the siege was "food insecurity" among the population, but denied that this consequence of Israeli policy constituted collective punishment because it "does not equate to 'starvation'". There was "no evidence", the Commission declared, that "Israel is denying objects essential for the survival of the civilian population". Yet there was "considerable evidence" that Israel "allows the passage of objects essential for the survival of the civilian population". Therefore, Israel was "in compliance with the requirement of proportionality provided in international humanitarian law, especially in view of the extensive steps that it took" following the attack on the flotilla to ease restrictions.[128]

In short, the commission's argument was that inflicting punishment on the civilian population by creating a condition of "food insecurity" was acceptable under international law so long the resulting humanitarian crisis didn't escalate to the point where Gazans began to actually drop dead from outright starvation.

This intention of Israel to collectively punish the people of Gaza was recognized in the November 2008 State Department cable, which was obtained by the organization Wikileaks and published just weeks before the Turkel Commission report was released. As previously noted, the cable stated that "Israeli officials have confirmed to Embassy officials on multiple occasions that they intend to keep the Gazan economy functioning at the lowest level possible consistent with avoiding a humanitarian crisis." They "intend to keep the Gazan economy on the brink of collapse without quite pushing it over the edge".[129]

Subsequently, the US State Department also privately observed that Israel was achieving its goal of collectively punishing the civilian population. Consul General of the US Mission in Jerusalem Daniel Rubinstein noted that Gaza's water and electricity infrastructure "suffer from a lack of supplies and basic maintenance", the "lack of variety and continuing price increases" of food in Gaza was "negatively impacting people's health", and the "lack of medicine is crippling the health sector." Yes, the population was malnourished, he acknowledged, but not "starving".[130]

But according to the logic of the Turkel Commission, enforcing a policy that caused hunger, malnutrition, stunted growth in children, etc., was all perfectly "legal". The Commission arrived at this conclusion by adopting it as its premise: "If the customary rules regarding the imposition of a naval blockade are followed," the Commission reasoned, "it is difficult to see how this could constitute collective punishment."[131]

Furthermore, "the fact that the fabric of economic life of the civilian population is adversely affected as a result of economic warfare does not, in itself, amount to 'collective punishment.'" This was, again, because the evidence didn't go as far as supporting a charge of outright genocide through mass starvation.[132]

The Commission acknowledged that "there is no doubt that the economic warfare Israel carries out with an intention of weakening the Hamas has an adverse impact on the daily life of the civilian population in Gaza." But there was "nothing in evidence" that would "suggest that Israel is *intentionally* placing restrictions on goods for the sole or primary purpose of denying them to the population of Gaza."[133] Perhaps Israel blocked the importation of toys and fishing nets because it believed that Hamas intended to manufacture weapons out of them, and livestock because, in lieu of tanks and jets, Hamas might ride into battle on the backs of donkeys and goats?

It is enough to observe the fact that, by this standard, so long as "*intentionally*" denying goods to the civilian population of Gaza was merely a *secondary* goal of Israel's policy, it would *still* not constitute "collective punishment" as redefined by the Turkel Commission.

On such premises, the Commission further judged that it had a right to intercept the flotilla. Moreover, the "captain of the *Mavi Marmara* was warned that if the ship did not stop, it would be responsible for the consequences". In this way, Israel relieved itself of any responsibility for its attack on a civilian vessel in international waters. When the boats refused to change course, the IDF moved to forcibly "take control of the ships", and its soldiers "were met with extreme violence" on the deck of the *Mavi Marmara*.

The Commission claimed that the passengers' attacks on Israeli soldiers included "the use of firearms" and that "two were shot". Its report included lengthy testimonies from IDF soldiers describing passengers as "terrorists". The two soldiers in question described coming to the realization that they had been shot and attributing this outcome to the "terrorists", dismissing the possibility of friendly fire, even though neither, evidently, had actually seen where the shots came from or identified their shooter. The commission admitted that "no firearms were found on the *Mavi Marmara*". The pistol confiscated by Ken O'Keefe was later recovered, but the other firearms taken from Israeli soldiers were not found. One soldier witnessed a passenger throwing a firearm overboard.[134]

The Turkel Commission further argued that since the civilian passengers aboard the *Mavi Marmara* were "clearly resisting capture", the ship became "a military objective" and thus "could have been attacked." That is, the act of resistance to an attack by Israeli soldiers provided *ex post facto* justification for the Israeli military having initiated that attack—logic any pirate would enthusiastically embrace. The commission then delved even deeper into absurdity by maintaining that, even though it would have been justified, "Israeli forces did *not* attack the flotilla vessels" because "they did not use force or 'violence' against the *ships*. Their efforts were focused exclusively on capturing the ships and diverting them"—by using force and violence against the *passengers* of the ships. By resisting, passengers were taking part in "hostilities". Therefore, they lost their civilian status and could be "targeted in the same manner as if they were combatants." That is to say, the passengers lost their right to self-defense by virtue of having attempted to exercise it. Ergo, any suggestions that the passengers "were acting in legitimate self-defense" were "not supported by the evidence".

The real victims, according to the Turkel Commission, were the Israeli soldiers, who "had to respond to the violence offered first" by the passengers. The commission described the tactics employed by the IDF as "non-aggressive".[135] It offered no explanation for how the threat and use of force from Israeli naval vessels, military helicopters, and armed commandos firing red paintballs—if not live ammunition—at civilian passengers while storming their boat in international waters did *not* qualify as aggressive behavior.

As for the IDF's claims that passengers had brought firearms on board, the Commission said it "did not find that the evidence point[s] conclusively to the fact that the IHH activists were using firearms which they brought on board the *Mavi Marmara* themselves." This was an odd way of putting it, given that the commission didn't present *any* evidence to support this claim and rather acknowledged that no such firearms were found. It was also quite beyond reason, obviously, to describe the allegation as a "fact" while admitting in the same breath that it couldn't be proven.

Unable to substantiate Israel's claims that the passengers brought firearms on board, the commission argued that the conclusion that passengers "used firearms against Israeli personnel" was supported by the fact that they captured Israeli weapons. The other possibility, of course, and the one actually supported by the evidence, is that the passengers instead threw the confiscated guns overboard, which was indicated by the IDF's own explanation of events, including the testimony of at least one Israeli soldier who witnessed this occur. It would follow that the two Israeli soldiers who reportedly received gunshot wounds were hit with friendly fire during what the commission itself described as the chaotic "fog of war". The report subsequently stated that it was a "fact" that some passengers "were using firearms"—which was accurate, provided that by "using" they meant "disarming" or "throwing overboard".[136]

Netanyahu declared that the Turkel Commission Report showed the "truth" that the soldiers who stormed the *Mavi Marmara* "were defending our country and defending their very lives." Defense Minister Barak proclaimed that the report's conclusions "prove that Israel is a law-abiding country that is capable of examining itself and that respects the norms and rules of the international system."[137] What else could the people of Earth expect from the most moral army on the planet?

The government of Turkey denounced the report and released details from its own inquiry, including its contention that two of the passengers killed were shot by Israeli forces from a helicopter even before they landed on the deck.[138]

Amnesty International issued a statement condemning the Turkel Commission's findings as a "whitewash" that "failed to account for the deaths of nine Turkish nationals". It detailed the unsupported conclusions of the commission and its other failings, such as its reliance on the written statements of Israeli soldiers and lack of authority to question them directly, the fact it heard testimony from only two of the flotilla passengers, and its exclusion of autopsy reports. The commission's findings did not support its conclusion that passengers had used firearms. Furthermore, Israel's analysis was also based on international humanitarian law governing armed conflict, which was not applicable in this case. The proper framework to assess the incident was rather international human rights law. Amnesty rejected the commission's assumption that it constituted "armed hostilities" in an "armed conflict", as well as its conclusions that passengers had lost their civilian status, that Israel was not the occupying power in Gaza, and that the blockade was lawful. It was, rather, an act of collective punishment, and Israel's so-called easing had "failed to end the humanitarian crisis".[139]

As Israel released the Turkel Commission Report, more Israeli soldiers were speaking out about the IDF's conduct during Operation Cast Lead. Allowing themselves to be named and appearing in the documentary *Concrete* by Israeli filmmaker Nurit Kedar (who received death threats for making the film), they spoke of how their commanders had encouraged disproportionate use of force. A twenty-four-year-old tank commander named Ohad testified, "We needed to cleanse the neighborhoods, the buildings, the area. It sounds really terrible to say 'cleanse', but those were the orders. . . . I don't want to make a mistake with the words."

In the IDF's defense, an Israeli spokesperson naturally invoked the findings of its self-investigations as proof of no wrongdoing.[140]

CHAPTER 8

THE 'SPECIAL RELATIONSHIP'

S HORTLY AFTER OBAMA AND Netanyahu had their "makeup session" on July 6, 2010, Saeb Erekat indicated that the Palestinians were preparing to abandon the US-led "peace process" and would look to the international community to recognize Palestine's independence, with East Jerusalem as its capital, in accordance with the international consensus on the two-state solution. "The Israelis have a choice," he said; "settlements or peace. They can't have both."[1]

The same day, Israel resumed demolitions of Palestinian homes in East Jerusalem.

"Israel has been given the choice between settlements and peace," Erekat responded, "and it is obvious that it chose settlements."[2]

The same week, a video from 2001 was made public showing Netanyahu bragging about how he had "stopped the Oslo Accords" and expressing how little Israel had to fear from the US. "I know what America is," Netanyahu boasted in the video. "America is something that can be moved easily."[3]

While the Obama administration was reaffirming the US-Israeli "special relationship", it warned the PA in a letter that the US would not be able to assist the Palestinians if they did not recommit to the "peace process". The PA reasonably interpreted the letter as a threat that US financial and political assistance might be ended if it did not comply with the ultimatum.[4] No letter was sent to Israel saying that the US would no longer be able to provide assistance if it did not end its illegal settlement activities or other criminal behavior.

In August, the PA agreed to recommit to negotiations if they were based on the Quartet statement of March 19, which called on Israel to "to freeze all settlement activity, including natural growth". This recommendation was instructively rejected by the Obama administration. Netanyahu likewise rejected the idea as constituting a "precondition".[5]

A *New York Times* editorial endorsed the US government's policy by criticizing *Abbas* for "stubbornly resisting". It was "time for him to talk." True, Abbas had "understandable reasons" for not wanting to participate. Netanyahu was "a master manipulator", and it wasn't known whether he "really wants a deal". Abbas feared that the Palestinians would "be blamed if negotiations fail" and that Netanyahu would "use the process to give the illusion of progress while never addressing Palestinian concerns". But Abbas deserved blame for "clinging to the maximalist position" that Israel should cease all settlement activity. Thus, the US-Israeli position that settlement activity could continue was the one deemed moderate by the *Times*, while the position held by the rest of the planet that Israel should cease this violation of international law was the one dubbed extreme.

The editorial also repeated the story that Netanyahu had "forced" Obama to "back down" from his own flirtation with the "maximalist" position (his "justified but poorly executed attempt to push the Palestinian position by playing hardball with Israel on settlements"). The truth, of course, was that the administration had from the very beginning pushed the *Israeli* position and demanded that the Palestinians enter negotiations "without preconditions". As for "playing hardball", the editors didn't explain what this was supposed to refer to. Repeatedly assuring Israel that US financial and military assistance would continue regardless of Israel's ongoing colonization? Biden's late arrival for dinner at Netanyahu's home? The reader was left to wonder.

But Obama was now "committed to playing a more balanced role", the *Times* assured—meaning he was pushing the Israeli position even more forcefully and with even less pretense of rhetorical opposition to the settlement policy. Accordingly, Obama was "losing patience with" Abbas, who would be "foolish" to "alienate" the US president. If Abbas didn't accept negotiations on the US and Israel's terms, then Netanyahu would have an "excuse" not to extend the partial moratorium when it expired on September 26. The Palestinians must agree to talks because, otherwise, "there is no serious way of testing Mr. Netanyahu's intentions". Mr. Netanyahu's refusal to cease Israel's illegal settlement activity, the recognition that he was looking for an "excuse" to end the moratorium, his explicit rejection of the two-state solution, his recently-publicized boast about derailing the so-called "peace process", his "disengagement plan" with its explicit goal of expanding settlements in the West Bank, etc., were all evidently not strong enough indications of Mr. Netanyahu's intentions for the *New York Times* to take seriously.[6]

Unsatisfied with the editors' endorsement of the US-Israeli policy, Ambassador Oren wrote a letter to the *Times* criticizing it for being unfair to Israel, such as having called Netanyahu a "'master manipulator' without adducing the slightest evidence to support this charge."[7]

Other reports and commentary on the prospects for negotiations generally stuck to the same script. True to form, Ethan Bronner wrote that Abbas had mistakenly hoped "that the Obama administration would impose a solution" in which Israel would "yield more land" to the Palestinians.[8] Adopting the same framework, Jackson Diehl in the *Washington Post* criticized Abbas for demanding "big concessions", while Netanyahu was being "flexible and more open to a peace settlement". This naturally presented "the real mystery about Abbas: Does he really want peace?" The same question was not asked of Netanyahu.[9]

Not one inch of the land in question, of course, was Israel's to "yield", but was already Palestinian territory under international law. One must not fail to remember that the framework for discussion in the US media is not what Israel has a *right* to under international law, but what it *wants*. Ergo, if Israel wants Palestinian land and the Palestinians don't want to meekly surrender it to them, then the Palestinians are demanding "big concessions" from Israel, which indubitably proves how uninterested in peace the Palestinians really are.

Abbas eventually capitulated. In late August, he agreed "under intense pressure" (*New York Times*) to resume direct negotiations.[10] Speaking at the White House alongside Obama and Netanyahu on September 1, Abbas—rather meaninglessly, in light of his capitulation—called on the Israelis to abide by prior agreements and their obligations under international law, "including a freeze on settlement activities" and an end to the siege of Gaza.[11]

The following day, Abbas joined Netanyahu and Secretary Clinton at the State Department, where the Israeli prime minister reiterated his demand, "We expect you to recognize Israel as the nation-state of the Jewish people."[12] Meanwhile, the director of the Israeli settlers' Yesha Council, Naftali Bennett, declared that settlers would not wait until the end of the moratorium on September 26, and construction activities resumed throughout the West Bank.[13]

It had really never stopped to begin with. The Israeli group Peace Now explained how Netanyahu had approved "an unusually large number" of housing developments just before the so-called "freeze" was implemented. Furthermore, in addition to the construction already exempted, hundreds of housing units that the government had "turned a blind eye to" were being built "in violation of the freeze". The ten-month moratorium on the whole was "insignificant" and amounted to "a meaningless, several month delay on some construction projects."[14] *Spiegel Online* similarly reported how construction was "proceeding at full speed". The legal ban on such activity was "being ignored" and the government was "looking away." There were "few signs that the moratorium has even been put in place" in the West Bank. While construction continued unabated, "no construction firm has been called to account over those violations", despite the ban being "enshrined in law—meaning that any violation should be legally punished." Dror Etkes, an Israeli who meticulously tracked Israel's settlement activities, described the freeze as "a fiction right from the outset."[15] Etkes subsequently penned an op-ed for *Haaretz* describing the "freeze" as "barely a slowdown" and a "PR stunt". Netanyahu would "probably not win the Nobel Peace Prize but he is certainly likely to win the Nobel Prize for Physics, or at least Chemistry," for discovering that "water is not the only substance that expands instead of contracting when it freezes."[16]

On September 4, Abbas said that if Israel did not extend the moratorium, he would quit the negotiations. By no means troubled by that outcome, Ehud Barak responded by affirming that the moratorium would not be renewed.[17] Obama weighed in that "it makes sense to extend that moratorium". But he offered this opinion only in the context of lecturing Abbas that he had to prove he was "serious" and would be "constructive in these talks so that the politics for Prime Minister Netanyahu, if he were to extend the settlements moratorium, would be a little bit easier." Obama credited Abbas for having already capitulated, but warned that "the window for creating a Palestinian state is closing." In other words, if Abbas did not desist from such rebellious statements as demanding Israel cease violating international law, the US would publicly blame Abbas for the failure of negotiations. The White House knew it had the political capital to get away with this absurdity, too, as the media had already adopted the basic assumption that if Abbas didn't bow down to Washington, it would prove how unserious he was about achieving a peace agreement with Israel.[18]

Knowing that he had the full political muscle of the US backing him, Netanyahu a couple of days later reiterated his position to Quartet envoy Tony Blair: Israel would not extend the moratorium.[19]

On September 23, Obama gave a speech before the UN General Assembly in which he bragged about having promised his "best efforts" to support a two-state solution. He recognized that there were "pessimistic" views about the US-led "process", but argued that the alternative would be for the "hard realities of demography" to take hold—an allusion to the problem that Palestinians existed and procreated, which troublingly meant that Israel would either remain "Jewish", as an apartheid state, or "democratic", but no longer demographically "Jewish".

From this premise, Obama praised both Netanyahu and Abbas for their expressions of commitment to the US-led process and demanded that their words "must now be followed by action". Obama repeated his opinion that the moratorium should be extended, but for his outstanding example of following words with actions, he pointed to Netanyahu, whose moratorium had "made a difference on the ground and improved the atmosphere for talks." As for the Palestinians, they must "stop trying to tear down Israel" and cease "efforts to chip away at Israel's legitimacy". (He had no words for Israel about trying to tear down Palestine, which it had quite more literally been doing since it came into existence.) They must cease their "slaughter of innocent Israelis" and firing of rockets "at innocent women and children" in Israel. (He had no words for the incomparably greater slaughter of innocent Palestinians or the firing of far more sophisticated and powerful—often US-supplied—weaponry on innocent women and children in Gaza.)

"This time," Obama theatrically orated, "we should reach for what's best within ourselves. If we do, when we come back here next year, we can have an agreement that will lead to a new member of the United Nations—an independent, sovereign state of Palestine, living in peace with Israel."[20] All that was left now was for words to be followed by actions. Netanyahu had done his part. What was hence needed was for Abbas to bow to the US and Israel's demands, surrender the internationally recognized rights of his people, and acquiesce to the theft of even more of their land.

As the so-called settlement "freeze" officially expired, Ambassador Oren offered the meaningless reassurance that "when construction resumes, it will be reserved, responsible and limited."[21]

When asked to comment, the best State Department Spokesman P. J. Crowley could muster was that the US's policy toward Israel's settlement activities "has not changed" (which was true enough).[22]

By contrast, while meeting with Abbas, French President Nicolas Sarkozy told the press that he deplored Israel's decision and insisted that its settlement activity "must stop."[23]

While the US continued to pressure Abbas to recommit to negotiations without a commitment from Israel to extend the moratorium, Hamas leader Khaled Meshal reminded Abbas of his vow to quit the talks.[24]

The US media played its part. Ethan Bronner wrote how the talks had been focused "on curbing Jewish settlements on land that would go to the Palestinians for a future state"—as though it wasn't Palestinian land to begin with. This mischaracterization he sustained by simply choosing not to mention the fact that the settlements were illegal under international law.[25]

Richard Cohen in the *Washington Post* did acknowledge that the settlements were illegal, but the only significance he attributed to this was that it represented a "poke in the eye" for the Palestinians, "an in-your-face reminder" of their "impotency" and their "inability to control life or fate". Hence, for the Obama administration to insist "as the prerequisite for peace talks" that Israel stop this activity "made no sense". Netanyahu's moratorium was already "a major concession" from Israel. Furthermore, Obama was failing to understand the "religious, cultural or historical importance" of the settlements "to some Jews". To suggest that Israel should freeze construction, Cohen continued, was "counterproductive" because it "foolishly demanded something Israel could not give."

The feelings Jews had about the land thus overrode anything international law had to say about it, in Cohen's equation, and also unquestionably trumped the religious, cultural, and historical importance of their homeland *to the Palestinians*. And only a fool could think it was not impossible for Israel to comply with international law. Only a fool could act so irresponsibly as to suggest that it should. Hence, the only sensible thing to do was to demand that the Palestinians acquiesce to the continued theft of their land out of consideration for the importance that same land had for "some Jews".[26]

Such was the nature of respectable opinion in the United States regarding Israel's colonization of the West Bank. Given the media's tendency to manufacture consent for US policy, it should come as no surprise that polls showed that Americans were far more sympathetic to Israel than the Palestinians.[27] A September poll showed that "18 percent of respondents think Barack Obama sympathizes more with the Palestinians, while 15 percent believe he is more considerate to the Israelis." That such a delusional belief could be so pervasive— reminiscent of the public's widespread belief before the US invasion of Iraq in 2003 that the country had weapons of mass destruction and that Saddam Hussein was behind the terrorist attacks of September 11, 2001—is another stark testimony about the nature of the US media's reporting. It should perhaps be not too surprising, then, that when Americans were asked their views about "the creation of an independent Palestinian state on the West Bank and Gaza strip living side-by-side with Israel", less than half expressed support for the two-state solution.[28]

Rewarding Israel for Violating International Law

Illustrating just how Obama would follow up his own words with deeds and how committed to peace his administration was, the *Wall Street Journal* reported in August 2010 how US military aid to Israel had "increased sharply" that year. This was accompanied by an "intensified partnership" between the US and Israeli armed forces, including more joint military exercises. US officials said that this might "help induce Israeli Prime Minister Benjamin Netanyahu to make concessions in talks with Palestinians"—an explanation for the increase in military aid that the *Journal* took seriously enough to relay without additional comment.[29]

Further "inducements" to Israel were revealed after the moratorium expired by David Makovsky of the Washington Institute for Near East Policy (WINEP), an influential think-tank founded by AIPAC. In a final effort to salvage prospects for direct talks, the Obama administration had sent a letter to Netanyahu promising additional US support in exchange for a two-month extension of the moratorium. Obama promised that, thereafter, he would not again ask Israel to show some restraint with its settlement activities. Furthermore, the US government would continue, as always, to regard the question of settlements as one to be decided only through negotiations—meaning that the US would continue to reject the applicability of international law. Obama also promised that the US would continue to use its veto at the UN Security Council to protect Israel from international censure for its criminal policies. Furthermore, the US would accept "the legitimacy of existing Israeli security needs and not seek to redefine them"—meaning that the US would continue to acquiesce to Israel's desire to annex whatever Palestinian territory it deemed necessary to establish "secure" borders, in accordance with its unilateral interpretation of Resolution 242. In this context, the US would support and help maintain a continued Israeli military presence in the Jordan Valley, as well as offer Israel additional military systems and hardware.

Netanyahu liked "the inducements of the US package", Makovsky reported, but was "not inclined to accept it."[30] The reason was obvious: the Prime Minister could decline, and Israel would still continue to get everything Obama promised anyway.

The White House denied that such a letter had been sent, but as *Haaretz* observed, even if this denial was technically true, "Obama could have made the offer via means other than a letter."[31] The *New York Times* corroborated that "the White House's senior Middle East advisers, Dennis B. Ross"—who also worked at WINEP—"and Daniel B. Shapiro, briefed Democratic representatives on Capitol Hill about what Mr. Ross described as a 'string of assurances in return for a two-month moratorium,' according to people who were in the meeting."[32] The *Times* subsequently reported as fact that the administration "offered Israel security guarantees and military hardware in exchange for a one-time 60-day extension of the building freeze."[33] The *Washington Post* also reported that despite the official denial, "Administration sources confirmed Makovsky's account was largely accurate."[34]

After Netanyahu declined the deal, the US proceeded to sign a contract with Israel for the sale of twenty F-35 stealth fighter jets worth $2.75 billion, paid for entirely by Foreign Military Financing grants to Israel—which is to say that the bill was entirely footed by the American taxpayers. In addition, Israel's defense industry was rewarded $1.4 billion in contracts to manufacture components to be integrated into the F-35s.[35]

"The Israelis get the weapons, but all the profits go to our war contractors," commented Dr. Francis Boyle, Professor of International Law at the University of Illinois, referring to the US practice of granting aid to Israel that served effectively as a subsidy to what President Dwight D. Eisenhower famously described in his farewell address as the "military-industrial complex". "Everyone's making money," Boyle commented, "and the American people are getting ripped off. This is nothing new."[36]

As a result of Israel's refusal to comply with international law, the PA announced on October 2 that there would be no talks, since "the resumption of negotiations requires tangible steps that demonstrate their seriousness, first and foremost halting settlement without qualifications or exceptions."[37] President Abbas also threatened to resign if settlement construction didn't stop.[38] He indicated to the Arab League that, with no prospects for serious talks, the PA might move forward with seeking international recognition of a Palestinian state. Saeb Erekat said the possibility of going to the UN Security Council "to get a resolution that calls upon member states to recognize the state of Palestine on the 1967 borders" was being considered.[39]

On October 10, the Israeli cabinet approved a draft amendment to Israel's citizenship law that required non-Jewish immigrants—but not Jewish immigrants—to pledge loyalty to Israel as a Jewish state. Netanyahu said non-Jewish residents of Israel must "recognize" the "Jewish identity and the democracy of the state of Israel"—the paradox of legally requiring non-Jews to make a pledge effectively declaring their status as second-class citizens while touting Israel as a "democracy" seemingly escaping him. The motion passed with a vote of twenty-two to eight. Isaac Herzog, a dissenting cabinet member from the Labor Party, said the draft amendment "borders on fascism."[40]

The following day, Netanyahu said he would agree to renew the moratorium if the Palestinians would recognize Israel as a "Jewish state".[41] The US State Department then urged the Palestinians to extend a counter-proposal, to which the PA appropriately replied, "We officially demand that the US administration and the Israeli government provide a map of the borders of the state of Israel which they want us to recognize. . . . If this map is based on the 1967 borders and provides for the end of the Israeli occupation over all Palestinian lands . . . then we recognize Israel by whatever name it applies to itself in accordance with international law."[42]

While demanding that Palestinians recognize Israel as a "Jewish state", Israel continued to refuse to recognize Palestine in any form. When Argentina announced that it would join Brazil and Uruguay in recognizing the independent state of Palestine within the 1967 lines, Israeli Foreign Ministry spokesman Yigal Palmor dismissed the recognition as "clearly meaningless".[43]

In mid-October, the *New York Times* published an op-ed by Mustafa Barghouti, a member of the Palestinian Legislative Council. Barghouti pointed out that "in the 17 years since the Oslo agreement . . . the number of settlers has increased by 300 percent and the number of settlements doubled." The settlements—along with "checkpoints, road segregation, security zones, the 'apartheid wall' and 'natural reserves'"—had "for years eaten up the land, water resources and the economic space of the independent Palestinian state supposedly being negotiated in this same period." Although the ICJ and numerous UN resolutions had affirmed the illegality of the settlements, and even though the Road Map itself called for the cessation of all settlement activity, "neither the United States nor the Quartet as a whole has had the guts to exert serious pressure on Israel to stop settlements." Barghouti concluded:

The only way to save the two-state solution is for the Palestinians to declare the establishment of an independent Palestinian state on the territories occupied by Israel in 1967, including East Jerusalem, and to demand that the world community recognize it and its borders—as it did in the case of Kosovo. . . . If the world community turns its back on such a declaration of independence by using the well-worn and insulting argument that every step should first be verified with the Israeli government, then the message will be clear: Peace based on two states is no longer an option.[44]

The following day, Israel announced plans to build another 238 housing units in occupied East Jerusalem. Saeb Erekat responded, "Netanyahu has once again demonstrated why there are no negotiations today."

Reporting this for the *Times*, Ethan Bronner, in a moment of rare candor, wrote that "The vast majority of governments accept what the United Nations and the International Court of Justice in The Hague have declared—that the settlements violate international law." Israel alone rejected the international consensus, he wrote, while the US and Japan "take no stand on the settlements' legality" but "oppose them on policy grounds."[45] Bronner was, however, mischaracterizing the US and Japanese positions; the "vast majority of governments" in fact meant every single government on the planet apart from Israel's own.

Japan was a non-permanent member of the Security Council when it unanimously passed Resolution 242 in 1967, and its position has since remained that "under international law, acquisition of land by force is not admissible and that measures undertaken under such acquisition do not constitute any basis for obtaining territorial title. Japan does not recognize, therefore, any changes to the pre-1967 borders other than those arrived at by agreement between the parties concerned."[46] Japan's policy has thus always been ipso facto one of opposition to the settlements as *illegal*. In more recent years, Japan has repeatedly and explicitly stated that Israel's settlements in East Jerusalem and the West Bank are "a violation of international law".[47]

The US, of course, also voted in favor of Resolution 242. And despite having since adopted a policy of accepting Israel's interpretation of that resolution and referring to settlements as "unhelpful" or some other euphemism, the US officially recognizes their illegality. On March 1, 1980, for instance, the US voted in favor of Security Council Resolution 465, which determined that "all measures taken by Israel to change the physical character, demographic composition, institutional structure of the Palestinian and other Arab territories occupied since 1967, including Jerusalem, or any part thereof, have no legal validity and that Israel's policy and practices of settling parts of its population and new immigrants in those territories constitute a flagrant violation of the Fourth

Geneva Convention".[48] That vote was in keeping with the State Department's definitive legal position, which remains that Israel's settlements are "inconsistent with international law."[49]

By November, the situation could be aptly summed up with the headline of another piece by Bronner: "Settlers Race to Build Units in West Bank". Construction had restarted at a rate "somewhat higher than in recent years", Bronner informed. Yesha Council Director Naftali Bennett described the settlements as a "necessary shield" to defend Israel and asked, "Why should there be any place in Israel"—by which he meant the occupied West Bank—"where we are barred from building?" In another rare departure, Bronner quoted the UN special envoy for Middle East peace, Robert H. Serry, providing the answer: "Renewed settlement construction, which is illegal under international law, runs contrary to the international community's repeated appeals to the parties to create conditions conducive to negotiations, and will only further undermine trust."[50]

Isabel Kershner wrote that 1,000 new housing units were planned for "a hotly contested area" of East Jerusalem, the Jewish settlement of Har Homa. State Department spokesman P. J. Crowley expressed that the US was "deeply disappointed" by Israel's "counterproductive" plans to build in "sensitive areas" in East Jerusalem. "Palestinians and much of the world consider it and similar developments across the 1967 lines as illegal settlements on occupied land", Kershner wrote, with "much of the world" again meaning every country on the planet. The area was "hotly contested", in the *Times'* lexicon, solely by virtue of the fact that Israel wanted to take it from the Palestinians.[51]

Obama responded to Israel's planned settlement expansion by describing it as unhelpful and illustrative that Israel was not making "the extra effort". Then he turned the focus back onto the Palestinians, criticizing them for not more readily acquiescing to Israel's theft of their land.

Netanyahu's reply to Obama was that "Israel sees no connection at all between the peace process and building plans in Jerusalem". This, of course, was in perfect accordance with the US policy of treating Jerusalem and settlements as "separate issues" (David Hale).[52]

A particularly inane commentary on the situation, even by US media standards, was offered by Michael Weiss in *Foreign Policy*. Weiss dismissed the settlements as "one of the least problematic obstacles" and instead criticized Abbas for having "used settlements as an excuse to disrupt the latest round of talks"—a reiteration of the theme that the Palestinians' reluctance to acquiesce to Israel's theft of their land proved their lack of interest in peace. Weiss took this a step further by arguing that Israel had only really intended to annex "minimal" areas of the West Bank following the June 1967 war, but "the escalation of Palestinian terrorist attacks" in the mid-1970s "provoked an equally hard-edged Israeli response, which gave the settlement project a more ideological underpinning".[53]

While Weiss would have his readers believe this "ideological underpinning" did not exist before "the mid-70s", Israel had in fact made known its intention to colonize the West Bank immediately after the occupation began in June 1967. The US Mission to the UN, for example, cabled the State Department on September 23, 1967, to inform that Israel had expressed its desire to annex occupied territory. "Israel would like to have the [Gaza] territory without the population but did not see how that could come about", the cable reported. Israel had a similar problem with the West Bank, because "Incorporation of [the] West Bank into Israel, with its large Arab population, would completely transform Israel's national existence and reason for being."[54]

A US National Intelligence Estimate (NIE) from 1968 similarly stated that "Israel's fundamental foreign policy is to secure the broadest possible support for itself as the rightful occupant of Palestine." But, again, demographics were an obstacle to Israel's desire for the land: "About 200,000 Arabs fled from the West Bank and Gaza during and immediately after the June war; the flow now is a few thousand monthly and relatively few have been allowed to return. But even so, incorporating the newly occupied territory into Israel would add a million Arabs to the population, of which they would then constitute one-third. Almost all Israelis would regard this as an unacceptably high proportion."

Foreshadowing the creation of the PA, the NIE continued: "An alternative would be to give occupied Palestine some form of autonomy. But it would be difficult to get enough cooperation from Palestinian leaders to make such a scheme workable. Most of them would fear that the territory might later be turned back to Jordan or Egypt as part of a broader settlement, in which case there would be reprisals against them for collaboration."

Israel therefore saw its options as either annexing the West Bank and Gaza or finding Palestinian leaders willing to collaborate under a scheme in which they exercised "some form of autonomy" within the framework of continued Israeli occupation and colonization.

The NIE also assessed that the consequence of continued Israeli occupation would be more violence: "[I]f Israel continues to occupy conquered territory for an extended period, say two to three years, it will find it increasingly difficult to relinquish control. . . . In the longer run, the frustration of the Arab States would almost certainly drive them to seek military means of compelling Israeli withdrawal. . . . [W]hatever the precise course of events, continued Israeli occupation will almost certainly lead to a new round of major hostilities in the future."[55]

But Israel didn't really want the land, Weiss insisted, they just needed it "as a bargaining chip" to get "the Palestinians to accept a territorial compromise based on the 1967 frontiers". The settler population had "tripled since the Madrid conference" only because it was fueled by this "logic" of trying to get the Palestinians to accept borders based on the 1967 lines. The issue of settle-

ments should therefore not be among the Obama administration's top priorities, Weiss concluded, and "fixation" on it was "a convenient distraction" from
the real obstacles of Palestinian terrorism and their inability to functionally
govern themselves.[56] Weiss didn't trouble himself to try to explain the paradox
of why, if the settlements were just a "bargaining chip" to get the Palestinians to
agree to a two-state solution "based on the 1967 frontiers", Israel then insisted
on continuing to expand them while rejecting the Palestinians' persistent plea
to negotiate on the basis of those very same "frontiers".

In November, Abbas reiterated that without a full settlement freeze, the
Palestinians would not return to talks. "If we fail in this," he added, "we want
to go to the United Nations Security Council to ask the world to recognize the
Palestinian state."[57]

The following week, Netanyahu and Secretary Clinton again discussed
a ninety-day extension of the moratorium in return for a promise from the
Obama administration not to repeat this request thereafter, to provide the additional twenty F-35s, and to oppose any Palestinian attempt to gain international recognition of statehood. Obama described Netanyahu's consideration of
the deal as "a signal that he is serious."[58]

The fact that the deal was even being offered was itself a monumental signal of just how "serious" the Obama administration was about achieving the
two-state solution, although mainstream media observers remained as self-disciplined as ever, with commentary descending into the abysmal depths of absolute asininity at both ends of the spectrum, whether favoring or opposing the
administration's policy.

Typical of the kind of cognitive dissonance that dominated the discussion,
Aaron David Miller wrote in *Foreign Policy* how Obama's proposal to Netanyahu was "good news". The ninety-day extension, he wrote, would "allow the
administration to shift focus from settlements (where it had no chance to succeed) to the substance of the negotiations (where it must go if it wants an Israeli-Palestinian agreement)."

This was certainly a puzzling argument. If the Obama administration had
"no chance to succeed" in getting Israel to temporarily implement a partial
freeze, much less to permanently end its illegal colonization, how could it succeed in getting the Israelis and Palestinians to an agreement on a two-state
solution, which required an agreement on borders? How was the issue of illegal
settlements on occupied Palestinian territory *not* of crucial substance to any
future negotiations purportedly designed to bring about the establishment of a
Palestinian state? Miller didn't bother to try to resolve such enigmas, evidently
because to ponder such simple and obvious questions would be a distraction
from the point.

Continuing, Miller observed that the Obama administration had "gener-
ously rewarded the Israelis with military hardware and political guarantees for

something (settlements) they shouldn't have been doing in the first place". He then urged readers to "skip over" this fact. It was, remember, "good news". The "bad news" was that the US would have only three months to achieve agreement on "the only realistic two-state solution possible": the establishment of a Palestinian state along the 1967 lines "with land swaps". This would be "very hard", Miller conceded, because it might "require a new Israeli government more capable of compromise".

This naturally presented some more riddles. Since the administration *was* stuck for the next three months with the rejectionist Netanyahu government, what, then, by Miller's own argument, would be the point of talks? And, if the two-state solution based on the 1967 lines was admittedly the only realistic one, how was Israel's ongoing colonization not a matter of substance for negotiations? Miller left his readers to puzzle over such conundrums for themselves.

What was even "more troubling" than the Netanyahu government's unwillingness to extend the moratorium, Miller continued, was that Israel's expansion of Jewish settlements in East Jerusalem would continue "presumably with US acquiescence." But, then, we must not mind such substanceless issues as the US's acquiescence to this illegal activity because, after all, Obama's proposal to reward Israel for it was a "breakthrough" and "good news" for the prospect of Middle East peace.[59]

On the other side of the debate, Elliot Abrams and Michael Singh contributed a piece to *Foreign Policy* falsely attributing to Obama a "quixotic quest for a total construction freeze", which was "a step backward" from peace, despite appearing "at first glance to be a sweetheart deal" for Netanyahu. Indeed, a reasonable case could have been made that the proposal was a step backward from peace, but the authors chose not to make it. Instead, they argued that the "most worrying aspect of Obama's package" was the "suggestion that unless there is a construction freeze", the US would "no longer" habitually veto "unconstructive, unhelpful, and unprincipled" UN Security Council resolutions critical of Israel. How dare the international community condemn Israel's violations of international law! (The fact that the Obama administration had suggested no such thing was of no consequence to Abrams and Singh, who knew they could simply invent whatever fictions they wished and still get published.)

"More disturbing still", they continued, was the "sweetener" of twenty F-35 jets, which came "at a cost of $3 billion to US taxpayers". The cost to the taxpayers, however, wasn't what they found disturbing about it; rather, they were distraught that the administration was willing to use the jets to "pressure" Israel to extend the moratorium. This was reprehensible, in the authors' view, according to whose logic the additional jets should just be given with nothing in return, as though the American taxpayers somehow owed the fruits of their labors to Israel.

Obama was also guilty of neglecting Israel's "political realities", Abrams and Singh charged, for having "sought a total freeze as a precondition for negotiations". All of these moves by the administration constituted "departures from sensible policy". The real issue was how to "prevent a barrage of rockets" against Israel from any future Palestinian state and how to prevent Hamas from "trouncing" the PA if Israel was to withdraw from the West Bank. Hence, the only "sensible" policy was one of dropping any pretenses of opposition to the settlements in favor of open and unconditional support for Israel's colonization, including showering Israel with exorbitant gifts from the American taxpayers to reward it for violating international law.[60]

Daniel Kurtzer offered his opposing view in an op-ed for the *Washington Post*, criticizing Obama's attempt at "bribing Israel" as "a very bad idea" since it was "the first time in memory" that the US was "poised to reward Israel for its bad behavior". US opposition to Israeli settlements had previously "resulted in penalties, not rewards, for continued construction". His example was the Bush administration's deduction from loan guarantees "an amount equivalent, dollar for dollar, to the money that Israel spent in the occupied territories."

Clearly, Kurtzer's memory had failed him. Recall that the money deducted wasn't even equivalent to the amount Israel spent on its illegal separation wall in the West Bank, much less the entire cost of the settlement regime. Recall further that this deduction came from an allocated amount that was $1 billion *greater* than Israel had requested in the first place. Thus, the Bush administration's "penalty" was in fact a considerable reward and financial incentive to Israel to continue its illegal construction. We may also recall that Kurtzer himself had dutifully carried out his assigned task of assuring Israel in no uncertain terms that the Bush administration supported its policy on settlements. His self-contradictions are not irreconcilable, however. They can be understood by recognizing that his real point was that to reward Israel for its illegal activities, as the US did on a regular basis, was perfectly fine; it just shouldn't be done in so conspicuous a manner because it harmed US efforts to manage "perceptions".

That this was his true underlying message was further exposed as Kurtzer proceeded to echo Abrams and Singh by condemning Obama's offer for "subjecting Israel's defense needs" to "political demands". In other words, Kurtzer was in agreement that US military assistance to Israel—such as the twenty additional F-35s—should be unconditional and continue with no strings attached, regardless of Israel's ongoing violations of international law. Obama had broken that cardinal rule by asking Israel for a temporary and partial cessation of its criminal activity in return for an arms package.[61]

One was hard-pressed to find any kind of sensible and coherent commentary on Obama's offer in the Western media, a fact pointed out in one of the rare exceptions. Writing in *The Independent*, the ever-undisciplined Robert Fisk put it most succinctly:

> In any other country, the current American bribe to Israel, and the latter's reluctance to accept it, in return for even a temporary end to the theft of somebody else's property would be regarded as preposterous. . . . The fact that the West and its political and journalistic elites—I include the ever more disreputable *New York Times*—take this tomfoolery at face value, as if it can seriously be regarded as another "step" in the "peace process", to put this mystical nonsense "back on track", is a measure of the degree to which we have taken leave of our senses in the Middle East.

In a "sane world", Fisk continued, offering to pay a country billions of dollars to temporarily scale back its violations of international law while promising to not speak a word against it when those violations were thereafter resumed would be recognized as "appeasement."[62]

In the end, Netanyahu predictably stuck to rejecting Obama's proposal, having been offered no real incentive to accept it, given the knowledge that he could reject it and still continue to receive everything Obama offered anyway.

The EU responded to Israel's decision not to extend the partial moratorium by reiterating its clear position that the settlements "are illegal under international law and an obstacle to peace."[63] The Obama administration, on the other hand, immediately rewarded Israel for its decision by abandoning altogether any further efforts to persuade Israel to freeze settlement activities.[64] It also moved forward on the deal to provide Israel with F-35 stealth fighter jets. Ambassador Oren said Israel was still seeking the additional jets and that negotiations were still underway. "The 90-day extension discussion is off the table but the 20 extra jets are very much on the table," informed Oren. "It's not attached to the 90-day freeze." He also disclosed that part of the negotiations was about finding a way to finance the arms deal, since Israel lacked the funding to purchase the jets.[65] So if the deal was concluded, the American taxpayers would just have to foot the bill, as usual.

When it was announced several weeks later that the production of F-35 jets would be frozen under Pentagon budget "cuts" (a euphemism used by government officials and the media for reductions from the projected baseline *increases* in government spending), *Ynetnews* reported that sources in Washington had reassured that "the halt in the production of the advanced stealth jets would not affect the expected delivery of 20 planes to Israel".[66]

Obama's 'Diplomatic Bind'

In January 2011, UN Special Rapporteur Richard Falk, in a report on the situation of human rights in the Palestinian territories, criticized Israel for its pattern of refusing to cooperate with his mission, which was contrary to its obligations as a UN member state. Evidence that Israel was willing to credibly investigate itself and hold its soldiers and leaders accountable remained absent. The international community had woefully failed to implement the recommendations of numerous UN reports, which fostered the perception that Israel was able to violate international law with impunity.

Falk did not refrain from identifying the reason for this, which was the "unconditional support of the United States of America" that Israel enjoyed. US officials such as Hillary Clinton used language that did not reflect the facts on the ground, but obfuscated the truth. The Obama administration's offers to provide Israel "with substantive benefits for temporarily and partially halting an unlawful activity" effectively rewarded Israel for its illegal settlements policy, which infringed on the rights of the Palestinians and raised "disturbing issues of principle and precedent." Obama was attempting to restart "a negotiating process that incorporates an acceptance and legitimization of Israeli settlements". Moreover, Netanyahu's "freeze" was not at all serious. "In fact, the rate of settlement construction quadrupled compared to what it had been during the two years before the moratorium."

Additionally, international aid "ostensibly aimed at improving the lives of Palestinians" was instead benefiting the occupying power. US financing for road construction in the West Bank, for example, served "to restrict Palestinian movement and access and, at the same time, to facilitate the movement of Israeli settlers." This meant that American taxpayers, through USAID, were "financing, and thereby further entrenching, the Israeli de facto annexation of the West Bank." This "could arguably result" in the US "being deemed complicit in the illegal occupation."

Israel's blockade was in violation of international law, and "action by humanitarian organizations to break an unlawful and cruel blockade of this sort is fully justified." Israel also had a policy of opening fire on Palestinians attempting to access their own land in Gaza. It was "particularly appalling" when Israeli soldiers arbitrarily opened fire on Palestinian children. Seventeen children had been shot in such incidents since March 2010.

Israel also continually arrested and detained children, mostly on "suspicion of stone-throwing". The children were often abused by their captors. Israel's policy of prosecuting Palestinian children aged sixteen or older as adults under its military court system, while Israeli children were prosecuted in the civilian courts and not as adults until the age of eighteen, was one example of the "apartheid dimension" of the occupation. The facts were "rendered more disturbing when account is taken that almost all of these arrests of children are generated by their resistance to unlawful patterns of Israeli settlement building and expansion, along with the related ethnic-cleansing measures being applied at an accelerating rate in East Jerusalem."

Falk renewed the call of his predecessor, John Dugard, to refer the situation to the ICJ for judgment on whether "elements of the (Israeli) occupation constitute forms of colonialism and of apartheid". In addition, the ICJ should rule on whether Israel's policies constituted ethnic cleansing. "There is no question that, with its policy of Palestinian expulsion and dispossession in Jerusalem," Falk concluded, "Israel continues to be responsible for a gradual, incremental, yet cumulatively devastating policy designed to achieve the ethnic cleansing of Palestinians."[67]

Meanwhile, the propaganda offensive against Palestinians' rights continued in *Foreign Policy* with an article by former IDF Chief of Staff Moshe Ya'alon titled "The Palestinians Are the Real Obstacle to Peace", which ventured still further into the realm of fantasy and psychological projection by preposterously asserting that Israel had repeatedly affirmed the Palestinians' right to self-determination, but that this had gone "unreciprocated". This, he declared, was the "fundamental problem" in the conflict.[68]

Outside of the rabbit hole, Israel's rejection of the Palestinians' right to self-determination was daily manifested in the ongoing occupation. Human Rights Watch presented case studies of Israel's discriminatory treatment of Palestinians, which was institutionalized and codified in law. While settlers were treated preferentially, Israeli practices toward Palestinians were intended to stifle growth in their communities, including by "forcibly displacing Palestinian residents." Such racist treatment "violates the fundamental prohibition against discrimination under human rights law." Additionally, every country except Israel itself recognized its settlements as illegal, and there was "nearly universal" agreement "that Israel should cease its violation of international humanitarian law by removing its citizens from the West Bank." In conclusion,

> Israel's allies—above all the United States—should strongly encourage the Israeli government to abide by its obligations and should themselves ensure that they are not contributing to or complicit in the violations of international law caused by the settlements, such as the discriminatory human rights violations that are the focus of this report. . . . The United States should consider suspending financing to Israel in an amount equivalent to the costs of the Israeli government's spending in support of settlements and the discriminatory policies documented in this report, since the US's $2.75 billion in annual military aid to Israel substantially offsets these costs. . . . The US Congress should request the General Accounting Office to prepare a report on the amounts and end-uses of tax-exempt funding flows to settlements, and the lawfulness of tax-exemp-

tions for such support according to the US's international obligations.[69]

But the Obama administration had already repeatedly made clear that it
would not consider ending its support for Israel's criminal and racist policies.
Secretary Clinton had reiterated this little more than a week before in no uncertain terms:

> We say it often, but it bears repeating: America's commitment
> to Israel's security and its future is rock solid and unwavering,
> and that will not change. From our first days in office, the
> Obama Administration has reaffirmed this commitment. For
> me and President Obama, this is not simply a policy position.
> It is also a deeply held personal conviction. Over the last two
> years under President Obama's leadership, the United States
> has expanded our cooperation with Israel and focused in par-
> ticular on helping Israel meet the most consequential threats
> to its future as a secure and democratic Jewish state. Our secu-
> rity relationship has grown broader, deeper, and more intense
> than ever before.

The Obama administration had "not just worked to maintain Israel's qualitative
military edge", she crowed, but "increased it".

Clinton acknowledged that the ongoing conflict "denies the legitimate aspirations of the Palestinian people" and that the occupation deprived them
"of dignity and self-determination". But she expressed equal concern that the
"long-term population trends that result from the occupation are endangering
the Zionist vision of a Jewish and democratic state". So the problem was that
the Palestinians existed in the land and had a habit of procreating. She then
showered Israel with praise for having slightly eased its collective punishment in
Gaza and professed how greatly "America is serious about peace."

Neither side should take "actions that prejudge the outcome of negotiations
or undermine good faith efforts to resolve final status issues", said Clinton. This
chiefly meant that the PA should not take the "unilateral" step of seeking international recognition of Palestine at the UN. This would be "not helpful" and
"undermine trust". As for Israel, she offered the carefully-worded criticism that
"[p]rovocative announcements" of additional settlement construction in East
Jerusalem were "counterproductive".[70]

As Falk observed, Clinton's language served to obfuscate. As with Joe Biden's
March 2010 visit to Israel, the criticism was not that Israel was continuing this
illegal construction, merely that it was making unnecessarily provocative announcements about it. And it must be noted that any effort on behalf of the
Palestinians to seek recognition of statehood along the 1967 lines in accordance

with the international consensus would not be a "unilateral", but a *multilateral* step, by definition. It is simply that mainstream media commentators mindlessly adopt the US and Israeli governments' use of the word to mean any action taken by the Palestinians without Israel's approval.

It is also instructive that Clinton, in leveling her criticisms, drew equivalence between (a) Palestinian announcements about taking the *multilateral* step of seeking international recognition of their rights in accordance with principles of international law and (b) Israeli announcements about taking the *unilateral* step of *rejecting* and *violating* international law. This speaks for itself, if we dare to allow our gaze to fall upon the form of the US's rejectionist policy scarcely hidden beneath the thin veil of rhetoric about how the US is "serious about peace".

The *New York Times* summarized the situation on December 22, 2010, with the headline, "After Freeze, Settlement Building Booms in West Bank"—one of the direct consequences of American seriousness.[71] The PA went ahead with preparation of a draft resolution for the UN Security Council condemning Israel for continuing its unilateral settlement activities in violation of international law and its obligations under the Road Map. Israeli Foreign Ministry spokesman Yigal Palmor described this as yet more proof that the Palestinians "renounce peace altogether."[72]

When Israel demolished the Shepherd's Hotel in occupied East Jerusalem in early January 2011, Secretary Clinton said the US was "very concerned" about this "disturbing development", which "undermines peace efforts to achieve the two state-solution." But what else did the Secretary of State expect, when the US position was identical to the Israeli position that Jerusalem and settlements were "separate issues", and when Obama himself had declared in Sderot that, if he had anything to say about it as president, an undivided Jerusalem would be the capital of Israel? Such statements were about managing "perceptions", nothing more.[73]

Two weeks later, Guyana became the seventh Latin American country to recognize Palestine as an independent state. The week after that, Peru became the eighth. Venezuela had recognized Palestine in 2000. Brazil had announced its recognition on December 3, 2010, followed by Uruguay, Argentina, Bolivia, Ecuador, and Chile. Additionally, around 100 other countries had recognized Palestine after the PLO's 1988 declaration of independence.[74]

With a firm understanding that the US must from time to time express meaningless rhetorical opposition to its actions, Israel meanwhile announced an additional 1,400 homes to be built in occupied East Jerusalem.[75] Such "counterproductive" behavior from Israel, however, wasn't what troubled members of the US Congress. They were instead concerned about the PA's draft UN resolution condemning such activity. Kirsten Gillibrand and sixteen other senators sent Clinton a letter urging the Obama administration to veto the "anti-Israel" resolution because it "hurts the prospects for a peace agreement".[76]

House majority leader Eric Cantor, Representative Ileana Ros-Lehtinen, and four other representatives likewise denounced the draft resolution as "anti-Israel" and "without merit" in a bipartisan letter to Obama. They lauded Israel for having "proven" its "steadfast commitment to peace" by making "painful sacrifices" (i.e., Netanyahu's moratorium farce). They backed the Obama administration's insistence that Palestinians must negotiate with Israel while it continued to prejudice the outcome with its ongoing colonization and deplored the Palestinians' position that Israel should cease this illegal activity. Illustrating their own contempt for international law and Palestinians' rights, they described Jerusalem as "Israel's undivided capital." The draft UN resolution must be opposed, they argued, because it would "isolate Israel" and instill a sense of hope in the Palestinians that would "undermine the peace process". They urged the administration to veto the resolution, pressure the Palestinian leadership to abandon their "one-sided measures", and punish the Palestinians with "significant negative consequences" if they disobeyed their orders from Washington, DC.[77]

Contrasting the attitude in Congress, thirty-four policy commentators, academics, and former government officials sent a letter to the administration encouraging it to support the resolution in order to send a "clear signal" to the international community that the US "can and will approach the conflict with the objectivity, consistency and respect for international law required if it is to play a constructive role in the conflict's resolution." The passage of the UN draft resolution would put "all sides on notice that the continued flouting of international legality will not be treated with impunity."[78]

The administration again made clear, however, that it had no interest in so reversing its policy. The State Department denounced the draft resolution as unproductive.[79] Deputy US Representative to the UN Rosemary A. DiCarlo affirmed that the US would "consistently oppose" Palestinian appeals to the international community for recognition of their rights.[80]

The Associated Press noticed that the draft UN resolution once again put the Obama administration "in a difficult position" because the US pretended to be opposed to Israeli settlements but didn't want "to endorse a resolution that is critical only of Israel, its main Mideast ally."[81] *Time* magazine likewise observed how the resolution put Obama in "a diplomatic bind". It was understood that the US would likely use its veto, but the act of "symbolically challenging unconditional US support for Israel" with "a vote of no-confidence in US peacemaking efforts" had created "a headache for the Obama Administration". The US had as a matter of tradition regularly vetoed UN resolutions critical of Israel, but there was a "twist this time" because this particular resolution was consistent with the administration's "own stated positions". The administration's rationale for opposing the resolution was that it would not move the parties closer to a negotiated settlement; but that argument, *Time* further perceived, was "unlikely to convince most of the international community".[82]

Ian Williams appropriately commented in *The Guardian*, "It is as if you have caught someone stealing your car and the police decide to overlook technical issues like the law and ownership and instead tell you to negotiate with the thief to get occasional access to the back seat."[83] The Egyptian ambassador to the UN, Maged A. Abdelaziz, accurately summarized the Obama administration as effectively saying, "We are against settlements and we are not going to do anything about it and we don't want you to do anything about it. We will let the Israelis do what they want."[84]

The Obama administration wasn't assisted in its dilemma when *Al Jazeera* and *The Guardian* published leaked documents dubbed "The Palestine Papers" showing how Palestinian negotiators had during and after the Annapolis process made enormous concessions to Israel, including agreeing to Israeli annexation of most of its settlements in East Jerusalem.

"We are building for you the largest Jerusalem in history", said Saeb Erekat on May 4, 2008, after proposing the land swaps and settlements to be annexed.

"I want to say that we do not like this suggestion", responded Tzipi Livni, "because it does not meet our demands, and probably it was not easy for you to think about it but I really appreciate it."[85]

On June 15, 2008, the Palestinian team reiterated its desire for a two-state solution with borders based on the 1967 lines and equal land swaps, indicating again its agreement that Israel would annex "all settlements in Jerusalem except Jabal Abu Ghneim (Har Homa)".[86] In January 2010, Saeb Erekat, using the Hebrew word for Jerusalem, told David Hale that Palestinians were offering Israel "the biggest *Yerushalaim* in Jewish history".[87] But these enormous Palestinian concessions were not enough for Israeli negotiators.

The leaked documents also further revealed how the US was effectively advocating for Israel and pressuring the Palestinians to agree to Israel's demands. "Far from sitting between the parties as an 'honest broker,'" wrote Ali Abunimah in the *Christian Science Monitor*, the documents showed that "the United States has continued to play its role as 'Israel's lawyer.'"[88] "The papers give the lie to Israel's claim that it yearns for peace but lacks a Palestinian 'partner'", wrote literary scholar Saree Makdisi in the *Los Angeles Times*. He excoriated the Palestinian negotiators for being "willing to bargain away" their rights under international law. "And all this was contemptuously turned down by the allegedly peace-seeking Israeli government, with the connivance of the United States, to whom the Palestinians kept plaintively appealing as an honest broker, even as it became clearer than ever that it is anything but."[89]

On February 18, 2011, the draft resolution, sponsored by seventy-nine nations, went to a vote in the UN Security Council. The text was completely uncontroversial. It reaffirmed that all Israeli settlements in the occupied Palestin-ian territory, including East Jerusalem, were illegal; demanded that Israel respect international law and comply with its legal obligations by ceasing settlement activities; and called for continued negotiations on a final status agreement. It failed with a vote of fourteen in favor and one opposed.[90] US Ambassador to the UN Susan Rice said that the Obama administration's veto should not be "misunderstood to mean we support settlement activity. On the contrary, we reject in the strongest terms the legitimacy of continued Israeli settlement activ-ity." The rationale offered for the veto was that the resolution would not "move the parties closer to negotiations and an agreement."[91]

Of course, demanding that the Palestinians negotiate without an end to set-tlement activity had decidedly not moved the parties closer to negotiations and an agreement. When the PA repeatedly announced that it would consequently abandon the "peace process" and turn to the UN, the administration did not veto its own policy, but persisted in it to the detriment of its own stated goal. Obviously, the true criteria was not whether an action moved the parties closer to negotiations, but whether the action helped or harmed the US and Israel in their mutual effort to force the Palestinians to capitulate to their demands.

With no misunderstanding about the reason for the US's veto, Israel wasted no time announcing more illegal construction of Jewish housing in occupied East Jerusalem and elsewhere throughout the West Bank. A headline in the *New York Times* summed up the situation by mid-March: "Israel to Step Up Pace of Construction in West Bank Areas"—yet more proof of America's seriousness about peace.[92]

Fatah-Hamas Reconciliation: 'A Formula for War'

At the UN Human Rights Council in February 2011, Richard Falk again re-newed the call of John Dugard to refer to the ICJ the question of whether elements of the occupation constituted "colonialism and apartheid", as well as the question of whether Israeli policies qualified as "ethnic cleansing".[93] Israel's UN envoy, Aharon Leshno Yaar, responded by calling Falk an "embarrassment to the United Nations".[94] In *Haaretz*, Daniel Blatman penned an op-ed that echoed Falk's statements, saying that the Knesset had passed a "tsunami of racist laws" aimed at "the gradual establishment of an apartheid state in Israel, and the future separation on a racial basis of Jews and non-Jews."[95] The Israeli govern-ment must have thought Professor Blatman a considerable embarrassment to the Hebrew University of Jerusalem, where he served as head of the Institute for Contemporary Jewry.

In March, Palestinian Foreign Affairs Minister Riyad al-Maliki described the "peace process" as "useless" and indicated the PA's intention to seek statehood recognition at the UN in September if Israel did not cease its settlement con-

struction and agree to negotiate borders on the basis of the 1967 lines.[96] Ehud
Barak warned that such a move by the Palestinians would be "a diplomatic-
political tsunami" and "a very dangerous situation, one that requires action."
Ethan Bronner explained to *Times* readers that while it "could place Israel into a
diplomatic vise", such an effort by the Palestinians would surely succeed in the
General Assembly, where "the United States cannot save Israel as it often has
in the Security Council"—the verb "save" being Bronner's gracious euphemism
for protecting Israel from being held accountable for violations of international
law.[97]

In early April, a group of about forty prominent Israelis announced a draft
peace plan dubbed the Israeli Peace Initiative. It was a response to the 2002 Arab
Peace Initiative, which called for implementation of the two-state solution. The
Israeli initiative alternatively proposed the establishment of a "demilitarized"
Palestinian state based on the 1967 lines with equal land swaps, with East Jerusalem as its capital. Israel would annex Jewish communities and have West
Jerusalem as its capital. The plan recognized "the suffering of the Palestinian
refugees since the 1948 war", but rejected the right of return. Refugees could
return "only to the Palestinian state", with "symbolic exceptions" who could
return to Israel. The group said their plan was intended to urge the Netanyahu
government to "immediately renew peace talks".[98]

Two weeks later, in another effort by Israeli citizens to persuade their government to reconsider its settlement policy, more than sixty of Israel's most
honored artists and intellectuals signed a declaration calling for the "end of the
occupation" and "welcoming and endorsing a newly born Palestinian state on
the basis of the 1967 borders".[99]

With its retention of demands for the Palestinians to surrender their rights,
the Israeli Peace Initiative was within the realm of tolerable dissent from government policy, but still too radical a departure for the Netanyahu regime to
contemplate. Shortly after the initiative was announced, on the day before President Obama was to meet Israeli President Shimon Peres at the White House,
the Netanyahu government announced more construction in the West Bank,
including 1,000 new housing units in East Jerusalem.[100]

With the Palestinians weighing the option of putting recognition of Palestinian statehood to a vote at the UN, world bodies began to weigh in. The
International Monetary Fund (IMF) issued a report affirming that the PA was
"now able to conduct the sound economic policies expected of a future well-
functioning Palestinian state". The World Bank similarly determined, "If the
Palestinian Authority maintains its performance in institution-building and
delivery of public services, it is well positioned for the establishment of a state
at any point in the near future".[101] A UN report concurred that "governmental
functions are now sufficient for a functioning government of a state."[102]

Toward that end, Fatah and Hamas announced at the end of April that they would create an interim unity government and hold elections within a year.[103] Former Mossad chief Efraim Halevy told the *New York Times* that "there will be no serious progress in the Israeli-Palestinian conflict without some way of including Hamas in the process so as to transform them from being part of the problem to being part of the solution." Ethan Bronner divined that such sensible talk was "a minority view in Israel".[104] A survey from November 2009 seemed to cast some doubt on Bronner's ability to read the public mind, however, having shown that 57 percent of Israelis supported engagement with Hamas.[105]

Under the reconciliation accord, Fatah and Hamas would agree to form a transitional government and prepare for parliamentary and presidential elections within a year. Khaled Meshal said that, when it was signed, Fatah and Hamas would speak with "one authority and one decision."[106] Meshal also reiterated Hamas's goal of a Palestinian state alongside Israel, with the 1967 lines for borders. In addition to affirming Hamas's commitment to the right of return, Meshal said, "Where there is occupation and settlement, there is a right to resistance. Israel is the aggressor. But resistance is a means, not an end."[107]

Responding to the prospect of Hamas-Fatah reconciliation, Israel immediately moved to punish the Palestinians, announcing that it would withhold nearly $90 million in tax revenues it collected in occupied territory on behalf of the PA (a move that proved temporary, since it weakened Israel's client regime in the West Bank while politically benefiting Hamas).[108] Netanyahu denounced any reconciliation as "a tremendous blow to peace and a great victory for terrorism." The PA, he declared, "must choose between peace with Israel or peace with Hamas."[109]

Hillary Clinton denounced the prospect of Hamas-Fatah reconciliation by reiterating the US's usual demands for Hamas to renounce the internationally recognized rights of the Palestinians.[110] Representative Eric Cantor introduced a resolution in the House denouncing the accord and again calling on the Obama administration to "veto any resolution on Palestinian statehood" in the UN Security Council and otherwise "oppose recognition of a Palestinian state".[111] A similar resolution was introduced in the Senate, which added that the administration should "consider restrictions on aid" to the PA "should it persist in efforts to circumvent direct negotiations by turning to the United Nations or other international bodies". It also urged the administration to "consider suspending assistance to the Palestinian Authority pending a review of the unity agreement between Fatah and Hamas".[112] Both resolutions were subsequently passed in their respective houses of Congress.

Clueing readers in about how they were supposed to perceive it, a *Washington Post* headline told how the reconciliation accord was "seen as [an] obstacle to peace". The headline of a *Times* piece by Bronner on May 5 read, "Hamas Leader Calls for Two-State Solution but Refuses to Renounce Violence".[113]

Far be it from the *New York Times* to explain to Americans that the right to armed resistance in self-defense against a foreign occupying military power is an inherent right recognized under international law. The UN Charter explicitly recognizes the "equal rights and self-determination of peoples" (Articles 1, 55) and "the inherent right of individual or collective self-defense" (Article 51). The UN Declaration on Principles of International Law concerning Friendly Relations and Cooperation among States in accordance with the Charter of the United Nations reaffirms the right to self-determination and states that "No territorial acquisition resulting from the threat or use of force shall be recognized as legal".[114] The Protocol I additional to the Geneva Conventions explicitly recognizes "armed conflicts in which peoples are fighting against colonial domination and alien occupation and against racist regimes" as falling within "the exercise of their right of self-determination" (Article 1). Naturally, though, the *New York Times* headline didn't read, "Hamas Leader Calls for Two-State Solution but Refuses to Renounce Right to Self-Defense", or even the perfectly neutral and non-interpretive alternative, ". . . but Refuses to Renounce 'Armed Resistance'". Naturally, no *New York Times* headline has ever proclaimed that the Israeli government "Refuses to Renounce Violence".

It also wasn't long before Bronner relegated the acknowledgment that Hamas accepted a two-state solution down the memory hole. He quickly returned to writing that Hamas "calls for Israel's destruction" in lieu of informing readers that Hamas had frequently and repeatedly, for at least half a decade, stated its acceptance of a Palestinian state alongside Israel.[115] Three days after publishing a headline acknowledging this longstanding position of Hamas's, a *Times* editorial was back to repeating the obligatory line that Hamas "has committed to Israel's destruction". The editors did acknowledge further down the page that, in an interview with the newspaper, Meshal had "declared himself fully committed to working for a two-state solution". But they argued that his statement could be disregarded because Hamas refused to renounce violence, and a few days earlier Ismail Haniyeh "was out there celebrating Osama bin Laden as a 'Muslim and Arab warrior.'"[116]

As one might expect, the *Times* was quoting Haniyeh completely out of context. The quote was pulled from a statement in which Haniyeh condemned the Obama administration's extrajudicial execution of the infamous Al-Qaeda leader: "*Despite the difference in opinions and agenda between us and them* [i.e., Al-Qaeda], *we condemn the assassination of* a Muslim and Arabic warrior and we pray to God that his soul rests in peace" (emphasis added).[117] Hamas had long made known its differences with bin Laden and his Al-Qaeda organization. In 2006, after the US froze aid to the Palestinian government for Hamas's election victory, Osama bin Laden issued a recording stating, "The blockade which the West is imposing on the government of Hamas proves that there is a Zionist crusaders war on Islam." In reply, Hamas spokesman Sami Abu Zuhri emphasized that "the ideology of Hamas is totally different from the ideology of Sheikh bin Laden."[118]

As one might also expect, the ever self-disciplined editors of the *New York Times* were just taking their cue from the State Department, which condemned Haniyeh's "outrageous" opposition to the US's practice of extrajudicial killing. As for describing bin Laden as a "warrior", the word Haniyeh used was "mujahed".[119] It's useful to recall that during the Soviet-Afghan war (1979-1989), Osama bin Laden was running the Maktab al-Khidamat (MAK)—the precursor organization to Al-Qaeda—out of Peshawar, Pakistan, where the US Central Intelligence Agency (CIA) also had its base of operations to finance, arm, and train radical "jihadists" to fight the US's proxy war against the occupying Soviet forces and the Soviet-backed government of Afghanistan. The MAK was backed by Pakistan's Inter-Services Intelligence agency (ISI), which was in turn the primary conduit through which the CIA funneled its resources in support of the war effort. While bin Laden was working under this arrangement alongside the CIA, he was among the "mujahedeen" whom President Ronald Reagan celebrated as "freedom fighters".[120]

Still taking their cue from government, the *Times* editors also shared the view that for the Palestinians to go to the UN was "not the answer", and if the PA continued to disobey orders and formed a unity government with Hamas, the Obama administration should "put the new government on notice that all support will be carefully scrutinized".[121]

On May 16, the *Times* published an op-ed by Mahmoud Abbas, who wrote that Palestinians had "cause for hope" as they commemorated the Nakba because Palestine would request international recognition along the 1967 lines, as well as admission into the UN. This "would pave the way for the internationalization of the conflict as a legal matter, not only a political one. It would also pave the way for us to pursue claims against Israel at the United Nations, human rights treaty bodies and the International Court of Justice."[122]

After publishing Abbas's piece, the *Times* described it as "the diplomatic equivalent of a declaration of war on the status quo".[123] Another editorial urged Obama to "put a map and a deal on the table" to jumpstart talks specifically for the purpose of heading off the UN bid.[124] Thomas Friedman remarked that in order to retain its Jewish majority, Israel must "cede" the West Bank, but that Netanyahu had "not spent his time in office using Israel's creativity to find ways to do such a deal. He has spent his time trying to avoid such a deal—and everyone knows it. No one is fooled." Friedman nevertheless concluded that it was "silly for the Palestinians to be going to the United Nations" and that they should instead be talking to the very same government he had just acknowledged was working so hard to prevent implementation of the two-state solution.[125]

The same day Abbas's op-ed was published, Netanyahu said in an address to the Knesset that "The root of the conflict is, and always has been, their refusal to recognize the Jewish state. It is not a conflict over 1967, but over 1948, over the very existence of the State of Israel."[126] Indeed, the problem was that the Palestinians refused to accept as legitimate their political disenfranchisement, the rejection of their self-determination and expropriation of their land by force, and the ethnic cleansing of Palestine by which the "Jewish state" came into existence. Netanyahu reiterated his demands that the Palestinians recognize Israel as a "Jewish state"; renounce the right of return, collective right to self-defense, and sovereignty over their own borders; and accept Israeli annexation of "the settlement blocs" and East Jerusalem. He stressed that Israel "must maintain the settlement blocs. There is widespread agreement that the settlement blocs must remain within the State of Israel".

Ethan Bronner waved his pen and magically transformed Netanyahu's words into a speech wherein the Prime Minister "showed more willingness to yield territory".[127] In the *Washington Post*, Jackson Diehl criticized the refusal "to make any concession". But this was directed not toward Netanyahu, but *Abbas*. Unlike Netanyahu, the Palestinian leader had committed the grave sin of "turning his back on American diplomacy". Diehl's headline described the reconciliation accord as "Mahmoud Abbas's formula for war".[128]

Israel meanwhile announced the approval of 1,500 additional Jewish homes in East Jerusalem.[129] There were no headlines in the opinion pages of America's top newspapers condemning "Netanyahu's formula for war" or news analyses criticizing Israel for "refusing to make any concessions", but demanding that the Palestinians show more willingness to yield territory.

Goldstone's Betrayal

On March 18, 2011, the UN committee of independent experts released its follow-up report assessing the investigations of Israel and Hamas into their conduct during Operation Cast Lead. The committee reported little progress with regard to Israel's investigations and reiterated the same concerns it had expressed in its first report.

With regard to the two soldiers who "received suspended sentences of three months each" for using a boy as a human shield, the committee said that it was "hard to square the apparent finding that the soldiers 'did not seek to degrade or humiliate the boy' with evidence that they intended to put him directly in harm's way at grave risk to his life." The committee also pointed out that these soldiers received a much more lenient penalty than the soldier who stole a credit card.

The committee reiterated the conclusions from its first report that Israel's investigations were not sufficiently prompt; there was no indication Israel had opened any investigations into the role of officials "who designed, planned, ordered and oversaw Operation Cast Lead"; and due to its role as legal advisor to the military, which presented a clear conflict of interest, the MAG's office was not "an appropriate mechanism for carrying out an independent and impartial analysis . . . into allegations that high-level decision-making related to the Gaza conflict violated international law." The committee also criticized Hamas for not conducting investigations into the allegations of war crimes by Palestinian militants.[130]

Richard Goldstone then penned an op-ed for the *Washington Post* characterizing the committee's report as though it had found Israel's self-investigations to be credible. "If I had known then what I know now," Goldstone wrote, "the Goldstone Report would have been a different document." To sustain this fiction that much more was now known, and that this new information exculpated Israel, he lied that the information the UN Fact-Finding Mission based its findings on "did not include any evidence provided by the Israeli government", whereas Israel's investigations were "recognized in the UN committee's report". In fact, the Fact-Finding Mission *did* take into consideration the reports the Israeli government had made public.

Goldstone next quoted from the committee's report: "Israel has dedicated significant resources to investigate over 400 allegations of operational misconduct in Gaza". He withheld from readers the fact that the results of these investigations were found by the committee to lack credibility.

Goldstone reminded that the Fact-Finding Mission concluded that Israeli soldiers in some instances had intentionally targeted civilians. He then sought to lead readers to believe that this conclusion had since been disproven, asserting that both Israel's investigations and the UN committee's report indicated "that civilians were not intentionally targeted as a matter of policy." It was the same strawman employed by Alan Dershowitz, and for the same purpose. Again, the UN Mission did *not* conclude in the instances it investigated where Israeli soldiers were found to have intentionally targeted Palestinian civilians that they were acting under policy directives to do so. What the Mission concluded with regard to Israel's policy, rather, was that it sought to punish the civilian population by using disproportionate force under its "Dahiya Doctrine".

Whereas Goldstone had previously noted Israel's "dismal" record of investigating itself, he now told a different story, expressing great confidence in Israel's ability and willingness to do so. Incredibly, the example he chose to support this characterization was the Samouni family. The deaths of twenty-nine members of the family, Goldstone wrote, "was apparently the consequence of an Israeli commander's erroneous interpretation of a drone image, and an Israeli officer is under investigation for having ordered the attack." In this and other instances, he argued, the Fact-Finding Mission would have arrived at different conclusions if this "evidence" from Israel's own self-investigations had been available to it.[131]

It warrants examining Goldstone's example to see how his characterization holds up. Recall that Israeli forces had forced the Samouni family to relocate to another building and then bombed the building and prevented rescuers from getting through to help survivors. What did the UN committee of experts actually have to say about Israel's investigation into this incident? The committee expressed "considerable concern" that it did "not have sufficient information to establish the current status of the ongoing criminal investigations into the killings" of members of the Samouni family. Of further concern was the fact that the killings may have been the result of not only "the actions and decisions of soldiers on the ground", but also "of senior officers located in a war room". There was a clear conflict of interest in the MAG's office investigating the attack on the Samouni family home: the MAG was involved in providing legal advice on "the rules of engagement *and the use of drones*" (emphasis added). The senior officer who apparently approved the airstrike denied having knowledge that civilians were in the home, telling the MAG's investigators "that he was not warned that civilians were at the location". Yet "some of those civilians had been ordered there by IDF soldiers from that same officer's unit, and air force officers reportedly informed him of the possible presence of civilians." After approving the drone strikes, *the very same officer* "insisted that ambulances not enter the sector under his control".[132]

But the actual facts didn't matter. The damage to the cause of justice was done. Goldstone's cowardly "retraction" op-ed was a gift to the "passionate defenders" of Israel's crimes. As Aluf Benn put it in *Haaretz*, Goldstone had given Israel "a major public relations coup".[133] "Everything we said has been proven to be true", Prime Minister Netanyahu proclaimed. "The fact that Goldstone backtracked must lead to the shelving of this report once and for all."[134] Defense Minister Barak complained that Goldstone had taken "such a long time to change his mind" despite having received Israel's reports as a member of the Fact-Finding Mission. Unsatisfied, Barak called on Goldstone to do more to "lessen the damage" he had caused to Israel's reputation.[135] Foreign Minister Avigdor Lieberman proclaimed that "the truth is clear, and cannot be questioned. . . . Today it is clear to everyone that the IDF is the most moral army."[136] Gabriela Shalev, Israel's former ambassador to the UN, drew the lesson that if Israel had to "defend" itself again, it would "be able to say there is no way to deal with this terror other than the same way we did in Cast Lead."[137]

The reaction was much the same in the US. Kirsten Gillibrand cosponsored a Senate resolution with thirty-four other senators "Calling on the United Nations to rescind the Goldstone report". It repeated the usual false claims that the Mission had "prejudged the outcome", "made numerous unsubstantiated assertions against Israel", "downplayed the overwhelming evidence that Hamas de-

liberately used Palestinian civilians and civilian institutions as human shields",
etc. On the grounds that "Justice Richard Goldstone publicly retracted the
central claims of the report", the resolution called on the UN to repudiate the
report and on the Obama administration to "take a leadership role in getting
the United Nations and its bodies to prevent any further action on the report's
findings and limit the damage that this libelous report has caused to our close
ally Israel". The resolution passed unanimously.[138]

A State Department spokesman announced:

> As we made clear when the Goldstone Report was initially
> presented and have maintained ever since, we did not see any
> evidence that the Israeli government had intentionally target-
> ed civilians or otherwise engaged in war crimes. Justice Gold-
> stone has now reached the same conclusion. . . . We would
> like to see the United Nations end its actions in relation to
> the Goldstone Report, and the other reports that have flowed
> from it. We will continue working for an end to the anti-Israel
> bias in the Human Rights Council and other UN bodies.[139]

The State Department's response wasn't exculpatory enough of Israel for Jennifer Rubin, who bemoaned in her blog at the *Washington Post*, "That's it? We'd
'like to see an end' to the UNHRC use of this defamatory attack on Israel's right
of self-defense? No call for groups, lawsuits and international bodies to retract
claims based on the false Goldstone Report? It's pathetically weak, a reflection
of the degree to which the administration shrinks from staunch defense of its
democratic ally. Our administration has much to say about the rights of Palestinians and the errors of Israel, not so much about the injustices suffered by
Israel."[140] Alan Dershowitz hailed that Goldstone's op-ed "made it clear" that
Israel had "fulfilled its obligation to carry out an independent report", which
"must take any possibility of launching an investigation against Israel off the
International Court's agenda." Israel, he proclaimed, had "acted correctly during the war and its investigation."[141] The American Jewish Committee called
on Goldstone to "present his updated conclusions to the UN Human Rights
Council, as well as to the General Assembly, which endorsed the skewed report,
and press for its rejection."[142]

The lead paragraph of an article by Ethan Bronner and Isabel Kershner
misinformed that Goldstone had "retracted the central and most explosive assertion" of the Fact-Finding Mission's report, "that Israel intentionally killed
Palestinian civilians there." Echoing Goldstone, they reported that the committee of independent experts found "that Hamas had not conducted any internal
investigations of its own but that Israel had devoted considerable resources in
looking into more than 400 accusations of misconduct". Like Goldstone, they
chose not to disclose to readers that the committee had found those inquiries

lacking in credibility. Toward the end of the article, they understatedly noted that the committee's report "was more critical of Israel than Mr. Goldstone acknowledged in his article", but declined to elaborate. In the very last paragraph, they perhaps unwittingly presented a possible explanation for what prompted Goldstone to write the op-ed; he had been "ostracized by Jewish communities in South Africa and elsewhere" for participating in the UN mission to the extent that "there was an attempt to bar him from his grandson's bar mitzvah in Johannesburg".[143]

In a second jointly-written article, Bronner and Kershner uncritically accepted as fact Goldstone's assertion that Israel had been largely vindicated. They attributed to "human rights organizations" the view that "much of" the UN Fact-Finding Mission's report "remains valid"—as though it was a *fact* that its main findings had been discredited. On the basis of this fiction, they propagated the US-Israeli government narrative that *Israel* had been the victim of injustice due to the ostensibly false findings of the Fact-Finding Mission. Despite Goldstone's "disavowal", they wrote, "the question remained whether the harm the Goldstone report caused—the ammunition it gave to those who view Israel as a pariah state and question its right to exist; the campaigns that have stopped some Israeli officials from traveling abroad for fear of arrest for war crimes—could be undone".[144]

In the *Washington Post*, Richard Cohen praised Goldstone for having "retracted his findings" and no longer believing "that Israel intentionally targeted civilians during the Gaza war". Israel was exonerated, and readers could rest assured that "Israel adheres to a morality we all recognize and admire".[145] Cohen had not at that time read the report of the committee of independent experts. However, after actually doing so, to his credit, he wrote a follow-up column noting that while Goldstone attributed his "volte-face" to the report's findings, "Goldstone and I have not been reading the same report." Goldstone's op-ed was a "mystery", Cohen wrote, in a reversal of his own. "Goldstone has moved but the evidence has not, really." This raised the question "of whether the jurist buckled under pressure so unrelenting it almost got him barred from his grandson's bar mitzvah in South Africa."[146]

Bolstering Cohen's conclusion, the *New York Times* informed that "The year and a half since the Gaza report was published have been hard on Mr. Goldstone." His participation in the UN Mission had caused his own daughter to be "furious with him" and "he was nearly unable to attend the bar mitzvah of his other daughter's son in South Africa because of plans by some members of the Jewish community there to demonstrate against his presence."[147]

Outside of the US mainstream media, alternative views of Goldstone's op-ed—according to which it *wasn't* deemed praiseworthy—could be found. Israeli author and historian Ilan Pappé described it as a "shameful U-turn" that resulted from "more than a year and a half of a sustained campaign of intimidation and character assassination against the judge", including threats by the South African Zionist Federation to picket outside the synagogue during his grandson's bar mitzvah if he showed up. The only new information upon which Goldstone drew his conclusion was the IDF's own self-exoneration, Pappé observed. "So it cannot be new evidence that caused Goldstone to write this article. Rather, it is his wish to return to the Zionist comfort zone that propelled this bizarre and faulty article." Goldstone had hoped "this would absolve him of Israel's righteous fury" and win "Zionist love", but this was "far less important than losing the world's respect in the long-run."[148]

Noura Erekat, a Palestinian human rights attorney and adjunct professor at the Center for Contemporary Arab Studies in Georgetown University, appropriately described Goldstone's op-ed an "act of negligence". He "should have known better" than to accept "Israel's investigatory findings at face value notwithstanding the Independent Committee of Experts' conclusions that they are structurally flawed and unlikely to yield effective measures of accountability and justice."[149]

Cedric Sapey, a spokesman for the Human Rights Council, responded to Goldstone's action by stating that "UN reports are not canceled on the basis of an op-ed in a newspaper". Various resolutions passed by the Council would have to be repealed by that body, and the same went for resolutions of the General Assembly. If Goldstone wished to request that the report with his name on it be withdrawn, he would have to submit a formal request. Goldstone subsequently told the Associated Press that he would not submit such a request to the Council.[150]

Goldstone's colleague Hina Jilani also expressed her disagreement. "Ultimately," she said, "the UN Report would not have been any different to what it was" given information that had since become available.[151] Ms. Jilani joined the two other members of the Mission, Christine Chinkin and Desmond Travers, in publishing a statement "to dispel any impression that subsequent developments have rendered any part of the mission's report unsubstantiated, erroneous or inaccurate." The demands that the Mission's report should be withdrawn were unjustified since "nothing of substance has appeared that would in any way change the context, findings or conclusions of that report. . . . We firmly stand by these conclusions." Goldstone's characterization of the report of the committee of independent experts as though it "somehow contradicts the fact-finding mission's report or invalidates it" was "a clear distortion of their findings".[152]

But what do facts actually matter to the US government or the mainstream media?

'The 1967 Lines'

On May 19, 2011, as Israel was announcing additional settlement construction, President Obama gave a speech at the State Department characterizing the Israeli-Palestinian conflict as follows: "For Israelis, it has meant living with the fear that their children could be blown up on a bus or by rockets fired at their homes, as well as the pain of knowing that other children in the region are taught to hate them. For Palestinians, it has meant suffering the humiliation of occupation, and never living in a nation of their own."

So Palestinians merely suffered "humiliation", compared to the much more serious consequences of "pain" and being "blown up" suffered by Israelis.

The reality was quite different. According to detailed statistics from B'Tselem, from the start of the First Intifada in December 1987 until September 2000, 1,551 Palestinians were killed by Israelis compared to 421 Israelis killed by Palestinians. From September 2000 until the start of Operation Cast Lead in December 2008, 4,905 Palestinians were killed compared to 1,041 Israelis. During that assault, 1,401 Palestinians were killed and 9 Israelis. From the end of that massacre until the time of Obama's speech, 215 Palestinians and 21 Israelis were killed. In total, from the start of the First Intifada until the month Obama spoke, 8,072 Palestinians had been killed by Israelis, compared to 1,492 Israelis killed by Palestinians, for a ratio of more than five Palestinians killed for every Israeli—including many who were "blown up".[153]

And surely the Palestinians also felt pain from knowing that Israeli children were taught to hate them. This was the lesson taught every day to Israeli children with Israel's ongoing occupation, its theft of Palestinian land and destruction of their homes, and its collective punishment and violence against them.

Palestinians surely also recall how Baruch Goldstein—the Jewish settler who murdered twenty-nine Muslims praying in a mosque in Hebron in 1994—is celebrated in Israel as a martyr, with a marble plaque at his grave reading, "To the holy Baruch Goldstein, who gave his life for the Jewish people, the Torah and the nation of Israel." They surely understand the lesson it teaches Israeli children when Jews gather annually at the grave to celebrate the anniversary of the massacre.[154]

There is no shortage of other examples of Israeli children learning the lesson of hate. Take the book *The King's Torah* (2009), which the Jewish daily *Forward* described as "a rabbinic instruction manual outlining acceptable scenarios for killing non-Jewish babies, children and adults. The prohibition 'Thou Shalt Not Murder' applies only 'to a Jew who kills a Jew,' write Rabbis Yitzhak Shapira and Yosef Elitzur of the West Bank settlement of Yitzhar. Non-Jews are 'uncompassionate by nature' and attacks on them 'curb their evil inclination,' while babies and children of Israel's enemies may be killed since 'it is clear that they will grow to harm us.'" The book had "wide dissemination and the enthusiastic endorsements of prominent rabbis". At the entrance to one bookstore, "copies

of 'The King's Torah' were displayed with children's books".[155] One passage in
the book read, "If we kill a Gentile who has sinned or has violated one of the
seven commandments—because we care about the commandments—there is
nothing wrong with the murder."[156]

But it was only Palestinians, as Obama told it, who committed deadly acts
of violence, and only Palestinians who taught their children to hate. Obama
continued to lecture the Palestinians for the sin of trying to "delegitimize" and
"isolate" Israel by seeking recognition of statehood at the UN. Once again
expressing the US's "unshakeable" commitment to "Israel's security", Obama
promised to "stand against attempts to single it out for criticism in international
forums", as his administration had done by vetoing an uncontroversial UN Security Council resolution condemning Israel's illegal settlement expansion.

Obama expressed his disapproval of the "status quo" solely on the grounds
that it was "unsustainable" because "a growing number of Palestinians live west
of the Jordan River" and "a Jewish and democratic state" could not exist at
the same time as "permanent occupation". So the main problem—as Secretary
Clinton had also already outlined—was that Palestinians existed and procreated.

As for how these two states would define their mutual border, Obama alluded to the US acceptance of the Israeli interpretation of Resolution 242: "We
believe the borders of Israel and Palestine should be based on the 1967 lines
with mutually agreed swaps, so that secure and recognized borders are established for both states."[157]

In the minds of Israeli officials, however, Obama had not advocated their
government's position strongly enough. The Prime Minister's office issued a
statement expressing Netanyahu's expectation that Obama should reaffirm "US
commitments made to Israel". This meant supporting Israel's position of "not
having to withdraw to the 1967 lines", rejecting the Palestinian right of return,
and demanding that Palestinians "recognize Israel as the nation state of the
Jewish people".[158] Ambassador Michael B. Oren said, "While there were many
points in the president's speech that we appreciate and welcome, there were
other aspects, like the return to the 1967 borders, which depart from longstanding American policy, as well as Israeli policy, going back to 1967."[159]

Of course, Obama had *not* said that Israel should withdraw to the 1967
lines, or that it should accept the armistice lines as a border. Rather, he had
simply reiterated longstanding US policy. Recall, for example, the Bush administration's policy that a solution must be "achieved on the basis of mutually
agreed changes that reflect" the "realities" of illegal Israeli colonization of Palestinian land. Indeed, in a BBC interview published the same day as his speech,
Obama elucidated, "The basis for negotiations will involve *looking at* that 1967
border, *recognizing that conditions on the ground have changed* and there are go-

ing to need to be swaps to accommodate the interest of both sides" (emphasis added).[160]

US commentators nevertheless responded to Obama's speech by unanimously describing it as a "shift" in US policy. Obama's "formula of land swaps" was "a new starting point for negotiations" hailed the *New York Times*. It was "a new benchmark for a diplomatic solution", and "a subtle, but significant shift, in American policy". The *Times* noted the how the administration maintained that land swaps would need "to account for large Jewish settlements that have taken root in the West Bank since 1967"—yet the newspaper neglected to illuminate how, exactly, this constituted a "shift" in US policy.[161]

Josh Rogin at *Foreign Policy* noted that Hillary Clinton had already said that the goal was two states "based on the 1967 lines, with agreed swaps". Clinton's statement, of course, had not been met with any declarations of a "shift" in policy (for the obvious reason that it wasn't). But Rogin maintained that a shift had occurred and assured his readers that Obama's remark went "one step further" than Clinton's—without troubling himself to explain what difference he perceived between the two, apart from the fact that they were made by two different senior members of the administration.[162]

The executive director of WINEP, Robert Satloff, shared his brilliant insight that Obama's speech constituted a "substantial shift" and "a major departure from long-standing US policy" because, although the Clinton parameters had also called for a settlement on the basis of the armistice lines with mutually agreed land swaps, Bill Clinton hadn't actually used the words "1967 lines" in his proposal.[163]

Glenn Kessler at the *Washington Post* attempted to explain to those perplexed individuals who were still having trouble perceiving this "shift" that the reason they found Obama's statement "unremarkable" was simply because they were "not trained in the nuances of Middle East diplomacy". The "experts", on the other hand, were enlightened enough to realize that it represented a "major shift" in US policy, even though it was admittedly "not news that the eventual borders of a Palestinian state would be based on land swaps from the 1967 dividing line", and even though President Bush had said in 2005 that a negotiated settlement must include mutually agreed "changes to the 1949 Armistice Lines"—synonymous with the pre-June 1967 lines.[164] The precise nature of this ostensible "shift" thus remained remarkably ambiguous, Kessler's earnest effort to explain it to the pitiable uninitiated notwithstanding.

In the *New York Times*, Roger Cohen offered further insights into what "major shift" the "experts" perceived by interpreting Obama's remark as having urged Netanyahu "to accept Israeli borders at or close to the 1967 lines". He added that Obama was "right" to shift policy away from Bush's acceptance of Israeli annexation of major settlement blocs. How Cohen took *this* away from Obama's statement, he declined to elucidate, but we must presume the *Times* columnist was trained well enough in the "nuances" of regional diplomacy to be able to take away what lesser mortals, in all their witlessness, failed to perceive.[165]

Setting aside the consensus that a "shift" had occurred, the transparent purpose of Obama's utterance of the "1967 lines" was to bait the Palestinians to abandon their aspirations of gaining international recognition of statehood and return to the US-led "peace process" by which the US and Israel had long prevented the two-state solution from being implemented. In other words, his statement represented absolute continuity of longstanding US policy.

Administration officials said as much to reporters. One official told the *Washington Post* that the Obama and Bush administrations' policies were "consistent". The official also emphasized, "We certainly know what the president's position doesn't mean—a return to the 1967 lines." Nevertheless, the *Post* inexplicably insisted that Netanyahu's reply that Israel would not withdraw to the 1967 lines "laid bare" the "fundamental differences" between his and Obama's positions.[166] No less enigmatically, a Reuters analysis described "a deep divide" between Obama and Netanyahu.[167]

Israeli commentor Aluf Benn (who soon thereafter became editor-in-chief of *Haaretz*) was among those apparently lacking the proper training "in the nuances of Middle East diplomacy" to correctly interpret Obama's remark. Netanyahu could be pleased with Obama's speech, Benn wrote, because it granted him "a major diplomatic victory". Obama had "scornfully rejected" the Palestinians' UN bid, demanded that they return to the "peace process", called for land swaps "without defining the size of these lands", and explained his support for a Palestinian state solely in terms of the Jewish "demographic inferiority".[168]

Similarly uninitiated was Sever Plocker, who wrote an analysis in *Ynetnews* titled "Obama the Zionist". Obama had "unequivocally adopted the essence of the Israeli-Zionist narrative in his speech" by leaving out any specifics "as to the size and locations of the territories to be swapped", as well as by requiring the Palestinians "to recognize Israel as the Jewish State and renounce, in practice, the right of return". There were efforts "to portray Obama as an Israel-hater who curries favor with the Arabs", but "none of the above is true". On the contrary, "No previous US president, including Israel's staunchest friends, had openly expressed the American position in a way that is so commensurate with the national Zionist-Jewish position."[169]

Perhaps the most important observation to be made about the reaction to Obama's speech among American commentators was the universal tacit acknowledgment that US policy had always been rejectionist. After all, logically, if the US had always supported the two-state solution, any remark by the president interpreted as calling for a final settlement based on a return to the 1967 lines with minor and mutually agreed revisions to the final border could not have constituted a "major shift" in policy. But such "nuances" as these were lost upon the American intelligentsia in all their glorious cognitive dissonance.

Obama Speaks to AIPAC

Three days after his remarks at the State Department, Obama gave another speech that received far less attention—at an AIPAC conference. He recalled for his audience having visited the Western Wall in the Old City of Jerusalem, touching his hand against it, placing his prayer "between its ancient stones", and thinking of "all the centuries that the children of Israel had longed to return to their ancient homeland." Far from his mind were the Palestinian children who were ethnically cleansed from the homes their families had lived in and the soil they had worked on for many generations in order to accommodate the "return" of immigrants who had never before set foot in the land. For these Arab children of Palestine, Obama had no words or prayers.

He reiterated the "unbreakable" bond and "America's commitment to Israel's security", which his administration had made "a priority". Military cooperation had been increased "to unprecedented levels" under his administration, and the US was making available to Israel its "most advanced technologies". This commitment to Israel was "why, despite tough fiscal times" for the American taxpayers footing the bill, his administration had "increased foreign military financing to record levels." "So make no mistake," he vowed, "we will maintain Israel's qualitative military edge."

He reiterated the US-Israeli policy of refusing to negotiate with a Palestinian government that included Hamas, describing the recent reconciliation accord as "an enormous obstacle to peace".

He repeated the usual demand that the Palestinians must essentially recognize that the Jews had a "right" to establish their state by ethnically cleansing three-quarters of a million Arabs from their homeland.

Obama also went out of his way to accommodate Israel's rejectionist position by carefully choosing his words. He described an area "west of the Jordan River", which fell short of publicly adopting "Judea and Samaria" while also avoiding the mental association "West Bank" has with "occupied Palestinian territory".

The fundamental problem, as Obama outlined it once more, was that Palestinians lived in the land and procreated. The unfortunate result was the "reshaping" of "demographic realities", which threatened Israel's existence "as both a Jewish state and a democratic state." *This*, he explained, was why it was so vitally important to achieve a "peace deal". He understood that there was "impatience with the peace process, or the absence of one". He understood that this was the reason the Palestinians were appealing to the international community, yet criticized them for "pursuing their interests at the United Nations" and pledged that "the United States will stand up against efforts to single Israel out at the United Nations or in any international forum." He promised to continue to protect Israel from efforts by the international community to hold it accountable for its violations of international law, described euphemistically as "the march to isolate Israel internationally". At the same time, he promised that the US would "hold the Palestinians accountable for their actions and for their rhetoric", meaning that they would be punished for disobeying orders by appealing to the international community to recognize Palestine.

Peace "cannot be imposed on the parties to the conflict", Obama said. Of course, to impose their will on the Palestinians through military force and political coercion was the name of the game for the US and Israel. What Obama really meant was that peace could not be achieved through bodies like the UN by applying international law. "No vote at the United Nations will ever create an independent Palestinian state", Obama professed, while bragging about how the US had recognized Israel just "moments" after the Zionist leadership announced its existence on the supposed authority of UN General Assembly Resolution 181.

Continuing, Obama said his speech a few days earlier had "generated some controversy", but he reemphasized that there had been no change in US policy, which had remained consistent "since at least the Clinton administration." He explained the necessity of having "a credible peace process" to prevent the Palestinians from abandoning negotiations and going to the UN. *This* was the purpose of his speech at the State Department. As for his mention of the "1967 lines", he stressed that it was just a reiteration of the US's "well-known formula" that the Palestinians must agree that Israel would annex territory so that the final outcome would be "a border that is different than the one that existed on June 4, 1967".

Obama proceeded to declare that "every state has the right to self-defense"— *except* Palestine. While "Israel must be able to defend itself", he argued, the *Palestinians* must effectively *renounce* their right to collective self-defense and accept a "non-militarized state."

He closed with, "God bless you. God bless Israel, and God bless the United States of America." Palestine and its people were left with the US president's curses.[170]

A final border based on mutually agreed changes to the 1967 lines is indeed a "well-known formula", but it warrants reemphasizing that the US's version of this formula is much different than the version in favor of which there is otherwise an international consensus. Again, it is crucial to differentiate between *the* two-state solution, which requires full Israeli withdrawal, and the formula for *a* two-state solution that Obama outlined, which was just a reiteration of the same formula adopted by previous administrations. Under the US formula, international law would not apply, and the Palestinians must negotiate while remaining under military occupation and while the Occupying Power continued to prejudice the outcome of talks by constructing "facts on the ground".

The *New York Times* pointed out how Obama told his AIPAC audience that his "1967 lines" comment reflected a consistent US policy since the Clinton administration. The newspaper attempted to reconcile this with its earlier reporting about a dramatic "shift" by rationalizing that this policy had "always been privately understood", but was "not spoken publicly, and certainly not publicly endorsed by a sitting American president".[171] This was nonsense, of course. *Ynetnews* attempted to set the record straight by pointing out, for example, that President Bush had publicly stated in 2005 "that both sides must agree on any changes to the 1949 armistice lines"—a.k.a. the "1967 lines".[172]

The *Times* did, however, inform its readers, near the end of the article, about the true meaning of Obama's "1967 lines" speech: "Administration officials argue that one way to try to derail the United Nations vote is to have a viable peace process under way between Israelis and Palestinians." Daniel Levy, a member of the Israeli delegation during the Taba negotiations, summarized Obama's accompanying AIPAC speech as communicating to the Israeli government, "I can continue defending you to the hilt, but if you give me nothing to work with, even America can't save you".[173]

Mr. Netanyahu Goes to Washington

Obama's AIPAC speech evidently satisfied the expectations of the Israeli prime minister, who affirmed his determination to work with the US president "to find ways to renew the peace negotiations."

Saeb Erekat, however, indicated that the Palestinian leadership would not take Obama's bait. "I am waiting to hear from Prime Minister Netanyahu", Erekat replied. "Does he accept the doctrine of two states on the 1967 lines with agreed swaps or not? Before we hear that acceptance, we are just grinding water."[174] If Netanyahu would agree to the two-state solution, Erekat also said, then "we shall turn over a new leaf. If he doesn't then there is no point talking about a peace process. . . . Once Netanyahu says that the negotiations will lead to a Palestinian state on the 1967 borders, then everything will be set". The Hamas foreign ministry similarly issued a statement saying, "The categorical rejection of 1967 lines and the right of return, and the hanging on to Jerusalem as Israel's capital destroy the foundations of peace negotiations".[175]

On May 25, Netanyahu gave a speech on the floor of the Capitol in Washington, DC. He expressed his deep appreciation for the US government's expropriation of wealth from American taxpayers (who were suffering through what was dubbed by some economists "the Great Recession") in order to redistribute it to Israel for purposes such as the war crimes committed during Operation Cast Lead. The US government had been "very generous" in giving

Israel such military aid, even though "economic times" were "tough". There were "many who rush to condemn Israel" for "defending itself", Netanyahu told his Congressional audience; "Not you," he praised. "Not America."

Israel was "what is right about the Middle East", Netanyahu boasted. It was a state that understood the values of "democracy" and "liberty". It was a state that George Eliot once described as "a bright star of freedom amid the despotisms of the East".

Then he turned his attention to Iran. Gaza's misery was Iran's fault, he charged, without elaborating, because it "subjugates" the Palestinians there. Invoking the Holocaust, he described Iran as a nation seeking nuclear weapons, a state with "genocidal aims" that was "calling for the annihilation of the Jewish state".

In fact, Israel's own intelligence community agreed with the US's assessment that Iran did not have an active nuclear weapons program. Iran had not threatened Israel with a military attack. Israel, on the other hand, had repeatedly threatened to bomb Iran to destroy its nuclear facilities. Israel is the only country in the Middle East possessing nuclear weapons, and unlike Israel, Iran is a signatory of the Nuclear Non-Proliferation Treaty (NPT) and has its nuclear program under the safeguards regime of the International Atomic Energy Agency (IAEA).[176] The Congress, however, was perfectly eager to allow their attention to be distracted from Israel's siege of Gaza and other violations of international law toward yet another manufactured threat.

Netanyahu declared his commitment "to a solution of two states for two peoples: a Palestinian state alongside a Jewish state." He was "willing to make painful compromises to achieve this historic peace." Having already explained in his Bar-Ilan speech, he repeated for the Congress what he meant by "compromises". While it was "not easy" for him, he understood that Israel would not be able to annex *all* of the West Bank or Gaza, which were both "parts of the ancestral Jewish homeland", in which "the Jewish people are not foreign occupiers." The Arabs who lived in the West Bank would be "neither Israel's subjects nor its citizens"; rather, Israel would, out of its great munificence, gift some portion of the West Bank to the Palestinians where they could live "in their own state" by the grace of the Jews of Israel.

Despite such incredible generosity on the part of Israel's leadership, peace had perplexingly "eluded" them. This was because the Palestinians were so uncompromising. They refused to recognize Israel as "a Jewish state" and had repeatedly "refused generous offers". Now Israel was again willing to "be generous about the size of the future Palestinian state", but, "as President Obama said, the border will be different than the one that existed on June 4, 1967." Israel would "be generous on the size of a Palestinian state," he stressed again, "but we'll be very firm on where *we* put the border with it" (emphasis added). In accordance with the US formula over multiple administrations, the "precise delineation" of the border "must be negotiated"—meaning that the Palestinians must be coerced into acquiescing to Israel's planned annexation and accept a border determined by Israel. Accordingly, as Obama had agreed in Sderot, an undivided Jerusalem "must remain the united capital of Israel".

In addition to handing over more of their land, the Palestinians must also renounce their right of return so that "the Palestinian refugee problem will be resolved outside the borders of Israel." Netanyahu sympathized that this would be "difficult" for the Palestinians, but they must accept it because Israel's "security" and the desires of its Jewish citizens trumped Palestinian rights and international law. Hence, it was "absolutely vital" to Israel that the Palestinians also renounce their collective right to self-defense and accept as a precondition a "fully demilitarized" state. They must also surrender sovereignty over their own borders since it was "absolutely vital" for Israel to "maintain a long-term military presence along the Jordan River."

He denounced the "Palestinian attempt to impose a settlement through the United Nations", which, he insisted, "will not bring peace"—only a settlement imposed by the US and Israel upon the Palestinians "around the negotiating table" would do that. Efforts to create a framework for peace talks based on international law "should be forcefully opposed by all those who want to see this conflict end".

Netanyahu closed by again expressing his appreciation for Obama's "clear position on this issue" and showering the Congress with praise and gratitude for the US support for Israel's endeavor to bring about "peace" by beating the Palestinians into submission. In closing, he said, "I speak on behalf of the Jewish people and the Jewish state when I say to you, representatives of America, thank you. Thank you. Thank you for your unwavering support for Israel. Thank you for ensuring that the flame of freedom burns bright throughout the world. May God bless all of you, and may God forever bless the United States of America. Thank you. Thank you very much. Thank you. Thank you."[177]

Far from being recognized as hate speech, Netanyahu's remarks were unsurprisingly met throughout with thunderous applause and standing ovations from the Congress.[178]

While Netanyahu's visit to Washington had been intended "to find a way to lure the Palestinians back to direct negotiations, thereby preempting their plan" to go to the UN, Ethan Bronner remarked in the *New York Times*, "hopes were dashed that his visit might advance peace negotiations with the Palestinians" because his speech "persuaded them that they had no negotiating partner." Nevertheless, the "praise" for Netanyahu's "oratory skill" among Congress members was "overwhelming"; "Disputes about his performance were limited to how many times he brought the senators and representatives to their feet (from 26 to 34)."[179]

The *Times* editors weren't as enthusiastic about Netanyahu's speech. They objected to it on the narrow grounds that it "wasted" an "opportunity" to head off the Palestinian plan to go to the UN, which had to be condemned since it would "further isolate Israel and Washington"—a very grave sin, indeed. There was no objection to the actual substance of Netanyahu's speech, no criticism of his rejection of the two-state solution, no acknowledgment that the Palestinians were certainly right to conclude that they had no negotiating partner.

The *Times* also performed an astonishing reversal from its earlier insistence that Obama's State Department speech indicated a dramatic "shift" in policy. The editors now found it convenient to acknowledge that the idea of an Israeli withdrawal to the "pre-1967 borders—with mutually agreed land swaps" had been "the basis of all negotiations for more than a decade, including those backed by President George W. Bush."[180] A second editorial illuminated the reason for dropping the façade of a "shift". The Republican presidential candidates had been condemning Obama's speech, the *Times* explained:

> "President Obama has thrown Israel under the bus," said Mitt Romney. Tim Pawlenty wrongly said Mr. Obama had called for Israel to return to its 1967 borders, which he called "a disaster waiting to happen." Rick Santorum said Mr. Obama "just put Israel's very existence in more peril." Others went even further. . . . Pandering on Israel in the hopes of winning Jewish support is hardly a new phenomenon in American politics, but there is something unusually dishonest about this fusillade. Most Republicans know full well that Mr. Obama is not calling on Israel to retreat to its 1967 borders.

This was accurate enough—except, of course, for the part about the dishonesty being "unusual". The criteria of the left-leaning newspaper was abundantly clear: if it was perceived as bold leadership to achieve peace on the part of the Democratic president, then Obama's speech represented a dramatic shift in policy from his Republican predecessor's; but if it was perceived as poor judgment that betrayed Israel, then the policy Obama outlined in his speech was consistent with the previous administration's.[181]

The manufactured controversy about Obama's loyalty to Israel served to distract public attention away from any kind of meaningful and substantive discussion about US policy in the Middle East. This was further illustrated by the fact that criticism of Obama for his ostensible "shift" had by no means been limited to Republicans. Democrats, too, had condemned his mention of the "1967 lines" on the exact same grounds. "To an overwhelming bipartisan majority of Congress," Stephen Zunes incisively noted, "Obama was simply not anti-Palestinian enough." The "bipartisan rebuke of Obama" was evident when Netanyahu "received the most enthusiastic applause" for declaring that

Israel would not return to the 1967 lines and pledging "to never end the Israeli occupation of Arab East Jerusalem."

Zunes also relayed an incident that occurred on the floor of the House during Netanyahu's speech:

> One of the most telling examples of the mindset of the bipartisan supermajority came when Israeli-American peace activist Rae Abileah, sitting in the visitor's gallery, began shouting, "Equal rights of Palestinians." Right-wing supporters of the Israeli prime minister began attacking her, until Capitol police rescued her and took her to a hospital, where her injuries were determined to be serious enough to require an overnight stay. After initially booing her for interrupting the speaker, virtually the entire House floor rose to its feet cheering while she was being manhandled and silenced. Videos show those who could see that section of the gallery were looking directly at the attack clapping and cheering, apparently well aware of what was happening, indicating how Congress believes such dissident voices should be treated.[182]

As the woman was being physically assaulted on the floor of the Capitol, Netanyahu told the Congress, "You know, I take it as a badge of honor, and so should you, that in our free societies you can have protests. You can't have these protests in the farcical parliaments in Tehran or in Tripoli. This is real democracy."[183]

The narrow criticism of Netanyahu's speech in the *Times* was contrasted by an editorial in *Haaretz* blasting him for having proven once again that he had no interest in peace. "Netanyahu wasted the generous credit he got from his American hosts", the editors wrote, "to cast accusations at the Palestinians and impose endless obstacles in connection with the core issues". The Prime Minister had "couched his readiness to make far-reaching concessions within endless conditions that have no relation to reality." Israelis "who seek peace", the editors opined, ought to seek "a different leader."[184]

Haaretz columnist Gideon Levy similarly criticized it as "the speech of the death of peace". It was "filled with lies on top of lies and illusions heaped on illusions". Netanyahu had attempted to sell the Congress "a pile of propaganda and prevarication" with "hypocrisy and sanctimony". Levy concluded, "The fact that the Congress rose to its feet multiple times to applaud him says more about the ignorance of its members than the quality of their guest's speech. . . . The man who explicitly said he would do his level best to destroy the Oslo Accords suddenly says he's in favor of peace with the Palestinians. Last night we saw that the Americans will buy anything, or at least their applauding legislators will."[185]

Challenging Netanyahu's description of Israel as "a bright star of freedom", Daniel Levy commented in *Foreign Affairs* that Israel's prideful claim about "being a democracy" was "a proposition that always appeared somewhat tenuous for the 20 percent of Israel's citizens who are Palestinian-Arab, who lived under a military governorate from 1948 to 1966 and continue to face entrenched structural discrimination." Under the "current governing coalition", there had been "a slew of anti-democratic and at times unashamedly racist legislative initiatives targeting the Palestinian-Arab community." This had "found great resonance in the Israeli public"—86 percent of whom, according to a survey by the Israel Democracy Institute, "believe that decisions critical to the state should be taken only by a Jewish majority".[186]

Freedom Flotilla II

In May 2011, three months after a popular revolution in Egypt resulted in the overthrow of President Hosni Mubarak (a regional strongman of Washington's whom Secretary Clinton once described as "family"), the interim Egyptian authorities prepared to partially reopen the Rafah border crossing into Gaza.[187]

In the *New York Times*, Ethan Bronner sympathetically offered Israel's perspective on this development under the headline "Israel Waits and Worries Before Gaza Border Opening". Israeli officials were "worried about weapons and militants flowing into the Hamas-controlled strip" when the Rafah crossing opened. He declined to relay the perspective of the Palestinians or the consensus of the international community. Instead, he limited criticism of Israel to the view that its policy of "suppressing economic growth in Gaza" was "largely viewed as a failure" because "Hamas seemed no weaker and Israel faced condemnation". So it wasn't that Israel's collective punishment was illegal and immoral, merely that it failed to achieve the goal of regime change and damaged Israel's image.[188]

In a subsequent article, Bronner quoted Christopher Gunness saying, "The policy of weakening Hamas seems to have failed, but the policy has been highly successful at punishing the people of Gaza." Presumably, UNRWA's principle concern was not how this might be affecting the world's perception of Israel.[189]

The decision by the military leadership of the interim Egyptian government was not an act of humanitarianism, but was intended to appease the public's opposition to their government's complicity in Israel's criminal siege. Under the new policy, the authorities permitted only 400 people to pass through the crossings daily and continued to blockade badly need goods, such as construction materials.[190]

Egypt's policy might have had something to do with the fact that the Egyptian military establishment annually received $1.3 billion in aid from Washington under the terms of the 1978 Camp David Accords and the peace treaty between Egypt and Israel signed the following year. Egypt has since been the second-largest recipient of US foreign assistance after Israel. Under the treaty, Israel agreed to withdraw its occupying forces from the Sinai Peninsula in exchange for an agreement from Egypt to keep the Sinai demilitarized and a normalization of trade relations, including sales of Egyptian oil to Israel.[191]

Following Mubarak's ousting in February, Senator Joseph Lieberman bragged that the US "should feel very good about the assistance we have given the Egyptian military over the years since the Camp David peace with Israel, because the Egyptian military really allowed this revolution in Egypt to be peaceful and let the people carry out their desires for political freedom and economic opportunity".[192] That is to say, Americans should pat themselves on the back since the response of the US-backed Egyptian military establishment to the popular uprising was mostly limited to using tear gas canisters marked "Made in USA" against peaceful protesters, while the number of people they injured was kept down to around 6,400 and the number killed to a mere 846—yet another shining example of how the US promoted democracy around the world.

With the Egyptian government's continued complicity in Israel's illegal blockade, conditions in Gaza remained desperate. "Gaza is more dependent than ever on outside aid", said Mathilde de Riedmatten, the deputy head of the ICRC's sub-delegation in Gaza. Israel's siege "makes economic recovery impossible."[193] UNRWA reported that while there had been job gains in the public sector as well as construction under the Hamas government, there had on the whole been a decrease in jobs in the private sector, which was dependent on external aid. Employment in the private sector was driven by external assistance funneled through UN agencies and NGOs. The unemployment rate was one of the highest in the world at 45.2 percent.[194] "It is hard to understand the logic of a man-made policy", said Christopher Gunness, "which deliberately impoverishes so many and condemns hundreds of thousands of potentially productive people to a life of destitution."[195]

While the *New York Times* relayed the concern that Israel's policy was damaging its image, the *Jerusalem Post* reported on "the second shopping mall to open in the Gaza Strip in a year", which was deemed further proof that concerns about the humanitarian situation in Gaza were unfounded.[196]

The first mall in Gaza, which had opened in July of the previous year, had been met with the same treatment. A *Ynetnews* op-ed described "The good life in Gaza" and proposed that "images from the new mall make one wonder about the humanitarian crisis all these international 'aid' ships are sailing to."[197] *Ynetnews* elsewhere cited the mall as an indication that "the Gaza market seems to be doing alright." The article went on to note that the mall was a mere 9,700 square feet over two floors, and visitors had to take the stairs when it opened because the only elevator wasn't working. Tens of thousands visited the mall in the first days after its opening, but, as one employee told *Ynetnews*, "Not everyone comes to shop. There are those who are curious who just come to see the place and others who come for the air conditioning."[198]

Indeed, among the details the *Jerusalem Post* left out were that the wares of Gaza's two malls were unaffordable for most of the population and that the prosperity of the territory's small number of wealthy people was largely dependent on the black market economy. The *Post* could just as well have cited other examples of how booming the Gazan economy was. Take Roots Club, described by *CBS News* as "one of Gaza's few upscale restaurants". With goods like cilantro and instant coffee being banned under "secret guidelines to differentiate between humanitarian necessities and nonessential luxuries", Roots Club used "a mixture of smuggled and legally imported goods for its menu." As CBS also explained, "Gaza's tiny elite and foreigners are well served by the handful of restaurants like Roots, where a meal costs more than a typical Gazan's daily wage. But such places are out of reach for virtually all of Gaza's residents, who overwhelmingly rely on UN-donated food aid."[199]

Or take Faisal Equestrian Club, which brought in some of its horses through the tunnels. The club had a membership of about 120, with monthly fees of 300 shekels, "a considerable commitment," as *The Guardian* pointed out, "even for Gaza's elite families." Next door to Faisal was Crazy Water Park, and a number of seafront cafes had opened up, in addition to the plan to open the first shopping mall. "The Israeli government says all this attests to the lack of an economic crisis in the territory", *The Guardian* observed, "But in reality, access to these facilities is limited to a tiny stratum of the population."[200]

In one later manifestation of the persistent hasbara theme, the IDF published a blog post titled "What Happened to the Humanitarian Crisis in Gaza?" It contained photos purportedly showing Gazans "out in force, enjoying themselves in sparkling new malls, beautiful beaches and hotels, and doing their shopping in pristine grocery stores and markets heaving with fresh produce."[201] The IDF posted to the online social network Twitter, "People say there is a humanitarian crisis in #Gaza. The hotels, beaches, malls & nightlife say otherwise. #MythBusted".[202] The *Times of Israel*, however, noted that "The pictures did indeed show a different reality to the Gaza the world has become accustomed to seeing over the past several years." This included a photo that the IDF captioned "The shopping mall for the latest fashion from overseas". The photo was actually of a mall in Kuala Lumpur, Malaysia. "More than once," pictures used by the IDF had "proven to be fictitious—whether photoshopped, taken at a different time and place than claimed, or purporting to show" something they didn't.[203]

Writing in January 2014, Daniella Peled commented on the theme of the malls as a "phenomenon beloved of right-wing bloggers and the hasbara machine". "According to this trope," Peled noted in *Haaretz*, "Gaza is more akin to a seaside holiday camp than a vast open-air prison." The reality was that, "In any impoverished country around the world, any war zone, amid any humanitarian crisis, these pockets of luxury can and will be found. Western journalists like to sleep at night between crisp sheets, especially if they're on expense (I certainly do); there are always powerbrokers with the money to buy fancy cars for themselves and plush toys for their children, regardless of the situation outside their privileged orbit. But the only constituencies these fancy hotels and lavishly-stocked supermarkets serve are the tiny elite minority who can afford them". Life was "utterly different" for most of Gaza's 1.7 million inhabitants, 70 percent of whom relied on humanitarian aid and at least a third of whom remained unemployed.[204]

Unconvinced that no humanitarian crisis existed in Gaza, in June 2011, a coalition of activist groups planned another flotilla, dubbed Freedom Flotilla II, to break the siege, including an American vessel dubbed *The Audacity of Hope* after the title of President Obama's second book. Alice Walker, the Pulitzer Prize-winning author of *The Color Purple*, was to be among the boat's thirty-four passengers. "We're sending a message to our own government", said Leslie Cagan, one of the organizers for the American boat, "that we think it could play a much more positive role in not only ending the siege of Gaza, but also ending the whole occupation".

The Israeli minister for public diplomacy, Noam Katz, lost no time in denouncing the activists' mission as "a political statement in order to support Hamas".[205]

Instead of warning Israel not to use violence against the boats and passengers, including American citizens, the US State Department warned the participants, "We have made clear through the past year that groups and individuals who seek to break Israel's maritime blockade of Gaza are taking irresponsible and provocative actions that entail a risk to their safety."[206] The US government also appealed to Turkey to stop IHH activists from joining the flotilla with an "offer" to host an Israeli-Palestinian "peace summit" in return.[207] The *Mavi Marmara* ultimately did not participate, having "been pressed by the Turkish government to shelve plans for the flotilla", by one account. According to Bulent Yildirim, the head of the IHH, the decision was rather made due to unrepaired damage to the ship from Israel's attack the previous year.[208]

Having been given the clear green light from the US State Department, Israel announced that it would intercept and hijack the boats and that force would be used if met with any resistance. An Israeli naval official warned that, if met with the same kind of welcome they'd received on the *Mavi Marmara*, there was "a pretty good chance" that passengers would get injured.[209] The Israeli Government Press Office warned journalists that if they joined the flotilla, they could be "liable" for punishment by "being denied entry into the State of Israel for ten years", as well as having their equipment impounded and being subjected to "additional sanctions." Israel's Foreign Press Association called on the government to reverse the decision, saying that journalists "covering a legitimate news event should be allowed to do their jobs without threat and intimidation."[210] Under public pressure, the government rescinded its warning to journalists, exempting them from the "regular policy against infiltrators and those who enter Israel illegally."[211]

Ethan Bronner reported the developing story in the usual manner. While informing about the warnings to passengers from the US and Israeli governments, Bronner relayed the Turkel Commission's conclusion that the blockade and attack on the *Mavi Marmara* were legal. He declined to inform readers of the international consensus to the contrary, as reflected in UN Security Council meeting records, the UN fact-finding mission on the attack, the ICRC's statements, reports from numerous international human rights organizations, etc. To Bronner and his editors at the *New York Times*, only the fact that Israel had declared itself innocent was important enough for readers to know.[212]

On June 22, the State Department issued a travel advisory warning US citizens against "traveling to Gaza by any means, including via sea. Previous attempts to enter Gaza by sea have been stopped by Israeli naval vessels and resulted in the injury, death, arrest, and deportation of US citizens."[213] The following day, Secretary Clinton, knowing full well that the flotilla planned to sail only through international and Gazan waters, condemned it with the duplicitous remark, "[I]t's not helpful for there to be flotillas that try to provoke actions *by entering into Israeli waters* and creating a situation in which the Israelis have the right to defend themselves" (emphasis added).[214] (Had they actually intended to enter Israeli waters, it is also difficult to see how this would have required Israelis to "defend themselves" from the unarmed peace activists.) Again the next day, the State Department warned: "Groups that seek to break Israel's maritime blockade of Gaza are taking irresponsible and provocative actions that risk the safety of their passengers." It further threatened that passengers could be criminally charged with providing support for "a designated terrorist organization" if their participation in the mission was interpreted by government prosecutors as "delivering or attempting or conspiring to deliver material support or other resources to or for the benefit of a designated foreign terrorist organization, such as Hamas".[215]

While the State Department repeatedly warned Americans not to participate in this effort to focus the world's attention on the plight of Gazans, it had yet to issue any warnings to Israel not to attack US citizens legally traveling in international waters on a peaceful humanitarian mission. An uncommon voice of reason in government, Representative Dennis Kucinich initiated a letter to Secretary Clinton urging her to do everything possible "to ensure the safety of the US citizens on board". Robert Naiman, the policy director of the organization Just Foreign Policy, who planned to travel aboard *The Audacity of Hope*, commented that Kucinich's letter "runs in stark contrast to the Secretary of State

Clinton's false accusation that we are trying to 'provoke action by entering into Israeli waters,' when in fact we have every intention of sailing to Gaza peacefully and avoiding Israeli waters entirely. We hope Secretary Clinton heeds this request from Congress and speaks out against threats from the Israeli authorities to attack us in our effort to break the illegal blockade on the Gaza Strip."

Kucinich was joined in signing the letter by only five other members of Congress. Needless to say, their request that the State Department act to protect Americans from threatened Israeli violence was ignored.[216]

The same day that the State Department threatened American participants with prosecution for assisting the people of Gaza, the World Food Program issued a report assessing the impact of Israel's "easing" of the siege the previous June, following its deadly attack on the *Mavi Marmara*. The slight change in policy had "only marginal positive impact in Gaza." The number of truckloads of goods into Gaza remained at 41 percent of what it was before the siege was implemented following Hamas's election victory in 2006. The continued blockade of construction materials and heavy restrictions on exports prevented jobs from being created and exacerbated poverty. Construction materials were permitted through the crossings "only if destined for projects under the supervision of the UN or international organizations". The number of construction jobs remained 42 percent below where it was before the siege. There was an estimated 15 percent "economic growth", but this was mainly driven by external aid. "With the private sector still moribund," this growth was "unsustainable" and had "not translated into poverty reduction". Sixty-six percent of households remained either "food insecure" or "vulnerable to food insecurity". Sixty-two percent of the income of those in the former category was devoted to food. Seventy-five percent of households continued to rely on humanitarian aid. Thirty-eight percent of the population remained "below the poverty line", and the unemployment rate remained "one of the highest in the world." Households were coping by deferring utility bill payments, buying food on credit, buying lower quality food, and eating less. The additional goods Israel decided to permit through the crossings remained "inaccessible" to the poorest families, who couldn't afford them and depended rather on poorer quality, lower priced goods brought in through the tunnels. Some households survived by selling their assets or using up their life savings, leaving only 7 percent of Gazans with any remaining assets and only 11 percent with any remaining savings. Consequently, the WFP called on the international community to act to bring about "a full lifting of the blockade".[217]

The health care situation was "nothing short of catastrophic", noted Richard Falk the following day. Ninety-five percent of Gaza's drinking water was "unsafe for human consumption." Falk again decried Israel's "deliberate policy of collective punishment" as "legally indefensible and morally reprehensible".[218]

Gisha reported that while there was "no shortage of food in Gaza," economic recovery was being "blocked by sweeping restrictions on the movement of goods and people", including a complete ban on goods destined for Israel or West Bank, which represented 85 percent of exports from Gaza before the siege.[219]

The situation could be aptly summed up by the words of Dov Weissglass on the purpose of Israel's blockade: "The Palestinians will get a lot thinner, but won't die."

Ethan Bronner, meanwhile, took his cue from Israel's hasbara campaign and chose to focus his reporting on how well Gaza was doing, thanks to Israel's easing of the blockade. "As pro-Palestinian activists prepare to set sail aboard a flotilla aimed at maintaining an international spotlight on Gaza and pressure on Israel," Gaza was "experiencing its first real period of economic growth since the siege they are protesting began in 2007." Gaza "has never been among the world's poorest places" and was enjoying "near universal literacy and relatively low infant mortality", with "health conditions" remaining "better than across much of the developing world." Israel had "allowed most everything into Gaza but cement, steel and other construction material—other than for internationally supervised projects—because they are worried that such supplies can be used by Hamas for bunkers and bombs."[220]

On the strength of Bronner's contribution to the hasbara effort, Ehud Rosen at the JCPA crowed that the "vast economic improvements" in Gaza showed that the activists' "claim" that their purpose was "to relieve the siege" rang "completely hollow". It was obvious, rather, that their sole motive was "to delegitimize Israel".[221]

In the ongoing hasbara campaign to delegitimize the flotilla, the IDF next declared that they had obtained "intelligence" that participants were planning to "murder Israeli soldiers" by pouring sacks of sulfur on them as they attempted to board the ships. This use of "a chemical weapon" could "paralyze" a soldier, an anonymous IDF source told the *Jerusalem Post*. "If the sulfur is then lit on fire, the soldier will light up like a torch."[222] "This is a dramatic development," another anonymous IDF source told *Haaretz*. "The picture emerging here is that some of the flotilla participants clearly intend a violent clash."[223] Netanyahu called it the "provocation flotilla" and declared Israel's "full right to operate against efforts to smuggle missiles, rockets and other weapons to Hamas's terror enclave."[224] The Ministry of Defense proposed establishing a military court to confiscate any boats that attempted to defy the naval blockade, as though this would legalize such piracy (not unlike how Israel's settlements in the West Bank are declared to be "legal" if "authorized" by the Israeli government). Defense Minister Barak said, "There's no doubt that impounding vessels is a deterrent measure that could prevent the need to use force against future violations." He decried the flotilla as an "unnecessary provocation" and once more reminded, "There is no humanitarian crisis in Gaza".[225]

"I just love Israel's 'hasbara' campaign against Freedom Flotilla 2", rejoined Larry Derfner in the *Jerusalem Post*. "If it were up to the government, Gazans would still be unable to receive terrorist infrastructure equipment such as toys, musical instruments, heaters, newspapers, fishing rods, tractor parts, irrigation pipes and, of course, coriander, on relief trucks coming across the border." It was only after killing nine civilian activists aboard the *Mavi Marmara* that "Israel was compelled by international outrage to begin allowing all those previously banned weapons of mass destruction—cumin, ginger, dried fruit, industrial margarine, clothing fabric, sewing machines and more—into the Strip."[226]

Security cabinet ministers meanwhile told the Israeli newspaper *Maariv* that they were not given any information about the supposed threat of flotilla activists planning to harm Israeli soldiers. "Netanyahu decided to change the version about the nature of the flotilla for two reasons that are connected to the international community," one of the ministers said. "The first is for reasons of covering himself—if, suddenly, in the course of the military operation something goes awry and there are casualties, Israel will be able to say that it warned of that in advance. The second reason is to apply pressure on the international community so that governments will prevent the ships from leaving for the flotilla from the outset." One minister said that it was "inconceivable" that the IDF "would produce for the media information that is the complete opposite of what we were told." Another observed, "There is increasing reason to fear that this is spin. Nothing of the information that was disseminated to the media was presented to us".[227] Alex Fishman, a military correspondent for Israel's *Yedioth Ahronoth* newspaper, noted,

> There isn't a shred of substance to the report that extremist elements will put up violent resistance to IDF soldiers aboard the flotilla. Neither is there any clear information regarding deadly weapons on any of the ships. It can be assumed that this is considered a possibility—along with many other scenarios and possibilities that come up in brainstorming sessions among military and intelligence officials preparing for the flotilla. But when a possibility such as this gets turned into a fact within the context of the Israeli hasbara campaign—this can boomerang and show Israel to be lacking in credibility.[228]

An Israeli participant in the flotilla, Dror Feiler, told the *Jerusalem Post* that such claims were "an attempt to justify in advance IDF violence". All passengers had "signed a pledge of non-violence", he informed, and had "no intention of confronting anyone. We just want to arrive in Gaza in peace."[229] In an interview with Amy Goodman on *Democracy Now!*, another Israeli participant, former air force pilot Yonatan Shapira, explained,

> We are committed to nonviolence, and these are just more and more lies of the Israeli propaganda machine. And people in 2011 that are still buying into this propaganda are not connected to reality. And mostly, these things, in my opinion, are directed in order to brainwash the Israeli public in order to justify any kind of harm that they are going to do to us. If someone is preparing a chemical and different other kind of weapons against someone, it's the Israeli army against us, it's not us against them.
>
> Our power, our advantage is our nonviolent message, our international message of peace, justice and equality. Their weapon is the chemical and the tear gas, the water cannon, the bullets, rubber-coated or not rubber-coated. We are with the message of peace and justice and nonviolence, and they are coming with violence. And the way they try to turn it upside down is just making them look even more ridiculous.
>
> . . . I see it as an obligation of me as an Israeli and as a Jew to help steer the wheel of this boat into Gaza in order to challenge these war criminals and send this message to the Palestinian people, to the Palestinian children in Gaza and the rest of the world, that they are not alone and we support them, and one day, one day, they will be free.
>
> And I do it also as an ex-military person, that finally, after too many years, but finally, I did it in 2003, eight years ago. I refused. And that's what I expect my former fellows in the squadron where I used to serve . . . that participated in the massacre on the *Mavi Marmara* a year ago. And my message to these pilots in this specific squadron is, if you want to be honest with yourself, if you want to be able to look into the eyes of your children in 10 and 20 years from now, refuse to be part of this illegal blockade. Refuse to obey these illegal orders to arrest us, to board our boats, to shoot us. It's up to them if this illegal operation is going to happen. And this is a direct call to these pilots to refuse their orders.[230]

As the flotilla participants were clearly undeterred by the threats from both the US and Israeli governments, Israel evidently turned to other means to stop them. The propeller shaft of the *Juliano* was sabotaged while docked in port in Piraeus, Greece. (The ship was named after Juliano Mer-Khamis, an Arab Israeli actor, director, and activist who had been shot dead in the West Bank that April.)[231] Shortly thereafter, the propeller shaft of the Irish ship *Saoirse* was sabotaged in the Turkish port of Göcek.[232]

In the *New York Times*, Ethan Bronner contributed once more with an "analysis" piece titled "Setting Sail on Gaza's Sea of Spin". The "Spin" he was referring to, naturally, was not the hasbara campaign he was participating in; rather, by his account, it was the flotilla organizers and other pro-Palestinian activists who were engaged in anti-Israel propaganda. Bronner brazenly lied that since the "easing of the siege" the previous year, "basic aid" like "food and cement" were "no longer needed" in Gaza. Hence, Bronner assessed, the flotilla couldn't be about helping the people of Gaza. "Almost everything about the flotilla" seemed rather to be "part of an unstated effort to recast the Israeli-Palestinian narrative in extreme terms." Bronner unquestioningly relayed the Israeli claims that "the flotilla is aimed at delegitimizing Israel and killing its soldiers", "flotilla participants plan to pour sacks of sulfur on Israeli commandos and set them afire", and "terror groups" were "on their way to join the flotilla"—all as though to be taken seriously. To further bolster his characterization of the situation, Bronner quoted an excerpt from the statement Gisha had recently released, as follows: "The focus on humanitarian aid by flotilla organizers and the Israeli government is infuriating and misleading. . . . There is no shortage of food in Gaza, but economic recovery is blocked by sweeping restrictions."

However, Bronner was misquoting by adding a full stop after "restrictions" where in his source there was none. What Gisha had said was that "economic recovery is blocked by sweeping restrictions *on the movement of goods and people*" (emphasis added). The very next sentence in the Gisha statement noted that Israel's "continued ban on export, *construction materials*, and travel" was contrary to its announcements that it would ease the siege (emphasis added). So while Bronner was claiming that basic goods, including cement, were "no longer needed", his own source, cited to support his claim, actually expressed the need to end the restrictions on such goods, including cement, precisely because they were very much needed. Of course, Bronner didn't need Gisha to inform him of this. He had reported just the week before how Israel continued to restrict importation of cement. Bronner's colleague David D. Kirkpatrick had recently reported how Egypt's regime "left in place a blockade on the shipment into Gaza of goods, *including concrete that is badly needed to repair buildings* damaged in clashes with Israel" (emphasis added).

Having so outdone himself, Bronner closed by characterizing "the Israeli-Palestinian dispute" as a battle between those who dismiss any criticism of Israel's blockade policy as an attempt to "delegitimize" Israel and "those claiming that Israel is a genocidal machine"—thus pitting an *accurate* characterization of Israel's apologists against a strawman *mis*-characterization of its critics.[233]

Robert Naiman responded to Bronner's disgraceful reporting by pointing out that Gisha's criticism was not a response to the actual goals of the flotilla organizers, "but to the flotilla organizers as portrayed by others, including Bronner." Contrary to Gisha's criticism, the focus of the flotilla was not on delivering humanitarian aid. The *Audacity of Hope*, in fact, was not even carrying any aid, only "letters of solidarity from Americans to the people of Gaza". Their purpose, rather, was to focus the world's attention on the need to end Israel's illegal siege. "I saw people wearing t-shirts that said, 'We sail until Palestine is free'", wrote Naiman. "I didn't see anyone wearing a t-shirt that said, 'We sail until Israel allows more humanitarian aid into Gaza.'" He also remarked on the fact that "Bronner managed to write a 'news analysis' that slammed the 'focus' of 'flotilla organizers' *without naming or quoting a single one of them.*"[234]

The same day the *New York Times* published Bronner's hasbara piece declaring that cement was "no longer needed" in Gaza, the US and its Quartet partners issued a statement allowing that "considerably more needs to be done to increase the flow of people and goods to and from Gaza, including a liberalization of the market in aggregate, steel bar and cement."

The purpose of the Quartet statement, however, was not to demand that Israel end its siege, but to warn the flotilla participants against sailing to Gaza and to demand that they deliver any goods "through established channels"—meaning to *cooperate* with and *legitimize* Israel's siege by delivering humanitarian aid to Israel for *it* to deliver (or not). The Quartet blamed the killing of civilians aboard the *Mavi Marmara* the previous year not on Israel, but on the victims ("the injury and deaths", it said, were "caused by the 2010 flotilla"). Only within this context did the statement urge "restraint". Instead of warning Israel against again violating international law and assaulting civilians, Washington's Quartet partners joined in calling on any concerned governments "to use their influence to discourage additional flotillas".[235]

The government of Greece promptly obeyed orders from Washington and refused to permit flotilla ships to leave port. The *Audacity of Hope* set sail anyways, but was chased down and prevented from leaving Greek waters by the coast guard. Forced back to port, the captain of the American vessel was arrested and held on charges of "trying to leave port without permission and of endangering the lives of the boat's passengers", the latter of which was a felony charge.[236] The Free Gaza Movement responded with a statement accusing Greece of being "now directly complicit in the immense suffering caused by the illegal blockade of Gaza. . . . Participating in Israel's naval blockade and illegal siege on the Gaza Strip is against international law and humanity."[237]

With eight boats blocked in Greek ports and the Irish ship undergoing repairs in Turkey, the only boat that was able to set sail to Gaza was the French vessel *Dignité-Al Karama*, which sailed from Corsica and was allowed to continue on its journey after refueling in Crete.[238] Passengers included Dror Feiler (musician and president of European Jews for a Just Peace), Jean Claude Lefort (former member of the European Parliament), and Amira Hass (the *Haaretz* reporter).[239] While the boat was at sea, the Knesset's Ethics Committee protested it by suspending Hanin Zoabi from parliamentary debates for having participated in the previous year's flotilla aboard the *Mavi Marmara*.[240] The French vessel was intercepted by Israel's Navy while in international waters, boarded, and forcefully redirected to Israel.[241]

After having prevented most of the flotilla vessels from sailing, the Greek government tried to save face by offering to deliver humanitarian aid to Gaza through "established channels". Numerous Palestinian civil society organizations sent a letter in reply to the Greek government:

> The people of Gaza are only in need of humanitarian aid because we are prevented from building our economy. . . .
>
> Your offer to deliver the cargo of the Freedom Flotilla entrenches the notion that humanitarian aid will solve our problems and is a weak attempt to disguise your complicity in Israel's blockade.
>
> We are so sorry not to accept your charity. The organizers and participants of the Freedom Flotilla recognize that our plight is not about humanitarian aid; it is about our human rights. They carry with them something more important than aid; they carry hope, love, solidarity and respect. Your offer to collude with our oppressors to deliver aid to us is strongly REJECTED.
>
> While it is clear that you have been under enormous political pressure to comply with the will of the Israeli regime, to collaborate with Israel in violating international law and legitimizing the siege, we refuse to accept your breadcrumbs. We crave freedom, dignity and the ability to make choices in our daily lives. We urge you to immediately reconsider and to let the Freedom Flotilla sail.[242]

The government of Greece, needless to say, declined the Palestinians' appeal to defy its marching orders from Washington, DC.

CHAPTER 9

THE STATEHOOD 'PLOY'

THE *WALL STREET JOURNAL* on June 3, 2011, ran an op-ed by former US ambassador to the UN John Bolton titled "How to Block the Palestine Statehood Ploy". The Palestinians' dastardly plan was to seek "to legitimize" Palestine's "claim to international status as a 'state'". It was "obvious" that their sinister objective was to make statehood a "fait accompli" by removing the issue from the existing framework, in which the US and Israel claimed veto power over the exercise of Palestinian self-determination. For the Palestinians to exercise this right was "[r]idiculous in the real word but not in the UN", where the PLO had "gained overwhelming support" from member nations for the 1988 Palestinian declaration of independence. The US, on the other hand, had objected that Palestine did not meet the definition of statehood because it did not have "a clearly defined territory" or exercise "a government's legitimate domestic and international responsibilities." The George H. W. Bush administration responded by threatening to cut off financing for international organizations that recognized Palestine.

"The lesson for today is plain," Bolton continued. President Obama should do what the Bush administration did in 1988 and announce that funding would be withdrawn from any UN body that recognized Palestine. But since Obama was unlikely to do the right thing, Americans "should turn to Congress, which has a rich history of dealing with UN actions it doesn't appreciate." In keeping with that legacy, the Congress "should legislate broadly that any UN action that purports to acknowledge or authorize Palestinian statehood will result in a cutoff of all US contributions to the offending agency."[1]

In fact, Congress had already passed legislation containing a clause clearly targeting Palestine: the Foreign Relations Authorization Act for Fiscal Years 1994 and 1995, signed by President Clinton into Public Law 103-326. The law "Prohibits US contributions to any affiliated organization of the United Nations or to the United Nations if they grant full membership as a state to a group that does not have internationally recognized attributes of statehood."[2]

Naturally, the US government does not apply this law to Israel, which by an equal measure lacks "clearly defined territory" and thus, according to the US's own argument, does not meet the definition of statehood.

Further illustrating the different standard applied to Israel, the following week, Senator Orrin Hatch with thirty-three cosponsors introduced a bill declaring that "it is the policy of the United States to support and facilitate Israel in creating and maintaining secure, recognized, and defensible borders; and . . . it is contrary to United States policy and our national security to have the borders of Israel return to the armistice lines that existed on June 4, 1967."

That is to say, the bill, if it were to become law, would make *official* the already *de facto* US policy of supporting the Israeli occupation and illegal colonization of Palestinian land with the rationale that Israel has a "sovereign right" to take whatever Palestinian land it deems necessary for its "security", without regard for the rights of the Palestinians, relegated under US policy to irrelevance.[3]

'Defensible Borders'

The argument that Israel's occupation and theft of Palestinian land is permissible because it has a "sovereign right" to "defensible borders" is standard Zionist propaganda. It is without basis in international law, prejudicial toward the equal rights of the Palestinians, and contrary to the international consensus that Israel must withdraw from the occupied territories in accordance with the principle that the acquisition of territory by war is inadmissible.

With June 5, 2011, marking the forty-fourth anniversary of the 1967 war, Israel's ambassador to the US and author of *Six Days of War*, Michael B. Oren, took the opportunity to promulgate this hasbara in the pages of *Foreign Policy*. The Arabs' plans at the time "called for obliterating Israel's army, conquering the country, and killing large numbers of civilians", Oren claimed. "The Arabs readied to strike—but Israel did not wait". In the face of this genocidal threat, the IDF "prepared to launch a pre-emptive strike to neutralize Egypt"; on the morning of June 5, "Israeli jets and tanks launched a surprise attack against Egypt". Oren boasted how, in "the most successful single operation in aerial military history", Israel obliterated the Egyptian air force. Then, "as feared, other Arab forces attacked"—obvious proof that Israel had indeed acted in "pre-emptive" self-defense.[4]

Oren knew perfectly well as he was writing this that the threat of an Egyptian attack on Israel in 1967 was virtually nonexistent. Rather, Egypt's forces in the Sinai had taken up defensive positions in preparation for anticipated Israeli aggression. Oren was well aware that the Egyptian government perceived the threat of an Israeli attack on Syria, with which Egypt had a defensive pact, to be very real. In *Six Days of War*, he explained that the Soviet Union had passed an intelligence assessment to Egypt about a planned Israeli attack. He attempted to downplay this assessment by attributing it to the tendency of Soviet leaders "to be influenced by their own propaganda" and "ideological myopia", which resulted in them "magnifying the threat Israel really posed to Syria."

But turning to Oren's footnote, one finds: "A similar interpretation of Soviet decision-making was posited by State Department Middle East expert Harold Saunders shortly after the war: 'The Soviet advice to the Syrians that the Israelis were planning an attack was not far off, although they seem to have exaggerated the magnitude. The Israelis probably were planning an attack—but not an invasion.'" One might be tempted to inquire why Oren would relegate to a footnote this seemingly important American assessment that the threat of an Israeli attack on Syria, despite being perhaps exaggerated by the Soviets, was nevertheless *real*.

Oren himself documented in his book that there was no imminent threat of an Egyptian first-strike on Israel, much less a genocidal threat to Israel's very existence. "Had Egypt intended to attack Israel immediately," he wrote a couple of pages later, "the army's advance into Sinai would have been conducted as quietly as possible, at night. Instead, by acting conspicuously, [Egyptian President Gamal Abdel] Nasser sent a double message to Israel: Egypt had no aggressive designs, but neither would it suffer any Israeli aggression against Syria." Oren admitted further that "By all reports Israel received from the Americans, and according to its own intelligence, Nasser had no interest in bloodshed". To launch an attack on Israel under present conditions, "Nasser would have to be deranged"; the conditions under which a sane Nasser might do so were "most unlikely" to occur.[5]

Indeed, on May 23, 1967, Director of Central Intelligence Richard Helms presented President Lyndon B. Johnson with the CIA's assessment that, in the event of war, Israel could "defend successfully against simultaneous Arab attacks on all fronts . . . or hold on any three fronts while mounting successfully a major offensive on the fourth." In a document titled "Military Capabilities of Israel and the Arab States", the CIA assessed that "Israel could almost certainly attain air supremacy over the Sinai Peninsula in less than 24 hours after taking the initiative or in two or three days if the UAR [the United Arab Republic, as Egypt was then known] struck first." The latter, however, was judged unlikely to occur. The CIA also assessed that the Egyptian military had taken up defensive positions in the Sinai Peninsula, which Israel's military would have little trouble breaching: "Armored striking forces could breach the UAR's double defense line in the Sinai in three to four days and drive the Egyptians west of the Suez Canal in seven to nine days. Israel could contain any attacks by Syria or Jordan during this period." Although the Arabs had numerical superiority in terms of military hardware, "Nonetheless, the IDF maintain qualitative superiority over the Arab armed forces in almost all aspects of combat operations."

The Mossad nevertheless relayed an intelligence estimate to Washington claiming that Israel would be outgunned. The CIA's response was to inform policymakers, "We do not believe that the Israeli appreciation . . . was a serious estimate of the sort they would submit to their own high officials"; rather, it was "probably a gambit intended to influence the US" to "provide military supplies", "make more public commitments to Israel", "approve Israeli military initiatives", and "put more pressure on Nasser." President Johnson wasn't buying it; he told Israeli Foreign Minister Abba Eban, "All of our intelligence people are unanimous that if the UAR attacks, you will whip hell out of them." But it was clear to the US intelligence community that it would be *Israel*, not Egypt, who would start the war. Helms sent a message to Johnson on June 2 correctly predicting that Israel would likely launch its planned attack within a matter of days.[6]

In a meeting with Nasser following the war, Johnson's special envoy to the UAR, Robert B. Anderson, expressed puzzlement over the decision to mass troops in the Sinai. "Whether you believe it or not," Nasser replied, "we were in fear of an attack from Israel. We had been informed that the Israelis were massing troops on the Syrian border with the idea of first attacking Syria, there [*sic*] they did not expect to meet great resistance, and then commence their attack on the UAR." Anderson then told Nasser "that it was unfortunate the UAR had believed such reports, which were simply not in accordance with the facts". Nasser retorted that his information had come from reliable sources. "[Y]our own State Department called in my Ambassador to the US in April or May", Nasser added, "and warned him that there were rumors that there might be a conflict between Israel and the UAR."[7]

That there was no real imminent threat of an Egyptian attack on Israel has been acknowledged by prominent Israelis, such as Prime Minister Menachem Begin, who was a member of the Israeli cabinet during that war. In 1982, he reminded an audience at Israel's National Defense College that Israel had attacked Egypt in 1956 and that, "In June 1967 we again had a choice. The Egyptian army concentrations in the Sinai approaches do not prove that Nasser was really about to attack us. We must be honest with ourselves. We decided to attack him."[8] According to Avraham Sela, a colleague of Oren's at the Shalem Center in Jerusalem (Oren wrote *Six Days of War* while a senior fellow there), "The Egyptian buildup in Sinai lacked a clear offensive plan, and Nasser's defensive instructions explicitly assumed an Israeli first strike."[9]

Well aware of the facts, Oren continued his fictional account in *Foreign Policy* by justifying Israel's occupation of the Palestinian territories with the ludicrous assertion that the 1949 armistice lines were "indefensible"—clearly not, given the fact of history (and Oren's own boasts about how the extraordinary might of the Israeli military crushed the combined Arab armies in less than a week). With logic plagiarized from George Orwell's *1984*, Oren reasoned that starting a war with its neighbors in 1967 "furnished Israel with the territory and permanence necessary for achieving peace with Egypt and Jordan".

Oren next offered the touching remark that this occupation "made us aware that another people—the Palestinians—inhabited that land and that we would have to share it."[10] Such a stunning reversal from the early days, as in May 1918, when Zionist leader Chaim Weizmann declared in a letter to Lord Arthur James Balfour that the "present state of affairs would necessarily tend towards the creation of an Arab Palestine, if there were an Arab people in Palestine"! Such enlightenment compared to the time when Israeli Prime Minister Golda Meir infamously remarked, "It was not as though there was a Palestinian people in Palestine considering itself as a Palestinian people and we came and threw them out and took their country away from them. They did not exist"![11] How exceptionally cognizant of Israelis to finally come to realize, following the June 1967 war, that the Palestinians did indeed exist and truly were a people! And how very generous of Israel to be willing "to share" land it occupied, during a war it started, with the land's native inhabitants and rightful owners!

Oren next lamented how ungrateful the Palestinians were to Israel, despite its wondrous munificence. He repeated the standard refrain about how they had rejected previous Israeli offers of statehood. Then he reiterated two of the demands Palestinians must gratefully accept from their benevolent Israeli masters: their state would have to be defenseless; and they could not exercise sovereignty over their own borders, but must consent to a continued long-term Israeli military presence along the Jordan River. The reason for these conditions, Oren explained, was that Israelis "need defensible borders to ensure that Israel will never again pose an attractive target for attack"—as in 1967, when Israel, after having assessed that Nasser would not attack, launched its own planned war on Egypt to "furnish" itself with more Palestinian land.

Oren expressed Israel's appreciation for "Obama's opposition to unilaterally declared Palestinian statehood", repeated the standard Zionist lie that UN Resolution 242 "indicated that Israel would not have to forfeit all of the captured territories", and concluded that "Israel's insistence on defensible borders is a prerequisite for peace and a safeguard against a return to the Arab illusions and Israeli fears of June 1967"—the word "peace" throughout his article being a euphemism for the submission of the Palestinians under force and violence to Israel's demands that they renounce their rights.

The obvious problem was that the unruly Palestinians, unlike the more civilized Israelis, had just never learned "to share".[12]

The Zionist hasbara about Resolution 242 was repeated by Dore Gold in *The Weekly Standard*, whose editors also had no problem printing the lie that "Resolution 242 made clear that Israel was not expected to withdraw from all the territories that came into its possession". Rejecting the idea of land swaps, Gold argued that the resolution did not require Israel "to pay for any West Bank land it would retain by handing over its own sovereign land in exchange"—which was certainly true enough, given that the resolution in fact required Israel to fully withdraw from all territory occupied during the war.

Gold claimed that the idea of land swaps originated in "the mid-1990s". In fact, Resolution 242 was passed with the explicit understanding among Security Council members that "mutual territorial adjustments" (to quote the Indian delegate just before the vote) could be expected in any final agreement on borders.

The pre-June 1967 line was "not a real international boundary", Gold continued, but "only an armistice line demarcating where Arab armies had been stopped when they invaded the nascent state of Israel in 1948."[13] This was the standard hasbara version, routinely propagated in Western media, of how the Zionist forces had been stopped after unilaterally declaring the existence of their "Jewish state" and carrying forward ethnic cleansing operations, with most of the combat occurring in areas that UN General Assembly Resolution 181 had recommended be apportioned to an Arab state. The Arab League Council didn't make a decision to send troops to Palestine until April 1948, by which time, as Israeli historian Ilan Pappé documented in his book *The Ethnic Cleansing of Palestine*, "a quarter of a million Palestinians had already been expelled, two hundred villages destroyed and scores of towns emptied." The strongest contingent sent by the Arab states was Jordan's Arab Legion, which only actively defended the territory today known as the West Bank. "When it was over, more than half of Palestine's native population, close to 800,000 people, had been uprooted, 531 villages had been destroyed, and eleven urban neighborhoods emptied of their inhabitants."[14]

As explained by Yigal Allon, then a commander of the Palmach, an elite force within the Zionist military organization the Haganah, "Thanks to the local offensive war, the continuity of the Jewish territories was accomplished and also the penetrating of our forces into Arab areas. . . . If it wasn't for the Arab invasion there would have been no stop to the expansion of the forces of Haganah who could have, with the same drive, reached the natural borders of western Israel, because in this stage most of the local enemy forces were paralyzed."[15]

Gold *did* mention ethnic cleansing in his article; he wrote that the Old City of Jerusalem "was ethnically cleansed of all its Jewish residents."[16] Indeed, some 2,000 Jews were expelled from the Jewish Quarter of the Old City—after Zionist forces had "cleansed" West Jerusalem of most of its Arab inhabitants, around 30,000 Palestinians.[17]

Gold, like Oren, characterized Israel's land-grabbing as necessary to reduce Israel's "vulnerability". Yes, Dore allowed, "Israel won the Six Day War from the 1967 lines"; but it "had to resort to a preemptive strike as four armies converged on its borders". From the false premise that the attack was "preemptive", he leaped to the conclusion that "defensible borders" for Israel were a necessary prerequisite for any "viable peace" to be achieved.[18] Palestine's borders, on the other hand, had to remain completely defenseless. In the *New York Times*, the same arguments were repeated by Ephraim Sneh. Israel must annex major portions of the West Bank, he wrote, because "the country's 1967 borders are not militarily defensible". Any Palestinian state must be "demilitarized" so as not to be able to "menace" Israel, as the Arab states had done in 1967, etc., ad nauseam.[19]

In his *Weekly Standard* piece, Dore Gold pointed out how Obama's AIPAC speech was accommodative of Israeli policy and its interpretation of Resolution 242. A perplexed Henry Siegman at *Foreign Policy* also took notice of this, asking, "Does Obama really prefer that Palestinians negotiate with Israel as a subject people rather than as a sovereign nation?" The "default settings" of UN Resolutions 242 and 338, he correctly reasoned, "could not conceivably be that the occupier may hold on permanently to the occupied territories or may determine unilaterally how much of those territories to annex."[20]

To answer Siegman's question: *Yes*, Obama *did* expect the Palestinians to negotiate as a subject people. This aspect of US policy is certainly hard to miss. It must take an extraordinary effort on the part of the American intelligentsia not to see it.

The Obama administration wasn't without its disagreements with the Netanyahu government, however. Israel was not being particularly cooperative in making it easier for the US to manage "perceptions" and maintain its "credibility". As *Haaretz* pointed out, "the Americans were very frustrated" with Netanyahu's refusal to resume talks on the basis of Obama's "1967 lines" speech because they felt "that he was impeding America's efforts to keep the Palestinians from unilaterally seeking UN recognition of a state in September".[21]

To that end, the Obama administration dispatched David Hale, who succeeded George Mitchell as special envoy after the latter's resignation the previous month, and Dennis Ross, who was head of the American team at the Camp David negotiations in 2000. They arrived in Israel in mid-June with the aim of "getting everyone back to the negotiating table". The US was also busy drumming up support for its position from its European partners. The main goal of pushing talks was summed up with the *Jerusalem Post* headline: "US, EU officials in Israel work to stop Palestinian UN move".[22]

As the US was busy condemning the Palestinians for the "unilateral" step of going to the UN, Israel was sharply increasing its demolitions of Palestinian homes in the West Bank. By mid-June 2011, Israel had already demolished more homes than in the entire previous year.[23] There were no headlines telling how the US was working to stop Israel's unilateral moves.

The 'Jewish' and 'Democratic' State of Israel

The Israeli government's discrimination against Palestinians was not limited to the occupied territories, but extended to its own Arab citizens. On March 23, 2011, the Knesset passed a law authorizing "admissions committees" to reject applicants for residency in Jewish-majority communities who did not meet "social suitability" criteria. Human Rights Watch pointed out that the measure codified into law the already existing practice of "unjustly rejecting applications by Palestinian Arab citizens of Israel", which was the declared intent of Knesset members who supported the law. David Rotem of the Yisrael Beiteinu party said the law would allow towns to be "established by people who want to live with other Jews." Yisrael Hasson of the Kadima party spoke of how it would "work to preserve the ability to realize the Zionist dream".

A second law was passed the same day banning any publicly-funded institution from commemorating the Nakba or any expression deemed by the government to "negate the existence of Israel as a Jewish and democratic state." Human Rights Watch pointed out that this included municipalities, theaters, and schools, and would make it illegal for such institutions to, for instance, put on plays or screen films about the Nakba. It was, in effect, another effort by the government to wipe the ethnic cleansing of Palestine from history and from memory. "Democracies shouldn't quash expression even if it's unpopular," said Sarah Leah Whitson, "and in this case, what's unpopular to some legislators is central to the historical narrative of a million and a half citizens."[24]

In response to the oppressive occupation and colonization of the West Bank, there was a growing global campaign calling for boycott, divestment, and sanctions against Israel (the BDS movement). The movement was reciprocated by some Israelis. Theater artists had protested their government's policy by refusing to perform in settlements. Israeli writers and academics had refused to conduct events such as lectures in the West Bank. So, on July 11, the Knesset passed a law making calls for a boycott against Israeli goods produced in West Bank settlements a punishable offense.[25] Under the law, any person or organization who called for a boycott of Israel or the settlements could be sued and ordered by a court to pay whatever compensation it determined, without the targets of the boycott even having to show that they had actually sustained any damages.

Protests broke out, and the peace organization Gush Shalom filed a petition with the Supreme Court to overturn the law for being unconstitutional. The law, the group said, was an attempt "to silence criticism against the government's policies in general and its policies in the occupied territories in particular, and prevent an open and productive political discourse, which is the backbone of a democratic regime." The Association of Civil Rights in Israel filed a petition similarly calling the law "unconstitutional and undemocratic". The legal rights group Adalah, Physicians for Human Rights, the Public Committee Against Torture, and the Coalition of Women for Peace all stated their intent to also challenge the law in court, saying it "gives protection to the illegal West Bank settlements in Israeli law by penalizing their opponents". Three dozen law professors sent a petition to Attorney General Yehuda Weinstein calling the ban unconstitutional, saying that it "conflicts directly with the principles established in Israel in the 1990s that entrench the right to freedom of speech in the legal system." The group Peace Now defied the law by creating a Facebook page calling for a boycott of products from the settlements that was joined by about 2,000 people within hours after the legislation was passed.[26]

Haaretz published an op-ed by Avirama Golan calling the law "unconstitutional and undemocratic". It had "one purpose only", which was "to completely eradicate open political debate".[27] A former Knesset member, veteran Israeli journalist, and founding member of Gush Shalom, Uri Avnery recalled how his peace group had declared a boycott of products made in the settlements back in 1997. At first, the boycott was ignored by the Israeli media, but it gained momentum. Hundreds of thousands of Israelis no longer bought settlement products. The EU began enforcing a clause under its trade agreement with Israel excluding settlement products from its privileges. But the Israeli government continued to favor the hundreds of factories in the settlements with generous subsidies and tax exemptions. The new boycott law meant that "each of the 300,000 settlers can claim millions from every single peace activist associated with the call for boycott, thus destroying the peace movement altogether."[28]

The *New York Times* was moved to denounce the law as a violation of free speech unbefitting a democracy; but the editors made sure to stress their own opposition to any "boycotts of Israel", by which they meant boycotts of products made in illegally-constructed settlements in the occupied West Bank.[29]

The Bias of the New York Times

The *New York Times'* coverage of Israel's Nakba law and the Palestinians' annual commemoration of their "Catastrophe" provides a useful case study. The newspaper reported on the Nakba law only once during March. Ethan Bronner explained that "Nakba" was a "reference to the Arabic word for 'catastrophe' commonly used by Arabs to describe the birth of Israel in 1948." Instead of celebrating Israeli independence, he wrote, Arab Israelis commemorate "the destruction of hundreds of villages and the exile of hundreds of thousands of Palestinians."[30] The word "Nakba" wasn't mentioned again until May, on the sixty-third anniversary of the declaration of the existence of the state of Israel. Bronner explained "Nakba" as an event "to mark the founding of Israel 63 years ago". He elaborated: "After Israel declared independence on May 14, 1948, armies from neighboring Arab states attacked the new nation; during the war that followed, hundreds of thousands of Palestinians fled or were driven from their homes by Israeli forces. Hundreds of Palestinian villages were also destroyed."[31] The following day, Bronner repeated that "Nakba" referred to "the anniversary of Israel's declaration of independence in 1948 and the war in which hundreds of thousands of Palestinians lost their homes through expulsion and flight."[32] Another *Times* article from May tossed in a passing reference to "the Nakba, or catastrophe, a day that marks for Palestinians the creation of Israel in 1948."[33] "Nakba" appeared again in a July article by Isabel Kershner, who similarly abridged the history down to a passing mention that May 15 is a day "which Palestinians have come to refer to as Nakba Day, marking the founding of Israel in 1948. Nakba means catastrophe."[34]

Thus, in two of the few instances where the word "Nakba" was mentioned at all, the *Times* withheld from readers the critical fact that the catastrophe was not "the founding of Israel" per se, but the ethnic cleansing of Palestine by which the "Jewish state" came into being. In the even fewer instances where the expulsion of Palestinians and destruction of their villages did receive a passing mention, it was only in the context of a war started by the Arab states when they sent armies to invade Israel. Thus relegated to irrelevancy by the *Times* was the fact that the Zionists' offensive military and ethnic cleansing operations had begun months before their May 14 declaration. By the time the neighboring Arab states managed to muster a military response, three-quarters of a million Arabs had already been made refugees. As David Ben-Gurion wrote in his book *Rebirth and Destiny of Israel*, already by the time the state of Israel was declared, "that part of Palestine where the Haganah could operate was almost clear of Arabs."[35]

It may be useful to recall Ethan Bronner's agreement with one critic that he "should not be a reporter" if he is "not telling the whole story". The explanations the *Times* provided to readers about the significance of the Nakba came quite far from telling the whole story.

It was not merely that Arab villages were destroyed, for instance. As Israeli Defense Minister Moshe Dayan commented in an interview with *Haaretz* in 1969,

> We came to this country which was already populated by Arabs, and we are establishing a Hebrew, that is a Jewish state here. In considerable areas of the country we bought the lands from the Arabs. Jewish villages were built in the place of Arab villages. You do not even know the names of these Arab villages, and I do not blame you, because these geography books no longer exist; not only do the books not exist, the Arab villages are not there either. Nahalal arose in the place of Mahalul, Gevat—in the place of Jibta, Sarid—in the place of Haneifs, and Kefar Yehoshua—in the place of Tell Shaman. There is

not one place built in this country that did not have a former
Arab population.[36]

The "considerable areas" where Jews legally purchased land amounted to less
than 7 percent of the territory of Palestine. The rest of the country was conquered through violence, with Arab villages cleansed of their inhabitants before
being wiped completely off the map. Yet, in the historical narrative of the *New
York Times* and the rest of the Western media, it was the *Arabs* who were the
invaders.

In January 2010, the online news publication *The Electronic Intifada* broke
the story that Bronner's son had joined the IDF. When Bronner was asked in
an email to confirm this, he declined to reply directly, but forwarded the query
to the foreign editor, Susan Chira. Her reply was that "Mr. Bronner's son is a
young adult who makes his own decisions." The editors considered his coverage to be "scrupulously fair", and they were "confident" that he would remain
unbiased. *The Electronic Intifada* pointed out, however, that the newspaper's
own ethics policy stated that the activities of the family member of a journalist
might constitute a conflict of interest. The example provided was that of the "a
business reporter or editor" having a brother or daughter with "a high-profile
job on Wall Street".[37]

The media watchdog group Fairness & Accuracy In Reporting (FAIR) then
picked up the story, noting that the *Times* was refusing to confirm or deny the
report and that Ms. Chira was treating the matter "as none of our business",
even though it "would pose a serious conflict of interest" if true. "When the
IDF goes into battle," FAIR asked, "might he be rooting for the side for which
his son is risking his life?" The conflict of interest was particularly troubling
in light of "what would appear to be a bias toward the Israeli government" in
Bronner's reporting for the *Times*.[38]

The *Times* then confirmed that Bronner's son had indeed joined the IDF.
Executive Editor Bill Keller defended Bronner by asserting that he would have
no conflict of interest even if his son was sent as a foot soldier into Gaza during
another Israeli military operation. His son would have to be a commanding
officer or his unit "accused of wrongdoing" before Keller would even begin to
consider the question of conflicting interests.

The public editor, Clark Hoyt, nevertheless recommended that Bronner be
reassigned for the duration of his son's service (which included a year of training and six months of active duty before he planned to return to the US for
college). This was not because Hoyt felt there was a conflict of interest, but on
the narrow grounds that asking whether a father might be affected by having a
son in the IDF, "especially if shooting broke out", could not be dismissed as an
entirely unreasonable question. Hoyt agreed with Keller that Bronner was "a su-
perb reporter" who was consistently "solid and fair". The only thing "relentlessly

unfair" was people's criticisms of his reporting. Anyone who dared to question his impartiality was simply "hostile to objective reporting."[39]

In the end, Bill Keller announced that Bronner would remain with the newspaper's Jerusalem bureau because his "expertise and integrity" was so greatly valued. He had "covered this most difficult of stories extraordinarily well", and his "fair-mindedness" was "precious and courageous". Bronner's critics were "savage partisans" and "zealots", hypocrites guilty of "blinding prejudice". Removing Bronner would mean "cheating readers who genuinely seek to be informed."[40]

In response to Bronner's reporting about the Nakba, one reader genuinely seeking to be informed wrote to the *Times* to express his view that Bronner was cheating his readers by failing to apprise them that the expulsions of Palestinians had begun before the May 14 declaration. The public editor, Arthur S. Brisbane, relayed Bonner's response that "space was limited in a short story and he wasn't trying to recite the full history." In other words, neither Mr. Bronner nor his editors considered this fact particularly relevant, and due to space limitations, nothing could be done but mislead readers into believing that the expulsions began only after the Arab states took up arms.[41]

Max Blumenthal subsequently revealed in the *Columbia Journalism Review* that Bronner had joined the Speakers Bureau of Lone Star Communications, a leading Israeli PR firm, in 2009. The firm arranged speaking dates for Bronner and pitched him stories. Bronner had also reported on some of the firm's other clients. The company's founder and director, Charley Levine, did PR work for top Israeli officials, including Shimon Peres and Ehud Olmert. Levine was also a reservist captain in the IDF's Spokesperson's Unit, which was "responsible for disseminating the military's point of view to the national press corps—and to international reporters like Bronner."

The *Times'* ethics guidelines stated that staff members "may not accept employment or compensation of any sort from individuals or organizations who figure in coverage they are likely to provide, prepare or supervise". Furthermore, they "may not collaborate in ventures with individuals or organizations that are likely to figure in their coverage." Yet Bronner insisted that he was "fully in keeping with *New York Times* ethical guidelines". Eileen Murphy, the *Times'* vice president of corporate communications, likewise maintained that his work conformed to the guidelines.[42] Arthur Brisbane defended Bronner by asserting that the case for a conflict of interest was "slender". There was only "the appearance of a conflict", not a real one. Nevertheless, Bronner had since severed his ties to the PR firm. Brisbane acknowledged that Bronner had not disclosed his business relationship and *had* violated the newspaper's ethics guidelines by failing to provide an accounting to his editors for having earned more than $5,000 in speaking fees from the firm. Bronner nevertheless had the audacity to accuse Blumenthal of trying to "discredit" him with an "attack" that was "ideologically motivated".[43]

Bronner was not the only *Times* journalist assigned to cover the Israeli-Pal-estinian conflict whose reporting was demonstrably biased and who had blatant conflicts of interest. An examination of Isabel Kershner's articles by FAIR re-vealed that she relied "overwhelmingly" on the Institute for National Security Studies (INSS) "for think tank analysis about events in the region." From 2009 to 2012, "there were 17 articles Kershner wrote or contributed to where officials from the INSS were quoted". One of the analysts for this Israeli think tank was Giora Eiland, a former head of the National Security Council and Army Reserve Major General who had supported the use of disproportionate force under the "Dahiya Doctrine".[44] (As an October 2008 *Haaretz* article noted, "Eiland recommends preemptive action: that Israel pass a clear message to the Lebanese government, as soon as possible, stating that in the next war, the Lebanese army will be destroyed, as will the civilian infrastructure."[45]) Eiland also headed a team tasked with presenting findings and conclusions to the IDF Chief of the General Staff, Lt. Gen. Gabi Ashkenazi, during Israel's self-investi-gation into the attack on the *Mavi Marmara*.[46]

Another person who worked for the INSS was Isabel Kershner's husband, Hirsh Goodman. FAIR noted that Goodman was "a senior research fellow and director of the Charles and Andrea Bronfman Program on Information Strat-egy, tasked with shaping a positive image of Israel in the media."[47] Goodman himself wrote about the purpose of this program: The media, he explained, was "of strategic importance in political and military conflict" because of its influ-ence on public perception. "The more convincing the 'story' that is portrayed in the international media regarding the justness of one side's struggle, the more legitimacy that side will gain in the eyes of the international community." The "military-media dynamic" was "especially complex" in the Israeli-Palestinian conflict because "much of the engagement takes place in densely populated urban environments". This created "the quintessential image" of "a state-of-the art army advancing on a beleaguered civilian population". The result was "fre-quently a public relations debacle for Israel." The goal of the INSS program he directed was to "propose and help implement a doctrine for managing media-military relations in Israel."[48]

At the end of Operation Cast Lead, Goodman blasted the Israeli govern-ment for failing in its hasbara campaign. Whereas it had kept the flow of infor-mation "tightly controlled" during the massacre, "on the morning after, when reporters from all over the world converged on the Gaza rubble, Israel had no convincing message that could explain the dimensions of the devastation, and no acceptable rationale for what the world perceived to be an excessive use of force and disregard for international convention."[49]

FAIR pointed out that according to the *Times*' code of ethics, "Staff members must be sensitive that direct political activity by their spouses . . . may well cre-ate conflicts of interest or the appearance of conflicts". Yet the *Times* had refused to disclose the fact that Kershner's husband was in the business of conducting hasbara for the IDF. Kershner, an immigrant to Israel, also had two sons who as Israeli citizens would be required to perform compulsory military service (in October 2014, she acknowledged that her oldest had joined the IDF).[50]

Ethan Bronner was married to an Israeli citizen, had a son in the IDF, had done business with an Israeli PR firm representing senior government officials, and had by the *Times'* own admission violated its ethical guidelines. Isabel Kershner was married to an Israeli whose job was to conduct PR to help manage the IDF's image in the media and had sons who would by law need to join the IDF. And yet, as far as the *Times* was concerned, the fact that two of its leading reporters on the Israeli-Palestinian conflict were so personally wedded—quite literally—to the Israeli side of the conflict did not constitute any conflict of interest. As far as the *Times* was concerned, none of this was relevant for their readers to know and could shed no illumination on why, for example, headlines appearing in the *Times* during Operation Cast Lead bore fawning titles like "Israel Reminds Foes That It Has Teeth" (Bronner) and "Despite Strikes, Israelis Vow to Soldier On" (Kershner)—headlines that might just as well have been written by the IDF itself.

Bronner gave an instructive talk about his reporting for the *Times* in October 2011 at the University of Maryland's School of Journalism. The title of his talk was "Can Anyone Get It Right? Reporting and Misreporting the Israeli-Arab Conflict". He discussed candidly how the *Times* deliberately manipulated perceptions through its choice of language. He explained, for example, how the illegal wall built by Israel inside of the West Bank "is to Palestinians a 'wall'". But the *Times* didn't call it that "because that sounds aggressive." It was a "fence" to the Israelis, which "sounds neighborly." The *Times* chose to call it "a 'barrier'" so that "it doesn't sound like anything."

This should raise an obvious question: Since it was a completely uncontroversial point of fact under international law that the wall was being built illegally on Palestinian territory, why would the *Times* wish to make it sound like *nothing*? Since the ICJ had affirmed that the wall was illegal, prejudiced Palestinians' rights, and caused them damages, how was it in any way *objective* for the *Times* to try to characterize it as non-aggressive?

Unwittingly offering another example of the patent lack of objectivity at the *Times*, Bronner pointed out that in European newspapers there was an "underlying question" in their coverage of the conflict about whether the founding of Israel was "really legitimate". In Europe, they asked whether what happened in 1948 was "okay", while American journalists "don't really have that question underlining their coverage." That is to say, in the American media, nobody questioned the legitimacy of establishing the "Jewish state" by cleansing Palestine of its Arab inhabitants.

Bronner made a number of insightful observations. He pointed out that the Netanyahu government and defense establishment were opposed to the US cutting off funding to the PA because it served as Israel's enforcer. Its security forces policed the Palestinians so that the Israelis "don't actually have to do the work themselves". What Israel wanted was "to continue the situation, the status quo, as long as possible." Following his talk, an audience member asked him, "What would have to happen domestically for there to be pressure put on Israel?" Bronner replied, "Thirty million evangelicals would have to, like, discover Buddhism, I think, right?" When the laughter subsided, he astutely added, "I mean, that's a strong, strong Christian—I mean, it's not the Jews, it's the Christian lobby in this country which deeply believes in this thing, and is not going to let the President do that thing." Perhaps someone should have asked him why such incisive and forthright analysis didn't seem to make its way into his *Times* articles.

When asked about being married to an Israeli and having a son in the IDF, Bronner insisted it didn't affect his view of the conflict. When asked what could be done to bring peace to the region, his reply was that this was "just not a major part of what I do". But when pressed further about his purpose in writing on the conflict, Bronner replied, "I feel like there is real value in truth telling. . . . I'm just trying to help you focus on—obviously, it's *my judgment* of what's going on. But my hope is that through that judgment, something real can emerge which will produce good. . . . I believe that sunshine and truth and frankness will produce good." One audience member challenged Bronner's penchant for "truth telling" by pointing out that there were already 300,000 Palestinian refugees *before* the declaration of Israel's existence in 1948. Bronner acknowledged the fact, but nevertheless defended his reporting by saying he was not persuaded that there had been a policy of ethnic cleansing.[51]

Perhaps to describe the destruction of Palestinian villages and expulsion of their inhabitants as "ethnic cleansing" would sound too aggressive for the *Times*? Was David Ben-Gurion's "compulsory transfer" also not neighborly-sounding enough? Whatever terminology the *Times* might choose, and regardless of whether it was a matter of policy, it remained willfully dishonest for Bronner to communicate to *Times* readers that this only occurred as a result of the war that followed the May 14 declaration.

But how plausible was Bronner's denial? Surely, he could not have convinced himself that the expulsion of more than half of the Arab population could occur without at least tacit approval from the leadership? Surely, he could not have been unaware that the desire to have Palestine free of Arabs was deeply embedded in Zionist thought? Surely, he could not have been unaware that the Zionists' desire to create a demographically "Jewish state" would *require* the removal of Palestine's majority Arab population?

Theodor Herzl infamously expressed the need to rid the land of its majority Arab inhabitants in his diary in 1895: "We shall have to spirit the penniless population across the border, by procuring employment for it in the transit countries, while denying it any employment in our own country. Both the process of expropriation and the removal of the poor must be carried out discreetly and circumspectly."[52]

When the British Peel Commission proposed in 1937 that Palestine be partitioned into separate Jewish and Arab states, David Ben-Gurion accepted the plan as a pragmatic first step toward establishing Eretz Yisrael in place of Palestine. On October 5, 1937, he wrote to his son (underlined emphasis in original):

> Of course the partition of the country gives me no pleasure. But the country that they are partitioning is not in our actual possession; it is in the possession of the Arabs and the English. What is in our actual possession is a small portion, less than what they are proposing for a Jewish state. If I were an Arab I would have been very indignant. But in this proposed partition we will get more than what we already have, though of course much less than we merit and desire. . . . What we really want is not that the land remain whole and unified. What we want is that the whole and unified land be Jewish. A unified Eretz Israeli [*sic*] would be no source of satisfaction for me—if it were Arab.

Acceptance of "a Jewish state on only part of the land", Ben-Gurion continued, was "not the end but the beginning." In time, the Jews would settle the rest of the land, "through agreement and understanding with our Arab neighbors, *or through some other means*" (emphasis added). If the Arabs did not acquiesce to the establishment of the Jewish state to rule over their land, then "we will have to talk to them in a different language"; the Jews might be "compelled to use force" to guarantee their "right" to settle the land if the Arabs didn't go along with the plan compliantly.[53]

As Israeli historian Benny Morris notes in his book *1948*, Zionist leaders first proposed "transfer" as the solution to the "Arab problem" only privately, but from August 1937, by "a virtual consensus", they "went on record in support of transfer".[54] Israeli journalist Ari Shavit likewise notes in his acclaimed book *My Promised Land* that from 1937, "the idea of 'transfer'—the removal of the Arab population—became part of mainstream Zionist thinking."[55]

In June 1938, Ben-Gurion said, "My approach to the solution of the question of the Arabs in the Jewish state is their transfer to Arab countries."[56] He told the Jewish Agency Executive, "I am for compulsory transfer. I do not see anything immoral in it."[57] In December 1940, the head of the forestry division of the Jewish National Fund wrote in his diary, "Just between us, it must be clear that there is no room in the land for the two people[s]. . . . There is no other way but to transfer the Arabs from here to the neighboring countries. To transfer all, except perhaps Bethlehem, Nazareth, Old Jerusalem. Not one village is to remain, not one tribe."[58] As Golda Myerson, the acting head of the Jewish Agency Political Department, diplomatically put it in 1947, "we are interested in less Arabs who will be citizens of the Jewish state." (She later changed her last name to Meir and in 1969 became Prime Minister.) Ben-Gurion argued that "it is better to expel them" than for Arabs to become citizens of the proposed Jewish state.[59]

On March 10, 1948, the Zionist leadership approved the codenamed "Plan D" (for *Dalet*, the fourth letter of the Hebrew alphabet), which formalized ethnic cleansing operations that had already been underway for several months. The plan detailed how Ben Gurion's "compulsory transfer" would be implemented. Brigade commanders were to use their own discretion in mounting operations against "enemy population centers" by choosing between the following options:

—Destruction of villages (setting fire to, blowing up, and planting mines in the debris), especially those population centers which are difficult to control continuously.

—Mounting combing and control operations according to the following guidelines: encirclement of the village and conducting a search inside it. In the event of resistance, the armed force must be wiped out and the population must be expelled outside the borders of the state.[60]

The operations were carried out by the Zionist paramilitary organization the Haganah, which became the Israel Defense Forces after the declaration of Israel's existence. Plan D was, as Israeli historian Benny Morris described it, a blueprint for the Zionists' "war of conquest".[61]

And, as Palestinian scholar Walid Khalidi has noted, "The ideological premises of Plan D are to be found in the very concept of Zionism."[62] In the words of Benny Morris, "It is impossible to evade it. Without uprooting of the Palestinians, a Jewish state would not have arisen here. . . . A Jewish state would not have come into being without the uprooting of 700,000 Palestinians. Therefore it was necessary to uproot them. There was no choice but to expel that population. . . ."[63]

While describing what occurred as "cleansing" may sound too "aggressive" for the *Times*, as Morris has also noted, "that's the term they used at the time".[64] Rehavam Zeevi, who served under Shimon Avidan, the commander of the Givati Brigade, did not shy away from using the word when he recalled in 1992 how Avidan had "cleansed his front from tens of villages and towns". Yitzhak Pundak, who commanded the Givati Brigade's 53rd Battalion, explained to *Haaretz* in 2004 that in the southern part of Palestine, "There were 200 villages . . . and these are gone. We had to destroy them, otherwise we would have had Arabs here . . . as we have in Galilee. We would have had another million Palestinians."[65]

Readers of the *New York Times*, though, cannot know that the destruction of Palestinian villages and expulsion of their inhabitants began months before the May 14 declaration. They cannot know that the expulsion of more than half of the Arab population was not somehow accidental, but an intended outcome. They cannot learn this because journalists like Ethan Bronner and Isabel Kershner and editorial boards like the one at the *Times* have decided that this information isn't particularly important for them to know. It isn't relevant enough to merit a mention because, after all, space is limited, and one cannot expect newspaper articles to recite the full history of what the Nakba means to Palestinians. And only "zealots" guilty of "blinding prejudice" would criticize the *Times* for not telling the whole story.

Israel Seeks a 'Moral Minority'

On July 7, 2011, the US House of Representatives passed a resolution introduced by Eric Cantor with 356 cosponsors reaffirming "its strong support for a negotiated solution" to the Israeli-Palestinian conflict. Accordingly, the Palestinians must recognize Israel as a "Jewish state" and "accept Israel's right to exist". There could be no "attempt to establish or seek recognition of a Palestinian state" without Israel's approval. The Obama administration should continue to exercise veto power in the Security Council to protect Israel from condemnation for its violations of international law and to oppose recognition of Palestine in the UN. The administration should also consider suspending financial assistance to the PA as punishment for defying orders from Washington.[66]

The resolution passed with 407 in favor and only 6 voting against, including Dennis Kucinich and Ron Paul. Rising in opposition to the resolution, Dr. Paul said that while he shared "the hope for peace in the Middle East and a solution to the ongoing conflict," peace would not result if the US continued "to do the same things while hoping for different results." Calling for a non-interventionist foreign policy, Dr. Paul remarked, "I must wonder how the US expects to be seen as an 'honest broker' when it dictates the terms of a solution in such a transparently one-sided manner? In the resolution before us, all demands are made of only one side in the conflict. Do supporters of this resolution really believe the actors in the Middle East and the rest of the world do not notice?"[67]

The leaders of the House Appropriations State and Foreign Operations subcommittee, Republican Kay Granger and Democrat Nita Lowey, also sent a letter to President Abbas to express their "serious concerns" about his "intentions to pursue recognition of a Palestinian state at the United Nations". They warned of "severe consequences" for abandoning talks; specifically, financial aid would "be jeopardized" if the PA disobeyed orders.[68]

Meanwhile, the US and Israel moved closer to signing a $2.7 billion contract for the twenty additional F-35s by agreeing to rewire the fighter jets so Israeli electronic warfare systems could be installed after delivery.[69]

A day before the Quartet was scheduled to meet, Saeb Erekat expressed his hope that the group would issue a statement calling for a solution "on the basis of the 1967 borders" and "an immediate cessation of settlement construction."[70] These were "harsh and stubborn conditions", replied Avigdor Lieberman, who accused the PA of being unwilling to compromise and "dictating the opening conditions of negotiations". He demanded that the Quartet refer to Israel as "the state of the Jewish people" in any statement produced from the meeting.[71]

The Quartet, however, failed to produce a statement since Russia refused to agree to this Israeli demand, which was apparently insisted upon by the US.[72] While the US and its Quartet partners remained silent on the matter, the EU denounced Israeli plans for additional illegal settlement construction in the West Bank.[73] The Quartet's failure to produce a statement confirmed the need to go to the UN, said the PLO's Executive Committee in a statement. "The only option facing the world today, especially the United States, is to use all tools to oblige the occupiers to halt their racist, expansionary policy. . . . The United States bears the prime responsibility for the continuation of this racist policy."[74]

If the UN bid was merely "symbolic", wondered Palestine's UN ambassador, Riyad Mansour, then why were the US and Israel fighting so hard to prevent it? Palestinian independence was "not a matter for negotiation", he said, pointing out that the Zionist leadership in 1948 "did not seek permission from anyone to declare their independence". Furthermore, the UN bid was "not a unilateral action" but a "multilateral" one since it would involve the engagement of many countries, 122 of which had already recognized the state of Palestine.[75] President Abbas encouraged Palestinians to participate in peaceful rallies in support of the UN bid.[76] The Arab League pledged to appeal to Security Council members to recognize Palestine and endorse its membership in the UN.[77]

The UN bid would put the US "in something of an awkward position", noted the *New York Times*, particularly since Obama had expressed his hope to the General Assembly the previous year that Palestine would be able to join the UN by September 2011.[78] Ron Prosor, the newly appointed Israeli ambassador to the UN, announced, "We are seeking a moral minority of countries who would oppose this move."[79]

Naturally, any countries that supported the aspirations and rights of the Palestinians were by definition wicked, having failed to gain enlightenment by following the shining example of that bastion of morality, the United States.

When Honduras joined the immoral majority in early August by announcing its intention to support Palestine's UN bid, its ambassador was summoned by the Israeli Foreign Ministry, which expressed its "surprise" and "disappointment" and demanded clarification.[80] Honduras went a step further later that month by recognizing Palestine as an independent state, prompting Israel's ambassador, Eliahu Lopez, to protest this deed as "a blow to the heart of Israel."[81] In August, Honduras was joined in its iniquity by El Salvador, whose president, Mauricio Funes, reminded the world of its sinfulness by pointing out that the majority of UN members had already recognized Palestine, including permanent Security Council member China.[82]

The morally superior state of Israel in the meantime continued to escalate its efforts to colonize Palestine. Demolitions of Palestinian homes in the West Bank had "escalated alarmingly" that year, UNRWA reported in early August. There had been 356 demolitions displacing 700 Palestinians in the first six months of 2011 compared to 431 demolitions with 594 displaced for the whole of 2010. "Most demolitions have targeted already vulnerable Bedouin and herding communities," said Christopher Gunness. "In many cases, demolition orders have been issued to virtually the whole community, leaving these communities facing a real danger of complete destruction."[83]

Israel proceeded to approve another 900 housing units in East Jerusalem. While the US remained silent, the EU condemned the move and reemphasized that all of Israel's settlement activities, "including in East Jerusalem", were "illegal under international law."[84]

The following week, Israel announced the approval of a 1,600 unit apartment complex and said it would approve 2,700 additional housing units in East Jerusalem in a matter of days.[85] The EU again condemned Israel's illegal actions.[86] Israel's announcement had come "a day after President Obama spoke with Prime Minister Benjamin Netanyahu of Israel by telephone", the *New York Times* perceived. The State Department's only comment was that Israel's settlement activities were counterproductive in terms of the goal of getting the Palestinians "back to the table". In another typical example of how the *Times* frames the discussion through deceptive language, it described East Jerusalem as "disputed" land solely on the grounds that "Israel's government has said it regards all of Jerusalem as its capital", thus lending equal weight to Israel's position as that of the rest of the planet that its annexation was illegal, null and void under international law.[87]

Three days later, Israel announced the approval of 277 new homes in Ariel, the settlement deepest inside the West Bank. Noting that "every single country in the world" recognized the settlements as "illegal and an obstacle to peace",

PA spokesman Ghassan Khatib called on the international community to hold Israel accountable for its actions.[88] The EU again issued a statement that "All settlement activities are illegal under international law and threaten the viability of an agreed two-state solution."[89] The Quartet, on the other hand, issued a statement expressing merely that it was "greatly concerned" by the latest announcement, without mentioning the settlements' illegality. The statement instead asserted that "unilateral action by either party cannot prejudge the outcome of negotiations and will not be recognized by the international community." To the US, of course, this applied exclusively to the Palestinians and their UN bid, with the Obama administration maintaining as a matter of policy that the outcome of negotiations must take Israel's settlements into account.[90]

The UN Bureau of the Committee on the Exercise of the Inalienable Rights of the Palestinian People issued a statement welcoming the Quartet's "expressions of concern" while emphasizing the need for more "credible and decisive action to compel Israel to abide by its legal obligations". Members of the Security Council bore "a special responsibility in this regard."[91] But the US was having none of that. Its plans to help Israel procure additional F-35s moved forward. Congressman Steny Hoyer assured that the dismal state of the US economy, including still rampant unemployment, would have no "adverse effect" on the government's "promise to Israel" to expropriate wealth from American taxpayers to help ensure its "qualitative (military) superiority" and "economic security".[92]

Stephen M. Walt, coauthor of the influential book *The Israel Lobby and US Foreign Policy*, translated: "we may be cutting Medicare and Social Security for US citizens, but Israelis—whose country has the 27th highest per capita income in the world—will continue to get generous subsidies from Uncle Sucker." Hoyer was one of eighty-one members of Congress who were enjoying a junket to Israel paid for by the American Israel Education Foundation (AIEF), an affiliate of AIPAC. Walt explained that "such junkets burnish a legislator's 'pro-Israel' credentials and facilitate campaign fundraising". They also exposed Congress members "to the policy preferences and basic worldview of Israel's leaders, which is of course why AIEF pays for them."[93]

Josh Ruebner at the think-tank Foreign Policy In Focus likewise commented that the US government treated "Israeli militarism as more sacrosanct than medical care for seniors", despite military aid being used "to commit human rights abuses against Palestinians" in violation of US law. It was also illegal for House members to accept a junket from a registered lobbyist or agent of a foreign country. AIPAC got around this by funding the trip through its AIEF spinoff, even though AIPAC directly contributed more than $3.2 million to cover AIEF's staff costs. "In other words," Ruebner elaborated, "a 501(c)(4) organization with registered lobbyists is paying for the staff of a 501(c)(3) organization to run congressional delegations that cannot be funded by an organization that employs registered lobbyists."[94]

"Looking for your member of Congress?" asked the *New York Times* in a story on the junket. Its advice was: "Try Jerusalem." The junket was all part of the "enduring efforts of Israel to court its most friendly ally, the United States Congress". A record-setting forty-seven members of "the freshman Congressional class" were participating. "It's my responsibility to be able to advocate on pro-Israel issues", declared New York Representative Michael Grimm, who was evidently quite confused about the location of his constituency.[95]

In late August, US Consul General and Chief of Mission in Jerusalem Daniel Rubinstein told Saeb Erekat that the Obama administration would veto any Security Council resolution on statehood or UN membership. He also relayed the explicit threat that if the PA sought "to upgrade its position at the UN through the General Assembly, the US Congress will take punitive measures against it, including a cut in US aid."[96]

Undaunted, the Fatah leadership worked on a draft General Assembly resolution containing the uncontroversial wording that the final borders of Palestine would need to be determined through negotiations with Israel on the basis of the pre-June 1967 lines. *Haaretz* observed that this wording would "make it difficult" for the US and Israel "to explain their votes against the proposal."[97]

Israel moved to punish the PA for its insubordination by withholding $106 million in Palestinian tax revenues. Instructively, Israeli Finance Minister Yuval Steinitz declared that the possibility of the Palestinians achieving recognition of statehood at the UN "represents a more serious threat than that posed by Hamas."[98]

The Palmer Report

In early September 2011, the office of the UN Secretary-General released the report of its Panel of Inquiry into the flotilla incident. The Panel was chaired by former Prime Minister of New Zealand Geoffrey Palmer and vice-chaired by former President of Colombia Alvaro Uribe. It also included Joseph Ciechanover from Israel and Özdem Sanberk from Turkey.[99] The "Palmer Report" constituted a shameful betrayal on the part of Secretary-General Ban Ki-moon, under whose auspices it was conducted. It was immediately hailed by apologists for Israel's collective punishment of the people of Gaza as vindication, for it erroneously concluded that "The naval blockade was imposed as a legitimate security measure in order to prevent weapons from entering Gaza by sea and its implementation complied with the requirements of international law." While thus vindicating Israel, the Panel accused the flotilla participants of having "acted recklessly in attempting to breach the naval blockade."

The Panel did not place the entirety of the blame on the victims. It also found that Israel's attack on the *Mavi Marmara* was "excessive and unreasonable" and that the loss of life was "unacceptable". Furthermore, the report stated, "No satisfactory explanation has been provided to the Panel by Israel for any of the nine deaths. Forensic evidence showing that most of the deceased were shot multiple times, including in the back, or at close range has not been adequately accounted for in the material presented by Israel." In addition, "There was significant mistreatment of passengers by Israeli authorities after the take-over of the vessels had been completed through until their deportation."[100]

The Panel explicitly emphasized that it "was not asked to make determinations of the legal issues" and "cannot make definitive findings either of fact or law." That is to say, the Panel's conclusion that Israel's naval blockade was lawful exceeded its mandate and was not an authoritative legal opinion. The Panel argued that it was nevertheless proper for it to "give its view", which it arrived at by examining the reports of Israel and Turkey, the former of which declared Israel's innocence and the latter that Israel's blockade and attack on the flotilla were illegal. Both reports' conclusions, the Panel noted, "are no more authoritative or definitive than our own". To put it another way, Turkey's conclusion that Israel's blockade was illegal was no *less* authoritative than the Panel's conclusion that it *wasn't*; the key difference was that Turkey's conclusion actually followed from the facts, while the Panel's emphatically did not.

The Panel revealed its political motive by stating that its purpose was to search for "solutions" that would "allow Israel, Turkey and the international community to put the incident behind them" and "move on." Its instructions from the Secretary-General were "to achieve a way forward." This was "the purpose of everything that follows."[101] To that end, the Panel went to great lengths to accommodate Israel's position on its naval blockade. The central means by which the Panel determined that the blockade was lawful was to treat it as completely separate from, and unrelated to, the "restrictions on the land crossings to Gaza". These were "two distinct concepts which require different treatment and analysis", the Panel asserted. Only by basing its argument on the *assumption* that the naval blockade was *not* part of a policy of collective punishment could it arrive at a conclusion that it was lawful. That is to say, the Panel employed the *petitio principii* fallacy, its desired conclusion being presupposed in the premise.

In its vain effort to support this premise, the Panel relied completely on Israel's own arguments. Citing the Turkel Commission Report as its only source, the Panel first asserted that "the land crossings policy has been in place since long before the naval blockade was instituted". The "border controls" were implemented in June 2007, the Panel stated, while "the naval blockade was imposed more than a year later, in January 2009".[102] But turning to the source, the Turkel Report made clear that the land-crossing restrictions imposed in

2007 were merely an *escalation* of an already existing policy. Israel had in fact imposed restrictions and implemented occasional total closures of the crossings since Hamas was elected in 2006. As the Turkel Report explicitly noted, what occurred in September 2007 were merely "*additional* restrictions" (emphasis added). It also admitted that these "restrictions" were "in the civilian sphere"— meaning that they targeted the *civilian* population, therefore by definition constituting collective punishment under international law.

Similarly, while the Turkel Report stated that the naval blockade "was imposed on January 3, 2009", it also made clear that this referred merely to the date that Israel formally announced it. The Panel chose to simply ignore the Turkel Report's acknowledgments that the blockade policy had been implemented well prior to that date. Indeed, the Turkel Report noted that the "military administration" of Gaza was established in 1967, from which time "the IDF operated with regard to the territorial waters off the Gaza Strip with all of the powers given to the party in control of a certain territory"—(that is, Israel operated as the Occupying Power under international law)—"with respect to the territorial waters adjoining that territory, including control of the passage of naval transportation for security reasons." The naval blockade of Gaza was established as a matter of policy in 1968, when the IDF "determined that the Gaza Strip was a closed area, and permission was required to enter it and depart from it in any way, including by sea." The Turkel Report cited examples of the Israeli navy enforcing this blockade and stopping ships it claimed were carrying weapons from 2001, 2002, and 2003. When Israel implemented its "disengagement plan" in 2005, it considered its occupation to be at an end, and with it, any powers pursuant to its role as Occupying Power. Israel nevertheless continued to enforce the naval blockade of Gaza, calling on flotilla organizers in 2008 to avoid Gaza's territorial waters, which it defined as an "exclusion zone". While a number of boats were "permitted" through, others were intercepted and prevented from reaching Gaza under this naval blockade policy.

We thus see how, to arrive at its desired conclusion, the Panel resorted to deliberate deception by presenting the formal declaration of the blockade as constituting the date it was initiated, even though it knew perfectly well from its own source that this was *false*.[103]

The Panel's second argument was no less willfully dishonest than its first. It declared that "Israel has always kept its policies on the land crossings separate from the naval blockade". How so? The restrictions on land "fluctuated", while at sea they were never "altered". This was merely a repetition of Israel's own argument, the only source cited once again being the Turkel Report.[104] But this distinction is absolutely irrelevant. The conclusion that the naval blockade could be considered "separate" from Israel's policy of collectively punishing the civilian population vis-à-vis the land crossings certainly does *not* follow from the observation that the naval blockade was even more consistent in preventing goods from entering Gaza! The Panel argued this non sequitur even while acknowledging that "there may be potential overlaps in the *effects* of the naval blockade and the land crossings policy" (their emphasis).

The Panel's third argument was no less illogical and equally disingenuous. Once again citing the Turkel Commission, it asserted that "the naval blockade as a distinct legal measure was imposed primarily to enable a legally sound basis for Israel to exert control over ships attempting to reach Gaza with weapons and related goods." So the Panel's circular reasoning was that the blockade was legal because it was separate from a policy of collective punishment, and it was not collective punishment because it was legally imposed. Never mind the "overlaps in the *effects*" of the blockade that admittedly included causing "food insecurity" among Gazans.[105]

The Panel relied entirely on Israel's own declarations of innocence to arrive at its conclusions elsewhere throughout the report, in a manner similarly dismissive of facts and reason. For instance, the Panel stated that the Turkel Commission report "makes it clear that the naval blockade as a measure of the use of force was adopted for the purpose of defending its territory and population, and the Panel accepts that was the case." The Panel accepted this, again, despite the admitted "overlaps in the *effects*", meaning that the naval blockade, like the land restrictions, caused harm to the civilian population.

The Panel allowed that "it would be illegal if its imposition was intended to starve or to collectively punish the civilian population". But it accepted Israel's denials that the purpose was to punish Gazans and stated further that there was "no material before the Panel that would permit a finding confirming the allegations that Israel had either of those intentions". No material, that is, other than the volumes concerning the admitted "overlap in the *effects*" between the naval blockade and the border control policy—designed to be "like an appointment" for Gazans "with a dietician", as Dov Weissglass had put it.

The Panel argued that, contrary to "allegations" that Israel's intent was to punish the Palestinians, "it is evident that Israel had a military objective. The stated primary objective of the naval blockade was for security." The Panel thus again unthinkingly took Israel's stated position at face value, as though it were not possible for a government to say one thing but intend another (certainly a curious oversight, given all of recorded history). They also overlooked the highly relevant fact that, even if Israel could be taken at its word about its *primary* objective, any *secondary* objective of collectively punishing civilians would, of course, still render the policy illegal under international law. Furthermore, the legality of Israel's policy was not a question of *intent* but of *fact*. Did the policy cause disproportionate harm to the civilian population that might be expected to be excessive in relation to any direct military advantage? The Panel seemed to answer that question in the affirmative by acknowledging the "overlap of effects", despite avoiding altogether the question of whether Israel's land blockade constituted collective punishment. But the question was deemed irrelevant by the Panel by virtue of its *petitio principii* fallacy. It was "wrong", the Panel circularly reasoned, "to impugn the blockade's legality based on another, separate policy." Having so begged the question, the Panel further asserted that it was "in the interests of the international community to actively discourage attempts to breach a lawfully imposed blockade."[106]

Notwithstanding how it was used by apologists for Israel's criminal policies, the fact of the matter is that the Panel *did not inquire* whether the naval blockade contributed to a policy of collective punishment. It rather went to great lengths indeed *to avoid doing so*. The Panel, in short, perpetrated a deliberate fraud.

It is telling that in all of the arguments the Panel used to arrive at its conclusion, the *only* source it cited to support either its opinions or its assertions of fact was Israel's Turkel Commission Report. At *no* point in the main body of its report did the Panel actually cite what international law had to say about the matter. The closest it came was to cite Turkey's report and relay its observation that the UNHCR and ICRC "have declared that the land restrictions constitute collective punishments"—authoritative judgments of the international community summarily dismissed by the Secretary-General's Panel in furtherance of the political goal of getting the world to "move on".[107]

The Panel relegated its discussion of applicable international law to an appendix, which warrants further examination. Citing Article 102 of the San Remo Manual, the Panel stated that "a blockade must have a lawful military objective" and that it would be "illegal to impose a blockade if the only purpose is to starve the civilian population or to deny the civilian population other objects for its survival." But this is *not* an accurate paraphrasing of Article 102, which emphatically does *not* say that denying goods to the civilian population must be the "only" purpose of a blockade for it to be illegal. On the contrary, it states:

> The declaration or establishment of a blockade is prohibited if:
>
> (a) it has the sole purpose of starving the civilian population or denying it other objects essential for its survival; *or*
>
> (b) the damage to the civilian population is, or may be expected to be, excessive in relation to the concrete and direct military advantage anticipated from the blockade.[108]

The Panel thus purposefully obfuscated the fact that merely having "a lawful military objective" did not make Israel's blockade legal. The obvious reason for this obfuscation, again, was to avoid inquiring whether the naval blockade could be expected to cause disproportionate harm to the civilian population.

This mischaracterization was no mere accidental oversight on the part of the Panel. Yet more proof of its deceptive intent was found in the very next paragraph, where the Panel adopted Israel's standard by asserting, "It is important to note that a 'blockade, in order to be of itself illegal, must have the *sole purpose* of starving the population.'" (The emphasis is theirs, as is, crucially, the full stop after "population".) To make it appear as though this standard of Israel's was in accordance with international law, the Panel was misquoting the San Remo Manual Explanation and its discussion of the meaning of Article 102.[109] Turning once again to the Panel's own source, one finds (emphasis added):

> The wording of subparagraph (a) as it stands reflects the view of the majority of the participants that the blockade, in order to be of itself illegal, must have the sole purpose of starving the population *or have a disproportionate effect as indicated in subparagraph (b)*. Whenever the blockade has starvation as one of its effects, the starvation effectively triggers the obligation, subject to certain limitations, to allow relief shipments to gain access to the coasts of the blockaded belligerent. This obligation is reflected in the next paragraph.[110]

On the following page, the Panel did acknowledge that "a blockade as a method of warfare is illegal if the damage to the civilian population is, or may be expected to be, excessive in relation to the concrete and direct military advantage obtained by the imposition of the blockade". But it mentioned this only in passing and, incredibly, offered no comment about its applicability to Israel's naval blockade of Gaza.[111]

The Panel's demonstrable lack of good faith did not end there. Citing Articles 67 and 98 of the San Remo Manual, it tried to further defend Israel's actions by stating, "If a vessel resists interception or capture, it may be attacked." Citing article 40, it continued, "At that moment, the vessel becomes a military object."[112]

Turning again to the Panel's own source, Article 67 in fact states that vessels "may not be attacked unless they . . . are believed on reasonable grounds to be carrying contraband or breaching a blockade" or "otherwise make an effective contribution to the enemy's military action". The context of the phrase "breaching a blockade" here can only refer to a case where there are "reasonable grounds" to believe that a vessel is making an effective military contribution, not merely that a vessel is entering a blockade zone. This is readily apparent because, logically, whether a vessel is entering a blockade zone or not is a question of fact, *not belief.* Either a ship is entering a blockade zone or it is not, and it makes no sense to say there must be "reasonable grounds" to *believe* that a ship is doing so. It does make sense, on the other hand, to say that there must be reasonable grounds to believe that a ship entering a blockade zone is making an effective military contribution. It can therefore be only in *this* sense that the phrase "breaching a blockade" was intended. Article 98 reiterates that only "vessels believed on reasonable grounds to be breaching a blockade may be captured". In other words, even assuming a lawful blockade to begin with, a vessel resisting capture may only be attacked "after prior warning" *if* there are reasonable grounds to believe it is making an effective military contribution. Further illustrating that the phrase "breaching a blockade" can only be intended to refer to ships reasonably suspected of making an effective military contribution, Article 40 states explicitly that, "In so far as objects are concerned, *military objectives are limited to those objects which by their nature, location, purpose or use make an effective contribution to military action* and whose total or partial destruction, capture or neutralization, in the circumstances ruling at the time, *offers a definite military advantage*" (emphasis added).[113] The Panel, however, simply interpreted the phrase "breaching a blockade" to mean attempting to reach Gaza by sea, notwithstanding the total absence of any reasonable grounds to believe that the flotilla was making an effective military contribution (or the fallacious reasoning by which they determined that the blockade was lawful in the first place).

The Panel pointed out that "the military advantage of the attack needs to be weighed against the collateral casualties" and that if the latter were "excessive", then "the attack would be illegal."[114] Yet, even though the Panel concluded that the loss of life on the *Mavi Marmara* was indeed "excessive and unreasonable", it nowhere in the report drew the unavoidable corollary that Israel's attack violated international law. Mr. Ciechanover, in a dissenting statement attached to the report, made sure to express that "Israel does not concur with the Panel's characterization of Israel's decision to board the vessels in the manner it did as 'excessive and unreasonable.'" In his own dissenting view, Mr. Sanberk correctly observed that the Panel's "Chairmanship and its report fully associated itself with Israel and categorically dismissed the views of the other, despite the fact that the legal arguments presented by Turkey have been supported by the vast majority of the international community."[115]

To encourage the resumption of diplomatic relations between Israel and Turkey, the Panel suggested that, "in light of its consequences", Israel should make an "appropriate statement of regret" about the "incident", as well as "offer payment for the benefit of the deceased and injured victims and their families".[116]

When Israel still refused to apologize following the release of the Palmer Report, Turkey, having already withdrawn its ambassador from Tel Aviv, took the additional step of expelling Israel's ambassador and cutting military ties. Foreign Minister Ahmet Davutoğlu pointed out that the Panel's judgment that Israel's blockade was legal had not been endorsed by the UN and was not authoritative. "What is binding is the International Court of Justice," he said.

"This is what we are saying: let the International Court of Justice decide. We are starting the necessary legal procedures this coming week." Turkey, however, never followed through with this pledge.

Davutoğlu's Israeli counterpart, Danny Ayalon, responded to Turkey's demand for an apology by saying that Israel had nothing to apologize for. Turkey, not Israel, was the problem, he insisted, for being unwilling to "compromise". As far as Israel was concerned, said Ayalon, "this saga is behind us."[117] "We need not apologize for the fact that naval commandos defended their lives against an assault by violent IHT activists," Netanyahu likewise declared. "We need not apologize for the fact that we acted to stop the smuggling of weapons to Hamas, a terrorist organization that has already fired over 10,000 missiles, rockets and mortar rounds at our civilians. We need not apologize for the fact that we acted to defend our people, our children and our communities."

All of which was to say that Israel need not apologize for attacking a humanitarian flotilla posing no threat to Israel in international waters and murdering nine civilian peace activists on board.[118]

The US mainstream media continued to play its usual role. The *New York Times* reported that "Turkey argued" that the Panel had no authority to issue a legal opinion—as though this was merely the opinion of Turkey's government and not a fact emphasized by the Panel itself.[119] A *Times* editorial used the occasion to blast the UN for having "long pummeled Israel" and applauded the Panel for being "even handed" by adopting Israel's position in defiance of what international law and the global consensus actually had to say about it. The *Times* further stated that Turkey "rejected the findings" of the report, while Israel "accepted" them. This served to obfuscate the relevance of the fact that the Panel *did* find Israel's attack to be "excessive and unreasonable"—a finding that Turkey certainly accepted. The editors agreed that "Israel should apologize for the deaths", but nevertheless criticized Turkey as the "irresponsible" party for "upping the ante" and "keeping this conflict going" simply "to burnish its standing in the Arab world". Thus summarily dismissed by the *Times* was any possibility that the government of Turkey had acted out of a principled stand against lawlessness and the murder of its citizens—something the US government refused to do despite Israel's murder of an American citizen.[120]

To his credit, *Times* columnist Roger Cohen actually read the report (which few others commenting about it seemed to have bothered to do) and pointed out that the Panel's findings with regard to the killing of civilian passengers "raise the possibility of an execution or something close". Informing readers that he had met the previous year with Furkan Doğan's father in Ankara, Cohen wrote,

> It's hard to imagine any other circumstances in which the slaying in international waters, at point-blank range, of a US citi-

zen by forces of a foreign power would prompt such a singular American silence. . . . But of course no US president, and certainly no first-term US president, would say what Prime Minister David Cameron of Britain said: "The Israeli attack on the Gaza flotilla was completely unacceptable." Even if there's an American citizen killed, raising such questions about Israel is a political no-no. So it goes in the taboo-littered cul-de-sac of US foreign policy toward Israel, a foreign policy that is in large measure a domestic policy.[121]

Turkey continued to escalate its woefully empty rhetoric by announcing that it would send naval forces to accompany and protect further flotillas to Gaza. "The eastern Mediterranean will no longer be a place where Israeli naval forces can freely exercise their bullying practices against civilian vessels," said one official. Prime Minister Erdoğan announced that it was the military's "duty" to protect Turkish ships and said, "This aid will no longer be subjected to any kind of attack as the Mavi Marmara was." This, too, was a pledge Turkey would not follow through on.[122]

"We'll exact a price from Erdoğan that will prove to him that messing with Israel doesn't pay off," threatened Israel's Foreign Minister Avigdor Lieberman in reply. He warned that "Turkey better treat us with respect and common decency." He apparently did not consider it respect and common decency to offer a simple apology for killing nine Turks.[123]

Amnesty International issued a statement in response to the Palmer Report reiterating that Israel must "end the collective punishment of Gaza's 1.5 million residents" and "completely lift its illegal siege of Gaza". This illegal blockade was a "comprehensive closure regime" that included the use of its navy to prevent Palestinian fishermen from accessing their own coastal waters. Amnesty also observed that the "question of the legality" of the siege "was not directly addressed by the Palmer report".[124]

Gisha likewise noted that the Panel did not actually consider the legality of the overall closure regime. It rejected Palmer and Uribe's view that the naval blockade must be considered a completely separate policy. On the contrary, Gisha argued, "the legality of the maritime closure must be considered in the context of the overall closure of the Gaza Strip, which is also enforced by air and land. In this context, Israel has failed to meet its legal obligations." Furthermore, Israel could lawfully prevent ships from reaching Gaza only if there was "a concrete reason for doing so". In this case, however, there was no military objective. Israel had rather acted to prevent "the passage of civilians and goods of a civilian nature", which "violated its obligations under international law, rendering its policy of closure—including the maritime closure—unlawful."[125] Gisha observed further that Israel's naval blockade of Gaza didn't begin in 2009, as the Panel had falsely claimed, but that "it has blocked sea access to Gaza since 1967" in its role as Occupying Power.[126]

A group of five UN independent experts under the auspices of the Office of the High Commissioner for Human Rights (OHCHR) likewise rejected the Panel's hollow opinion that Israel's naval blockade was legal. In a report to the Human Rights Council, the group criticized the Palmer Report for failing to recognize that the naval blockade was "an integral part of Israel's closure policy towards Gaza which has a disproportionate impact on the human rights of civilians". This closure policy constituted "collective punishment, in flagrant contravention of international human rights and humanitarian law." Richard Falk noted additionally that the Palmer Report "was aimed at political reconciliation between Israel and Turkey" rather than justice for the victims. "It is unfortunate", Falk commented, "that in the report politics should trump the law."[127]

Falk also criticized the Panel on his blog for having "failed to address the central international law issues in a credible and satisfactory manner." In a scathing indictment, Falk wrote,

> The Panel as appointed was woefully ill-equipped to render an authoritative result. Geoffrey Palmer, the Chair of the Panel, although a respected public figure, being the former Prime Minister of New Zealand and an environmental law professor, was not particularly knowledgeable about either the international law of the sea or the law of war. And incredibly, the only other independent member of the Panel was Alvaro Uribe, the former President of Colombia, with no professional credentials relevant to the issues under consideration, and notorious both for his horrible human rights record while holding office and forging intimate ties with Israel by way of arms purchases and diplomatic cooperation that was acknowledged by 'The Light Unto The Nations' award given by the American Jewish Committee that should have been sufficient by itself to cast doubt on his suitability for this appointment. His presence on the panel compromised the integrity of the process, and made one wonder how could such an appointment can be explained, let alone justified.

Furthermore, Palmer and Uribe's conclusion "contradicted the earlier finding of a more expert panel established by the Human Rights Council, as well as rejected the overwhelming consensus that had been expressed by qualified international law specialists on these core issues." The Panel's decision to separate its assessment of the naval blockade "as if exclusively concerned with Israeli security" while ignoring "its essential role in imposing an intolerable regime of collective punishment on the population of Gaza" was a "gross inadequacy". The Palmer Report was

> a step backward from the fundamental effort of international law to limit permissible uses of international force to situations of established *defensive necessity,* and even then, to ensure that the scale of force employed, was *proportional,* respectful of civilian innocence, and weighed security claims against harmful humanitarian effects. It is a further step back to the extent that it purports to allow a state to enforce on the high seas a blockade, condemned around the world for its cruelty and damaging impact on civilian mental and physical health. . . .[128]

Falk offered further criticisms of the Panel in an article co-authored with journalist Phyllis Bennis. The Palmer Report gave "considerable attention to the illegal rockets fired in Israel" while completely ignoring "the crucial fact that a unilateral ceasefire had been observed by Hamas" since the end of Operation Cast Lead in January 2009, as well as the fact that the ceasefire between Israel and Hamas "was broken by Israel in November of that year". The report "cannot be legally persuasive on the central issue of self-defense without addressing the relevance of these ceasefires that gave Israel a viable security alternative to blockade and force." It also lacked credibility due to its refusal to examine Israel's closure regime—a particularly woeful omission given the fact that the flotilla's purpose was to help bring about an end to this illegal policy of collective punishment. The report's acceptance of this policy as "legal" was "a sad day for both the global rule of law and the well-being of some of the most vulnerable and abused people on the planet."[129]

In a subsequent report to the UN Human Rights Council, Falk reminded that he was still unable to discharge his obligations under the mandate given to him due to Israel's refusal to permit him entry into Israel or the occupied territories. He noted that the recommendations of the report of the UN Fact-Finding Mission on the Gaza Conflict had not been implemented and that the Committee of Independent Experts had noted "the failure by Israel to conduct investigations of alleged war crimes in a manner that accords with international standards." The international community had similarly failed to take "appropriate action" in light of the findings and recommendations of the Fact-Finding Mission on the Flotilla Incident. Such "failure to follow through on initiatives recommended by competent international experts under the auspices of the United Nations contributes to a lack of accountability for serious allegations of war crimes and human rights violations." Falk recommended that the General Assembly call for the immediate lifting of "the unlawful blockade of Gaza" and "request that the International Court of Justice issue an advisory opinion on the legal status of prolonged occupation". But this remained yet another sensible recommendation that the world's governments failed to follow through on.[130]

Averting the 'Sideshow' at the UN

Although it was initially unclear what the PA actually intended to do at the UN in September, whether it would seek membership in the Security Council or seek an upgrade from observer status to non-member state in the General Assembly, by mid-August, the PA made clear it would go to the Security Council. The purpose, Abbas emphasized, was to "reinforce the two-state solution".[131]

One of Israel's stated objections to the UN bid, and the principle basis for characterizing it as a "unilateral" action, was a clause in the 1995 Interim Agreement (Oslo II) that stated, "Neither side shall initiate or take any step that will change the status of the West Bank and the Gaza Strip pending the outcome of the Permanent Status negotiations." Israel, of course, had perpetually violated this very same clause, which was, after all, what had compelled the Palestinians to go to the UN in the first place.[132]

Another objection was that a vote on Palestinian statehood at the UN would lead to a new wave of violence throughout the Middle East. In August, the US State Department delivered a diplomatic message to more than seventy countries instructing them to oppose the UN bid on the grounds that it would destabilize the region.[133] Former US ambassador to Israel Martin S. Indyk said that the "most powerful argument" against the UN bid is that it would "provoke a Palestinian awakening, that there will be a new violence and that we'll be blamed".[134] Jackson Diehl in the *Washington Post* parroted that a vote at the UN "may be the trigger for another violent upheaval in the Arab Middle East". "If the world is lucky," he opined, the UN bid "will turn out to be just another Palestinian dud", and the status quo would be happily preserved.[135]

While objections about "unilateral" Palestinian moves and the threat of violent upheaval in the region dominated the narrative, more credible explanations for the US-Israeli opposition to the UN bid were scarcely concealed in the Western media. One problem was the damage it would do to the US's "credibility" if it had to resort to using its veto power in the Security Council. This, the London *Telegraph* noted, "would only confirm in the eyes of many that the United States—just like Israel—is the enemy of the Arab people and their aspirations."[136] Given the "broad international support" for the UN bid, the *New York Times* observed, a US veto "would be an awkward setback for American diplomacy in the Arab world". The US's opposition to international recognition of Palestinian statehood "threatens to leave the United States increasingly isolated."[137]

Illustrating the point, the *Times* published an op-ed by Prince Turki al-Faisal, a former Saudi ambassador to the US and former director of Saudi Arabia's intelligence services, who argued that the US would "risk losing the little credibility it has in the Arab world" if it did not support the bid. This would have consequences for "the 'special relationship' between Saudi Arabia and the United States." He warned that "Saudi leaders would be forced by domestic and regional pressures to adopt a far more independent and assertive foreign policy."[138]

The "special relationship" he was referring to is the partnership in which Saudi Arabia agrees to sell oil in dollars, which creates demand for the US dollar, props up its value, and helps maintain its status as the world's reserve currency. This in turn also allows the US government to finance its operations by borrowing at low interest rates as countries use excess dollar reserves to purchase US Treasuries. If countries ceased trading in dollars and it lost its status as the world's reserve currency, the decreased demand for both dollars and US government debt would result in dollar devaluation (and hence price inflation), as well as rising interest rates, thus hampering the government's ability to finance its deficit spending. The world has witnessed what happens to countries that threaten dollar hegemony. One of Saddam Hussein's gravest sins was to start trading Iraq's oil for euros rather than dollars. Iran, too, has threatened the world order by ceasing to accept dollars in exchange for oil and proposing that the Organization of Petroleum Exporting Countries (OPEC) denominate oil sales in a basket of other currencies. This contrasts with the US-Saudi "special relationship", in which the OPEC giant supplies the US with oil and recycles petrodollars back into US Treasuries in exchange for US support for the oppressive Saud regime, including lucrative arms deals.[139]

In addition to the threat to US "credibility", the *Telegraph* explained that the UN bid would be "disastrous" for the Israelis "because it could pave the way for the Palestinians to pursue them in international courts."[140] The Associated Press pointed out that the Palestinians would gain access to the ICJ and the ICC to pursue legal claims against Israel. Although Israel was not a member of the ICC, 116 other countries were, and "Israeli soldiers or officials could face threat of arrest in any of them." This would make it "much more difficult to sustain" the status quo, in which Israel "bombards Gaza more or less at will, regularly killing militants but leaving considerable collateral destruction in its wake."[141] The *New York Times* likewise pointed out on numerous occasions that a successful UN bid would allow the Palestinians to pursue legal cases against Israel, "an outcome that Israel dreads".[142] David Makovsky noted in a WINEP report that, far from the bid being merely "symbolic", Israel feared that the Palestinians would gain the ability "to exploit the UN machinery to its fullest advantage at Israel's political expense. For example, this could mean seeking prosecution of Israeli officials by the International Criminal Court for alleged war crimes related to either the Palestinian intifada of 2000–2004 or the Gaza war of 2008–2009. Israel takes this scenario very seriously . . . ."[143]

The US was also taking that scenario very seriously. As John Bolton had observed, there were "important implications for America" because "to convoke the International Criminal Court is like putting a loaded pistol to Israel's head—or, in the future, to America's." The US, too, had a stake in making sure that the Palestinians could have no recourse to international legal mechanisms to seek remedy for violations of their rights by Israel and its chief benefactor.

The US government's rejection of Palestinian statehood was contrasted by public opinion not only in the Arab world, but around the globe. A poll showed that the majority of the population in Germany (71 percent), France (69 percent), and the UK (59 percent) wanted their government to vote in favor of recognizing a Palestinian state if a resolution was brought before the UN. Support for an independent Palestine was even higher without reference to a UN vote, with 86 percent in Germany, 82 percent in France, and 71 percent in the UK supporting the Palestinians' right to self-determination.[144] A Globescan poll conducted for the BBC found that in all of the nineteen countries it surveyed, "more citizens would prefer to see their government vote to support the resolution than vote against it". This was true even in the US.[145]

A poll by the Pew Research Center showed that a far greater number of Americans sympathized with Israel (40 percent) than with the Palestinians (21 percent). Far more believed that the Obama administration favored the Palestinians too much (20 percent) than thought he was biased in favor of Israel (5 percent). More than one-quarter of Americans were opposed to the US government recognizing Palestine as an independent state. While an earlier poll had shown that less than half of Americans supported the two-state solution, the number who thought the US government should recognize Palestine still constituted a plurality at 42 percent.[146] According to a Gallup poll, support for Palestinian statehood was 81 percent among Muslim Americans and 78 percent among Jewish Americans.[147]

A poll conducted in the occupied territories found that 83 percent of Palestinians supported the UN bid, with 59 percent considering it to be "the most vital Palestinian goal" for ending the Israeli occupation.[148] A poll conducted jointly by the Harry S. Truman Research Institute for the Advancement of Peace at Hebrew University and the Palestinian Center for Policy and Survey Research in Ramallah likewise found that 83 percent of Palestinians supported the UN bid. A considerable majority of Israelis, 69 percent, thought Israel should accept the UN decision if it recognized Palestinian statehood, compared to 16 percent who thought Israel should reject it and intensify settlement construction in the West Bank.[149]

The bid also provided a popularity boost for Abbas, with 59 percent saying they would vote for Abbas if new presidential elections were held, compared to 34 percent for Haniyeh. If new legislative elections were held, 67 percent said they would vote, among whom 45 percent said they would vote for Fatah and

29 percent for Hamas.[150] As David Makovsky noted in his WINEP report, it was largely Palestinian public opinion that was driving Abbas's decision to pursue the statehood bid: "Abbas is also driven by fear that if he backs down from this initiative, the Palestinian public may interpret it as a capitulation and a sign of weakness. Reinforcing this belief is his bitter memory of 2009, when Hamas ridicule in the Arab media forced him to reverse course on his initial decision to delay a controversial UN Human Rights Council vote regarding an investigation of the 2008–2009 Gaza war (i.e., the Goldstone report). Abbas is not eager to repeat that experience."[151]

Hamas officials, however, rejected the bid on the grounds that it would prejudice the Palestinians' right of return. "Hamas and other factions are not part of this step and do not support it," said Salah al-Bardaweel, a senior Hamas official in Gaza. Ismail Haniyeh reiterated that Hamas supported "the establishment of a Palestinian state on any liberated part of Palestinian land that is agreed upon by the Palestinian people, without recognizing Israel or conceding any inch of historical Palestine." But he rejected the UN bid because there was "no mandate for any Palestinian leadership to infringe on Palestinian national rights, nor is there a mandate for any Palestinian actor to make historic concessions on Palestinian land or the right of the Palestinians, foremost among them the right of return."[152]

It is not clear on what reasoning Hamas officials were basing their conclusion that recognition of the state of Palestine by the UN would prejudice the internationally recognized right of return of refugees to their homeland. This objection seemed intended to appeal to the Palestinian public by portraying Hamas as the greater defender of their rights while masking the true reason for opposing the bid, which was that Hamas wasn't involved in it. This was evident in Hamas's additional and more valid criticism that Abbas was going to the UN without first having come to a reconciliation agreement with the elected Hamas government. In an authoritarian show of protest, Hamas banned public demonstrations in Gaza in support of the bid.[153]

There were legitimate objections to the bid relating to the failure of Fatah and Hamas to come to a reconciliation agreement. Steven J. Rosen rightly pointed out in *Foreign Policy* that Hamas did not consider Abbas to be the president and that "Hamas has Palestine's own laws on its side". Indeed, Abbas's term had expired in January 2009, and he had since remained in office by unilaterally and illegally extending his own term for another year—which extension had also since expired. In fact, the "legally empowered president of Palestine" since January 2009, according to Article 65 of the Basic Law, was Palestinian Legislative Council Speaker and Hamas representative Abdul Aziz Dweik. A similar situation existed with regard to Abbas's appointment of Salam Fayyad as prime minister, which was also illegal since Abbas was "not legally the president of Palestine under Article 65 and because Fayyad has not been empowered as prime minister by the PLC as required by Article 66 of the Basic Law. Neither his first appointment, on June 15, 2007, nor his reappointment on May 19, 2009, was confirmed by the PLC as required." Hamas insisted that Ismail Haniyeh remained the elected prime minister, and in this case, too, "Hamas has the law on its side." Rosen concluded that if Palestinian statehood was recognized in the General Assembly, it would be "an imaginary state that has two incompatible presidents, two rival prime ministers, a constitution whose most central provisions are violated by both sides, no functioning legislature," and "no ability to hold elections".[154]

Guy Goodwin-Gill, a professor of public international law at Oxford University, raised similar concerns about the status of Abbas's government in an influential legal opinion published in August. His concern was related to "problems potentially affecting the right of the Palestinian people to self-determination and the manner by which that right can or may be exercised, due account being taken of the will of the people." The PA, he noted, was a subsidiary body receiving its authority from the Palestinian National Council, the legislative body of the PLO, which was recognized by the international community as the sole legitimate representative of the Palestinian people. The PA "does not have the capacity to assume greater powers, to 'dissolve' its parent body, or otherwise to establish itself independently of the Palestinian National Council and the PLO."

Goodwin-Gill concluded that Palestine did not meet the requirements for statehood because having "*representative* and democratic government" was an "inherent aspect of the principle of self-determination today", with legitimate governance established "through elections which are based on the enfranchisement of the people at large".[155] In an interview with *Al Jazeera*, Goodwin-Gill reiterated that the important question was "whether a state will in fact be truly representative of the popular will of all the people of Palestine, or whether the change in representation will in fact undermine their ability to claim their rights."[156]

Despite the merits of his argument, however, the Montevideo Convention merely requires there to be "government" in order for a political body to qualify under the definition of statehood. It says nothing about what *kind* of government, and, needless to say, there are numerous political constructs universally recognized as states despite *not* having truly representative government. (Indeed, with a ratio of one House representative for every 700,000-plus Americans, the argument could easily be made—on that criteria alone—that the US is not a state.) Furthermore, what Abbas was effectively seeking was recognition by the UN of the Palestinian state declared by the PLO in 1988, before the PA even existed, as most countries had already done in their individual capacity outside of the UN. It was also evident that despite his government's illegitimacy, Abbas had overwhelming public support among Palestinians for the UN bid, which therefore met Goodwin-Gill's requirement that government action be "representative of the popular will". If Abbas did one thing right, the UN bid was arguably it.

Fearful of losing "credibility" and of Palestinians gaining legal mechanisms to pursue their rights and seek remedy for US-supported Israeli crimes against them, the Obama administration "initiated a last-ditch diplomatic campaign" (*New York Times*) in early September to derail the UN bid.[157] David Hale and Dennis Ross were dispatched to talk with Israeli and Palestinian officials. Despite pressure from the US, however, the PA stayed the course.[158] "History will judge us", said Saeb Erekat, who reemphasized that the goal was "to preserve the two-state solution". Abbas reiterated that addressing the international community was "not unilateral" and that the goal was not to bypass meaningful negotiations, but to facilitate them.[159] Abbas also reminded that Obama in his 2010 speech before the General Assembly had said that if the world's rhetoric about peace was supported by actions, it would witness the membership of the "independent, sovereign state of Palestine" in the UN in 2011. "If he said it," Abbas quipped, "he must have meant it".[160]

Illustrating further how Obama supported his own rhetoric with actions, his administration on September 8 announced its intention to veto any resolution that came before the Security Council. It "should not come as a shock" that the US opposed the bid, State Department spokeswoman Victoria Nuland reasonably supposed. "So yes, if something comes to a vote in the UN Security Council, the US will veto".[161] She also warned the Palestinians that if they proceeded with the bid, the Congress could cut aid to the PA. "We don't threaten", said Nuland. "But we are making sure that they are hearing the voices in Congress, which are getting increasingly loud on this subject."[162]

Abbas replied that the US's efforts were "too late" and dismissed the idea of returning to negotiations under the status quo as unworkable. If the UN recognized Palestinian statehood, he said, "we will be a state under occupation, and we will talk accordingly and negotiate accordingly with the Israelis". He also assured that Palestinian rallies in support of the bid would remain peaceful and that the PA's security forces would maintain law and order.[163]

The US Congress responded to the PA's disobedience by making sure its voice was heard loud and clear. The House passed an appropriations bill including language requiring the US to sever aid to punish the Palestinians for "going outside the peace process", as Representative Kay Granger explained.[164] "If the Palestinians continue on their current path," warned Representative Steve Chabot, head of the Middle East subcommittee of the House Foreign Affairs Committee, "the question before the Congress will not be what portion of our aid will be cut, but rather what portion will remain."[165]

In mid-September, under the headline "US Scrambles to Avert Palestinian Vote at UN", the *New York Times* reported that the Obama administration would again dispatch negotiators to meet with Netanyahu and Abbas "in a final effort to avert a vote on the matter."[166] Secretary of State Clinton asserted that a UN vote was "not going to result in the kind of changes that the *United States* wishes to see that will move us toward the two-state solution that we strongly support." What the US strongly supported, of course, differed fundamentally from the international consensus. The US's alternative "solution" could only come about "through direct negotiations between the parties".[167] State Department spokesman Mark Toner stressed that the US was "working hard to get both parties back to the negotiating table and avert any sideshow in New York on statehood." The world mustn't forget that the main attraction was the freak show at center ring in the self-imposed capital of the world.[168]

In its continued attempt to avert the "sideshow", the Obama administration told the PA that it would agree to support recognition of "some of the attributes of a state". This would allow the PA to receive funding from the World Bank as a quid pro quo for scrapping the plan to seek UN membership. Another offer from Washington, according to a Palestinian official who spoke to the *New York Times*, "was for a resumption of negotiations based on the 1967 lines, but it didn't include an Israeli settlement freeze. We rejected both ideas."[169]

A senior aide to Abbas, Nimmer Hammad, however, told the IDF's broadcast network, Army Radio, that the PA did agree to return to talks if Israel *either* immediately ceased all settlement activity *or* agreed to accept the 1967 lines as the basis for negotiations on a border. This proposal was rejected by Netanyahu, who professed that their appeal to the international community was evidence that the Palestinians were not serious about negotiations.[170] Foreign Minister Lieberman proclaimed that Israel had "shown great generosity towards the Palestinians" and warned that the pursuit of statehood through "unilateral" moves would have "dire consequences".[171]

The US mainstream media played its usual role of manufacturing consent for government policy, with few exceptions.[172] As always, America's "newspaper of record" was the standard bearer. In August, the *New York Times* editors criticized the Palestinian leadership for committing the grave sin of pursuing a course of action that would "further isolate both Israel and Washington". They blamed Arab leaders for not giving Israel any "incentive" to cease violating international law ("to compromise", as they euphemistically put it). They mindlessly scolded Abbas for going to the UN instead of returning to talks with Israel despite acknowledging that Netanyahu had "used any excuse he can find . . . to avoid negotiations". They described Abbas's effort to seek a peaceful way forward at the UN as an action that "seemed to give up on diplomacy"—with "diplomacy" being another euphemism referring specifically to the negotiating framework Washington insisted upon, to the *exclusion* of any diplomatic effort that was contrary to US policy. The editors also repeated the standard fiction that the bid was a response to Obama's supposed inability to "deliver a promised settlement freeze". The *Times* explicitly endorsed the US policy of trying to "move the peace process forward" by "inducing the Palestinians to drop their statehood bid" and advocated that the US veto the Security Council resolution if they refused to obey.[173]

The following month, as the annual General Debate of the General Assembly approached, another *Times* editorial repeated the criticism that a vote on statehood in the Security Council "would be ruinous" since it would force the US to use its veto, thus "ensuring the further isolation of Israel and Washington". An alternative course was an upgrade of status in the General Assembly, "which the Palestinians are sure to win". By doing so, they could "pursue cases against Israel at the International Criminal Court". The *Times* cloaked its opposition to this outcome in a thin veil of concern for the feelings of the Palestinians, arguing that a successful bid would not result immediately in an Israeli withdrawal, "leaving the Palestinians disaffected after the initial euphoria". Well within the boundaries of allowable dissent, the editors criticized the Obama administration only on the grounds that it had "shown insufficient urgency or boldness" in trying to derail the UN bid and getting the Palestinians to agree to enter negotiations with the same Israeli Prime Minister who, they again reminded, "has used any excuse to thwart peace efforts". In another illustration of the limits of the debate within the mainstream media, the editorial also warned against the US and Israel cutting off funding to the PA solely on the grounds that it would be "counterproductive" to "bring down the most moderate leadership the Palestinians have had, empower Hamas and shred vital security cooperation between Israel and the authority." That is to say, cutting off funding would harm *Israel's* interests by undermining the role of the PA as "Israel's collaborator" (the goal of Oslo, as Shlomo Ben-Ami pointed out), a client regime that would "keep the Palestinians under control" (Natan Sharansky) by acting as "Israel's Enforcer" (Israel Shahak).[174]

Even more mind-numbing commentary could be found at *Foreign Policy*, where one could read David Aaron Miller opining that "Israeli-Palestinian peacemaking isn't and shouldn't be Barack Obama's top priority. Getting re-elected is." Miller described Obama's rejectionist policy as "smart", despite being "bad for American interests" because of the damage to the US's "credibility in the Arab and Muslim world" (which was "already low"); and since doing so would help him win votes, if a resolution on statehood was presented to the Security Council, "Obama should veto it and sleep well that night".[175]

There were also the usual repetitions in the Western media of the myth that the UN had either directly created Israel or conferred some kind of legal authority to the Zionists for their unilateral declaration of May 14, 1948. The *Telegraph* described the UN bid as "one of the most momentous taken at the world body for decades, and arguably the most dramatic since it approved the creation of Israel in 1947."[176] A CNN op-ed by WINEP senior fellow David Makovsky falsely suggested that "the United Nations created Israel". At the same time, Makovsky argued that the UN should not recognize Palestinian statehood, a goal that "can only be reached between an agreement between the two sides". In an attempt to explain why these different standards applied, Makovsky rationalized that the UN "created the state of Israel in 1947 because Britain sought an exit from the region". The Palestinians' present circumstances, on the other hand, were "very different". As an example, Makovsky brilliantly observed that, unlike the British in 1947, "Neither the Palestinians nor the Israelis are seeking to exit the region". How his conclusion followed from this observation was something he left lesser minds to puzzle over on their own. He went on to repeat the obligatory false claims about how "the Palestinians never miss an opportunity to miss an opportunity", as he quoted Abba Eban famously saying, and to characterize their rejection of the 1947 partition plan and Israel's offers at Camp David and Annapolis as having been somehow unreasonable.[177]

The extreme difficulty the intelligentsia was having rationally justifying the US government's rejectionism was impressively illustrated in an article in *Foreign Affairs* by former State Department official Robert M. Danin. Likewise ignoring all the relevant facts, he inexplicably blamed not Israel, but *the Palestinians* for having "rejected" the "option" under Phase II of the Road Map of creating "an independent Palestinian state with provisional borders". He criticized the PA's plan for being "aimed at enhancing their leverage in future negotiations with Israel", such as by gaining "legal recourse at the UN Security Council, the International Court of Justice, and possibly the International Criminal Court." His argument against this was that the Palestinians were "pursuing this goal outside of any international diplomatic effort, rather than within one"—meaning that they were pursuing it through an international diplomatic effort, rather than within the US's alternative framework that rejected such participation of the international community and the applicability of international law. Admittedly, the Palestinians had "good reasons to be reluctant to return to the negotiating table without a clear reference point". But they should do so anyway, he enigmatically reasoned, because a successful bid to gain UN recognition of Palestinian statehood "would likely set back, rather than advance, their national aspirations". For the UN to recognize the state of Palestine "would undermine Palestinians' moral and historical claims to being a stateless people". The conflict "would effectively become a border dispute" rather than "an existential challenge". Furthermore, since Israel had a "preponderance of power and control" in the occupied territories and "would likely take harsher countermeasures on the ground, such as withholding tax remittances, restricting Palestinian movement, and possibly annexing some West Bank territory", the Palestinians should just follow orders rather than invite such punishment for having "defied Israel".

Hence, by Danin's dizzying reasoning, in order to advance their national aspirations, the Palestinians must *not* seek to gain international recognition of statehood, but must rather choose to remain a stateless people; they must not seek remedy from the international community through application of international law, but must rather choose to remain powerless in negotiations with the Occupying Power illegally colonizing their land; they must not defy their occupiers, but must rather choose to be subservient to them, as a slave to his master. "By adopting a publicly confrontational approach toward the Israelis," Danin concluded, "the Palestinians risk undermining the goodwill and security on the ground that is the sine qua non for any further progress."[178]

This claimed "goodwill and security on the ground", however, was not in abundant evidence, and no arguments the politicians or intelligentsia could come up with would persuade the Palestinians to reverse course.

Israel's Benevolent Occupation

The day after Danin's *Foreign Affairs* article was published, Amnesty International issued a report illustrating just what Israel's "goodwill and security on the ground" meant for Palestinians. IDF bulldozers had "demolished three homes and water cisterns in 'Aqaba village in the northern West Bank" earlier that morning, leaving twenty-two Palestinians homeless, including twelve children. Their numbers were added to the more than 750 Palestinians who had been displaced by Israeli demolitions so far that year, a fivefold increase from the same period the previous year.[179]

"What we want to achieve", explained Abbas as the UN General Debate approached, "is to end the occupation and delegitimize the occupation and its measures, practices, that is a nightmare that we face every day. And these measures continue in the form of arrests—breaking into our cities, destroying houses, increasing settlement activities, and attacks by settlers who uproot trees and torch mosques."[180]

Israeli settlers defaced mosques, burned cars, and damaged other Palestinian property in what they called "price tag" attacks. As Isabel Kershner explained, they were meant "to exact a price from local Palestinians for violence against settlers or from Israeli security forces for taking action against illegal construction in Jewish outposts in the West Bank."[181] Reporting on "price tag" attacks in Qusra, Ethan Bronner pointed out that the village was under Israel's security jurisdiction, but that "few violent settlers have been caught or prosecuted." The son of former Prime Minister Menachem Begin and a minister in Netanyahu's government, Benny Begin remarked that Israel had "not been terribly successful in catching them."[182]

The government of Israel nevertheless proclaimed its "goodwill" on the ground by characterizing itself as a benevolent occupying power whose presence on their land was beneficial for the Palestinians. On September 18, Israel issued a report titled "Measures Taken by Israel in Support of Developing the Palestinian Economy and Socio-Economic Structure". The same day, the Office of the United Nations Special Coordinator for the Middle East Peace Process (UNSCO) published a report on the situation in the occupied territories titled "Palestinian State-Building: An Achievement At Risk", which reached dramatically different conclusions.[183]

The Israeli report claimed that its policies had "contributed significantly to growth in the past year" in the West Bank and had "made a substantial contribution to the Gaza economy on the ground." Israel's policy, it declared, was "aimed at improving the quality of life in Gaza" and "has enabled an economic and humanitarian recovery".[184]

The UNSCO report, on the other hand, observed that Palestinian institutions were "ready to assume the responsibilities of statehood", but "constrained in realizing their full potential" due "primarily" to "the persistence of occupation". The economic growth seen in Gaza was not driven by the private sector and was not occurring on a sustainable basis. Israel continued to defy calls from the UN to comply with Resolution 1860. The blockade was preventing sustainable growth from occurring, and the continued ban of goods such as construction materials was preventing "the revitalization of the private sector". Israel's restrictions on exports was also holding the economy back and negating the positive impact of its increase in imports. A black market economy had arisen as a result of the siege, with goods being imported from Egypt through the tunnels, which were dangerous and posed a serious risk, including to children. Wages were falling. Over one-third of Gaza's farmland remained inaccessible due to Israel's "security zone", undermining the productivity of the agricultural sector. Thirty-eight percent of Gazans were living in poverty and 75 percent depended on humanitarian assistance, without which an additional 10 percent of the population would be below the poverty line. The report concluded that "To arrest the de-development in Gaza, a full lifting of the closure is needed."

As for the West Bank, UNSCO reported that there had been a "significant increase in settlement activity", particularly in East Jerusalem. There had also been an increase in the "confiscation of private Palestinian land". Demolition of Palestinian homes and other property had increased "at an alarming rate" and was "increasingly targeting livelihood and basic service structures". All this was continuing in violation of international law and Israel's obligations under the Road Map.

Also of growing concern was Israeli settler violence against Palestinians, which since April had resulted in fifty-nine injuries and the death of a seventeen-year-old. In addition, about 2,777 agricultural trees had been damaged in over 109 incidents and four mosques desecrated in the same period. The settler violence underscored Israel's failure in its responsibility under international law as the Occupying Power to enforce the rule of law.

The illegal separation wall, if completed along the approved route, would cut off 9.4 percent of the West Bank. Palestinians' livelihoods continued to be undermined by Israel's regime of permits and gates, which hindered construction and infrastructure maintenance and obstructed access to their own land and resources, as well as services, including schools.

Palestinians had no access to most of the land under total Israeli control in in Area C, which comprised more than 60 percent of the West Bank. "More Palestinians lost their homes in Area C in the first half of 2011 than in either of the past two years", the report noted, and "such demolitions and consequent displacement and dispossession have a devastating impact on livelihoods."

East Jerusalem was becoming increasingly cut off from the rest of the West Bank. Palestinians living there were increasingly restricted from access to hospitals and schools. Families were increasingly separated from each other. Israel's policies were "threatening to undermine the Palestinian presence in East Jerusalem". To put it another way, Israel was engaged in a process of gradual ethnic cleansing of the city. The report called on Israel to end all of these illegal practices that were hindering economic development and gave cause for serious humanitarian concern.[185]

Returning to the Israeli report, the opening paragraph instructively prefaced that Israel "wishes to maintain the existing legal framework, as long as circumstances allow." It complained that "security in southern Israel along the border with Gaza has been under constant threat", with an "escalation" beginning in July 2011 and peaking from August 15–25, during which time Israel "was subjected to a continuous, almost daily, barrage of heavy rocket and mortar fire". "Three Israeli civilians were murdered in these attacks" the report stated, "while numerous civilians have been wounded and have suffered trauma."[186]

The UNSCO report provided some additional relevant information happily omitted by Israel. Between April 21 and September 4, "Israel conducted 22 incursions and 78 airstrikes" into Gaza, killing 14 Palestinian civilians and injuring 158, in addition to 18 militants killed and 21 injured. On August 18, militants entered Israel from Egypt and attacked several civilian vehicles and a military vehicle. Two Israeli soldiers and six civilians were killed in the attack. "Claiming that the attacks were linked to Palestinian militants based in Gaza, Israel conducted air strikes on Gaza," UNSCO noted, which "damaged a range of civilian infrastructure". It was in retaliation for these attacks that "militants indiscriminately fired rockets and projectiles into Israel"[187] While omitted from Israel's report, one of its own sources noted that the escalation in violence "ended on August 26", when Islamic Jihad agreed to cease fire, followed by a similar commitment from the Popular Front for the Liberation of Palestine (PFLP). Hamas's security forces "were instructed to enforce the lull and prevent

rocket fire into Israeli territory, 'even by force,' when they identified rocket firing squads".[188]

"Unfortunately," the Israeli report complained, with regard to Palestinians'
access to water, "over the past year the Palestinians have politicized this topic,
instead of increasing cooperation"—that is, as Robert M. Danin had advised,
the Palestinians were supposed to *cooperate* with the Occupying Power in its
confiscation of their resources instead of objecting to it. Israel stated that in
addition to the 135 million cubic meters of water produced by the Palestinians
each year, "Israel supplies another 52 million cubic meters annually", boasting
that this was "over 20 million cubic meters more than Israel is obligated to supply". The report neglected to mention that the water that "Israel supplies" came
from the mountain aquifer recharged by rainfall in and lying predominantly
under the West Bank, a fact only hinted at further into the report, where it
noted that "Israel and the Palestinian Authority share their water resources".[189]

The UNSCO report painted a much different picture by noting that "a
Humanitarian Response Plan for Area C" had "not been fully facilitated" by
Israel.[190] Here, UNSCO referred to another report from OCHA, which noted
that Palestinians in Area C faced "ongoing water shortages" in part due to "lack
of equitable distribution of water resources". Limited access to water, education, and health services was "widespread throughout Area C". This was caused
by "the lack or inadequate public service infrastructure due to the restrictive
planning and permitting process", "closure obstacles," "inadequate roads and
the lack of transport systems in remote areas", and the "threat of physical violence from settlers, especially against students on their way to school". The
Humanitarian Response Plan was intended, among other things, "to ensure
that communities have access to minimum amounts of water", but "the Israeli
authorities' failure to facilitate implementation of the Plan will result in Palestinian communities left with a chronic lack of water". The transfer of parts of
Area C to the PA "as envisaged in the Interim (Oslo) Agreement" was an "important complementary step towards addressing the economic, agricultural and
water needs of Palestinians in the West Bank".[191]

Four days prior to Israel's release of its report, *The Guardian* described the
situation in the West Bank village of Al-Amniyr near Hebron:

> The Palestinian village of al-Amniyr looks from afar like a rub-
> bish tip until you realize that the rubbish is people's dwellings,
> which have been destroyed in attacks targeting their water cis-
> terns. The villager Mohammed Ahmad Jabor's water cistern
> has been destroyed three times this year. The last time was by
> the settlers. The settler attacks come generally at night and
> where they cannot destroy water cisterns they poison them
> by putting chicken carcasses in them. The second time Jabor's

cistern was destroyed was by Israeli soldiers who destroyed seven tent dwellings and a sheep pen. . . . The land has been declared as agricultural, a designation which prohibits residents from constructing structures of any kind, especially cisterns. Construction needs permits, which are all but impossible to obtain. . . . And under another law, if the land is not used for three years, it reverts to Israel. So the inhabitants . . . are faced with a catch-22. If they comply with the law they cannot build cisterns and collect even rainwater. But if they fail to use their land agriculturally, they lose it anyway.

The Guardian explained further that "The Oslo accords created a Joint Water Management Committee, which grants Israel a veto over water resources and infrastructure in the West Bank." In the past two years, Israel had destroyed "100 water, sanitation and hygiene structures, 44 cisterns, 20 toilets and sinks, [and] 28 wells. This year alone, 20 cisterns have been destroyed. Most of this is happening in Area C, which is under full Israeli military control." A source from the Israeli embassy in London responded, "Unfortunately, there is a limited supply of water in the region. This is the fairest system for allocation through a bilateral committee."[192]

In fact, as Amnesty International has similarly reported, the problem of lack of access to water for Palestinians "arises principally because of Israeli water policies and practices which discriminate against the Palestinian population". As an Amnesty report from October 2009 elaborated, "inequality in access to water between Israelis and Palestinians is striking." While the WHO recommended daily water consumption of 100 liters per capita, Palestinian consumption was about 70 liters a day per person, with some surviving on as little as 20 liters a day, "the minimum amount recommended by the WHO for emergency situations response." Furthermore:

> Access to water resources by Palestinians in the OPT [Occupied Palestinian Territory] is controlled by Israel and the amount of water available to Palestinians is restricted to a level which does not meet their needs and does not constitute a fair and equitable share of the shared water resources. Israel uses more than 80 percent of the water from the Mountain Aquifer, the only source of underground water in the OPT, as well as all of the surface water available from the Jordan River of which Palestinians are denied any share.[193]

"Israel allows the Palestinians access to only a fraction of the shared water resources," explained Donatella Rovera, "which lie mostly in the occupied West

Bank, while the unlawful Israeli settlements there receive virtually unlimited supplies."[194]

With the evidence for Israel's "goodwill" on the ground indeed remaining hard to come by, the Palestinians forged ahead with their dastardly "ploy" to obtain international recognition of the state of Palestine at the UN.

CHAPTER 10

THE QUESTION OF PALESTINE

URING THE FALL OF 2011, the discussion in the American mainstream media ranged from praising Obama for his staunch support for Israel, on one end of the spectrum, to criticizing him for not being supportive enough, on the other extreme. One had to turn to the alternative or international media to read any suggestions that the US should *not* support Israel's criminal policies. Such a proposal would have been heretical in the US mainstream, especially during a presidential election campaign season in which Republican contenders were competing to outdo Obama, as well as each other, in their professions of loyalty to Israel.

The inability of Obama to prevent the Palestinians from going to the UN was a "failure of leadership", blasted former Massachusetts governor Mitt Romney. It "could have been avoided" if only Obama had "made it clear from the very outset that we stand by Israel, that we lock arm and arm", instead of communicating to the Palestinians that "there may be some distance between us and Israel."[1] The UN bid was "an unmitigated diplomatic disaster" and "the culmination of President Obama's repeated efforts over three years to throw Israel under the bus".[2]

Romney described himself as being "guided by one overwhelming conviction and passion: This century must be an American Century". He vowed to "never, ever apologize for America."[3] That was a line borrowed from former President George H. W. Bush, who had used it frequently.[4] "I will never apologize for the United States of America," then Vice President Bush said, for instance, in response to the shoot-down by a US warship of an Iranian civilian passenger airliner on July 3, 1988. "I don't care what the facts are."[5] The facts were that the Aegis cruiser *USS Vincennes*, under the command of Captain Will Rogers III, had entered Iran's territorial waters and opened fire on Iranian

gunboats posing no threat. At that time, as a Navy investigation later acknowledged, the *Vincennes* detected a plane ascending "on a normal commercial air
flight plan profile" and squawking a transponder signal identifying itself as a
commercial aircraft. Lieutenant William Montford warned Rogers that the
plane was "possible COMAIR", but Rogers nevertheless convinced himself that
his ship was under attack from an F-14 fighter plane (which the US had sold
to Iran in the early 1970s while it was under the thumb of Washington's man,
Mohammad Reza Shah Pahlavi, whose brutal regime was overthrown in the
1979 Islamic revolution). Rogers ordered his gunner to open fire on the plane,
Iran Air Flight 655, killing all 290 civilians aboard. The Navy investigation
attributed the discrepancy between the facts and Rogers' actions to "scenario
fulfillment" caused by "an unconscious attempt to make available evidence fit a
preconceived scenario."[6]

Also not one to apologize for murdering 290 civilians, President Ronald
Reagan justified the shoot-down as "a proper defensive action".[7] Campaigning
for the presidency, Vice President Bush called it "just an unhappy incident" and
reassured Americans that "life goes on."[8] Scheduled to speak before the UN
Security Council about the incident, Bush said, "I can't wait to get up there
and defend the policy of the United States government" by presenting "the free
world's case" for why 290 innocent civilians were dead.[9] Justifying the attack
before the Council, Bush blamed Iran for allowing a civilian airliner to go about
its business carrying passengers to Dubai at a time when an American warship
was "engaged in battle". He declined to explain how the pilot, Captain Mohsen
Rezaian, or the air traffic controllers at the airport in Bandar Abbas, where
Flight 655 had taken off, could possibly have known that a US warship was in
Iran's territorial waters firing at anything that moved. Bush lied to the Council
that the *Vincennes* had "acted in self-defense" against "a naval attack initiated by
Iranian vessels" on the American ship when it "came to the aid" of an "innocent
ship in distress."[10]

Also not wont to question the actions of the US government, the *New York
Times* in an editorial described the incident as unavoidable and defended Captain Rogers by saying he "had little choice" but to shoot down the civilian
airliner.[11] Rogers was later presented with the Legion of Merit award "for exceptionally meritorious conduct in the performance of outstanding service" during
his time as commanding officer when the shoot-down occurred. His weapons
and combat systems officer, Lieutenant Commander Scott E. Lustig, received
two commendation medals and was praised for "heroic achievement" for his
conduct during the incident. The entire crew of the *Vincennes* received combat
action ribbons.[12]

But Romney, like Bush, would "never apologize" for anything the US did,
no matter what the facts were. The US was "an exceptional country" that, with
"the strongest military in the world", had the "unique destiny" of leading "the

free world". With the US's leadership, there was "credibility" and "faith in the ultimate success of any action". Without it, the world would be "a far more dangerous place". Under a Romney administration, "American leadership will also focus multilateral institutions like the United Nations on achieving the substantive goals of democracy and human rights enshrined in their charters." Illustrating just how the US would support those goals if he was president, he announced that he would "begin discussions with Israel to increase the level of our military assistance and coordination" and "reaffirm as a vital national interest Israel's existence as a Jewish state."[13]

Texas Governor Rick Perry similarly criticized that the US would not be "at the precipice of such a dangerous move if the Obama policy in the Middle East wasn't naive, arrogant, misguided and dangerous." It was "wrong" for the Obama administration "to suggest the 1967 borders should be the starting point for Israel-Palestinian negotiations" since to apply international law would "put Israel in a position of weakness".[14] Perry penned an op-ed for the *Wall Street Journal* on one hand dismissing the UN bid as mere "theatrics" while on the other warning that it "threatens Israel and insults the United States". Echoing Romney's criticism, he said that Obama had "encouraged the Palestinians to take backward steps away from peace" by having made the "mistake" of calling for "an Israeli construction freeze, including in Jerusalem, as an unprecedented precondition for talks." Translated into meaningful terms, his central criticism, like Romney's, was that Obama had bothered to go through the motions of pretending to be opposed to Israel's colonization instead of openly declaring US policy to be one of unapologetic support for this illegal activity. While condemning the fictional Obama "precondition" of expecting Israel to cease violating international law, Perry demanded that the Palestinians recognize Israel "as a Jewish state" as "the precondition for any properly negotiated future settlement". He added that the US should withhold aid to the Palestinians if they continued to disobey orders from their overlords in Washington, DC.[15]

The *New York Times* rushed to Obama's defense by pointing out that when his administration wanted to prevent Congress from blocking $50 million in new aid to the PA, it fought the move by turning to "a singularly influential lobbyist: Israel's prime minister, Benjamin Netanyahu." At the administration's request, Netanyahu urged members of Congress not to cut off funding to the PA because "Israel views the money as helping to foster stability by supporting Palestinian government services and professionalizing security forces"—which is to say, cutting funding would undermine the PA's role as "Israel's Enforcer".[16]

The charge from Republicans that the Obama administration had acted "to throw Israel under the bus" was consistent with the dominant media narrative of the president as being "tough" on Israel. Challenges by American commentators to that narrative did appear, but only in the context of praising Obama for his overwhelming support for Israel's criminal policies. Robert Wexler, a former

Florida Congressman and president of the S. Daniel Abraham Center for Middle East Peace, sought to assure Israelis in a *Jerusalem Post* op-ed that Obama had "consistently acted to protect Israel's safety and interests over his entire time in office", including his efforts to head off the Palestinians' UN bid. His administration was making "relentless efforts at the highest levels to block the resolution", including issuing instructions to over 150 countries "to vote against or abstain from a vote if there should be one." Furthermore, the administration was warning the Palestinians of "grave consequences" for disobedience. Wexler bragged how the administration had "voted against every anti-Israel resolution at the UN", including vetoing the "anti-Israel" Security Council resolution condemning it for its illegal settlement activity. Among its other good deeds, the Obama administration had "condemned the UN's Goldstone Report", "lobbied heavily against the report advancing beyond the Human Rights Council", "supported Israel after the Gaza flotilla incident", and ushered in an era of "unprecedented military and security cooperation with Israel".[17]

Offering similar reassurances to its American audience, the cover of the September issue of *New York* magazine featured a photo of the back of Obama's yarmulke-covered head with the headline "THE FIRST JEWISH PRESIDENT" (a reference to a 2008 quip from "Obama mentor" Abner Mikva). The cover story argued that Obama was "the best thing Israel has going for it right now." Yes, Obama "was furious with Netanyahu" for having "twisted" his mention of the 1967 lines "beyond recognition". But Obama had "never wavered in going balls-out for Israel" and had repeatedly shown that the US "had Israel's back". This included opposing the Palestinians' UN bid, "despite the damage thwarting that bid might do to America's standing in the region", as well as backing Israel after its deadly attack on the *Mavi Marmara*. The "security relationship" between the US and Israel had "never been more robust". It was "perplexing" that Obama was portrayed as "ardently anti-Israel", which misperception was hurting his poll numbers among Jewish voters. This was a consequence of Obama trying "to preserve the Zionist dream" by applying "tough love to Israel". He was playing the role of "the caring and sober brother slapping his drunken sibling", which was intended "not to hurt the guy but to get him to sober up." Beyond that, such misperceptions about Obama stemmed from "superficial" and "misguided" prejudices, such as the fact that "his middle name was Hussein", or that he considered Palestinian scholar Rashid Khalidi to be a friend. Obama had also made the rhetorical "blunder" of promising a new beginning with the Arab world in his June 2009 Cairo speech. It was not Obama's fault that people perceived a distancing between the US and Israel, but Netanyahu's. Examples included his "flagrant ill-treatment" and "cold-cocking of Joe Biden" in March 2010; or the way he "threw a nutty" about Obama's mention of the 1967 lines in May 2011, delivering an "on-camera lecture to Obama" characterized by "impudence" and "dishonesty". In conclusion, Obama was "every bit as pro-Israel as the country's own prime minister—and, if you look from the proper angle, maybe even more so."[18]

Some Israeli officials also sought to combat misperceptions about Obama by underscoring that the "special relationship" was as strong as ever under his administration. When asked in August about the supposed "rift" between Obama and Netanyahu, Deputy Foreign Minister Danny Ayalon advised people to not pay attention to such reports and reassured that "we have not had a better friend than President Obama".[19] When asked on CNN if there was any "daylight" between the Obama administration and Israel, Michael B. Oren replied that the US's positions on issues were probably closer to Israel's than at any time before. The administration's position on "direct negotiations and dealing with all the core issues" was "precisely the Israeli position." They were "totally eye to eye on that." The US and Israel were "pretty much on that same page".[20]

The coordinated effort to block the UN bid continued right up to the last minute. Netanyahu expressed his concern to Dennis Ross and David Hale that if the UN recognized Palestinian statehood, they would gain recourse to the ICC over Israel's settlement construction.[21] Accordingly, Ross and Hale met with Abbas in a final unsuccessful attempt to pressure him to back down.[22] Nabil Shaath, a senior member of the Palestinian negotiating team, said a proposed Quartet statement presented to them by American negotiators included acceptance of continued colonization, recognition of Israel as a "Jewish state", rejection of any discussion of the right of return, and rejection of any reconciliation efforts with Hamas. Furthermore, the statement only mentioned Israeli settlements in terms of "demographic changes since 1967" and "new facts on the ground". "This was the statement that was supposed to persuade President Abbas not to go?" Shaath rhetorically inquired. This was, in his view, "the final blow, the final straw" that made Abbas even more determined to go to the UN.[23]

On September 15, Israel's Foreign Ministry "summoned the ambassadors of five key EU members", *Haaretz* reported, in order "to rebuke them over their countries' policy on the Palestinians' bid". France and Spain had sinned by straying from Washington's leadership and launching an initiative of their own under which EU member states would join the US in opposing a vote in the Security Council but support a General Assembly resolution upgrading Palestine's status from observer to nonmember state on the condition that Palestinians agree not to file charges against Israel at the ICC. But even this limited recognition of Palestinians' right to self-determination was deemed unacceptable to the US, which pressured the EU's foreign policy chief, Catherine Ashton, to "quash" the initiative. As a result, Ashton "raised a proposal of her own that conformed to Netanyahu's position", under which the UN would create "a new legal status less than that of a state" that "would not give the PA the standing it would need to take Israelis to the ICC."[24]

The *New York Times* observed once more how the situation posed "an acute dilemma" for the Obama administration: the US had "struggled" to maintain the perception of being "on the side of those seeking justice and freedom", but vetoing a statehood resolution "would intensify Arab perceptions of American double standards."[25] Thomas L. Friedman opined that having to use its veto "could be disastrous in an Arab world increasingly moving toward more popular self-rule." He sympathized with the Obama administration, which was "scrambling to defuse the crisis", and criticized the Israeli government for giving the US "nothing to defend it with". He advised that Netanyahu adopt more "subtle diplomacy" before he "plunges Israel into deeper global isolation and drags America along with it."[26]

The good news was that "the effort could also get lost for months in a bureaucratic thicket," the *Times* reported, which would give the US time "to try to restart negotiations", which in turn might help avoid "an embarrassing veto". With unusual candidness, the *Times* explained that "as long as Arab despots endorsed American control over the peace process", which the US "began monopolizing" in 1991, then "officials in Washington usually ignored how they treated their citizens." In order "to overcome that legacy", political analyst Mouin Rabbani explained, the Obama administration had tried repainting the US "as the main ally and sponsor of democratization in the region, the friend of the people's aspirations". This effort would be "undermined" by the UN bid, since the US would be "seen as pro-Israeli" if "actively forced to show its cards by vetoing."[27] The *Times* additionally noted that Obama's scheduled speech to the General Assembly would be "a high-wire act for him" since, as administration officials privately acknowledged, "the president risks appearing hypocritical".[28]

The only problem with US policy, as far as the mainstream media was concerned, was that it was increasingly difficult for the unapologetic leaders of the free world to manage "perceptions" about Washington's role in the Middle East.

Championing the Status Quo

Obama put forth his best effort at managing perceptions in his speech to the UN General Assembly on September 21, 2011. His main theme was the US's support for democracy in the Arab world. As examples, he cited the US's illegal use of force to overthrow the Gaddafi regime in Libya and its support for armed rebels seeking to overthrow the Assad regime in Syria.

Then there was Egypt, where the world had witnessed "the moral face of non-violence" and "knew that change had come". He didn't mention how the Egyptian revolution had forced the US to abandon its three-decades-old policy of supporting the Mubarak dictatorship, or how the policy of supporting the Egyptian military establishment continued unabated.[29]

Indeed, the Obama administration subsequently supported a military coup d'etat that overthrew President Mohamed Morsi, who was democratically elected into office in June 2012. Following the overthrow of Morsi on July 3, 2013, despite US law requiring that aid be cut off to any government that takes power through a coup, the Obama administration illegally continued $1.5 billion in annual aid, mostly for the military.[30] The Egyptian military proceeded to crack down violently on demonstrators protesting the coup, resulting in a massacre of more than sixty people on July 8.[31]

On July 25, the White House announced its official determination that the aid would continue. "Among the potential dangers" that government officials perceived with any cut-off of military aid, the *New York Times* explained, was "a reduction in the ability of the Egyptian military to halt smuggling of weapons to Hamas, which could use them against Israel. The aid program is also a pillar of the 1979 peace treaty between Egypt and Israel, and Israeli officials have urged the United States not to suspend it."[32]

Two days later, the military massacred over seventy demonstrators in Cairo, bringing the total killed since Morsi's ouster to over 200.[33] Next, the generals threatened to quash sit-in protests taking place in several squares in the city, deemed hotbeds of "terrorism".[34] With another massacre looming, the *New York Times* expressed its support for the US government's policy, weighing in that "American military aid to Egypt should not be cut off".[35] Defending US policy, Secretary of State John Kerry (who replaced Clinton in February 2013) announced that the Egyptian military was busy "restoring democracy".[36] The predictable consequence was a third massacre, beginning on August 15 and continuing for several days. As the death toll passed 1,000, the *New York Times* described it as "a ferocious assault" and "the worst bloodletting in modern Egyptian history."

The *Times* astutely noted how "The generals in Cairo felt free to ignore" calls from US officials for the release of political prisoners and diplomatic engagement with the opposition, "in a cold-eyed calculation that they would not pay a significant cost—a conclusion bolstered when President Obama responded by canceling a joint military exercise but not $1.5 billion in annual aid."[37] The response to the massacre from the Obama administration was to make clear once more that Egyptian military aid would not be suspended as required by US law, prompting the ruling junta to extend its crackdown to include rounding up "dissenters" like political activists and journalists—"a chilling warning", noted the *Times*, "that no Egyptians should feel safe if they dare to challenge authority."[38]

The massacre finally prompted the *Times* to call for "immediately suspending military aid and canceling joint military exercises"—a welcome reversal, but too late for the editors to wash the blood from their own hands.[39] Under growing criticism for its complicity in the generals' oppression and killing, the

Obama administration announced the following month that it would temporarily withhold $260 million in non-military economic assistance, as well as freeze delivery of military hardware, including Apache helicopters, missiles, tank parts, and F-16 fighter jets—a clear green light for the generals signaling that, while they ought to avoid any further mass murders, the US would continue to provide $1.3 billion in financing for them to carry on with "restoring democracy".[40]

Haaretz relayed the Israeli government's fear that a cutoff of military aid could affect the 1979 peace treaty, which had "brought Cairo into Washington's sphere of influence." Israel had been making the case to the White House "that punishing Egypt for the latest violence between the government and protesters was secondary to preserving the peace deal. 'As long as the American aid flows to Cairo, the Egyptian regime can ward off criticism against preserving the peace treaty with Israel,' Israeli officials told their US counterparts."[41] That is to say, as long as the American aid continued to flow to the generals, they could continue to suppress the Egyptian people, whose popular will posed a threat to the status quo. If the people managed to establish an Egyptian government that actually respected public opinion, it might, for example, cease its complicity with Israel in collectively punishing the civilian population of Gaza by permanently and completely opening the Rafah border crossing.

After just having praised the US's own recourse to violence to change governments it didn't like, Obama continued his address to the UN by insisting on "a peaceful transition" in Yemen, where there were similar protests against the US-backed government of President Ali Abdullah Saleh.[42] He likewise insisted on "a meaningful dialogue that brings peaceful change that is responsive to the people" in Bahrain, where the US-backed monarchy had cracked down harshly on peaceful protesters with the help of Saudi Arabia, which had been given the green light from Washington to send in its own US-supplied military to assist the Bahrain regime in crushing the uprising. "America is a close friend of Bahrain", Obama remarked—perhaps not so much a friend of its people, but certainly of its autocratic government, which was sagacious enough to make the country useful to Washington by allowing the US Navy's Fifth Fleet to be based there.[43]

Notwithstanding the actual historical record, Obama proclaimed that the US had "sanctioned those who trample on human rights" and would "always serve as a voice for those who've been silenced." The standard was clear: if the US supported a tyrannical regime, the oppressed people living under it must not take up arms to overthrow it, but must strictly adhere to non-violent protests, which those same regimes could then violently crush, including with US-supplied military hardware; if, however, Washington opposed a foreign government, then, regardless of the resulting massive destruction and civilian casualties, it was a praiseworthy deed to violently overthrow it.

After citing these, the best examples the White House could come up with of US support for democracy in the Arab world, Obama reminded the General Assembly that he had stood the year before at that same podium and called for an independent state of Palestine—but only if established on Israel's terms. Palestinian statehood could not be achieved through the UN, but only through the US-led "peace process", in which the US and Israel exercised effective veto power over the Palestinians' exercise of self-determination. After expressing his commitment to Palestinian statehood in these terms, he continued,

> But understand this as well: America's commitment to Israel's security is unshakeable. Our friendship with Israel is deep and enduring. And so we believe that any lasting peace must acknowledge the very real security concerns that Israel faces every single day. Let us be honest with ourselves: Israel is surrounded by neighbors that have waged repeated wars against it. Israel's citizens have been killed by rockets fired at their houses and suicide bombs on their buses. Israel's children come of age knowing that throughout the region, other children are taught to hate them. Israel, a small country of less than eight million people, looks out at a world where leaders of much larger nations threaten to wipe it off of the map. The Jewish people carry the burden of centuries of exile and persecution, and fresh memories of knowing that six million people were killed simply because of who they are. Those are facts. They cannot be denied.[44]

Obama's "facts", however, left much to be desired in the way of accuracy. In truth, it was Israel that had waged repeated wars against its neighbors, including in 1948, when Palestine was ethnically cleansed of its Arab population, and 1967, when Israel launched a surprise attack on Egypt and began its occupation of Gaza and the West Bank. Obama was also alluding to the oft-repeated claim that Iran's President Mahmoud Ahmadinejad had threatened to "wipe Israel off the map"—a fabrication of Western propaganda that refused to die despite repeated debunking.[45] Tellingly, Obama withheld other crucial facts from his audience that truly could not be denied: that the Palestinians even more so faced very real security concerns every single day, that a far greater number of Palestinians had been killed by Israeli bombs and bullets, that Palestinian children came of age knowing that Israeli children were taught to hate them, and that the Palestinians were not responsible for the Nazi Holocaust during World War II and therefore should not be made to pay the penalty for it.

Netanyahu was not in attendance during Obama's speech. He was too busy meeting with the Colombian President Juan Manuel Santos in order to convince him to vote against the Palestinians' request for membership in the Security Council. Netanyahu also met with Canadian Prime Minister Stephen Harper and Gabon President Ali Bongo Ondimba. *Haaretz* reported how Foreign Minister Lieberman, who was also in attendance, was instructed by a senior American official via text message "to refrain from making statements to the media about the pressure Israel is applying on various other states." According to Ambassador Oren, when Netanyahu was handed a transcript of Obama's speech, "he skipped straight to the part concerning Israel and the Palestinians and nodded in satisfaction".[46]

Following his speech, Obama joined Netanyahu in a press conference, where he reiterated the US's "unbreakable" bonds with Israel and boasted that the US's "security cooperation" with Israel was "stronger than it has ever been" and would "never waiver". The US's idea of "a just and lasting peace" was one that "puts Israel's security at the forefront". After thanking Obama, Netanyahu criticized the Palestinians for wanting to achieve statehood without being prepared "to give peace to Israel in return". Turning to Obama, he said, "I think that standing your ground, taking this position of principle, which is also, I think, the right position to achieve peace—I think this is a badge of honor and I want to thank you for wearing that badge of honor, and also to express my hope that others will follow your example, Mr. President. So I want to thank you."[47]

Obama next met with Abbas—to try to persuade him one last time not to submit an application for statehood the next day at the Security Council.[48]

Responding to Obama's speech, Michael Oren echoed Netanyahu's remark that it was a "badge of honor" that the US sided with Israel. "It's the best speech Obama has made so far," acclaimed Avigdor Lieberman, "and I am ready to sign this speech with both hands."[49] Obama's speech was "billed in the media as his most pro-Israel yet", the BBC noted.[50] Ethan Bronner, writing from Jerusalem, remarked that the speech "could have been written by any [Israeli] official here."[51] Obama experienced a surge in popularity among Israelis, with one poll showing that a 54 percent majority considered his policies to be "pro-Israel" and 19 percent "pro-Palestinian" (compared to 12 percent and 40 percent, respectively, in May).[52]

Unsurprisingly, the speech was not so well received among Palestinians. "I couldn't believe what I heard," said Hanan Ashrawi, a member of the Palestinian delegation to the UN. "It sounded as though the Palestinians were the ones occupying Israel. There wasn't one word of empathy for the Palestinians. He spoke only of the Israelis' troubles. We understand Obama is facing elections, but what we heard from him—that's exactly why we're going to the UN."[53] Palestine Legislative Council member and former presidential candidate Mustafa Barghouti said, "It clearly shows the double standards of the US when it comes to the Palestinian issue. Obama spoke about freedom, human rights, justice in South Sudan, Tunisia, Egypt—but not for the Palestinians. . . . He doesn't see that this is not a struggle between two equal sides, but between an oppressor and the oppressed, an occupier and the occupied." Marwan Jubeh, a shop owner in Ramallah, expressed the conclusion he drew from Obama's speech to *The Guardian*: "Israel and the US are one and the same: the US is Israel, and Israel is the US."[54]

The *New York Times* managed to pick up on the irony. Obama was "throwing the weight of the United States directly in the path of the Arab democracy movement even as he hailed what he called the democratic aspirations that have taken hold throughout the Middle East and North Africa."[55]

President Abbas had "delivered on the threat" to go the UN, the *Times* further explained, thus "putting Mr. Obama in the position of having to stand in the way." Obama "did exactly what he had to do", the *Times* quoted former Clinton administration official David Rothkopf as saying. "He made a clear statement for what is a clear US position and put himself squarely as a champion of the status quo."[56]

The *Times* editors agreed, celebrating the speech and arguing that "Mr. Obama had no choice but to stand by Israel, this country's historic ally." In a remarkable display of cognitive dissonance, even by mainstream media standards, the editors managed somehow to convince themselves that "there can be no solution without strong American leadership."[57] Far be it from the *New York Times* to question the assumption that championing the status quo in the Middle East by standing in the way of legitimate aspirations of the Palestinian people was the proper role for the federal government of the United States of America.

Also addressing the General Assembly on September 21 was French President Nicolas Sarkozy, who took the opportunity to try to assert France into a leadership role. The "method used up to now" in the US-led "peace process" had "failed", so there was a need to "change the method!" The US could not resolve this problem on its own; France had its own proposal to help move the "process" forward. He agreed with the US position that the Palestinians must enter negotiations while Israel continued stealing their land. He parroted the fear that a US veto would precipitate "a cycle of violence in the Middle East"; but instead of arguing that the US should therefore support the bid (or at least abstain), he expressed his readiness to help the Obama administration head off a vote in the Security Council. He proposed as an alternative that the Palestinians could seek an upgrade of status to non-member observer state in the General Assembly. He made clear, however, that France would only support such a move if the Palestinians pledged "to avoid using this new status to undertake actions incompatible with the continuation of negotiations"—meaning they must not actually take advantage of the legal mechanisms that would become available to them to seek remedy for the crimes against them.[58]

It was an alternative plan the US was already familiar with and, as previously noted, Washington was not prepared to allow even such a narrow recognition of the Palestinians' right to self-determination in the UN. In a photo-op with

Sarkozy following the French president's speech, Obama "refused to engage with reporters", the *New York Times* noted. "'Do you support the French one-year timeline?' one reporter asked. Mr. Obama responded, 'I already answered a question from you before.' Another reporter asked Mr. Obama if he agreed with the French position on Palestine. Mr. Obama smiled and replied, 'Bonjour.' A third reporter queried if that response constituted a 'no comment.' The president's response: 'No comment.'"[59]

Despite the extremely limited nature of Sarkozy's criticism of US policy and his assurances that the slight change in tactics he proposed was intended to achieve the same goals, the *New York Times* reported that Sarkozy "broke sharply" with the Obama administration's efforts to "quash" the Palestinians' UN bid.[60] Sarkozy had "stepped forcefully into the void, with a proposal that pointedly repudiated Mr. Obama's approach." The French leader's speech was a "challenge to the status quo" and underscored the "stark new reality" that the US might have "to share, or even cede, its decades-long role as the architect of Middle East peacemaking."[61] Magnifying France's supposed sharp break from Washington, the *Times* noted Israel's concern that a successful bid in the General Assembly would allow the Palestinians access to the ICC, where they could "pursue Israeli leaders through 'lawfare.'" Withheld from readers was the fact that Sarkozy had qualified France's support for such a move on the condition that Palestinians essentially renounce their right to do so.[62]

Championing the status quo as ever, the Obama administration persuaded Germany to announce that it would not vote in favor of a resolution in the Security Council. At the same time, twenty-five of the EU's twenty-seven members, including Germany, Spain, and the UK, pledged their support for the French initiative, which required the Palestinians to pledge not to file charges against Israel at the ICC as well as withdraw a complaint it filed with the Court in 2009 over Operation Cast Lead.[63]

The Palestinians, however, had no intention of making such a pledge. "We will give some time to the Security Council to consider first our full membership request", Nabil Shaath told reporters, "before heading to the General Assembly."[64] Abbas was receiving "rare praise" from the Palestinian public for his unusual willingness to disobey orders, the *New York Times* noticed. While he had "mostly been seen as Hamlet-like in his indecision, trying too hard to please the Americans and the Israelis", now he seemed "to have found a kind of liberation, evident in a spring in his step, in deciding to defy Washington and force his people's plight into international consciousness."[65]

Palestine's Application for UN Membership

On September 23, 2011, President Mahmoud Abbas took his turn at the podium in the UN General Assembly. The central issue, he said, was Israel's refusal to commit to negotiations premised on international law and UN resolutions while "it frantically continues to intensify building of settlements on the territory of the State of Palestine." It was a "policy of colonial military occupation" that entailed "all of the brutality of aggression and racial discrimination". This policy was "the primary cause for the failure of the peace process". Abbas cited Israel's confiscation of Palestinian land, demolitions of Palestinian homes, illegal settlement construction in East Jerusalem and throughout the West Bank, the illegal construction of the annexation wall, raids and arrests, killings, checkpoints, settler attacks and destruction of property, and the ongoing siege of Gaza. Israel's actions constituted "a multi-pronged policy of ethnic cleansing". All of these were "unilateral actions" illustrating Israel's "selective application" of its previous agreements with the aim of "perpetuating the occupation." Unlike Israel, the Palestinians had made major concessions, having already "agreed to establish the State of Palestine on only 22 percent of the territory of historical Palestine".

Speaking on behalf of the PLO, Abbas affirmed that the Palestinians were seeking "the realization of their inalienable national rights" in accordance with the international consensus on a two-state solution, including a just solution to the Palestinian refugee problem in accordance with General Assembly Resolution 194 of December 1948. The Palestinians were ready to immediately resume negotiations "on the basis of the adopted terms of reference based on international legitimacy and a complete cessation of settlement activities". In the meantime, they would "continue their popular peaceful resistance to the Israeli occupation and its settlement and apartheid policies and its construction of the racist annexation Wall".

Stressing that the UN bid was itself a confirmation of the Palestinian commitment to diplomacy and rejection of unilateral actions, he continued:

> Our efforts are not aimed at isolating Israel or de-legitimizing it; rather we want to gain legitimacy for the cause of the people of Palestine. We only aim to delegitimize the settlement activities and the occupation and apartheid and the logic of ruthless force, and we believe that all the countries of the world stand with us in this regard. . . . Negotiations will be meaningless as long as the occupation army on the ground continues to entrench its occupation, instead of rolling it back, and continues to change the demography of our country in order to create a new basis on which to alter the borders. . . . It is a moment of truth and my people are waiting to hear the answer of the world. Will it allow Israel to continue its occupation . . . ? Will it allow Israel to remain a State above the law and accountability? Will it allow Israel to continue rejecting the resolu-

tions of the Security Council and the General Assembly of the
United Nations and the International Court of Justice and the
positions of the overwhelming majorities of countries in the
world?

Abbas closed by informing the Assembly that he had delivered Palestine's
application for UN membership to Secretary-General Ban Ki-moon and calling on members to recognize Palestinian statehood. As he held up a copy of the
Palestinian application for membership, the Assembly erupted into a standing
ovation and sustained thunderous applause, cheers, and whistles.[66]

In the West Bank, as Abbas addressed the Assembly, Palestinians were in
the streets to show their support for the UN bid. "I am here to tell the Americans that we are with Abu Mazen," Issa al-Rafati, a forty-six-year-old construction worker, told the *New York Times*. "America took Israel's side against our
people."[67]

The UN Secretary-General, in keeping with his duty, forwarded Palestine's
application for membership to the Security Council. It stated:

> This application for membership is being submitted based on
> the Palestinian people's natural, legal and historic rights and
> based on United Nations General Assembly resolution 181 (II)
> of 29 November 1947 as well as the Declaration of Indepen-
> dence of the State of Palestine of 15 November 1988 and the
> acknowledgment by the General Assembly of this Declaration
> in resolution 43/177 of 15 December 1988.

> In this connection, the State of Palestine affirms its commit-
> ment to the achievement of a just, lasting and comprehensive
> resolution of the Israeli-Palestinian conflict based on the vi-
> sion of two-States living side by side in peace and security, as
> endorsed by the United Nations Security Council and General
> Assembly and the international community as a whole and
> based on international law and all relevant United Nations
> resolutions.

Abbas included a declaration "that the State of Palestine is a peace-loving nation and that it accepts the obligations contained in the Charter of the United
Nations and solemnly undertakes to fulfill them." He also included a letter to
the Secretary-General recalling the 1988 Palestinian Declaration of Independence and international recognition of the "right of the Palestinian people to
self-determination". The letter stated further that

Palestine's application for membership is made consistent with the rights of the Palestine refugees in accordance with international law and the relevant United Nations resolutions, including General Assembly resolution 194 (III) (1948), and with the status of the Palestine Liberation Organization (PLO) as the sole legitimate representative of the Palestinian people. . . . Further, the Palestinian leadership stands committed to resume negotiations on all final status issues—Jerusalem, the Palestine refugees, settlements, borders, security and water— on the basis of the internationally endorsed terms of reference, including the relevant United Nations resolutions, the Madrid principles, including the principle of land for peace, the Arab Peace Initiative and the Quartet Roadmap, which specifically requires a freeze of all Israeli settlement activities.[68]

The US responded by immediately issuing a joint statement with its Quartet partners taking note of the application and affirming "its determination to actively and vigorously seek a comprehensive resolution of the Arab-Israeli conflict, on the basis of UN Security Council Resolutions 242, 338, 1397, 1515, 1850, the Madrid principles including land for peace, the Roadmap, and the agreements previously reached between the parties". It called upon both parties "to refrain from provocative actions" and "reiterated the obligations of both parties under the Roadmap". It then rendered this all meaningless by reiterating its call for the resumption of negotiations "without delay or preconditions", the standard code letting Israel know that it could feel free to continue violating previous agreements and international law with impunity.[69] Reporting on the Quartet statement, the *New York Times* perceived how, "before the thunderous applause greeting his announcement in the General Assembly had faded, international powers laid out a new plan to resume direct Israeli-Palestinian peace talks that was designed to delay a contentious vote on the Palestinian request as long as possible." The text of the statement was nevertheless still "heavily diluted" from what the US would have liked, having "failed to achieve a consensus" among its Quartet partners.[70]

The government of Israel, however, was satisfied with what the US was able to accomplish on its behalf. "We were pleased to see that the Quartet has called for an immediate return of the Palestinians to the negotiating table with us, without preconditions," lauded Michael Oren. "The US and Israel are more closely coordinated now than they have been at any time in the last two years, or more," he added. "We see things very much eye-to-eye on how to move forward."[71]

A 'Theatre of the Absurd'

The day after Abbas's address, Prime Minister Netanyahu took the podium. Days earlier, he had announced his intention to address the Assembly by saying that, while it was "not a place where Israel usually receives a fair hearing", he had "still decided to tell the truth before anyone who would like to hear it."[72] Truth, however, was in very short supply in his speech. He declared that "Israel has extended its hand in peace from the moment it was established 63 years ago"—at a time when the ethnic cleansing of the Arab population of Palestine was well underway. He touted Israel as "the one true democracy in the Middle East", which was "unjustly singled out for condemnation" annually at the UN, a "theater of the absurd" that had the audacity to "cast Israel as the villain". He had come "to speak the truth", which was that Israel wanted a "peace" that "must be anchored in security"; a "peace" that could not be achieved through UN resolutions, but only through negotiations. The Palestinians' refusal to negotiate while the theft of their land continued indicated that they did not want peace, as did their stubborn repeated rejection of Israel's "sweeping" peace offers "that met virtually all of the Palestinian demands".

In attempting to justify Israel's ongoing colonization of Palestinian land, Netanyahu repeated the usual hasbara. After Israel's withdrawal from Gaza, "thousands of rockets" were fired "from the very territories we vacated". Sharon's "disengagement plan" was "a bold act of peace", but with Hamas taking over Gaza, all Israel got in return was war. If Israel withdrew from the West Bank, it would become "another Gaza", which was why Israel needed "real security arrangements", which "the Palestinians simply refuse to negotiate". Resolution 242 "didn't require Israel to leave all the territories it captured in the Six-Day War. It talked about withdrawal from territories, to secure and defensible boundaries." To this end, Israel needed to "maintain a long-term Israeli military presence in critical strategic areas in the West Bank." Why did Abbas refuse to accept this? After all, the US had troops "in Japan, Germany and South Korea for more than half a century"; the UK had an air base in Cyprus; France had forces in three African countries; yet, none of these host countries complained "that they're not sovereign countries". Israel's "security" further required that it maintain control over Palestine's airspace and borders. Israel would be "the first" country "to welcome a Palestinian state as a new member of the United Nations", just as soon as they surrendered their rights by accepting all of his preconditions.

Netanyahu next turned to the theme of Israel being the region's only "democracy". Israel protected the rights of its Arab minorities, while Palestinians were calling for the "ethnic cleansing" of Israelis from a future Palestinian state. While Israel believed in equality, the Palestinian government was guilty of "racism" for a law forbidding land sales to Israeli settlers. And it was time for the Arabs who were ethnically cleansed from Palestine in order for the "Jewish state" to be established to "give up the fantasy" of ever returning to their homeland. Israel's occupation and theft of Palestinian land was "a result of the conflict", not a cause of it. Rather, the "core of the conflict" had always been "the refusal of the Palestinians to recognize a Jewish state in any border". Israel was "prepared to make painful compromises" by permitting the Palestinians to keep some of their land. It was now up to the Palestinians to show that they, too, were "ready for compromise and for peace" by "taking Israel's security requirements seriously" and recognizing the Jews' "historical connection" to their "ancient homeland". Instead of showing that he was ready for peace, Abbas did not respond to his offer to negotiate "without preconditions"; to his "vision of peace of two states for two peoples"; to his generous willingness "to ease freedom of movement" in occupied territory, which had "facilitated a fantastic growth in the Palestinian economy"; or to his "unprecedented" settlement freeze. He could not "make peace alone"; it was time for Abbas to take the hand he was extending "in peace".[73]

Netanyahu's comment about Palestinians calling for ethnic cleansing alluded to a recent statement from the Palestinian ambassador to Washington, Maen Rashid Areikat, who had said in an interview that Israelis and Palestinians "need to divorce. After we divorce, and everybody takes a period of time to recoup, rebound, whatever you want to call it, we may consider dating again." Asked whether this meant "it would be necessary to first transfer and remove every Jew", he replied, "I'm saying transfer Jews who, after an agreement with Israel, fall under the jurisdiction of a Palestinian state." He later clarified that by "Jews" he meant "Israelis" living in illegally built settlements inside of Palestine and that he was not opposed to Jews returning legally to live as citizens of Palestine. "Why can't you be Palestinian Jews?" he asked rhetorically of the settlers. Palestinians were "not against Jews or Judaism", he said, but "against Zionism as a political theory." In a second interview shortly thereafter, Areikat made similar remarks, making clear that he was expressing his own personal view, and not an official position of the PA. "I personally still believe that as a first step we need to be totally separated," he said, "and we can contemplate these issues in the future. But after the experience of the last 44 years of military occupation and all the conflict and friction I think it would be in the best interests of the two peoples to be separated at first." After his words were characterized by the media as a call for ethnic cleansing, Areikat gave a third interview in which he clarified once more that he was not saying "that no Jews can be in Palestine", but was referring to soldiers and settlers, "persons who are amid an occupation, who are in my land illegally".[74]

Meanwhile in the US, Republican presidential candidates were debating what to do about individuals labeled "illegal immigrants", and the Obama administration was busy conducting nationwide sweeps to arrest and deport the largest number of immigrants since the Bureau of Immigration and Customs

Enforcement was established under the Homeland Security Act in 2003—more than two-thirds of whom were guilty of nothing more than setting foot across the border without Washington's permission.[75]

Netanyahu also referred to a Palestinian law under which selling land to "occupiers" is considered an act of treason punishable by death, a sentence that had never been enforced.[76] Israel, of course, has a complex system of laws dating back to the Mandate period designed precisely in order to prevent Arabs from buying back land in Israel.[77] The Constitution of the Jewish Agency established in 1929, for example, stated that "Land is to be acquired as Jewish property . . . [and] held as the inalienable property of the Jewish people. The Agency shall promote agricultural colonization based on Jewish labor, and in all works or undertakings carried out or furthered by the Agency, it shall be deemed to be a matter of principle that Jewish labor shall be employed . . . ."[78]

Netanyahu's speech, unsurprisingly, was not as well received by the world as Abbas's. "It was clear for which one the audience had greater sympathy", noted the BBC. "Scores of envoys leaped to their feet applauding" when Abbas held up Palestine's letter of application, while Netanyahu displayed his "characteristic combativeness" and "was rewarded with sparse and often partisan applause".[79] *The Economist* perceived that, despite his professed desire for a negotiated peace deal, Netanyahu's demand that Palestinians recognize Israel as a "Jewish state" seemed "intended merely to prevent talks restarting."[80]

Abbas was not without his detractors, of course; nor Netanyahu his admirers. Elliot Abrams harshly denounced Abbas's speech as "a nasty piece of work filled with harshly worded denunciations". The "rapturous applause" it received was "deceiving" since "any real commitment to telling truths to the Palestinian people was absent".[81] A poll conducted by *Haaretz* revealed that among Israelis, "Netanyahu significantly improved his public standing after his speech".[82] Daniel Levy observed at *Foreign Policy* that while Netanyahu was not greeted with parades like Abbas, and while the Israeli media "had few kind words" for him, he nevertheless "could take comfort in a sight even more edifying to a politician—a boost in his poll numbers." Yet, while Netanyahu was being hailed by his admirers for embracing a two-state solution, "his idea of what Palestinian statehood would entail is exactly the same as his previous vision for Palestinian autonomy, the only difference being his recognition that it makes more sense to say that if the Palestinians are willing to call this bantustanization statehood, then why on Earth should Israel oppose it?" Netanyahu's additional precondition that Palestinians must accept Israel "as a Jewish state" required the Palestinians to "embrace their own dispossession". This is what Netanyahu meant when he once said, "It is not a conflict over 1967, but over 1948." Levy closed with the astute observation that "the status quo holds only for as long as the PLO leadership believes there is some hope to return to that old Oslo model. That era seems to be passing."[83]

As Abbas arrived in Ramallah a few days after his speech, thousands of Palestinians took to the streets to celebrate his return from New York. His popularity had "skyrocketed" for "defying the Obama administration" (Associated Press). The streets in Gaza, however, remained mostly empty due to the ban on demonstrations by Hamas, whose leadership continued to criticize Abbas for not having consulted with them about the effort. In another attempt at reconciliation, however, talks between Fatah and Hamas were scheduled to resume in Cairo.[84]

Less than a week since Obama's address to the General Assembly, Israel announced plans to construct 1,100 new housing units in the Gilo neighborhood of occupied East Jerusalem. The EU issued a statement deploring the move and calling on Israel to reverse its plan.[85] German Chancellor Angela Merkel responded with a telephone call to Netanyahu to express her anger over the announcement in light of "the prodigious efforts she had made on Israel's behalf to thwart the Palestinians' UN recognition bid" (*The Independent*).[86]

The White House limited its own criticism to the statement that it was "deeply disappointed" by this anticipated consequence of its own policy.[87] Defense Secretary Leon Panetta expressed his concern that "it is not a good situation for Israel to become increasingly isolated", while also making sure to reiterate the US's commitment to maintaining Israel's "qualitative military edge".[88] *New York Times* columnist Nicholas D. Kristof similarly criticized Netanyahu solely on the grounds that he was "isolating his country" by continuing to expand settlements instead of showing proper respect for the Obama administration for having suffered through the humiliation of promising "to veto the Palestinian statehood that everybody claims to favor".[89]

On September 29, the Security Council referred Palestine's application for UN membership to its Committee on the Admission of New Members.[90] The following day, the EU Parliament passed a resolution affirming the "right of Palestinians to self-determination and to have their own state". It called for a two-state solution on the basis of the 1967 lines, with east Jerusalem as Palestine's capital, as well as for a complete halt to Israel's settlement construction.[91] Eight Security Council members reportedly favored admitting Palestine, one short of the nine states required. By early November, the states expected to vote in favor included Russia, China, Brazil, India, Lebanon, South Africa, Gabon, and Nigeria. Expected to abstain were the UK, France, Germany, Portugal, Colombia, and Bosnia. The US, of course, had promised to use its veto. Germany and Colombia later that month were reportedly persuaded to join the US in opposition.[92]

Richard N. Haass, a former State Department official and President of the Council on Foreign Relations, outlined in *Time* magazine why the world should oppose the UN bid. It wouldn't help the Palestinians, he argued, because "Israelis could make life far more difficult" for them—an effort in which Israel would be joined by the US, which might cut off aid to the PA. But the US and Israel "would lose as well", since a US veto "would be wildly unpopular in the Arab world", and popular protests "would also prove costly to Israel." These "dire outcomes" must be prevented, Haass argued, not by holding Israel accountable for its illegal and oppressive policies or by supporting Palestinian self-determination at the UN, but rather by getting the Palestinians to obey their oppressors, accept their powerlessness, give up their aspirations, drop their bid, and return to talks under the old status quo.[93]

The US Congress reminded the PA of its dependence on US aid by pushing for a substantial cut as punishment for what Representative Ileana Ros-Lehtinen called the "dangerous Palestinian scheme". She chaired the House Foreign Affairs Committee, which, along with the Senate Foreign Relations Committee, imposed a freeze on $200 million of the $500 million the PA received annually from the US. "There may need to be a total cut-off of all aid to the Palestinians," warned Representative Gary Ackerman, for their "dangerous and ill-advised" move to seek statehood recognition. Congressional cuts in aid to the PA, which mainly affected infrastructure and development projects, were widely opposed, but only on the usual narrow grounds that it would harm *Israel's* interests. "If they were to cut off the Palestinian Authority," charged Elliot Abrams, "Israel would have to pick up a lot of its responsibilities, so who would they be helping and who would they be hurting?" As Daniel Levy explained, "American aid to the Palestinians is not a favor to them". It was rather given "largely because the structures that are kept in place—aid and security cooperation—serve Israeli and American interests." It was for this reason that the Obama administration requested that the Congress unblock the funds. "We think it is money that it not only in the interests of the Palestinians," explained State Department spokeswoman Victoria Nuland, "it's in US interests and it's also in Israeli interests."[94]

Mustafa Barghouti responded that Palestinians would not "sell our freedom for some aid" and would "need to find ways to be self-reliant rather than dependent on foreign aid".[95] This, unfortunately, was easier said than done while Palestine remained under the thumb of the occupying regime.

In the end, the matter of Palestine's membership in the UN remained in committee and was never brought to a vote in the Security Council.

Palestine's UNESCO Membership

Under Article 4 of the UN Charter, "membership in the United Nations will be effected by a decision of the General Assembly upon the recommendation of the Security Council."[96] While Palestine's request for the Council to do so was held up in committee, the PA unexpectedly issued a request to be admitted into the UN Educational, Scientific and Cultural Organization (UNESCO).[97]

UNESCO was established under Article 22 of the UN Charter, which authorizes the General Assembly to "establish such subsidiary organs as it deems necessary for the performance of its functions". According to UNESCO's Constitution, states that are not members of the UN may be admitted into UNESCO upon recommendation of its Executive Board and by a two-thirds majority vote of the agency's General Conference. On November 30, 2011, UNESCO's Executive Board agreed by a vote of forty to four to recommend that the General Conference admit Palestine as a member (there were fourteen abstentions; the US, needless to say, along with Germany, Latvia, and Romania, voted in opposition).[98] A successful membership bid would allow Palestine to benefit from UNESCO's protection of its historical sites, including in East Jerusalem.[99]

This was yet another "dangerous Palestinian scheme", cried Representative Ros-Lehtinen, who unnecessarily urged the Obama administration to oppose it, as well as to "make clear" that if Palestine was admitted, the US would cut off funds to UNESCO. "Unfortunately", grumbled Secretary of State Clinton, "there are those who, in their enthusiasm to recognize the aspirations of the Palestinian people, are skipping over the most important step, which is determining what the state will look like, what its borders are, how it will deal with the myriad issues that states must address"—none of which issues had prevented the US sixty-three years earlier from recognizing the state of Israel only *minutes* after the Zionist leadership unilaterally declared its existence without defined borders and mostly on land they had no rights to.[100]

The US prepared to cut off its share of funding for UNESCO, which amounted to 22 percent of the organization's annual budget, on the basis of two laws from the 1990s. Public Law 101-246 (1990) prohibited funds "for the United Nations or any specialized agency thereof which accords the Palestine Liberation Organization the same standing as member states." Public Law 103-236 (1994) stated that the US "shall not make any voluntary or assessed contribution . . . to any affiliated organization of the United Nations which grants full membership as a state to any organization or group that does not have the internationally recognized attributes of statehood". State Department lawyers, the *New York Times* reported, "see no way around the laws"—even though the PLO had been removed from the State Department's list of foreign terrorist organizations in 1994 and most countries, as well as international organizations like the UN, IMF, and World Bank, considered Palestine to have met the requirements for statehood.[101]

On October 31, the General Conference voted to admit Palestine as a member by a vote of 107 in favor and 14 opposed (with 52 abstentions).[102] As the Israeli delegate grumpily voiced his "no" vote, there was laughter in the room. When the votes were tallied and the decision declared, the room erupted in sustained applause, with most delegates present rising to their feet to rejoice Palestine's new membership in UNESCO.[103]

Hanan Ashrawi, a member of the PLO's Executive Committee, described the UNESCO vote as "a significant victory" that "sends a clear message to those who are trying to hold history and deny the rights of Palestinians that there are a majority of nations with conscience who refuse to be intimidated and blackmailed". Those who voted against Palestine's membership were "isolating themselves along with Israel on the wrong side of justice and the law."[104]

Israel's ambassador to the organization, Nimrod Barkan, lamented the vote as "a tragedy for UNESCO" and "a great disservice to international law". Netanyahu complained that while Israel was "trying to form a Palestinian state with a peace agreement", the Palestinians were "trying to form a state without an agreement"—an agreement being something the Zionists hadn't cared too much about sixty-three years prior when they established their "Jewish state" by cleansing the land of most of its Arab population. The Prime Minister immediately convened a meeting of senior ministers to consider how to punish the Palestinians for their insubordination. Among the ideas considered, according to *Haaretz*, were "cancelling the VIP status of senior Palestinian officials which enables them to cross through Israeli checkpoints, increasing settlement construction, and halting the transfer of tax money which Israel collects for the Palestinian Authority."[105]

Victoria Nuland expressed the US State Department's view that the vote was "regrettable, premature and undermines our shared goal of a comprehensive just and lasting peace in the Middle East." White House spokesman Jay Carney repeated the same talking point. US Ambassador to the UN Susan Rice denounced the vote as "deeply damaging to UNESCO." Representative Ros-Lehtinen deplored it as a "reckless action" that was "anti-Israel and anti-peace" because it rewarded the Palestinians for their "dangerous scheme". The US must take "strong action", she urged, "to deter other UN bodies from following in UNESCO's footsteps, and to prevent US taxpayer dollars from paying for biased entities at the UN"[106] Former Secretary of State Condoleezza Rice sniped that if the UN wanted "to go down this road, let them see how well they do without US support."[107]

As promised, the Obama administration cut off funding to UNESCO. While the US said it would remain a member, the decision meant that it would lose its voting privileges in the General Conference. The cutoff meant a shortfall of $80 million out of UNESCO's general 2011 budget of $643 million, which affected programs deemed in the US government's own interests, such as water resource management, education, and literacy training projects in Iraq and Afghanistan. "The ramifications are serious," said the American former head of the UNESCO office for Iraq, George Papagiannis. "The larger issue is how a law has undermined our capacity to deliver in a place very critical to American interests. We've invested gazillions of dollars in Iraq, and we can't put a price on the lives of the Americans and Iraqis who died, and we promised to help build a new Iraq, something fresh and new in the Middle East, and then we hamstrung ourselves."[108]

On November 1, Israel announced that it would accelerate its housing construction in the West Bank and East Jerusalem to punish the Palestinians. Victoria Nuland said the US was "deeply disappointed" by the announcement and continued to make its opposition to settlements clear to Israel. When one reporter pressed Nuland about what the US was actually *doing* to make this clear and pointed out that the $3 billion in annual military aid gave the administration "leverage", Nuland snapped, "I think we're engaged in a policy polemic here rather than questions for the podium." When a follow-up question was asked about the US being unwilling to use its influence, Nuland responded, "I don't think that anybody here believes you can bludgeon parties to the peace table. That is not the exercise that we're engaged in"—which must certainly have come as news to the Palestinians. Nuland explained the cutoff of funding for UNESCO by saying the administration "obviously" had to "comply with US law". Equally obvious, the White House just *had* to violate the spirit, if not the letter, of the Foreign Assistance Act, the US Arms Export Control Act, and the Leahy Law by continuing to provide military assistance to Israel despite its egregious record of human rights abuses and violations of international law. The US government certainly wouldn't want to "bludgeon" Israel, after all, by obeying its own laws and professed moral principles. Different standards had to apply, owing to the US's "special relationship" with the "Jewish state".[109]

In addition to announcing more settlement construction, Israel tried to further bludgeon the Palestinians by withholding more than $100 million in taxes it owed to the PA, despite protests from Israel's Defense Ministry. An aide to Netanyahu told the *New York Times* that Israel was "trying to send a clear message" to the Palestinians. Ever merciful, Israel would release the money once the Palestinians started showing more obedience to their masters by pledging not to try to join other UN agencies. To release the money would not be an entirely selfless deed for Israel, however. As Ethan Bronner illuminated, "it is widely agreed in the Israeli military establishment that a functioning Palestinian Authority is in Israel's interest because, without it, Israel would have to police and provide civilian services to millions of Palestinians."[110]

By the end of the month, Israel released the money with the explanation that the PA had "stopped taking unilateral moves", but also with the warning: "If the Palestinians return to taking unilateral steps, we will weigh again the transfer of funds."[111]

On November 3, there was a meeting of the Group of Twenty (G-20), a forum for the governments and central banks of major economic powers, following which there occurred another "hiccup" in the US-Israeli relationship. A diplomatic row broke out when Obama, following a G-20 press conference, scolded French President Sarkozy for not warning him that France would vote in favor of Palestine's UNESCO membership. Obama thought he was having a private conversation, but unbeknownst to the two presidents, their microphones were still on. Sarkozy was overheard expressing his frustration that Israel had decided to accelerate settlement construction even after he had gone out on a limb for the country with his effort to head off a vote in the Security Council, as well as to condition France's support for a vote in the General Assembly on a demand that would defeat the purpose, as far as the Palestinians were concerned. He told Obama that he could not stand Netanyahu and called the Israeli leader "a liar." Obama sympathetically replied, "You're fed up with him, but I have to deal with him every day!" But it wasn't Israel's penchant for violating international law that primarily concerned Obama. His instructions for the French president were, "You have to pass the message along to the Palestinians that they must stop this immediately."[112]

Naturally, the overheard conversation was regarded as scandalous for all the wrong reasons. In keeping with the dominant narrative, it was deemed yet more proof that Obama was not supportive enough of Israel. The pro-Israel Anti-Defamation League (ADL) said the incident was "decidedly unpresidential". The group's national director, Abraham Foxman, hoped the Obama administration would do "everything it can to reassure Israel" that the US-Israeli relationship was "on a sure footing".[113] Elliot Abrams wailed that Obama had disgracefully "joined the chorus of assaults on the Jewish state".[114] Mitt Romney issued a statement condemning Obama's "derisive remarks" about Netanyahu, which "confirm what any observer would have gleaned from his public statements and actions toward our longstanding ally, Israel. At a moment when the Jewish state is isolated and under threat, we cannot have an American president who is disdainful of our special relationship with Israel."[115]

Israeli officials once more attempted to set the record straight. "You know, when I judge by his actions," informed President Shimon Peres, "he really has shown friendship. I don't judge a person just by what he says, but rather by what he does. And so in fact he was friendly to Israel and we appreciate it."[116] Ehud Barak assured that Obama's devotion to Israel's security was unquestionable. Indeed, Obama was an "extremely strong supporter of Israel" and was "excelling" at "taking care of its security needs."[117]

What that implied for the security needs of *the Palestinians* was, as ever, something neither US government officials nor mainstream media commentators could be bothered to contemplate.

'A Lost Year'

In October 2011, Israel and Hamas announced an agreement for the release of Gilad Shalit, the Israeli soldier captured in 2006, in exchange for more than 1,000 Palestinian prisoners.[118] The prisoner swap deal was supported by an overwhelming majority of Israelis, according to polls. The Netanyahu government agreed to it after intense campaigning on the part of Gilad's parents, Noam and Aviva Shalit. Upon his release, Gilad told Egyptian state television, "I hope this deal will help with the conclusion of a peace deal with the Israelis and Palestinians and I hope that cooperation links between the two sides will be consolidated."[119]

Around 200 of the released Palestinian prisoners would not be permitted to return to their homes in the West Bank. Instead, they would be sent to Gaza—and thus from one imprisonment to another. Others were to be completely exiled from Palestine, most of them permanently. According to Israel, most of the prisoners were convicted of manslaughter, attempted murder, or homicide. However, many had been convicted in Israeli military trials on the basis of secret evidence, and many others were being held without charge.[120] As Human Rights Watch has pointed out, "Israel's international legal obligations require it to inform those arrested of the reasons for the arrest at the time, to promptly inform them of any charges against them, and to bring them before a judge, and in criminal cases, to provide a fair and public trial in which the defendant may challenge any witnesses against them." Furthermore, Israel's practice of removing Palestinians from the West Bank and imprisoning them in Israel, as well as its practice of expelling detainees to Gaza instead of returning them to the West Bank, were in violation of the Geneva Conventions.[121]

The United Nations Children's Fund appealed to Israel to also release all 164 Palestinian children who were then being held in Israeli military detention, mostly on charges of stone throwing. While Palestinian children from East Jerusalem were tried in civil courts, those from elsewhere in the West Bank were tried in military courts. "Juvenile justice standards are clear", said Radhika Coomaraswamy, UN special representative for children in armed conflict: "children should not be tried before military tribunals." UNICEF spokesperson Catherine Weibel pointed out that it was also a violation of Article 76 of the Fourth Geneva Convention to remove children under military occupation from occupied territory. Article 76 states, "Protected persons accused of offences shall be detained in the occupied country, and if convicted they shall serve their sentences therein."[122]

According to Hamas official Mahmoud Zahar, who was a member of the negotiating team, Israel had also agreed as part of the deal to ease the blockade of Gaza. An Israeli official denied any agreement to cease its collective punishment.[123] A *Haaretz* editorial criticized Israel's unwillingness to end its "arbitrary restrictions on the entry of consumer goods". In addition to calling for an end to the siege, *Haaretz* called on the Israeli government to engage with Hamas and put an end to assassinations and airstrikes.[124]

The *New York Times* covered the news of Shalit's release in its customary manner. Some historical context was obviously needed, so the *Times* recounted how an earlier ceasefire between Israel and Hamas "endured on and off until late 2008, when clashes broke out between Hamas and the IDF along the Gaza border." Then, "after the cease-fire was broken, Israel launched Operation Cast Lead".[125]

The US presidential candidates continued to try to outdo each other in professing their devotion to Israel and support for its criminal policies. "Support for Israel has become something of a litmus test for evangelical Christians in early voting states", the *New York Times* observed.[126] "One reason Republicans seek to sound serious on Israel is to appeal to evangelical Christians", in addition to "Jewish voters", the *Times* also noted. The headline informed, "GOP Candidates, at Jewish Coalition, Pledge to Be Israel's Best Friends".[127] Candidate Rick Santorum was eager enough for votes to declare that "all the people who live in the West Bank are Israeli; they're not Palestinians. There is no 'Palestinian.' This is Israeli land."[128] Newt Gingrich tried to one-up Santorum by saying that they were "an *invented* Palestinian people" who "had a chance to go many places" very early on. They should have taken that opportunity to leave their homes and their land to make room for "the Jewish people", who, unlike invented peoples, "have the right to have a state".[129] When his comments were raised during a presidential debate, he defended them as "factually correct" and "historically true".[130] This prompted commendations from others equally proud of their bigotry. "I jumped up out of my chair and cheered for Newt", former New York City mayor Rudolph Giuliani exulted on *Fox News*. Guiliani added that it was not in "the interest of the United States of America" for the Palestinians to exercise self-determination.[131]

As for historical truth, Gingrich was appealing to the ignorance of the substantial population of conservative Christian Zionists by mindlessly parroting racist Zionist propaganda dating to before Israel's existence. In May 1918, as previously noted, Chaim Weizmann contended in a letter to Lord Arthur Balfour that "the democratic principle" must be applied to Palestine to resolve the growing conflict between Jews and Arabs. There were "five Arabs to one Jew", so "the brutal numbers operate against us", and the "present state of affairs would necessarily tend towards the creation of an Arab Palestine, if there were an Arab people in Palestine." His meaning was not that there were no Arabs inhabiting the land. He had, after all, just acknowledged that they were a large majority. Rather, he meant that they didn't meet the criteria for a "people". Hence their right to self-determination could be denied under this racist and colonialist application of "the democratic principle".[132] In 1936, David Ben-Gurion, head of the Labor faction of the Zionist movement, similarly declared that "there is no conflict between Jewish and Palestinian nationalism because the Jewish Nation is not in Palestine and the Palestinians are not a nation."[133] It was this racist sentiment Prime Minister Golda Meir was invoking when she infamously remarked in 1969, "It was not as though there was a Palestinian people in Palestine considering itself as a Palestinian people and we came and threw them out and took their country away from them. They did not exist."[134]

On December 19, 2011, the UN General Assembly voted on its annual resolution reaffirming "The right of the Palestinian people to self-determination". It was adopted by a vote of 182 to 7. The US and Israel were joined in their rejectionism by Canada, the Marshall Islands, Micronesia, Nauru, and Palau.[135]

At the same time, the US blocked a Security Council statement condemning another Israeli announcement of plans to expand settlements. In lieu of a Security Council statement, the EU members of the Council (the UK, France, Germany, and Portugal) issued a joint statement demanding an end to all settlement activity, including in East Jerusalem, which activity was "illegal under international law".[136] When asked whether the Obama administration concurred with the joint statement, Victoria Nuland's casual reply was that the US "declined to join that statement for all the usual reasons". While it was the US's "longstanding policy" not to recognize the "legitimacy" of Israeli settlements, "shouting from the rooftops of the Security Council is not going to change the situation on the ground". A reporter wondered why this was true for Israel, but not countries like Syria, Libya, Yemen, North Korea and elsewhere, where "screaming and yelling at the Security Council" was deemed "a good thing" by the US. Nuland enlightened the reporter, without feeling it necessary to elaborate, that the situation with Israel was "different".[137]

The siege of Gaza persisted. In November, peace activists planned to sail two ships to Gaza: the Irish vessel *Saoirse*, Gaelic for "Freedom", and the Canadian *Tahrir*, Arabic for "Liberation". The US State Department again threatened American citizens with criminal penalties if they participated, while the Canadian government dutifully took Washington's cue to also warn its own citizens not to challenge the existing order. On November 4, the ships were hijacked and the twenty-seven civilians on board were kidnapped, taken under threat of force to Ashdod.[138]

In the *New York Times*, Isabel Kershner educated Americans about the legality of the blockade by relaying Israel's position that it was "in accordance with international law" and asserting that this was "backed up by the Palmer report". That, in the judgment of Kershner and her editors, was all *Times* readers needed to know about the matter.[139]

On March 22, 2012, the UN Human Rights Council voted to create an independent international fact-finding mission "to investigate the implications of the Israeli settlements on the civil, political, economic, social and cultural rights of the Palestinian people throughout the Occupied Palestinian Territory, including East Jerusalem."[140] There was only one vote against the resolution. Denouncing it as "one-sided and biased", Susan Rice cursed that it wouldn't help to achieve peace. Netanyahu denounced the Council as "hypocritical" and

said it "should be ashamed of itself". Announcing that Israel would not cooperate with the investigation, Israel's Foreign Ministry expressed its defiance by
ordering its ambassador to the UN to ignore phone calls from the Chief Commissioner of the UN Human Rights Council, Navi Pillay.[141] The US pressured
Pillay to delay the establishment of the fact-finding mission.[142]

At the end of the month, the Defense Ministry's Civil Administration released maps of its plans for the West Bank. *Haaretz* reported that in some places, parcels allotted to Jewish settlements coincided with the route of the illegal
wall. This suggested the wall was not "based on Israel's security needs", as Israel
had argued to the ICJ, but rather "intended to increase the area and population
of the settlements." The total land area marked for settlement expansion on
the maps amounted to about 10 percent of the West Bank, mostly classified as
"state lands".[143]

In April, the ICC turned down a longstanding request from the PA to investigate accusations of Israeli war crimes during Operation Cast Lead on the
grounds that it had no jurisdiction to do so until either the UN or the ICC's
Assembly of State Parties made a legal determination that Palestine qualified as
a state for the purposes of acceding to the Rome Statute, the Court's founding
treaty. That, of course, was an outcome the US and Israel were determined to
prevent.[144]

On April 11, the Quartet issued a statement describing Israel's "continued
settlement activity" as being among "unilateral and provocative actions by either party"—thus drawing equivalence between Palestinian appeals for recognition of their rights and Israeli violations of international law. The statement
asserted that such actions "cannot prejudge the outcome of negotiations". Then
it rendered that meaningless, insofar as it applied to Israel, by declaring that
talks under the existing framework—in which international law was deemed
immaterial and Palestinians' rights subject to negotiation—were "the only way
to a just and durable solution to the conflict."[145]

In the US House of Representatives, a bill was passed stating, "It is the
policy of the United States: (1) To reaffirm the enduring commitment of the
United States to the security of the State of Israel as a Jewish state. . . . (2) To
provide Israel the military capabilities necessary to deter and defend itself by
itself against any threats. (3) To veto any one-sided anti-Israel resolutions at
the United Nations Security Council."[146] Congressman Ron Paul, one of only
two representatives to vote against the bill, opposed it as "another piece of one-
sided and counterproductive foreign policy legislation" that "undermines US
diplomatic efforts by making clear that the US is not an honest broker seeking
peace for the Middle East."[147] While that bill was never passed by the Senate,
an alternative version containing the same declarations of policy was passed and
signed by President Obama into Public Law 112-150.[148]

US media coverage of Israel's colonization continued to mislead, such as news reports that Israel had "legalized" settlement outposts. This referred to residences that settlers had initially established without authorization from the Israeli government, but which the government later gave its stamp of approval for. The US media consistently referred to these as having been "legalized" despite the fact that they remained illegal under international law. Instead of properly informing its audience of this, the *New York Times* falsely suggested that the question of their legality was controversial by saying there was "disagreement over the basic facts" because the "international community broadly views settlement in the West Bank as illegal".[149] The *Washington Post* similarly reported that Palestinians "view the housing developments as Israeli land-grabbing" and "most foreign governments consider all settlements illegal".[150] Neither the *Times* nor the *Post* named any of the countries that dissented from the view that Israel's settlements violate international law—which was not too surprising an omission for the simple reason that *there weren't any.*

Reconciliation between Hamas and Fatah remained elusive. The previous year, there was an agreement in Egypt to hold presidential and legislative elections. In February 2012, talks in Qatar led to an agreement to follow through with the elections. Ever supportive of democracy in the Arab world, the US warned that if a unity government was formed with Hamas, aid would be cut off.[151] In May, Hamas and Fatah signed yet another agreement in Cairo that would ostensibly pave the way for the long-delayed elections.[152]

On June 13, Isabel Kershner reminded *Times* readers once more all they needed to know about Israel's naval blockade of Gaza: Israel said it was legal, and "a United Nations panel" agreed.[153] The next day, fifty international aid groups, including seven UN organizations, issued the statement, "For over five years in Gaza, more than 1.6 million people have been under blockade in violation of international law. More than half of these people are children. We the undersigned say with one voice: 'End the blockade now.'" Signatories included Amnesty International, CARE International, Christian Aid, Oxfam, and Save the Children, as well the UN Humanitarian Coordination/Resident Coordinator of the occupied Palestinian territory, the OHCHR, UNICEF, UNESCO, UNRWA, United Nations Women, and the WHO. The Associated Press had a sixteen-paragraph wire story about it; the *New York Times* ran with it—after abridging it down to two.[154]

On June 18, Islamic militants from Egypt attacked Israeli construction workers building a security fence along the border, killing Said Fashapshe, an Arab Israeli. Two of the attackers were also killed. Israel responded by launching airstrikes into Gaza, claiming that the attack was planned from there. At least eight people, including a fourteen-year-old boy, were killed in the strikes. Hamas's military wing, the Izz ad-Din al-Qassam Brigades, retaliated by launching rockets into Israel. The group issued a statement on Twitter claiming responsibility for the rocket fire and condemning Israel's "aggression against our people in Gaza Strip", including most recently, "the airstrikes that targeted police stations and other areas, [which] resulted in killing a child in Khan Younis city and wounding many other civilians." The BBC noted that it was "unusual" for Hamas to have participated in rocket attacks. The group had "largely refrained from carrying out attacks" since it declared a ceasefire following Operation Cast Lead. It was the first rocket fire from Hamas in over a year.[155]

Having declined to press its membership bid to a vote in the Security Council, the PA decided instead to go the General Assembly to seek an upgrade of status to non-member observer state. US Secretary of State Hillary Clinton reportedly warned Abbas in Paris that if a bid was submitted before the US presidential election in November, the administration would cut off aid. Abbas agreed, which meant the Palestinians would lose the opportunity to bring the matter to a vote during the General Assembly's annual General Debate in New York in September.[156]

The campaign season wore on, with Mitt Romney emerging as the presumptive Republican nominee. Speaking to an AIPAC conference in March, Romney vowed never to call for Israel to withdraw from the occupied territories.[157] In June, he said that in order to formulate his own Middle East policy, he would "just look at the things the president has done and do the opposite".[158]

An Obama campaign spokesman responded by requesting Romney to be more specific, appropriately wondering whether that meant Romney would let Israel "stand alone" at the UN and reverse the policy of sending Israel "the largest security assistance packages in history".[159] A clearly delusional Romney next insisted that Obama, "to the enthusiastic applause of Israel's enemies," had spoken to the General Assembly "as if our closest ally in the Middle East was the problem". Obama had joined in "the chorus of accusations, threats, and insults" against Israel at the UN. A more sober Vice President Joe Biden set the record straight that Obama had "stood up repeatedly, publicly and often alone" in the UN against efforts to hold Israel accountable for its violations of international law ("to delegitimize Israel", in Biden's parlance).[160]

On July 27, Obama signed into law the US-Israel Enhanced Security Cooperation Act, which, among other things, made it explicit policy that the US would veto any Security Council resolutions critical of Israel. Observers suggested the timing of the signing was intended "to upstage" Romney, who had planned to arrive in Jerusalem the following day. Michael Oren expressed Israel's "profound gratitude" to Obama for signing the bill, and various Jewish American organizations, including the National Jewish Democratic Council and the Orthodox Union, joined in the praise. Romney countered by accusing Obama of "evasiveness" for not clarifying whether he "recognizes Jerusalem as the capital of Israel".[161]

In his quest for votes, Romney traveled to Jerusalem, where he held a fund-raiser attended by settler leaders, former Netanyahu aides, American citizens living in Israel, and American Jews who flew from the US for the event (including billionaire Sheldon Adelson). The press was barred from the event. A common ritual for US politicians, he also visited the Western Wall, where he wore a yarmulke and participated in the Jewish tradition of inserting a prayer note into a crack between the stones.[162] In a speech before the backdrop of the walls of the Old City, Romney said it was "a deeply moving experience to be in Jerusalem," which he called "the capital of Israel." He praised Israel's economy by comparing its gross domestic product (GDP) with that of the West Bank. He had studied the reasons for the economic disparity, and it was clear to him that, "Culture makes all the difference. Culture makes all the difference." Culture, the "hand of providence", and "the human spirit" of "a species created in the image of God" were his explanations for why the West Bank was not as prosperous as Israel.[163]

"It is a racist statement," Saeb Erekat replied. He reminded Romney that "the Palestinian economy cannot reach its potential because there is an Israeli occupation."[164] A *New York Times* editorial slammed Romney for gratuitously insulting the Palestinians "by declaring that cultural differences—not decades under Israeli occupation—are the reason Israelis are more successful economically."[165] Romney's bigotry also compelled Thomas L. Friedman to put in a good word for the Palestinians. Had Romney visited Ramallah, "he would have seen a Palestinian beehive of entrepreneurship, too, albeit small, but not bad for a people living under occupation."[166] Zahi Khouri, a Palestinian American, wrote in the *Washington Post*, "If Romney had any historical perspective, he would dispose of his racist judgments about Palestinian culture and instead imagine our potential without Israel's imposed hindrances."[167]

At a September fundraiser in Florida, an unapologetic Romney accused the Palestinians of having "no interest whatsoever in establishing peace". Moreover, suggestions that the US should pressure Israel to cease its violations of international law ("to give something up", as he put it) was "the worst idea in the world."[168]

Saeb Erekat replied, "No one stands to gain more from peace than the Palestinians, and no one stands to lose from the absence of peace like the Palestinians." It was people like Romney who tolerated Israel's continued occupation who were "working against democracy and peace".[169]

Romney's vice-presidential running mate, Representative Paul Ryan, was also deemed "a strong supporter of Israel" (*Israel National News*).[170] On his official website, Ryan listed "Israel" under matters of "Homeland Security". His "first priority" was "keeping America safe", which included such deeds as co-sponsoring the United States-Israel Strategic Partnership Act, as well as a bill to collectively punish the civilian population of Iran for their government's disobedience in refusing to surrender their "inalienable right" under the NPT to enrich uranium for civilian purposes.[171]

The Romney-Ryan campaign, however, just couldn't compete with Obama-Biden for the votes of Americans supportive of Israel's crimes against the Palestinians. At *Foreign Policy*, Colin H. Kahl quipped that Romney's attacks on Obama were "a kind of election-year Jedi mind trick".[172] In a *New York Times* op-ed, Haim Saban, an Israeli American and a founder of the Saban Center for Middle East Policy at the Brookings Institution, extolled how Obama, unlike his Republican predecessor, had never opposed Israeli settlements by withholding loan guarantees. On the contrary, he had "increased aid to Israel and given it access to the most advanced military equipment, including the latest fighter aircraft". Obama had also thankfully blocked the Palestinians' attempts to seek international recognition of their right to self-determination. Had he not done so, critics of Israel's violations of international law ("Israel's foes") would have been able to hold it accountable for its crimes ("criminalize its policies"). To protect Israel, Obama had "even vetoed a Security Council resolution on Israeli settlements". "When I enter the voting booth," Saban concluded, "I'm going to ask myself, what do I prefer for Israel and its relationship with the United States: meaningful action or empty rhetoric? To me the answer is clear: I'll take another four years of Mr. Obama's steadfast support over Mr. Romney's sweet nothings."[173] Romney's charges against Obama for not being pro-Israel enough "don't seem to be helping garner Jewish support for the Republican candidate", observed *Haaretz*. A Gallup poll showed that 70 percent of Jewish voters planned to vote for Obama and only 25 percent for Romney.[174]

Looking more broadly at Americans' views on the topic, only 40 percent thought that the US should have a neutral policy on the conflict. Four percent wanted the US to lean toward Palestine while 29 percent wanted the government to favor Israel—a number that rose to 50 percent among Republicans. Only 34 percent supported the right of Palestinians to return or receive compensation for being "forced to leave Israel as a result of the 1948 war". Only 32 percent thought the US government should try to stop Israel's expansion of settlements. An astonishing 31 percent did not agree that "Israelis and Palestinians are equal people entitled to equal rights".[175]

The Obama administration continued its effort to get the Palestinians to return to the "peace process". Dennis Ross, who had resigned as Obama's National Security Adviser on the Middle East in November 2011, proposed a twelve-step plan that explicitly endorsed continued construction in major settlement blocks that Israel was "expected to retain". Israel was "expected to retain" the settlements, of course, by virtue of the fact that the Palestinians' acquiescence to the theft of their land was one of the US and Israel's preconditions for negotiations.[176]

In August, UNRWA published a report titled "Gaza in 2020: A liveable place?" It concluded that without an end to Israel's illegal blockade, the answer was negative. The *New York Times* ran a story on it by Isabel Kershner, who naturally withheld from readers the fact that the blockade was illegal. On the other hand, she relayed Israel's position that it was "necessary to prevent the smuggling of weapons".[177]

Breaking the Silence also released another report of soldiers' testimonies about the harsh treatment of Palestinian children in the occupied West Bank, including harassment, humiliation, physical violence, child arrests, cruel treatment of children in custody, and the use of children as human shields. The report received headline attention internationally. It went unmentioned in the US.[178]

Abbas affirmed that the PA would submit an application for an upgrade of status at the General Assembly on September 27, but would not seek a vote until after the US presidential election in November. "Blackmail is how I'd put it impolitely," said PLO Executive Committee member Dr. Hanan Ashrawi about the decision on the timing. "I don't know what else to call it when you are told Congress will suspend all funding for the Palestinians, suspend all relations with us and close our representative's office in Washington."[179]

Abbas once again found himself facing criticism at home for bowing to the US and Israel's demands instead of adamantly pursuing Palestinians' rights through the legitimate mechanisms available to him. "There is no Palestinian leadership," criticized Omar Barghouti, a prominent activist for the growing BDS movement. Describing the lack of a unity government with Hamas as Abbas's biggest failure, political analyst and economist Omar Shabban wrote, "He should go today. In fact he should have gone yesterday."[180] The Palestinian leadership had "wasted a whole year" since the UNESCO victory, lamented Nabil Shaath, "and that waste cost us a lot in the circumstances of our people, in the support of our people." It was, said Shaath, a "lost year". In the face of pressures from abroad and criticisms at home, Abbas once again threatened to resign and to abandon Oslo altogether, thus implying he might dissolve the PA. But he was just "posturing", recognized a former legal adviser for the Palestinian negotiating team, who told the *New York Times*, "The threat of canceling Oslo is always a reactionary threat, just the same way that Abbas is always threatening to quit."[181]

Appealing for support for the new UN bid, PLO Executive Committee member Hanan Ashrawi described it as a "test of global consensus and rule of law". In addition to political support, the Palestinians were also in need of a financial "safety net" in case the US cut off aid.[182]

Deputy Israeli Prime Minister Dan Meridor counseled that a successful UN bid would be fruitless. "Nothing will change on the ground", he cursed.[183]

Saeb Erekat answered, "Yes, occupation will continue, settlements will continue, the crimes of settlers may continue. But there will be consequences."[184]

Netanyahu's chief spokesman Mark Regev needlessly reminded that for the Palestinians to gain access to international bodies like the ICC was "not what we had in mind."[185]

At the UN General Debate

On September 25, 2012, President Obama addressed the General Assembly during the General Debate at the UN headquarters in New York. He devoted much of his speech to the message that "this violence and intolerance has no place among our United Nations." But what he was referring to, specifically, was the killing two weeks before of Ambassador Chris Stevens by terrorists in Benghazi, Libya, where the US had overthrown the government by waging a bombing campaign in support of armed rebels whose ranks included Islamic extremist groups. With Western assistance, the rebels on October 20, 2011, captured Libyan leader Muammar al-Gaddafi and executed him in cold blood.[186]

Obama also preached the message of the "universal values" of "freedom and self-determination". Specifically, he was referring again to NATO's bombing of Libya in the name of "freedom", as well as the situation in Syria, where the US was once more engaged in regime change by backing armed rebels whose ranks included Islamic extremist organizations.[187] The CIA was coordinating the flow of arms from Gulf countries Saudi Arabia and Qatar to the rebel forces, with the Al-Qaeda affiliated Jabhat al-Nusra taking on a key role as "one of the uprising's most effective fighting forces", as the *New York Times* described the group.[188] As the *Times* reported in October 2012, most of the arms funneled to the rebels ended up in the hands of the "hard-line Islamic jihadists".[189]

Obama dedicated one paragraph of his speech to the Israeli-Palestinian conflict, condemning "those who reject the right of Israel to exist" and again endorsing Netanyahu's precondition that the Palestinians must recognize Israel as a "Jewish state".[190]

Mahmoud Abbas in his own speech on September 27 minced no words, condemning "the racist Israeli settlement" of Palestine and escalation of settler attacks on Palestinians and their property. In occupied East Jerusalem, "a campaign of ethnic cleansing against the Palestinian people" was underway. Israel's rejection of the two-state solution was evident from its actions. Instead, what Israel envisioned as the outcome of negotiations was a series of "small Palestinian enclaves surrounded by large Israeli settlement blocs and walls, checkpoints and vast security zones and roads devoted to the settlers." While the Palestinians' bid in the Security Council the previous year had been unsuccessful, the Palestinians would continue to pursue UN membership. The next step to that end would be for the General Assembly to adopt a resolution upgrading Palestine's status to non-member state.[191]

Taking his turn at the podium, Netanyahu preferred to use the opportunity to distract attention from the Palestine issue with melodramatic fearmongering about the supposed "threat" from Iran's nuclear program, complete with invocation of the Holocaust and a cartoon drawing of a bomb showing different levels of uranium enrichment on which he drew a symbolic "red line" at weapons-grade enrichment with a marker. He did allow time in his speech, however, for answering Abbas's address to the Assembly by calling it "libelous" and insisting once more that the Palestinians must negotiate away their right to collective self-defense and recognize Israel as "the one and only Jewish State."[192]

While world leaders were gathered in New York for the UN General Debate, the US issued a memorandum to European governments urging them to stand in opposition to the Palestinians' General Assembly bid. The memo asserted that UN recognition of the state of Palestine "would be extremely counterproductive" and threatened "significant negative consequences" for the PA, including a cutoff of aid, if it continued its intransigence.[193] The PA fought back, dispatching envoys to European countries to persuade them to vote in favor of Palestine's status upgrade in the General Assembly.[194] On November 11, following an election victory that granted him a second term in office, Obama personally called Abbas to pressure him to abandon the UN bid.[195] US Senators Ben Cardin and Susan Collins sent Abbas a letter reminding him of "significant consequences" for disobeying his overlords.[196] On November 21, Secretary of State Clinton met with Abbas in Ramallah in yet another attempt to get him to drop the bid, all of which ultimately proved futile.[197]

Israel, too, continued its efforts to head off the bid. "We are trying to make the case with all United Nations members that this vote is not what it seems," said Israeli Foreign Ministry spokesman Yigal Palmor. "It is not a vote for Palestinian reconciliation with Israel but for a continuation of the confrontation with Israel by other means."[198] The Foreign Minister's office prepared a draft document suggesting that Israel should overthrow Abbas and dismantle the PA to punish the Palestinians for "breaking the rules".[199] Israel's ambassadors around the world, in coordination with their American counterparts, were instructed to deliver the message that Israel would consider canceling the Oslo Accords. Foreign Minister Lieberman and Finance Minister Yuval Steinitz said that if the bid was successful and the Palestinians approached the ICC, it would constitute "a declaration of war" against Israel.[200]

Former Prime Minister Ehud Olmert, on the other hand, dissented from the government's position and publicly expressed his support for the bid. "I believe," he told journalist Bernard Avishai, "that the Palestinian request from the United Nations is congruent with the basic concept of the two-state solution. Therefore, I see no reason to oppose it. Once the United Nations will lay the foundation for this idea, we in Israel will have to engage in a serious process of negotiations, in order to agree on specific borders based on the 1967 lines, and resolve the other issues. It is time to give a hand to, and encourage, the moderate forces amongst the Palestinians."[201]

The *New York Times*, for its part, disagreed with Olmert and took up the position of the US and Israeli governments. It editorialized that the bid would be good for no one, including the Palestinians, who should avoid punishment from the US and Israel by ceasing their rebellious "unilateral" attempt to gain a status upgrade. The editors continued to insist that the Palestinians could not have a state without the approval of the Israeli government—even while pointing out once more that Netanyahu had "refused to make any serious compromises".[202] At the end of November, the day before the vote in the General Assembly, the editors noted that the resolution was sure to pass; they argued hence that the Obama administration needed to get the Palestinians to return to negotiations and that "Mr. Abbas would be wise to do so."[203] After all, as another *Times* article observed the same day, "A major concern for the Americans is that the Palestinians might use their new status to try to join the International Criminal Court"—and Abbas would surely be unwise to anger his masters by taking a step in that direction.[204]

The date chosen for the vote on the Palestinians' application for an upgrade of status in the General Assembly was November 29, the anniversary of the passage of Resolution 181 in 1947, a day also recognized by the UN since 1977 as the International Day of Solidarity with the Palestinian People.[205]

Operation 'Pillar of Defense'

On November 14, 2012, Israel launched another military operation against the Gaza Strip. Lasting eight days, it was dubbed "Operation Pillar of Defense". Once again, the mainstream media simply parroted Israel's own version of events. The triggering event, according to the government of Israel, was an attack on November 10 by Palestinian militants on an IDF jeep, resulting in the injury of four soldiers.[206] This account was parroted uncritically by mainstream media sources like Reuters, the *Washington Post*, and the journal *Foreign Affairs*. Elsewhere, the media attributed the initiation of violence to various other incidents—but by all accounts, it was the Palestinians who were responsible. To the *New York Times* editors, it was the destruction of another Israeli jeep two days earlier, on November 8. To *Times* columnist Roger Cohen, it began even earlier, on November 3, when Palestinian militants launched rockets at Israel. Frequently, it was deemed unnecessary to pinpoint any one incident. The abridged version preferred by the US government was simply that Israel's operation was in response to weeks of rocket attacks by Palestinian armed groups.

The truth was an entirely other matter. Absent from US mainstream accounts was any mention of the fact that when the jeep was destroyed on November 10, it was an attack on Israeli forces that had invaded Gaza. Nor did the media explain that the November 8 attack, too, was against Israeli forces invading Gaza—much less that it was retaliation for the murder of a thirteen-year-old Palestinian boy by the IDF earlier that morning. Numerous other relevant facts were likewise simply omitted from the narrative presented to the public by government officials and the mainstream media. A closer examination of the context in which Operation Pillar of Defense occurred is warranted.

In March 2012, Israel assassinated a senior leader of the Popular Resistance Committee (PRC), Zuhir Musa Ahmed Qaisi, along with his deputy, Mahmoud Ahmed Mahmoud Hanani. Palestinian armed groups responded by launching over 200 rockets into Israel. Egypt then brokered a ceasefire that held until June, when violence once again erupted.[207] Mid-month, two Grad rockets landed in the Negev desert in Israel. The IDF determined that they were most likely fired from Egypt, although possibly from Jordan.[208] On June 17, three mortars were fired at an IDF patrol that was preparing to enter Gaza.[209] Although Hamas remained committed to the ceasefire, Israel declared that it was holding Hamas responsible for all attacks and launched airstrikes into Gaza.[210]

On Monday, June 18, as previously noted, terrorists operating out of Egypt murdered Said Fashapshe, a thirty-six-year-old Arab Israeli and father of four who was doing contract work for the IDF on the border fence between Israel and Egypt.[211] Israel attributed the attack to an Al-Qaeda inspired Salafist group known as Al-Tawhid wal-Jihad, which had been active in Gaza since 2008.[212] (Salafism is a small sect of fundamentalist Islam that since the 1970s has spread from Saudi Arabia to other countries in the Middle East.[213]) The Salafists in Gaza were no friends of Hamas. The leader of Al-Tawhid wal-Jihad, Hisham al-Saidani, was released from prison in August 2012 after having been arrested by Hamas in March 2011. A month after his arrest, members of the group kidnapped Italian reporter and peace activist Vittorio Arrigoni, threatening to execute him the following afternoon unless Saidani was released. The next morning, Hamas security forces raided the house where Arrigoni was being held, but found him already dead. Hamas followed up with subsequent raids, killing or arresting others involved in the kidnapping.[214]

In response to the cross-border attack from Egypt, Israel again launched airstrikes into Gaza, which continued through the week.[215] As a consequence, for the first time in over a year, Hamas responded by launching rockets into Israel, while also making clear that it was interested in a return to calm. On June 20, after eight Palestinians had been killed in Israeli attacks, Hamas announced that it would commit to an Egyptian-brokered ceasefire.[216] Israel, however, continued its airstrikes, citing continued rocket fire from Salafist militants. "We regard Hamas as fully responsible for everything that is happening in the Gaza area", informed Israeli Civil Defense Minister Matan Vilnai. Although Hamas remained committed to the ceasefire, on June 23, Israel struck Hamas "security targets", killing two and wounding thirty Palestinians. The attack prompted another wave of rocket attacks, one of which injured a factory worker in Sderot. An Israeli security source told Reuters that Salafists were responsible for the rocket fire.[217] The following day, with at least fifteen Palestinians killed since the airstrikes began, Hamas once again declared its commitment to an Egyptian-brokered ceasefire.[218]

Facts notwithstanding, in the US media, the public could read how the recent violence had begun with Hamas rocket fire, which "violated an unofficial truce that had stood since April 2011" and "prompted an Israeli counter-attack that killed up to 15 Palestinians, and that's where it stopped" (*The Atlantic*).[219]

The next "serious escalation"—as it was described to the Security Council by UN Undersecretary-General for Political Affairs Jeffrey Feltman—occurred on October 7, when Israel launched an airstrike into Gaza targeting two men on a motorcycle described by the IDF as "Global Jihad" operatives. One was "a senior operative involved in the planning and execution" of the cross-border attack from Egypt in June, according to the IDF. The attack resulted in the death of one of the men and serious injury to the other. Eight civilians were also killed.[220] Early the next morning, Palestinian armed groups launched rocket and mortar attacks into Israel, damaging a residential building and killing and injuring goats in a petting zoo. For the first time since Hamas declared its commitment to a renewed ceasefire on June 20, the Qassam Brigades claimed responsibility for rocket fire in retaliation for the "Israeli aggression on civilians" the previous evening. Israel in turn struck a mosque with tank fire, injuring five. A second mosque was also targeted, reported the Hamas Interior Ministry, as well as a factory. An IDF spokeswoman confirmed that mosques were targeted, calling them "Hamas posts" without elaboration.[221]

The *New York Times* acknowledged that this "latest flare-up" in violence "began with a missile strike" on Gaza that prompted retaliatory rocket fire. But its headline didn't read "Gaza Militants Launch Rocket Attacks After Airstrikes from Israel". Instead, what any readers skimming headlines took away was "Israel Launches Airstrikes After Attacks From Gaza".[222] The following week, the *Times* again acknowledged that Israel was responsible for initiating this round of violence; but it did so by reporting that the airstrike "killed another militant in Gaza and wounded at least nine others", thus implying that everyone injured was a militant, rather than properly informing readers that eight of them were civilians.[223]

On October 13, Israel assassinated Hisham Saidani, the leader of Al-Tawhid wal-Jihad.[224] Two civilians were also killed in the attack on Saidani, one of them a ten-year-old child. It was described by Jeffrey Feltman to the Security Council as "[a]nother serious escalation".[225] The Meir Amit Intelligence and Terrorism

Information Center assessed that Hamas's view of Saidani's assassination was that "it has rid itself of a tough opponent who refused to obey its 'rules of the game'", such as deliberately attempting "to undermine the ceasefire agreed upon by Hamas and Israel" in January 2009.[226] Hamas's view of the Salafist group was irrelevant, however, to the Israeli government; the IDF issued a statement about the assassination reminding that Israel held Hamas "solely responsible for any terrorist activity emanating from the Gaza Strip."[227]

During ensuing violence, an incident occurred that provides a useful snapshot of the schizophrenic nature of US policy in the region: the IDF confirmed the firing of an SA-7 anti-aircraft missile at an Israeli helicopter operating over Gaza.[228] The Soviet-made SA-7 is among a number of weapons known as man-portable air defense systems, or MANPADS, such as the US-made Stinger missiles provided to the Mujahedeen during the Soviet-Afghan war.[229] According to the IDF, this was the first time an SA-7 was fired in Gaza. However, according to the private Israeli military intelligence publication *DEBKAfile*, an SA-7 smuggled from Libya had been fired on March 10, making this the second time one had been used.[230] *Haaretz* likewise reported that SA-7s had been smuggled into Gaza from Libya, their proliferation being one of the consequences of the US-backed overthrow of the Gaddafi regime.[231]

The SA-7s were also reportedly delivered to Syrian rebels as part of a covert CIA operation.[232] Following Gaddafi's execution, the CIA ran another operation under the cover of the State Department out of the consulate building in Benghazi—the same building where Ambassador Chris Stevens was later killed. "The US effort in Benghazi was at its heart a CIA operation, according to officials briefed on the intelligence", the *Wall Street Journal* reported. A "main concern" of the operation "was the spread of weapons and militant influences throughout the region, including in Mali, Somalia and Syria".[233] Reuters similarly reported that Benghazi was the base of an operation for, "among other things, collecting information on the proliferation of weaponry looted from Libyan government arsenals, including surface-to-air missiles".[234]

But the CIA was evidently not interested in rounding up the weapons to prevent their proliferation. CNN reported that, on the contrary, there was speculation in Congress that "the US agencies operating in Benghazi were secretly helping to move surface-to-air missiles out of Libya, through Turkey, and into the hands of Syrian rebels."[235] Indeed, SA-7s were among the weapons delivered on board a Libyan ship to the Syrian rebels just five days before the killing of Ambassador Stevens on September 11, 2012.[236] According to *Business Insider*, the shipment was organized by the head of the Tripoli Military Council, Abdelhakim Belhadj, who was known to have met with leaders of the Free Syrian Army (FSA) in Turkey with an offer of money and weapons to assist in the overthrow of Bashar al-Assad.[237] As the Obama administration's liaison with the Libyan rebels during the US-NATO campaign, Stevens had worked directly with Belhadj to coordinate the overthrow of Gaddafi.[238] In November, a Syrian helicopter was for the first time brought down by a MANPAD, and analysts expressed concern that the SA-7s from Libya could fall into the hands of the Al-Qaeda affiliated extremists who were among the ranks of the armed rebels being supported by Washington.[239]

In sum, it seems that SA-7s delivered by the US first to Libyan rebels to help overthrow the Gaddafi regime and then to Syrian rebels to overthrow the Assad regime wound up in the hands of extremists in Gaza, who fired them at helicopters of the US's own Middle East partner. The director of Israel's Ministry of Strategic Affairs, Yosef Kuperwasser, acknowledged that large quantities of arms from Libya had been smuggled into Gaza. He also pointed out that Islamic Jihad, not Hamas, was responsible for most rocket attacks and cautioned that an Israeli military operation in Gaza "is not going to really solve the problem. There is a wide and deep problem of hate indoctrination that produces more and more terrorists all the time."[240]

The round of violence initiated by Israel's assassination of Saidani continued through the week. The New York Times acknowledged that Al-Qaeda inspired Salafists were "challenging" Hamas's ceasefire with Israel while Hamas was "working to suppress the more radical Islamic militant groups" in Gaza, such as making arrests and confiscating arms from a group known as Jaish al-Umma. Hamas had "crushed" another Salafist group that went by the name of Jund Ansar Allah in 2009, the Times also noted.[241] Notwithstanding Hamas's long-standing opposition to the Salafist groups, Israel maintained its policy of holding Hamas responsible for all attacks. It wasn't until October 24, after several Hamas members had been killed in Israeli airstrikes, that the Qassam Brigades joined in the rocket fire, which that day wounded three migrant workers and damaged a number of homes.[242]

Israel's siege of Gaza, meanwhile, was unrelenting. On October 20, the Israeli navy hijacked the Estelle in international waters and diverted it to Ashdod. "As Americans," said passenger Robert Naiman (who had sailed on The Audacity of Hope the previous year), "we call on the US government to stop enabling Israeli government violations of international law." The thirty passengers on board the ship included three Israelis and members of parliament from Canada, Norway, Sweden, Greece, and Spain.[243] The IDF said the decision to hijack the ship was made because its civilian passengers "made it clear that they would not cooperate or accept the invitation to sail to the southern port of Ashdod".[244] Passengers reported that Israeli soldiers had used Tasers against them during the hijacking of their ship, while Spokeswoman Avital Leibovich insisted that the IDF had only threatened to use force.[245] Netanyahu praised the IDF for its "efforts in safeguarding the naval blockade of the Gaza Strip in accordance with international law." Since "there is no humanitarian crisis in Gaza", it was clear that the ship's passengers only wanted "to create a provocation and to slander

Israel's name"—a devilish plan that Israel could have easily outwitted, had any of this been true, by simply allowing the ship to uneventfully reach its destination.[246]

Seriously challenging Netanyahu's characterization of the situation, several days before the hijacking of the *Estelle*, a slideshow presentation prepared by the Coordinator of Government Activities in the Territories under the Israeli Ministry of Defense was made public. The document, titled "Food Consumption in the Gaza Strip—Red Lines", noted that the Ministry of Health was "calculating the minimal subsistence" level at which Palestinians could live "without the development of malnutrition." It calculated a target number of calories and then determined how many truckloads of food would be required to maintain subsistence at that level. This worked out on average to be 2,279 calories per person per day. Gisha noted that according to UN data, the number of trucks allowed into Gaza often fell below that required to maintain subsistence at even that level.[247]

Euphemistically describing Israel's collective punishment as "imposing austerity on Gaza", the *Washington Post* observed that the policy was "strongly backed" by the US government.[248]

On October 25, an Egyptian-brokered ceasefire went into effect. Three days later, the IDF launched an airstrike in the city of Khan Younis that killed twenty-seven-year-old Hamas member Suleiman Qarra, whom Israel accused of firing mortars at Israeli troops. Twenty-six rockets were subsequently fired into Israel, causing no injuries.[249]

On November 5, Israeli soldiers shot and killed an unarmed twenty-three-year-old Palestinian man named Ahmad Nabhani. An IDF spokeswoman said he was shot because he ignored warnings not to approach the border fence. But according to Ahmad's older brother, Hazem, "He was sick, he had a mental illness. . . . My brother didn't understand anything. Sometimes you'd speak to him and he wouldn't understand. It is like he wasn't there."[250] After shooting the unarmed mentally ill young man, Israeli forces prevented a Palestinian ambulance from reaching him for two hours. The medics judged that had they been able to give him rapid treatment for his injuries, he might have survived. His death brought the total number of Palestinians killed by Israeli forces in Gaza so far that year to seventy-one. There were at least three additional incidents that week in which Israeli soldiers fired warning shots at Gazan farmers working their own land. The Israeli navy also continued to open fire on fishing boats to force them back to shore.[251]

On November 6, the IDF began regular incursions into Gaza on the pretext of locating and disarming improvised explosive devices (IEDs). Three Israeli soldiers on patrol near the border fence east of Khan Younis were injured when an IED exploded near their vehicle.[252]

On November 8, a number of IDF bulldozers and tanks invaded Gaza on another "patrol". During the incursion, an Israeli helicopter opened fire, killing a thirteen-year-old boy named Hamid Younis Abu Daqqa while he was playing soccer with his friends, three of whom were wounded. Hamid was evacuated to a hospital but pronounced dead fifteen minutes later. The IDF claimed that its forces had been fired upon and returned fire "towards open areas in the vicinity" deemed to be "suspicious locations". But according to witnesses, it was the helicopter attack that sparked an exchange of fire with Palestinian militants.[253] A few hours later, there was another Israeli incursion, again undertaken on the pretext of dismantling explosives. While 200 meters inside Gaza during what the IDF described as "a routine activity", an explosion went off in a tunnel underneath a parked IDF jeep, blasting it into the air and injuring a nearby soldier with shrapnel. Hamas claimed responsibility for the blast as retaliation for the killing of young Hamid.[254]

On November 10, Israeli forces once again invaded Gaza. While operating about 200 meters beyond the fence near the Karni border crossing, they came under fire from an anti-tank missile, which struck another jeep. Four soldiers were wounded, two seriously. The Abu Ali Mustafa Brigades, the armed wing of the Popular Front for the Liberation of Palestine (PFLP), claimed responsibility, but the IDF and media were skeptical and suspected Islamic Jihad. According to the Saudi-owned news network Al Arabiya, the armed wing of Hamas also claimed responsibility, again as retaliation for the murder of Hamid two days before.[255]

The IDF responded to the attack with tank fire and airstrikes. An artillery shell struck a field where children were playing soccer in a neighborhood east of Gaza City, killing two teenage boys and wounding dozens of others. According to the Palestinian Center for Human Rights, when others rushed to the scene to help, the IDF fired additional shells, killing two more teenagers.[256] "Targeting civilians is a dangerous escalation that cannot be tolerated", responded Hamas spokesman Fawzi Barhoum. He added that Israeli soldiers were "legitimate" targets and vowed to retaliate against the "Zionist escalation". At least thirty rockets were fired into Israel, all of which fell into open fields, causing no casualties. Responsibility for the rocket fire was claimed by Islamic Jihad and the PFLP.[257]

The IDF retaliated, killing a local Islamic Jihad commander.[258] Israel's attacks continued through the afternoon and evening. Eleven civilians were injured, including women and children, when a municipal water tank was struck with artillery. East of Gaza City, an office of the Gaza Electricity Distribution Company was shelled and a brick factory was destroyed in an airstrike. Another attack destroyed a metalwork shop, damaging a neighboring home and injuring a woman and her seventeen-year-old son.[259]

Israeli airstrikes continued the following day, with civilian objects such as homes and a poultry farm again coming under fire.[260] Israeli government officials indicated that another major military operation in Gaza was imminent. Cabinet Minister Yisrael Katz called for assassinating Hamas leaders.[261] "Israel must perform a reformatting of Gaza, and rearrange it", said Home Front Defense Minister Avi Dichter, the ostensible goal being to reestablish military deterrence to rocket fire.[262] A spokesperson for the Prime Minister's office briefed the press that Netanyahu was "interested in preparing international public opinion for an Israeli military operation in Gaza"—or "conducting hasbara", as *Haaretz* put it—because "he understands that Israel does not have the international legitimacy to launch an operation in Gaza at the moment."[263]

While Israel was preparing for war, Hamas was preparing for peace. At the request of Hamas officials, Egyptian intelligence officials successfully brokered another ceasefire agreement. Citing senior Egyptian sources, *Ynetnews* reported that "both Hamas and Islamic Jihad have agreed to hold their fire if Israel suspends its airstrike [*sic*] on Gaza."[264] *Yedioth Ahronoth* also reported that the US had given Israel a green light for the planned operation in Gaza and that Netanyahu had convened foreign ambassadors to coordinate the hasbara effort.[265] On November 12, Palestinian militant groups issued a joint statement announcing their agreement to comply with the Egyptian-mediated ceasefire, conditional upon "the end of Israeli aggression" and an end to the illegal blockade. The statement added that the "resistance has a right to respond to any Israeli breach."[266] Ismail Haniyeh praised the main armed factions in Gaza for showing "a high sense of responsibility" by joining Hamas in agreeing to the ceasefire.[267] As a result of Palestinian armed groups committing to the ceasefire, only one rocket was fired into Israel the following day.[268]

The day Palestinian groups agreed to the ceasefire, UN Secretary-General Ban Ki-moon saw fit to issue a statement condemning indiscriminate rocket attacks by Palestinians, but not attacks resulting in the killing of Palestinian civilians by Israel. Instead, the US's Quartet partner essentially provided Israel a green light of his own, calling on its government to merely "exercise maximum restraint" in its operations in Gaza.[269] The media parroted Israel's hasbara narrative; Reuters pinpointed the anti-tank missile attack on the jeep as the initiating event, withholding from readers the fact that the Israeli forces had invaded Gaza, as well as the fact that the IDF had killed a thirteen-year-old Palestinian boy during another incursion two days earlier.[270]

On November 14, Israel commenced its military assault on Gaza, which it dubbed in Hebrew "Operation Pillar of Cloud", an allusion to the biblical story of Moses and the divine cloud that shielded the Israelites from the Pharaoh's army during the exodus from Egypt. Worried that the reference might not be widely understood abroad, Israel gave it the English name of "Operation Pillar of Defense".[271] The Al Mezan Center for Human Rights reported that the initial wave of attacks resulted in sixty-six casualties, mostly civilians, including seven deaths. An airstrike in Zeytoun killed a nineteen-year-old girl and an eleven-month-old baby—the sister-in-law and son, respectively, of a journalist for the BBC Arabic Service. Another young girl, Ranan Arafat, was killed in a separate airstrike in the same neighborhood.[272]

One initial target of Israel's offensive was Hamas commander Ahmed al-Jabari, who was assassinated in a strike on his car. Jabari was the alleged mastermind of the 2006 capture of Gilad Shalit, as well as the leading Hamas official responsible for negotiating Shalit's release. Jabari had made a rare public appearance alongside Shalit when he was freed.[273] Israel's purpose in assassinating him, Netanyahu explained, was to send "a clear message" to Hamas and other armed groups.[274] The IDF posted on Twitter, "We recommend that no Hamas operatives, whether low level or senior leaders, show their faces above ground in the days ahead." IDF spokesman Yoav Mordechai threatened, "If I were a senior Hamas activist, I would look for a place to hide."[275]

In a repeat from the playbook for "Operation Cast Lead", Netanyahu attempted to justify the offensive by saying, "We will not accept a situation in which Israeli citizens are threatened by the terror of rockets. No country would accept this."[276] Ehud Barak claimed that the goal was to strengthen Israeli "deterrence" and to "reinstitute the calm"—the very calm that Israel had shattered with its airstrikes.[277] Likewise claiming that the primary goal was "to bring back quiet to southern Israel", Yoav Mordechai warned the Israeli "home front" that it "must brace itself" for the consequence of Israel having violated the ceasefire in the name of protecting the home front.[278]

Uri Avnery, in a Gush Shalom press release, slammed the Israeli government for putting its own citizens at risk by deliberately ending the ceasefire. "The inhabitants of the communities of southern Israel, who just started to breathe freely," Avnery noted, were "sent right back to air raid alarms and to running to shelters."[279] Israel had used the ceasefire as a "disinformation ruse", Barak Ravid explained in *Haaretz*, in order to "lull Hamas and other terror organizations in Gaza into a false sense of security, in the hope that they would lower their level of preparedness for an Israeli attack and return to their normal routines in a fashion which would help the IDF identify the head of Hamas's military wing Ahmed Jabari, and assassinate him."[280]

The implausibility of Israel's claim that its operation was aimed at restoring calm was underscored by the fact that Jabari was a key figure responsible for enforcing previous ceasefires among other armed groups. He was, in effect, Israel's "subcontractor", as *Haaretz* editor-in-chief Aluf Benn described him.[281] In another *Haaretz* commentary, Reuven Pedatzur noted that Jabari's assassination showed that the Israeli government had "decided a cease-fire would be undesirable for Israel at this time, and that attacking Hamas would be preferable."[282]

Jabari's assassination was "a pre-emptive strike against the possibility of a long term ceasefire", commented Gershon Baskin, who in his capacity as a private Israeli citizen had been responsible for negotiating the release of Gilad

Shalit. The founder of the Israel/Palestine Center for Research and Information, Baskin was also a key player in the Egyptian-brokered negotiations with Hamas over a ceasefire agreement. He pointed out that when Hamas had participated in recent rocket fire under pressure from its public and other armed groups to respond to Israeli attacks, "it almost always aimed its rockets at open spaces in Israel and their damage was minimal. It was clear to all involved that Hamas was not interested in escalating the situation." He further explained how Jabari, on the morning of his assassination, had received the draft of an extended cease-fire agreement. It was Jabari who was to present the agreement to other armed groups and to encourage them to accept it. Israel's assassination of Jabari was an act of "extreme irresponsibility". Netanyahu had "endangered the people of Israel and struck a real blow against the few important more pragmatic elements within Hamas. He has given another victory to those who seek our destruction, rather than strengthen those who are seeking to find a possibility to live side-by-side, not in peace, but in quiet."[283] Baskin emphasized to *Haaretz* that senior Israeli leaders were well aware of this effort to achieve an extended ceasefire.[284] In an op-ed published by the *New York Times*, Baskin further observed that Israel had frequently tried violence, with no success in achieving its ostensible aim of stopping rocket fire. The only thing Israel had not tried was achieving a long-term truce. "Instead, Mr. Jabari is dead—and with him died the possibility of a long-term cease-fire."[285]

As always, the response of the US government to the escalation of hostilities was to reflexively blame the Palestinians and express firm support for Israel's violence, including by defending its deadly attacks on civilians. The White House issued a statement informing the public that Obama had spoken with Netanyahu to express his support for Israel's military assault on Gaza.[286] State Department spokesman Mark Toner said the violence was initiated by the "cowardly acts" of Palestinians with "the barrage of rocket fire from Gaza into southern Israel". While there was "no justification for the violence that Hamas and other terrorist organizations are employing against the people of Israel", the US gave its blessing to the no-less-cowardly and far more murderous violence that the IDF was inflicting on the people of Gaza under the guise of Israel's "right to defend itself". Using the same language, Susan Rice defended Israel's assault in an emergency closed session of the UN Security Council.[287] "We stand by our Israeli partners", Pentagon spokesman Stephen Warren refrained, "in their right to defend themselves against terrorism."[288]

Playing its usual role, the *New York Times* summed up the situation with the statement that Israel had "launched the most ferocious assault on Gaza in four years after persistent Palestinian rocket fire". With Isabel Kershner as lead author, the article recalled Operation Cast Lead with the same deceitfulness, asserting that Israeli forces had in that case, too, entered Gaza "after years of rocket attacks by Palestinian militants into Israel". Far be it from Isabel Kershner to resurrect the fact that there had been a ceasefire—Israel's violation of which was tossed down the memory hole by Kershner and the rest of her colleagues within mere weeks of its occurrence. For context, the article cited the anti-tank missile attack on the IDF jeep as the triggering event while continuing to withhold from readers the fact that the truck was in Gaza at the time. Also left undisclosed was the fact that Israeli forces had two days earlier killed thirteen-year-old Hamid. The *Times* noted how Palestinian rockets had "hit homes, caused injuries and frightened the population" of Israel. But the only indication that Israel had by then already not only "frightened" Palestinians but *killed* them was a passing mention near the end of the article that Hamas had been observing a ceasefire, but that, "under pressure from some of the Gaza population *for not avenging deadly Israeli airstrikes*, Hamas has claimed responsibility for participating in the firing of rockets" (emphasis added).[289]

The *Times* editors took it a step further by exonerating Israel and placing full blame on the Palestinians for the violence on the grounds that Hamas was responsible for violating its "informal cease-fire with Israel after the war there in the winter of 2008–09." To support this allegation, they selected as the triggering event Hamas's bombing of the IDF jeep on November 8, with no mention of the killing of the Palestinian boy. Rather than disclosing that the IDF forces were inside Gaza at the time, the editors disingenuously described the attack as occurring "along the Israel-Gaza border while Israeli soldiers were working nearby". While condemning the rocket attacks that Israelis had endured in recent days, the editors offered no comment about Palestinians having to endure Israeli airstrikes during the same period of time. Nor did they disclose the fact that Palestinian armed groups had recently joined Hamas in accepting another ceasefire that was immediately shattered by Israel; on the contrary, by their account, this ceasefire never occurred. They offered the mild criticism that it was "hard to see" how Israel's military operation "could be the most effective way of advancing its long-term interests". After all, the IDF had tried this already with Operation Cast Lead, which not only invited international condemnation, but "did not solve the problem." There were options available to Israel other than military action, such as seeking an Egyptian-mediated ceasefire—a possibility, the editors bewilderingly added, that Hamas had "hinted that it was open to".[290]

The following day, Isabel Kershner likewise reported how the Obama administration had "asked friendly Arab countries with ties to Hamas" to "seek a way to defuse the hostilities". She declined to mention the fact that Egypt had already done precisely that by successfully brokering a ceasefire that was then used by Israel as an opportunity to draw out and assassinate Ahmed al-Jabari.[291]

Reporting on his assassination, the *Washington Post* offered a slightly different but equally disingenuous account: the "latest round of fighting" began on

November 10, "when militants from a non-Hamas faction fired an antitank missile at an Israeli jeep traveling along the Israel-Gaza border, injuring four Israeli soldiers." That the Israeli forces were not just near the border but had invaded Gaza was information the *Post* judged its readers needn't know. That article was originally published online on November 14 under the headline "Hamas Leader in Gaza Killed by Israeli Strike". But that perhaps risked giving away that it was Israel who violated the ceasefire; the piece was updated and the title changed the following day to "Three Israelis killed by rocket fired from Gaza Strip; Israel intensifies air offensive". Four Palestinian civilians had already been killed in airstrikes by November 14, but unlike the deaths of Israelis, this was just not headline-worthy news, as far as the *Post* was concerned. Not until seventeen paragraphs down the page could readers learn that, "After mediation from Egypt, the flare-up appeared to have waned" just the previous day (November 13). Like the *Times*, the *Post* decided not to divulge that this was because Palestinian armed groups had agreed to join Hamas in a ceasefire that was violated the following morning by Israel.[292]

By contrast, Human Rights Watch reported that "The current round of fighting began on November 8, during an incursion by Israeli forces into southern Gaza . . . that left a 13-year-old Palestinian boy dead."[293] *The Guardian* informed that there had been an Egyptian-mediated "ceasefire between Israel and Hamas" that was "short-lived" because it "broke down with the air strikes" that Israel launched that morning.[294] But as far as the US mainstream media was concerned, such details were unfit to print; all the American public needed to know was that Israel launched its operation in self-defense after relentless rocket fire and attacks on its soldiers near the border fence. As during Operation Cast Lead, media outlets like the *New York Times* and the *Washington Post* chose to serve effectively as the US government's very own Ministry of Propaganda with highly disciplined self-censorship.

To cite a few additional examples, in *Foreign Affairs*, Barak Mendelsohn repeated the version that the latest round of violence was initiated by Hamas on November 10, but with the added lie that the IDF forces were "inside Israeli territory" at the time.[295] Writing in *Foreign Policy*, Daniel Kurtzer likewise blamed the "brewing war" on "rocket fire from Gaza", with no mention of Israel's deadly attacks on Palestinians. The consequence for Israelis, he assessed, would be that "Hamas will have killed some Israeli civilians" and "disrupted life in southern Israel". On the other hand, the killing of Palestinians and disruption of their lives just didn't factor into the equation; the only consequence on the Palestinian side worth considering was that the IDF's operation, when all said and done, "will have degraded Hamas's military capacity".

Kurzter further opined that anyone suggesting that the US government should take "a hands-off approach" was "blind toward history" since it was an article of faith that "inactivity by the United States allows the situation on the ground to heat up until it boils over—and that active agile, and persistent diplomacy by the United States actually has a chance of making things better." This was illustrated by the latest round of violence, he declared, as though self-evident and requiring no elaboration. Obviously, Kurtzer concluded, the Middle East was in need of "a fresh American initiative."[296]

Taking a fresh initiative in the US Senate, Kirsten Gillibrand introduced a resolution with sixty-six co-sponsors: "Expressing vigorous support and unwavering commitment to the welfare, security, and survival of the State of Israel as a Jewish and democratic state with secure borders, and recognizing and strongly supporting its right to act in self-defense to protect its citizens against acts of terrorism." The resolution reiterated the usual euphemistic demands of Hamas and urged the UN Security Council to condemn only the Palestinian violence. Needless to say, it passed. The House passed its own version introduced by Ileana Ros-Lehtinen the following day, which naturally drew praise for the Congress from AIPAC.[297]

By November 15, the anniversary of the PLO's 1988 Declaration of Independence, the Palestinian death toll had risen to nineteen, including six children and a teacher. UNRWA closed all its schools so they could be used as shelters if necessary.[298] The three Israelis killed on November 15, all of them civilians, were killed in a single rocket strike on an apartment in the southern Israeli town of Kiryat Malachi.[299] According to the IDF, more than 275 rockets had been fired at Israel since Jabari's assassination, including two Iranian-made, long-range Fajr-5 rockets fired at Tel Aviv that landed in the sea. Notwithstanding the fact that this threat to Israel's civilian population was precipitated by its violation of the ceasefire, the IDF claimed success in damaging Hamas's long-range rocket capability. "We managed to destroy most of the long-range Fajr rockets and other Hamas infrastructure", boasted Ehud Barak.[300]

By November 16, twenty-nine Palestinians had been killed, including eight children and a pregnant woman.[301] It was all part of Israel taking a "Tougher Approach" to reestablish "deterrence", Ethan Bronner reported. "The operative metaphor is often described as 'cutting the grass,' meaning a task that must be performed regularly and has no end."[302] Roger Cohen criticized this Israeli policy with the appropriate retort, "But of course bombing Gaza is potent fertilizer to the grasses of hatred."[303] The Israeli cabinet, meanwhile, authorized the mobilization of up to 75,000 reservists in preparation for a possible ground invasion.[304] Egyptian Prime Minister Hesham Qandil arrived in Gaza to meet with Ismail Haniyeh to discuss a long-term ceasefire. A three-hour cessation of violence that was arranged to accommodate his visit, however, never fully transpired as sporadic airstrikes and rocket fire continued. Jodi Rudoren in the *New York Times* remarked that this failed lull "began a day of highs and lows across Gaza, where the largely impoverished population of 1.5 million people has become somewhat inured to violence after years of battle with Israel, and where resistance is an honored part of the culture."[305]

The following day, the Palestinian death toll rose past forty, including at least six children.[306] The WHO warned that Gaza's hospitals were already "severely over stretched mainly as a result of the siege of Gaza" and now were "having to deal with the growing number of casualties with severely depleted medical supplies."[307] In the north and east of Gaza, people began fleeing their homes—among them the Samouni family of Zeytoun.[308] The IDF expanded its operation to include government buildings and bombed the office of Ismail Haniyeh, where the day before the Hamas prime minister had met with his Egyptian counterpart for the purpose of achieving a ceasefire.

In furtherance of that goal, Egyptian President Mohamed Morsi was scheduled to meet in Cairo with Hamas leader Khaled Meshal, the emir of Qatar, and the prime minister of Turkey.[309] But while Hamas was working to achieve peace, Israel was focused on an entirely different goal; the purpose of the IDF's operation, said Interior Minister Eli Yishai, was "to send Gaza back to the Middle Ages."[310] The editors of *Haaretz* rejoined that "Destroying Gaza's already meager civil infrastructure isn't only inhuman and a war crime, it doesn't do Israel any good. Israel has tried it more than once. It has demolished roads and bridges, destroyed power stations and water supplies and turned the lives of Gaza's 1.5 million people into hell. As a result, Hamas has only grown stronger, the people's suffering has worsened and with it the hatred for Israel. Israel should seek the complete opposite: Gaza's prosperity."[311]

As an additional consequence of Israel's previous attempt to bomb Gaza back to the Middle Ages, it was this time around faced with more constraints. Netanyahu privately assured Obama that despite Israel's mobilization, no ground operation was imminent, according to Eli Lake in the *Daily Beast*, citing two US officials briefed on the call. One prominent reason why Israel might be hesitant to launch a full-scale invasion, Lake explained, was because it "paid a significant political cost in the aftermath of what was called Operation Cast Lead in 2008 and 2009."[312]

As during that assault, the Israeli government was also waging an information war. As part of its hasbara campaign, the IDF posted on Twitter, "Video: These are the tactics #Hamas uses in the #Gaza Strip".[313] The post linked to a video that had been published on the IDF's YouTube channel on November 10, 2011. The IDF claimed the video was "based on intelligence and other findings gathered in the field during Operation Cast Lead". It featured an animation of Hamas militants firing rockets from a school yard, with "UNRWA" and its logo painted in blue on the side of the building.[314] In response, UNRWA issued a statement noting that the IDF's allegation was false and expressing its concern "about the creation and use of footage that wrongly suggests that UNRWA is allowing its premises to be used for terrorist activities in the current conflict and the unauthorized use of its logo in computer-generated material."[315]

Combating Israel's hasbara was an ongoing struggle for the UN agency. Just three weeks before Israel launched its military operation, UNRWA reported,

> Israel's highest-rating news program, Channel Two News, has published a statement correcting false claims that rockets were fired from schools operated by the United Nations Relief and Works Agency for Palestine Refugees (UNRWA) during the Gaza war in 2008–2009. The statement makes clear that Israeli officials themselves acknowledged that such claims were false and that there was no evidence to support them.

> "We heard this misinformation during the war when there was shelling on and around the Agency's schools and our main warehouse in Gaza", said UNRWA Spokesperson Chris Gunness, "but Israeli officials made it clear to the UN during the war itself that they knew claims about militants in UNRWA installations were completely false. Constant, unchecked repetition of this misinformation has been very damaging to the Agency and has produced some very poor and biased journalism, which I will continue to confront. This is the third time in just a few months that a major news organization has issued a public retraction because of false information about UNRWA."[316]

With Israel's latest military operation, the population of Gaza was living in "constant fear", UNRWA reported. No place was safe as the IDF continued to target residential buildings. With more than half the population under eighteen years of age, Gaza's children had been "constantly exposed to violence. The additional severe military escalation that is currently ongoing will only add to their already-existing psychological trauma."[317]

The US government continued to give its blessing to Israel's traumatization of Gaza's children. "Let's understand what the precipitating event here was that's causing the current crisis," Obama inculcated on November 18, "and that was an ever-escalating number of missiles; they were landing not just in Israeli territory, but in areas that are populated. And there's no country on Earth that would tolerate missiles raining down on its citizens from outside its borders. So we are fully supportive of Israel's right to defend itself from missiles landing on people's homes and workplaces and potentially killing civilians. And we will continue to support Israel's right to defend itself."[318]

As Representative Ron Paul retorted, "Considering that this president rains down missiles on Yemen, Afghanistan, Pakistan, and numerous other countries on a daily basis, the statement was so hypocritical that it didn't pass the laugh test. But it wasn't funny."[319]

To Obama, it was quite tolerable for US-provided military hardware to rain down death and destruction on the population of Gaza. As he defended the on-slaught, the *New York Times* reported how an Israeli bomb "pummeled a home deep into the ground" in Gaza City, "killing 11 people, including nine in three generations of a single family, in the deadliest single strike since the cross-border conflict between Israel and the militant faction Hamas escalated on Wednes-day." Following the strike, "it took emergency workers and a Caterpillar digger more than an hour to reveal the extent of the devastation under the two-story home of Jamal Dalu, a shop owner. Mr. Dalu was at a neighbor's when the blast wiped out nearly his entire family . . . . "[320]

Human Rights Watch subsequently reported that twelve people were killed in the attack, including ten from that household: Mohamed Jamal al-Dalu; five women; and four children, ages seven, six, four, and one. The head of the house-hold, Jamal al-Dalu, along with his son Abdallah, had gone to market, where he ran a shop, and then to mosque for afternoon prayers, where he received a call that his home had been destroyed and his family killed. A young man and elderly woman from the Muzannar family next door were also killed. The attack was, the rights group observed, "a clear violation of the laws of war."[321]

The IDF claimed that the home was "a hideout of [a] senior militant op-erative in Hamas's rocket-launching infrastructure" and blamed the deaths on "terror operatives who use the civil population as [a] human shield when using civilian buildings as hideouts or to store weaponry."[322] Initially, the IDF claimed its target was a Hamas fighter named Yahia Abayah. More than a week later, it changed its story, claiming that the target had been Mohamed Jamal al-Dalu, who was a police officer under the Interior Ministry—a job description that was enough for the IDF to describe him as a "known terror operative affiliated with the military wing of Hamas".[323]

When Palestinians gathered the next day to mourn those killed in the at-tack, *New York Times* reporter Jodi Rudoren remarked that such funerals were "a punctuating rhythm of life" in Gaza.[324] On her Facebook page, Rudoren re-marked that "while death and destruction is far more severe in Gaza than in Is-rael, it seems like Israelis are almost more traumatized. The Gazans have a deep culture of resistance and aspiration to martyrdom, they're used to it from Cast Lead and other conflicts, and they have such limited lives than [*sic*] in many ways they have less to lose." In another Facebook post, Rudoren informed that she had just shed her own "first tears in Gaza"—after reading an article "about what it's like to be in Jerusalem" during the latest round of violence."[325]

In addition to residential and government buildings, Israel also admittedly targeted two media buildings that housed offices of Reuters, Fox News, Sky News, CBS, ARD television, RT, Press TV, Abu Dhabi TV, Al Arabiya, Ma'an

News Agency, and the Al-Quds Satellite Channel. Thirteen journalists were injured, including Khader az-Zahar, whose leg required amputation as a result. Israel's Vice Prime Minister, Moshe Ya'alon, defended the attack by saying the IDF was targeting "Hamas military antenna" and characterizing the injury of journalists as merely incidental.[326] "By placing communication infrastructure on roofs of media buildings," said an IDF spokesman, "Hamas uses the foreign journalists as human shields."[327] The organization Reporters Without Borders reminded Israeli authorities that "under humanitarian law, the news media enjoy the same protection as civilians and cannot be regarded as military targets."[328]

By the day's end, the number of Palestinians killed had risen to seventy, including twenty children, and the number of wounded had nearly doubled. The number of Israelis killed remained at three, all civilians, with seventy-nine injured in rocket attacks.[329] Ban Ki-moon issued a statement deploring the deaths of civilians on both sides and urging all parties to cooperate with Egypt to achieve a ceasefire.[330] In pursuit of that goal, Egyptian officials met separately with Israeli and Hamas officials in Cairo. According to Egyptian Member of Parliament Reda Fahmy, Hamas had "one clear and specific demand: for the siege to be completely lifted from Gaza".[331] Israel was participating in the negotiations, Stratfor assessed, because its leaders feared the high political cost of a ground invasion, with "the political fallout of Operation Cast Lead" weighing heavily on their minds.[332]

There were, of course, those who did not share such concerns about committing war crimes. Gilad Sharon, son of former Prime Minister Ariel Sharon, wrote an op-ed for the *Jerusalem Post* stating, "We need to flatten entire neighborhoods in Gaza. Flatten all of Gaza. The Americans didn't stop with Hiroshima—the Japanese weren't surrendering fast enough, so they hit Nagasaki, too. There should be no electricity in Gaza, no gasoline or moving vehicles, nothing. Then they'd really call for a ceasefire."[333]

He was indulging in "the old Israeli dream", Roger Cohen appropriately explained in the *New York Times*, "that the Palestinian people should just disappear."[334]

By November 19, the civilian toll in Gaza was at least fifty-seven killed, including eighteen children. Over one-third of the 740 Palestinian civilians injured were children. OCHA reported that "The increased targeting by the Israeli military of residential properties in Gaza, which have resulted in multiple civilian casualties, is of increasing concern."[335] Amnesty International condemned both sides for "violating international humanitarian law" and called on the UN Security Council to impose an arms embargo on Palestinian armed groups and Israel.[336] A group of thirty-eight aid and development agencies urged the international community to put pressure on both sides to end the violence and on Israel to end its blockade in accordance with UN Security Council Resolution 1860.[337]

At the UN Security Council, however, the US blocked a statement calling for an immediate ceasefire on the grounds that it didn't identify "the continuing barrage of rocket attacks from Gaza against Israel" as "the root cause of the current escalation".[338]

The US mainstream media continued to accommodate the US government's account by systematically wiping from the record Israel's repeated attacks and killing of Palestinians in Gaza prior to its launch of Operation Pillar of Defense, as well as the ceasefire to which Hamas and other armed groups had committed. The *New York Times* repeatedly offered the abridged account that the IDF's operation began on November 14 after "months of Palestinian rocket fire into Israel."[339] A *Times* editorial on November 20 described Hamas as "so consumed with hatred for Israel that it has repeatedly resorted to violence, no matter what the cost to its own people." The editors judged that all their readers needed to know was that Israel assassinated a Hamas leader and "began its artillery and air campaigns" only after hundreds of rockets were fired into Israel.[340] The Associated Press echoed that "Israel launched the offensive on Nov. 14 in a bid to end months of rocket attacks".[341] At the website of the Council on Foreign Relations, Steven A. Cook dutifully retold, "It started with rockets being fired from Gaza into southern Israel, and the Israelis have responded with air attacks."[342]

Amira Hass in a *Haaretz* column expressed her puzzlement over this dominant media narrative, which she described as a tremendous propaganda victory for the Israeli government. She recounted how young Hamid Abu Daqqa was killed while playing soccer two days before the anti-tank missile attack on an Israeli jeep, following which four more teenagers were killed by the IDF. Then she appropriately wondered, "So why shouldn't the count of aggression start with a child?"[343]

In Cairo to negotiate a ceasefire, Khaled Meshal called Israel's bluff to launch a ground invasion by taunting, "If you wanted to launch it, you would have done it." Hamas was seeking a cessation of hostilities, he explained, in accordance with the "legitimate demands" of the people of Gaza "for Israel to be restrained from its aggression, assassinations and invasions, and for the siege over Gaza to be ended."[344]

Anxious to avoid a repeat of the political fallout from Operation Cast Lead, Hillary Clinton arrived in Jerusalem to meet with Netanyahu to discuss wrapping up Israel's operation, after which she was scheduled to travel to Cairo to consult with Egyptian officials attempting to broker a ceasefire, as well as with Ban Ki-moon.[345]

One consequence of Israel's operation was increased support for Hamas at the expense of Abbas. The PA, observed the *New York Times*, was "rapidly losing credibility, even relevance."[346] Chemi Shalev in *Haaretz* agreed that the "big loser" was Abbas and the PA, "who have been pushed even further to the side-lines as Hamas celebrates what will be widely perceived in the Arab world and in the Palestinian street as its victory."[347] The *Jerusalem Post* concurred, "There is little doubt the fighting boosted Hamas's standing in the region . . . ."[348] A poll the following month indicated "a dramatic change in public attitude" and "a significant boost" for Hamas, showing that Haniyeh would defeat Abbas if new presidential elections were held. (Even more popular was imprisoned Fatah leader Marwan Barghouti.) When it came to the question of who would gain more support if legislative elections were held, Hamas or Fatah, the numbers were near even.[349]

On November 20, a meeting of the Committee to Protect Journalists was held at the Waldorf-Astoria hotel in New York City, where the practice of states targeting journalists was discussed and condemned. The same day, the IDF targeted a car carrying two cameramen for the Hamas TV station, Al-Aqsa. A journalist from the Al-Quds Educational Radio station was also killed. IDF spokeswoman Avital Leibovich said the journalists were targeted because they had "relevance to terror activity."[350] On Twitter, the IDF warned: "Advice to reporters in #Gaza, just like any person in Gaza: For your own safety, stay away from #Hamas positions and operatives."[351]

Human Rights Watch condemned the killings as a war crime, reminding that "Civilian broadcasting facilities are not rendered legitimate military targets simply because they broadcast pro-Hamas or anti-Israel propaganda." Report-ers Without Borders called the attacks a "clear violation of international stan-dards." In the *New York Times*, David Carr noted that a translator and driver for the newspaper was in the vehicle just in front of the one Israel targeted, "so the execution hit close to our organization." Describing the killings as "deeply troubling", he commented, "So it has come to this: killing members of the news media can be justified by a phrase as amorphous as 'relevance to terror activity.'" He also reminded that "such attacks are hardly restricted to Israel: recall that in the United States assault on Baghdad, television stations were early targets."[352]

While working near the border fence, an Israeli civilian military contrac-tor was killed, and an Israeli soldier was also killed, bringing the total number of Israeli deaths to five.[353] The Palestinian civilian death toll rose to seventy, including twenty-three children and twelve women, according to OCHA. The IDF began dropping leaflets across Gaza City with the warning, "For your own safety, you are required to immediately evacuate your homes and move toward Gaza City center." OCHA reported that this was "adding to the sense of fear and uncertainty among civilians" and causing widespread displacement—although many Gazans, recollecting Israeli attacks on civilian persons and locations dur-ing Operation Cast Lead, chose to remain in their homes rather than flee to the shelter of UNRWA schools.[354] An hour after the leaflets were distributed, at around four in the afternoon, Israel launched airstrikes around the city. Among those killed were two children kicking a soccer ball in the street.[355]

On November 21, a bomb exploded on a bus in Tel Aviv. While causing no fatalities, many passengers had to be taken to the hospital for shock and to treat injuries. Passenger Amira Castro told the *Jerusalem Post* that she had four sons in the military and understood that Israel would "pay a price" if it launched a ground invasion, but that she wanted the government to "do something to make our suffering stop." The lesson drawn by paramedic Israel Kornik was that there was no point in stopping the operation; the IDF needed to "keep working until they finish the job."[356]

Immediately issuing a statement denying responsibility for the bombing, Khaled Meshal blamed the violence on Israel for invading Gaza and killing a child on November 8 and then assassinating Jabari a day after Hamas had accepted the Egyptian-brokered ceasefire. Hamas was ready for "a peaceful way" forward "without blood or weapons", he said, and reiterated Hamas's acceptance of a Palestinian state along the 1967 lines, with Jerusalem as its capital and without prejudice to the refugees' right of return.[357]

It was subsequently learned that the bus bombing was organized by a terrorist cell as an act of revenge for Jabari's assassination and the IDF's bombardment of Gaza.[358]

In the end, Israel did not follow through with its threat to launch a ground invasion. Egypt's efforts finally paid off as a ceasefire agreement was reached. It consisted of a one-page memorandum of understanding that Israel and all Palestinian factions would cease hostilities. The MOU also stated that procedures to implement an opening of the crossings and facilitation of free movement of goods and people "shall be dealt with after 24 hours from the start of the ceasefire."[359] In Israel's understanding, however, "after 24 hours" evidently meant something perhaps just short of never. When the agreement was being debated within the Israeli government, Ehud Barak argued in favor by saying, "A day after the cease-fire, no one will remember what is written in that draft. The only thing that will be tested is the blow Hamas suffered."[360]

Barak Ravid pointed out that the terms of the ceasefire were "almost identical to those reached following Operation Cast Lead at the start of 2009."[361]

The US government, for its part, had played a role in convincing Israel to accept the agreement, including a number of phone calls between Obama and Netanyahu.[362] Chemi Shalev explained in *Haaretz* that the Obama administration was eager

> to prevent the absolute worst-case scenario: an Israeli ground
> incursion that might have sparked a regional chain reaction
> that could de-stabilize the Middle East and damage Ameri-
> can strategic interests." He explained that "the specter of angry

Arab masses converging on US embassies throughout the Arab world is a nightmare for an administration that is still criticized for, and traumatized by, the recent September 11 riots and the deadly terrorist attack on the American consulate in Benghazi.[363]

To prevent such an outcome, the Obama administration offered Israel a quid pro quo for ending its operation in the form of additional funding for its Iron Dome missile defense system. Each battery cost about $50 million, and each interceptor missile cost tens of thousands of dollars. The promised funds would be in addition to the hundreds of millions of dollars that had already been expropriated from the American people to pay for the system.[364]

American money also helped explain why Egypt, despite its efforts to achieve a ceasefire, remained complicit in Israel's policy of collective punishment. While the IDF bombarded Gaza, Egypt kept the Rafah border crossing closed and prevented Palestinians from escaping the violence, with the exception of evacuating the injured for medical attention. Egypt was not only dependent on the US's $1.5 billion in aid, but was also seeking Washington's support to secure a $4.8 billion loan from the IMF.[365]

Palestinian casualties from Operation Pillar of Defense, according to the UN and WHO, included 175 dead, mostly civilians, and 1,399 injured, also mostly civilians. Among the dead were 24 women and 43 children, including 15 younger than five. Among the wounded were 431 children, including 141 younger than five. The Israeli casualties included 6 dead, 4 of them civilians, and 224 wounded, also mostly civilians.[366] A later B'Tselem report put the final number of Palestinian deaths at 167, of whom at least 87—more than half— were civilians. Among the known non-combatants killed were 31 minors, including 20 children under age twelve.[367]

Approximately 450 Palestinian homes were destroyed or severely damaged. At the height of the violence, about 15,000 Gazans were displaced from their homes to seek refuge elsewhere, such as emergency shelters set up in sixteen schools, fourteen of which were run by UNRWA.[368] At least 136 schools were damaged by Israel's bombardment. When they reopened, UNICEF and the UN Mine Action Service (UNMAS) placed posters in the courtyards showing explosive remnants and warning children not to pick up anything from the rubble that looked similar. "The trauma is reflected in children's drawings", reported UNICEF. "Many have produced violent images, such as families waiting in houses as military aircraft drop bombs from the sky."[369]

The *New York Times* commented that "Hamas faces an enormous rebuilding effort, with at least 10 of its government buildings—including the ministries of culture, education and interior; the prime minister's headquarters; and police stations—now reduced to rubble littered with payroll sheets and property tax rolls."[370]

Oxfam urged Israel to take the opportunity presented by the ceasefire to lift its blockade, "which has had a devastating impact on the lives and well-being of Gaza's civilian population and on Palestinian development."[371] But as Gazan fisherman tried to venture out beyond the three-nautical-mile limit Israel had imposed since 2006, some were met by Israeli navy ships firing warning shots towards their boats and warning them through loudspeakers to turn back. Others were kidnapped and transported to Ashdod.[372] In the weeks that followed the ceasefire, the IDF also continued to fire at Palestinians in Gaza and conduct sweeping raids in the West Bank, arresting fifty-five Palestinians with ties to Hamas or Islamic Jihad.[373]

Emboldened by the ceasefire, Gazans began to venture nearer to the border. Just two days after the ceasefire, on the morning of November 23, Israeli soldiers shot and killed twenty-year-old Anwar Qudaih. Israeli officials maintained that the wide strip of land along the border remained off-limits to the people of Gaza, prompting the *New York Times* to remark that this "was clearly not the understanding of the hundreds of Gazans who thought that they would have access to the so-called buffer zone".[374]

While Hamas maintained the ceasefire, IDF spokeswoman Avital Leibovich attempted to justify the shooting by claiming in a Twitter message that the Gazans were breaking the ceasefire by trying to breach the border fence and that the IDF responded with "warning shots". When challenged on this claim, Leibovich posted a photo showing a crowd of Palestinians near the fence with their arms in the air, an apparent expression of both celebration and defiance. Leibovich's comment was, "as you can see, they are very close to the fence". When one Twitter user observed that there was a difference between breaching the fence and being near it, Leibovich replied, "indeed there is. In our case, they breached it. One man even infiltrated." She made no further attempt to support the claim with evidence.[375] Speaking on the condition of anonymity, however, a Hamas police officer told the *New York Times* that some Palestinians had indeed crossed the fence to stand on the Israeli side—at the location where IDF forces had downed the fence on November 10 during their incursion into Gaza.[376] Anwar Qudaih was evidently not among those guilty of standing on Israeli soil; rather, his sentence of being shot in the head was executed for the crime of approaching the fence to plant a Hamas flag on it.[377]

Within a month of the ceasefire, in addition to Qudaih's killing, some thirty Gazans were injured in at least ten incidents where Israeli soldiers fired across the border, including five farmers shot and wounded on December 21.[378]

In the aftermath of Operation Pillar of Defense, analysts questioned both the effectiveness of the IDF's assault in reaching its ostensible goals and the government's motives. When Ehud Barak resigned as defense minister, *Time* magazine probed for an explanation, commenting that while the IDF had "clearly met its military goals", Hamas nevertheless "seems to have emerged stronger politically."[379] The *New York Times* astutely assessed that the operation was "something of a practice run for any future armed confrontation". Specifically, if Israel was to launch an attack on Iran's nuclear facilities, Palestinian armed groups might be expected to retaliate; hence "Israel was using the Gaza battle to learn the capabilities of Hamas and Islamic Jihad".[380] Israel was "preparing the ground for a wider military assault against Iran", Nafeez Mosaddeq Ahmed similarly noted in *Le Monde Diplomatique*. But the Israeli government was also motived by its need to deal a blow to Hamas for standing in the way of an agreement with the PA to develop gas reserves in Gaza's territorial waters. Then Israeli Vice Prime Minister and Minister of Strategic Affairs, Moshe Ya'alon had written, "It is clear that without an overall military operation to uproot Hamas control of Gaza, no drilling work can take place without the consent of the radical Islamic movement." Ya'alon subsequently replaced Ehud Barak as Minister of Defense.[381]

Perhaps the most incisive analysis came from American political scientist Norman G. Finkelstein, who agreed that Israel's goal was to establish "deterrence" but questioned the nature of the threat it sought to deter. Netanyahu had humiliated himself trying to rally international support for a military attack on Iran at the UN with his cartoon bomb drawing. Hezbollah had acquired a drone capability. Hamas had gained respectability. In sum, "The natives were getting restless. It was time to take out the big club again and remind the locals who was in charge."

Jabari's assassination was intended to provoke a violent response as a pretext for the planned attack on Gaza, but this time, there were major political constraints. Israel, with the US's help, had avoided prosecution at the ICC for war crimes during Operation Cast Lead, but it might not be so lucky a second time around. Whereas Israel had successfully blocked journalists from entering Gaza during Cast Lead, this time, "Gaza was swarming with foreign reporters" who could "report Israeli atrocities in real-time." Israel ended up becoming "caught between a rock and a hard place. It couldn't subdue Hamas without a ground invasion, but it couldn't launch a ground invasion without incurring a politically unacceptable price in IDF casualties and global opprobrium."

Finkelstein continued, "It is possible to pinpoint the precise moment when the Israeli assault was over: Hamas leader Khaled Meshal's taunt to Israel at a 19 November press conference, *Go ahead, invade!*" Once Netanyahu's bluff was called, "Secretary of State Hillary Clinton was summoned to bail Israel out".[382]

Bailing Israel out, however, was hardly a selfless act on the part of the Obama administration, which was no doubt mindful of its complicity and the possibility of future prosecution for war crimes at the ICC. As John Bolton had warned, "to convoke the International Criminal Court is like putting a loaded pistol to Israel's head—or, in the future, to America's."

Returning from a week-long UN mission to assess the impact of Israel's blockade on Gaza, Richard Falk condemned Israel for attacks during Operation Pillar of Defense that "killed and harmed civilians in a grossly disproportionate manner". Alluding to the US role, he relayed the "widespread feeling among Palestinians that Israel is above the law, and that it is likely to continue to have the benefits of impunity even when it flagrantly and repeatedly violates international human rights and humanitarian laws."[383]

In a *New York Times* op-ed, the executive director of the Jerusalem Fund, Yousef Munayyer, blasted US policy for being "founded on the assumption that American hard power, through support for Israel and other Middle Eastern governments, can keep the legitimate grievances of the people under wraps." Its policies had "sent counterproductive messages to the Palestinians that have only increased the incentives for using violence." The message Palestinians took away "from observing America's reflexively pro-Israel policy was that the peace process was merely a cover for endless Israeli colonialism." Given the US's financial, military, and diplomatic support despite Israel's continued settlement projects, "it is no wonder that some in Israel continue to believe that perpetual occupation, or de facto apartheid, is a viable policy option."[384]

Representative Ron Paul likewise observed that "without changes in US foreign policy it is only a matter of time before the killing begins again." A rare voice of reason in the Congress, he wrote that

> as long as Israel can count on its destructive policies being underwritten by the US taxpayer it can continue to engage in reckless behavior. And as long as the Palestinians feel the one-sided US presence lined up against them they will continue to resort to more and more deadly and desperate measures. Continuing to rain down missiles on so many increasingly resentful nations, the US is undermining rather than furthering its security. We are on a collision course with much of the rest of the world if we do not right our foreign policy. Ending interventionism in the Middle East and replacing it with friendship and even-handedness would be a welcome first step.[385]

But no amount of reason could convince American policymakers to change course. Less than three weeks after the November 22 ceasefire agreement, the US proceeded with a $647 million arms deal with Israel. According to *Haaretz*, the package included "10,000 bombs of various kinds—3,450 bombs weighing a ton each, 1,725 bombs weighing 250 kilograms each, 1,725 BLU-109 bunker-buster bombs, and 3,450 GBU-39 bunker-buster bombs". The purpose of the arms sale was "to renew the inventory of the Israel Defense Forces following the massive bombings in Gaza during Operation Pillar of Defense."[386]

A Historic Vote

On November 29, 2012, the sixty-fifth anniversary of the passage of Resolution 181 and the International Day of Solidarity with the Palestinian People, Palestine's application for an upgrade of status in the UN General Assembly went to a vote. Addressing the Assembly, President Abbas had the following to say:

> What permits the Israeli Government to blatantly continue with its aggressive policies and the perpetration of war crimes stems from its conviction that it is above the law and that it has immunity from accountability and consequences. . . .
>
> The moment has arrived for the world to say clearly: Enough of aggression, settlements and occupation.
>
> This is why we are here now. . . .
>
> We will not give up, we will not tire, and our determination will not wane and we will continue to strive to achieve a just peace.
>
> However, above all and after all, I affirm that our people will not relinquish their inalienable national rights, as defined by United Nations resolutions. And our people cling to the right to defend themselves against aggression and occupation and they will continue their popular, peaceful resistance and their epic steadfastness and will continue to build on their land. And they will end the division and strengthen their national unity. We will accept no less than the independence of the State of Palestine, with East Jerusalem as its capital, on all the Palestinian territory occupied in 1967, to live in peace and security alongside the State of Israel, and a solution for the refugee issue on the basis of resolution 194 (III), as per the operative part of the Arab Peace Initiative. . . .
>
> The world is being asked today to undertake a significant step in the process of rectifying the unprecedented historical injustice inflicted on the Palestinian people since Al-Nakba of 1948.

Every voice supporting our endeavor today is a most valuable voice of courage, and every State that grants support today to Palestine's request for non-member observer State status is affirming its principled and moral support for freedom and the rights of peoples and international law and peace.

Your support for our endeavor today will send a promising message—to millions of Palestinians on the land of Palestine, in the refugee camps both in the homeland and the Diaspora, and to the prisoners struggling for freedom in Israel's prisons—that justice is possible and that there is a reason to be hopeful and that the peoples of the world do not accept the continuation of the occupation.

This is why we are here today.

Your support for our endeavor today will give a reason for hope to a people besieged by a racist, colonial occupation. Your support will confirm to our people that they are not alone and their adherence to international law is never going to be a losing proposition.[387]

Netanyahu chastised Abbas's address as being "full of dripping venom and false propaganda against the IDF and Israeli citizens". It was clear proof, he posited, that Abbas had no interest in peace.[388]

The submitted draft resolution recalled Resolution 181, reaffirmed "the right of the Palestinian people to self-determination and to independence in their State of Palestine on the Palestinian territory occupied since 1967", accorded to Palestine "non-member observer State status in the United Nations", and expressed the hope that the Security Council would favorably consider Palestine's application from the previous year for full membership.[389] It was adopted as Resolution 67/19 by the General Assembly on November 29, 2012, by a vote of 138 to 9 (with 41 abstentions). Joining the US and Israel in opposition were Canada, the Czech Republic, the Marshall Islands, Micronesia, Nauru, Palau, and Panama. Secretary Clinton lamented it as an "unfortunate and counterproductive" resolution that "places further obstacles in the path to peace."[390]

The woeful rhetoric emanating from Washington was matched only by that from Israeli officials. "The UN was founded to advance the cause of peace," responded Israeli Ambassador to the UN Ron Prosor. "Today the Palestinians are turning their back on peace. Don't let history record that today the UN helped them along on their march of folly."[391] Barak Ravid noted in *Haaretz* how "Israel's leaders competed with each other" to "utter the most disparaging remark" about the UN bid. "Never have so many press releases been issued over an event that they themselves characterized as meaningless. Deputy Foreign Minister Danny Ayalon outdid his peers. 'This day is the day of the historic rout of the Palestinians,' Ayalon declared in tones reminiscent of Iraq's propaganda minister's boasting victory over the Americans as tanks poured through the streets of Baghdad." Israel's political leadership was not blind, however, to the resolution's true significance. The UN vote was

> the international community's warning light to Israel, as much
> as a show of support for the Palestinians. Germany, France,
> Britain, Italy and other friendly countries delivered messages
> to Israel with their votes—their patience with the occupation
> of the West Bank has worn off, they have had enough of settle-
> ment construction and there's no faith in Israeli declarations
> of hands outstretched in peace and a desire to advance toward
> a Palestinian state.[392]

The denunciations of the vote from the US and Israel served to mask their real concern, which was that Palestine's status upgrade meant it could pursue legal actions against Israel at the ICC. This was perfectly well understood. The *New York Times* noted that the vote was "a sharp rebuke to the United States and Israel", whose "major concern" was that the Palestinians might use their new status to join the ICC and pursue legal action against Israel for viola-tions of international law.[393] Yet political commentators and analysts in the US media still dutifully parroted the government's rhetoric and exerted consider-able effort to feign ignorance about the vote's significance. In *Foreign Affairs*, Robert Blecher, too, acknowledged that it would allow the Palestinians access to international bodies where they could pursue legal actions against Israel, yet nevertheless dismissed it as "little more than an act of political theater". Rather than advising the US government to support Palestinians' rights, he advised the PA not to pursue legal remedy through international mechanisms lest the US and Israel harshly punish the Palestinians for this sin.[394]

Human Rights Watch, on the other hand, urged Palestinian leaders to pur-sue ratification of international human rights treaties and the Rome Statute of the ICC. It also urged governments "that have pressed Palestine to forgo membership in the ICC" or threatened sanctions to reverse their policies. "This could help Palestinian and Israeli victims of human rights abuses and war crimes obtain a measure of justice," said Sarah Leah Whitson, "something other gov-ernments should not try to block."[395] In addition to the Rome Statute, Palestine had the option of joining the Statute for the ICJ, as well as treaties such as the Law of the Sea Convention and the Geneva Conventions, which would allow Palestine to file complaints and pursue legal claims against Israel for its illegal settlements and blockade of Gaza.[396]

"Those who worry about the International Criminal Court", as Saeb Erekat appropriately put it, "should not commit acts that will take them there."[397]

Israel's response to the vote was to withhold from the PA more than $100 million confiscated from Palestinian taxpayers on its behalf, as well as to announce an expansion of settlements in occupied East Jerusalem.[398] The plan included the construction in an area designated "E1" of 3,000 new housing units in order to prevent the territorial contiguity of Palestine.[399] Condemning the settlements as "illegal under international law", Ban Ki-moon described the plan as "an almost fatal blow to remaining chances of securing a two-State solution."[400] The UK likewise condemned the plan as "illegal under international law" and joined France, Spain, Sweden, and Denmark in summoning the Israeli ambassador to register its protest—"an unusually sharp diplomatic step that reflected the growing frustration abroad with Israel's policies on the Palestinian issue", as Isabel Kershner pointed out.[401] In the UN Security Council, a resolution was proposed condemning Israel's announcement, but while supported by every other member, it never went to a vote due to the US's opposition. So, instead, a non-binding statement condemning Israel's declared intent to further violate international law was proposed; but the US blocked it, too, prompting the Council's EU members to go ahead and issues a joint statement of their own.[402]

The US government reissued its usual meaningless declaration of "long-standing opposition to settlements" solely on the grounds that it was "counter-productive" in terms of convincing the Palestinians to return to the negotiating table. By issuing such rhetoric, Victoria Nuland argued, the US government proved that its policy was "evenhanded". But when pressed several times about what the US would actually *do* about it in terms of consequences for Israel's illegal actions, Nuland first dodged the question and then informed that she had no further comment. Challenged yet further on the US's alleged even-handedness, the best she could do was to repeat the demand that the Palestinians could not exercise self-determination without Israel's approval, which they must achieve by reentering negotiations while Israel continued to prejudice the outcome.[403]

Israel's reaction to the UN vote was "puzzling", the *New York Times* editors commented, given how Israel had "disparaged the United Nations vote as insignificant." But there was no real mystery about it; further down the page, they pointed out that it was well understood that for Israel to develop the E1 area with Jewish settlements would be "fatal to a two-state solution."[404] In a subsequent editorial, they stated that Israel's plan "would split the West Bank and prevent the creation of a viable contiguous Palestinian state." Accordingly, there was "increasing talk" of "a one-state future". This would be "disastrous to both sides", they opined. It would be disastrous for Israel, they explained, because annexing the West Bank would "risk its character as a Jewish state because

Israeli Jews could become a minority in their own country." Furthermore, Israel would be forced "to decide whether to give Palestinians equal rights". The only problem the *Times* editors saw with Israel not treating Arabs equally was that it "would harm Israel's standing as a democracy." They didn't bother elaborating on why they thought a single democratic state recognizing the equal rights of all of its inhabitants would be a disaster for the Palestinians, for the obvious reason.[405]

The *Times* editors commented further on how every other member of the Security Council condemned Israel's announcement while "the Obama administration has resisted joining criticism of Israel." They didn't bother to explain *why* the international community condemned the announcement.[406] Their own criticism was limited to the complaint that it made it "nearly impossible to restart peace negotiations". Even worse, it was "a terrible distraction from the Iranian nuclear issue" and "unwisely alienated the European Union". The fact that Israel's settlement construction infringed on the rights of Palestinians and violated international law was, of course, of no consideration. Accordingly, they parroted the US government's position that Abbas must "forgo applying for Palestinian membership in United Nations affiliates or trying to bring cases against Israel in the International Criminal Court."[407]

Yet more proof of just how "evenhanded" the Obama administration was, the day after the UN vote, Secretary Clinton gave a speech for a gala dinner at the Saban Center for Middle East Policy. Included on the guest list were Israel's Foreign Minister Lieberman, Deputy Prime Minister Meridor, and Ambassador Oren. Clinton opened her remarks by stating that those in attendance had "a lot to celebrate" because "America has Israel's back". She bragged that the US had "proved it again" by voting against the General Assembly resolution upgrading Palestine's status at the UN. "America and Israel are in it together", she assured, including the US government's racist commitment to Israel as a "Jewish state".

The usual euphemistic demands were made of Hamas to renounce the right of armed opposition to foreign occupation, accept their framework for negotiations that rejected the application of international law, and renounce the right of Palestinian refugees to return to their homeland. By doing so, Hamas could "rejoin the international community"—a standard euphemism meaning to comply with Washington's dictates.

The PA, on the other hand, deserved some measure of praise for being much more acquiescent. Clinton praised Abbas for dutifully fulfilling the PA's intended role by building a security force that worked daily with the IDF to keep Israel and its settler communities safe. But Abbas, too, was prone to fits of disobedience, such as by taking "a step in the wrong direction" by appealing to the world community to help resolve the conflict through the recognition of Palestinians' rights and application of international law.

Yes, the Palestinians were suffering, Clinton admitted. She proceeded with the usual tripe about how their suffering was nobody's fault but their own. They could have already had a state, she asserted, if only they had "made the right decision in 1947". If only the majority population would have submissively acquiesced to surrendering their right to self-determination and to having their land expropriated for redistribution to the more worthy minority in order for the "Jewish state" to be established there . . . .

Then again at Camp David, the Palestinians could have made the "right decision". If only Yasser Arafat had been willing to acquiesce to Israel's demand for additional territorial concessions, rather than so stubbornly insisting that the Palestinian state should be established in the remaining 22 percent of former Palestine comprising the West Bank and Gaza Strip . . . . If only he had not failed to appreciate Israel's generosity in offering to annex all major settlement blocks, in addition to East Jerusalem, and to leave the Palestinians with a series of Bantustan-like enclaves separated by Jewish-only highways and surrounded by Israeli military forces, which enclaves they were welcome to call a "state" if they so pleased . . . .

Yet again at Annapolis, the Palestinians had missed another opportunity by refusing to go along with what Ehud Olmert and Tzipi Livni wanted. If only the Palestinians could have appreciated Livni's animosity toward international law and accepted that there was no place for it in the framework for negotiations . . . . If only they had been more willing to negotiate future borders while Israel insisted on prejudicing the outcome, and while Israel made clear that, thanks to US backing, it would continue to violate both international law and the terms of the Road Map with impunity . . . . [408]

In the General Assembly, immediately following the vote, US Ambassador to the UN Susan Rice issued the Obama administration's denunciation, castigating both the Palestinian leadership and the international community. "Today's grand pronouncements will soon fade," she cursed, "and the Palestinian people will wake up tomorrow and find that little about their lives has changed, save that the prospects of a durable peace have only receded." [409]

It was a promise the US would continue to do its best to fulfill.

CONCLUSION

SINCE PALESTINE HAS BEEN recognized by the UN as a state, the siege of Gaza and the violence have continued, including another full-scale military assault by Israel against the Gaza Strip that exceeded Operation Cast Lead in both duration and civilian deaths. Of the 2,192 Palestinians killed, at least 1,523—well over two-thirds—were civilians, including 287 women and 519 children.[1] The fifty-day operation, dubbed "Protective Edge", was launched on July 8, 2014, and ended with a ceasefire on August 26. The US mainstream media once again blamed the Palestinians, although even Washington recognized its limited ability this time to manage perceptions and joined the rest of the world in criticizing Israel for bombing UN schools.

The "peace process" has worn on, with Abbas backing down and agreeing to return to talks despite Israel's ongoing colonization of the West Bank, and with the US playing its usual role of pressuring the Palestinians to accept Israel's demands, including recognition of Israel as a "Jewish state". Abbas reentered negotiations with an agreement from Israel for a series of prisoner releases in exchange for his commitment not to seek membership in any additional international organizations. After Israel announced additional housing construction in East Jerusalem and reneged on the agreement by refusing to release the final group of prisoners unless Abbas agreed to extend the talks beyond their deadline of April 29, 2014, a reconciliation agreement between Fatah and Hamas was signed and Abbas submitted Palestine's application for membership in fifteen international conventions and treaties. This prompted the US media to largely blame the Palestinians for the failure of talks, although, once again, even the government recognized that it could not conceal the fact that the Palestinians' actions were a direct response to Israel's. With extreme prejudice to the Palestinians, Secretary of State John Kerry was careful to blame both sides equally.

It wasn't until after yet another year was lost that Mahmoud Abbas finally moved forward with submitting the request to accede to the Rome Statute of the International Criminal Court. Bringing the number of state parties to the Rome Statute to 123, Palestine's accession was effected on January 2, 2015, and entered into force on April 1, 2015. Had Abbas acted sooner, he might very well have been able to deter yet another massacre of his people in Gaza.

For the Palestinian Authority to play a constructive role in achieving a peaceful resolution, it must be legitimate in the eyes of its own people, cease acting as "Israel's Enforcer", and exercise leadership by defying the US and Israel and pursuing legal recourse through international organizations such as the United Nations, the International Criminal Court, and the International Court of Justice. If the US and Israel punish the PA by cutting off funding, they risk collapsing the very regime they established under the Oslo accords to block implementation of the two-state solution. Palestinians cannot gain their independence so long as the PA leadership is content to remain financially dependent on their oppressors. To achieve the economic growth necessary to attain independence from Washington and Tel Aviv, there must be an end to Israel's occupation, settlement regime, and siege of Gaza. If Abbas fails to exercise his duties to his own people, the Palestinians must find new leadership less hesitant to uphold their rights before the international community. If the way forward requires the dissolution of the PA, so be it. Indeed, this would seem to be a prerequisite.

If Hamas continues to seek this leadership role for itself, it must also end its crimes against both its own people and the residents of Israel. It must recognize that indiscriminate rocket attacks are not only war crimes and cost it legitimacy in the eyes of the world, but are also a strategic mistake. Not only are such attacks illegal and immoral, but it is utter foolishness to provide the Israeli government with the very pretext it requires to be able to continue its criminal policies. Furthermore, Palestine's leadership must remain united and not allow itself to become a willing victim to the US and Israel's divide-and-conquer strategy, as occurred following Hamas's 2006 election victory.

On the question of Israeli settlements, having been established in violation of international law, the fact of their existence does not confer to the state of Israel rights to the land upon which they have been built. All private land stolen for their development should be returned to its rightful owners, whose options would include selling or allowing the current residents to continue living there as tenants. In the case of housing developments on land considered to be public Palestinian property, any Jews who wish to continue their residence there following the complete withdrawal of occupying military forces should be allowed to do so, to live side by side with their Arab neighbors as fellow Palestinians. Those who would prefer not to remain as residents of Palestine would be equally free to move to Israel, or elsewhere. Any abandoned housing units could be utilized to provide shelter to Palestinian refugees as part of an organized resettlement program. Israel would have an incentive to coordinate with the government of Palestine under such a program if the transfer of Israel's improvements and developments on that stolen land was considered part of a compensation package in furtherance of the goal of a just resolution to the refugee problem and settlement of all claims against Israel.

A few words should also be said about the growing advocacy for a one-state solution—a single, democratic state in all of former Palestine in which the equal rights of all its citizens are respected. There is, at present, a pointless division among supporters of Palestinian rights over the question of whether a single state or two states would be the preferable solution. If a single democratic state is the ultimate goal, the first step towards its realization must be the implementation of the two-state solution in accordance with the international consensus. Acceptance of a state within the 22 percent of former Palestine comprised of Gaza, the West Bank, and East Jerusalem does not constitute a renunciation of the right of Palestinian refugees to return to their homeland, whereas it is unrealistic to focus on achieving the exercise of that right so long as the occupation and settlement regime continues. Only once the occupation is ended, the accommodation of lawlessness and racism by world governments is ceased, and Palestine's independence is realized will the focus on achieving a just resolution to the refugee problem have a chance of bearing fruit. Not until Palestinians exercise their sovereignty will they have the political leverage required to realize the return of any refugees who still cling to that hope, as well as to come to terms with Israel on the matter of compensation for the victims of ethnic cleansing.

Once the root causes and reasons for the persistence of the Israeli-Palestinian conflict are understood, the solutions become more readily apparent. While difficult problems would remain to be worked out, it is self-evident that to achieve a way forward, the primary obstacle to peace must be removed. For peace to be realized, the US government's support for Israel's crimes against the Palestinian people must end. Israel's violations of international law could not continue without this US support. It is not the purpose of this book to instruct concerned individuals on what steps they can take to help achieve that goal. It is up to every person who chooses to take up political activism to decide what role they can play based on their own unique abilities. Certainly, Americans have a special responsibility in this regard. Our collective efforts must be focused on rendering it politically infeasible for the US government to continue its complicity in crimes against humanity, which must start with educating ourselves and others. The lies must be exposed and the truth about the conflict must be brought to light.

It is to that end that this book was written. It is my sincere hope that it may contribute to the cause and that you will have found it valuable for your own efforts to help achieve peace and justice in the Middle East. It is up to you how to utilize the knowledge and any insights you may have found within its pages to help eliminate the single greatest obstacle to a peaceful resolution: the criminal policies of the government of the United States of America.

NOTES

A note on quotations and references: Certain names in this book are spelled variously by different sources cited, but, for consistency and to avoid confusion, have been standardized throughout this book. For example, the spelling "Jabaliya" has been adopted; if the source for a quote spelled the word "Jabaliyah", "Jabalia", or "Jabalya", it has been changed. "Yasser" Arafat is used where the work cited may have been "Yasir", and so on. British English has been replaced with American English spellings. Certain other conventions have also been standardized for consistency throughout, and obvious typos or grammatical errors in source material at times have been corrected to make for a better reading experience. No substantive alterations have been made and quotes are otherwise verbatim from sources cited. If you are reading an electronic version of this book, links are provided wherever possible to original sources. Web addresses have, with some exceptions, been excluded from notes in the print edition because to include them would significantly increase the length of the book and hence printing costs and book price. In most cases, sources may be easily found online by simply doing a search for the title.

There are a number of useful resources online for finding and accessing UN documents. The main UN website, where information about the organization and its bodies as well as Security Council and General Assembly resolutions can be found, is www.un.org. Voting records are available at the UN Bibliographic Information System website, http://unbisnet.un.org. For historical documents specific to the topic, see the United Nations Information System on the Question of Palestine at http://unispal.un.org. A searchable database is located at the Official Documentation System of the United Nations, http://documents. un.org. Another useful resource is http://undocs.org. If you know the document symbol you are searching for, it can often be found by adding it to the URL following a backslash. For example, to find UN Security Council Resolution 242, you would enter "http://undocs.org/S/RES/242(1967)". For a guide to UN document symbols, see http://research.un.org/en/docs/symbols.

Introduction

1.   See Chapter 9: The Statehood 'Ploy': The Bias of the New York Times.
2.   Shlomo Ben-Ami, "A War to Start All Wars: Will Israel Ever Seal the Victory of 1948?" *Foreign Affairs*, September/October 2008.
3.   See Chapter 9: The Statehood 'Ploy': The Bias of the New York Times.
4.   Ben-Ami, "A War to Start All Wars."
5.   See Chapter 9, footnote 63.
6.   Ari Shavit, *My Promised Land: The Triumph and Tragedy of Israel* (New York: Spiegel & Grau, 2013).
7.   See Chapter 9: The Statehood 'Ploy': 'Defensible Borders'.
8.   See Chapter 8: The 'Special Relationship': 'The 1967 Lines'.
9.   Ken Silverstein and Michael Scherer, "Born-Again Zionists," *Mother Jones*, September/October 2002.
10. See Chapter 4: Obama's 'New Beginning'.
11. See Chapter 8: The 'Special Relationship': Rewarding Israel for Violating International Law.
12. See Chapter 2: 'Operation Cast Lead': The US's Rejection of a Ceasefire.

Preface

1.   "Remarks by the President on the Middle East and North Africa," *The White House*, May 19, 2011.
2.   Glenn Kessler, "Understanding Obama's shift on Israel and the '1967 lines,'" *The Fact Checker*, *Washington Post*, May 20, 2011. Josh Rogin, "Obama alters U.S. policy, tells Israel to start with '67 borders," *The Cable*, *Foreign Policy*, May 19, 2011. Mark Landler and Steven Lee Myers, "Obama Sees '67 Borders as Starting Point for Peace Deal," *New York Times*, May 19, 2011. The *Times* stated, "Mr. Obama's statement represented a subtle, but significant shift, in American policy." See further discussion in Chapter 8.
3.   See, for example, Noam Chomsky's essential analysis of the Israeli-Palestinian conflict and the US role: *Fateful Triangle: The United States, Israel & The Palestinians* (Cambridge: South End Press, 1999).
4.   Jeremy R. Hammond, "Cease-Fire Will End With Israeli Attack on Gaza," *JeremyRHammond.com*, June 30, 2008.
5.   See story number 9, "US Arms Used for War Crimes in Gaza," in *Censored 2010: The Top 25 Censored Stories of 2008-09* (New York: Seven Stories Press, 2009), 42-46. Additionally, I wrote the update for this story, which is also available online at *ProjectCensored.org*, May 8, 2010.
6.   Jeremy R. Hammond, *The Rejection of Palestinian Self-Determination: The Struggle for Palestine and the Roots of the Israeli-Arab Conflict* (Raleigh: Lulu Press Inc., 2009).
7.   Jeremy R. Hammond, "The Myth of the U.N. Creation of Israel," *Foreign Policy Journal*, October 26, 2010. Dr. Mordechai Nisan, "Is UN Creation of Israel a Myth? Ask Foreign Policy Journal," *Arutz Sheva*, October 27, 2010. Jeremy R. Hammond, "Rejoinder to 'Is UN Creation of Israel a Myth? Ask Foreign Policy Journal,'" *Foreign Policy Journal*, October 28, 2010. See also: Jeremy R. Hammond, "The Role of the U.N. in Creating the Israeli-Palestinian Conflict," *Washington Report on Middle East Affairs*, August 2013, 20-21.

Chapter 1

1.   John Kifner, "Islamic Fundamentalist Group Splitting Palestinian Uprising," *New York Times*, September 17, 1988. Zachary Laub, "Backgrounders: Hamas," *Council on Foreign Relations*, August 1, 2014.
2.   Richard Sale, "Hamas history tied to Israel," *United Press International*, June 18, 2002. Andrew Higgins, "How Israel Helped to Spawn Hamas," *Wall Street Journal*, January 24, 2009.
3.   US Department of State, "Fundamentalism and the Intifada: Defining the Issues," cable from the American Consulate in Jerusalem to the Secretary of State, September 23, 1988; published at *Wikileaks.org*, accessed August 7, 2014.
4.   US Department of State, "Islamic Group, Hamas, Outlawed," cable from the American Embassy in Tel Aviv to the Secretary of State; published at *Wikileaks.org*, accessed August 7, 2014.
5.   "Jewish settler kills 40 at holy site," *BBC*, February 25, 1994. "Palestinian suicide attacks," *BBC*, January 29, 2007.

6.   Francis A. Boyle, "The Creation of the State of Palestine," *European Journal of International Law,* January 1, 1990. UN General Assembly, *Letter dated 18 November 1988 from the Permanent Representative of Jordan to the United Nations Addressed to the Secretary-General*, A/43/827 (November 18, 1988).

7.   Boyle, "The Creation of the State of Palestine."

8.   UN General Assembly, 43rd Session, *Provisional Verbatim Record of the Seventy-Eighth Meeting* (December 13, 1988), A/43/PV.78 (January 3, 1989).

9.   Jeremy R. Hammond, "The Myth of the U.N. Creation of Israel," *Foreign Policy Journal*, October 26, 2010.

10.   UN General Assembly Resolution 106 (S-1), *Special Committee on Palestine*, A/RES/106 (S-1) (May 15, 1947).

11.   UN General Assembly, *United Nations Special Committee on Palestine Report to the General Assembly, Volume 1*, A/364 (September 3, 1947). Hereafter "UNSCOP Report."

12.   UN General Assembly, *Ad Hoc Committee on the Palestinian Question: Report of Sub-Committee 2*, A/AC.14/32 (November 11, 1947), 41, 43. Hereafter "Report of Sub-Committee 2."

13.   Anglo-American Committee of Inquiry, *A Survey of Palestine: Prepared in December 1945 and January 1946 for the information of the Anglo-American Committee of Inquiry* (Washington, DC: Institute for Palestine Studies, 1991), Volume II, 566. The entire three-volume *Survey of Palestine* is available for purchase at www.palestine-studies.org and can also be viewed online at www.palestineremembered.com/Acre/Books/Story831.html. A dunam is 1,000 square meters, or about a quarter acre.

14.   Report of Sub-Committee 2, 43-44; Appendix 5: "Palestine Land Ownership by Sub-Districts (1945)." A higher quality image of the map is available at http://domino.un.org/maps/m0094.jpg. Statistics were as follows (Arab/Jewish land ownership in percentages): Safad: 68/18; Acre: 87/3; Tiberias: 51/38; Haifa: 42/35; Nazareth: 52/28; Beisan: 44/34; Jenin: 84/1, Tulkarm: 78/17; Nablus: 87/1; Jaffa: 47/39; Ramle: 77/14; Ramallah: 99/less than 1; Jerusalem: 84/2; Gaza: 75/4; Hebron: 96/less than 1; Beersheeba: 15/less than 1.

15.   Walid Khalidi, "Revisiting the UNGA Partition Resolution," *Journal of Palestine Studies*, Vol. XXVII, No. 1 (Autumn 1997). Khalidi writes that "Jewish-owned land on the eve of the partition resolution amounted, according to Jewish sources, to 1,820,000 dunams, or less than 7 percent of the total land area of the country" (13). This would be 6.9 percent, although Khalidi puts the total area of Palestine at the higher figure of 27 million dunams, which would put it at about 6.7 percent. His source cited is: Jewish National Fund, "Jewish Settlements in Palestine" (Jewish National Fund, Jerusalem, March 1948, Mimeographed), p. ii. See also Edward W. Said, *The Question of Palestine* (New York: Vintage Books Edition, 1992), 98. Said writes that, by the end of 1947, the Jewish community had legally acquired 1,734,000 dunams, or about 6.6 percent of the territory of Palestine. He cites a slightly different number of 26,323,000 dunams for the total land area of Palestine, which still rounds to 6.6 percent. Said also notes, "After 1940, when the mandatory authority restricted Jewish land ownership to specific zones inside Palestine, there continued to be illegal buying (and selling) within the 65 percent of the total area restricted to Arabs." According to Abraham Granott, "The total area of land in Jewish possession at the end of June 1947 amounted to 1,850,000 dunams. . . ." See: Abraham Granott, *The Land System in Palestine* (London: Eyre and Spottiswoode 1952), 278. This number would put the amount of land in Jewish possession at 7 percent. Israeli historian Ilan Pappé puts the figure lower, writing, "By the end of the Mandate in 1948, the Jewish community owned around 5.8% of the land in Palestine." See: Ilan Pappé, *The Ethnic Cleansing of Palestine* (Oxford: Oneworld Publications, 2006), Kindle Edition, Location 655. However, this is evidently an error; Pappé seems to have cited the statistic from 1943, which was no longer accurate by the end of the Mandate. Benny Morris likewise puts the amount of land owned by the Jewish community at "7 percent". See: Benny Morris, *1948: A History of the First Arab-Israeli War* (New Haven and London: Yale University Press, 2008), Kindle Edition, Location 957.

16.   UNSCOP Report.

17.   Report of Sub-Committee 2, 43.

18.   Khalidi, "Revisiting the UNGA Partition Resolution," 11, 13. Khalidi cites rounded figures of 12 million dunams for the Arab state and 15 million dunams for the Jewish state, totaling 27 million dunams. Additionally, Jerusalem was to be an international enclave of 187,000 dunams. From this, we arrive at 44.1 percent and 55.2 percent, respectively. Note that Khalidi offers the figures of 45.5 percent and 55.5 percent, respectively, which is apparently either a typographical or rounding error as this totals 101 percent. According to Benny Morris, the plan called for about 55 percent of Palestine to go to the Jewish state and about 42 percent to the Arab state, which would indicate a significantly larger international zone for Jerusalem. Morris, *1948*, Locations 945-952.

19. UNSCOP Report.

20. UN General Assembly Resolution 106 (S-1). UNSCOP Report. UNSCOP consisted of representatives from Australia, Canada, Czechoslovakia, Guatemala, India, Iran, Netherlands, Peru, Sweden, Uruguay and Yugoslavia. Pakistan and Yemen were admitted as members to the UN in 1947, bringing the total to fifty-seven members.

21. UN General Assembly, Ad Hoc Committee on Palestinian Question, 2nd Meeting, *U.K. Accepts UNSCOP General Recommendations; Will Not Implement Policy Unacceptable to Both Arabs and Jews*, Press Release, GA/PAL/2 (September 26, 1947).

22. UN General Assembly, Ad Hoc Committee on Palestinian Question, 3rd Meeting, *The Arab Case Stated by Mr. Jamal Husseini*, Press Release GA/PAL/3 (September 29, 1947). India, Iran, and Yugoslavia dissented from the majority UNSCOP recommendation, proposing instead a federal state plan, which was "in every respect the most democratic solution" and "most in harmony with the basic principles of the Charter of the United Nations". Moreover, while the partition plan was supported by no Arabs, the federal state plan was supported by "a substantial number of Jews" and would therefore "best serve the interests of both Arabs and Jews." See UNSCOP Report.

23. Report of Sub-Committee 2.

24. UN Security Council, 253rd Meeting, *The Palestine Question*, S/PV.253 (February 24, 1948).

25. UN Security Council, 271st Meeting, *Continuation of the discussion of the Palestine question*, S/PV.271 (March 19, 1948).

26. Pappé, *Ethnic Cleansing of Palestine*, Location 267-270. See footnote 12. Pappé refers to Benny Morris's *The Birth of the Palestinian Refugee Problem, 1947-1949*, in which Morris mentions a figure of 200,000-300,000 refugees by this time. Pappé remarks, "There were in fact 350,000 if one adds all of the population from the 200 towns and villages that were destroyed by 15 May 1948."

27. The Declaration of the Establishment of the State of Israel, May 14, 1948; published at the Israel Ministry of Foreign Affairs website (www.mfa.gov.il), accessed October 16, 2014.

28. Pappé, *Ethnic Cleansing of Palestine*, Locations 220, 881. As Pappé documents, ethnic cleansing operations began in early December, 1947.

29. Rashid Khalidi, *Brokers of Deceit: How the U.S. Has Undermined Peace in the Middle East* (Boston: Beacon Press, 2013), Kindle Edition, Location 191.

30. Greg Myre, "Israel's Chief of Staff Denounces Policies Against Palestinians," *New York Times*, October 30, 2003. Justin Huggler, "Disaster looms for Israel, says ex-security chiefs," *The Independent*, November 15, 2003.

31. James Bennet, "Leader of Hamas Killed by Missile in Israeli Strike," *New York Times*, March 22, 2004.

32. Esther Pan, "The Assassination of Sheik Yassin," *Council on Foreign Relations*, March 24, 2004.

33. Ibid.

34. Justin Huggler, "Israel rejects 'insincere' Hamas offer of 10-year truce," *The Independent*, January 27, 2004.

35. Conal Urquhart, "Hamas hints at ceasefire as the Palestinians vote," *The Guardian*, January 9, 2005.

36. US Department of State Office of Research, "Hamas and Fateh Neck and Neck As Palestinian Elections Near," January 19, 2005; published at www.fas.org, accessed August 16, 2014.

37. Chris McGreal, "Islamists halt attacks on Israel," *The Guardian*, January 24, 2005.

38. Arnon Regular, "Hamas wins overwhelming victory in Gaza vote," *Haaretz*, January 29, 2005. Molly Moore, "In Gaza, New Hamas-Dominated Council Attends to Basics," *Washington Post*, May 16, 2005. "Palestinian, Israeli leaders announce cease-fire," *CNN*, February 9, 2005. "Palestinian militants say they will hold to truce," *CNN*, February 12, 2005.

39. Moore, "In Gaza."

40. "Demolition of Gaza homes completed," *Ynetnews*, September 1, 2005.

41. "Truck Explodes At Gaza Hamas Rally," *CBS News*, September 23, 2005. Shmulik Hadad, "Rockets fired at western Negev," *Ynetnews*, September 23, 2005.

42. Hadad, "Rockets fired at western Negev." Ali Waked, "Gaza: Blast during Hamas rally kills 19," *Ynetnews*, September 23, 2005. Amos Harel, "Abbas: Hamas irresponsibility caused Gaza rally blast Friday," *Haaretz*, September 23, 2005. Khaled Abu Toameh, "PA, Hamas argue over blast," *Jerusalem Post*, September 24, 2004. Tova Dadon, "3 hurt in rocket barrage on South," *Ynetnews*, September 24, 2005. Greg Myre, "Truckful of Rockets Explodes at Hamas Rally in Gaza, Killing 15 and Injuring Dozens," *New York Times*, September 24, 2005. "Police, fearing terror bids, boost alert status nationwide," *Haaretz*, September 25, 2005. "Israel kills Islamic Jihad leader in Gaza offensive," *Associated Press*, September 25, 2005. "Hamas pledges end to Gaza rockets," *BBC*, September 26, 2005. "Hamas

says it will stop attacks from Gaza," *CNN*, September 26, 2005. Greg Myre, "Hamas calls cease-fire after 3 days of attacks," *New York Times*, September 26, 2005. Holly Fletcher, "Al-Aqsa Martyrs Brigade," *Council on Foreign Relations*, April 2, 2008.

43. Laura King, "Hamas makes strong showing in elections," *Los Angeles Times*, September 30, 2005.

44. Chris McGreal, "Hamas drops call for destruction of Israel from manifesto," *The Guardian*, January 12, 2006.

45. Greg Myre, "Israel Threatens to Hinder Palestinian Vote," *New York Times*, December 22, 2005. "Israel bars Hamas from voting in East Jerusalem," *National Public Radio*, January 16, 2006.

46. Steven Erlanger, "U.S. Spent $1.9 Million to Aid Fatah in Palestinian Elections," *New York Times*, January 23, 2006.

47. "Hamas at the Helm," *New York Times*, February 2, 2006.

48. Ibid.

49. Steven Erlanger, "Hamas Routs Ruling Faction, Casting Pall on Peace Process," *New York Times*, January 27, 2006.

50. "Hamas faces a terrible dilemma," OUPblog, *Oxford University Press*, January 26, 2006.

51. "Hamas leader sets conditions for truce," *CNN*, January 29, 2006.

52. Khalid Mish'al, "We will not sell our people or principles for foreign aid," *The Guardian*, January 31, 2006.

53. Aluf Benn, "U.S. backs Israel on aid for humanitarian groups, not Hamas," *Haaretz*, February 16, 2006. Shmuel Rosner, Aluf Benn, and Amos Harel, "U.S. asks Palestinians to return $50 million in aid," *Haaretz*, February 17, 2006.

54. Gideon Levy, "As the Hamas team laughs," *Haaretz*, January 19, 2006.

55. Steven Erlanger, "U.S. and Israelis Are Said to Talk of Hamas Ouster," *New York Times*, February 14, 2006.

56. Ibid.

57. Sarah El Deeb, "Hamas Cabinet ministers face financial crisis on first day in office," *Associated Press*, March 30, 2006. Anne Barnard, "Israel to sever all links with Palestinians," *Sydney Morning Herald*, April 11, 2006.

58. Steven Erlanger and Greg Myre, "Hamas and Abbas Clash Over Path for Palestinians," *New York Times*, February 19, 2006.

59. "Hamas revokes Abbas's wider powers," *Reuters*, March 6, 2006. "Senior aide to Mahmoud Abbas accuses Hamas of coup attempt," *Haaretz*, March 6, 2006.

60. "'We Do Not Wish to Throw Them Into the Sea,'" *Washington Post*, February 26, 2006.

61. Rachelle Marshall, "Israel and the U.S. Take Aim at Palestinian Democracy," *Washington Report on Middle East Affairs*, April 2006, 7-9.

62. Steven Erlanger, "Hamas Fires Rockets at Israel After Calling Off Truce," *New York Times*, June 10, 2006.

63. "Beach strike shakes Hamas cease-fire," *CNN*, June 9, 2006.

64. Sarah El Deeb and Ibrahim Barzak, "Hamas Military Wing Calls of Israel Truce," *Associated Press*, June 9, 2006. "Palestinians killed on Gaza beach," *BBC*, June 9, 2006.

65. Erlanger, "Hamas Fires Rockets at Israel."

66. "Israel captures pair in Gaza raid," *BBC*, June 24, 2006. "Administrative Detention," *B'Tselem.org*, January 1, 2011; accessed October 16, 2014.

67. Ian Fisher and Steven Erlanger, "Israel Threatens to Widen Conflict Over Captured Soldier," *New York Times*, June 28, 2006. "Israeli troops invade Gaza, attack bridges, knock out power," *Associated Press*, June 28, 2006.

68. B'Tselem, *Act of Vengeance: Israel's Bombing of the Gaza Power Plant and its Effects*, September 2006.

69. "Israel seizes Hamas legislators," *BBC*, June 29, 2006.

70. "Hamas Provokes a Fight," *New York Times*, June 29, 2006.

71. Steven Erlanger, "With Israeli Use of Force, Debate Over Proportion," *New York Times*, July 19, 2006.

72. Gideon Levy, "Gaza's darkness," *Haaretz*, September 3, 2006.

73. "Report: 307 Palestinians killed in Gaza since Shalit's kidnapping," *Ynetnews*, September 13, 2006.

74. Avi Issacharoff and Yoav Stern, "Poll: 67% of Israelis want talks with PA gov't including Hamas," *Haaretz*, September 27, 2006.

75. Avi Issacharoff and Aluf Benn, "PA's Abbas to demand Hamas honor Oslo Accords," *Haaretz*, September 26, 2009. "Poll: Most Palestinians think Hamas should not recognize Israel," *Deutsche Presse-Agentur*, September 18, 2006.

76. Rory McCarthy, "Gaza sliding into civil war," *The Guardian*, October 12, 2006.

77. Diaa Hadid, "Hamas: Fatah Acting As U.S. Stooge," *Associated Press*, October 15, 2006. Scott Wilson, "Fatah Troops Enter Gaza With Israeli Assent," *Washington Post*, May 18, 2007. Aaron Klein, "Abbas asks Rice for weapons from U.S.," *World Net Daily*, October 4, 2006. A version of the WND article was also published by *Ynetnews*.

78. Yoav Stern, "Abbas lacks majority in Fatah to oust Hamas government," *Haaretz*, October 17, 2006. "Hamas: No recognition of Israel," *BBC*, November 14, 2006.

79. Greg Myre, "Israel and Palestinians Reach Truce After Months of Fighting in Gaza," *New York Times*, November 26, 2006. Dina Kraft, "Israel Withdraws From Gaza as Truce Begins, Unsteadily," *New York Times*, November 26, 2006.

80. Scott Wilson, "Hamas Rejects Plan by Abbas To Call Elections," *Washington Post*, December 17, 2006. "Hamas to boycott early elections," *BBC*, December 18, 2006.

81. Tim Butcher, "Hamas and Fatah agree unity government deal," *The Telegraph*, February 9, 2007.

82. Ronny Sofer, "Arabs decide to revive peace plan," *Agence France-Presse*, March 29, 2007. John Crowley, "Israel rejects Arab peace initiative," *The Telegraph*, March 29, 2007.

83. Isabel Kershner, "Hamas militants declare end to cease-fire with Israel," *New York Times*, April 24, 2007.

84. Steven Erlanger, "Israelis Bomb Hamas Targets in Gaza, Killing 5," *New York Times*, May 27, 2007.

85. Scott Wilson, "Gaza Fighting Intensifies, Leaving at Least 21 Dead," *Washington Post*, May 17, 2007. Steven Erlanger, "Fatah and Hamas Chiefs Meet on Cease-Fire," *New York Times*, May 24, 2007.

86. Wilson, "Fatah Troops Enter Gaza."

87. Aaron Klein, "Hamas seizes US weapons," *World Net Daily*; republished by *Ynetnews*, May 14, 2007.

88. Steven Erlanger and Isabel Kershner, "Attacks Escalate as Palestinians Fight for Power," *New York Times*, June 12, 2007.

89. Isabel Kershner and Teghreed El-Khodary, "9 Die in Fierce Palestinian Factional Fighting," *New York Times*, June 11, 2007.

90. Erlanger and Kershner, "Attacks Escalate."

91. Steven Erlanger, "Hamas Seizes Broad Control in Gaza Strip," *New York Times*, June 13, 2007.

92. "Abbas dismisses government, declares emergency," *Reuters*, June 14, 2007.

93. Scott Wilson, "Abbas Appoints Crisis Cabinet," *Washington Post*, June 18, 2007.

94. "Opinion of lawyer who drafted Palestinian law," *Reuters*, July 8, 2007.

95. Scott Wilson, "Abbas Appoints Crisis Cabinet," *Washington Post*, June 18, 2007.

96. Glenn Kessler, "U.S. Lifts Embargo To Help Abbas," *Washington Post*, June 19, 2007.

97. Helene Cooper, "U.S. Unfreezes Millions in Aid to Palestinians," *New York Times*, June 19, 2007.

98. David Rose, "The Gaza Bombshell," *Vanity Fair*, April 2008.

99. "Guide: Gaza under blockade," *BBC*, July 6, 2010.

100. US Department of State, "Cashless in Gaza?" cable from the American Embassy in Tel Aviv to the Secretary of State, November 3, 2008; published at *Wikileaks.org*, accessed August 8, 2014. "Israel said would keep Gaza near collapse: WikiLeaks," *Reuters*, January 5, 2011.

101. UN General Assembly, Human Rights Council, 7th Session, *Human Rights Situation in Palestine and Other Occupied Territories: Report of the Special Rapporteur on the situation of human rights in the Palestinian territories occupied since 1967, John Dugard*, A/HRC/7/17 (January 21, 2008).

102. Isabel Kershner, "Olmert Warns of a Major Military Thrust in Gaza," *New York Times*, June 7, 2008.

103. "Report: Abbas informed of Israel's plan to retake Gaza," *Ynetnews*, June 7, 2008.

104. Griff Witte and Ellen Knickmeyer, "Israel, Hamas Agree on Gaza Strip Truce," *Washington Post*, June 18, 2008.

105. Isabel Kershner, "Truce Is Strained as Militants Launch Rockets and Israel Keeps Goods Out of Gaza," *New York Times*, June 27, 2008. Roi Mandel, "UN: Israel violated truce 7 times in one week," *Ynetnews*, June 27, 2008.

106. Avi Issacharoff, "Gaza truce shaken as four Qassams slam into west Negev," *Haaretz*, June 24, 2008.

107. Barak Ravid, et al, "Jihad threatens to continue rocket attacks, despite truce," *Haaretz*, June 25, 2008.

108. Ibid.

109. "Islamic Jihad Pledges To Observe Ceasefire With Israel," *Agence France-Presse*, June 25, 2008.

110. Isabel Kershner, "Rockets Hit Israel, Breaking Hamas Truce," *New York Times*, June 25, 2008.

111. "Fatah-allied militants fire rocket into Israel from southern Gaza," *Agence France-Presse*, June 27, 2008.

112. Fadi Eyadat and Avi Issacharoff, "Top Hamas official: We'll stop anyone who breaks Gaza truce," *Haaretz*, June 28, 2008.

113. "Gaza truce under strain as rocket lands in Israel," *Reuters*, June 30, 2008.

114. "Israel's Diplomatic Offensive," *New York Times*, June 30, 2008.

115. Jeremy R. Hammond, "Cease-Fire Will End With Israeli Attack on Gaza," *JeremyRHammond.com*, June 30, 2008. This analyst wrote at the time: "In the event of any such invasion, Israel will claim that it had exhausted diplomacy. Israel has made sure that the cease-fire is unsustainable. But it is beneficial as it would be used as political cover for future military action. Coupled with Israel's agreement to a prisoner exchange with Hezbollah, the New York Times calls this 'Israel's Diplomatic Offensive'. The exchange is Israel's effort to wrap-up its 2006 war with Hezbollah before engaging in another war. The 'Diplomatic Offensive' will more likely than not be followed in coming months by a military offensive."

116. Amos Harel, "Palestinians who approach Gaza fence will be shot, says IDF," *Haaretz*, July 1, 2008. "Haniyeh: Israel must lift Gaza siege, open crossings," *Ynetnews*, July 4, 2008.

117. "Hamas officials say group arrested rocket-launcher operators in Gaza," *Jerusalem Post*, July 7, 2008. "Hamas slams Israeli actions targeting Hamas-affiliated charities," *Xinhua*, July 7, 2008.

118. "Israeli troops kill Palestinian in Gaza," *Associated Press*, July 10, 2008. "Hamas arrests Gaza rocket squad after two Qassams hit Negev," *Haaretz*, July 10, 2008. "Israeli troops abduct 12 Hamas members in West Bank," *Agence France-Presse*, July 16, 2008.

119. Amnesty International, *Gaza Blockade—Collective Punishment*, July 4, 2008.

120. "Israel warns Hezbollah war would invite destruction," *Reuters*, October 3, 2008. Amos Harel, "IDF plans to use disproportionate force in next war," *Haaretz*, October 5, 2008. US Department of State, "IDF Regional Commanders Speak Out in Press Interviews," cable from the American Embassy in Tel Aviv to the Secretary of State, October 15, 2008; published at *Wikileaks.org*, accessed August 8, 2014.

121. Gabi Siboni, "Disproportionate Force: Israel's Concept of Response in Light of the Second Lebanon War," *Institute for National Security Studies*, October 2, 2008.

122. Jeremy R. Hammond, "Rogue State: Israeli Violations of U.N. Security Council Resolutions," *Foreign Policy Journal*, January 27, 2010.

123. International Court of Justice, *Legal Consequences of the Construction of a Wall in the Occupied Palestinian Territory*, Advisory Opinion, July 9, 2004.

124. "Obama's Speech in Sderot, Israel," *New York Times*, July 23, 2008.

125. Isabel Kershner, "Israel Moves Toward Building More Settler Homes," *New York Times*, July 25, 2008.

126. Peter Wallsten, "Allies of Palestinians see a friend in Obama," *Los Angeles Times*, April 10, 2008.

127. Richard Pérez-Peña, "McCain attacks Los Angeles Times over its refusal to release '03 Obama video," *New York Times*, October 30, 2008. Hilary Leila Krieger, "McCain camp pushes Obama-Khalidi ties," *Jerusalem Post*, October 29 2008.

128. Matthew Berger, "Palin keeps up the hits," First Read, *MSNBC*, October 29, 2008.

129. Seth Colter Walls, "McCain Funded Work of Palestinian His Campaign Hopes To Tie To Obama," *Huffington Post*, October 28, 2008.

130. Natasha Mozgavaya, "Biden voices 'unshakeable commitment' to strong Israeli-U.S. ties," *Haaretz*, October 28, 2008. The "special relationship", as it was described by President John F. Kennedy, was cemented following Israel's victory in the 1967 war. The name has stuck. See: Douglas Little, "The Making of a Special Relationship: The United States and Israel, 1957 – 68," *International Journal of Middle East Studies*, Vol. 25, No. 4, November 1993, 563-585.

131. The Meir Amit Intelligence and Terrorism Information Center (ITIC), *The Six Months of the Lull Arrangement*, December 2008. This source puts the number of Hamas militants killed in the attack at seven. The more commonly reported number was six, such as the subsequent Amnesty International report cited below. The ITIC is part of the Israel Intelligence Heritage & Commemoration Center (IICC), which characterizes itself as a non-governmental organization but maintains an office at the Defense Ministry and receives government financing. See: Amy Teibel, "Hezbollah Accused of Using Human Shields," *Associated Press*, December 5, 2006. Steven Erlanger, "Militant Zeal," *New York Times*, June 25, 2006.

132. "Rocket From Gaza Lands in Israel," *Reuters*, August 20, 2008.

133. ITIC, *Six Months of the Lull Arrangement*.

134. "Gaza Ceasefire at Risk," *Amnesty International*, November 5, 2008.

135. Julie Stahl, "Israel Considering Military Operation in Gaza," *CNSNews.com*, November 14, 2008.

136. "UNRWA chief: Gaza on brink of humanitarian catastrophe," *Haaretz*, November 21, 2008.

137. Gisha, *Gaza Closure Defined: Collective Punishment*, December 2008.

138. "Gaza Reduced to Bare Survival," *Amnesty International*, December 5, 2008.

139. UN Office of the High Commissioner for Human Rights, "Gaza: Silence is not an option," Statement by the Special Rapporteur on the situation of human rights on Palestinian territories occupied since 1967, Richard Falk, December 9, 2008.

140. Isabel Kershner, "U.N. Rights Investigator Expelled by Israel," *New York Times*, December 15, 2008. Richard Falk, "My expulsion from Israel," *The Guardian*, December 19, 2008.

141. "Hamas declares Gaza truce with Israel is at an end," *Associated Press*, December 19, 2008. Roni Sofer, "Israel in favor of extending Gaza lull," *Ynetnews*, December 13, 2008.

142. Ethan Bronner, "A Gaza Truce Undone by Flaws May Be Revised by Necessity," *New York Times*, December 20, 2008.

143. Matti Friedman, "Hamas Orders Fighters to Hold Fire, Says True With Israel Could Be Renewed," *Associated Press*, December 23, 2008.

144. Larry Derfner, "Rattling the Cage: Accept Hamas's offer," *Jerusalem Post*, December 24, 2008.

145. Adam Entous and Ari Rabinovitch, "Olmert issues 'last-minute' warning to Hamas," *Reuters*, December 25, 2008.

Chapter 2

1. Amos Harel, "IAF strike on Gaza is Israel's version of 'shock and awe,'" *Haaretz*, December 27, 2008.

2. Norman G. Finkelstein, *'This Time We Went Too Far': Truth and Consequences of the Gaza Invasion* (New York: OR Books, 2010), revised and expanded Kindle edition, Location 370.

3. "UN official says Israel responsible for breaking truce with Gaza," *Associated Press*, December 30, 2008. "United Nations: Hamas Did Not Break the Truce, Israel Did," *YouTube* video, 3:31, C-SPAN clip posted by "AntiHypocrisy," January 3, 2009.

4. UN Office of the High Commissioner for Human Rights, "Statement by Prof. Richard Falk, United Nations Special Rapporteur for Human Rights in the Occupied Territories," December 27, 2008.

5. Amos Harel, "After IAF strike kills at least 230 in Gaza, Hamas chief vows third Intifada has come," *Haaretz*, December 28, 2008. Sami Abdel-Shafi, "Inside Gaza: 'The hospital morgues were already full. The dead were piled on top of each other outside,'" *The Independent*, December 28, 2008.

6. "Civilians must be protected in Gaza and Israel," *Amnesty International*, December 28, 2008.

7. Nicola Smith, "Britain and US refuse to demand end to Israeli airstrikes on Gaza," *Sunday Times*, December 28, 2008. Taghreed El-Khodary and Ethan Bronner, "Israelis Say Strikes Against Hamas Will Continue," *New York Times*, December 28, 2008.

8. Robert Pear, "White House Puts Onus on Hamas to End Escalation of Violence," *New York Times*, December 28, 2008.

9. "IDF mobilizes tanks, reinforces troops along Gaza border," *Haaretz*, December 28, 2008.

10. Yaakov Katz, "IAF hits Islamic University targets," *Jerusalem Post*, December 28, 2008. "IFJ Condemns Israel for Strike on Television During Gaza Blitz," *International Federation of Journalists*, December 28, 2008. "Israel destroys Islamic University in new wave of strikes on Gaza," *Haaretz*, December 29, 2008. Taghreed El-Khodary and Isabel Kershner, "Israeli Troops Mass Along Border; Arab Anger Rises," *New York Times*, December 28, 2008. Amira Hass, "'Little Baghdad' in Gaza—bombs, fear and rage," *Haaretz*, December 28, 2008. Abdel-Shafi, "Inside Gaza."

11. UN Security Council, *Press Statement on Situation in Gaza*, SC/9559 (December 28, 2008).

12. "Barak: This is an all out war," *Jerusalem Post*, December 29, 2008.

13. "Barak to MKs: Obama said he would do all to prevent rocket fire on his own home," *Haaretz*, December 29, 2008.

14. Steven Lee Myers and Helene Cooper, "Gaza Crisis Is Another Challenge for Obama, Who Defers to Bush for Now," *New York Times*, December 28, 2008.

15. "Obama closely monitoring Gaza, adviser says," *CNN*, December 28, 2008.

16. Yaakov Katz, "IAF uses new US-supplied smart bomb," *Jerusalem Post*, December 29, 2008.

17. "UN: Over 50 civilians killed in Gaza op," *Jerusalem Post*, December 29, 2008.

18. *Haaretz*, December 29, 2008.

19. Johann Hari, "The true story behind this war is not the one Israel is telling," *The Independent*, December 29, 2008.

20. Ethan Bronner, "Israel Reminds Foes That It Has Teeth," *New York Times*, December 28, 2008.

21. El-Khodary and Kershner, "Israeli Troops Mass Along Border."

22. Rory McCarthy, "Israel pounds Hamas in Gaza," *The Guardian*, December 30, 2008.

23. Ethan Bronner and Taghreed El-Khodary, "No Early End Seen to 'All-Out War' on Hamas in Gaza," *New York Times*, December 30, 2008.

24. McCarthy, "Israel pounds Hamas."

25. Witte and Raghavan, "Israel vows 'all-out war.'"

26. "War Over Gaza," *New York Times*, December 30, 2008.

27. Isabel Kershner, "Despite Strikes, Israelis Vow to Soldier On," *New York Times*, December 30, 2008.

28. Stephen Farrell, "Hamas Credo Led It to End Cease-Fire," *New York Times*, December 29, 2008.

29. "Americans Closely Divided Over Israel's Gaza Attacks," *Rasmussen Reports*, December 31, 2008.

30. Anshel Pfeffer, "Israel claims success in the PR war," *Jewish Chronicle*, December 31, 2008.

31. "Immediate Access to Humanitarian Workers and Observers Essential," *Amnesty International*, December 31, 2008.

32. Barak Ravid, "Disinformation, secrecy and lies: How the Gaza offensive came about," *Haaretz*, December 31, 2008.

33. William Sieghart, "We must adjust our distorted image of Hamas," *The Times*, December 31, 2008. The author was chairman of Forward Thinking, an independent conflict resolution agency.

34. Mark Landler, "U.S. Presses Israel on Cease-Fire," *New York Times*, December 30, 2008. Ethan Bronner and Taghreed El-Khodary, "Amid a Buildup of Its Forces, Israel Ponders a Cease-Fire," *New York Times*, December 30, 2008.

35. Barak Ravid, Amos Harel, and Avi Issacharoff, "Cabinet debating 48-hour Gaza truce as int'l pressure grows," *Haaretz*, December 31, 2008.

36. "White House: Hamas must cease rocket fire as first step to truce," *Haaretz*, December 31, 2008. A Google search at the time of this writing turned up numerous references to the quote from the White House's statement in the international media, none in the US.

37. Amnesty International, December 31, 2008.

38. UN Security Council, 6060th Meeting, *The situation in the Middle East, including the Palestinian question*, S/PV.6060 (December 31, 2008).

39. Ibid.

40. Sudarsan Raghavan, "Israel Rejects Proposal for 48-Hour Truce," *Washington Post*, January 1, 2009.

41. Yaakov Katz, "IDF coordination chief: There is no humanitarian crisis," *Jerusalem Post*, January 2, 2009.

42. Barak Ravid, "Livni: Cease-fire in Gaza would grant Hamas legitimacy," *Haaretz*, January 1, 2009.

43. "Arab League slams Livni remark 'there's no humanitarian crisis in Gaza,'" *Reuters*, January 3, 2009.

44. Amos Harel and Ruth Sinai, "IDF admits to overestimating Gaza rocket severity, but warns worst may be yet to come," *Haaretz*, January 2, 2009.

45. "Livni: Israel should strike Hamas again to halt arms smuggling," *Haaretz*, January 1, 2009.

46. Ethan Bronner, "Israel Rejects Cease-Fire, but Offers Gaza Aid," *New York Times*, January 1, 2009.

47. Taghreed El-Khodary, "In Dense Gaza, Civilians Suffer," *New York Times*, January 1, 2009. It should be noted that since English was not her first language, the *Times* editors would receive El-Khodary's reports and revise or rewrite them, or combine her reports with those of other correspondents such as Bronner and Kershner. See: "Q. and A. With Taghreed El-Khodary in Gaza," The Lede, *New York Times*, January 19, 2009. It may well have been the case that her editors embellished upon her original reporting with the remarks about the "ambiguity" between civilian and military objects.

48. Ibrahim Barzak and Amy Teibel, "Israel kills top Hamas figure, escalating campaign," *Associated Press*, January 1, 2009. Isabel Kershner, "In a Broadening Offensive, Israel Steps Up Diplomacy," *New York Times*, January 2, 2009.

49. Protocol Additional to the Geneva Conventions of 12 August 1949, and relating to the Protection of Victims of International Armed Conflicts (Protocol I), 8 June 1977, Art. 50. Israel is a party to the Geneva Conventions. It is not a party to the Additional Protocols, but many of their provisions, including this one, are considered customary international law that Israel is legally obligated to comply with.

50. Amos Harel and Avi Issacharoff, "IDF sending Hamas a message: Now it's personal," *Haaretz*, January 2, 2009.

51. Charles Krauthammer, "Moral Clarity in Gaza," *Washington Post*, January 2, 2009.

52. Amos Harel and Yoav Stern, "IDF targets senior Hamas figures," *Haaretz*, January 2, 2009. *Haaretz* notes that "In some cases, residents of suspected houses have been able to prevent bombings by climbing up to the roof to show that they will not leave, prompting IDF commanders to call off the strike."

It's worth noting this as such occurrences were absurdly cited as examples of Hamas's use of "human shields" by defenders of Israel's killing of Palestinian civilians.

53. Krauthammer, "Moral Clarity."
54. Alan M. Dershowitz, "Israel's Policy Is Perfectly 'Proportionate,'" *Wall Street Journal*, January 2, 2009.
55. Dershowitz, "Israel's Policy."
56. Natasha Mozgovaya, "Bush calls Hamas attacks 'acts of terror', says working on truce," *Haaretz*, January 3, 2009.
57. "U.S. blocks U.N. statement on Gaza," *Associated Press*, January 3, 2009. "U.S. blocks UN cease-fire resolution, diplomats say," *Associated Press*, January 4, 2009. Yitzhak Benhorin, "UN: US foils Libyan ceasefire proposal," *Ynetnews*, January 4, 2009. Shlomo Shamir and Barak Ravid, "U.S. quashes Arab-backed Gaza cease-fire resolution in UN Security Council meet," *Haaretz*, January 4, 2009.
58. Gareth Porter, "Bush Plan Eliminated Obstacle to Gaza Assault," *Inter Press Service*, January 5, 2009.
59. Arnon Regular, "Jihad denies reports it struck ceasefire deal with Abbas," *Haaretz*, January 21, 2005.
60. CNN, January 29, 2006. See Chapter 1 notes.
61. Washington Post, February 26, 2006. See Chapter 1 notes.
62. "Report: Hamas chief Meshal calls for 10-year cease-fire," *Haaretz*, December 11, 2006.
63. "Q&A with Hamas leader Khaled Meshaal," *Reuters*, January 10, 2007.
64. "Carter Mideast trip: Few tangible results," *Associated Press*, April 21, 2008.
65. Griff Witte, "Carter: Hamas Ready To Live Beside Israel," *Washington Post*, April 22, 2008.
66. Roee Nahmias, "Hamas says accepts Palestinian statehood," *Ynetnews*, April 21, 2008.
67. Barak Ravid, "Meshal offers 10-year truce for Palestinian state on '67 borders," *Haaretz*, April 21, 2008.
68. Amira Hass, "Haniyeh: Hamas willing to accept Palestinian state with 1967 borders," *Haaretz*, November 9, 2008.
69. Isabel Kershner and Taghreed El-Khodary, "Israeli Troops Launch Attack on Gaza," *New York Times*, January 4, 2009. The *Times* only vaguely alluded to the US's role in blocking the UN statement by remarking that the Bush administration, "rather than calling for a halt to military action, urged Israel to be 'mindful of the potential consequences to civilians.'" Isabel Kershner, "Israeli Strike Is First in Gaza Since Start of Cease-Fire," *New York Times*, November 4, 2008.
70. "Israel and Hamas: Conflict in Gaza," an interactive graphic published at www.nytimes.com, January 4, 2009; accessed January 5, 2009. "Palestinians: Mother, 4 children killed in IDF Gaza offensive," *Haaretz*, January 4, 2009.
71. "Deaths as Israel hits Gaza mosque," *Al Jazeera*, January 4, 2009. "Israel launches ground offensive, kills more civilians," *Agence France-Presse*, January 4, 2009. Kershner and El-Khodary, "Israeli Troops Launch Attack on Gaza." UN Office for the Coordination of Humanitarian Affairs, "Gaza Humanitarian Situation Report," January 4, 2009.
72. Barak Ravid, "Shin Bet Chief: Hamas has eased its demands for Gaza truce with Israel," *Haaretz*, January 4, 2009.
73. OCHA Situation Report, January 4, 2009.
74. "Red Cross says its medical team denied access to Gaza," *Deutsche Press-Agentur*, January 4, 2009.
75. Edith M. Lederer, "UN chief to meet Arab ministers on Gaza," *Associated Press*, January 4, 2009.
76. Barak Ravid, "No Gaza truce right now, Hamas needs a 'real lesson,'" *Haaretz*, January 4, 2009.
77. "Dick Cheney: Israel didn't seek U.S. okay before Gaza invasion," *Associated Press*, January 4, 2009.
78. James Bone and Francis Elliot, "Gordon Brown calls for an immediate ceasefire in Gaza," *The Times*, January 5, 2009.
79. US Department of State, Daily Press Briefing by Spokesman Sean McCormack, January 5, 2009.
80. Bone and Elliot, "Gordon Brown."
81. State Department Press Briefing, January 5, 2009.
82. Ibid.
83. Taghreed El-Khodary, "Gaza Hospital Fills Up, Mainly With Civilians," *New York Times*, January 5, 2009.
84. Sheera Frenkel and Michael Evans, "Israel rains fire on Gaza with phosphorus shells," *The Times*, January 5, 2008.
85. World Health Organization, "Health Situation in Gaza," January 5, 2009.
86. United Nations Children's Fund, "UNICEF Statement on the crisis in Gaza," January 5, 2009. The UN International Children's Emergency Fund was established in 1946. The organization's name was changed in 1953, though it retained the original acronym.

87. Nic Robertson, "Gaza horrors sow seeds for future violence," *CNN*, January 5, 2009.

88. "Media Ban in Gaza a Recipe for Censorship, Ignorance and Fear, Says IFJ," *International Federation of Journalists*, January 5, 2009. "IFJ Calls on Israel to Release Journalists Arrested in Gaza," *International Federation of Journalists*, January 13, 2009.

89. "Media rights group slams Israel's treatment of press in conflict," *Agence France-Presse*, January 5, 2009.

90. Arthur Max, "Frustrated reporters locked out of Gaza war zone," *Associated Press*, January 5, 2009.

91. Taghreed El-Khodary and Isabel Kershner, "Warnings Not Enough for Gaza Families," *New York Times*, January 6, 2009.

92. Ethan Bronner, "Israel Deepens Gaza Incursion as Toll Mounts," *New York Times*, January 6, 2009.

93. UN Special Coordinator for the Middle East Peace Process, "Statement of the UN Humanitarian Coordinator for the occupied Palestinian territory Mr. Maxwell Gaylard," January 6, 2009. Gaylard, an Australian, served this role in his capacity as Deputy Special Coordinator for the Middle East Peace Process, appointed by the Secretary-General. UN Relief and Works Agency for Palestine Refugees in the Near East, "Direct Hit on UNRWA School Kills Three in Gaza," Press Release, January 6, 2009.

94. World Health Organization, "Health Situation in Gaza," January 6, 2009. There was initial confusion as to the specifics of the attack. It would later be learned that Israel's mortar fire had struck just outside the school, and that those killed were among a large crowd going out to buy food from the market. See: Griff Witte, "U.N. Says School in Gaza Where 43 Died Wasn't Hit by Israeli Fire," *Washington Post*, February 7, 2009.

95. UN Secretary-General Ban Ki-moon, "Statement by the Secretary-General on strike on UN Relief and Works Agency (UNRWA) School in Gaza," January 6, 2009.

96. UN High Commissioner for Refugees, "Gaza: 'The only conflict in the world in which people are not even allowed to flee'—High Commissioner Guterres," January 6, 2009.

97. UN Office for the Coordination of Humanitarian Affairs, "Situation Report From the Humanitarian Coordinator," January 6, 2009.

98. United Nations News Service, "Security Council meets on Gaza fighting, Ban renews ceasefire call," January 6, 2009.

99. International Committee of the Red Cross, "Gaza: plight of civilians traumatic in 'full-blown humanitarian crisis,'" Press Briefing, January 6, 2009. International Committee of the Red Cross, "Gaza: access to the wounded remains top priority," Operational Update, January 7, 2009.

100. Amira Hass, et al, "UN rejects IDF claim Gaza militants operated from bombed-out school," *Haaretz*, January 7, 2009.

101. UN Office of the Spokesperson for the Secretary-General, "Highlights of the Noon Briefing by Michele Montas," January 6, 2009.

102. UN Relief and Works Agency for Palestine Refugees in the Near East, "Remarks by John Ging, UNRWA Director of Operations in Gaza," January 7, 2009.

103. "Israel condemned for attacks on UN schools," *Australian Broadcasting Corporation* (ABC), January 7, 2009.

104. Griff Witte and Sudarsan Raghavan, "Israel Hits U.N.-Run School in Gaza," *Washington Post*, January 7, 2009.

105. Hass, et al, "UN rejects IDF claim."

106. UNRWA Spokesman Johan Eriksson, comments in an online Q&A, "Israel Halts Operations To Allow Aid Shipments," *Washington Post*, January 7, 2009.

107. UN Relief and Works Agency for Palestine Refugees in the Near East, Statement by Chris Gunness, January 8, 2009.

108. Brenda Gazzar and Tovah Lazaroff, "UNRWA: IDF knows gunfire didn't emanate from Jabalya school," *Jerusalem Post*, January 8, 2009.

109. The White House, Press Briefing by Press Secretary Dana Perino, January 6, 2009.

110. Amos Harel, "Four of six IDF soldiers killed in Gaza were victims of friendly fire," *Haaretz*, January 7, 2009. Note that this ratio is an underestimate of Palestinian deaths as it doesn't include adult male civilians, only women and children.

111. UN Security Council, 6061st Meeting, *The situation in the Middle East, including the Palestinian question*, S/PV.6061 (January 6, 2009).

112. Ethan Bronner, "Israeli Attack Splits Gaza; Truce Calls Are Rebuffed," *New York Times*, January 4, 2009.

113. "Gaza Crisis Sees its Deadliest Attack Yet," Anderson Cooper 360 Degrees, *CNN*, January 6, 2009.

114. Ethan Bronner, "Israel Puts Media Clamp on Gaza," *New York Times*, January 6, 2009.

115. Avi Issacharoff, "IDF ban on reporters in Gaza combat zones leads to limited coverage," *Haaretz*, January 7, 2009.

116. "IFJ Condemns Killings of Journalists and Backs Media Protests over Israeli Actions," *International Federation of Journalists*, January 7, 2009.

117. Gideon Levy, "And there lie the bodies," *Haaretz*, January 5, 2009.

118. Avi Shlaim, "How Israel brought Gaza to the brink of humanitarian catastrophe," *The Guardian*, January 7, 2009.

119. Gideon Lichfield, "Israel's PR war," *Haaretz*, January 8, 2009.

120. "Death of innocents," *Jerusalem Post*, January 6, 2009.

121. Shashank Bengali, "Israelis, sipping Pepsi, watch bombardment of Gaza town," *McClatchy*, January 5, 2009.

122. Amira Hass, "Lucky my parents aren't alive to see this," *Haaretz*, January 7, 2009.

123. World Health Organization, "Health Situation in Gaza," January 7, 2009.

124. United Nations Children's Fund, "During short ceasefire, some life-saving supplies delivered in Gaza," January 7, 2009.

125. UN Office for the Coordination of Humanitarian Affairs, "Situation Report from the Humanitarian Coordinator," January 7, 2009.

126. "Israel accepts truce 'principles,'" *BBC*, January 7, 2009.

127. Washington Post, January 7, 2009.

128. "UN rights body calls special Gaza session," *Reuters*, January 7, 2009. UN Human Rights Council, "Human Rights Council to Hold Special Session on Human Rights Situation in Gaza on 9 January 2009," January 7, 2009.

129. UN Office for the Coordination of Humanitarian Affairs "Situation Report on the Humanitarian Situation in the Gaza Strip—No. 6," January 8, 2009.

130. UN General Assembly, *Troubled by Escalating Gaza Violence, Palestinian Rights Committee Calls Situation "Unacceptable and Untenable,"* statement by the Bureau of the Committee on the Exercise of the Inalienable Rights of the Palestinian People, GA/PAL/1110 (January 8, 2009).

131. "Babies cling to life in stricken hospital," *The Independent*, January 8, 2009,

132. Michael Evans and Sheera Frenkel, "Gaza victims' burns increase concern over phosphorus," *The Times*, January 8, 2009.

133. UN Secretary-General Ban Ki-moon, "Secretary-General Condemns Israeli Firing on United Nations Aid Convoy in Gaza, Again Calls for Immediate Ceasefire to Allow Full Humanitarian Access," SG/SM/12040/Rev.1 (January 8, 2009). United Nations News Centre, "Major UN agency suspends Gaza relief operations after Israeli strike kills two drivers," January 8, 2009.

134. "Gaza civilians endangered by the military tactics of both sides," *Amnesty International*, January 8, 2009.

135. International Committee of the Red Cross, "Gaza: ICRC demands urgent access to wounded as Israeli army fails to assist wounded Palestinians," January 8, 2009.

136. Barak Ravid and Shlomo Shamir, "UN Security Council calls for immediate Gaza truce," *Haaretz*, January 9, 2009.

137. UN Security Council, 6063rd Meeting, Resolution 1860 (2009), *Middle East, including the Palestinian question*, S/RES/1860(2009), (January 8, 2009).

138. UN Security Council, 6063rd Meeting, *The situation in the Middle East, including the Palestinian question*, S/PV.6063 (January 8, 2009).

139. "Rice shame-faced by Bush over UN Gaza vote: Olmert," *Agence France-Presse*, January 12, 2009.

140. Barak Ravid, "U.S.: Olmert never asked us to abstain from UN vote on Gaza truce," *Haaretz*, January 14, 2009.

141. "Rice: Olmert's claims regarding my Gaza UN resolution vote are 'fiction,'" *Haaretz*, January 15, 2009.

142. Akiva Eldar, "Inquiries show Olmert version of UN Gaza vote spat closer to the truth than Rice's," *Haaretz*, January 16, 2009. The article closed by criticizing Olmert for publicly bragging about persuading Bush to tell Rice to instead abstain.

143. S.RES.10, 111th Congress (2009-2010). H.RES.34, 111th Congress (2009-2010). See also: Jeremy R. Hammond, "US Senate Endorses Israel's War on Gaza," *Foreign Policy Journal*, January 9, 2009. Peter Phillips and Mickey Huff, ed., *Censored 2010: The Top 25 Censored Stories of 2008-09*, (New York: Seven Stories Press, 2009), 42-46. This author was a recipient of the Project Censored 2010 Award for Outstanding Investigative Journalism for reporting on the Israeli assault on Gaza and the US role. The

relevant chapter of the book, including this author's update of the situation, is also available online. See: "US Arms Used for War Crimes in Gaza," available at www.projectcensored.org.

144. Stephen Zunes, "Virtually the Entire Dem-Controlled Congress Supports Israel's War Crimes in Gaza," *AlterNet*, January 13, 2009. For the HRW report Zunes refers to, see: Human Rights Watch, *Why They Died: Civilian Casualties in Lebanon during the 2006 War*, September 5, 2007.

145. Rory McCarthy, "Gaza bloodshed continues despite UN calls for ceasefire," *The Guardian*, January 9, 2009.

146. Nidal al-Mughrabi, "Israel rebuffs U.N. resolution, pursues Gaza war," *Reuters*, January 9, 2009.

147. Shlomo Shamir and Barak Ravid, "Israel rejects UN truce resolution, says Gaza operation to continue," *Haaretz*, January 10, 2009.

148. Barak Ravid, "IDF: Hamas rocket fire down 50% since start of Gaza offensive," *Haaretz*, January 12, 2009.

149. United Nations Children's Fund, "UNICEF: Number of Child Casualties Still Rising in Gaza," January 9, 2009.

150. IFJ, January 13, 2009.

151. United Nations Department of Public Information, "Press Conference on Humanitarian Situation in Gaza," January 9, 2009.

152. United Nations Relief and Works Agency for Palestine in the Near East, "UNRWA Statement on Its Operations in Gaza," January 9, 2009.

153. "'Hard' for Israel to spare Gaza civilians: Rice," *Agence France-Presse*, January 9, 2009.

154. World Health Organization, "Health Situation in the Gaza Strip," January 11, 2009.

155. "Israel: Stop Unlawful Use of White Phosphorus in Gaza," *Human Rights Watch*, January 10, 2009. See also: "Q & A on Israel's Use of White Phosphorus in Gaza," *Human Rights Watch*, January 10, 2009.

156. "Israel is using phosphorus illegally in Gaza Strip bombings," *B'Tselem*, January 12, 2009.

157. HRW, January 10, 2009.

158. "Group accuses Israel of firing white phosphorus into Gaza," *CNN*, January 12, 2009.

159. Ibid.

160. "Israel denies banned weapons use," *BBC*, January 11, 2009.

161. "Israel's bombardment of Gaza is not self-defence—it's a war crime," *Sunday Times*, January 11, 2009.

162. Steven Erlanger, "A Gaza War Full of Traps and Trickery," *New York Times*, January 11, 2009.

163. Ethan Bronner, "Israelis United on Gaza War as Censure Rises Abroad," *New York Times*, January 13, 2009.

164. "Attack on UNRWA school firing of indiscriminate weapon," *B'Tselem*, January 11, 2009.

165. International Committee of the Red Cross, "Gaza: ICRC strives to evacuate and treat the wounded despite limited access," January 12, 2009. United Nations News Service "Gaza: UN official reports horrific hospital scenes of casualties," January 12, 2009.

166. Rami Abdou, Iyah Romm, Davida Schiff, et al, "In solidarity with Gaza," *The Lancet*, January 12, 2009.

167. UN Human Rights Council, *The Grave Violations of Human Rights in the Occupied Palestinian Territory particularly due to the recent Israeli military attack against the occupied Gaza Strip*, A/HRC/S-9/L.1/Rev.2 (January 12, 2009).

168. Lisa Schlein, "UN Rights Council Condemns Israeli Action in Gaza," *Voice of America*, January 12, 2009.

169. United Nations Office for the Coordination of Humanitarian Affairs, "Field Update on Gaza from the Humanitarian Coordinator," January 13, 2009.

170. United Nations Children's Fund, "'I wish the war would end'—Gaza's children pay psychological cost of conflict," January 12, 2009.

171. International Committee of the Red Cross, "Gaza: ICRC president demands greater respect for civilians and humanitarian workers," January 13, 2009.

172. International Committee of the Red Cross, "Gaza crisis: joint public statement by the International Red Cross and Red Crescent Movement," January 13, 2009.

173. OCHA Field Update, January 13, 2009.

174. Human Rights Watch, *Deprived and Endangered: Humanitarian Crisis in the Gaza Strip*, January 13, 2009.

175. IFJ, January 13, 2009.

176. Bradley S. Klapper, "ICRC: Israel's use of white phosphorus not illegal," *Associated Press*, January 13, 2009. The AP report was widely published, including by the *Jerusalem Post*, *CBS News*, *FOX News*, *Seattle Times*, and *The Huffington Post*.

177. Michael B. Farrell, "Red Cross: No evidence Israel is using white phosphorus illegally," *Christian Science Monitor*, January 14, 2009.

178. Robert Marquand, "Gaza: Israel under fire for alleged white phosphorus use," *Christian Science Monitor*, January 14, 2009. Marquand also noted that doctors treating unusual wounds in Gaza had also raised questions "about the possible use of another weapon called Dense Inert Metal Explosives, or DIME, that was created by the US Air Force. DIME is designed to be used in crowded urban areas since the weapons are highly lethal but have an extremely limited range of explosive force that can reduce collateral damage."

179. Taghreed El-Khodary and Sabrina Tavernise, "U.N. Warns of Refugee Crisis in Gaza Strip," *New York Times*, January 13, 2009.

180. Sheera Frenkel, "Amnesty International: Gaza white phosphorus shells were US made," *The Times*, February 14, 2009.

181. Ethan Bronner, "Egypt Cites Progress Toward Truce as Gaza Toll Exceeds 1,000," *New York Times*, January 15, 2009.

182. Ethan Bronner, "The Bullets in My In-Box," *New York Times*, January 24, 2009.

183. Thomas L. Friedman, "Israel's Goals in Gaza?" *New York Times*, January 13, 2009.

184. William Douglas, "American public backs Israel firmly in war with Hamas, poll finds," *McClatchy*, January 13, 2009.

185. Ethan Bronner, "Israelis United on Gaza War."

186. Etgar Lefkovits, "Overwhelming Israeli support of Gaza op," *Jerusalem Post*, January 14, 2009.

187. Douglas, "American public backs Israel."

188. OCHA Field Update, January 13, 2009.

189. United Nations Office for the Coordination of Humanitarian Affairs, "Field Update on Gaza from the Humanitarian Coordinator," January 14, 2009.

190. UN Security Council, 6066th Meeting, *Protection of civilians in armed conflict*, S/PV.6066 (January 14, 2009).

191. "Gaza Conflict—Full Arms Embargo Vital as US Munitions Reported on Way to Israel," *Amnesty International*, January 14, 2009. "U.S. arms shipment to Israel canceled due to Gaza conflict," *Reuters*, January 13, 2009.

192. United Nations Office for the Coordination of Humanitarian Affairs, "Field Update on Gaza from the Humanitarian Coordinator," January 15, 2009.

193. UN Department of Public Information, "Senior official gives eyewitness account of Israeli shelling of UN Gaza compound," January 15, 2009.

194. Isabel Kershner, "Israel Shells U.N. Site in Gaza, Drawing Fresh Condemnation," *New York Times*, January 16, 2009.

195. Griff Witte, "On Day of Heavy Fighting, Moves Toward Gaza Peace," *Washington Post*, January 16, 2009. Kershner, "Israel Shells U.N. Site."

196. United Nations Department of Public Information, "Press Conference on Gaza Humanitarian Situation," January 15, 2009.

197. Witte, "Moves Toward Gaza Peace."

198. Sheera Frenkel and Philippe Naughton, "UN headquarters in Gaza hit by Israeli 'white phosphorus' shells," *The Times*, January 15, 2009. "UN accuses Israel over phosphorus," *BBC*, January 15, 2009.

199. "Rice cautions Israel over IDF shelling of UN facilities in Gaza," *Reuters*, January 16, 2009.

200. "Brown condemns Gaza attack on UN," *BBC*, January 15, 2009.

201. European Parliament, "Hans-Gert Pöttering condemns attack on UN Relief Work in Gaza," January 15, 2009.

202. "European Parliament resolution of 15 January 2009 on the situation in the Gaza Strip," published at http://unispal.un.org; accessed October 16, 2014.

203. Ethan Bronner, "Egypt Cites Progress Toward Truce as Gaza Toll Exceeds 1,000," *New York Times*, January 15, 2009.

204. "Shelling of UN Compound Must Be Investigated," *Amnesty International*, January 15, 2009.

205. United Nations Department of Public Information, "Press Conference on Humanitarian Situation in Gaza," January 16, 2009. Three-hundred seventy children were reported killed and 1,745 injured.

206. "Israel attacks UN compound, hospitals," *Reuters*, January 16, 2009.

207. Lisa Schlein, "UN: Gaza Conflict Will Have Long-Lasting Psychological Impact on Children," *Voice of America*, January 16, 2009.
208. World Food Programme, "Gaza: Operational Update," January 16, 2009.
209. "Israel: Stop Shelling Crowded Gaza City," *Human Rights Watch*, January 16, 2009.
210. United Nations General Assembly Resolution ES-10/18, *General Assembly resolution supporting the immediate ceasefire according to Security Council resolution 1860 (2009)*, A/RES/ES-10/18 (January 16, 2009). Patrick Worsnip, "U.N. assembly urges Gaza truce, drops radical text," *Reuters*, January 17, 2009.
211. Amira Hass, "Is Israel using illegal weapons in its offensive on Gaza?" *Haaretz*, January 16, 2009.
212. UN General Assembly, Tenth Emergency Special Session, 34th & 35th Meetings, *General Assembly Demands Full Respect for Security Council Resolution 1860 Calling for Immediate Gaza Ceasefire, as Emergency Session Concludes*, GA/10809 (January 16, 2009). "US urges General Assembly not to undermine Gaza truce bid," *Agence France-Presse*, January 16, 2009.
213. Worsnip, "U.N. assembly urges Gaza truce." US Department of State, "Signing Ceremony of the U.S.-Israel Memorandum of Understanding with Israeli Foreign Minister Tzipi Livni," January 16, 2009. "U.S., Israel sign pact to battle Iran arms smuggling into Gaza," *Associated Press*, January 17, 2009.
214. Robert Bryce, "Gaza invasion: Powered by the U.S.," *Salon*, January 16, 2009.
215. United Nations Department of Public Information, "As Third United Nations School Hit by Israel Force, Secretary-General Condemns 'Outrageous Attack', Demands Investigation, Punishment of Those Responsible," January 19, 2009.
216. United Nations Office for the Coordination of Humanitarian Affairs, "Field Update on Gaza from the Humanitarian Coordinator," January 18, 2009. Steven Erlanger, "Israel Declares Cease-Fire; Hamas Says It Will Fight On," *New York Times*, January 18, 2009.
217. OCHA Field Update, January 18, 2009.
218. Tamer Saliba and Patrick Quinn, "UN says Gaza hospitals in crisis," *Associated Press*, January 16, 2009.
219. "The medical conditions in Gaza," *The Lancet*, January 17, 2009.
220. Jan McGirk, "Medical facilities under intense pressure in Gaza," *The Lancet*, January 27, 2009. "DIME" is an acronym for Dense Inert Metal Explosive.
221. OCHA Field Update, January 18, 2009.
222. Al Jazeera English, "Gaza doctor's tragedy caught on Israeli TV," *YouTube* video, 2:49, January 18, 2009; archived by "Agence Web à Paris," January 18, 2009.
223. Dina Kraft, "Gazan Doctor and Peace Advocate Loses 3 Daughters to Israeli Fire and Asks Why," *New York Times*, January 18, 2009.
224. "Gaza doctor in mobile phone plea," *YouTube* video, 2:22, *Reuters* clip posted by "freedomisjoy," January 17, 2009.
225. Noah Kosharek, "IDF bomb kills three daughters, niece of Gaza MD working at Tel Hashomer," *Haaretz*, January 18, 2009. Lucy Ash, "Gaza doctor's loss grips Israelis," *BBC*, January 19, 2009.
226. Kraft, "Gazan Doctor."
227. Fida Qishta and Peter Beaumont, "Israel accused of war crimes over 12-hour assault on Gaza village," *The Guardian*, January 18, 2009.

Chapter 3

1. United Nations Department of Public Information, "UN already assessing Gaza relief needs on first full day of halt to fighting," January 19, 2009.
2. United Nations Security Council, 6077th Meeting, *The situation in the Middle East, including the Palestinian question*, S/PV.6077 (January 27, 2009).
3. United Nations Office for the Coordination of Humanitarian Affairs, "Field Update on Gaza from the Humanitarian Coordinator," January 29, 2009.
4. B'Tselem statistics on fatalities during Operation Cast Lead, accessed from www.btselemn.org on September 7, 2014.
5. "Israel Used White Phosphorus in Gaza Civilian Areas," *Amnesty International*, January 19, 2009.
6. "The Conflict in Gaza: A Briefing on Applicable Law, Investigations and Accountability," *Amnesty International*, January 19, 2009.
7. Dion Nissenbaum, "Israeli troops killed Gaza children carrying white flag, witnesses say," *McClatchy*, January 27, 2009.

8. "Israeli army used flechettes against Gaza civilians," *Amnesty International*, January 27, 2009.

9. "Attacks on ambulance workers in Gaza," *Amnesty International*, January 28, 2009.

10. Jonathan Finer, "At a Flash Point in Gaza, A Family's Deadly Ordeal," *Washington Post*, January 27, 2009.

11. Sheera Frenkel, "Israeli soldiers recall Gaza attack orders," *The Times*, January 28, 2009.

12. Rod Nordland, "The Smell of Death," *Newsweek*, January 18, 2009. "Report: IDF probing racist graffiti left by soldiers in Gaza," *Haaretz*, January 28, 2009. "IDF soldiers leave racist graffiti on Gaza homes," *Ynetnews*, January 28, 2009.

13. Reuven Pedatzur, "The war that wasn't," *Haaretz*, January 25, 2009.

14. "U.S. envoy to UN calls on Israel to investigate Gaza war crimes claims," *Reuters*, January 30, 2009.

15. "Israeli jets target Gaza tunnels," *BBC*, January 28, 2009. "Israel warplanes bomb Gaza smuggling tunnels," *The Guardian*, January 28, 2009. Daniel Luban, "Peace Recedes as Israeli Settlements Expand," *Inter Press Service*, January 28, 2009.

16. "Hamas: We will accept long-term truce if Gaza borders opened," *Associated Press*, January 1, 2009.

17. "Clinton: Hamas must abide by preconditions to be included in talks," *Haaretz*, February 3, 2009.

18. US Department of State, *Sharm El-Sheikh Fact-Finding Committee Report* (The Mitchell Report), April 30, 2001. *Israeli-PLO Declaration of Principles*, September 13, 1993; republished in the *Journal of Palestine Studies*, Vol. XXIII, No. 1 (Autumn 1993), 115-121.

19. "Rightists in Israel predict dismal fate for Obama envoy's efforts," *Haaretz*, January 28, 2009.

20. United Nations Security Council, 1382nd Meeting, *Resolution 242 (1967)*, S/RES/242(1967) (November 22, 1967).

21. Yehuda Blum, "The Territorial Clauses of Security Council Resolution 242," *Jerusalem Center for Public Affairs*, June 4, 2007. Blum is a former Israeli Ambassador to the UN and Professor Emeritus of International Law at the Hebrew University of Jerusalem.

22. United Nations Security Council, 1382nd Meeting, *The situation in the Middle East*, S/PV.1382 (OR) (November 22, 1967).

23. United Nations General Assembly, 1529th Plenary Meeting, *Fifth Emergency Special Session*, A/PV.1529 (June 21, 1967).

24. Ibid.

25. United Nations Security Council, 1379th Meeting, *The situation in the Middle East*, S/PV.1379 (November 16, 1967).

26. United Nations Security Council, 1381st Meeting, *The situation in the Middle East*, S/PV.1381 (November 20, 1967).

27. US Department of State, *Foreign Relations of the United States* (FRUS), Vol. XIX, "Arab-Israeli Crisis and War, 1967," Document 380, "Telegram From the Mission to the United Nations to the Department of State," July 21, 1967. The full text of two draft resolutions prepared jointly by the US and USSR was included in the telegram. The discussions between the Americans and Soviets also reveal that, although it did not appear in the final draft, the US was not opposed to a resolution calling Israel to withdraw "without delay", so long as the section also calling for an end of states of belligerency also contained that wording. See Document 377, "Telegram From the Mission to the United Nations to the Department of State," July 20, 1967. When Arthur Goldberg transmitted this text to the State Department, he expressed no concern about the fact that the wording "positions . . . before June 5, 1967" was included. Instead, his primary concern was that the US-USSR proposals "will be unacceptable to [the] Arabs". See Document 380. A later communication from Goldberg noted that the Soviets had transmitted the text of the first version to the Arabs, but that they had changed it by introducing "reference to [the] June 5 date", which Goldberg said "was not acceptable" because "it had not been included in that version as given". That is, the only objection was that the reference was added without prior consultation with the US. Instructively, again, the second version did contain the date reference, without objection from Goldberg. Furthermore, Goldberg noted that after expressing his disapproval of the USSR having transmitted an altered version of the text without having first discussed the change with the US, "I said we agreed to [the] text with one understanding"—which concerned the inclusion of a clause calling for a reconvening of the General Assembly and had nothing whatsoever to do with the extent of withdrawal sought by the US, thus further demonstrating US acceptance on principle of a full withdrawal to the 1949 armistice lines. See Document 384, "Telegram From the Mission to the United Nations to the Department of State," July 22, 1967. Underscoring this point, the Soviet Foreign Minister Anatoliy Dobrynin praised the bilateral discussions with the US, expressing pleasure at having reached "common ground" with regard to "the withdrawal of Israeli troops". See Document 392, "Memorandum of Conversation," July 27, 1967.

28. United Nations General Assembly, 1544th Plenary Meeting, *Fifth Emergency Special Session*, A/PV.1554 (July 14, 1967).

29. US Department of State, FRUS, Vol. XIX, Document 415, "Memorandum From the President's Special Consultant (Bundy) to President Johnson," August 11, 1967.

30. S/PV.1379.

31. Ibid.

32. US Department of State, FRUS, Vol. XIX, Document 541, "Editorial Note."

33. As the ICJ has also observed, "it is an established principle that the right of giving an authoritative interpretation of a legal rule (*le droit d'interpréter authentiquement*) belongs solely to the person or body who has power to modify or suppress it." See: Michael C. Wood, "The Interpretation of Security Council Resolutions," *Max Planck Yearbook of United Nations Law Volume 2*, 1998.

34. ICJ Advisory Opinion, July 9, 2004.

35. US Department of State, FRUS, Vol. XIX, Document 506, "Telegram From the Department of State to the Embassy in Israel," November 30, 1968.

36. Chomsky, *Fateful Triangle*, 40-41.

37. Ibid., 64.

38. Ibid., 67.

39. The phrase "state religion" is borrowed from Noam Chomsky, who has explained that "There is indeed something truly religious in the fervor with which responsible American intellectuals have sought to deny plain fact and to secure their dogmas concerning American benevolence, the contemporary version of the 'civilizing mission.'" He goes on to describe these dogmas as "the doctrines of the state religion". See his 1977 essay "Intellectuals and the State," reprinted in *Towards a New Cold War: Essays on the Current Crisis and How We Got There* (Pantheon, 1982). Chomsky is also co-author with Edward S. Herman of *Manufacturing Consent: The Political Economy of the Mass Media* (Pantheon, 2002), the title phrase in turn being borrowed from Walter Lippmann, who in his book *Public Opinion* (1921) described "the manufacture of consent" by government officials through the media. The public is brought on board with policies through "manipulation" of the facts and under "the impact of propaganda". Lippmann further observed that "The creation of consent is not a new art. It is a very old one which was supposed to have died out with the appearance of democracy. But it has not died out." (Public domain, Kindle edition, 131-32.) Manufacturing consent is the purpose of all propaganda, which was reinvented in the 1920s as the public relations industry by Edward L. Bernays, the nephew of Sigmund Freud, the founder of psychoanalysis. In his 1947 essay "The Engineering of Consent," Bernays recognized the media "as a potent force for social good or possible evil." Whereas authoritarian governments used force to achieve their goals, government leaders in democratic societies are "faced with the problem of engineering the public's *consent* to a program or goal." See Edward L. Bernays, "The Engineering of Consent," *Annals of the American Academy of Political and Social Science*, March 1947, 113-120. See also the BBC TWO documentary series, "The Century of the Self," aired starting March 17, 2002.

40. United Nations Security Council, *Letter Dated 29 November 1948 from Israel's Foreign Minister to the Secretary-General Concerning Israel's Application for Admission to Membership of the United Nations and Declaration Accepting Obligations under the Charter*, S/1093 (November 29, 1948). Israel's letter of request notably also asserted that the state of Israel had been declared "in pursuance of" General Assembly Resolution 181.

41. United Nations Security Council, *Letter Dated 6 December 1948 from the Chairman of the Membership Committee to the President of the Security Council Concerning Israel's Application for Admission to the Membership of the United Nations*, S/1110 (December 7, 1948). United Nations General Assembly, 3rd Session, 1st Committee, *Progress Report of the UN Mediator on Palestine - Syria: Draft Resolution*, A/C.1/405 (November 30, 1948). Syria had also suggested that the Assembly establish a commission to study the issue and "prepare proposals for the establishment of a single State of the whole of Palestine" in which Arabs and Jews alike would "participate in rights and duties as loyal citizens of a democratic State with wide autonomous privileges." See United Nations General Assembly, 3rd Session, 1st Committee, *Progress Report of the United Nations Mediator on Palestine - Syria: Draft Resolution*, A/C.1/402 (November 26, 1948).

42. United Nations General Assembly, 220th Meeting, *Continuation of the discussion on the progress report of the United Nations Mediator on Palestine*, A/C.1/SR.220 (December 1, 1948). Syria had also drafted a resolution correctly pointing out that the General Assembly had no authority to partition Palestine. The draft would have established a commission "to prepare proposals for the establishment of a single State of the whole of Palestine on cantonization or federal basis in which all sections of population in

Palestine will participate in rights and duties as loyal citizens of a democratic State with wide autonomous privileges in cantons or areas to be assigned to each of them." See: United Nations General Assembly, 3rd Session, 1st Committee, *Progress Report of the United Nations Mediator on Palestine—Syria: Draft Resolution*, A/C.1/402 (November 26, 1948).

43. United Nations General Assembly, *Progress Report of the United Nations Mediator on Palestine Submitted to the Secretary-General for Transmission to the Members of the United Nations*, A/648 (September 16, 1948).

44. Donald Neff, "Jewish Terrorists Assassinate U.N. Peacekeeper Count Folke Bernadotte," *Washington Report on Middle East Affairs*, September 1995, 83-84. Donald MacIntyre, "Israel's forgotten hero: The assassination of Count Bernadotte – and the death of peace," *The Independent*, September 18, 2008.

45. United Nations General Assembly, 186th Plenary Meeting, *194 (III). Palestine—Progress Report of the United Nations Mediator*, A/RES/194 (III) (December 11, 1948).

46. United Nations General Assembly, 186th Plenary Meeting, *Continuation of the discussion on the Progress Report of the United Nations Mediator on Palestine: reports of the First Committee (A/776) and of the Fifth Committee (A/786)*, A/PV.186 (December 11, 1948). The vote was 35 to 15, with 8 abstentions.

47. United Nations Security Council, *Draft Resolution Submitted by Syria at the 385th Meeting on the Application of Israel for Admission to the United Nations*, S/1125 (December 17, 1948).

48. United Nations Security Council, 386th Meeting, *Continuation of the discussion on the application of Israel for admission to membership in the United Nations*, S/PV.386 (December 17, 1948). It should be noted that the Security Council in 1948 consisted of only eleven members: the five permanent members (China, France, the USSR, the UK, and the US) and six non-permanent members (Argentina, Belgium, Canada, Colombia, Syria, and the Ukrainian Soviet Socialist Republic). Membership can be searched by year at www.un.org/en/sc/members/search.asp. An amendment to the UN Charter to increase the number of Council members to fifteen was adopted by the General Assembly on December 17, 1963 and came into force on August 31, 1965. See the "Introductory Note" to the UN Charter at http://www.un.org/en/documents/charter/index.shtml.

49. United Nations Security Council, 385th Meeting, *Continuation of the discussion on the application of Israel for admission to membership in the United Nations*, S/PV.385 (December 17, 1948). United Nations Security Council, *Draft Resolution Submitted by the United Kingdom at the 384th Meeting on the Application of Israel for Admission to the United Nations*, S/1121 (December 15, 1948). United Nations Security Council, *Draft Resolution Submitted by France at the 385th Meeting on the Application of Israel for Admission to the United Nations*, S/1127 (December 17, 1948). For the voting record, see S/PV.386.

50. S/PV.385.

51. The US and USSR, for example, were of like mind on this issue, albeit for opposing reasons. The Soviets charged that the UK was seeking to advance its own interests in the region by limiting the territory in which the state of Israel would be recognized so that Transjordan—Britain's former protectorate, which "played the role of a puppet of the United Kingdom"—could annex much of Palestine for its own. The Soviets argued that the US had colluded with the UK in its aims by suggesting amendments to an earlier UK draft resolution, which originally proposed annexation by Transjordan, in order for it to gain more support in the Assembly. In furtherance of its own goal of challenging this perceived Western plot, the USSR opposed Syria's proposal to refer the matter to the ICJ. The Soviet delegate attempted to rationalize this opposition with the circular argument that since Resolution 181 "granted" the Zionists "the right" to create Israel, therefore there was "no need to appeal to the International Court on this matter." His argument for admitting Israel into the UN similarly begged the question: its admission would be "consistent with the provisions of international law. There is therefore no need to consult the International Court." See A/PV.186.

52. United Nations Conciliation Commission for Palestine, *Summary Record of a Meeting Between the Conciliation Commission and His Excellency Mr. Shertok, Minister for Foreign Affairs of Israel* (February 7, 1949), A/AC.25/SR/G/1 (February 9, 1949).

53. United Nations Conciliation Commission for Palestine, *Summary Record of a Meeting Between the Conciliation Commission and His Excllency Ibrahim Dessouki Abaza Pasha, Minister for Foreign Affairs of Egypt*, A/AC.25/SR/G/3 (February 3, 1949).

54. United Nations Conciliation Commission for Palestine, *Summary Record of a Meeting Between the Conciliation Commission and His Excellency Mr. Moshe Shertok, Foreign Minister of Israel*, A/A.C.25/SR/G/14 (February 24, 1949). The Commission urged Israel "to make a gesture accepting in principle the right of the refugees to return to their homes" in order to "facilitate" negotiations over a permanent peace settlement, which proposal Shertok repeatedly rejected.

55. United Nations Conciliation Commission for Palestine, *The Refugee Problem in Concrete Terms*, A/AC.25/W/3 (March 17, 1949).

56. United Nations Conciliation Commission for Palestine, *Summary Record of the Twelfth Meeting*, A/AC.25/SR.12 (February 7, 1949). It should be noted that the UN itself sought to alter the status quo of Jerusalem by implementing the recommendation of Resolution 181 to place it under an international regime. This was one of the reasons Egypt and other Arab states voted against Resolution 194, which reiterated this proposal. As the Egyptian foreign minister expressed to the Commission, "he saw no reason why Jerusalem should not remain under Arab control as it had been for so many centuries." See: A/AC.25/SR/G/3.

57. A/AC.25/SR/G/3.

58. United Nations Conciliation Commission for Palestine, *The Work of the Conciliation Commission in connection with the Refugee Problem*, A/AC.25/CCP.RWA/2 (April 17, 1950).

59. United Nations Security Council, 414th Meeting, *Continuation of the discussion on the application of Israel for membership in the United Nations*, S/PV.414 (March 4, 1949).

60. United Nations General Assembly, *Application of Israel for Membership in the United Nations*, A/818 (March 9, 1949).

61. United Nations General Assembly, 45th Meeting, *Application of Israel for admission to membership in the United Nations*, A/AC.24/SR.45 (May 5, 1949).

62. United Nations General Assembly, 48th Meeting, *Application of Israel for admission to membership in the United Nations*, A/AC.24/SR.48 (May 7, 1949).

63. United Nations General Assembly, 51st Meeting, *Application of Israel for admission to membership in the United Nations*, A/AC.24/SR.51 (May 9, 1949).

64. United Nations General Assembly, 207th Plenary Meeting, *Application of Israel for admission to membership in the United Nations: report of the Ad Hoc Political Committee*, A/PV.207 (May 11, 1949). United Nations General Assembly Resolution 273 (III), *Admission of Israel to membership in the United Nations*, A/RES/273 (III) (May 11, 1949).

65. Charter of the United Nations, Article 4.

66. International Court of Justice, *Conditions of Admission of a State to Membership in the United Nations*, Advisory Opinion, May 28, 1948.

67. Convention on the Rights and Duties of States, signed in Montevideo, Uruguay, on December 26, 1933 and entered into force on December 26, 1934; published at www.cfr.org, accessed October 16, 2014.

68. Israel Ministry of Foreign Affairs, *The Camp David Accords: Documents Pertaining to the Conclusion of Peace*, April 1979; available at the Birzeit University Institute of Law website (http://muqtafi.birzeit.edu/), accessed January 21, 2015.

69. "1987: First Intifada," *BBC*, May 6, 2008. See also: Avraham Sela, "The first intifada: How the Arab-Israeli conflict was transformed," *Haaretz*, December 13, 2012. Sonja Karkar, "The first intifada 20 years later," *The Electronic Intifada*, December 10, 2007. "The First Intifada," *Ma'an News*, August 16, 2009.

70. Shlomo Ben-Ami, *Scars of War, Wounds of Peace: The Israeli-Arab Tragedy* (New York: 2006), 191, 211; cited in Finkelstein, *'This Time We Went Too Far'*, Location 127.

71. Andy Levy-Ajzenkopf, "Sharansky on Tour Promoting Identify, Freedom," *Canadian Jewish News*, July 1, 2008; cited in Finkelstein, *'This Time We Went Too Far'*, Location 127.

72. Dr. Israel Shahak, "Oslo Agreement Makes PLO Israel's Enforcer," *Washington Report on Middle East Affairs*, November/December 1993, 7-16.

73. The UN General Assembly in 1974 recognized the PLO as "the representative of the Palestinian people" and invited it "to participate in the deliberations of the General Assembly on the question of Palestine in plenary meetings." See: United Nations General Assembly, 2268th Plenary Meeting, *Invitation to the Palestine Liberation Organization*, A/RES/3210(XXIX) (October 14, 1974). The PLO was further recognized as "the sole legitimate representative of the Palestinian people" by the Arab League in 1974. See: League of Arab States, Seventh Arab League Summit Conference, *Resolution on Palestine*, October 28, 1974. This international standing of the PLO did not change with the establishment of the PA by the Oslo process.

74. Camille Mansour, "The Palestinian-Israeli Peace Negotiations: An Overview and Assessment," *Journal of Palestine Studies*, Vol. XXII, No. 3 (Spring 1993), 5-31.

75. Chomsky, *Fateful Triangle*, 537. Prior to the signing of the Israel-Egypt peace treaty, in a letter to President Carter dated September 17, 1978, Sadat expressed his (correct) understanding of Resolution 242 that "All the measures taken by Israel to alter the status of the City [of Jerusalem] are null and void and

should be rescinded." Begin the same day wrote to Carter, "I have the honor to inform you, Mr. President, that on 28 June 1967—Israel's parliament (The Knesset) promulgated and adopted a law to the effect: 'the Government is empowered by a decree to apply the law, the jurisdiction and administration of the State to any part of Eretz Israel (Land of Israel—Palestine), as stated in that decree.' On the basis of this law, the government of Israel decreed in July 1967 that Jerusalem is one city indivisible, the capital of the State of Israel." See "Exchanges of Letters" in State of Israel, *The Camp David Accords*.

76.   United Nations General Assembly, 49th Session, *The Situation in the Middle East*, A/49/180 – S/1994/727 (June 20, 1994); Annex, *Agreement on the Gaza Strip and the Jericho Area*, May 4, 1994.

77.   Israeli-Palestinian Interim Agreement on the West Bank and the Gaza Strip (the Oslo II Accord, or the Taba Agreement), September 28, 1995; full text including a map of the proposed zones of control published in the *Journal of Palestine Studies*, Vol. XXV, No. 2 (Winter 1996), 123-137. For additional analysis, see also Chomsky, *Fateful Triangle*, 540-558.

78.   Prime Minister Yitzhak Rabin, Speech to the Extraordinary Knesset Session on the Interim Agreement, Jerusalem, 5 October 1995; published in the *Journal of Palestine Studies*, Vol. XXV, No. 2 (Winter 1996), 137-139.

79.   The Wye River Memorandum, October 23, 1998; published in the *Journal of Palestine Studies*, Vol. XXVIII, No. 2 (Winter 1999), 135-139.

80.   US Secretary of State Madeleine K. Albright, "Letter of Assurance to PLO Chairman Yasir Arafat," October 23, 1998; JPS Vol. XXVIII, No. 2, 139-140.

81.   "Letter from U.S. Ambassador to Israel Edward S. Walker, Jr. to the Office of the Prime Minister," October 29, 1998"; JPS Vol. XXVIII, No. 2, 144-145. The issue of the settlements was mentioned in neither letter.

82.   "Letter from U.S. Ambassador to Israel Edward S. Walker, Jr. to the Office of the Prime Minister, October 30, 1998"; JPS Vol. XXVIII, No. 2, 144.

83.   "President William Clinton Remarks at the White House Signing Ceremony, Washington, 23 October 1998"; JPS Vol. XXVIII, No. 2, 140-141.

84.   Israeli Cabinet, "Government Decision on the Wye River Memorandum," November 11, 1998; JPS Vol. XXVIII, No. 2, 145-146.

85.   Amnesty International, *Demolition and Dispossession: The Destruction of Palestinian Homes*, December 8, 1999.

86.   Robert Malley and Hussein Agha, "Camp David: Tragedy of Errors," *New York Review of Books*, August 9, 2001; republished in the *Journal of Palestine Studies*, Vol. XXXI, No. 1 (Autumn 2001), 62-75.

87.   Seth Ackerman, "The Myth of the Generous Offer: Distorting the Camp David negotiations," *Fairness & Accuracy in Reporting* (FAIR), July/August 2002.

88.   Carol Migdalovitz, "Israeli-Arab Negotiations: Background, Conflicts, and U.S. Policy," *Congressional Research Service*, October 30, 2008. Although CRS reports are not made public by the government, many are obtained and made available by the Federation of American Scientists on their website, www.fas.org.

89.   Dr. Ron Pundak, "From Oslo to Taba: What Went Wrong?" *Survival: Global politics and Strategy*, Vol. 43, Issue 3, No. 3, Autumn 2001.

90.   Akram Hanieh, "The Camp David Papers," *Journal of Palestine Studies*, Vol. XXX, No. 2 (Winter 2001), 75-97.

91.   "Ehud Barak on Camp David: 'I Did Not Give Away a Thing,'" *Journal of Palestine Studies*, Vol. XXXIII, No. 1 (Fall 2003), 84-87.

92.   The Mitchell Report.

93.   "The Clinton proposal," *Haaretz*, March 25, 2002. *Haaretz* published "the minutes of former U.S. president Bill Clinton's comments at a meeting with Israeli and Palestinian representatives at the White House on December 23, 2000, as given to *Haaretz* by Palestinian sources."

94.   "The Israeli-Palestinian Joint Statement at Taba," January 27, 2001; published in the *Journal of Palestine Studies*, Vol. XXXI, No. 3 (Spring 2002), 80-81.

95.   "The Moratinos Nonpaper on the Taba Negotiations," Summer 2001; JPS Vol. XXXI, No. 3, 81-89.

96.   Migdalovitz, "Israeli-Arab Negotiations."

97.   The White House, "President Bush Calls for New Palestinian Leadership," President George W. Bush remarks to the press in the Rose Garden, June 24, 2002.

98.   "A Performance-Based Road Map to a Permanent Two-State Solution to the Israeli-Palestinian Conflict" (The Road Map), April 30, 2003; published in the *Journal of Palestine Studies*, Vol. XXXII, No. 4 (Summer 2003), 88-94.

99. Secretary of State Colin Powell and National Security Adviser Condoleezza Rice Statement on Israel's Reservations on the Road Map, May 23, 2003; JPS Vol. XXXII, No. 4, 96.

100. Israeli Prime Minister Ariel Sharon Statement Accepting the Road Map, May 23, 2003; JPS Vol. XXXII, No. 4, 96-97.

101. "Israel's Road Map Reservations," *Haaretz*, May 27, 2003; JPS Vol. XXXII, No. 4, 97-99.

102. Chris McGreal, "Sharon goes back on settlements pledge," *The Guardian*, November 28, 2003. John Ward Anderson, "Israel Approves Construction of More Homes At Settlements," *Washington Post*, December 3, 2003.

103. Richard W. Stevenson, "U.S. Cutting Loan Guarantees To Oppose Israeli Settlements," *New York Times*, September 17, 2003.

104. US Department of State, Embassy in Tel Aviv, "U.S. Deducts $289.5 Million From Israeli Loan Guarantees," November 26, 2003.

105. "US Tax-Exempt Charitable Contributions to Israel: Donations, Illegal Settlements and Terror Attacks against the US," *Institute for Research: Middle Eastern Policy* (IRmep), October 5, 2005.

106. David Ignatius, "A Tax Break Fuels Middle East Friction," *Washington Post*, March 26, 2009.

107. Jim Rutenberg, Mike McIntire, and Ethan Bronner, "Tax-Exempt Funds Aid Settlements in West Bank," *New York Times*, July 5, 2010.

108. "Prime Minister's Speech at the Herzliya Conference, December 18, 2003," *Arutz Sheva*, December 19, 2003. The English online version of the Israeli media network Arutz Sheva is also known as *Israel National News* (www.israelnationalnews.com).

109. "Prime Minister Sharon's Letter to President Bush (April 14, 2004)," *JewishVirtualLibrary.org*, accessed October 16, 2013.

110. The White House, Letter from US President George W. Bush to Israel Prime Minister Ariel Sharon, April 14, 2004.

111. Ari Shavit, "Top PM aide: Gaza plan aims to freeze the peace process," *Haaretz*, October 6, 2004.

112. Glenn Kessler, "Bush Sees 'Opening' for Mideast Peace in Arafat's Death," *Washington Post*, November 11, 2004.

113. "Mr. Sharon's Giant Step," *New York Times*, February 24, 2005.

114. ICJ Advisory Opinion, July 9, 2004.

115. "Sen. Clinton: I support W. Bank fence, PA must fight terrorism," *Haaretz*, November 13, 2005.

116. "Israel admits West Bank fence will form part of the border," *The Telegraph*, December 2, 2005. Donald Macintyre, "Sharon 'sees wall as Israel's new border,'" *The Independent*, December 2, 2005.

117. The full text of Israeli Prime Minister Ariel Sharon's declaration of a ceasefire with the Palestinians at the Sharm al-Sheikh summit, published by *BBC News*, February 8, 2005; accessed October 16, 2014.

118. U.S. Ambassador Daniel Kurtzer Interview with Israel Television Channel Ten, March 25, 2005; transcript published by *Independent Media Review Analysis* (IMRA), accessed September 4, 2014.

119. Steven Erlanger, "Rice Says U.S. Opposes Israeli Plan for Settlement Expansion," *New York Times*, March 26, 2005.

120. Aluf Benn, "PM: We can't expect explicit U.S. okay to build in settlements," *Haaretz*, March 28, 2005.

121. Jackson Diehl, "Sharon's Gamble Rides on Bush," *Washington Post*, April 11, 2005.

122. Donald Macintyre, "Sharon pledges to expand West Bank settlements as last Israelis leave Gaza," *The Independent*, August 23, 2005.

123. Aluf Benn, "PM to UN: Israel's responsibility for Gaza Strip has ended," *Haaretz*, September 13, 2005.

124. United Nations General Assembly Resolution 60/39, *Peaceful settlement of the question of Palestine*, A/RES/60/39 (December 1, 2005). United Nations Department of Public Information, "General Assembly Underscores Need for International Support to Revitalize Middle East Peace Process," summary of General Assembly 60th Plenary Meeting, December 1, 2005.

125. "Bolton Says Palestinian Resolutions Demonstrate UN Irrelevance," *Bloomberg*, December 1, 2005.

126. "President Bush Discusses the Middle East," *The White House*, July 16, 2007.

127. Minutes from 8th Negotiation Team Meeting (In Preparation for Annapolis), November 13, 2007; part of "The Palestine Papers" collection published by *Al Jazeera*, accessed September 4, 2014.

128. Israel and the PLO "Joint Understanding," November 27, 2007; published in the *Journal of Palestine Studies*, Vol. XXXVII, No. 3 (Spring 2008), 76-77.

129. US President George W. Bush, Opening Statement to the Annapolis Conference, November 27, 2007; JPS Vol. XXXVII, No. 3, 77-80.

130. Israeli Prime Minister Ehud Olmert, Statement to the Annapolis Conference, November 27, 2007; JPS Vol. XXXVII, No. 3, 83-85. Sharon suffered a stroke on January 4, 2006, from which time Olmert was acting Prime Minister. Olmert's official term started on April 14, 2006.
131. Israeli Foreign Minister Tzipi Livni, Statement to the Annapolis Conference, November 27, 2007; JPS Vol. XXXVII, No. 3, 85-88.
132. Israeli Prime Minister Ehud Olmert, Cabinet Report on Annapolis, December 2, 2007; JPS Vol. XXX-VII, No. 3, 91. To reconcile the apparent contradiction, Israel viewed its commitments as "stemming from" the Road Map, rather than being direct obligations of the agreement.
133. Israeli Foreign Minister Tzipi Livni, Cabinet Report on Annapolis, December 2, 2007; JPS Vol. XXX-VII, No. 3, 91-92.
134. "Housing Min. rejects Rice warning against E. J'lem construction," *Haaretz*, December 7, 2007.
135. "From Annapolis to Har Homa," *Haaretz*, December 12, 2007.

Chapter 4

1. Hirsh Goodman, "Analysis: The effective public diplomacy ended with Operation Cast Lead," *Jerusalem Post*, February 5, 2009. Note that the author was the husband of *New York Times* reporter Isabel Kirshner, as will be discussed in Chapter 9.
2. Alaa Al Aswany, "Why the Muslim World Can't Hear Obama," *New York Times*, February 8, 2009.
3. Glenn Kessler and Griff Witte, "In Israeli Vote Results, A Setback for Obama: Prospects for Peace Deal Appear to Dim," *Washington Post*, February 11, 2009.
4. Akiva Eldar, "U.S. expected to pressure Israel on settlement construction," *Haaretz*, February 15, 2009.
5. "Profile: Tzipi Livni," *BBC*, February 3, 2009.
6. Profile of Menahem Begin, www.etzel.org.il, accessed September 16, 2014.
7. Profile of Yitzhak Shamir, www.knesset.gov.il, accessed September 16, 2014.
8. Eldar, "U.S. expected to pressure Israel."
9. "Foreign-Supplied Weapons Used Against Civilians by Israel and Hamas," *Amnesty International*, February 20, 2009.
10. Amnesty International, *Fuelling Conflict: Foreign Arms Supplies to Israel/Gaza*, February 2009.
11. "U.S. official: Obama won't cut military aid to Israel," *Deutsche Presse-Agentur*, March 11, 2009.
12. Anthony H. Cordesman, "The 'Gaza War': A Strategic Analysis," *Center for Strategic and International Studies*, February 2, 2009. For additional critical analysis of Cordesman's report, see: Finkelstein, *This Time We Went Too Far*, Chapter 3.
13. "Israel troops admit Gaza abuses," *BBC*, March 19, 2009.
14. Roi Mandel, "Soldiers say IDF immoral in Gaza," *Ynetnews*, March 19, 2009.
15. Donald Macintyre, "Israel's dirty secrets in Gaza," *The Independent*, March 20, 2009.
16. Amos Harel, "IDF in Gaza: Killing civilians, vandalism, and lax rules of engagement," *Haaretz*, March 19, 2009.
17. Cliff Churgin, "Religioius war in Gaza? Israeli soldier says rabbis said 'get rid of the gentiles,'" *Chicago Tribune*, March 21, 2009.
18. Uri Blau, "Dead Palestinian babies and bombed mosques – IDF fashion 2009," *Haaretz*, March 20, 2009.
19. Macintyre, "Israel's dirty secrets." BBC, March 19, 2009.
20. Ethan Bronner, "Soldiers' Accounts of Gaza Killings Raise Furor in Israel," *New York Times*, March 19, 2009.
21. "Chief of staff responds to claims against IDF in Gaza," *Ynetnews*, March 23, 2009.
22. Gideon Levy, "IDF ceased long ago being 'most moral army in the world,'" *Haaretz*, March 22, 2009.
23. Josef Federman, "Israel army: No charges in Gaza probe," *Associated Press*, March 30, 2009.
24. "Rights group: Israeli troops broke medical ethics," *Ynetnews*, March 23, 2009.
25. Human Rights Watch, *Rain of Fire: Israel's Use of White Phosphorus in Gaza*, March 2009.
26. United Nations Human Rights Council, *Human Rights Situation in Palestine and Other Occupied Arab Territories: Report of the Special Rapporteur on the situation of human rights in the Palestinian territories occupied since 1967, Richard Falk*, A/HRC/10/20 (March 17, 2009).
27. Natasha Mozgovaya, "'IDF troops used 11-year-old boy as human shield in Gaza,'" *Haaretz*, March 23, 2009.

28. Ibid.
29. "Israel bows to U.S. pressure, lifts food restrictions on Gaza," *Reuters*, March 24, 2009.
30. United Nations Human Rights Council, "Richard J. Goldstone Appointed to Lead Human Rights Council Fact-Finding Mission on Gaza Conflict," Press Release, April 3, 2009.
31. "Israel will not cooperate with UN Gaza inquiry," *Reuters*, April 15, 2009.
32. Sebastian Van As, Alicia Vacas Moro, Ralf Syring, et al, "Final Report: Independent fact-finding mission into violations of human rights in the Gaza Strip during the period 27.12.2008 – 18.01.2009," *Physicians For Human Rights-Israel*, April 2009.
33. Israel Ministry of Foreign Affairs, *IDF: Conclusion of Investigation into Central Claims and Issues in Operation Cast Lead—Part 1*, April 22, 2009. Israel Ministry of Foreign Affairs, *IDF: Conclusion of Investigation into Central Claims and Issues in Operation Cast lead—Part 2*, April 22, 2009.
34. Anshel Pfeffer, "Barak: Gaza probe shows IDF among world's most moral armies," *Haaretz*, April 23, 2009.
35. Ibid.
36. "Israeli Army Probe Lacks Credibility and Is No Substitute for Independent Investigation," *Amnesty International*, April 23, 2009.
37. Isabel Kershner, "Israeli Military Says Actions in Gaza War Did Not Violate International Law," *New York Times*, April 23, 2009.
38. "Letter to Secretary Clinton on Blockade of Gaza Strip," *Human Rights Watch*, April 30, 2009.
39. Ethan Bronner, "Misery Hangs Over Gaza Despite Pledges of Help," *New York Times*, May 29, 2009.
40. United Nations Secretary-General, *Secretary-General's Summary of the Report of the United Nations Headquarters Board of Inquiry into certain incidents in the Gaza Strip between 27 December 2008 and 19 January 2009*, May 5, 2009.
41. Rory McCarthy, "UN accuses Israel of Gaza 'negligence or recklessness,'" *The Guardian*, May 5, 2009.
42. Column Lynch, "U.N. Inquiry Finds Israel Purposely Fired on School in Gaza," *Washington Post*, May 6, 2009.
43. US Department of State, "Ambassador Rice's May 4 Telcons with UN Secretary-General on Gaza Board of Inquiry Report," cable from the US Mission to the UN to the Secretary of State, May 9, 2009; published at *Wikileaks.org*, accessed September 10, 2014.
44. US Department of State, "Gaza Board of Inquiry and Next Steps," cable from the US Mission to the UN to the Secretary of State, May 7, 2009; published at *Wikileaks.org*, accessed September 10, 2014.
45. US Department of State, "Security Council and Gaza Board of Inquiry: Council Decides to Let the Secretary-General Maintain the Lead," cable from the US Mission to the UN to the Secretary of State, May 13, 2009; published at *Wikileaks.org*, accessed September 10, 2014. It's useful to also note, with regard to Ban Ki-moon's role as a tool of US foreign policy, that after a delegation of Arab foreign ministers met with the permanent members of the Security Council on January 5, 2009, to press for an immediate ceasefire resolution, the Secretary-General assured the US Ambassador to the UN, Zalmay Khalilzad, that "he was sympathetic to Israel's position, even if he would then be forced to shore up his image in the Arab world by reacting to Israel's ground operation in Gaza." The fact that the Secretary-General expressed his sympathies not for the victims, but the perpetrator of the massacre, and would only speak out against Israel's war crimes because he was "forced" to under public pressure is a remarkable illustration of his willingness to serve US interests in a manner conflicting with the duties of his office. See: US Department of State, "Calls in New York for Security Council to Act on Gaza," cable from the US Mission to the UN to the Secretary of State, January 6, 2009; published at *Wikileaks.org*, accessed September 10, 2014.
46. "Israel compensation payment to UN ignores rights of Gaza victims," *Amnesty International*, February 23, 2010.
47. "Israel: Misuse of Drones Killed Civilians in Gaza," *Human Rights Watch*, June 30, 2009. Human Rights Watch, *Precisely Wrong: Gaza Civilians Killed by Israeli Drone-Launched Missiles*, June 30, 2009. Sheera Frenkel, "At least 29 killed unlawfully by Israeli drones in Gaza, report says," *The Times*, June 30, 2009.
48. "Barack Obama hints at tougher line on Israel," *The Times*, May 5, 2009. Aluf Benn, "Obama team readying for confrontation with Netanyahu," *Haaretz*, April 9, 2009.
49. Benn, "Obama team readying for confrontation."
50. The Times, May 5, 2009.
51. Akiva Eldar, Amos Harel, and Avi Issacharoff, "Livni to Mitchell: We don't gain from stagnant peace process," *Haaretz*, April 16, 2009.

52. Jeffrey Heller and Adam Entous, "Obama envoy tells Israel U.S. wants Palestinian state," *Reuters*, April 16, 2009.

53. "Netanyahu Ready For Peace Talks," *Reuters*, May 5, 2009.

54. "Poll: Most Palestinians, Israelis want two-state solution," *Associated Press*, April 22, 2009.

55. "Transcript: Interview With Khaled Meshal of Hamas," *New York Times*, May 5, 2009.

56. Scott Wilson, "Obama, Peres Discuss Israeli-Palestinian Peace," *Washington Post*, May 5, 2009.

57. George Friedman, "An Israeli Prime Minister Comes to Washington Again," *Stratfor*, May 18, 2009.

58. Helene Cooper, "World Watches for U.S. Shift on Mideast," *New York Times*, May 17, 2009.

59. "Remarks by President Obama and Prime Minister Netanyahu of Israel in Press Availability," *The White House*, May 18, 2009.

60. Barak Ravid, "Netanyahu: We'll build only in existing settlements," *Haaretz*, May 24, 2009.

61. "Israel 'will not bow' to US settlement freeze call," *Sydney Morning Herald*, May 31, 2009.

62. Yossi Verter and Barak Ravid, "Barak: We didn't bow to Obama on West Bank outpost evacuation," *Haaretz*, May 21, 2009.

63. Mark Landler and Isabel Kershner, "Israeli Settlement Growth Must Stop, Clinton Says," *New York Times*, May 27, 2009.

64. "Obama 'confident' on two-state solution," *BBC*, May 29, 2009.

65. Meeting Minutes: Saeb Erekat with NSU on US Meetings, June 2, 2009; from "The Palestine Papers," *Al Jazeera*, accessed September 16, 2014.

66. Ethan Bronner, "Israelis Say Bush Agreed to West Bank Growth," *New York Times*, June 4, 2009.

67. Elliot Abrams, "Hillary Is Wrong About the Settlements," *Wall Street Journal*, June 26, 2009.

68. Elliot Abrams, "The Settlement Freeze Fallacy," *Washington Post*, April 8, 2009.

69. Aluf Benn, "PA rejects Olmert's offer to withdraw from 93% of West Bank," *Haaretz*, August 12, 2008.

70. Aluf Benn, "Olmert's plan for peace with the Palestinians," *Haaretz*, December 17, 2009. See also the map provided by *Haaretz* based on sources who received reports of Olmert's offer.

71. Benn, "PA rejects Olmert's offer."

72. Charles Krauthammer, "The Settlements Myth," *Washington Post*, June 5, 2009.

73. Dan Kurtzer, "The Settlement Facts," *Washington Post*, June 14, 2009. Kurtzer was also an adviser to the Obama campaign and was a coauthor with Dennis Ross of a speech Obama gave to the Israeli lobby group AIPAC in June 2008. See: Jay Solomon, "Obama's Mideast Experts Emphasize Talks," *Wall Street Journal*, June 16, 2008.

74. The White House, "Remarks by the President on a New Beginning," June 4, 2009.

75. The White House, "Remarks by the President at the Acceptance of the Nobel Peace Prize," December 10, 2009. Regarding his denunciation of armed resistance, to illustrate that liberties are not being taken with interpretation, his actual words were, "*Resistance* through violence and killing is wrong and it does not succeed" (emphasis added). This obviously includes not only acts of terrorism and war crimes, but also legitimate armed resistance, which falls under "the inherent right of individual or collective self-defense" recognized in Chapter VII, Article 51 of the UN Charter.

76. White House, "Remarks by the President on a New Beginning."

77. "Full text of Netanyahu's foreign policy speech at Bar Ilan," *Haaretz*, June 14, 2009.

78. Howard Schneider, "Netanyahu Backs 2-State Goal," *Washington Post*, June 15, 2009.

79. Isabel Kershner, "Netanyahu Backs Palestinian State, With Caveats," *New York Times*, June 15, 2009.

80. Schneider, "Netanyahu Backs 2-State Goal."

81. The White House, "Remarks by President Obama and Prime Minister Berlusconi of Italy in Press Availability," June 15, 2009.

82. Saud Abu Ramadan, "Haneya tells Carter Hamas accepts a state on 1967 border," *Xinhua*, June 16, 2009.

83. International Committee of the Red Cross, *Gaza: 1.5 million people trapped in despair*, June 29, 2009.

84. "IDF Navy intercepts Gaza-bound ship," *Jerusalem Post*, June 30, 2009.

85. "Israelis intercept Gaza aid ship," *BBC*, June 30, 2009.

86. Statement from Cynthia McKinney, Press Release, *Green Party of the United States*, July 2, 2009. "Cynthia McKinney calls WBAIX from Israeli prison," *YouTube* video, 2:46, WBAIX radio interview posted by "RunCynthiaRun," July 2, 2009. Rhonda Cook, "McKinney, still in jail, expected to see judge Sunday," *Atlanta Journal-Constitution*, July 4, 2009. "Israel Attacks Justice Boat; Kidnaps Human Rights Workers; Confiscates Medicine, Toys and Olive Trees," Press Release, *Free Gaza Movement*, June 30, 2009.

87. "Nobel Peace Laureate Mairead Maguire Speaks from Israeli Jail Cell After Arrest on Boat Delivering Humanitarian Aid to Gaza," *Democracy Now!*, July 2, 2009.

88. BBC, June 30, 2009.

89. "Israel navy intercepts boat with ex-U.S. Rep. McKinney," *CNN*, June 30, 2009.

90. Isabel Kershner, "Activists Held by Israel for Trying to Break Gaza Blockade," *New York Times*, July 2, 2009.

91. David Lewkowict, "Cynthia Mckinney Does it Again," LIVEshots, *Fox News*, July 2, 2009.

92. Mary Ann Akers, "Where Are They Now: Cynthia McKinney Strikes Again," The Sleuth, *Washington Post*, July 1, 2009.

93. "McKinney Says Police Officer Touched Her 'Inappropriately,'" *Associated Press*, April 1, 2006. "McKinney apologizes for scuffle with officer," *CNN*, April 6, 2006. McKinney apologized that for the "escalation" of the situation, describing it as a "misunderstanding" and maintaining, "There should not have been any physical contact in this incident."

94. Thomas B. Edsall and Molly Moore, "Pro-Israel Lobby Has Strong Voice," *Washington Post*, September 4, 2004. See also: Stephen Zunes, "Don't Blame the Jews for Cynthia McKinney's Defeat," *CommonDreams.org*, August 25, 2002. Zunes didn't think Jewish support for her opponent was the primary reason she lost the race, but acknowledged that she was indeed "a target of the so-called 'Jewish lobby'", which financed her opponent's campaign because of her willingness to criticize Israel.

95. Amnesty International, *Operation 'Cast Lead': 22 Days of Death and Destruction*, July 2, 2009.

96. Dan Izenber and Yaakov Katz, "Hamas, Israel reject Amnesty claims," *Jerusalem Post*, July 1, 2009.

97. Yaakov Katz, "Israel hopes Congress will lift F-22 ban," *Jerusalem Post*, July 3, 2009.

98. Donald Macintyre, "Britain punishes Israel for Gaza naval bombardment," *The Independent*, July 14, 2009.

99. Breaking the Silence, *Soldier's Testimonies from Operation Cast Lead, Gaza 2009*, June 2009 (released in July 2009). The US State Department noted that "by far the strongest reverbration [*sic*] in Israel was that created by the Israeli organization 'Breaking the Silence', which collected testimony from 26 unnamed IDF soldiers. All of the soldiers had been involved in Operation Cast Lead in the Gaza Strip, and testified to instances where Gazans were used as human shields, incendiary phosphorous shells were fired over civilian population areas, and other examples of excessive firepower that caused unnecessary fatalities and destruction of property." While IDF spokesman Brig. Gen. Avi Benayahu was "a seasoned player when it comes to handling the media", the testimonies "constituted a very different challenge" as the soldiers' "allegations were not easy to dismiss". See: US Department of State, "IDF to Investigate Complaints of Criminal Conduct by Its Forces During Operation Cast Lead," July 30, 2009, cable from the American Embassy in Tel Aviv to the Secretary of State, published at *Wikileaks.org*, accessed September 16, 2014.

100. "Israel soldiers speak out on Gaza," *BBC*, July 15, 2009.

101. "Gaza war lacked restraint, some Israeli troops say," *Reuters*, July 15, 2009.

102. "Council on Foreign Relations Address by Secretary of State Hillary Clinton," *Council on Foreign Relations*, July 15, 2009.

103. Natasha Mozgovaya, "U.S.: We won't exert economic pressure on Israel," *Haaretz*, July 24, 2009. "US dispels fears over Israel sanctions," *Jerusalem Post*, July 24, 2009.

104. "Israel envoy: No crisis with U.S. over settlements," *Haaretz*, July 22, 2009.

105. Ibid.

106. "Israel doesn't see U.S. limiting loan guarantees," *Reuters*, July 23, 2009.

107. United States Code, Title 22, Chapter 32 – Foreign Assistance, Subchapter II – Military Assistance and Sales, Sections 2302, 2304, accessible at www.law.cornell.edu.

108. Under international law, the only legitimate use of force is when exercised in self-defense against armed aggression or when authorized by the UN Security Council. The US's war on Iraq was neither, hence a war of aggression, defined at Nuremberg as "not only an international crime; it is the supreme international crime differing only from other war crimes in that it contains within itself the accumulated evil of the whole." See: *Trial of the Major War Criminals before the International Military Tribunal, Nuremberg, 14 November 1945 – 1 October 1946* (Nuremberg 1947), 186; available online at the Library of Congress. For more on the US's false pretexts for war, see: Jeremy R. Hammond, "The Lies that Led to the Iraq War and the Persistent Myth of 'Intelligence Failure,'" *Foreign Policy Journal*, September 8, 2012.

109. Jeremy M. Sharp, "U.S. Foreign Aid to Israel," *Congressional Research Service*, September 16, 2010.

110. "U.S. re-approves Israel loan guarantees program," *Reuters*, June 30, 2009. The article states that $1 billion was deducted from the total amount of loan guarantees, but does not clarify that this was

done previously, under the Bush administration, with no deductions under the Obama administration for fiscal year 2009—or any other year of his administration, for that matter.

111.   Eli Lake, "Obama Sold Israel Bunker-Buster Bombs," *The Daily Beast*, September 23, 2011. Eli Lake, "Inside Obama's Israel Bomb Sale," *The Daily Beast*, September 25, 2011.

Chapter 5

1.   State of Israel, Ministry of Foreign Affairs, *The Operation in Gaza 27 December 2008 – 18 January 2009: Factual and Legal Aspects*, July 2009, paras. 6, 10, 17, 20, 23, 26.
2.   Ibid., paras. 40, 41, 81.
3.   Ibid., para. 119.
4.   Israel Security Agency (Shabak), "Selected Examples of Interrogations Following Operation Cast Lead," accessed October 2, 2011.
5.   Amnesty International, *Israel/OPT: Briefing to the Committee Against Torture*, September 30, 2008.
6.   Israel, *The Operation in Gaza*, para. 119.
7.   United Nations General Assembly/Security Council, *Children and armed conflict: Report of the Secretary-General*, A/63/785-S/2009/158 (March 26, 2009).
8.   Hanan Greenberg, "Mofaz: IDF to appeal 'human shield' ruling," *Ynetnews*, October 11, 2005.
9.   Israel, *The Operation in Gaza*, paras. 159-162.
10.   Rod Nordland, "Hamas and Its Discontents," *Newsweek*, January 19, 2009.
11.   Israel, *The Operation in Gaza*, paras. 164-166.
12.   Foreign Policy Journal, "Israel Issues False Propaganda to Cover Up War Crimes," *YouTube* video, 3:40, January 16, 2009. This author produced this video rebuttal to the IDF's claimed evidence of weapons stored in the mosque. The IDF also pointed to a flash in the video following the second bomb dropping to suggest it was a secondary explosion from arms stored in the mosque. However, this flash is merely the thermal imaging monitor being switched from "black hot" to "white hot" as clouds of smoke and heat escape the building, which obscured the operator's view. After adjusting the settings, the operator zoomed in to get a closer view of the damage caused by the two Israeli bombs.
13.   United Nations Office for the Coordination of Humanitarian Affairs, *LOCKED IN: The Humanitarian Impact of Two Years of Blockade on the Gaza Strip*, August 2009.
14.   Human Rights Watch, *White Flag Deaths: Killings of Palestinian Civilians during Operation Cast Lead*, August 2009.
15.   B'Tselem, *B'Tselem's investigation of fatalities in Operation Cast Lead*, September 9, 2009.
16.   United Nations Human Rights Council, *Report of the United Nations Fact-Finding Mission on the Gaza Conflict* (The Goldstone Report), A/HRC/12/48 (September 25, 2009), para. 11.
17.   Ibid., paras. 29-31. The Mission confirmed that four Israelis were killed by rocket or mortar fire by Palestinian armed groups against southern Israel: three civilians and one soldier. In addition, nine Israeli soldiers were killed in Gaza, four by friendly fire.
18.   Ibid., para. 69.
19.   Ibid., paras. 65-67, 322, 1219, 1315.
20.   Ibid., paras. 1268, 1271.
21.   Ibid., paras. 1318, 1326, 1331, 1929.
22.   Ibid., para. 62.
23.   Ibid., para. 1893.
24.   Ibid., paras. 62, 1192-1216.
25.   Ibid., paras. 32-34.
26.   Ibid., paras. 37, 48, 500-542.
27.   Ibid., paras. 38, 543-595.
28.   Ibid., paras. 39, 596-629.
29.   Ibid., paras. 630-652.
30.   Ibid., paras. 41-42, 653-703.
31.   Ibid., paras. 43, 811. Part XI of the report deals with these incidents and is titled "Deliberate Attacks Against the Civilian Population".
32.   Ibid., paras. 706-744.
33.   Ibid., paras. 770-779.
34.   Ibid., paras. 822-843.
35.   Ibid., paras. 844-866.

36.   Ibid., paras. 867-885.

37.   Ibid., paras. 50-54.

38.   Ibid., paras. 439-498.

39.   Ibid., paras. 103-110, 1594-1691.

40.   Ibid., paras. 55, 1032-1106.

41.   Ibid., paras. 1804-1835.

42.   Ibid., para. 1969.

43.   Richard Goldstone, "Justice in Gaza," *New York Times*, September 17, 2009.

44.   US Department of State, "U.S. Response to the Report of the United Nations Fact-Finding Mission on the Gaza Conflict," Statement by Michael Posner, United States Assistant Secretary of State for Democracy, Human Rights and Labor, at the 12th Session of the Human Rights Council, Geneva, Switzerland, September 2009.

45.   US Department of State, "Remarks by Ambassador Susan E. Rice, U.S. Permanent Representative to the United Nations, on Somalia, the Middle East and the 2009 H1N1 influenza pandemic, at the Security Council Stakeout," September 17, 2009.

46.   Neil MacFarquhar, "A U.S. Envoy Makes a Case for the U.N.," *New York Times*, September 21, 2009.

47.   United States Senate, Office of Senator Kirsten Gillibrand, "Gillibrand, Senate Colleagues Urge U.S. to Block Inflammatory Anti-Israel Report from Reaching U.N. Security Council," Press Release, September 29, 2009

48.   Stephen Zunes, "The Gaza War, Congress and International Humanitarian Law," *Middle East Policy Council*, March 22, 2010.

49.   Goldstone Report, para. 1883.

50.   Ibid., para. 183.

51.   Natasha Mozgovaya and Barak Ravid, "Netanyahu calls UN Gaza probe a 'kangaroo court' against Israel," *Haaretz*, September 16, 2009.

52.   Barak Ravid, "Netanyahu asks world to reject Goldstone findings," *Haaretz*, October 3, 2009.

53.   Barak Ravid, "Netanyahu rejects inquiry, sets up special panel to counter Goldstone," *Haaretz*, October 26, 2009.

54.   Mozgovaya and Ravid, "UN Gaza probe a 'kangaroo court.'"

55.   Ravid, "Netanyahu rejects inquiry."

56.   Larry Derfner, "Rattling the Cage: Our exclusive right to self-defense," *Jerusalem Post*, October 7, 2009.

57.   "Israel must investigate army's conduct in Operation Cast Lead," *B'Tselem*, October 19, 2009.

58.   "UN: US, EU Undermine Justice for Gaza Conflict," *Human Rights Watch*, September 30, 2009.

59.   United Nations Human Rights Council, Draft Resolution 12/L.12 (A/HRC/12/L.12), September 25, 2009. Egypt Ministry of Foreign Affairs, "Members, Observers and Guests," Summit of the Non-Aligned Movement, Sharm El Sheikh, July 11-16, 2009; archived at http://web.archive.org, January 11, 2012, accessed October 16, 2014.

60.   Israel Ministry of Foreign Affairs, "Cabinet communique," remarks by Israel Prime Minister Benjamin Netanyahu to the Cabinet, October 1, 2009.

61.   Neil MacFarquhar, "Palestinians Halt Push on War Report," *New York Times*, October 1, 2009. United Nations Office at Geneva, "Human Rights Council Adopts Six Resolutions and One Decision on Discrimination Against Women and Freedom of Expression, Among Others," October 2, 2009. Howard Schneider and Column Lynch, "U.N. Human Rights Council Shelves Divisive Report on Gaza War," *Washington Post*, October 3, 2009. Amira Hass, "PA move to thwart Goldstone Gaza report shocks Palestinian public," *Haaretz*, October 6, 2009. "UN Security Council: Demand Justice for Gaza Victims," *Human Rights Watch*, October 12, 2009.

62.   Schneider and Lynch, "Council Shelves Divisive Report."

63.   "The Nobel Peace Prize for 2009," Press Release, *NobelPrize.org*, October 9, 2009.

64.   The White House, "Remarks by the President on Winning the Nobel Peace Prize," October 9, 2009.

65.   "UN Security Council: Demand Justice for Gaza Victims," *Human Rights Watch*, October 12, 2009.

66.   United Nations Human Rights Council, Draft Resolution S-12/L.1, A/HRC/S-12/L.1 (October 14, 2009). United Nations Office of the High Commissioner for Human Rights, "Human Rights Council Endorses Recommendations in Report of Fact-Finding Mission Led by Justice Goldstone and Calls for Their Implementation," October 16, 2009.

67.   Ibid. See also United Nations Human Rights Council, Resolution S-12/1, A/HRC/RES/S-12/1 (October 16, 2009).

68.   John Bolton, "Israel, the U.S. and the Goldstone Report," *Wall Street Journal*, October 19, 2009.
69.   United Nations Department of Public Information, "Crimes within the Court's Jurisdiction," May 1998.
70.   "U.N. Finds Evidence of War Crimes in Gaza Fighting," NewsHour, *PBS*, September 15, 2009.
71.   "Goldstone dares US on Gaza report," *Al Jazeera*, October 22, 2009.
72.   Bill Moyers Journal, *PBS*, October 23, 2009.
73.   H.RES.867.IH, 111th Congress, as introduced into the House of Representatives, October 23, 2009.
74.   United Nations Office of the High Commissioner for Human Rights, "UN Fact-Finding Mission on the Gaza Conflict Holds First Meeting in Geneva," May 8, 2009. United Nations Human Rights Council, "Richard J. Goldstone Appointed to Lead Human Rights Council Fact-Finding Mission on Gaza Conflict" April 3, 2009. United Nations Human Rights Council, 12th Session, *Statement by Richard Goldstone on behalf of the Members of the United Nations Fact Finding Mission on the Gaza Conflict before the Human Rights Council*, September 29, 2009.
75.   H.RES.867.IH.
76.   Sunday Times, January 11, 2009. See Chapter 2.
77.   H.RES.867.IH.
78.   E-mail from Maurice Ostroff to Justice Richard Goldstone, September 18, 2009; published at http://www.2nd-thoughts.org/id230.html, accessed July 5, 2011.
79.   "International Law and Military Operations in Practice," Address by Colonel Richard Kemp to the Jerusalem Center for Public Affairs Joint International Conference on Hamas, the Gaza War and Accountability Under International Law, June 18, 2009; published at *JCPA.org* July 7, 2009, accessed October 16, 2014.
80.   BBC Interview with British Army Colonel Richard Kemp, January 9, 2009; video clip published on the website of the Britain Israel Communications & Research Centre (www.bicom.org.uk), accessed July 5, 2011; archived at https://web.archive.org, January 22, 2009, accessed May 23, 2015.
81.   "UK Commander Challenges Goldstone Report," *UN Watch*, October 16, 2009. "About Us > Mission & History," *UNWatch.org*, accessed October 10, 2011. Peter Capella, "UN Gaza probe chief underlines balanced approach," Agence France-Presse, July 7, 2009. "Who We Are > What Others Are Saying > Israel Advocacy," *AJC.org*, accessed September 26, 2014.
82.   E-mail from Richard Goldstone to Maurice Ostroff.
83.   H.RES.867.IH.
84.   "Goldstone: 'If This Was a Court of Law, There Would Have Been Nothing Proven,'" *Forward*, October 7, 2009.
85.   H.RES.867.IH.
86.   Letter to Chairman of the House Committee on Foreign Affairs Howard Berman and Ranking Member of the House Committee on Foreign Affairs Ileana Ros-Lehtinen from Justice Richard J. Goldstone regarding H.RES.867, published at the website of the American Association for Palestinian Equal Rights (AAPER), www.aaper.org, October 29, 2009; accessed November 3, 2009; archived copy accessible at https://web.archive.org.
87.   H.RES.867.EH, 111th Congress, as passed in the House of Representatives, November 3, 2009.
88.   United Nations General Assembly, Resolution 64/10, A/RES/64/10 (December 1, 2009).
89.   United Nations General Assembly, 64th Session, 38th and 39th Plenary Meetings, "By Recorded Vote, General Assembly Urges Israel, Palestinians to Conduct Credible, Independent Investigations into Alleged War Crimes in Gaza," Press Release, GA/10883 (November 5, 2009).
90.   Ian Black and Ian Cobain, "British court issued Gaza arrest warrant for former Israeli minister Tzipi Livni," *The Guardian*, December 14, 2009.
91.   Gil Hoffman, "'Guardian' confirms Livni warrant," *Jerusalem Post*, December 14, 2009.
92.   James Hider, "Israel fury over British war crimes warrant for Tzipi Livni," *The Times*, December 15, 2009.
93.   Barak Ravid, "Israel confirms U.K. arrest warrant against Livni," *Haaretz*, December 19, 2009.
94.   "Anti-Israel is the new anti-Semitism," *Jerusalem Post*, December 16, 2009.
95.   Ravid, "Israel confirms U.K. arrest warrant."
96.   Ian Williams, "The NS Interview: Richard Goldstone," *The New Statesman*, December 30, 2009.
97.   Noam Chomsky, *The New Military Humanism: Lessons from Kosovo* (Monroe: Common Courage Press, 1999), 20-21.
98.   Ibid.
99.   "The Nightmare," *Newsweek*, April 11, 1999. Panorama, *BBC*, April 19, 1999.

100. Human Rights Watch, *Civilian Deaths in the NATO Air Campaign*, February 2000.

101. Independent International Commission on Kosovo, *The Kosovo Report* (New York: Oxford University Press, 2000), 4; available at http://reliefweb.int, accessed October 16, 2014.

102. Biography of Anne-Marie Slaughter from the website of the Woodrow Wilson School of Public and International Affairs at Princeton University, http://www.princeton.edu/~slaughtr, accessed July 5, 2011. Anne-Marie Slaughter, "Good Reasons for Going Around the U.N.," *New York Times*, March 18, 2003. US Central Intelligence Agency, *Comprehensive Report of the Special Advisor to the DCI on Iraq's WMD*, September 30, 2004.

103. David Jolly, "Britain Sends Supplies to Libyan Rebels," *New York Times*, June 30, 2011.

104. The White House, "Remarks by the President on the Situation in Libya," March 18, 2011.

105. The White House, "Remarks by the President in Address to the Nation on Libya," March 28, 2011.

106. Stewart Patrick, "A New Lease on Life for Humanitarianism," *Foreign Affairs*, March 24, 2011.

107. Steve Chapman, "Did Obama avert a bloodbath in Libya?" *Chicago Tribune*, April 3, 2011.

108. Richard N. Haass, "What Next in Libya?" *Huffington Post*, April 6, 2011.

109. Anne-Marie Slaughter, "Fiddling While Libya Burns," *New York Times*, March 13, 2011.

110. Robert E. Hunter, "What Intervention Looks Like," *Foreign Affairs*, March 16, 2011.

111. Helene Cooper and Steven Lee Myers, "Obama Takes Hard Line With Libya After Shift by Clinton," *New York Times*, March 18, 2011.

112. David D. Kirkpatrick and Elisabeth Bumiller, "Allies Target Qaddafi's Ground Forces as Libyan Rebels Regroup," *New York Times*, March 20, 2011.

113. Michael W. Doyle, "The Folly of Protection: Is Intervention Against Qaddafi's Regime Legal and Legitimate?" *Foreign Affairs*, March 20, 2011. Doyle was Harold Brown Professor of International Affairs, Law, and Political Science at Columbia University and Chair of the United Nations Democracy Fund Advisory Board.

114. Kareem Fahim and David D. Kirkpatrick, "Rebel Advance Halted Outside Qaddafi's Hometown," *New York Times*, March 28, 2011.

115. Patrick, "A New Lease on Life."

116. Rachel Donadio, "Italy Says Death Toll in Libya Is Likely Over 1,000," *New York Times*, February 23, 2011.

117. "Libya death toll 'reaches 10,000,'" *Al Jazeera*, April 19, 2011.

118. "U.S.: Libya death toll as high as 30,000," *CBS News*, April 27, 2011.

119. Kim Sengupta, "Rebel leaders put Libya death toll at 50,000," *The Independent*, August 31, 2011.

120. Amnesty International, *The Battle for Libya: Killings, Disappearances and Torture*, September 2011.

121. United Nations High Commissioner for Refugees, "UNHCR concerned as sub-Saharan Africans targeted in Libya," August 26, 2011.

122. Richard Spencer, "Libya: the West and al-Qaeda on the same side," *The Telegraph*, March 18, 2011. Praveen Swami, "Libyan rebel commander admits his fighters have al-Qaeda links," *The Telegraph*, March 25, 2011. "Libya: Al Qaeda flag flown above Benghazi courthouse," *The Telegraph*, November 1, 2011. "Libya: Detainees killed by al-Gaddafi loyalists," *Amnesty International*, August 26, 2011. Simon Denyer, "Libyan rebels carry out reprisal attacks," *Washington Post*, August 26, 2011. "Libya: Fears for detainees held by anti-Gaddafi forces," *Amnesty International*, August 30, 2011. Mohammed Abbas, "African workers live in fear after Gaddafi overthrow," *Reuters*, August 31, 2011.

123. Amnesty International, *Libya: Militias threaten hopes for new Libya*, February 16, 2012.

124. Kareem Fahim, Anthony Shadid, and Rick Gladstone, "Violent End to an Era as Qaddafi Dies in Libya," *New York Times*, October 20, 2011.

125. Stephanie Nebehay, "Mass graves still being found in Libya: Red Cross," *Reuters*, October 20, 2011. Kareem Fahim and Adam Nossiter, "In Libya, Massacre Site Is Cleaned Up, Not Investigated," *New York Times*, October 24, 2011. "Libya: Apparent Execution of 53 Gaddafi Supporters," *Human Rights Watch*, October 24, 2011.

126. United Nations Human Rights Council, *Report of the International Commission of Inquiry on Libya*, A/HRD/19/68 (March 2, 2012), paras. 86-87, 89.

127. C. J. Chivers and Eric Schmitt, "In Strikes on Libya by NATO, an Unspoken Civilian Toll," *New York Times*, December 17, 2011. Human Rights Watch, *Unacknowledged Deaths: Civilian Casualties in NATO's Air Campaign in Libya*, May 14, 2012.

128. "UN chief says former Libya rebels still hold 7,000 people, some reportedly tortured," *Associated Press*, November 29, 2011. "Libya: Deaths of detainees amid widespread torture," *Amnesty International*, January 26, 2012.

129. Amnesty International, *Libya: Militias threaten hopes for new Libya*, February 16, 2012.

130. David D. Kirkpatrick, "Braving Areas of Violence, Voters Try to Reshape Libya," *New York Times*, July 7, 2012.

131. Frederic Wehrey, "Libya's Militia Menace," *Foreign Affairs*, July 15, 2012.

132. Mel Frykberg, "Human Rights Worse After Gaddafi," *Inter Press Service*, July 14, 2012.

133. Scott Shane, "Western Companies See Prospects for Business in Libya," *New York Times*, October 28, 2011.

134. "MI5 warns of terror-trained Britons," *Press Association*, August 2, 2012. Scott Stewart, "Will Libya Again Become the Arsenal of Terrorism?" *Stratfor*, March 10, 2011. Tim Dickinson, "U.S. Bombs Libya, Helps . . . Jihadists?!" *Rolling Stone*, March 21, 2011.

135. Scott Stewart, "Mali Besieged by Fighters Fleeing Libya," *Stratfor*, February 2, 2012. Anthony Shadid, "Libya Struggles to Curb Militias as Chaos Grows," *New York Times*, February 8, 2012.

136. Ross Douthat, "Libya's Unintended Consequences," *New York Times*, July 7, 2012.

137. Yahia H. Zoubir, "Qaddafi's Spawn," *Foreign Affairs*, July 24, 2012.

138. John Mueller, "The Iraq Syndrome Revisited: U.S. Intervention, From Kosovo to Libya," *Foreign Affairs*, March 28, 2011.

139. Michael O'Hanlon, "Winning Ugly in Libya: What the United States Should Learn From Its War in Kosovo," *Foreign Affairs*, March 30, 2011.

140. Eric A. Posner, "Outside the Law: From flawed beginning to bloody end, the NATO intervention in Libya made a mockery of international law," *Foreign Policy*, October 25, 2011.

141. Doyle, "The Folly of Protection."

142. "Dershowitz: Goldstone is a traitor to the Jewish people," *Haaretz*, January 31, 2010.

143. Alan Dershowitz, "The case against the Goldstone Report," *Jerusalem Post*, January 28, 2010.

144. Alan Dershowitz, *The Case Against the Goldstone Report: A Study in Evidentiary Bias*, Harvard Law School, Public Law & Legal Theory Working Paper Series, Paper No. 10-26, January 2010.

145. Ibid., 2, 5, 6, 7.

146. Ibid., 2.

147. Goldstone Report, paras. 1884, 1895.

148. Dershowitz, *The Case Against the Goldstone Report*, 6.

149. Goldstone Report, para. 1893.

150. Ibid., 19-20.

151. Ibid., 20-21.

152. Ibid., 26.

153. Ibid., 27.

154. Dershowitz, *The Case Against the Goldstone Report*, 10.

155. Goldstone Report, para. 1196.

156. Dershowitz, *The Case Against the Goldstone Report*, 11.

157. Goldstone Report, para. 1199.

158. "Customary IHL > Chapter 4. Proportionality in Attack > Rule 14. Proportionality in Attack," from the website of the International Committee of the Red Cross (www.icrc.org), accessed October 2, 2014.

159. Rome Statute of the International Criminal Court, Article 8; available at the website of the International Criminal Court (www.icc-cpi.int), accessed October 16, 2014. The Statute entered into force on July 1, 2002.

160. Dershowitz, *The Case Against the Goldstone Report*, 12.

161. Ibid., 35. Tim McGirk and Jebel al-Kashif, "Voices from The Rubble," *Time*, January 29, 2009.

162. Amnesty International, *Operation 'Cast Lead'*. See Chapter 4 notes.

163. Human Rights Watch, *White Flag Deaths: Killings of Palestinian Civilians during Operation Cast Lead*, August 13, 2009.

164. Goldstone Report, para. 773.

165. McGirk and al-Kashif, "Voices from The Rubble."

166. Israel did discuss the attack on the Abd Rabbo family in a subsequent report, which we will come to.

167. Goldstone Report, 448-449.

168. Dershowitz, *The Case Against the Goldstone Report*, 5. For the AP article cited, see: "UN's Gaza war crimes investigation faces obstacles," *Associated Press*, June 9, 2009.

169. Dershowitz, *The Case Against the Goldstone Report*, 7.

170. Ibid., 23.

171. Ibid., 14-15.

172. Israel, *The Operation in Gaza*, paras. 398-400. Israel Ministry of Foreign Affairs, *Gaza Operation Investigations: An Update*, January 2010, para. 104 (see footnote 99).

173. Goldstone Report, para. 1187 (see footnote 574).

174. Dershowitz, *The Case Against the Goldstone Report*, 15.

175. Goldstone Report, para. 1187.

176. Dershowitz, *The Case Against the Goldstone Report*, 17, 20.

177. Goldstone Report, para. 483.

178. Dershowitz, *The Case Against the Goldstone Report*, 37.

179. Goldstone Report, para. 674.

180. Dershowitz, *The Case Against the Goldstone Report*, 37.

181. Goldstone Report, para. 449.

182. Dershowitz, *The Case Against the Goldstone Report*, 36, 38.

183. Goldstone Report, para. 623.

184. Dershowitz, *The Case Against the Goldstone Report*, 39.

185. Goldstone Report, paras. 472-473.

186. Dershowitz, *The Case Against the Goldstone Report*, 39.

187. Goldstone Report, para. 465.

188. Dershowitz, *The Case Against the Goldstone Report*, 40. Steven Erlanger, "Weighing Crimes and Ethics in the Fog of Urban Warfare," *New York Times*, January 16, 2009. Sebastian Rotella, "Hamas rocket teams continue to launch," *Los Angeles Times*, January 15, 2009 (cited by Dershowitz under the title "Hamas' Weapon of Choice"). Craig Whitlock and Reyham Abdel Kareem, "Gaza Clan Finds One Haven After Another Ravaged in Attacks," *Washington Post*, January 16, 2009.

189. Ibid., 40-41. Israel Defense Forces, "Precision Airstrikes on Hamas Terror Targets," *IDFblog.com*, January 7, 2009. Israel Defense Forces, "Weapons Hidden in Mosque Neutralized by Israel Air Force," *YouTube* video, 0:48, posted on the official IDF YouTube channel ("idfnadesk"), December 31, 2008. Israel Defense Forces, "IAF Strike on Mosque used as Weapon Storage Site," *IDFblog.com*, January 2, 2009. Israel Defense Forces, "Weaponized Mosque," *IDFblog.com*, January 13, 2009. Israel Defense Forces, "Weapons Discovered in Zeitoun Mosque," *IDFblog.com*, January 13, 2009. Meir Amit Intelligence and Terrorism Information Center, *Evidence from Operation Cast Lead Shows Hamas Uses Mosques to Store Weapons and as Sites Launch Rockets and Mortar Shells File No. 3*, February 16, 2009. Israel Defense Forces, "Intelligence Maps: Hamas Uses Mosques and Schools for Cover," *IDFblog.com*, January 22, 2009. Israel Defense Forces, "IDF Maps Reveal Hamas Exploitation of Gazan Residents," *IDFblog.com*, January 19, 2009. Israel Defense Forces, "Captured Hamas Intelligence," *IDFblog.com*, January 9, 2009. US Department of State, Secretary of State Colin L. Powell Remarks to the U.N. Security Council, February 5, 2003; archived at http://web.archive.org, February 4, 2005, accessed October 16, 2014.

190. Dershowitz, *The Case Against the Goldstone Report*, 41. Goldstone Report, para. 495.

191. Dershowitz, *The Case Against the Goldstone Report*, 41-42. Erlanger, "Weighing Crimes and Ethics". Joel Greenberg, "Israeli Army's conduct questioned," *Chicago Tribune*, January 26, 2009.

192. Dershowitz, *The Case Against the Goldstone Report*, 43.

193. Sheera Frenkel, "'Human shields forced into Gaza front line by Israelis and Hamas,'" *The Times*, February 2, 2009.

194. Dershowitz, *The Case Against the Goldstone Report*, 43-44.

195. Ibid., 44. Israel Defense Forces, "Cast Lead Video: Hamas Terrorist uses Children as Human Shield," *YouTube* video, 0:52, posted on the official IDF YouTube channel ("idfnadesk"), September 17, 2009. Israel Defense Forces, "Cast Lead Video: Civilians Flee Hamas Terrorist as He Attempts to Use Them as Human Shields," *YouTube* video, 1:25, posted on the official IDF YouTube channel ("idfnadesk"), September 17, 2009.

196. Dershowitz, *The Case Against the Goldstone Report*, 44-45, 47-48.

197. Goldstone Report, para. 483.

198. Dershowitz, *The Case Against the Goldstone Report*, 49.

Chapter 6

1. The White House, "Statement by the Press Secretary on Israeli Settlements," September 4, 2009.

2. Rory McCarthy, "US fails to broker deal with Israel over settlements," *The Guardian*, September 18, 2009. "Israel OKs nearly 400 settlement units: ministry," *Agence France-Presse*, September 7, 2009.

3. "Obama's Speech to the United Nations General Assembly," *New York Times*, September 23, 2009.
4. Meeting Minutes: Saeb Erekat and George Mitchell, September 24, 2009; "The Palestine Papers," *Al Jazeera*, accessed November 4, 2014.
5. Meeting Summary: Saeb Erekat and George Mitchell, October 2009; "The Palestine Papers," *Al Jazeera*, accessed November 4, 2014.
6. Meeting Minutes: Saeb Erekat and George Mitchell, October 2, 2009; "The Palestine Papers," *Al Jazeera*, accessed November 4, 2014. Gregg Carlstrom, "Deep frustrations with Obama," *Al Jazeera*, January 24, 2011.
7. Neil MacFarquhar, "Palestinians Halt Push on War Report," *New York Times*, October 2, 2009. Howard Schneider, "Defiant Abbas Reiterates Conditions Before Talks," *Washington Post*, October 12, 2009.
8. Meeting Minutes: Saeb Erekat and George Mitchell, October 21, 2009; "The Palestine Papers," *Al Jazeera*, accessed November 4, 2014.
9. Karen DeYoung and Howard Schneider, "Israel putting forth 'unprecedented' concessions, Clinton says," *Washington Post*, November 1, 2009. "Abbas spokesman: Netanyahu has more influence in US than in Israel," *Jerusalem Post*, November 1, 2009. Adrian Blomfield, "US drops demand for Israeli settlement freeze," *The Telegraph*, November 1, 2009.
10. Yana Dlugy, "Netanyahu savours victory after US drops settlement demand," *Agence France-Presse*, November 1, 2009.
11. Blomfield, "US drops demand."
12. Dlugy, "Netanyahu savours victory."
13. Ibid. David Usborne, "Clinton backtracks on Israeli settlements after Arab anger," *The Independent*, November 3, 2009.
14. Dlugy, "Netanyahu savours victory."
15. Ibid.
16. DeYoung and Schneider, "Israel putting forth 'unprecedented' concessions."
17. Dlugy, "Netanyahu savours victory."
18. Jerusalem Post, November 1, 2009.
19. Blomfield, "US drops demand."
20. DeYoung and Schneidger, "Israel putting forth 'unprecedented' concessions."
21. Ethan Bronner and Mark Landler, "Israel Offers a Pause in Building New Settlements," *New York Times*, November 26, 2009.
22. Isabel Kershner, "Palestinian Leader Maps Plan for Separate State," *New York Times*, August 26, 2009.
23. Barak Ravid and Natasha Mozgovaya, "PM heads to U.S. under threat of Palestinian statehood declaration," *Haaretz*, November 8, 2009.
24. Bronner and Landler, "Israel Offers a Pause."
25. Mel Frykberg, "Abbas Produces a Dubious Twist," *Inter Press Service*, November 6, 2009.
26. Gil Hoffman, "Freeze may be nixed if PA won't talk," *Jerusalem Post*, December 14, 2009.
27. "Abbas Sets Terms for Resuming Stalled Peace Talks," *Reuters*, December 15, 2009.
28. Khaled Abu Toameh, "Recognition of '67 border before talks," *Jerusalem Post*, December 15, 2009
29. Danny Ayalon, "Deputy FM to Arab world: Israel extends its hand in peace," *Haaretz*, December 15, 2009.
30. "Fmr. Israeli Foreign Minister Shlomo Ben Ami Debates Outspoken Professor Norman Finkelstein on Israel, the Palestinians, and the Peace Process," *Democracy Now!*, February 14, 2006.
31. Council of the European Union, "Council conclusions on the Middle East Peace Process," December 8, 2009.
32. "Israel's revealing fury towards EU," *Financial Times*, December 13, 2009.
33. Avi Issacharoff, "Abbas to Haaretz: Peace in 6 months if Israel freezes all settlements," *Haaretz*, December 16, 2009.
34. "Top UN official: Moratorium insufficient," *Associated Press*, December 18, 2009.
35. Sharp, "U.S. Foreign Aid to Israel". See Chapter 4 notes.
36. Ilene R. Prusher, "Israel shrugs off Mitchell's loan threat," *Christian Science Monitor*, January 10, 2010.
37. Natasha Mozgovaya, "State Dept.: U.S. not planning to withhold Israel loan guarantees," *Haaretz*, January 11, 2010.
38. Prusher, "Israel shrugs off Mitchell's loan threat."
39. "Israel Rations Palestinians to Trickle of Water," *Amnesty International*, October 27, 2009.

40. "Israel: Stop Blocking School Supplies From Entering Gaza," *Human Rights Watch*, October 11, 2009.

41. "One and a Half Million People Imprisoned," *B'Tselem*, December 27, 2009.

42. United Nations Relief and Works Agency, "OPT: UNRWA says Israeli blockade continues to cause suffering to Palestinians," Press Release, January 21, 2010.

43. Natasha Mozgovaya, "U.S. lawmakers to Obama: Press Israel to ease Gaza siege," *Haaretz*, January 26, 2010.

44. Howard Schneider, "Contrasts between Gaza, West Bank show Palestinian divide," *Washington Post*, December 15, 2009.

45. State of Israel, Ministry of Foreign Affairs, *Gaza Operation Investigations: An Update*, January 2010, para. 10.

46. Ibid., paras. 107, 112.

47. Ibid., para. 118.

48. Ibid., para. 100. "Israeli officers get 'slap on wrist' for white phosphorus use in Gaza," *The Times*, February 2, 2010.

49. Anshel Pfeffer, "IDF denies disciplining top officers over white phosphorus use in Gaza war," *Haaretz*, February 1, 2010.

50. Israel, *Gaza Operations Investigations: An Update*, para. 137, footnote 112.

51. Ibid., paras. 144, 147.

52. Goldstone Report, paras. 975, 985-986.

53. Israel, *Gaza Operations Investigations: An Update*, para. 160.

54. Goldstone Report, paras. 973-974.

55. Israel, *Gaza Operations Investigations: An Update*, paras. 164, 166-167, 173.

56. Goldstone Report, paras. 927, 929.

57. Israel, *Gaza Operations Investigations: An Update*, para. 176.

58. Goldstone Report, para. 654 (see footnote 380).

59. Barak Ravid, "Israel slams Goldstone 'misrepresentations' of internal probes into Gaza war," *Haaretz*, January 29, 2010.

60. "Barak: Goldstone report 'false, distorted, and irresponsible,'" *Haaretz*, January 28, 2010.

61. "Latest Israeli Response to Gaza Investigations Totally Inadequate," *Amnesty International*, February 2, 2010. Malcolm Smart, the Director of Amnesty International's Middle East and North Africa Program, also noted that more than a year after its assault on Gaza, "only one soldier has been convicted of an offence as a result of the Israeli investigations, and that was the theft of a credit card."

62. "Turning a Blind Eye: Impunity for Laws-of-War Violations during the Gaza War," *Human Rights Watch*, April 10, 2010.

63. "U.K. officer slams 'Pavlovian' criticism of IDF after Gaza war," *Haaretz*, February 22, 2010.

64. Jeffrey Heller, "Israeli envoy sees 'historic crisis' with U.S.: report," *Reuters*, March 15, 2010.

65. Ronen Medzini, "1,600 housing unites in east J'lem approved," *Ynetnews*, March 9, 2010

66. Janine Zacharia, "U.S. condemns Israel's plans to build housing in east Jerusalem," *Washington Post*, March 10, 2010.

67. Akiva Eldar, "U.S. gave Israel green light for East Jerusalem construction," *Haaretz*, March 12, 2010

68. Mark Perry, "The Petraeus briefing: Biden's embarrassment is not the whole story," *Foreign Policy*, March 13, 2010.

69. US Congress, *Statement of General David H. Petraeus, U.S. Army Commander, U.S. Central Command, Before the Senate Armed Services Committee on the Posture of U.S. Central Command*, March 16, 2010.

70. Dore Gold, "Diplomatic dispute obscures Israel's invaluable help to U.S. military," *Washington Examiner*, March 23, 2010.

71. Bernd Debusmann, "U.S. aid, Israel and wishful thinking," *Reuters*, April 12, 2010. Haig was Deputy National Security Advisor under Nixon, White House Chief of Staff under Nixon and Ford, the Supreme Allied Commander of Europe under Ford and Carter, and Secretary of State under Reagan.

72. Akiva Eldar, "Netanyahu and Obama are at point of no return," *Haaretz*, March 26, 2010.

73. US Department of State, *Joint Statement by the Quartet*, March 19, 2010.

74. George Friedman, "The Netanyahu-Obama Meeting in Strategic Context," *Stratfor*, March 23, 2010.

75. "81% of Americans Agree Israeli-Palestinian Conflict Negatively Impacts U.S. Interests," *Zogby International*, March 25, 2010.

76. David Frum, comments in an online debate, "Honest Broker," *The Economist*, July 21, 2009.

77. David Horowitz and Jacob Laksin, "Obama and the War Against the Jews," *FrontPageMag.com*, June 25, 2010.

78.   Natasha Mozgavaya, "Nearly 300 Congress members declare commitment to 'unbreakable' U.S.-Israel bond," *Haaretz*, March 25, 2010.

79.   Glenn Kessler, "Obama, Netanyahu meet for hours as U.S. pushes for outreach to Palestinians," *Washington Post*, March 25, 2010.

80.   Hilary Leila Krieger, "Dispute won't harm $3b. aid to Israel," *Jerusalem Post*, March 26, 2010.

81.   Amos Harel, "Despite U.S. anger over settlements, defense ties are flourishing," *Haaretz*, March 26, 2010.

82.   United Nations Human Rights Council, 13th Session, 41st Meeting, Resolution 13/6, *Right of the Palestinian people to self-determination*, A/HRC/RES/13/6 (adopted March 24, 2010).

83.   US Department of State, Permanent Mission of the United States of America to the United Nations and Other International Organizations in Geneva, "Explanation of Vote: Item 7 Resolutions Related to Israel and the Occupied Territories," Delivered by Ambassador Eileen Chamberlain Donahoe to the 13th Session of the UN Human Rights Council, March 24, 2010.

84.   United Nations Human Rights Council, 13th Session, 42nd Meeting, Resolution 13/9, *Follow-up to the report of the United Nations Independent International Fact-Finding Mission on the Gaza Conflict*, A/HRC/RES/13/9 (adopted March 25, 2010).

85.   US Department of State, Permanent Mission of the United States of America to the United Nations and Other International Organizations in Geneva, "Explanation of Vote: Follow-up to the Report on the UN Fact-Finding Mission on the Gaza Conflict," Delivered by Ambassador Donahoe to the UN Human Rights Council, 13th Session, March 25, 2010.

86.   "UN rights chief unveils members of independent probe into Gaza conflict," *UN News Centre*, June 14, 2010.

87.   Anne Gearan, "Obama: US can't force Mideast peace deal," *Associated Press*, April 13, 2010.

88.   Mark Landler and Helene Cooper, "Obama Speech Signals a U.S. Shift on Middle East," *New York Times*, April 14, 2010.

89.   Rory McCarthy, "US gives Abbas private assurances over Israeli settlements," *The Guardian*, April 29, 2010.

90.   Janine Zacharia, "Israeli construction in East Jerusalem adds to difficulties facing negotiators," *Washington Post*, May 7, 2010.

91.   Mortimer B. Zuckerman, "Israel Is a Key Ally and Deserves U.S. Support," *U.S. News & World Report*, May 21, 2010.

Chapter 7

1.   International Committee of the Red Cross, "Israel and the occupied territories: violence claims more lives as blockade continues to stifle Gaza," April 29, 2010.

2.   World Health Organization, "Health conditions in the occupied Palestinian territory, including east Jerusalem, and in the occupied Syrian Golan," May 13, 2010.

3.   United Nations Development Program, "One Year After," May, 2010.

4.   "Partial List of Items Prohibited/Permitted into the Gaza Strip," *Gisha*, May 2010.

5.   Amira Hass, "Why won't Israel allow Gazans to import coriander," *Haaretz*, May 7, 2010.

6.   Natasha Mozgovaya, "Obama: Jews' outlook on the future should be a lesson to all Americans," *Haaretz*, May 28, 2010.

7.   "Israel is lost at sea," *Financial Times*, May 31, 2010. The editorial also pointed out that Hamas was "an example of that rarest of Middle Eastern species: a popularly elected government" that had "signed up to the 2002 comprehensive peace offer by the Arab League and the Organisation of the Islamic Conference. If this is a bluff, it is one Israel has yet to call."

8.   Barak Ravid, "Netanyahu: I regret Gaza flotilla deaths, but Israeli troops had right to self-defense," *Haaretz*, May 31, 2010.

9.   Ibid.

10.   Amos Harel, Avi Issacharoff, and Anshel Pfeffer, "Israel Navy commandos: Gaza flotilla activists tried to lynch us," *Haaretz*, May 31, 2010.

11.   "Israel attacks Gaza aid fleet," *Al Jazeera*, May 31, 2010.

12.   Israel Ministry of Foreign Affairs, "IDF forces met with pre-planned violence when attempting to board flotilla," May 31, 2010.

13.   "Deaths as Israeli forces storm Gaza aid ship," *BBC*, May 31, 2010.

14. United Nations Security Council, 6325th Meeting, *The situation in the Middle East, including the Palestinian question*, S/PV.6325 (May 31, 2010).

15. United Nations Security Council, "Security Council Condemns Acts Resulting in Civilian Deaths During Israeli Operation Against Gaza-Bound Aid Convoy," Press Release, May 31, 2010. Neil Mac-Farquhar, "Security Council Debates Criticism of Israeli Raid," *New York Times*, May 31, 2010. Chris McGreal, "Israel should lead investigation into attack on Gaza flotilla, says US," *The Guardian*, June 1, 2010.

16. United Nations Human Rights Council, 14th Session, Resolution 14/1, *The grave attacks by Israeli forces against the humanitarian boat convoy*, A/HRC/RES/14/1 (June 2, 2010).

17. Barak Ravid and Natasha Mozgovaya, "U.S.: UN council rushing to blame Israel for Gaza flotilla deaths," *Haaretz*, June 2, 2010.

18. Shlomo Shamir, "Lieberman to UN chief: International community is two-faced for condemning Israel," *Haaretz*, May 31, 2010.

19. Barak Ravid, "Netanyahu: World hypocritical for condemning Gaza flotilla raid," *Haaretz*, June 2, 2010.

20. "Israel attack on gaza aid ship: US 'deeply regrets' loss of life," *The Telegraph*, May 31, 2010.

21. Natasha Mozgovaya, "White House urges 'credible and transparent' probe of Gaza flotilla raid," *Haaretz*, June 1, 2010.

22. "Top US lawmaker: No 'biased' UN resolution in flotilla raid," *Agence France-Presse*, June 1, 2010.

23. Greg Mitchell, "Biden Defends Israel—to the Max—on 'Charlie Rose' Tonight," *The Nation*, June 2, 2010. Yitzhak Benhorin, "Biden in 2007 interview: I am a Zionist," *Ynetnews*, August 23, 2008.

24. Yaakov Katz, "Next time we'll use more force," *Jerusalem Post*, June 1, 2010.

25. Isabel Kershner, "Deadly Israeli Raid on Aid Flotilla Draws Condemnation," *New York Times*, May 31, 2010.

26. Glenn Kessler, "Israel gives its account of raid on aid ship headed for Gaza," *Washington Post*, June 4, 2010.

27. "Deadly Israeli raid on aid fleet," *Al Jazeera*, June 1, 2010.

28. Helena Smith, "Israelis opened fire before boarding Gaza flotilla, say released activists," *The Guardian*, June 1, 2010. "Witnesses cast doubt on Israel's convoy raid account," *BBC*, June 1, 2010.

29. Yaakov Katz, "Analysis: Israel's PR machine fails yet again," *Jerusalem Post*, June 1, 2010.

30. Israel Ministry of Foreign Affairs, "Weapons found on Mavi Marmara," *Flickr*, June 1, 2010. "Gaza flotilla: How Israel's ministry of foreign affairs fakes photos of seized weapons," *IbnKafkasObiterDicta. WordPress.com*, June 2, 2010. This author confirmed that the metadata of the images showed they had been taken well before the attack on the *Mavi Marmara*.

31. Israel Defense Forces, "Attackers of the IDF Soldiers Found Without Identification Papers," June 2, 2010. As of the time of this writing, the IDF web page's meta title still maintains the original title with the claim of a link to al-Qaeda (accessed November 5, 2014). Max Blumenthal, "Under Scrutiny, IDF Retracts Claims About Flotilla's Al Qaeda Links," *MaxBlumenthal.com*, June 3, 2010.

32. Daniel Gordis, "A Botched Raid, a Vital Embargo," *New York Times*, June 2, 2010.

33. Michael B. Oren, "An Assault, Cloaked in Peace," *New York Times*, June 2, 2010.

34. Gordis, "A Botched Raid." Oren, "An Assault, Cloaked in Peace."

35. Natasha Mozgovaya, "Will the Gaza flotilla attack affect U.S.-Israeli ties?" *Haaretz*, June 1, 2010.

36. Jonathan Lis, "Mossad chief: Israel gradually becoming burden on U.S.," *Haaretz*, June 1, 2010.

37. Helene Cooper and Ethan Bronner, "Israeli Raid Complicates U.S. Ties and Push for Peace," *New York Times*, May 31, 2010.

38. Glenn Kessler, "Analysis: Condemnation of Israeli assault complicates relations with U.S.," *Washington Post*, June 1, 2010.

39. "Israel and the Blockade," *New York Times*, June 1, 2010.

40. Nicholas D. Kristof, "Saving Israel From Itself," *New York Times*, June 2, 2010.

41. Anthony H. Cordesman, "Israel as a Strategic Liability?" *Center for Strategic and International Studies*, June 2, 2010. The reader may recall that Cordesman had written the analysis in the immediate aftermath of Israel's massacre in Gaza that its assault did not violate international law.

42. Rachel Shabi, "Israel forced to apologise for YouTube spoof of Gaza flotilla," *The Guardian*, June 6, 2010.

43. Israel Defense Forces, "Specific Flotilla Passengers are Active Terror Operatives Linked to Al-Qaeda, Hamas, and Other Organizations," *IDFSpokesperson.com*, June 6, 2010. Al Jazeera English, "Al Jazeera talks to US activist named by Israel as a 'terrorist,'" *YouTube* video, 5:53, June 6, 2010.

44. Yassin Musharbash, "A Close Look at Israel's Terror Accusations," *Spiegel Online*, June 9, 2010.

45.   Janine Zacharia, "Nations decry Israel's blockade of Gaza," *Washington Post,* June 2, 2010.

46.   "A Credible Investigation," *New York Times,* June 3, 2010.

47.   Zoe Magee, "American, 19, Among Gaza Flotilla Dead," *ABC News,* June 3, 2010.

48.   Robert Booth, "Gaza flotilla activists were shot in head at close range," *The Guardian,* June 4, 2010.

49.   Sheera Frenkel, "Israel, denouncing flotilla as 'terrorist,' braces for next ship," *McClatchy,* June 2, 2010.

50.   "Presentation Speech by Egil Aarvik, Vice-Chairman of the Norwegian Nobel Committee, on the occasion of the awarding of the Nobel Peace Prize for 1976 in the University Festival Hall, Oslo, December 10, 1977," *NobelPrize.org,* accessed January 21, 2015.

51.   Carol Migdalovitz, "Israel's Blockade of Gaza and the *Mavi Marmara* Incident," *Congressional Research Service,* June 5, 2010.

52.   Thomas L. Friedman, "When Friends Fall Out," *New York Times,* June 1, 2010.

53.   Bernard-Henri Lévy, "It's time to stop demonizing Israel," *Haaretz,* June 8, 2010.

54.   Danny Ayalon, "The Flotilla Farce," *Wall Street Journal,* July 29, 2010.

55.   Ruth Lapidoth, "The Legal Basis of Israel's Naval Blockade of Gaza," *Jerusalem Center for Public Affairs,* Vol. 10, No. 4, July 18, 2010.

56.   The UN Charter is accessible at www.un.org.

57.   Fourth Geneva Convention Relative to the Protection of Civilian Persons in Time of War, August 12, 1949; available at www.icrc.org.

58.   Lapidoth, "The Legal Basis."

59.   San Remo Manual on International Law Applicable to Armed Conflicts at Sea, June 12, 1994; available at ICRC.org.

60.   Lapidoth, "The Legal Basis."

61.   San Remo Manual.

62.   Lapidoth, "The Legal Basis."

63.   Charles Levinson, "Israel's Foes Embrace New Resistance Tactics," *Wall Street Journal,* July 2, 2010.

64.   Isabel Kershner, "Israel Widens Supplies Allowed Into Gaza," *New York Times,* June 9 2010. Sheera Frenkel, "Israeli document: Gaza blockade isn't about security," *McClatchy,* June 9, 2010.

65.   Erica Werner, "Obama calls for new approach on Gaza blockade," *Associated Press,* June 9, 2010.

66.   "Obama makes remarks after bilateral meeting with President Abbas of the Palestinian Authority," *Washington Post,* June 9, 2010.

67.   "Obama calls for new approach on Gaza blockade," *USA Today,* June 9, 2010.

68.   Ethan Bronner, "A Rising Urgency in Israel for a Gaza Shift," *New York Times,* June 10, 2010.

69.   International Committee of the Red Cross, "Gaza closure: not another year!" June 14, 2010.

70.   Isabel Kershner and Fares Akram, "Israel Backs Panel to Examine Raid," *New York Times,* June 14, 2010. Stephanie Nebehay, "Israel's Gaza blockade breaks law, says ICRC," *Reuters,* June 13, 2010. For a sampling of coverage of the ICRC statement outside of the U.S., by comparison, see: "Israel's Gaza blockade breaks law, says International Red Cross," *Haaretz,* June 14, 2010. Imogen Foulkes, "ICRC says Israel's Gaza blockade breaks law," *BBC,* June 14, 2010. "ICRC joins call for lifting Gaza siege," *The Hindu,* June 14, 2010. "Red Cross: Israel's Gaza Blockade Breaks International Law," *Voice of America,* June 14, 2010. Ironically, the *Voice of America* (VOA), while an official news agency of the US government, was forbidden from broadcasting within the United States under the Smith-Mundt Act of 1948, an act intended to protect the American public from US government propaganda.

71.   Edmund Sanders, "Israel takes small step toward easing Gaza blockade," *Los Angeles Times,* June 20, 2010. Joel Greenberg, "U.S. envoy welcomes Israeli steps to relax Gaza blockade," *Washington Post,* June 30, 2010. "Israeli Government's Statement on Gaza blockade," *Oxfam International,* July 5, 2010. Israel Ministry of Defense, "The Civilian Policy Towards the Gaza Strip: The implementation of the Cabinet decision," June, 2010; published by *McClatchy,* accessed November 5, 2014.

72.   Janine Zacharia, "Israel eases restrictions on goods bound for Gaza Strip," *Washington Post,* June 18, 2010.

73.   Mel Frykberg, "Israel Chokes Gaza Despite Announced Easing," *Inter Press Service,* July 15, 2010.

74.   "Gaza is a prison camp, says David Cameron," *The Telegraph,* July 27, 2010.

75.   Greenberg, "U.S. envoy welcomes Israeli steps."

76.   Janine Zacharia, "Israel's feeling of isolation is becoming more pronounced," *Washington Post,* June 22, 2010.

77.   Stephen Zunes, "Israel's Dubious Investigation of Flotilla Attack," *Foreign Policy in Focus,* June 24, 2010.

78.   Marc Lynch, "Good Deal for Gaza," *Foreign Policy,* June 20, 2010.

79. Isabel Kershner, "East Jerusalem Building Plan Advances," *New York Times*, June 21, 2010.

80. Samuel Sockol, "Palestinian politicians reject Israeli deportation order," *Washington Post*, June 21, 2010.

81. B'Tselem, *By Hook and by Crook: Israeli Settlement Policy in the West Bank*, July 2010.

82. Anne E. Kornblut, "Obama, Netanyahu meet again," *Washington Post*, July 6, 2010.

83. The White House, "Remarks by President Obama and Prime Minister Netanyahu of Israel in Joint Press Availability," July 6, 2010.

84. Dana Milbank, "Netanyahu hears no discouraging words from Obama," *Washington Post*, July 7, 2010.

85. Anne E. Kornblut and Michael D. Shear, "Obama and Netanyahu met to thaw relations, discuss Middle East peace process," *Washington Post*, July 7, 2010.

86. United Nations Office for the Coordination of Humanitarian Affairs and World Food Programme, "Between the Fence and a Hard Place," August 2010.

87. Amnesty International, et al, *Dashed Hopes: Continuation of the Gaza Blockade*, November 30, 2010.

88. Palestinian Center for Human Rights, *The Illegal Closure of the Gaza Strip: Collective Punishment of the Civilian Population*, December 10, 2010.

89. Isabel Kershner, "Indictments in Gaza War Are Announced," *New York Times*, July 6, 2010.

90. State of Israel, Ministry of Foreign Affairs, *Gaza Operations Investigations: Second Update*, July 2010, paras. 79-88, footnote 38.

91. Ibid., paras. 61-66.

92. Ibid., paras. 92-97.

93. Ibid., paras. 67-78.

94. Ibid., paras. 99-102.

95. Ibid., paras. 103-107.

96. Ibid., paras. 108-109.

97. Ibid., paras. 113-117.

98. Ibid., paras. 122-129.

99. Ibid., paras. 130-134.

100. Ibid., paras. 135-140.

101. Ibid., paras. 141-145.

102. Ibid., para. 10. "Soldiers' Punishment for Using Boy as 'Human Shield' Inadequate," *Human Rights Watch*, November 26, 2010.

103. B'Tselem, *Void of Responsibility: Israel Military Policy Not to Investigate Killings of Palestinians by Soldiers*, October 2010.

104. United Nations Human Rights Council, 15th Session, *Report of the Committee of independent experts in international humanitarian and human rights laws to monitor and assess any domestic, legal or other proceedings undertaken by both the Government of Israel and the Palestinian side*, A/HRC/15/50 (September 23, 2010), paras. 30, 43, 51.

105. Ibid., paras 53-55, 63.

106. Ibid., para. 64.

107. Ibid., paras. 91, 95.

108. Ibid., para. 86.

109. US Department of State, "IDF to Investigate Complaints". See Chapter 4 notes.

110. Mark Steel, "No guns? They must be terrorists," *The Independent*, August 5, 2010.

111. Harriet Sherwood, "Ehud Barak accepts responsibility for Gaza flotilla raid," *The Guardian*, August 10, 2010.

112. Harriet Sherwood, "Israeli military chief defends Gaza flotilla raid," *The Guardian*, August 11, 2010.

113. United Nations Department of Public Information, "Secretary-General Announces Launch of Panel of Inquiry on 31 May Flotilla Incident After Intensive Consultation With Leaders of Israel, Turkey," August 2, 2010.

114. Center for Constitutional Rights, *Legal Aspects of the Gaza Flotilla Attack*, September 2010.

115. "Israeli raid on Gaza aid flotilla broke law – UN probe," *BBC*, September 23, 2010.

116. United Nations Human Rights Council, 15th Session, *Report of the international fact-finding mission to investigate violations of international law, including international humanitarian and human rights law, resulting from the Israeli attacks on the flotilla of ships carrying humanitarian assistance*, A/HRC/15/21 (September 27, 2010), paras. 53-54, 261, 275.

117. Ibid., paras. 56-58, 66.

118. Ibid., paras. 79, 88-89.

119. Ibid., paras. 98-99, 101-104.

120. Ibid., paras. 106-117.

121. Ibid., paras. 118, 120.

122. Ibid., paras. 163, 165, 167, 170.

123. Ibid., paras. 174, 187-188, 203.

124. United Nations Human Rights Council, 15th Session, 30th Meeting, Resolution 15/6, *Follow-up to the report of the Committee of independent experts in international humanitarian and human rights law established pursuant to Council resolution 13/9*, A/HRC/RES/15/6 (adopted September 29, 2010). There were nineteen abstentions.

125. United Nations Human Rights Council, 15th Session, 30th Meeting, Resolution 15/1, *Follow-up to the report of the independent international fact-finding mission on the incident of the humanitarian flotilla*, A/HRC/RES/15/1 (adopted September 29, 2010). There were fifteen abstentions.

126. Colum Lynch, "U.N. council endorses report accusing Israel of executions aboard aid flotilla," *Washington Post*, September 29, 2010.

127. State of Israel, *The Public Commission to Examine the Maritime Incident of 31 May 2010* (The Turkel Commission Report), Part I, January 23, 2011, paras. 45, 47.

128. Ibid., paras. 76-77, 80, 97.

129. US Department of State, *Cashless in Gaza?*, cable from the US embassy in Tel Aviv, March 11, 2008; the document was obtained by Wikileaks and published by the Norwegian newspaper *Aftenposten* on January 5, 2011.

130. US Department of State, *Gaza: Limited Food, Fuel, and Medicine; Infrastructure Under Stress*, cable from the US consulate in Jerusalem to the Secretary of State, et al, September 18, 2009; published at *Wikileaks.org*, accessed November 5, 2014.

131. Turkel Commission Report, para. 103.

132. Ibid., para. 104.

133. Ibid., para. 106.

134. Ibid., paras. 112-113, 121, 124, 132-134, 145.

135. Ibid., paras. 171, 175, 177, 193, 200, 227, 254.

136. Ibid., paras. 221-222, 238, 254.

137. Isabel Kershner, "Israeli Panel Rules Flotilla Raid Legal," *New York Times*, January 23, 2011.

138. Sebnem Arsu, "Turkey Says Israelis Used Excess Force in Flotilla Raid," *New York Times*, January 24, 2011.

139. "Israeli inquiry into Gaza flotilla deaths no more than a 'whitewash,'" *Amnesty International*, January 28, 2011. Scott Sayare, "Stuck in Dock, Flotilla Activists See the Hand of Israel," *New York Times*, July 1, 2011. Although living in Turkey, Furkan Doğan was not a Turkish citizen, but an American citizen of Turkish descent, although early news stories misreported him as having dual citizenship.

140. Alex Thomson, "Israeli soldiers ordered to 'cleanse' Gaza," *Channel 4 News*, January 24, 2011. "Revealed: story of Israeli troops told to 'cleanse' Gaza," *Channel 4 News*, January 26, 2011. "Israeli filmmaker receives death threats over Gaza report," *Channel 4 News*, January 27, 2011.

Chapter 8

1. "Erekat: No unilateral declaration of Palestinian state," *Haaretz*, July 13, 2010.

2. Diaa Hadid, "Israeli bulldozers raze 6 east Jerusalem buildings," *Associated Press*, July 13, 2010.

3. Gideon Levy, "Tricky Bibi," *Haaretz*, July 15, 2010. "Bibi Netanyahu 2001 'America is something that can easily be moved,'" *YouTube* video, 8:44, posted by "MrMokeyboy," July 17, 2010.

4. Karin Laub, "Obama letter to Palestinian leader included warning, PLO says," *Washington Post*, August 1, 2010.

5. Maher Abukhater, "Is Mitchell getting any closer to bringing Palestinians to negotiating table?" Babylon & Beyond, *Los Angeles Times*, August 11, 2010. Christa Case Bryant and Joshua Mitnick, "Israeli-Palestinian peace talks look less likely as settlers fret over freeze," *Christian Science Monitor*, August 12, 2010. Douglas Hamilton, "Major powers drawing up framework for Mideast talks," *Reuters*, August 12, 2010. Avi Issacharoff and Barak Ravid, "Netanyahu rejects peace talks based on 1967 borders," *Haaretz*, August 12, 2010.

6. "President Abbas and Peace Talks," *New York Times*, August 10, 2010.

7. Michael B. Oren, "Mideast Peace Talks," Letter to the Editor, *New York Times*, August 12, 2010.

8. Ethan Bronner, "In Mideast Talks, Scant Hopes From the Beginning," *New York Times*, August 20, 2010.

9. Jackson Diehl, "Why doesn't Abbas want peace talks?" PostPartisan, *Washington Post*, August 12, 2010.

10. Helene Cooper and Mark Landler, "Palestinians Resuming Talks Under Pressure," *New York Times*, August 20, 2010.

11. The White House, "Remarks by President Obama, President Mubarak, His Majesty King Abdullah, Prime Minister Netanyahu and President Abbas Before Working Dinner," September 1, 2010.

12. Scott Wilson, "As Mideast talks begin, Clinton urges Israelis, Palestinians to seek 'future of peace,'" *Washington Post*, September 2, 2010.

13. "Settlers defy peace talks with new construction across West Bank," *Reuters*, September 2, 2010.

14. "Eight months into the settlement freeze," *Peace Now*, August 2, 2010.

15. Juliane von Mittelstaedt, "An Unsettled Issue: Israeli Settlement Construction Booms Despite Ban," *Spiegel Online*, September 3, 2010. *Spiegel* described Etkes as "perhaps the Israeli who knows the most about the settlements" since he "has been documenting settlement construction and submitting complaints against illegal projects". The *Times of Israel* similarly described him: "No one outside the settlement movement and Israeli defense establishment—and few inside—knows more about the ongoing evolution of settlements than Dror Etkes." Matti Friedman, "Houses, fences and fruit trees: A decade of watching settlements grow," *Times of Israel*, May 20, 2013.

16. Dror Etkes, "Settlement freeze? It was barely a slowdown," *Haaretz*, September 28, 2010.

17. Karin Laub and Mohammed Daraghmeh, "Mideast crisis looms over Israeli settlements," *Associated Press*, September 5, 2010.

18. Helene Cooper, "U.S. Urges Israel to Extend Settlement Moratorium," *New York Times*, September 10, 2010.

19. Isabel Kershner, "Israel Bends Slightly on Settlement Building," *New York Times*, September 12, 2010.

20. The White House, "Remarks by the President to the United Nations General Assembly," September 23, 2010.

21. Joel Greenberg, "Israeli building ban ends," *Washington Post*, September 27, 2010.

22. "Israel defies building freeze calls," *Al Jazeera*, September 27, 2010.

23. "Abbas delays decision on talks," *Al Jazeera*, September 27, 2010.

24. "Palestinian leadership delays decision on peace talks," *BBC*, September 27, 2010.

25. Ethan Bronner and Mark Landler, "Diplomats Try to Save Mideast Talks," *New York Times*, September 27, 2010.

26. Richard Cohen, "Obama demands more than Israel can give," *Washington Post*, September 28, 2010.

27. "Americans' Support for Israel Unchanged Since Gaza Conflict," *Gallup*, March 3, 2009.

28. "Americans, Britons and Canadians Hesitant on Middle East Talks," *Angus-Reid*, September 21, 2010.

29. Charles Levinson, "U.S., Israel Build Military Cooperation," *Wall Street Journal*, August 14, 2010.

30. David Makovsky, "Dear Prime Minister: U.S. Efforts to Keep the Peace Process on Track," *Washington Institute for Near East Policy*, September 29, 2010. MJ Rosenberg, "Does PBS Know That 'The Washington Institute' Was Founded By AIPAC?" *Huffington Post*, April 12, 2010.

31. Natasha Mozgovaya, Jack Khoury, and Barak Ravid, "White House: Obama did not send letter to Netanyahu," *Haaretz*, September 30, 2010.

32. Mark Landler, Helene Cooper, and Ethan Bronner, "U.S. Presses Israelis on Renewal of Freeze," *New York Times*, September 30, 2010. Stephen M. Walt, "Robert Satloff doth protest too much," *Foreign Policy*, April 9, 2010.

33. Ethan Bronner, "Palestinian Leaders Urge End to Talks With Israel," *New York Times*, October 2, 2010.

34. Glenn Kessler, "White House offers Israel a carrot for peace talks," *Washington Post*, September 30, 2010.

35. Sharp, "U.S. Foreign Aid to Israel" (see Chapter 4 notes). Lockheed Martin, "Israeli Ministry of Defense Selects Lockheed Martin F-35 For Its Next-Generation Fighter," Press Release, October 7, 2010. "Israel to buy 20 F-35 fighter jets in deal with US," *Agence France-Presse*, October 8, 2010. "Israel, US sign $2.75 bn F-35 fighter deal," *Reuters*, October 8, 2010. "Israel buys F-35 jets with eyes on Iran," *United Press International*, October 8, 2010.

36. Nora Barrows-Friedman, "Israel Seals Unprecedented Weapon Deals With the US," *Truthout*, October 20, 2010. The White House, "Text of the Address by President Eisenhower, Broadcast and Tele-

vised from His Office in the White House, Tuesday Evening, January 17, 1961, 8:30 to 9:00 P.M. EST," January 17, 1961; archived at the Dwight D. Eisenhower Presidential Library, Museum, and Boyhood Home.

37. Joel Greenberg, "Palestinians: Peace talks hinge on Israeli settlement construction," *Washington Post*, October 3, 2010.

38. Akiva Eldar, "Abbas to Mitchell: I will resign if settlement construction continues," *Haaretz*, October 8, 2010.

39. "Abbas may circumvent Israel, ask U.S. to recognize Palestinian state," *Reuters*, October 9, 2010

40. Isabel Kershner, "Israeli Cabinet Approves Citizenship Amendment," *New York Times*, October 10, 2010.

41. Ethan Bronner, "Netanyahu's Moves Spark Debate on Intentions," *New York Times*, October 11, 2010.

42. Nasser Abu Bakr, "Palestinians call on US, Israel to set borders," *Agence France-Presse*, October 13, 2010.

43. Mark Landler, "U.S. Drops Bid to Sway Israel on Settlements," *New York Times*, December 7, 2010.

44. Mustafa Barghouthi, "Smothered by Settlements," *New York Times*, October 14, 2010.

45. Ethan Bronner, "Israel Plan to Build Clouds Peace Talks," *New York Times*, October 15, 2010

46. John McGlynn, "Japan, Israeli Settlements, and the Future of a Palestinian State," *The Asia-Pacific Journal*, December 28, 2009.

47. Ministry of Foreign Affairs of Japan, "Statement by the Press Secretary, Ministry of Foreign Affairs of Japan, on the decision regarding the construction of housing units in East Jerusalem and the West Bank," December 20, 2011. Ministry of Foreign Affairs of Japan, "Statement by the Press Secretary, Ministry of Foreign Affairs of Japan, on the decision regarding the construction of housing units for Jewish people in East Jerusalem and West Bank," November 8, 2012. Ministry of Foreign Affairs of Japan, "Statement by the Press Secretary, Ministry of Foreign Affairs of Japan, on the decision regarding the construction of housing units for Jewish people in East Jerusalem," December 19, 2012. Ministry of Foreign Affairs of Japan, "Démarche by Dr. Makio Miyagawa, Director-General, Middle Eastern and African Affairs Bureau, to Mr. Nisim Ben-Shitrit, Ambassador Extraordinary and Plenipotentiary of the State of Israel to Japan," December 21, 2012. Ministry of Foreign Affairs of Japan, "Statement by the Press Secretary, Ministry of Foreign Affairs of Japan, on the decision regarding the construction of housing units in the West Bank," May 10, 2013. Ministry of Foreign Affairs of Japan, "Statement by the Press Secretary, Ministry of Foreign Affairs of Japan, on the decision regarding the construction of housing units for Jewish people in East Jerusalem," June 3, 2013. Ministry of Foreign Affairs of Japan, "Statement by the Press Secretary, Ministry of Foreign Affairs of Japan, on the decision regarding the construction of housing units in the West Bank," June 17, 2013. Each of these statements describes Israel's settlements as "a violation of international law".

48. United Nations Security Council, 2203rd Meeting, Resolution 465, March 1, 1980. The resolution passed unanimously. See also the voting record at http://unbisnet.un.org; search UN Resolution Symbol "S/RES/465(1980)".

49. United States Senate, 95th Congress, *The Colonization of the West Bank Territories by Israel*, Subcommittee on Immigration and Naturalization of the Committee on the Judiciary, First Session on the Question of West Bank Settlements and the Treatment of Arabs in the Israeli-Occupied Territories, October 17 and 18, 1977; Testimony of Alfred L. Atherton, Jr., Assistant Secretary of State for the Near East and South Asia, 115-116. See also: Glenn Kessler, "1979 State Dept. Legal Opinion Raises New Questions About Israeli Settlements," *Washington Post*, June 17, 2009. Note that Kessler got the year wrong.

50. Ethan Bronner, "Settlers Race to Build Units in West Bank," *New York Times*, October 21, 2010.

51. Isabel Kershner, "Israel Plans 1,000 Housing Units in East Jerusalem," *New York Times*, November 8, 2010. No country, not even the US, considers Israel's annexation legal.

52. "Bibi: Jerusalem building, peace unconnected," *Jewish Telegraphic Agency*, November 9, 2010.

53. Michael Weiss, "The Settlement Fixation," *Foreign Policy*, November 10, 2010.

54. US Department of State, FRUS, Vol. XIX, Document 442, "Telegram From the Mission to the United Nations to the Department of State," September 23.

55. Director of Central Intelligence, National Intelligence Estimate Number 35-68, "Israel," April 11, 1968; available at *TheJerusalemFund.org*, accessed January 21, 2015.

56. Weiss, "The Settlement Fixation."

57. Khaled Abu Toameh, "Abbas: Israel seeking to 'close door to right of return,'" *Jerusalem Post*, November 8, 2010.

58. Ethan Bronner and Mark Landler, "A 90-Day Bet on Mideast Talks," *New York Times*, November 14, 2010. "Israel ponders US incentive offer on settlement freeze," *BBC*, November 14, 2010. Joel Greenberg, "Netanyahu moves on U.S. incentives for construction freeze in West Bank," *Washington Post*, November 15, 2010.

59. Aaron David Miller, "The Price of Success," *Foreign Policy*, November 15, 2010.

60. Elliot Abrams and Michael Singh, "Obama's Peace Process to Nowhere," *Foreign Policy*, November 20, 2010.

61. Daniel Kurtzer, "With settlement deal, U.S. will be rewarding Israel's bad behavior," *Washington Post*, November 21, 2010.

62. Robert Fisk, "An American bribe that stinks of appeasement," *The Independent*, November 20, 2010.

63. European Union, "Statement by EU High Representative Catherine Ashton on the Peace Process," December 8, 2010.

64. Karen DeYoung, "U.S. abandons push for renewal of Israeli settlement freeze," *Washington Post*, December 8, 2010.

65. Gopal Ratnam and Viola Gienger, "Israel Pursues 20 Added F-35 Jets Offered in U.S. Peace Swap," *Bloomberg*, December 14, 2010.

66. Yitzhak Benhorin, "F-35 production frozen due to cutbacks," *Ynetnews*, January 7, 2011. Government officials and the media constantly spoke of spending "cuts" when there were none, only spending increases. The Congressional Budget Office (CBO) had in fact put "Defense" spending for 2010 at $689 billion and projected increasing spending through 2021: $712 billion (2011), $710 billion (2012), $725 billion (2013), $738 billion (2014), $752 billion (2015), $773 billion (2016), $787 billion (2017), $801 billion (2018), $827 billion (2019), $848 billion (2020), $869 billion (2021). See: Congressional Budget Office, *The Budget and Economic Outlook: Fiscal Years 2011 to 2021*, January 26, 2011, 54.

67. United Nations Human Rights Council, *Report of the Special Rapporteur on the situation of human rights in the Palestinian territories occupied since 1967, Richard Falk*, A/HRC/16/72 (January 10, 2011).

68. Moshe Ya'alon, "The Palestinians Are the Real Obstacle to Peace," *Foreign Policy*, December 14, 2010. Ya'alon was a former IDF Chief of Staff, Likud Member of the Knesset, Vice Prime Minister, and Minister of Strategic Affairs.

69. Human Rights Watch, *Separate and Unequal: Israel's Discriminatory Treatment of Palestinians in the Occupied Palestinian Territories*, December 19, 2010.

70. US Department of State, "Remarks by Secretary of State Hillary Clinton at the Brookings Institution's Saban Center for Middle East Policy Seventh Annual Forum," December 10, 2010.

71. Ethan Bronner, "After Freeze, Settlement Building Booms in West Bank," *New York Times*, December 22, 2010.

72. Mohammed Daraghmeh, "Palestinians to take settlement battle to U.N.," *Associated Press*, December 29, 2010.

73. Isabel Kershner, "Israeli Demolition Begins in East Jerusalem Project," *New York Times*, January 9, 2011. US Department of State, "Demolition of the Shepherd's Hotel," Press Statement from Secretary of State Hillary Rodham Clinton, January 9, 2011.

74. Pierre Klochendler, "Latin America Deepens Israeli Isolation," *Inter Press Service*, January 16, 2011. Klochendler repeated the popular myth that with the passage of Resolution 181 by the UN General Assembly, "Israel was created". "Peru formally recognizes Palestinian state," *Reuters*, January 24, 2011.

75. "Israel eyes huge east Jerusalem settlement project," *Agence France-Presse*, January 17, 2011.

76. US Senate, Office of Kirsten Gillibrand, "Gillibrand Urges Administration To Oppose Latest Anti-Israel Action At U.N.," January 18, 2011.

77. US House of Representatives, Committee on Foreign Affairs, "Ros-Lehtinen, Cantor, Other Senior Members of Congress Send Bipartisan Letter Asking President to Pledge Veto of Anti-Israel UN Resolution," January 27, 2011.

78. "Pickering, Hills, Sullivan, Beinart, Dobbins, More Ask Obama Administration to Support UN Resolution Condemning Illegal Israeli Settlements," *The Washington Note*, January 19, 2011.

79. Matthew Lee, "Palestinians raise flag at Washington office," *Associated Press*, January 18, 2011.

80. Anita Snow, "UN council considers Israeli settlement issue," *Associated Press*, January 19, 2011.

81. "Palestinians raise flag at Washington office," *Associated Press*, January 18, 2011.

82. Tony Karon, "U.N. Resolution on Israeli Settlements Puts Obama in a Diplomatic Bind," *Time*, January 20, 2011.

83. Ian Williams, "Obama must call Israeli settlements illegal," *The Guardian*, January 21, 2011.

84. Ethan Bronner and Neil MacFarquhar, "Word of Palestinian Concession in 2008 Roils Mideast," *New York Times*, January 23, 2011.

85. "Meeting Minutes: Borders with Erekat, Qurei and Livni," May 4, 2008; "The Palestine Papers," *Al Jazeera*, accessed January 21, 2015.

86. "Meeting Minutes: Trilateral – United States, Israel and Palestine," June 15, 2008; "The Palestine Papers," *Al Jazeera*, accessed November 25, 2014.

87. Seumas Milne, "Palestinian leaders weak—and increasingly desperate," *The Guardian*, January 23, 2011.

88. Ali Abunimah, "Palestine Papers: If US can't be 'honest broker' in Middle East, get out of the way," *Christian Science Monitor*, January 27, 2011.

89. Saree Makdisi, "The Palestinian people betrayed," *Los Angeles Times*, January 27, 2011.

90. United Nations Security Council, Draft Resolution, S/2011/24 (February 18, 2011).

91. United Nations Security Council, 6484th Meeting, *The situation in the Middle East, including the Palestinian question*, S/PV.6484 (February 18, 2011).

92. Amy Teibel, "Housing for Jews approved in east Jerusalem," *Associated Press*, March 2, 2011. Isabel Kershner, "Israel to Step Up Pace of Construction in West Bank Areas," *New York Times*, March 13, 2011.

93. Richard Falk, "Report of Special Rapporteur to the UN Human Rights Council on Occupied Palestinian Territories," *RichardFalk.Wordpress.com*, February 14, 2011. "U.N. investigator: Israel engaged in ethnic cleansing with settlement expansion," *Reuters*, March 21, 2011.

94. Shlomo Shamir, "Israel UN envoy slams Falk over accusation of 'ethnic cleansing,'" *Haaretz*, March 21, 2011.

95. Daniel Blatman, "Heading toward an Israeli apartheid state," *Haaretz*, April 4, 2011.

96. Tovah Lazaroff, "'The widow for a negotiated peace ends in September,'" *Jerusalem Post*, March 23, 2011.

97. Ethan Bronner, "In Israel, Time for Peace Offer May Run Out," *New York Times*, April 2, 2011.

98. "The Israeli Peace Initiative (IPI) – in response to the Arab Peace Initiative (API) Proposal," March 31, 2011; published by the *New York Times*, accessed November 25, 2014. Ethan Bronner, "Prominent Israelis Will Propose a Peace Plan," *New York Times*, April 4, 2011. Natasha Mozgovaya, "Former Israeli defense chiefs draft new Mideast peace plan," *Haaretz*, April 5, 2011. The group included former army chief Amnon Lipkin-Shahak, former Mossad head Danny Yatom, former Shin Bet directors Yaakov Perry and Ami Ayalon, former Labor Party chief and 2002 candidate for prime minister Amram Mitzna, and the son and daughter of former Prime Minister Yitzhak Rabin.

99. Ethan Bronner, "Israeli Luminaries Press for a Palestinian State," *New York Times*, April 19, 2011. "Israeli Intellectuals Welcome and Endorse an Independent Palestinian State Next to Israel;" published by the *New York Times*, accessed November 25, 2014.

100. Isabel Kershner, "On Eve of Meeting in Washington, Israel Announces More Housing Construction," *New York Times*, April 4, 2011.

101. Ethan Bronner, "Bid for State of Palestine Gets Support From I.M.F." *New York Times*, April 6, 2011.

102. Office of the United Nations Special Coordinator for the Middle East Peace Process, *Palestinian State-Building: A Decisive Period*, April 13, 2011.

103. Ethan Bronner and Isabel Kershner, "Fatah and Hamas Announce Outline of Deal," *New York Times*, April 27, 2011.

104. Ethan Bronner, "Palestinian Factions Give Differing Views of Unity Pact," *New York Times*, April 28, 2011.

105. Yossi Verter, "Haaretz poll: 57% of Israelis support plan to talk to Hamas," *Haaretz*, November 13, 2009.

106. Ethan Bronner, "Palestinian Factions Sign Accord to End Rift," *New York Times*, May 4, 2011.

107. Ethan Bronner, "Hamas Leader Calls for Two-State Solution, but Refuses to Renounce Violence," *New York Times*, May 5, 2011.

108. Isabel Kershner, "Israel Holds Palestinian Funds as Deal Nears," *New York Times*, May 1, 2011. Hussein Ibish, "Penniless Palestine: How Fiscal Woes Are Making the PA's Political Problems Even Harder to Deal With," *Foreign Affairs*, August 11, 2011.

109. Joel Greenberg, "Palestinian rivals Fatah, Hamas reach accord seen as obstacle for peace with Israel," *Washington Post*, April 28, 2011.

110. Ethan Bronner and Steven Lee Myers, "Accord Brings New Sense of Urgency to Israeli-Palestinian Conflict," *New York Times*, May 5, 2011.

111. H.RES.268, 112th Congress, *Reaffirming the United States' commitment to a negotiated settlement of the Israeli-Palestinian conflict through direct Israeli-Palestinian negotiations, and for other purposes*, introduced May 13, 2011 (passed July 7, 2011).

112. S.RES.185, 112th Congress, *A resolution reaffirming the commitment of the United States to a negotiated settlement of the Israeli-Palestinian conflict through direct Israeli-Palestinian negotiations, reaffirming opposition to the inclusion of Hamas in a unity government unless it is willing to accept peace with Israel and renounce violence, and declaring that Palestinian efforts to gain recognition of a state outside direct negotiations demonstrates absence of a good faith commitment to peace negotiations, and will have implications for continued United States aid*, introduced May 16, 2011 (passed June 28, 2011).

113. Bronner, "Hamas Leader." Greenberg, "Palestinian rivals."

114. United Nations General Assembly, 1883rd Plenary Meeting, Resolution 2625 (XXV), *Declaration on Principles of International Law concerning Friendly Relations and Cooperation among States in accordance with the Charter of the United Nations*, A/RES/2625(XXV) (October 24, 1970).

115. Ethan Bronner, "Israeli-Hamas Agreement to Trade Prisoners May Reshape Politics in Region," *New York Times*, October 12, 2011.

116. "A Fatah-Hamas Deal," *New York Times*, May 8, 2011.

117. "Gaza Hamas leader condemns US killing of bin Laden," *Associated Press*, May 2, 2011.

118. "Hamas seeks to distance itself from latest bin Laden comments," *Associated Press*, April 23, 2006.

119. "US, UK condemn Hamas for mourning death of Osama bin Laden," *Jerusalem Post*, May 3, 2011.

120. Michael Moran, "Bin Laden comes home to roost: His CIA ties are only the beginning of a woeful story," *MSNBC*, August 24, 1998. Reuel Marc Gerecht, "The Counterterrorist Myth," *The Atlantic*, July/August 2001. Steve Galster, "Afghanistan: The Making of U.S. Policy, 1973-1990," October 9, 2001; from The National Security Archive at George Washington University, *The September 11th Sourcebooks, Volume II: Afghanistan: Lessons from the Last War*. "U.S. Analysis of the Soviet War in Afghanistan: Declassified," October 9, 2001; GWU, *The September 11th Sourcebooks*. President Ronald Reagan, "Proclamation 4908—Afghanistan Day," March 10, 1982; archived at the Ronald Reagan Presidential Library website.

121. New York Times, May 8, 2011.

122. Mahmoud Abbas, "The Long Overdue Palestinian State," *New York Times*, May 16, 2011.

123. Mark Landler and Helene Cooper, "As Uprisings Transform Mideast, Obama Aims to Reshape the Peace Debate," *New York Times*, May 17, 2011.

124. "President Obama and the Arab Spring," *New York Times*, May 17, 2011.

125. Thomas L. Friedman, "Bibi and Barack," *New York Times*, May 17, 2011.

126. Israel Ministry of Foreign Affairs, "PM Netanyahu's address at the opening of the Knesset summer session," May 16, 2011.

127. Ethan Bronner, "Israel Leader Outlines Points Before U.S. Trip," *New York Times*, May 16, 2011. Bronner noted that the occasion for Netanyahu's speech "was Nabka Day, when Palestinians mark Israel's creation and mourn the expulsion and flight of hundreds of thousands of Palestinians in 1948."

128. Jackson Diehl, "Mahmoud Abbas's formula for war," *Washington Post*, May 19, 2011.

129. Steve Weizman, "Israel approves 1,500 settler homes in east Jerusalem: NGO," *Agence France-Presse*, May 19, 2011.

130. United Nations Human Rights Council, 16th Session, *Report of the Committee of independent experts in international humanitarian and human rights law established pursuant to Council resolution 13/9*, A/HRC/16/24 (March 18, 2011), paras. 30, 32, 41-44, 79.

131. Richard Goldstone, "Reconsidering the Goldstone Report on Israel and war crimes," *Washington Post*, April 2, 2011. On Goldstone's lie, recall that the UN fact-finding mission did, in fact, consider Israel's initial published findings of its self-investigation ("IDF: Conclusion of Investigation into Central Claims and Issues in Operation Cast Lead," parts 1 and 2, Israel Ministry of Foreign Affairs, April 22, 2009), which were later followed up by two subsequent papers responding to specific incidents cited by the UN mission.

132. UNHRC, "Report of the Committee of independent experts," para. 27.

133. Aluf Benn, "Goldstone retraction shows West's changed attitude toward Israel in light of Arab world turmoil," *Haaretz*, April 3, 2011.

134. "Israel urges UN to cancel Goldstone Report on Gaza war," *BBC*, April 2, 2011.

135. "Barak: Goldstone should retract Gaza report in international forum," *Haaretz*, April 3, 2011.

136. Atilla Somfalvi, "PM: UN must retract Goldstone report," *Ynetnews*, April 3, 2011.

137. Jessica Montell, "Beyond Goldstone: A truer discussion about Israel, Hamas and the Gaza conflict," *Washington Post*, April 6, 2011.

138. S.RES.138, 112th Congress, *A resolution calling on the United Nations to rescind the Goldstone report, and for other purposes*, introduced April 8, 2011 (passed April 14, 2011).

139. Jennifer Rubin, "State Dept.'s restrained response to Goldstone's reversal," Right Turn, *Washington Post*, April 5, 2011.

140. Ibid.

141. Yitzhak Benhorin, "US groups want Goldstone Report retracted," *Ynetnews*, April 3, 2011.

142. Ibid.

143. Ethan Bronner and Isabel Kershner, "Head of U.N. Panel Regrets Saying Israel Intentionally Killed Gazans," *New York Times*, April 2, 2011.

144. Ethan Bronner and Isabel Kershner, "Israel Grapples With Retraction on U.N. Report," *New York Times*, April 3, 2011.

145. Richard Cohen, "The Goldstone Report and Israel's moral standing," *Washington Post*, April 5, 2011.

146. Roger Cohen, "The Goldstone Chronicles," *New York Times*, April 7, 2011.

147. Ethan Bronner and Jennifer Medina, "Past Holds Clue to Goldstone's Shift on the Gaza War," *New York Times*, April 19, 2011.

148. Ilan Pappé, "Goldstone's shameful U-turn" *The Electronic Intifada*, April 4, 2011.

149. Noura Erekat, "Goldstone: An act of negligence," *Al Jazeera*, April 4, 2011.

150. "UN council: Goldstone regret not enough to rescind Gaza war report," *Associated Press*, April 4, 2011. Steven R. Hurst, "Goldstone won't seek Gaza report nullification," *Associated Press*, April 6, 2011.

151. "Member of UN Fact Finding mission on Gaza conflict insists report stands unchanged," *Middle East Monitor*, April 4, 2011.

152. Hina Jilani, Christine Chinkin, and Desmond Travers, "Goldstone report: Statement issued by members of UN mission on Gaza war," *The Guardian*, April 14, 2011.

153. B'Tselem statistics are available on the group's website at http://www.btselem.org/statistics. From December 9, 1987, until September 28, 2000, the number of Palestinians killed in the occupied territories by Israeli security forces was 1,376, including 281 minors under age 17. An additional 115, including 23 minors, were killed by Israeli civilians. Furthermore, 33 were killed by security forces and 27 by Israeli civilians within Israel. The number of Israelis killed by Palestinians was 271, including 18 minors, and 150 security personnel. From September 29, 2000 until December 26, 2008, the number of Palestinians killed by Israeli security forces in the occupied territories was 4,789, in addition to 47 killed by Israeli civilians. The number of Israelis killed by Palestinians was 710 civilians, in addition to 331 security force personnel. From December 27, 2008 until January 18, 2009, the number of Palestinians killed by Israeli security forces in the occupied territories was 1,398, in addition to 3 killed by Israeli civilians in Israel. The number of Israelis killed by Palestinians was 3, in addition to 6 security force personnel. From January 19, 2008 until the end of April 2011, the number of Palestinians killed by Israeli security forces in the occupied territories was 209, in addition to 5 killed by Israeli civilians in occupied territory and 1 killed by an Israeli civilian in Israel. The number of Israelis killed by Palestinians was 17 civilians and 4 security force personnel.

154. "Graveside party celebrates Hebron massacre," *BBC*, March 21, 2000. Shmulik Grossman, "Goldstein legacy continues," *Ynetnews*, February 26, 2010.

155. Daniel Estrin, "The King's Torah: a rabbinic text or a call to terror?" *The Forward*; republished in *Haaretz*, January 22, 2010.

156. "West Bank rabbi: Jews can kill Gentiles who threaten Israel," *Haaretz*, November 9, 2009. In July 2011, Rabbis Dov Lior and Yacob Yousef, who had endorsed the book, were questioned by police investigating allegations of incitement. Hundreds protested their brief detention outside of the Supreme Court. "Both men have strong support among ideological Jewish settlers in the occupied West Bank," the BBC explained, "but the wider religious community also took up their cause." Yolande Knell, "King's Torah splits Israel's religious and secular Jews," *BBC*, July 20, 2011. The protests against their detention turned violent, and the Attorney General closed the case, issuing a statement that there was insufficient evidence to try the authors for incitement. See: "Case closed against 'The King's Torah' authors," *Jewish Telegraphic Agency*, May 28, 2012.

157. The White House, "Remarks by the President on the Middle East and North Africa," May 19, 2011.

158. Israeli Prime Minister's Office, "Statement on US President Obama's Speech," May 19, 2011.

159. Helene Cooper, "Obama and Netanyahu, Distrustful Allies, Meet," *New York Times*, May 19, 2011.

160. "Obama insists 1967 'basis' for Israel-Palestinian peace," *BBC*, May 19, 2011.

161. Mark Landler and Steven Lee Myers, "Obama Sees '67 Borders as Starting Point for Peace Deal," *New York Times*, May 19, 2011.

162. Josh Rogin, "Obama alters U.S. policy, tells Israel to start with '67 borders," The Cable, *Foreign Policy*, May 19, 2011.

163. Robert Satloff, "A substantial shift toward the Palestinian position," *Jerusalem Post*, May 20, 2011.

164. Glenn Kessler, "Understanding Obama's shift on Israel and the '1967 lines,'" The Fact Checker, *Washington Post*, May 20, 2011.

165. Roger Cohen, "Obama Draws the Line," *New York Times*, May 20, 2011.

166. Scott Wilson, "In meeting with Obama, Netanyahu rules out Israeli withdrawal to 1967 boundaries," *Washington Post*, May 21, 2011.

167. Jeffrey Heller and Matt Spetalnick, "Israeli rebuke of Obama exposes divide on Mideast," *Reuters*, May 20, 2011.

168. Aluf Benn, "Obama granted Netanyahu a major diplomatic victory," *Haaretz*, May 19, 2011.

169. Sever Plocker, "Obama the Zionist," *Ynetnews*, May 20, 2011.

170. The White House, "Remarks by the President at the AIPAC Policy Conference 2011," May 22, 2011.

171. Helene Cooper, "Obama Presses Israel to Make 'Hard Choices,'" *New York Times*, May 22, 2011.

172. Elior Levy, "PA challenges Netanyahu to accept 1967 lines," *Ynetnews*, May 22, 2011.

173. Cooper, "Obama Presses Israel."

174. Ibid.

175. Elior Levy, "PA Challenges Netanyahu." "Palestinians: Israel must accept 1967 border as basis for negotiations," *Jewish Telegraphic Agency*, May 22, 2011.

176. "Transcript: Israeli Prime Minister Binyamin Netanyahu's address to Congress," *Washington Post*, May 25, 2011. On the agreement between Israeli and US intelligence assessments that Iran is not developing nuclear weapons, see: James Risen, "U.S. Faces a Tricky Task in Assessment of Data on Iran," *New York Times*, March 17, 2012. Tabassum Zakaria and Mark Hosenball, "Special Report: Intel shows Iran nuclear threat not imminent," *Reuters*, March 23, 2012. It is often claimed that Iran has threatened to attack Israel, almost invariably attributed to a statement by Iranian President Mahmoud Ahmadinejad that Israel must be "wiped off the map". The media know this claim is a fabrication, and yet repeat it constantly anyway. See: Jeremy R. Hammond, "Turning Back from the Point of No Return," *Foreign Policy Journal*, August 26, 2010. See also, for example: Robert Mackey, "Israeli Minister Agrees Ahmadinejad Never Said Israel 'Must Be Wiped Off the Map,'" The Lede, *New York Times*, April 17, 2012. Notice such admissions may make it into the blog, but are otherwise deemed unfit to print, unlike the *Times*' propagandistic repetition of the fabricated quote.

177. *Washington Post*, May 25, 2011.

178. "Prime Minister of Israel Benjamin Netanyahu Speech at the Joint Session of Congress – May 24, 2011," *YouTube* video, 46:36, posted by "RepJoeWalsh," May 24, 2011.

179. Ethan Bronner, "Israelis See Netanyahu Trip as Diplomatic Failure," *New York Times*, May 25, 2011.

180. "The Mideast Peace Process: No Plan for Talks," *New York Times*, May 26, 2011.

181. "The Mideast Peace Process: Washington Makes Things Worse," *New York Times*, May 26, 2011. On the political leaning of the *Times*, see: Daniel Okrent, "Is The New York Times a Liberal Newspaper?" *New York Times*, July 25, 2004. The public editor's reply to this question was, "Of course it is." Don Irvine, "NY Times Public Editor Admits Paper Has a Liberal Bias [Video]," *Accuracy In Media*, August 21, 2013.

182. Stephen Zunes, "Netanyahu's Speech and Congressional Democrats' Embrace of Extremism," *Truthout*, June 3, 2011.

183. *Washington Post*, May 25, 2011.

184. "Netanyahu wasted his chance to present a vision for peace," *Haaretz*, May 25, 2011.

185. Gideon Levy, "Netanyahu's speech to Congress shows America will buy anything," *Haaretz*, May 25, 2011.

186. Daniel Levy, "Same Netanyahu, Different Israel," *Foreign Affairs*, May 24, 2011.

187. Kirit Radia, "Secretary Clinton in 2009: 'I really consider President and Mrs. Mubarak to be friends of my family,'" Political Punch, *ABC News*, January 31, 2011.

188. Ethan Bronner, "Israel Waits and Worries Before Gaza Border Opening," *New York Times*, May 27, 2011.

189. Ethan Bronner, "U.N. Charts High Jobless Rate in Gaza, Despite Israel's Easing of Blockade," *New York Times*, June 14, 2011.

190. David D. Kirkpatrick, "Egypt Lifts Blockade, Along With the Gazan's Hopes," *New York Times*, May 28, 2011. Fares Akram, "Open Border at Gaza Is Not So Open, Palestinians Find," *New York Times*, June 1, 2011.

191. Aram Roston and David Rohde, "Egyptian Army's Business Side Blurs Lines of U.S. Military Aid," *New York Times*, March 5, 2011. Jeremy M. Sharp, "Egypt: Background and U.S. Relations," *Congressional Research Service*, June 27, 2013. *Peace Treaty Between Israel and Egypt*, March 26, 1979; available at The Avalon Project online collection of Yale Law School.

192. G. Robert Hillman, "Lieberman optimistic about Egypt," Politico Live, *Politico*, February 27, 2011. Marian Wang, "State Department Approved Export of U.S.-Made Tear Gas to Egyptian Gov't," *ProPublica*, February 4, 2011. "Egypt unrest: 846 killed in protests – official toll," *BBC*, April 19, 2011.

193. International Committee of the Red Cross, "Gaza: no end in sight to hardship and despair," May 20, 2011.

194. United Nations Relief and Works Agency, "Labour Market Briefing," April 2011.

195. United Nations Relief and Works Agency, "UNRWA: Gaza blockade anniversary report," June 13, 2011.

196. Khaled Abu Toahmeh, "Biggest Palestinian shopping mall being built in Gaza," *Jerusalem Post*, May 24, 2011.

197. Jacob Shrybman, "The good life in Gaza," *Ynetnews*, July 20, 2010.

198. Ali Waked, "1st Gaza mall attracts thousands," *Ynetnews*, July 20, 2010.

199. "Israel's Gaza Blockade Baffles Both Sides," *CBS News*, May 28, 2010.

200. Harriet Sherwood, "Gaza's elite enjoy riding at Faisal," *The Guardian*, September 6, 2010.

201. Israel Defense Forces, "What Happened to the Humanitarian Crisis in Gaza?" *IDFblog.com*, August 12, 2013; archived at http://web.archive.org on August 14, 2013, accessed November 18, 2014.

202. "Altered Images: Malaysian mall 'illustrated life in Gaza,'" *BBC*, August 16, 2013.

203. Asher Zeiger, "IDF shows life in Gaza—in Malaysia," *Times of Israel*, August 16, 2013.

204. Daniella Peled, "So, did you see the malls in Gaza?" *Haaretz*, January 8, 2014.

205. Laurie Goodstein, "Americans Are Joining Flotilla to Protest Israeli Blockade," *New York Times*, June 1, 2011.

206. US Department of State, Briefing by Deputy Department Spokesman Mark C. Toner, June 1, 2011.

207. "Report: U.S. to offer Turkey major role in Mideast talks if it stops Gaza flotilla," *Haaretz*, June 3, 2011.

208. Joel Greenberg, "Turkish charity says its ship won't be part of flotilla," *Washington Post*, June 17, 2011.

209. Ethan Bronner, "Israel Warns of Using Force if New Flotilla Heads to Gaza," *New York Times*, June 16, 2011.

210. Ethan Bronner, "Avoid Gaza Flotilla, Israel Warns Foreign Journalists," *New York Times*, June 26, 2011.

211. Isabel Kershner, "Israel Rescinds Its Warning to Gaza-Bound Journalists," *New York Times*, June 27, 2011.

212. Bronner, "Israel Warns of Using Force."

213. US Department of State, Bureau of Consular Affairs, "Travel Warning: Israel, the West Bank and Gaza," June 22, 2011.

214. US Department of State, Secretary of State Hillary Clinton, "Remarks With Philippines Foreign Secretary Albert del Rosario After Their Meeting," June 23, 2011.

215. US Department of State, Press Statement by Spokesperson Victoria Nuland, "Gaza 'Anniversary' Flotilla," June 24, 2011.

216. Jordana Horn, "Congressmen ask Clinton to protect Americans in flotilla," *Jerusalem Post*, June 28, 2011.

217. World Food Program, *Gaza: eased or un-eased? Changes on Gaza Market and Household Conditions following Israel's 20 June 2010 New Access Regime*, June 2011.

218. United Nations Office of the High Commissioner for Human Rights, "'Blockade of Gaza denies Palestinians humanity and dignity,' says UN Special Rapporteur," June 23, 2011.

219. "As the flotilla approaches, Gisha warns: Gaza residents don't need more aid, they need to export and travel," *Gisha*, June 29, 2011.

220. Ethan Bronner, "Building Boom in Gaza's Ruins Belies Misery That Remains," *New York Times*, June 25, 2011.

221. Ehud Rosen, "Who Is Behind the Second Gaza Flotilla?" *Jerusalem Center for Public Affairs*, June 29, 2011.

222. Yaakov Katz, "IDF: Some flotilla activists planning to kill soldiers," *Jerusalem Post*, June 28, 2011.

223. Amira Hass, et al, "Israel's Defense Ministry proposes confiscating boats that breach Gaza blockade," *Haaretz*, June 28, 2011.

224. "PM: Israel fully entitled to stop 'arms-smuggling flotilla," *Jerusalem Post*, June 30, 2011.
225. Hass, et al, "Defense Ministry proposes confiscating boats."
226. Larry Derfner, "Hysteria, 'hasbara' and the flotilla," *Jerusalem Post*, June 29, 2011.
227. "Israel ministers slam flotilla threat as 'spin,'" *Agence France-Presse*, June 29, 2011.
228. Derfner, "Hysteria, 'hasbara' and the flotilla."
229. Katz, "IDF: Some flotilla activists planning to kill soldiers."
230. "Debunking the Israeli-U.S. Effort to Thwart Gaza Freedom Flotilla: 'We Are Committed to Nonviolence,'" *Democracy Now!*, June 30, 2011.
231. Hass, et al, "Defense Ministry proposes confiscating boats." Dahr Jamail, "Gaza flotilla ship 'sabotaged by divers,'" *Al Jazeera*, June 28, 2011.
232. Kevin Flower and Kareem Khadder, "Gaza flotilla sabotaged, organizer says," *CNN*, June 30, 2011. "Sabotage of M.V. Saoirse in Turkey 'an act of international terrorism,'" Press Release, *Free Gaza Movement*, June 30, 2011. "MV Saoirse Sabotage Photos and Video," *IrishShipToGaza.org*, June 30, 2011.
233. Ethan Bronner, "Setting Sail on Gaza's Sea of Spin," *New York Times*, July 2, 2011. Gisha, June 29, 2011. Bronner, "Building Boom in Gaza's Ruins." Kirkpatrick, "Egypt Lifts Blockade."
234. Robert Naiman, "Reading Ethan Bronner in Athens: How the New York Times Gets It Right – and Very Wrong – on the Gaza Flotilla," *Truthout*, July 9, 2011.
235. US Department of State, Quartet Statement on the Situation in Gaza, July 2, 2011.
236. Scott Sayare, "Stuck in Dock, Flotilla Activists See the Hand of Israel," *New York Times*, July 1, 2011.
237. "Don't let Israel export the blockade of Gaza to Greece," *Free Gaza Movement*, July 3, 2011.
238. Bego Astigarraga, "French Ship Carries Freedom Flotilla's 'Dignity' to Gaza," *Inter Press Service*, July 12, 2011.
239. "French boat Dignité of Freedom Flotilla II leaves Greece," *Free Gaza Movement*, July 17, 2011.
240. "French 'aid ship' sails towards Gaza," *Al Jazeera*, July 18, 2011.
241. Isabel Kershner, "Protest Yacht, Bound for Gaza, Is Diverted by Israeli Forces," *New York Times*, July 19, 2011. Amira Hass and Anshel Pfeffer, "Israel intercepts sole remnant of flotilla heading for Gaza," *Haaretz*, July 19, 2011.
242. "Gaza rejects Greek government charity," *Free Gaza Movement*, July 15, 2011

Chapter 9

1. John Bolton, "How to Block the Palestine Statehood Ploy," *Wall Street Journal*, June 3, 2011. Bolton was also a senior fellow at the American Enterprise Institute. The definition of statehood is provided under the Montevideo Convention on the Rights and Duties of States, signed December 26, 1933. A state possesses "a) a permanent population; b) a defined territory; c) government; and d) capacity to enter into relations with the other states." Bolton reminded how "Secretary of State James Baker warned publicly: 'I will recommend to the President that the United States make no further contributions, voluntary or assessed, to any international organization which makes any changes in the PLO's status as an observer organization.'"
2. H.R.2333, 103rd Congress (1993–1994), *Foreign Relations Authorization Act, Fiscal Years 1994 and 1995*, Introduced June 8, 1993; became Public Law No: 103-236 April 30, 1994.
3. S.CON.RES.23, 112th Congress (2011–2012), *A concurrent resolution declaring that it is the policy of the United States to support and facilitate Israel in maintaining defensible borders and that it is contrary to United States policy and national security to have the borders of Israel return to the armistice lines that existed on June 4, 1967*, Introduced June 9, 2011.
4. Michael Oren, "Remembering Six Days in 1967," *Foreign Policy*, June 6, 2011.
5. Michael B. Oren, *Six Days of War: June 1967 and the Making of the Modern Middle East* (New York: Presidio Press, 2003), 55, 59-60, 356 (footnote 52). Oren naturally ignored the fact that Israel's own intelligence assessment was that Egypt would *not* attack throughout most of the book, acknowledging it here only in passing, apparently in the hopes its significance would be lost upon his readers in the face of his overwhelming fictional narrative that Israel was facing imminent doom.
6. David S. Robarge, "Getting It Right: CIA Analysis of the 1967 Arab-Israeli War," *CIA Center for the Study of Intelligence*, Vol. 49, No. 1 (2005), Posted April 15, 2007.
7. US Department of State, FRUS, Volume XIX; Document 500, "Telegram [*text not declassified*] to the White House," July 21, 1967.
8. Israel Ministry of Foreign Affairs, Address by Prime Minister Begin at the National Defense College, August 8, 1982. Begin's admission didn't prevent him from declaring in his very next sentence, "This

was a war of self-defense in the noblest sense of the term"; nor did his further admission that Israel did not launch its attack "for lack of an alternative". "Who knows if there would have been an attack against us?" he asked. "There is no proof of it." Begin's declaration that Israel was acting in "self-defense" notwithstanding, under international law, such "preventive" (not "preemptive") warfare is indistinguishable from aggression, "the supreme international crime", as defined at Nuremberg. See Chapter 4 notes.

9. The Shalem Center, "Our History," from www.shalem.org.il, accessed April 24, 2012; archived copy accessible at https://archive.org/. Their timeline notes for the year 1998: "Shalem launches a senior fellows program to encourage the research and writing of agenda-shaping books, initially in the field of Zionist history and thought. The first to join is historian Michael Oren, who embarks on an ambitious project: the writing of the definitive history of the Six-Day War, based on archival sources from Israel, the U.S., Europe, the Soviet Union, and the Arab world." Norman G. Finkelstein, "Abba Eban with Footnotes," *Journal of Palestine Studies*, Vol. 32, No. 3 (Spring 2003), 81.

10. Oren, "Remembering Six Days."

11. Said, *The Question of Palestine*, 26-28. Chomsky, *Fateful Triangle*, 51.

12. Oren, "Remembering Six Days."

13. Dore Gold, "'Land Swaps' and the 1967 Lines," *The Weekly Standard*, June 20, 2011.

14. Pappé, *The Ethnic Cleansing of Palestine*, Locations 220, 2601, 2626, 2668.

15. Walid Khalidi, "Plan Dalet: Master Plan for the Conquest of Palestine," *Journal of Palestine Studies*, Vol. 18, No. 1, Special Issue: Palestine 1948, (Autumn, 1988), 19. The paper was republished for this special issue twenty-five years after its original publication in the *Middle East Forum*.

16. Gold "'Land Swaps' and the 1967 Lines."

17. Edward W. Said, "Projecting Jerusalem," *Journal of Palestine Studies*, Vol. XXV, No. 1 (Autumn 1995), 7. Nathan Krystall, "The De-Arabization of West Jerusalem 1947-50," *Journal of Palestine Studies*, Vol. XXXVII, No. 2 (Winter 1998), 19-20.

18. Gold, "Land Swaps."

19. Ephraim Sneh, "Bad Borders, Good Neighbors," *New York Times*, July 10, 2011.

20. Henry Siegman, "What have Obama and Netanyahu wrought?" *Foreign Policy*, June 8, 2011.

21. Barak Ravid, "U.S. pressuring Netanyahu to accept Obama's peace plan," *Haaretz*, June 13, 2011.

22. "George Mitchell resigns as Middle East envoy," *CNN*, May 13, 2011. T. Lazaroff, G. Hoffman, and H. Leila Kreiger, "US, EU officials in Israel work to stop Palestinian UN move," *Jerusalem Post*, June 15, 2011.

23. "Sharp increase in West Bank home demolition," Press Release, B'Tselem, June 22, 2011.

24. "Israel: New Laws Marginalize Palestinian Arab Citizens," *Human Rights Watch*, March 30, 2011.

25. Isabel Kershner, "Israel Bans Boycotts Against the State," *New York Times*, July 11, 2011.

26. Jonathan Lis and Tomer Zarchin, "Israeli Left launches public campaign against new law banning boycotts," *Haaretz*, July 12, 2011. Harriet Sherwood, "Israel's ban on boycotts faces legal challenge from civil rights groups," *The Guardian*, July 12, 2011. Harriet Sherwood, "Israel's boycott ban draws fire from law professors," *The Guardian*, July 14, 2011.

27. Avirama Golan, "The boycott law is unconstitutional and undemocratic," *Haaretz*, July 12, 2011.

28. Uri Avnery, "It Can Happen Here!" *Gush Shalom*, July 15, 2011.

29. "Not Befitting a Democracy," *New York Times*, July 17, 2011.

30. Ethan Bronner, "U.S. Group Stirs Debate on Being 'Pro-Israel,'" *New York Times*, March 24, 2011.

31. Ethan Bronner, "Tensions Rise as Palestinians Mourn Israel's Founding," *New York Times*, May 14, 2011.

32. Ethan Bronner, "Israeli Troops Fire as Marchers Breach Borders," *New York Times*, May 15, 2011.

33. Nada Bakri, "Bombing Attack on Peacekeepers in Lebanon Adds Another Jolt to a Region in Upheaval," *New York Times*, May 27, 2011.

34. Isabel Kershner, "U.N. Report Criticizes Israel for Actions at Border," *New York Times*, July 7, 2011. The only other mention of "Nakba" during this period of time was in Mahmoud Abbas's *Times* op-ed "The Long Overdue Palestinian State", in which he pointed out that "Nakba" refers to "our expulsion", as opposed to "the birth of Israel" per se.

35. Pappé, *The Ethnic Cleansing of Palestine*, Location 5294 (footnote 6). Pappé quotes from page 530 of Ben-Gurion's book. Benny Morris notes that the Zionist's military operations resulted in "the complete destruction of Palestinian Arab military power and the shattering of Palestinian society", and that by May 14, 1948, "hundreds of thousands of townspeople and villagers had fled or been forcibly displaced from their homes." Morris, *1948*, Location 1383. (See Chapter 1 notes.)

36. *Haaretz*, April 4, 1969; cited in Said, *The Question of Palestine*, 14. See Chapter 1 notes.

37. "New York Times fails to disclose Jerusalem bureau chief's conflict of interest," *The Electronic Intifada*, January 25, 2010.

38. "Does NYT's Top Israel Reporter Have a Son in the IDF?" *Fairness & Accuracy In Reporting*, January 27, 2010.

39. Clark Hoyt, "Too Close to Home," *New York Times*, February 6, 2010.

40. Clark Hoyt, "Bill Keller Takes Exception to 'Too Close to Home,'" *New York Times*, February 6, 2010.

41. Arthur S. Brisbane, "Where Words Can Never Do Justice," *New York Times*, June 11, 2011. The reader was writing in response to Bronner's May 14 "Tensions Rise" article. Recall that Bronner had written: "After Israel declared independence on May 14, 1948, armies from neighboring Arab states attacked the new nation; during the war that followed, hundreds of thousands of Palestinians fled or were driven from their homes by Israeli forces. Hundreds of Palestinian villages were also destroyed." Illustrating what nonsense Brisbane's argument was, the following alternative contains the exact same number of words (forty-four): "When the state of Israel was declared on May 14, 1948, armies from neighboring Arab states were sent to stop the ethnic cleansing operations that had already been underway for several months. Hundreds of thousands of Palestinians fled or were expelled from their homes."

42. Max Blumenthal, "Conflict in Israel? A problematic speaking deal at *The New York Times*," *Columbia Journalism Review*, September 14, 2011.

43. Arthur S. Brisbane, "Tangled Relationships in Jerusalem," *New York Times*, September 24, 2011.

44. Alex Kane, "New Conflict of Interest at NYT Jerusalem Bureau: Isabel Kershner's family tie to pro-government think tank," *Fairness & Accuracy In Reporting*, May 2012.

45. Amos Harel, "IDF plans to use disproportionate force." See Chapter 1 notes.

46. Israel Defense Forces, "Maj. Gen. (Res.) Eiland Submits Conclusions of Military Examination Team Regarding Mavi Marmara," *IDFblog.com*, July 12, 2010.

47. Kane, "New Conflict of Interest."

48. Hirsh Goodman, "Bronfman Program on Information Strategy," *Institute for National Security Studies*, accessed August 12, 2012; archived at https://archive.org/, accessed December 3, 2014.

49. Jerusalem Post, February 5, 2009. See Chapter 4 notes.

50. Kane, "New Conflict of Interest." Philip Weiss and Adam Horowitz, "Another New York Times' reporter's son is in the Israeli army," *Mondoweiss*, October 27, 2014.

51. Ethan Bronner, "Can Anyone Get It Right? Reporting and Misreporting the Israeli-Arab Conflict," Lecture at the University of Maryland, October 26, 2011. The full talk is viewable online: The Joseph and Alma Gildenhorn Institute for Israel Studies, "Ethan Bronner on the Israeli-Arab Conflict," *Vimeo* video, 1:22:04, October 27, 2011.

52. Theodor Herzl, *Complete Diaries*, ed. Raphael Patai, trans. Harry Zohn (New York: Herzl Press and T. Yoseloff, 1960), vol. I, 88; cited in Said, *The Question of Palestine*, 13. See Chapter 1 notes.

53. Letter from David Ben-Gurion to his son Amos written on October 5, 1937. The original letter written in Hebrew (archived at http://web.archive.org, May 12, 2012, accessed May 23, 2015) was obtained from the Ben-Gurion Archives and translated into English (archived at PalestineRemembered. com) by the Institute of Palestine Studies. See also: "JPS Responds to CAMERA's Call for Accuracy: Ben-Gurion and the Arab Transfer Reviewed work(s)," *Journal of Palestine Studies*, Vol 41, No. 2 (Winter 2012), 245-250.

54. Morris, *1948*, Locations 297-300.

55. Ari Shavit, *My Promised Land: The Triumph and Tragedy of Israel* (New York: Random House, 2013) Kindle Edition, Locations 1235-1236. Morris and Shavit both point out that the reason for this shift was the proposal of the British Peel Commission to partition Palestine with an exchange of populations. Once the British had endorsed the idea of "transfer" of the Arab population, the Zionist leadership felt comfortable enough to advocate it openly.

56. Shavit, *My Promised Land*, Location 1241.

57. Ibid. Pappé, *Ethnic Cleansing of Palestine*, Location 183.

58. Shavit, *My Promised Land*, Location 1241.

59. Morris, *1948*, Locations 780-786.

60. Walid Khalidi, "Plan Dalet"; Appendix B, "Text of Plan Dalet (Plan D), 10 March 1948: General Section," 29. Pappé, *Ethnic Cleansing of Palestine*, Locations 201-216, 1894-1923. Morris, *1948*, Location 1782.

61. Morris, *1948*, Location 1758.

62. Khalidi, "Plan Dalet," 9.

63.   Ari Shavit, "Survival of the Fittest," Interview with Benny Morris, *Haaretz*, January 8, 2004. The full interview is available online at Counterpunch.org. Morris opined that "Ben-Gurion was right. If he had not done what he did, a state would not have come into being. That has to be clear. It is impossible to evade it. Without uprooting of the Palestinians, a Jewish state would not have arisen here. . . . There is no justification for acts of rape. There is no justification for acts of massacre. Those are war crimes. But in certain conditions, expulsion is not a war crime. I don't think that the expulsions of 1948 were war crimes. You can't make an omelet without breaking eggs. You have to dirty your hands. . . . There are circumstances in history that justify ethnic cleansing. . . . That was the situation. That is what Zionism faced. A Jewish state would not have come into being without the uprooting of 700,000 Palestinians. Therefore it was necessary to uproot them. There was no choice but to expel that population. . . . But I do not identify with Ben-Gurion. I think he made a serious historical mistake in 1948. Even though he understood the demographic issue and the need to establish a Jewish state without a large Arab minority, he got cold feet during the war. In the end, he faltered." Ben-Gurion's error, Morris expounded, was in expelling too few Arabs: "If he was already engaged in expulsion, maybe he should have done a complete job. . . . If the end of the story turns out to be a gloomy one for the Jews, it will be because Ben-Gurion did not complete the transfer in 1948. Because he left a large and volatile demographic reserve in the West Bank and Gaza and within Israel itself. . . . The non-completion of the transfer was a mistake." Morris's interviewer, Ari Shavit, holds a similar view. In his critically acclaimed book, *My Promised Land*, he candidly explains how the Zionist project of establishing a demographically "Jewish state" required the removal of the Arab population. In the wake of the Holocaust, this was a necessary step to create a home for the Jews that would ensure their salvation. He interviewed a brigade commander, for example, who "says plainly that the mission was the cleansing of the Galilee before the invasion of Arab armies. The Jewish state about to be born would not survive the external battle with the armed forces of the Arab nations if it did not first rid itself of the Palestinian population that endangered it from within." Illustrating his agreement, Shavit expresses his view that the means by which Israel came into existence was irrefutable "Zionist justice", despite the admitted "injustice caused to native Arabs by the Zionist project". Ari Shavit, *My Promised Land*, Locations 903-917, 1824. See also this author's review of Shavit's book: Jeremy R. Hammond, "Flawed Reason: Insight via inconsistency," *Barron's*, March 1, 2014.
64.   Shavit, "Survival of the Fittest."
65.   Pappé, *Ethnic Cleansing of Palestine*, Locations 425-427.
66.   H.RES.268, 112th Congress (2011–2012), *Reaffirming the United States' commitment to a negotiated settlement of the Israeli-Palestinian conflict through direct Israeli-Palestinian negotiations, and for other purposes*, Introduced May 13 and passed on July 7, 2011.
67.   US House of Representatives, Statement by Ron Paul on H.RES.268, July 6, 2011; archived at http://web.archive.org, December 11, 2012, accessed May 23, 2015.
68.   Letter from Kay Granger and Nita Lowey to President Mahmoud Abbas, July 11, 2011. Josh Rogin, "House leaders to Palestine: seek U.N. recognition, forget foreign aid," The Cable, *Foreign Policy*, July 15, 2011.
69.   Alon Ben-David, et al, "Israel, U.S. Strike F-35 Technology Deal," *Aviation Week*, July 7, 2011.
70.   Khaled Abu Toameh, "PA to Quartet: Tell Israel to stop building over Green Line," *Jerusalem Post*, July 11, 2011.
71.   Herb Keinon, "Lieberman urges Quartet to call Israel a Jewish state," *Jerusalem Post*, July 11, 2011.
72.   Barak Ravid, "Officials: Mideast Quartet talks failed due to disagreement over Israel as Jewish state," *Haaretz*, July 12, 2011.
73.   "EU Denounces Israeli Plans for New Settlement Homes," *Voice of America*, July 19, 2011.
74.   "PLO: U.S. responsible for 'racist' Israeli policies that sabotage peace process," *Reuters*, July 13, 2011.
75.   Barak Ravid, "Palestinian envoy to UN: European states will recognize Palestine before September," *Haaretz*, July 13, 2011.
76.   Mohammed Daraghmeh, "Palestinian leader wants rallies to back UN bid," *Associated Press*, July 27, 2011.
77.   "Palestinians get Arab League boost for UN drive," *Associated Press*, July 14, 2011.
78.   Neil MacFarquhar, "Security Council Debate Offers Preview of Palestinian Bid," *New York Times*, July 26, 2011.
79.   Colum Lynch, "Israeli ambassador seeks 'moral minority' at U.N.," Turtle Bay, *Foreign Policy*, July 21, 2011. Lynch, in a welcome rare departure from the standard media myth that Resolution 181 created Israel, pointed out that the partition plan "was never implemented", but that Israel was created with a unilateral declaration the following year.

80. Herb Keinon, "J'lem protests Honduran support for PA statehood bid," *Jerusalem Post*, August 4, 2011.

81. "Honduras recognizes Palestine as independent state," *Reuters*, August 26, 2011.

82. "El Salvador recognizes Palestine as independent state," *Reuters*, August 26, 2011. "China announces support for Palestinian UN statehood bid," *Haaretz*, August 25, 2011.

83. "West Bank home demolitions up 'alarmingly': UN," *Agence France-Presse*, August 2, 2011.

84. Akiva Eldar, "EU slams Israel's decision to build new East Jerusalem housing project," *Haaretz*, August 6, 2011.

85. Rick Gladstone, "Israel Approves New Housing in East Jerusalem," *New York Times*, August 11, 2011.

86. European Union, "Statement by EU HR Ashton on Settlement Expansion in East Jerusalem," August 12, 2011.

87. Gladstone, "Israel Approves New Housing."

88. "Israel approves 277 new homes in West Bank settlement," *Associated Press*, August 15, 2011.

89. European Union, "Statement by EU HR Ashton on settlement expansion in the West Bank," August 17, 2011.

90. US Department of State, "Joint Statement by the Quartet," August 16, 2011.

91. United Nations General Assembly, Press Release, "Statement by Bureau of Committee on Exercise of Inalienable Rights of Palestinian People on Upsurge in Israeli Settlement Activity," GA/PAL/1209 (August 19, 2011).

92. "Israel 'seeks 20 more F-35 stealth jets,'" *United Press International*, August 9, 2011. Herb Keinon, "American congressman: US economic woes won't affect Israel," *Jerusalem Post*, August 11, 2011.

93. Stephen M. Walt, "The greatest elected body that money can buy," *Foreign Policy*, August 11, 2011.

94. Josh Ruebner, "Robbing Peter to Pay Israel," *Foreign Policy in Focus*, August 12, 2011.

95. Jennifer Steinhauer, "A Recess Destination With Bipartisan Support: Israel and the West Bank," *New York Times*, August 15, 2011.

96. "U.S.: We will stop aid to Palestinians if UN bid proceeds," *Deutsche Presse-Agentur*, August 26, 2011.

97. Akiva Eldar, "New Palestinian strategy document will make it difficult for U.S. to oppose UN vote," *Haaretz*, August 30, 2011.

98. "'Palestinian U.N. bid greater threat than Hamas,'" *Agence France-Presse*, September 1, 2011.

99. "UN chief receives report of panel of inquiry into Gaza flotilla incident," *UN News Centre*, September 2, 2011.

100. United Nations, *Report of the Secretary-General's Panel of Inquiry on the 31 May 2010 Flotilla Incident* (Palmer Report), September 2011, 4-5.

101. Ibid., paras. 5-6, 11, 14, 17.

102. Ibid., para. 70.

103. Turkel Commission Report, paras. 13, 14, 18, 20, 22, 24-25.

104. Palmer Report, para. 70.

105. Ibid., para. 70.

106. Ibid., paras. 72, 77, 81, 159.

107. Ibid., para. 77 (see footnote 274).

108. San Remo Manual. See Chapter 7 notes.

109. Palmer Report., Appendix I, paras. 33, 34 (see footnote 119).

110. International Institute of Humanitarian Law (Louise Doswald-Beck, ed.), *San Remo Manual on International Law Applicable to Armed Conflicts at Sea* (Cambridge: Cambridge University Press, 1995), 179.

111. Palmer Report, Appendix I, para. 36.

112. Ibid., Appendix I, para. 46.

113. San Remo Manual.

114. Ibid., Appendix I, para. 47.

115. Ibid., 104-105.

116. Ibid., 6.

117. David Batty, "Turkey to challenge Gaza blockade at International Court of Justice," *The Guardian*, September 3, 2011.

118. "Netanyahu pledges to defend Marmara commandos," *Jewish Telegraphic Agency*, September 4, 2011.

119. Neil MacFarquhar and Ethan Bronner, "Report Finds Naval Blockade by Israel Legal but Faults Raid," *New York Times*, September 1, 2011.

120. "Turkey, Israel and the Flotilla," *New York Times*, September 2, 2011.

121. Roger Cohen, "Israel Isolates Itself," *New York Times*, September 5, 2011.

122. Barak Ravid, "Turkey to refer Israel's blockade of Gaza Strip to The Hague," *Haaretz*, September 3, 2011. "Turkish Prime Minister Says Navy Will Escort Aid Ships to Gaza," *Associated Press*, September 9, 2011.

123. Shimon Shiffer, "Israel to 'punish' Turkey," *Ynetnews*, September 9, 2011.

124. "Gaza blockade must be lifted following UN panel finding on flotilla raid," *Amnesty International*, September 2, 2011.

125. "Q&A on the Palmer report," *Gisha*, September 1, 2011.

126. "Myths and Facts on the Palmer Report," *Gisha*, September 7, 2011.

127. United Nations Office of the High Commissioner for Human Rights, "How can Israel's blockade of Gaza be legal? – UN independent experts on the 'Palmer Report,'" September 13, 2011. The group consisted of Special Rapporteur on the right to food, Olivier De Schutter; Special Rapporteur on the right of everyone to the enjoyment of the highest attainable standard of physical and mental health, Anand Grover; Special Rapporteur on the human right to safe drinking water and sanitation, Catarina de Albuquerque; Special Rapporteur on extreme poverty and human rights, María Magdalena Sepúlveda Carmona; and Special Rapporteur on the situation of human rights on Palestinian territories occupied since 1967, Richard Falk.

128. Richard Falk, "Another UN Failure: The Palmer Report on the Flotilla Incident of 31 May 2010," *RichardFalk.Wordpress.com*, September 11, 2011.

129. Richard Falk and Phyllis Bennis, "The legal flaws of the Palmer Commission flotilla report," *RichardFalk.Wordpress.com*, September 13, 2011.

130. United Nations General Assembly, 66th Session, "Situation of human rights in the Palestinian territories occupied since 1967," A/66/358 (September 13, 2011).

131. Ali Sawafta, "Palestinians to seek U.N. statehood vote next month: foreign min," *Reuters*, August 13, 2011. Matthew Kalman, "Palestinians to apply for UN statehood next month," *The Independent*, August 15, 2011.

132. Dore Gold, "A Bad Deal: Why Palestinian unity won't lead to peace," *Foreign Policy*, April 28, 2011.

133. David Makovsky, "The Palestinian Bid for UN Membership: Rationale, Response, Repercussions," *Washington Institute for Near East Policy*, September 2011.

134. Steven Lee Myers and Mark Landler, "U.S. Is Appealing to Palestinians to Stall U.N. Vote," *New York Times*, September 3, 2011.

135. Jackson Diehl, "Will Abbas's desperate gambit trigger a third intifada?" *Washington Post*, August 15, 2011.

136. Adrian Blomfield, "Israel watches its old alliances crumble," *The Telegraph*, September 12, 2011.

137. Kirkpatrick, "Palestinians Pressured." David D. Kirkpatrick and Rick Gladstone, "Turkish Leader Urges Vote for Palestinian Statehood," *New York Times*, September 13, 2011.

138. Turki al-Faisal, "Veto a State, Lose an Ally," *New York Times*, September 11, 2011.

139. Marin Katusa, "Ditching the Dollar," *LewRockwell.com*, April 20, 2012. William Dowell, "Foreign Exchange: Saddam Turns His Back on Greenbacks," *Time*, November 13, 2000. Faisal Islam, "Iraq nets handsome profit by dumping dollar for euro," *The Guardian*, February 15, 2003. "Iran stops selling oil in U.S. dollars – report," *Reuters*, December 8, 2007. "Iran Ends Oil Transactions In U.S. Dollars," *CBS News*, April 30, 2008. Ian Black, "Barack Obama to authorize record $60bn Saudi arms sale," *The Guardian*, September 13, 2010. US Congress, Letter from Secretary of Defense Robert M. Gates and Secretary of State Hillary Rodham Clinton to Chairman of the House Committee on Foreign Affairs Steven R. Rothman, November 16, 2010; published by Steven Aftergood, "US-Saudi Arms Deal Defended by Gates, Clinton," Secrecy News, *Federation of American Scientists*, November 19, 2010. For more on the US regime change policy towards Iraq and Iran, see also: Jeremy R. Hammond, "The Reasons for Regime Change in Iraq," *JeremyRHammond.com*, September 6, 2007. Kourosh Ziabari, "Jeremy R. Hammond: US Should End Criminal Sanctions Regime Against Iran," *Fars News*, August 21, 2013.

140. Blomfield, "Israel watches."

141. Dan Perry and Josef Federman, "Palestinians' UN gambit could spur changes," *Associated Press*, September 12, 2011.

142. David D. Kirkpatrick, "Palestinians Pressured to Seek General Assembly Vote on Statehood," *New York Times*, September 13, 2011.

143. David Makovsky, "The Palestinian Bid."

144. Harriet Sherwood, "UN recognition of a Palestinian state receives public approval in Europe," *The Guardian*, September 12, 2011.
145. "Public Narrowly Backs UN Recognition of Palestine: Global Poll," *Globescan*, November 2, 2011. The countries surveyed were the US (45 percent in favor of recognizing Palestine compared to 36 percent opposed), Canada (46 percent to 25 percent), Mexico (45 percent to 15 percent), Brazil (41 percent to 26 percent), Chile (39 percent to 9 percent), Peru (38 percent to 18 percent), Turkey (60 percent to 19 percent), France (54 percent to 20 percent), Germany (53 percent to 28 percent), the UK (53 percent to 26 percent), Russia (37 percent to 13 percent), Egypt (90 percent to 9 percent), Ghana (41 percent to 33 percent), China (56 percent to 9 percent), the Philippines (56 percent to 36 percent), Pakistan (52 percent to 12 percent), Indonesia (51 percent to 16 percent), Australia (50 percent to 17 percent), and India (32 percent to 25 percent). In total, 49 percent of those surveyed said their government should vote in favor of a UN resolution recognizing Palestinian statehood compared to less than half that number (21 percent) who opposed doing so. Inexplicably, the poll's headline declared, "Public Narrowly Backs UN Recognition of Palestine", even though more than twice as many people thought that their government should support the bid than thought should oppose it—hardly a "narrow" margin.
146. "Palestinian Statehood: Mixed Views, Low Visibility," *Pew Research Center*, September 20, 2011. Twenty-one percent of respondents said they sympathized with neither party, and 25 percent had no opinion. Thirty-seven percent thought Obama was "striking the right balance" between Israel and the Palestinians, and 38 percent had no opinion. Thirty-two percent had no opinion about the US recognizing Palestinian statehood. Angus-Reid, September 21, 2010 (see Chapter 8 notes).
147. Shlomo Shamir, "Gallup poll reveals common ground for Jewish and Muslim Americans," *Haaretz*, August 2, 2011. The same poll showed Christians and Jews were more prone to support violence against civilians than Muslims, with 89 percent of Muslim Americans saying there is never a justification for attacks on civilians, compared to 79 percent of Mormon, 75 percent of Jewish, and 71 percent of Christian Americans.
148. "Massive Palestinian Support for Going to UN," *Konrad-Adenauer-Stiftung*, September 19, 2011.
149. "Joint Israeli-Palestinian Poll," *Palestinian Center for Policy and Survey Research*, September 21, 2011.
150. KAS, "Massive Palestinian Support."
151. David Makovsky, "The Palestinian Bid."
152. "Hamas: We may back Palestinian state that does not recognize Israel's existence," *Haaretz*, September 18, 2011.
153. Ethan Bronner and Isabel Kershner, "Palestinians Set Bid for U.N. Seat, Clashing With U.S.," *New York Times*, September 16, 2011.
154. Steven J. Rosen, "The Palestinians' Imaginary State," *Foreign Policy*, August 3, 2011.
155. Guy S. Goodwin-Gill, "Opinion Re The Palestine Liberation Organization, the future State of Palestine, and the question of popular representation," *DocumentCloud.org* (contributed by "haroon meer" of *Al Jazeera English*), August 10, 2011.
156. "Legal opinion challenges PLO statehood bid," *Al Jazeera*, August 25, 2011.
157. Steven Lee Myers and Mark Landler, "U.S. Is Appealing to Palestinians to Stall U.N. Vote," *New York Times*, September 3, 2011.
158. "Palestinians: We won't surrender to U.S. pressure to drop UN bid," *Associated Press*, September 6, 2011.
159. Ethan Bronner, "Abbas Affirms Palestinian Bid for U.N. Membership," *New York Times*, September 5, 2011.
160. Tom Perry, "Palestinians deploy Obama speech in U.N. campaign," *Reuters*, September 7, 2011.
161. "US says will veto Palestinian state bid at UN," *Agence France-Presse*, September 8, 2011.
162. Joel Greenberg, "Abbas vows to proceed with statehood bid despite U.S. warnings," *Washington Post*, September 9, 2011.
163. Ibid.
164. Ibid.
165. Joel Greenberg, "Anxieties mount over Palestinian statehood bid," *Washington Post*, September 15, 2011.
166. Steven Lee Myers and David D. Kirkpatrick, "U.S. Scrambles to Avert Palestinian Vote at U.N.," *New York Times*, September 13, 2011.
167. Meyers and Kirkpatrick, "U.S. Scrambles." Note Clinton's emphasis. See the video of her remarks: "Hillary Clinton: 'The road to Palestine does not lie through the UN,'" *The Telegraph*, September 13, 2011.

168. Greenberg, "Anxieties mount."

169. Ethan Bronner, "Palestinians Resist Appeals to Halt U.N. Statehood Bid," *New York Times*, September 15, 2011.

170. "Abbas aide: PA will renew talks if 1 of 2 conditions met," *Jerusalem Post*, September 14, 2011. Bronner, "Palestinians Resist Appeals."

171. Ilana Curiel, "FM: Unilateral Palestinian moves will have dire consequences," *Ynetnews*, September 14, 2011.

172. For two examples of the rare exception to the rule, see: Keith Ellison, "Support the Palestinian Bid for Statehood," *The New York Times*, September 22, 2011. John B. Judis, "Why the U.S. Should Support Palestinian Statehood at the U.N.," *The New Republic*, September 28, 2011.

173. "Palestinians and the U.N.," *New York Times*, August 7, 2011.

174. "Palestinian Statehood," *New York Times*, September 11, 2011.

175. Aaron David Miller, "The Do-Nothing Strategy," *Foreign Policy*, September 22, 2011.

176. Alex Spillius, "The Palestinian vote at the UN – how it would work," *The Telegraph*, September 16, 2011.

177. David Makovsky, "Why the U.N. cannot create Palestine," *CNN*, September 23, 2011.

178. Robert M. Danin, "The UN Vote and Palestinian Statehood," *Foreign Affairs*, September 14, 2011.

179. "Palestinians left homeless as Israel demolishes West Bank houses," *Amnesty International*, September 15, 2011.

180. The Situation Room, *CNN*, September 16, 2011.

181. Isabel Kershner, "Mosque Set on Fire in Northern Israel," *New York Times*, October 3, 2011.

182. Ethan Bronner, "Amid Statehood Bid, Tensions Simmer in West Bank," *New York Times*, September 23, 2011.

183. Both reports were presented to the Ad-Hoc Liaison Committee (AHLC), which was established in 1993 following the signing of the Declaration of Principles in Oslo to coordinate assistance efforts of donors to the Palestinian people. The fifteen-member committee is sponsored by the US and the EU, with participation also from the UN and World Bank.

184. Israel Ministry of Foreign Affairs, *Measures Taken by Israel in Support of Developing the Palestinian Economy and Socio-Economic Structure*, Report to the Ad Hoc Liaison Committee, September 18, 2011.

185. Office of the UN Special Coordinator for the Middle East Peace Process, *Palestinian State-Building: An Achievement At Risk*, Report to the Ad Hoc Liaison Committee, September 18, 2011.

186. Israel, *Measures Taken by Israel*. The report specified that the deaths and injuries occurred between August 18 and 25 and put the number of injured at twenty-seven. The UNSCO report stated that one Israeli civilian had died, while a footnote in the Israeli report stated: "A 62-year-old woman became the second victim to lose her life as a result of the rocket fire on Beer Shev when she passed away on August 24, 2011 at the Soroka Medical Center in Beer Sheba. A third victim, a 79 year old man, passed away at the Hadassah Medical Center in Jerusalem on September 4, 2011."

187. UNSCO, *Palestinian State-Building*.

188. "News of Terrorism and the Israeli Palestinian Conflict August 23-30, 2011," *The Meir Amit Intelligence and Terrorism Information Center*, August 30, 2011.

189. Israel, *Measures Taken by Israel*.

190. UNSCO, *Palestinian State-Building*.

191. United Nations Office for the Coordination of Humanitarian Affairs, "Area C Humanitarian Response Plan Fact Sheet," August 2010.

192. David Hearst, "West Bank villagers daily battle with Israel over water," *The Guardian*, September 14, 2011.

193. Amnesty International, *Troubled Waters – Palestinians Denied Fair Access to Water*, October 27, 2009.

194. "Israel Restricts Water Availability in West Bank and Gaza," Press Release, *Amnesty International*, October 27, 2009.

Chapter 10

The title of this chapter is taken from the historical description for the subject when it has been brought up on the agenda of the United Nations. For an overview of this history, see: United Nations Department of Public Information, *The Question of Palestine and the United Nations*, April 2008. See also the website of the United Nations Information System on the Question of Palestine (UNISPAL): http://unispal.un.org/. The chapter title is also a homage to Edward W. Said's classic work of the same name (see Chapter 1, footnote 15).

1. The Situation Room, *CNN*, September 16, 2011.
2. Paul Adams, "Why Obama has turned towards Israel," *BBC News*, September 22, 2011.
3. "Text of Mitt Romney's Speech on Foreign Policy at The Citadel," Washington Wire, *Wall Street Journal*, October 7, 2011.
4. Gerald M. Boyd, "THE 1988 ELECTIONS MAN IN THE NEWS: George Herbert Walker Bush; A Victor Free to Set His Own Course," *New York Times*, November 9, 1988.
5. Michael Kingsely, "Rally Round the Flag, Boys," *Time*, June 24, 2001. *Newsweek*, August 15, 1988; cited in William Blum, *Rogue State: A Guide to the World's Only Superpower* (Monroe: Common Courage Press, 2000), 227.
6. John Barry and Roger Charles, "Sea of Lies," *Newsweek*, July 12, 1992. Lieutenant Colonel David Evans, U.S. Marine Corps (Retired), "*Vincennes*: A Case Study," Naval Reserve Officer Training Corps Unit, University of Pennsylvania; Presented as "Lesson 20: Crisis Decision Making: USS Vincennes Case Study," part of the course "Naval Science 302: Navigation and Naval Operations II," offered by the Naval Reserve Officer Training Corps Unit at the University of Pennsylvania.
7. George C. Wilson, "Navy Missile Downs Iranian Jetliner," *Washington Post*, July 4, 1988; Page A01.
8. Tom Raum, "Bush's U.N. Speech Seen as Political Address, Too," *Associated Press*, July 14, 1988.
9. Ellen Warren, "Bush To Speak On Iran Jet Attack Will Address U.n. [*sic*] Council Today In Debate On Navy Downing," *Philadelphia Inquirer*, July 14, 1988.
10. "Excerpts of Vice President George Bush's Remarks to U.N. Security Council," *Associated Press*, July 14, 1988. "Downing of Iranian Airliner," *C-SPAN*, July 14, 1988.
11. "In Captain Rogers's Shoes," *New York Times*, July 5, 1988.
12. Molly Moore, "2 Vincennes Officers Get Medals; Citations Do Not Mention Downing of Iranian Airliner That Killed 290," *Washington Post*, April 23, 1990. Barry and Charles, "Sea of Lies." Evans, "*Vincennes*: A Case Study."
13. Wall Street Journal, October 7, 2011.
14. Yitzhak Benhorin, "Perry: Obama policy naïve, dangerous," *Ynetnews*, September 20, 2011.
15. Rick Perry, "The U.S. Must Support Israel At the U.N.," *Wall Street Journal*, September 16, 2011.
16. Jennifer Steinhauer and Steven Lee Myers, "House G.O.P. Tightens Its Bond With Netanyahu," *New York Times*, September 20, 2011.
17. Robert Wexler, "Defending Obama's pro-Israel credentials," *Jerusalem Post*, September 22, 2011.
18. John Heilemann, "The Tsuris," *New York*, September 18, 2011.
19. Democratic National Committee, "No Better Friend," *YouTube* video, 0:43, posted by "DemRapidResponse" (the YouTube channel of Democrats.org), September 8, 2011. For a partial transcript of the video clip, see: "President Obama and Israel: The Facts," *National Jewish Democratic Council*, August 24, 2012.
20. The Situation Room, *CNN*, September 16, 2011.
21. Barak Ravid, "Netanyahu: Israel will agree to upgrade of Palestinian status, not statehood," *Haaretz*, September 16, 2011.
22. Avi Issacharoff, "Palestinian foreign minister confirms PA will go to UN in quest for statehood," *Haaretz*, September 16, 2011.
23. Ethan Bronner and Isabel Kershner, "Palestinians See U.N. Bid as Their Most Viable Option," *New York Times*, September 17, 2011.
24. Ravid, "Israel will agree to upgrade."
25. Bronner and Kershner, "Palestinians Set Bid for U.N. Seat".
26. Thomas L. Friedman, "Israel: Adrift at Sea Alone," *New York Times*, September 17, 2011.
27. Neil MacFarquhar, "Palestinians Turn to U.N., Where Partition Began," *New York Times*, September 18, 2011.
28. Helene Cooper and Neil MacFarquhar, "Obama Praises Libya's Post-Qaddafi Leaders at U.N.," *New York Times*, September 20, 2011.
29. The White House, "Remarks by President Obama in Address to the United Nations General Assembly," September 21, 2011.
30. Public Law 112-74, 112th Congress, *Consolidated Appropriations Act, 2012*, Sec. 7008. The law forbids financial assistance "to the government of any country whose duly elected head of government is deposed by military coup d'etat or decree". Aid may only be resumed "if the President determines and certifies to the Committees on Appropriations that subsequent to the termination of assistance a democratically elected government has taken office. . . . "
31. Kareem Fahim and Mayy El Sheikh, "Crackdown in Egypt Kills Islamists as They Protest," July 27, 2013.

32. Mark Landler, "Aid to Egypt Can Keep Flowing, Despite Overthrow, White House Decides," *New York Times*, July 25, 2013. Note that the *Times* accepts unquestioningly the false assumption that since the White House said it was okay, therefore the continuation of aid did not violate US law. For further discussion, see: Jeremy R. Hammond, "Executive Branch: U.S. Law Does Not Require Executive Branch to Execute or Obey U.S. Law," *JeremyRHammond.com*, August 6, 2013.

33. Fahim and El Sheikh, "Crackdown in Egypt." "Egypt: Many Protesters Shot in Head or Chest," *Human Rights Watch*, July 28, 2013.

34. Kareem Fahim and Rick Gladstone, "Egypt Vows to End Sit-Ins by Supporters of Deposed President," *New York Times*, July 31, 2013.

35. "Egypt's Dangerous Slide," *New York Times*, July 30, 2013.

36. US Department of State, Secretary of State John Kerry Interview with Hamid Mir of Geo TV, August 1, 2013.

37. Alastair Beach, "Egypt's day of shame: Scores killed and hundreds more injured as government declares war on Islamists," *The Independent*, August 15, 2013. David D. Kirkpatrick, Peter Baker, and Michael R. Gordon, "How American Hopes for a Deal in Egypt Were Undercut," *New York Times*, August 17, 2013.

38. Kirkpatrick, et al, "How American Hopes." "Who Will Be Left in Egypt?" *New York Times*, September 12, 2013. The administration took preliminary steps to withhold some economic assistance to Egypt, but not military aid. The White House had requested $1.55 billion in aid for Egypt for 2014, $1.3 billion of which was military, all but $585 million of which had already been deposited in Egypt's account at the Federal Reserve Bank of New York. See: Mark Landler and Thom Shanker, "Leaving Military Aid Intact, U.S. Takes Steps to Halt Economic Help to Egypt," *New York Times*, August 18, 2013.

39. "Military Madness in Cairo," *New York Times*, August 14, 2013.

40. Michael R. Gordon and Mark Landler, "In Crackdown Response, U.S. Temporarily Freezes Some Military Aid to Egypt," *New York Times*, October 9, 2013. The *Times* noted that the $260 million was for "the general Egyptian budget", meaning non-military aid. The *Times* didn't clarify this explicitly for readers, but hinted at it further down the page; e.g., "But in a sign of how the administration is balancing its interests, senior officials said the United States would continue aid for counterterrorism programs.... American officials have long doubted that cutting back military aid would have any effect on the behavior of Egypt's military-backed government." Etc. See also: Landler and Shanker, "Leaving Military Aid Intact."

41. Jonathan Lis, "Washington cuts Egypt aid despite intense Israeli lobbying," *Haaretz*, October 10, 2013.

42. As *The Telegraph* notes, "For years, the Americans saw President Ali Abdullah Saleh as a key ally in the fight against al-Qaeda. He allowed his air bases to be used by US drones to strike at the movement's operatives, and gladly received Western aid in development cash and arms supplies." Richard Spencer, "How Yemen's US-backed ex-dictator is tearing his country apart," *The Telegraph*, March 28, 2015.

43. White House, September 21, 2011. Ethan Bronner and Michael Slackman, "Saudi Troops Enter Bahrain to Help Put Down Unrest," *New York Times*, March 14, 2011. The *Times* noted that according to a Saudi official, "the United States was informed Sunday that the Saudi troops would enter Bahrain on Monday" and that its military "would protect infrastructure, government offices and industries, even though the protests had largely been peaceful", which "would allow Bahrain to free up its own police and military forces to deal with the demonstrators".

44. White House, September 21, 2011.

45. Jeremy R. Hammond, "Turning Back From the Point of No Return," *Foreign Policy Journal*, August 26, 2010. The idiom "to wipe off the map" does not even exist in the Persian language, and as Farsi experts have pointed out, what Ahmadinejad said was that "This regime that is occupying Qods [Jerusalem] must be eliminated from the pages of history", which was a quote from Ayatollah Khomeini. The context was a speech in which Ahmadinejad spoke of the need for oppressive regimes to come to an end, and the examples he cited were the collapse of the Soviet Union and the regime of the US-backed Shah in Iran, neither of which were overthrown by military force from without, but collapsed from within. He also cited Saddam Hussein's regime in Iraq, though nobody in the Western media condemned him for suggesting that Saddam's dictatorship should also have been "wiped off the map", as it was, by the US, in an illegal war of aggression based on a pretext of lies.

46. Natasha Mozgovaya and Barak Ravid, "Israeli officials: PA will take statehood bid to UN General Assembly within weeks," *Haaretz*, September 22, 2011.

47. Israel Ministry of Foreign Affairs, "Statements by President Obama and PM Netanyahu before meeting at UN General Assembly," September 21, 2011.

48. Mozgovaya and Ravid, "Israeli officials".

49. Ibid.

50. Paul Adams, "Why Obama has turned towards Israel," *BBC*, September 22, 2011.

51. Ethan Bronner, "Israelis Happy at Home but Glum About Peace," *New York Times*, September 28, 2011.

52. Gil Hoffman, "'Post' poll finds surge in Obama popularity in Israel," *Jerusalem Post*, September 28, 2011.

53. Mozgovaya and Ravid, "Israeli officials".

54. Chris McGreal and Harriet Sherwood, "Palestinians ready to put statehood on backburner in favour of peace talks," *The Guardian*, September 22, 2011.

55. Helene Cooper, "Obama Says Palestinians Are Using Wrong Forum," *New York Times*, September 21, 2011.

56. Helene Cooper and Steven Lee Myers, "Obama Rebuffed as Palestinians Pursue U.N. Seat," *New York Times*, September 21, 2011.

57. "The Palestinians' Bid," *New York Times*, September 22, 2011.

58. Permanent Mission of France to the United Nations in New York, Speech by President Nicolas Sarkozy to the 66th Session of the UN General Assembly, September 21, 2011.

59. Cooper and Myers, "Obama Rebuffed."

60. Neil MacFarquhar, "France Breaks With Obama on Palestinian Statehood Issue," *New York Times*, September 21, 2011.

61. Cooper and Myers, "Obama Rebuffed."

62. MacFarquhar, "France Breaks With Obama."

63. Natasha Mozgovaya and Barak Ravid, "Abbas to seek full UN recognition despite Western pressure," *Haaretz*, September 23, 2011.

64. "PLO to give UN council time to mull bid," *Reuters*, September 22, 2011.

65. Neil MacFarquhar and Ethan Bronner, "Taking a Stand, and Shedding Arafat's Shadow," *New York Times*, September 21, 2011.

66. "Full transcript of Abbas speech at UN General Assembly," *Haaretz*, September 23, 2011. A video of the speech as well as a transcript is available at http://gadebate.un.org/66/palestine.

67. Isabel Kershner and Ethan Bronner, "Palestinians Rally in West Bank for Abbas Speech; Clashes Reported," *New York Times*, September 23, 2011.

68. UN General Assembly, *Application of Palestine for admission to membership in the United Nations*, A/66/371—S/2011/592 (September 23, 2011).

69. United Nations, "Quartet Statement," September 23, 2011.

70. Neil MacFarquhar and Steven Lee Myers, "Palestinians Request U.N. Status; Powers Press for Talks," *New York Times*, September 23, 2011.

71. Tovah Lazaroff, "Oren: PA's unilateralism may cost them post-Oslo gains," *Jerusalem Post*, September 27, 2011.

72. Bronner, "Palestinians Resist Appeals".

73. "Full transcript of Netanyahu speech at UN General Assembly," *Haaretz*, September 24, 2011.

74. David Samuels, "Q&A: Maen Rashid Areikat," *Tablet*, October 29, 2010. Oren Dorell, "PLO ambassador says Palestinian state should be free of Jews," *USA Today*, September 13, 2011. Joshua Hersh, "Report of Palestinian State Free Of Jews Was Misinterpretation, Official Says," *The Huffington Post*, September 14, 2011.

75. Jim Rutenberg and Jeff Zeleny, "Perry and Romney Come Out Swinging at Each Other in G.O.P. Debate," *New York Times*, September 22, 2011. US Immigration and Customs Enforcement, Department of Homeland Security, "FY 2011: ICE announces year-end removal numbers, highlights focus on key priorities," October 18, 2011.

76. Khaled Abu Toameh, "PA affirms death penalty for land sales to Israelis," *Jerusalem Post*, September 20, 2010; Mohammed Daraghmeh, "Palestinian official dies after fall from security compound window," *Times of Israel*, July 16, 2012.

77. Geremy Forman and Alexandre Kedar, "From Arab land to 'Israel Lands': the legal dispossession of the Palestinians displaced by Israel in the wake of 1948," *Environment and Planning D: Society and Space*, 2004, Vol. 22, 809-830. Also available at the website of the Faculty of Law at Haifa University.

78. See Stephen P. Halbrook, "The Alienation of a Homeland: How Palestine Became Israel," *Journal of Libertarian Studies*, Vol. V, No. 4 (Fall 1981), 363.

79. "Mid-East crisis: Abbas vs Netanyahu at UN," *BBC*, September 24, 2011.

80. "The war over statehood," *The Economist*, September 24, 2011.

81. Elliot Abrams, "Abbas Strikes Out," *National Review*, September 26, 2011.

82. Yossi Verter, "Haaretz poll: More Israelis approve of Netanyahu after UN speech," *Haaretz*, September 26, 2011.

83. Daniel Levy, "Will the Real Benjamin Netanyahu Please Stand Up?" *Foreign Policy*, October 7, 2011.

84. "President Abbas Declares 'Palestinian Spring' in Return to Middle East," *Associated Press*, September 25, 2011. "Analysis: UN speech gives Abbas a stronger hand," *Associated Press*, September 27, 2011. "OPT: Top Hamas official criticizes Palestinian bid for statehood," *Integrated Regional Information Networks* (IRIN, a service of OCHA), September 23, 2011.

85. European Union, "Statement by EU Ashton on the settlement expansion in Gilo, East Jerusalem," September 27, 2011.

86. Donald Macintyre, "Angela Merkel reads Benjamin Netanyahu the riot act over settlement plan," *The Independent*, October 3, 2011.

87. Isabel Kershner, "Israel Angers Palestinians With Plan for Housing," *New York Times*, September 28, 2011.

88. Julian E. Barnes, "Panetta Warns of Israeli Isolation," *Wall Street Journal*, October 2, 2011.

89. Nicholas D. Kristof, "Is Israel Its Own Worst Enemy?" *New York Times*, October 5, 2011.

90. United Nations Security Council, 6624th Meeting, "Security Council Refers Palestinian Application for United Nations Membership to Its Committee on Admission of New Members," Press Release, September 28, 2011.

91. European Union, "EU Parliament supports Palestine's 'legitimate' bid for statehood," September 29, 2011.

92. "Palestine has eight Security Council votes, says FM," *Agence France-Presse*, September 29, 2011. Khaled Abu Toameh, "France, Britain expected to abstain from PA UNSC vote," *Reuters*, November 4, 2011. Barak Ravid, "Security Council report reveals discord over fate of Palestinian statehood bid," *Haaretz*, November 9, 2011.

93. Richard N. Haass, "The Debate on a Palestinian State: Why Talks Are the Only Way Forward," *Time*, October 3, 2011.

94. "US Congress freeze on $200m Palestinian aid criticized," *BBC*, October 4, 2011. Anna Fifield, "US in push to cut off aid to Palestinians," *Financial Times*, October 10, 2011.

95. BBC, October 4, 2011.

96. Charter of the United Nations, Chapter II: Membership, Article 4.

97. Amira Hass, "Palestinians to pursue UNESCO bid despite political pressure," *Haaretz*, October 31, 2011.

98. Charter of the United Nations, Chapter IV: The General Assembly, Article 22. United Nations Educational, Scientific and Cultural Organization, "Request for the admission of Palestine to UNESCO," November 30, 2011. Scott Sayare and Steven Erlanger, "Palestinians Win a Vote on Bid to Join Unesco," *New York Times*, October 5, 2011.

99. Sayare and Erlanger, "Palestinians Win a Vote".

100. "Palestinians seek full member status at UNESCO," *Associated Press*, October 5, 2011. Sayare and Erlanger, "Palestinians Win a Vote". US National Archives and Records Administration, "The U.S. Recognition of the State of Israel," August 23, 2006.

101. UNESCO's budget for 2010-11 was $643 million. The US decision meant about $60 million would be cut off for the remainder of the year. The budget for 2011-12 was projected to be $653 million, so a loss of 22 percent would mean a shortfall of about $154 million. See Richard Falk, "Welcoming Palestine to UNESCO," *Al Jazeera*, December 13, 2011. Steven Erlanger, "Palestinian Bid for Full Unesco Membership Imperils American Financing," *New York Times*, October 23, 2011. See also the PDF file linked to in the aforementioned *Times* article online, "Limitations on Contributions to the United Nations and Affiliated Organizations." Michael Moran, "Terrorist Groups and Political Legitimacy," *Council on Foreign Relations*, March 16, 2006.

102. United Nations Educational, Scientific and Cultural Organization, "General Conference admits Palestine as UNESCO Member," October 31, 2011.

103. Euronews, "UNESCO gives Palestinians full membership," *YouTube* video, 1:06, October 31, 2011. Reuters, "UNESCO gives Palestinians full membership," *YouTube* video, 1:34, October 31, 2011.

104. Josh Levs, "U.S. cuts UNESCO funding after Palestinian membership vote," *CNN*, November 1, 2011.

105. Levs, "U.S. cuts UNESCO funding." Barak Ravid and Natasha Mozgovaya, "Israel to mull sanctions on Palestinian Authority following UNESCO vote," *Haaretz*, October 31, 2011.

106. Natasha Mozgovaya, "U.S. cuts funding for UNESCO after Palestinian vote," *Haaretz*, October 31, 2011. Levs, "U.S. cuts UNESCO funding."

107. Josh Rogin, "The FP Interview: Condoleezza Rice on Obama, 'Leading from Behind,' Iraq, and More," *Foreign Policy*, November 3, 2011.

108. Steven Erlanger, "Cutting Off Unesco, U.S. May Endanger Programs in Iraq and Afghanistan," *New York Times*, November 16, 2011.

109. US Department of State, Daily Press Briefing by Victoria Nuland, November 2, 2011.

110. Amy Teibel, "Israel to hold $100 million in taxes owed to Palestinians," *Associated Press*, November 14, 2011. Ethan Bronner, "Israel Halts Payments to Palestinians, Adding to Fiscal Woes," *New York Times*, November 23, 2011.

111. Ethan Bronner, "Palestinians to Receive Payments, Israel Says," *New York Times*, November 30, 2011.

112. "Report: Sarkozy calls Netanyahu 'liar,'" *Ynetnews*, November 7, 2011. Marcy Oster, "ADL calls Sarkozy-Obama exchange 'unpresidential,'" *Jewish Telegraphic Agency*, November 8, 2011.

113. Ibid.

114. Elliot Abrams, "Obama Joins the Chorus," Pressure Points, *Council on Foreign Relations*, November 8, 2011.

115. "Romney and Perry attack Obama handling of Israel and Iran," Security Clearance, *CNN*, November 9, 2011.

116. Interview with Israeli President Shimon Peres, Piers Morgan Tonight, *CNN*, November 14, 2011.

117. "Coming up on GPS: Ehud Barak praises Obama's support for Israel; Miliband slams UK austerity," Global Public Square, *CNN*, November 18, 2011.

118. Ethan Bronner, "Israel and Hamas Agree to Swap Prisoners for Soldier," *New York Times*, October 11, 2011.

119. Anne Barker, "Israeli soldier Shalit freed from captivity," *Australian Broadcasting Corporation* (ABC), October 18, 2011. Isabel Kershner, "Soldier's Family Led Campaign for His Release," *New York Times*, October 19, 2011. Daniel Gordis, "Why Netanyahu Made the Prisoner Swap Deal with Hamas," *Foreign Affairs*, October 17, 2011.

120. Ethan Bronner and Stephen Farrell, "Israel Releases Names of 477 Prisoners to Be Freed in Trade," *New York Times*, October 16, 2011.

121. "Israel: Stop Jailing People Without Charge or Trial," *Human Rights Watch*, May 2, 2012.

122. United Nations Children's Fund, "UNICEF Appeals For Release of Palestinian Detainees," October 17, 2011. "ISRAEL-OPT: Concerns over Palestinian children in Israeli custody," *IRIN*, October 19, 2011.

123. Amos Harel and Avi Issacharoff, "Hamas: Israel pledged to lift Gaza blockade as part of Shalit swap deal," *Haaretz*, October 18, 2011. Ernesto Londoño, "After Gilad Shalit prisoner swap, Hamas hopes for eased Gaza blockade," *Washington Post*, October 19, 2011.

124. "Israel must end the Gaza blockade," *Haaretz*, October 31, 2011.

125. Ronen Bergman, "Gilad Shalit and the Rising Price of an Israeli Life," *New York Times*, November 9, 2011.

126. Richard A. Oppel Jr., "Republican Candidates Aim at Obama Foreign Policy," *New York Times*, December 6, 2011.

127. Richard A. Oppel Jr., "G.O.P. Candidates, at Jewish Coalition, Pledge to Be Israel's Best Friends," *New York Times*, December 7, 2011.

128. Grace Kiser, "Rick Santorum claims everyone who lives in the West Bank is Israeli," *Reuters*, November 22, 2011.

129. "The Jewish Channel Exclusive Interview With GOP Front-Runner and former Speaker of the House Newt Gingrich," *The Jewish Channel*, December 9, 2011.

130. Jeremy R. Hammond, "Newt's Invented History of the Israeli-Palestinian Conflict," *Foreign Policy Journal*, December 13, 2011.

131. Tanya Somanader, "Giuliani: 'I Jumped Up Out Of My Chair And Cheered' When Gingrich Said Palestinians Are An 'Invented People,'" *Think Progress*, December 15, 2011.

132. Said, *The Question of Palestine*, 26-28.

133. Simha Flapan, *Zionism and the Palestinians* (Barnes & Noble, New York, 1979) 134; cited in Chomsky, *Fateful Triangle*, 51.

134. London Sunday Times, June 15, 1969; cited in Chomsky, *Fateful Triangle*, 51.

135. United Nations General Assembly, 66th Session, Draft Resolution, *The right of the Palestinian people to self-determination*, A/C.3/66/L.61 (November 1, 2011). United Nations Department of Public Information, "General Assembly Adopts More Than 60 Resolutions Recommended by Third Committee," December 19, 2011.

136. Edith M. Lederer, "US targeted over failure to condemn Israel," *Associated Press*, December 20, 2011. United Kingdom Mission to the United Nations, "Joint statement by European Union Security Council members," December 20, 2011. The statement also condemned Israeli settler violence.

137. US Department of State, Press Briefing by Victoria Nuland, December 21, 2011.

138. "Israel intercepts 2 Gaza-bound aid ships," *RIA Novosti*, November 4, 2011. Carmen Chai, "Ships aim to breach Israeli blockade at Gaza," *Calgary Herald*, November 4, 2011. Derek Abma, "Canadian detained after Gaza-bound ship intercepted 'basically OK,'" *National Post*, November 6, 2011. Isabel Kershner, "Israel Intercepts Two Boats Bound for Gaza," *New York Times*, November 4, 2011.

139. Kershner, "Israel Intercepts Two Boats." Kershner could have cited, for example, a report from OCHA that had been released just a few weeks prior, which stated that "The Gaza blockade (through the land, air and sea) is a denial of basic human rights in contravention of international law and amounts to collective punishment." United Nations Office for the Coordination of Humanitarian Affairs, "Humanitarian Situation in the Gaza Strip," October 18, 2011.

140. UN Human Rights Council, 19th Session, Resolution 19/17, Israeli settlements in the Occupied Palestinian Territory, including East Jerusalem, and in the occupied Syrian Golan, A/HRC/RES/19/17 (April 10, 2012).

141. Barak Ravid, "UN human rights body to probe Israel's settlement activities in West Bank," *Haaretz*, March 22, 2012. Barak Ravid, "Israel cut contact with UN rights council, to protest settlements probe," *Haaretz*, March 26, 2012.

142. Barak Ravid, "U.S. pressing UN Human Rights Commissioner to put off West Bank settlements probe," *Haaretz*, May 2, 2012.

143. Akiva Eldar, "Israel Defense Ministry plan earmarks 10 percent of West Bank for settlement expansion," *Haaretz*, March 30, 2012.

144. "ICC rejects bid for Gaza war crimes tribunal," *Al Jazeera*, April 3, 2012.

145. United Nations Secretary-General, "Statement by Middle East Quartet," Press Release, April 11, 2012.

146. H.R.4133, 112th Congress, *United States-Israel Enhanced Security Cooperation Act of 2012*, Passed in the House May 9, 2012.

147. Ron Paul, "Bad for America, Bad for Israel, Bad for the World," *Antiwar.com*, May 10, 2012.

148. S.2165, 112th Congress, *United States-Israel Enhanced Security Cooperation Act of 2012*, Introduced March 6, 2012. The bill was passed by the Senate on June 29, by the House on July 17, and signed into Public Law 112-150 by President Obama on July 27. The only difference between the two bills in this regard was the rewording in the one that became law of the second policy as follows: "To help the Government of Israel preserve its qualitative military edge amid rapid and uncertain regional political transformation".

149. Jodi Rudoren, "Israel Retroactively Legalizes 3 West Bank Settlements," *New York Times*, April 24, 2012.

150. Karin Brulliard, "Israel legalizes three West Bank outposts," *Washington Post*, April 24, 2012.

151. Ethan Bronner, "Unity Deal Brings Risks for Abbas and Israel," *New York Times*, February 6, 2012.

152. Jodi Rudoren and Fares Akram, "Palestinians Sign Deal to Set Up Elections," *New York Times*, May 20, 2012.

153. Isabel Kershner, "Israeli Watchdog Criticizes Government Over Gaza Flotilla Raid," *New York Times*, June 13, 2012.

154. "International pressure mounts over Gaza blockade," *Oxfam International*, June 14, 2012. "Aid Groups and U.N. Agencies Urge Israel to Lift Gaza Blockade," *Associated Press*, June 14, 2012; published by the *New York Times*. Compare the two-paragraph version published by the *Times* with the unabridged sixteen-paragraph AP article: Ibrahim Barzak, "50 aid groups demand Israel lift Gaza blockade," *Associated Press*, June 14, 2012.

155. Jon Donnison, "Hamas flexes muscle after period of 'calm,'" *BBC*, June 21, 2012. "Tentative talk of ceasefire after Gaza terrorists fire 25 rockets at Sderot area," *Times of Israel*, June 23, 2012. Ezzedeen Al Qassam Brigades Information Office (@AlqassamBrigade), "If Enemy doesn't Understand our Message . . . We Have More," image posted to Twitter, June 23, 2012.

156. "Arab League backs Palestinian plan to seek recognition at UN," *Associated Press*, July 23, 2012. "Abbas to delay Palestinian UN bid until after US elections," *Times of Israel*, July 24, 2012.

157. Jodi Rudoren, "Romney, an Eye on Campaign, Plans a Trip to Israel," *New York Times*, July 2, 2012.

158. Matt Williams, "Mitt Romney vows to do 'the opposite' of Obama on Middle East policy," *The Guardian*, June 17, 2012.

159. Rudoren, "Romney."

160. Natasha Mozgovaya, "Romney: Obama undermines Israel's global standing, Israelis deserve better," *Haaretz*, July 24, 2012.

161. Barak Ravid, "One day before Romney's visit, Obama to sign act expanding military cooperation with Israel," *Haaretz*, July 26, 2012. Natasha Mozgovaya, "Obama announces new military assistance to Israel on eve of Romney trip," *Haaretz*, July 27, 2012. Julie Pace, "Obama Releases $70M in Additional Military Funding," *Associated Press*, July 27, 2012.

162. Jodi Rudoren and Ashley Parker, "Romney Faces Perils and Opportunities in Israel," *New York Times*, July 27, 2012. Ashley Parker, "Fund-Raiser for Romney in Israel Bars Media," *New York Times*, July 29, 2012. Jodi Rudoren and Ashley Parker, "In Jerusalem, Romney Delivers Strong Defense of Israel," *The Caucus*, *New York Times*, July 29, 2012. Barak Ravid, "In Jerusalem speech, it was Romney's voice but Netanyahu's words," *Haaretz*, July 30, 2012.

163. Harriet Sherwood, "Mitt Romney 'providence comments in Israel outrage Palestinians," *The Guardian*, July 30, 2012. Philip Rucker and Joel Greenberg, "Romney faces Palestinian criticism for Jerusalem remarks as he heads to Poland," *Washington Post*, July 30, 2012.

164. Sherwood, "Mitt Romney."

165. "Mr. Romney Stumps in Israel," *New York Times*, July 30, 2012.

166. Thomas L. Friedman, "Why Not in Vegas?" *New York Times*, July 31, 2012.

167. Zahi Khouri, "The Palestine Romney doesn't know," *Washington Post*, August 9, 2012.

168. David Corn, "Secret Video: On Israel, Romney Trashes Two-State Solution," *Mother Jones*, September 18, 2012.

169. Mohammed Daraghmeh, "Palestinians Condemn Romney Mideast Peace Comment," *Associated Press*, September 20, 2012.

170. David Lev, "Officials: Romney VP Choice Very Pro-Israel," *Arutz Sheva*, August 11, 2012.

171. Philip Weiss, "Paul Ryan describes Israel as issue of 'Homeland Security,'" *Mondoweiss*, August 11, 2012. US Congressman Paul Ryan, "Homeland Security," US House of Representatives, accessed September 26, 2013. While the topic of Iran's nuclear program is beyond the scope of this book, I've written on it extensively elsewhere. The bottom line is that there is no credible evidence Iran has a nuclear weapons program; in fact, this is the assessment of the US's own intelligence community—an assessment with which Israeli intelligence concurs. See especially Jeremy R. Hammond, "Turning Back From the Point of No Return: Implications of the Threat to Bomb Iran," *Foreign Policy Journal*, August 26, 2010. Jeremy R. Hammond, "Preparing Minds for an Israeli Attack on Iran," *Foreign Policy Journal*, January 28, 2012. Jeremy R. Hammond, "The U.S. and Israel's 'Overreaction' to Iran's Nuclear Program: Another Mythical 'Intelligence Failure,'" *Foreign Policy Journal*, March 3, 2013. Jeremy R. Hammond, "The U.S.'s 'Coercive Diplomacy with Iran and Lessons Unlearned from Iraq," *Foreign Policy Journal*, February 3, 2013. *Fars News*, August 21, 2013 (Ziabari interview, Chapter 9 notes). For a definitive account, see: Gareth Porter, *Manufactured Crisis: The Untold Story of the Iran Nuclear Scare* (Charlottesville, Virginia: Just World Books, 2014).

172. Colin H. Kahl, "Obama Has Been Great for Israel: Anyone who tells you otherwise is distorting reality," *Foreign Policy*, August 16, 2012.

173. Haim Saban, "The Truth About Obama and Israel," *New York Times*, September 4, 2012.

174. "Obama lead over Romney grows among Jewish voters," *Haaretz*, September 15, 2012.

175. "American Opinions on the Israeli-Palestinian Conflict – 2012," *Arab American Institute*, August 2012. The full survey results are available online at http://b.3cdn.net/aai/0e61f1a90e5a6064ed_szm6bn949.pdf.

176. "President Obama's Mid-East adviser Dennis Ross resigns," *BBC*, November 10, 2011. Douglas Bloomfield, "A 12-step plan to sober up for peace," *Jerusalem Post*, July 25, 2012.

177. United Nations Relief and Works Agency, *Gaza In 2020: A Liveable Place?*, August 28, 2012. Isabel Kershner, "U.N. Sees Bleak Outlook for Gaza Unless Services Are Improved," *New York Times*, August 28, 2012. Note also that the headline of the *Times* article deflects blame away from the illegal blockade onto Gazans' own "Services".

178. Breaking the Silence, *Breaking the Silence: Children and Youth – Soldier's Testimonies 2005-2011*, August 2012. For examples of international coverage, see: Donald MacIntyre, "Israel breaks silence over army abuses: Ex-soldiers admit to appalling violence against Palestinian children," *Independent*, August 26, 2012. Harriet Sherwood, "Former Israeli soldiers disclose routine mistreatment of Palestin-

ian children," *The Guardian*, August 26, 2012. John Lyons, "Israeli soldiers break silence on abuse," *The Australian*, August 25, 2012. Pierre Klochendler, "Israeli Soldiers Show No Mercy to Palestinian Children," *Inter Press Service*, August 26, 2012. "Israel ex-soldiers say troops abused Palestinian kids," *Agence France-Press*, August 26, 2012. A search by this author for articles containing the phrase "Breaking the Silence" in articles from August 2012 turned up no results at the *Washington Post* and the *Los Angeles Time*, one at the *New York Times*—in a blog post about scientists conducting research in Antarctica.

179. Mohammed Daraghmeh, "Abbas to move on UN membership bid in September," *Times of Israel*, August 4, 2012. John Donnison, "Faded hopes of Palestinian place at UN," *BBC*, September 14, 2012.

180. Donnison, "Faded hopes."

181. Jodi Rudoren, "Year After Effort at U.N., New Aim for Palestinians," *New York Times*, September 20, 2012.

182. "Palestinians appeal for support for UN member-state bid," *BBC*, August 14, 2012.

183. Jodi Rudoren, "Before Palestinians Act at U.N., Israeli Officials Urge Other Steps," *New York Times*, September 24, 2012.

184. Rudoren, "New Aim for Palestinians."

185. Ibid.

186. The White House, "Remarks by the President to the UN General Assembly," September 25, 2012. Human Rights Watch, *Death of a Dictator: Bloody vengeance in Sirte*, October 17, 2012.

187. White House, September 25, 2012.

188. Karen DeYoung and Liz Sly, "Syrian rebels get influx of arms with gulf neighbors' money, U.S. coordination," *Washington Post*, May 15, 2012. Jay Solomon and Nour Malas, "U.S. Bolsters Ties to Fighters in Syria," *Wall Street Journal*, June 13, 2012. Eric Schmitt, "C.I.A. Said to Aid in Steering Arms to Syrian Opposition," *New York Times*, June 21, 2012. Mark Hosenball, "Exclusive: Obama authorizes secret U.S. support for Syrian rebels," *Reuters*, August 1, 2012. "UN warns 'foreign fighters' filtering into Syria, echoing Jordanian fears," *Reuters*, December 20, 2012. Rod Nordland, "Al Qaeda Taking Deadly New Role in Syria's Conflict," *New York Times*, July 24, 2012. Tim Arango, Anne Barnard, and Hwaida Saad, "Syrian Rebels Tied to Al Qaeda Play Key Role in War," *New York Times*, December 8, 2012.

189. David E. Sanger, "Rebel Arms Flow Is Said to Benefit Jihadists in Syria," *New York Times*, October 14, 2012.

190. White House, September 25, 2012.

191. Permanent Observer Mission of Palestine to the United Nations, "Statement by H.E. Mr. Mahmoud Abbas, President of the State of Palestine, Chairman of the Executive Committee of the Palestine Liberation Organization, President of the Palestinian National Authority, before the United Nations General Assembly Sixty-seventh Session, General Debate," *GADebate.UN.org*, September 27, 2012.

192. "Full Text: Benjamin Netanyahu's Speech at the United Nations General Assembly," *National Journal*, September 27, 2012.

193. Harriet Sherwood, "US warns European governments against supporting Palestinians at UN," *The Guardian*, October 1, 2012.

194. "Palestinians send envoys to Europe to campaign for UN recognition," *Associated Press*, October 31, 2012.

195. "Palestinians set November 29 as date for UN bid for status upgrade," *Associated Press*, November 12, 2012.

196. US Senate, Office of Maryland Senator Ben Cardin, "Cardin, Collins Send Letter To Abbas Opposing Attempts By Palestinians To Pursue Non-Member State Status At The United Nations," November 21, 2012.

197. Barak Ravid, "Clinton warns Netanyahu not to punish Palestinian Authority for UN bid," *Haaretz*, November 23, 2012.

198. Isabel Kershner, "Palestinians Renew Push for Enhanced U.N. Status," *New York Times*, November 9, 2012

199. Ori Lewis, "Invoking 'the rules', Israel mulls toppling Abbas," *Reuters*, November 14, 2012.

200. Barak Ravid, "Israel: We will annul Oslo Accords if Palestinians seek upgraded UN status," *Haaretz*, November 14, 2012.

201. Bernard Avishai, "Former Israeli PM Olmert Supports Palestine U.N. Bid," *Daily Beast*, November 28, 2012.

202. "Palestinians at the U.N., Again," *New York Times*, November 4, 2012.

203. "The Palestinians' U.N. Bid," *New York Times*, November 28, 2012.

204. Michael R. Gordon and Mark Landler, "U.S. and Israel Look to Limit Impact of U.N. Vote on Palestinian Authority," *New York Times*, November 28, 2012.

205. Ravid, "We will annul Oslo Accords." United Nations General Assembly, 32nd Session, 91st Plenary Meeting, Resolution 32/40, *Question of Palestine*, A/RES/32/40 (December 2, 1977).

206. Israel Ministry of Foreign Affairs, "Israel under fire-November 2012," November 22, 2012.

207. Elad Benari, "IAF Strikes Terror Targets in Gaza," *Arutz Sheva*, June 18, 2012.

208. Gil Ronen, "Grad Rocket Fired from Jordan?" *Arutz Sheva*, June 16, 2012. "Gaza Terrorists Fire Rockets at IDF Patrol," *Arutz Sheva*, June 17, 2012.

209. Arutz Sheva, June 17, 2012.

210. Benari, "IAF Strikes."

211. Ron Friedman and Mitch Ginsburg, "Haifa man killed in ambush at Egyptian border," *Times of Israel*, June 18, 2012.

212. "Implications of the death of Hisham Saidani, a top global jihad operative in the Gaza Strip, who died in a targeted killing carried out by the IDF," *Meir Amit Intelligence and Terrorism Information Center*, October 18, 2012.

213. Jacob Høigilt and Frida Nome, "Egyptian Salafism in Revolution," *Journal of Islamic Studies*, Vol. 26, Issue 1, January 2015, 35. Salafism is heavily inspired by Wahhabism, another radical sect originating from Saudi Arabia.

214. Levy, "2 terrorist killed." Fares Akram, "Israeli Airstrike Kills 2 Militants in Gaza," *New York Times*, October 13, 2012.

215. Benari, "IAF Strikes." Maayana Miskin, "Rocket Onslaught; Residents Ordered Into Shelters," *Arutz Sheva*, June 19, 2012.

216. "Hamas 'ready for truce' following fighting with Israel," *BBC*, June 20, 2012. Isabel Kershner, "Hamas Military Wing Accepts a Cease-Fire," *New York Times*, June 20, 2012. The *Times* acknowledged that "Hamas had joined in the latest round of fighting after a break of more than a year during which the group largely adhered to an informal cease-fire. . . . " Harriet Sherwood, "Hamas ready for ceasefire 'if Israel stops its aggression' in Gaza," *The Guardian*, June 21, 2012. "Israeli air strike kills Gaza militant, breaks truce," *Reuters*, June 22, 2012. "Tentative talk of ceasefire after Gaza terrorists fire 25 rockets at Sderot area," *Times of Israel*, June 23, 2012.

217. Saleh Salem, "Israel kills two in strikes on Gaza as truce falters," *Reuters*, June 23, 2012. Yaakov Katz, Yaakov Lappin, and Herb Keinon, "IDF: Quiet, violence to be met in kind," *Jerusalem Post*, June 23, 2012. The *Post* acknowledged that other groups, "although not Hamas", were responsible for the rocket fire for which Israel retaliated by striking Hamas targets.

218. Calev Ben-David and Gwen Ackerman, "Egypt-Brokered Cease-Fire With Israel Declared by Hamas," *Bloomberg*, June 24, 2012.

219. Moran Stern, "The Unlikeliest Peace: Why Israel and Hamas Have (Mostly) Stopped Fighting," *The Atlantic*, July 3, 2012. The truth, of course, was that Israel's so-called "counter-attack" *preceded* the Hamas rocket fire.

220. Israel Defense Forces, "IAF Targets Terrorist Operatives in the Gaza Strip," October 7, 2012. Office of the United Nations Special Coordinator for the Middle East Peace Process, "Jeffrey Feltman, Under Secretary-General for Political Affairs: Briefing to the Security Council on the Situation in the Middle East," October 15, 2012.

221. "Hamas fires dozens of rockets, mortars into Israel, vows to launch more if Israel strikes again," *Times of Israel*, October 8, 2012. The *Times* noted it was unusual for Hamas to claim responsibility for rocket fire and that this was the first time since June that it had done so. Ezzedeen Al-Qassam Brigades Information Office, "Abu Obedia: Aggression will bring a stronger response," www.qassam.ps, October 8, 2012.

222. Isabel Kershner and Fares Akram, "Israel Launches Airstrikes After Attacks From Gaza," *New York Times*, October 8, 2012. The headline appearing in the print edition the following day was "Israel: Military Strikes in Gaza After Rocket Attacks". The *Times* also noted that "Hamas had largely adhered to an informal, if fragile, cease-fire with Israel and has acted in the past to rein in smaller groups," this being the first time since June "that Hamas joined in firing rockets at Israel", mostly striking "uninhabited areas". A petting zoo was also struck, killing several goats.

223. Fares Akram, "Israeli Airstrike Kills 2 Militants in Gaza," *New York Times*, October 13, 2012.

224. Elior Levy, "2 terrorist killed in IAF strikes in Gaza," *Ynetnews*, October 13, 2012. "Israeli airstrike targets terror operatives in Gaza," *CNN*, October 13, 2012 (updated October 15).

225. UNSCO, Feltman Briefing, October 15, 2012. CNN, "Israeli airstrike."

226. "Implications of the death of Hisham Saidani, a top global jihad operative in the Gaza Strip, who died in a targeted killing carried out by the IDF," *Meir Amit Intelligence and Terrorism Information Center*, October 18, 2012.

227. Israel Defense Forces, "IAF Targets Terrorist Operatives in the Gaza Strip," October 13, 2012.

228. Amos Harell, "For first time, Palestinians in Gaza fire missile at IAF helicopter," *Haaretz*, October 16, 2012.

229. "Man-Portable Air Defense System (MANPADS) Proliferation," *Federation of American Scientists*, accessed at www.fas.org February 19, 2014. Steve Galster, "Afghanistan: The Making of U.S. Policy, 1973-1990," *George Washington University National Security Archive*, October 9, 2001.

230. "Libyan multiple-rocket launchers and SA-7 anti-air missiles from Gaza," *DEBKAfile*, March 10, 2012.

231. Harell, "For first time."

232. Christina Lamb, "Covert US plan to arm rebels," *Sunday Times*, December 9, 2012. Geoffrey Ingersoll and Michael Kelley, "REPORT: The US Is Openly Sending Heavy Weapons From Libya To Syrian Rebels," *Business Insider*, December 9, 2012.

233. Adam Entous, Siobhan Gorman, and Margaret Coker, "CIA Takes Heat for Role in Libya," *Wall Street Journal*, November 1, 2012.

234. Mark Hosenball, "U.S. intelligence set back when Libya base abandoned," *Reuters*, October 13, 2012.

235. Drew Griffin and Kathleen Johnston, "Exclusive: Dozens of CIA operatives on the ground during Benghazi attack," The Lead, *CNN*, August 1, 2013.

236. Catherine Herridge and Pamela Browne, "Was Syrian weapons shipment factor in ambassador's Benghazi visit?" *Fox News*, October 25, 2012.

237. Michael Kelley, "There's A Reason Why All Of The Reports About Benghazi Are So Confusing," *Business Insider*, November 3, 2012. Ruth Sherlock, "Leading Libyan Islamist met Free Syrian Army opposition group," *The Telegraph*, November 27, 2011.

238. "US Names Chris Stevens Liaison to Libyan Opposition," *ABC News Radio*, March 14, 2011. Michael Kelley, "How US Ambassador Chris Stevens May Have Been Linked To Jihadist Rebels In Syria," *Business Insider*, October 19, 2012.

239. Julian Borger, "Arms and the Manpads: Syrian rebels get anti-aircraft missiles," *The Guardian*, November 28, 2012. Rowan Scarborough, "Missiles flow into Syria, risk falling into hands of al Qaeda," *Washington Times*, November 6, 2013.

240. Crispian Balmer, "War will not resolve Gaza problem: Israeli official," *Reuters*, October 17, 2012.

241. Fares Akram and Isabel Kershner, "Hamas Finds Itself Aligned With Israel Over Extremist Groups," *New York Times*, October 19, 2012. In August 2009, Hamas confronted the group in a shootout at a mosque in Rafah, where 100 of the group's men were holed up; 28 were killed, including the group's leader, Abdel Latif Moussa.

242. Amos Harel and Avi Issacharoff, "Hamas policy on attacking Israel has changed," *Haaretz*, October 24, 2012.

243. "Israel Seizes Gaza-bound boat in International Waters, Defying International Law Kidnaps Parliamentarians and activists," *The Free Gaza Movement*, October 20, 2012.

244. "Israeli Navy boards Gaza-bound ship 'Estelle,'" *Jerusalem Post*, October 20, 2012.

245. "Gaza boat activists accuse Israel navy of using Tasers," *Agence France-Presse*, October 21, 2012.

246. Yoel Goldman and Michal Shmulovich, "Netanyahu says Gaza-bound activists aimed to provoke, slander Israel," *Times of Israel*, October 20, 2012.

247. Amira Hass, "2,279 calories per person: How Israel made sure Gaza didn't starve," *Haaretz*, October 17, 2012. A full translation of the document provided by Gisha is available at *Haaretz.com*.

248. Joel Greenberg, "Israel reckons with unraveling Gaza policy," *Washington Post*, October 30, 2012.

249. "Violence ends Israel-Gaza truce," *BBC*, October 29, 2012.

250. "Gaza: Israeli Forces Kill Palestinian Man," *Associated Press*, November 5, 2012.

251. "IDF kills Palestinian approaching Gaza security fence," *Reuters*, November 5, 2012. Office for the Coordination of Humanitarian Affairs, "Protection of Civilians Weekly Report: 31 October – 6 November 2012," November 6, 2012.

252. OCHA, November 6, 2012. Gili Cohen, Yaniv Kubovich, Jack Khoury, and Avi Issacharoff, "Four IDF soldiers wounded when Gaza anti-tank missile hits jeep on border," *Haaretz*, November 10, 2012.

253. "Israeli gunfire kills Palestinian boy in Gaza clash: medics," *Reuters*, November 8, 2012. Ilan Ben Zion, "Gaza boy reportedly killed by Israeli troops," *Times of Israel*, November 8, 2012. "Gaza boy killed by Israel dreamed of becoming soccer player," *Ma'an News Agency*, November 10, 2012. "New Israeli

Escalation against the Gaza Strip, 7 Palestinians, Including 3 Children, Killed and 52 Others, Including 6 Women and 12 Children, Wounded," *Palestinian Centre for Human Rights*, November 11, 2012. "Israel's Barack pledges response," *Agence France-Presse*, November 9, 2012.

254. Cohen, et al, "Four IDF soldiers wounded." AFP, November 9, 2012. Ben Zion, "Gaza boy reportedly killed."

255. Cohen, et al, "Four IDF soldiers wounded." Ilan Ben Zion and Elhanan Miller, "Four soldiers injured, two seriously, by anti-tank missile fired at their jeep from Gaza; rocket fire on South," *Times of Israel*, November 10, 2012.

256. Cohen, et al, "Four IDF soldiers wounded." Ben Zion and Miller, "Four soldiers injured." Ilan Ben Zion and Elhanan Miller, "Southern Israel comes under rocket attack from Gaza, IDF strikes back from the air," *Times of Israel*, November 11, 2012. Nidal Al-Mughrabi, "Gaza flares as Israel hits back killing five," *Reuters*, November 10, 2012. PCHR, November 11, 2012.

257. Cohen, et al, "Four IDF soldiers wounded." Ben Zion and Miller, "Four soldiers injured." Ben Zion and Miller, "Southern Israel comes under rocket attack."

258. Al-Mughrabi, "Gaza flares."

259. PCHR, November 11, 2012.

260. Ibid.

261. "'We Have to Take Out Hamas Leadership,'" *Arutz Sheva*, November 11, 2012.

262. "Minister Dichter: We need to reformat Gaza," *Ynetnews*, November 11, 2012.

263. Barak Ravid, "PMO: Netanyahu wants to prepare international public opinion for Gaza operation," *Haaretz*, November 11, 2012.

264. Elior Levy, "Report: Egypt brokers lull between Israel, Gaza terror groups," *Ynetnews*, November 11, 2012.

265. "Gaza factions meet over Israeli threats," *Ma'an News Agency*, November 12, 2012.

266. Avi Issacharoff, "Palestinian militants agree to Gaza truce if Israel ends all military operations," *Haaretz*, November 12, 2012.

267. "Israel, Gaza agree to hold fire after latest round of fighting," *Reuters*, November 13, 2012.

268. Ibid.

269. United Nations, "Statement Issued by the Spokesperson for U.N. Secretary-General Ban Ki-moon," November 12, 2012.

270. Reuters, November 13, 2012.

271. Yair Rosenberg, "Here's What 'Pillar of Defense' Actually Means," *Tablet Magazine*, November 14, 2012.

272. "66 killed and wounded in a series of Israeli attacks on Gaza, Al Mezan condemns IOF escalation and calls for urgent international intervention," *Al Mezan Center for Human Rights*, November 14, 2012. Robert Mackey, "Israel's Military Begins Social Media Offensive as Bombs Fall on Gaza," The Lede, *New York Times*, November 14, 2012. "New Israeli Military Escalation against the Gaza Strip," *Palestinian Centre for Human Rights*, November 15, 2012. There were contradictory reports regarding Ranan's age. The PCHR initially reported that she was three, then revised her age to five. According to the caption of an AFP/Getty Images photo of her taken by Mahmud Hams at her funeral the following day, she was four. The *New York Times*, apparently in reference Ranan, said a seven-year-old girl was killed. See: Isabel Kershner and Fares Akram, "Ferocious Israeli Assault on Gaza Kills a Leader of Hamas," *New York Times*, November 14, 2012. HRW likewise reported that she was seven: "Israel/Gaza: Avoid Harm to Civilians," *Human Rights Watch*, November 15, 2012.

273. Kershner and Akram, "Ferocious Israeli Assault."

274. Lapping and Lazaroff, "Gazans fire 95 rockets."

275. Kershner and Akram, "Ferocious Israeli Assault."

276. Ibid.

277. Yaakov Lappin and Tovah Lazaroff, "Gazans fire 95 rockets after Jabari hit," *Jerusalem Post*, November 15, 2012.

278. Lappin and Lazaroff, "Gazans fire 95 rockets."

279. "Avnery On the Deliberate Cynicism," Press Release, *Gush Shalom*, November 14, 2012.

280. Barak Ravid, "Ahead of Gaza offensive, Netanyahu's Israel did its best to lull Hamas to sleep," *Haaretz*, November 15, 2012.

281. Aluf Benn, "Israel killed its subcontractor in Gaza," *Haaretz*, November 14, 2012.

282. Reuven Pedatzur, "Why did Israel kill Jabari?" *Haaretz*, December 4, 2012.

283. Gershon Baskin, "Assassinating The Chance For Calm," *Daily Beast*, November 15, 2012. See also: Gershon Baskin, "Israel's Shortsighted Assassination," *New York Times*, November 16, 2012.

284. Nir Hasson, "Israeli peace activist: Hamas leader Jabari killed amid talks on long-term truce," *Haaretz*, November 15, 2012.

285. Gershon Baskin, "Israel's Shortsighted Assassination," *New York Times*, November 16, 2012.

286. David Lev, "Obama to PM: Green Light, But Watch Out for Civilians," *Arutz Sheva*, November 15, 2012.

287. Elad Benari, "Panetta to Barak: Israel Has the Right to Defend Itself," *Arutz Sheva*, November 16, 2012.

288. Peter Beaumont, "Egypt condemns Israeli air strikes in Gaza and demands ceasefire," *The Guardian*, November 14, 2012.

289. Kershner and Akram, "Ferocious Israeli Assault."

290. "Another Israel-Gaza War?" *New York Times*, November 14, 2012.

291. Isabel Kershner and Rick Gladstone, "Israel and Hamas Step Up Air Attacks in Gaza Clash," *New York Times*, November 15, 2012.

292. Karin Brulliard and Joel Greenberg, "Three Israelis killed by rocket fired from Gaza Strip; Israel intensifies air offensive," *Washington Post*, November 15, 2012. The original title can still be seen in the article's URL on the *Washington Post* website, as well as on websites that archived it before it was changed.

293. HRW, November 15, 2012.

294. Beaumont, "Egypt condemns Israeli air strikes."

295. Barak Mendelsohn, "Hamas's Miscalculation," *Foreign Affairs*, November 18, 2012.

296. Daniel Kurtzer, "The Peace Process Isn't Dead," *Foreign Policy*, November 15, 2012.

297. S.RES.599 and H.RES.813, 112th Congress, *Expressing vigorous support and unwavering commitment to the welfare, security, and survival of the State of Israel as a Jewish and democratic state with secure borders, and recognizing and strongly supporting its right to act in self-defense to protect its citizens against acts of terrorism*, November 15, 2012. Ron Kampeas, "Senate, House resolutions back Israel's actions in Gaza," *Jewish Telegraphic Agency*, November 16, 2012.

298. Nidal Al-Bughrabi, "Rockets hit near Tel Aviv as Gaza death toll rises," *Reuters*, November 15, 2012. UN Relief and Works Agency, "Death of UNRWA Teacher In Gaza," November 15, 2012. UN Relief and Works Agency, "Gaza Situation Report," November 15, 2012.

299. Fares Akram, Jodi Rudoren, and Alan Cowell, "Hamas Leader Dares Israel to Invade Amid Gaza Airstrikes," *New York Times*, November 19, 2012.

300. "LIVE BLOG: Day 2 of Israel-Gaza conflict 2012," *Haaretz*, November 15, 2012. Barak Ravid, Gili Cohen, Avi Issacharoff, Amos Harel, and Allison Kaplan Sommer, "Rocket barrage on Israel's south continues overnight, IDF striking in Gaza," *Haaretz*, November 15, 2012.

301. Nidal Al-Mughrabi and Jeffrey Heller, "Israel authorizes more reservists after rockets target cities," *Reuters*, November 16, 2012. "28 Palestinians killed and 292 injured in continued IOF attacks on Gaza," *Al Mezan Center for Human Rights*, November 16, 2012.

302. Ethan Bronner, "As Battlefield Changes, Israel Takes Tougher Approach," *New York Times*, November 16, 2012.

303. Roger Cohen, "Gaza Without End," *New York Times*, November 19, 2012.

304. Al-Mughrabi and Heller, "Israel authorizes more reservists."

305. United Nations Relief and Works Agency, "Gaza Situation Report," November 16, 2012. UNRWA noted that "sporadic air strikes and rocket firing were reported" during the three-hour lull. Jodi Rudoren and Fares Akram, "Mistaken Lull, Simple Errand, Death in Gaza," *New York Times*, November 16, 2012. The *Times* reported that rocket fire continued during Qandil's visit and that, while Israel said it had suspended airstrikes, "at least two of the familiar booms of F-16 bombardments were heard in Gaza City".

306. "On the 4th day of IOF aggression, casualties on the rise: 37 killed, 398 injured, and houses directly attacked," *Al Mezan Center for Human Rights*, November 17, 2012. Amira Hass, "Fear and loathing in Gaza as offensive continues," *Haaretz*, November 17, 2012. Nidal Al-Mughrabi and Jeffrey Heller, "Israel hits Hamas buildings, shoots down Tel Aviv-bound rocket," *Reuters*, November 17, 2012. Jodi Rudoren and Isabel Kershner, "Israel Broadens Its Bombing in Gaza to Include Government Sites," *New York Times*, November 17, 2012.

307. World Health Organization, "World Health Organization concerned over the emergency situation in Gaza," November 17, 2012.

308. Hass, "Fear and loathing."

309. Al-Mughrabi and Heller, "Israel hits Hamas buildings." Rudoren and Kershner, "Israel Broadens Its Bombing."

310. "Live Blog: Day 4 of Israel-Gaza conflict 2012," *Haaretz*, November 17, 2012.

311. "Israel's minister of incitement," *Haaretz*, November 20, 2012.

312. Eli Lake, "Netanyahu: No Current Plans for Gaza Ground War," *The Daily Beast*, November 17, 2012.

313. The Israel Defense Forces (@IDFSpokesperson), Twitter post, November 17, 2012, 3:16 pm.

314. Israel Defense Forces, "Hamas Terrorist Tactics in the Gaza Strip," *YouTube* video, 4:32, November 10, 2011.

315. United Nations Relief and Works Agency, "False Social Media Allegations About UNRWA," November 20, 2012.

316. United Nations Relief and Works Agency, "No Rockets from UNRWA Schools in Gaza During the Gaza War of 2008-2009," October 24, 2012.

317. United Nations Relief and Works Agency, "Gaza Situation Report, 20 November," November 20, 2012.

318. The White House, "Remarks by President Obama and Prime Minister Shinawatra in a Joint Press Conference," November 18, 2012.

319. Ron Paul, "How To End the Tragedy in Gaza," *LewRockwell.com*, November 27, 2012.

320. Jodi Rudoren, Fares Akram, and Isabel Kershner, "Israeli Airstrike Kills Three Generations of a Palestinian Family," *New York Times*, November 18, 2012.

321. "Israeli Airstrike on Home Unlawful," *Human Rights Watch*, December 7, 2012.

322. Harriet Sherwood, "Gaza: 'My child was killed and nothing has changed,'" *The Guardian*, December 11, 2012.

323. HRW, December 7, 2012.

324. Jodi Rudoren, "Hoisting Dead Children, Gazans Mourn Family Killed by Israeli Strike," *New York Times*, November 19, 2012. Recall that Rudoren is the same reporter who'd earlier described Palestinians as "somewhat inured to violence".

325. Philip Weiss, "Gazans are 'ho-hum' about the deaths of relatives—NYT's Rudoren," *Mondoweiss*, November 20, 2012.

326. Rudoren, et al, "Israeli Airstrike Kills Three Generations." "Direct IOF airstrike targets media offices and workers in Gaza," *Human Rights Watch*, November 18, 2012.

327. Alex Thomson, "Journalists among the injured in Gaza," Alex Thomson's View, *Channel 4*, November 18, 2012.

328. "RWB Condemns Air Strikes on News Media in Gaza City," *Reporters Without Borders*, November 18, 2012.

329. Rudoren, et al, "Israeli Airstrike Kills Three Generations."

330. United Nations, "Statement by the Secretary-General on the situation in the Middle East," November 18, 2012.

331. David D. Kirkpatrick and Mayy El Sheikh, "An Outgunned Hamas Tries to Tap Islamists' Growing Clout," *New York Times*, November 18, 2012.

332. George Friedman, "A Pause for Negotiations in the Israeli-Hamas Conflict," *Stratfor*, November 18, 2012.

333. Gilad Sharon, "A decicive conclusion is necessary," *Jerusalem Post*, November 18, 2012.

334. Cohen, "Gaza Without End."

335. United Nations Office for the Coordination of Humanitarian Affairs, "Escalation in Hostilities in Gaza and Southern Israel," November 19, 2012.

336. "Israel/Gaza conflict: UN must impose arms embargo, send international monitors immediately," *Amnesty International*, November 19, 2012.

337. "38 aid agencies warn of humanitarian disaster in Gaza if military confrontation is not stopped," *Oxfam International*, November 19, 2012.

338. Matt Bradley, Sam Dagher, and Joshua Mitnick, "Gaza Toll Rises as a Top Militant Is Targeted," *Wall Street Journal*, November 19, 2012. "US blocks UN Security Council call for Gaza cease-fire as unbalanced against Israel," *Associated Press*, November 20, 2012.

339. Akram, et al, "Hamas Leader Dares Israel." Rudoren, "Gazans Mourn Family."

340. "Hamas's Illegitimacy," *New York Times*, November 19, 2012.

341. Josef Federman and Ibrahim Barzak, "Israel Gaza Attacks Intensify Despite Truce Talks," *Associated Press*, November 20, 2012.

342. "Israel's Latest War With Hamas," *Council on Foreign Relations*, November 19, 2012.

343. Amira Hass, "Israel's 'right to self-defense' – a tremendous propaganda victory," *Haaretz*, November 19, 2012.

344. Akram, et al, "Hamas Leader Dares Israel."

345. Bronner and Kirkpatrick, "U.S. Seeks Truce." David D. Kirkpatrick and Jodi Rudoren, "Israel and Hamas Agree to a Cease-Fire, After a U.S.-Egypt Push," *New York Times*, November 21, 2012.

346. Ethan Bronner, "Gaza Crisis Poses Threat to Faction Favored by U.S.," *New York Times*, November 19, 2012.

347. Chemi Shalev, "A triple-crown achievement for Obama's Middle East policies," *Haaretz*, November 22, 2012.

348. "Mashaal vows to Gaza crowds Hamas will not concede land," *Jerusalem Post*, December 8, 2012.

349. "Gaza: War Gives Hamas an Electoral Victory in the West Bank and the Gaza Strip if Elections Are Held Today," Palestinian Center for Policy and Survey Research, *Konrad Adenauer Stiftung*, December 17, 2012.

350. David Carr, "Using War as Cover to Target Journalists," *New York Times*, November 25, 2012. See also: Federman and Barzak, "Israel Gaza Attacks Intensify."

351. Israel Defense Forces (@IDFSpokesperson), Twitter post, November 18, 2012, 7:28 a.m.

352. "Unlawful Israeli Attacks on Palestinian Media," *Human Rights Watch*, December 20, 2012. Carr, "Using War as Cover to Target Journalists."

353. "Timeline: Israel launches Operation Pillar of Defense amid Gaza escalation," *Haaretz*, November 20, 2012. Ethan Bronner and David D. Kirkpatrick, "U.S. Seeks Truce on Gaza as Enemies Step Up Attacks," *New York Times*, November 20, 2012.

354. United Nations Office for the Coordination of Humanitarian Affairs, "Escalation in Hostilities in Gaza and Southern Israel," November 20, 2012. "Israel army leaflet warns Gazans to leave homes," *Agence France-Presse*, November 20, 2012. "IOF target more civilians and spark wide-scale displacement in Gaza," *Al Mezan Center for Human Rights*, November 20, 2012.

355. Jodi Rudoren, "Missile's Firing, Bomb Blasts and Sirens Shatter Gaza Calm," *New York Times*, November 20, 2012.

356. Ben Hartman, "Terror attack rocks Dan bus in central Tel Aviv," *Jerusalem Post*, November 21, 2012.

357. Elad Benari, "Hamas Not Behind Tel Aviv Attack, Claims Mashaal," *Arutz Sheva*, November 22, 2012. "Mashaal: I accept a Palestinian state on '67 borders," *Jerusalem Post*, November 22, 2012.

358. "Hamas cries victory; truce with Israel holds," *USA Today*, November 22, 2012. "Tel Aviv bus bomber sentenced to 25 years," *Haaretz*, March 10, 2014.

359. Anup Kaphle, "Full text: Terms of Israel-Palestinian cease-fire," WorldViews, *Washington Post*, November 21, 2012.

360. Barak Ravid, "Behind the scenes of Israel's decision to accept Gaza truce," *Haaretz*, November 22, 2012.

361. Barak Ravid, "Cease-fire agreement almost identical to that reached in Operation Cast Lead," *Haaretz*, November 22, 2012.

362. Kirkpatrick and Rudoren, "Israel and Hamas Agree to a Ceasefire."

363. Chemi Shalev, "A triple-crown achievement for Obama's Middle East policies," *Haaretz*, November 22, 2012.

364. David E. Sanger and Thom Shanker, "For Israel, Gaza Conflict Is Test for an Iran Confrontation," *New York Times*, November 22, 2012.

365. "Egypt, Gaza and the Sinai Peninsula," *Stratfor*, November 16, 2012. Peter Baker and David D. Kirkpatrick, "Egyptian President and Obama Forge Link in Gaza Deal," *New York Times*, November 21, 2012.

366. United Nations Office for the Coordination of Humanitarian Affairs, "Occupied Palestinian Territory: Escalation in hostilities," November 22, 2012. World Health Organization, "Situation Report: Gaza," November 27, 2012.

367. Gili Cohen, "B'Tselem: More than 50% of Palestinians killed in Israel's last Gaza operation were civilians," *Haaretz*, May 9, 2013.

368. United Nations Office for the Coordination of Humanitarian Affairs, "Gaza Initial Rapid Assessment: Final Report," November, 2012.

369. Catherine Weibel, "In Gaza, children returning to school are scarred by violence," *United Nations Children's Fund* (UNICEF), November 27, 2012.

370. Jodi Rudoren and Isabel Kershner, "Factions in Gaza Make Unity Vow After Cease-Fire," *New York Times*, November 22, 2012.

371. Martin Hartberg, "Beyond Ceasefire: Ending the blockade of Gaza," *Oxfam International*, December 6, 2012.

372. "Ceasefire re-awakens dreams of Gaza fisherman," *International Solidarity Movement*, November 27, 2012. "OPT: Call for freer access to Gaza land and sea," *IRIN*, December 11, 2012. UN Office of the High Commissioner for Human Rights, "Israel must deliver on cease-fire agreement in the Gaza Strip – UN Special Rapporteur," December 5, 2012. Steven Erlanger and Fares Akram, "Gaza Cease-Fire Helps Fisherman, but Risks Remain," *New York Times*, December 24, 2012.

373. "Five Palestinians wounded by IDF fire on Gaza border," *Reuters*, December 21, 2012. Gili Cohen and Chaim Levinson, "IDF arrests 55 Palestinians in West Bank, on heels of Gaza truce," *Haaretz*, November 22, 2012.

374. Jodi Rudoren and Isabel Kershner, "Tension and Confusion Linger in Gaza Strip After Cease-Fire," *New York Times*, November 23, 2012.

375. Avital Leibovich (@AvitalLeibovich), Twitter post, November 23, 2012, 5:55 a.m. Leibovich, Twitter post, 6:12 a.m. Leibovich, Twitter post, 8:18 a.m.

376. Rudoren and Kershner, "Tension and Confusion Linger."

377. "Israeli gunfire kills Palestinian near border after truce," *Reuters*, November 23, 2012.

378. Reuters, "Five Palestinians wounded."

379. Karl Vick, "Politics and the Defense Minister: Why Ehud Barak Resigned," *Time*, November 26, 2012.

380. Sanger and Shanker, "Gaza Conflict Is Test."

381. Nafeez Mosaddq Ahmed, "Israel's War for Gaza's Gas," *Le Monde Diplomatique*, November 2012. Moshe Yaalon, "Does the Prospective Purchase of British Gas from Gaza Threaten Israel's National Security?" *Jerusalem Center for Public Affairs*, October 19, 2007.

382. Norman Finkelstein, "Israel's Latest Assault on Gaza – What Really Happened," *New Left Project*, November 28, 2012.

383. OHCHR, December 5, 2012.

384. Yousef Munayyer, "America's Failed Palestinian Policy," *New York Times*, November 23, 2012.

385. Paul, "How To End the Tragedy in Gaza."

386. Barak Ravid, "U.S. to sell Israel munitions to renew stock after Operation Pillar of Defense," *Haaretz*, December 11, 2012.

387. "Abbas' Speech to the UN General Assembly, November 2012," *Council on Foreign Relations*, November 29, 2012.

388. Barak Ravid, Chemi Shalev, and Natasha Mozgovaya, "In historic vote, Palestine becomes non-member UN state with observer status," *Haaretz*, November 30, 2012.

389. United Nations General Assembly, 67th Session, Draft Resolution, *Status of Palestine in the United Nations*, A/67/L.28 (November 26, 2012).

390. United Nations General Assembly, 67th Session, 44th Plenary Meeting, Resolution 67/19, *Status of Palestine in the United Nations*, A/RES/67/19 (November 29, 2012). US Department of State, Embassy in Warsaw, "Secretary Clinton's Remarks at the Foreign Policy Group's 'Transformational Trends 2013' Forum," November 29, 2012.

391. Ravid, et al, "In historic vote."

392. Barak Ravid, "Israel suffers humiliating defeat at UN," *Haaretz*, November 30, 2012.

393. Ethan Bronner and Christine Hauser, "U.N. Assembly, in Blow to U.S., Elevates Status of Palestine," *New York Times*, November 29, 2012.

394. Robert Blecher, "Abbas' New York Minute," *Foreign Affairs*, December 1, 2012.

395. "Palestine: Newest 'Observer State' Should Act on Rights Treaties," *Human Rights Watch*, November 29, 2012.

396. "Could Israel be Brought Before the International Criminal Court?" *Institute for Public Accuracy*, November 29, 2012.

397. Isabel Kershner, "After Vote, Palestinians and Israel Search for the Next Step," *New York Times*, November 29, 2012.

398. Joel Greenberg, "Abbas returns home to hero's welcome, but faces fresh punishment from Israel," *Washington Post*, December 2, 2012.

399. The Israeli peace group Peace Now pointed out that the E1 plan "could be the death blow to the two states solution. It is meant to prevent the territorial continuity of the Palestinian state, to cut between the north and south of the West Bank and to isolate East Jerusalem from the Palestinian territories". "The Government Announced 3,000 Units in Settlements and the Promotion of Plans in E1," *Peace Now*, December 1, 2012. *Haaretz* noted that the E1 plan "would prevent territorial contiguity between the northern and southern West Bank, making it difficult for a future Palestinian state to function." Barak Ravid, "In response to UN vote, Israel to build 3,000 new homes in settlements," *Haaretz*,

November 30, 2012. The *New York Times* acknowledged that it "could prevent the creation of a viable, contiguous Palestinian state." Jodi Rudoren and Mark Landler, "Housing Move in Israel Seen as Setback for a Two-State Plan," *New York Times*, November 30, 2012. The *Washington Post* noted that the area designated "E1" was "critical for the territorial contiguity of a future Palestinian state." Greenberg, "Abbas returns home." Etc.

400. UN Department of Public Information, "Secretary-General Says Israel's Settlement Expansion Would Be 'Almost Fatal Blow' to Two-State Solution; Urges All Stakeholders to Resume Negotiations," December 2, 2013.

401. United Kingdom, "Foreign Secretary extremely concerned at proposed new housing settlements in the West Bank and East Jerusalem," December 1, 2012. Isabel Kershner, "5 European Nations Summon Envoys of Israel," *New York Times*, December 3, 2012.

402. Barak Ravid and Nir Hasson, "UN Security Council members blast Israel over settlement construction plans," *Haaretz*, December 20, 2012.

403. John Ray, "US slams Israel's decision to expand settlements," *NBC News*, November 30, 2012. US State Department, Daily Press Briefing by Victoria Nuland, November 30, 2012.

404. "Mr. Netanyahu's Strategic Mistake," *New York Times*, December 3, 2012.

405. "The Fading Mideast Peace Dream," *New York Times*, December 20, 2012.

406. Ibid.

407. New York Times, December 3, 2012.

408. US Department of State, Secretary of State Hillary Rodham Clinton, "Remarks at the Saban Center for Middle East Policy 2012, Saban Forum Opening Gala Dinner," November 30, 2012.

409. UN General Assembly, 67th Session, 44th Plenary Meeting, *Question of Palestine*, A/67/PV.44 (November 29, 2012).

Conclusion

1. United Nations Office for the Coordination of Humanitarian Affairs, *Protection of Civilians Weekly Report: 30 September – 13 October 2014*, published October 17, 2014.

INDEX

C

ABOUT THE AUTHOR

JEREMY R. HAMMOND IS an independent political analyst and publisher and editor of *Foreign Policy Journal* (www.foreignpolicyjournal.com). In 2009, he received the Project Censored Award for Outstanding Investigative Journalism for his coverage of the US's support for Israel's 22-day full-scale military assault on the Gaza Strip, "Operation Cast Lead" (Dec. 27, 2008–Jan. 18, 2009). He is the author of *The Rejection of Palestinian Self-Determination: The Struggle for Palestine and the Roots of the Israeli-Arab Conflict* and *Ron Paul vs. Paul Krugman: Austrian vs. Keynesian Economics in the Financial Crisis*. Find him on the web at JeremyRHammond.com.

CPSIA information can be obtained
at www.ICGtesting.com
Printed in the USA
BVHW03*0734150218
508196BV00011B/8/P